POEMS, POETS, POETRY

An Introduction and Anthology

THIRD EDITION

Helen Vendler

HARVARD UNIVERSITY

Bedford/St. Martin's

Boston ▮ New York

For Bedford/St. Martin's

Developmental Editor: Joelle Hann
Project Editor: Peter Jacoby
Production Supervisor: Andrew Ensor
Marketing Manager: Adrienne Petsick
Editorial Assistants: Nina Gantcheva, Andrew Flynn
Art Director: Lucy Krikorian
Text Design: Anna George
Copy Editor: Sarah Zobel
Indexer: Kirsten Kite
Cover Design: Sara Eisenman
Composition: Macmillan Publishing Solutions
Printing and Binding: Haddon Craftsmen, Inc., an RR Donnelley & Sons Company

President: Joan E. Feinberg
Editorial Director: Denise B. Wydra
Editor in Chief: Karen S. Henry
Director of Development: Erica T. Appel
Director of Marketing: Karen R. Soeltz
Director of Editing, Design, and Production: Marcia Cohen
Assistant Director of Editing, Design, and Production: Elise S. Kaiser
Managing Editor: Shuli Traub

Library of Congress Control Number: 2009932162

4   3
k   j   i   h   g

For information, write: Bedford/St. Martin's, 75 Arlington Street, Boston, MA 02116
(617-399-4000)

ISBN-10: 0-312-46319-7
ISBN-13: 978-0-312-46319-9

Acknowledgments

Acknowledgments and copyrights appear at the back of the book on pages 680–88, which constitute an extension of the copyright page.

Preface:
About This Book

This book offers ways to read and understand poems with the pleasure they deserve. The ten chapters in Part I approach the poem from various directions, in the conviction that any artwork invites consideration from different perspectives. Chapter 1, "The Poem as Life," uses several short poems to show how a poetic utterance springs from a life-moment — sometimes a private one (falling in love), sometimes a public one (the decline of aristocracy). Chapter 2, "The Poem as Arranged Life," considers the same poems that appear in Chapter 1 but treats them as arrangements, rather than as utterances; it asks why the poem takes the imaginative shape it does and how its elements have been ordered. In Chapter 3, "Poems as Pleasure," aspects of poetry that give pleasure are mentioned and illustrated: formal aspects such as rhythm and rhyme, of course, but also construction and images. Thematic aspects such as poignancy and wisdom are included, too, as is the individual, personal language proper to each poet. Chapter 4, "Describing Poems," and Chapter 5, "The Play of Language," suggest some useful ways of describing poems — by the class of poems to which they belong, by the little plots they act out through grammar and syntax, by the speech acts in which they engage, by the agents the poets choose to do the work of the poem, and so on.

Chapter 6, "Constructing a Self," moves on to the psychological world of the poem. Given that each poem is a fictive speech by an imagined speaker, how is that speaker made convincing by the author? How is a credible self constructed on the page? The more abstract lyric self of Chapter 6 — ungendered, of no specified age or race, of no determined country — is contrasted in Chapter 7, "Poetry and Social Identity," with the lyric self that is socially marked, as we encounter a speaker making clear her sex, or his race, or his age, or her sexual orientation. Our sense of the purpose and the audience of a poem depends to a great extent on how the self of the speaker is defined. Chapter 8, "History and Regionality," takes up the topics of time and space — the two great axes on which all literature turns — as they apply to lyric poetry. In Chapter 9, "Attitudes, Values, Judgments," the largest questions we can put to a literary work — fundamentally, questions of ethical value — are raised and discussed with respect to some crucial examples, old and new. And finally, to close Part I, Chapter 10, "Poets on Poetry," investigates what poets themselves have said about poems, poetry, and the act of creating.

Each chapter takes up several poems by way of illustration, and ends with a section called "Reading Other Poems" that introduces a small group of poems that can be usefully read in the light of that chapter. These poems are usually short and range from the canonical to the recent.

Part II, "Writing about Poetry," introduces some techniques by which readers can convey what they discover in poems to other readers. Chapter 11, "Writing about Poems," looks closely at two poems about daffodils, one by Robert Herrick and one by William Wordsworth, and suggests some general methods for shaping a paper about Wordsworth's poem. Chapter 12, "Studying Groups of Poems," is divided into two parts: the first examines a suite of poems by Walt Whitman commemorating Abraham Lincoln, and the second probes the theme of time in several Emily Dickinson poems.

The anthology in Part III is intended to provide a wide sampling — more than 280 poems — from the literature of lyric, including some poems longer and more complex than those cited in the chapters. Arranged alphabetically by author, the anthology includes poems by more than 140 poets, many of them represented in significant depth so as to suggest the range of an individual poet's work. Finally, my appendices on prosody, grammar, speech acts, rhetorical devices, and lyric subgenres provide further illustration of points taken up substantively but not exhaustively in individual chapters. They can help consolidate and extend — when assigned as home reading — the demonstrations given in class.

For the second edition, I assented to a few changes in the format of the book. In the first edition, none of the poems had their lines numbered. Poets tend to conceive of their poems stanzaically, not line by line, and they prefer that their poems not be encumbered by elements (such as line numbers) that they themselves have not introduced. Therefore, my own classroom preference is to specify by referring to stanzas and page numbers. ("Look at the third stanza on page 42.") But many instructors pointed out how difficult it is to talk about long poems such as T. S. Eliot's "The Love Song of J. Alfred Prufrock" without some minimal line numbering to help navigate the turns of the discussion. In deference to them, every fifth line in poems of more than 50 lines is now numbered (unless the stanzas in those longer poems are already numbered — see, for example, Robert Browning's "Childe Roland to the Dark Tower Came").

Finally, I have indicated the poets' birth and death dates in the text, as well as in the chronological table of contents, so that readers will have a broad sense of when the poems were written and which poets were contemporaries — who might have read whom, and when.

New to This Edition

Based on the publisher's survey of instructors who have taught with *Poems, Poets, Poetry,* I have introduced about 70 new poems to this edition, many of them by contemporary poets. In Part I and in the anthology, several works by favorite poets such as John Donne, Marianne Moore, E. E. Cummings, Gwendolyn Brooks, Robert Creeley, and Lucille Clifton are new. I have also included in this third edition a much higher number of young poets and poets of various social backgrounds who are doing interesting work today: Victoria Chang, Eduardo Corral, Timothy Donnelly, Shara McCallum, Harryette Mullen, D. A. Powell, Srikanth Reddy, Aleida Rodríguez, Tracy K. Smith, Adrienne Su, Natasha Trethewey, Joshua Weiner, and John Yau.

In addition, the new Chapter 10 surveys the many ways in which poets themselves have described poetry or the act of creating it. Beginning with Philip Sidney's defense of poetic fiction in the sixteenth century, and arriving at such modern statements as William Carlos Williams's definition of a poem as "a small (or large) machine made of words," the chapter suggests that poets view their work from any number of different perspectives, and that poetry is not a single concept, but rather a name for many things that bear a "family resemblance" to each other.

Additional Resources for Teaching and Learning

RE: WRITING FOR LITERATURE: As online resources are becoming increasingly relevant for classroom work, a new Web site, *Re:Writing for Literature,* accessible at **bedfordstmartins.com/rewritinglit**, supplements the poems and explications of this book. *Re:Writing for Literature* provides students and instructors with free access to tutorials for close reading, links to over 800 author biographies — including those of all poets included in this book — and a glossary of over 200 literary terms. Links to additional resources, including (where available) audio of the poets reading their work, are included here, as well as further help with reading and writing about literature, model papers, and resources for finding and citing sources.

AUTHOR'S NOTES FOR TEACHING *POEMS, POETS, POETRY:* I have prepared a brief instructor's manual, available for download from **bedfordstmartins.com/vendler/catalog**, in which I discuss some of the issues of teaching poetry and suggest exercises that have, over the years, helped my students understand and appreciate poetry. The manual also comments on most of the poems in Part I that are not discussed in the text's ten chapters.

Acknowledgments

I'd like to thank once more all the reviewers who helped shape earlier editions by their detailed and incisive suggestions, among them Charles Altieri, University of California at Berkeley; Paul Fry, Yale University; Vincent B. Leitch, Purdue University; Jeredith Merrin, The Ohio State University; Robert Phillips, University of Houston; Susan Schweik, University of California at Berkeley; Paul Sofield, Amherst College; and George Stade, Columbia University. My latest debt of gratitude is to all the teachers who used the first two editions, but especially to those who took the time to fill out the publisher's survey about the second edition of *Poems, Poets, Poetry:* David Bruzina, Ohio University; Robert Chodat, Boston University; Paul Dolan, Boston University; Andrew DuBois, University of Toronto at Scarborough; Matthew Hartman, Ball State University; Ann R. Hawkins, Texas Tech University; Michael S. Holko, Texas Tech University; James Maynard, State University of New York at Buffalo; Steven Monte, College of Staten Island; Rowan Ricardo Phillips, State University of New York at Stony Brook; Maxine Weaver, Florida Atlantic University; Camille-Yvette Welsch, Pennsylvania State University.

Once more I am grateful to Charles Christensen, Joan Feinberg, Stephen Scipione, and Joelle Hann at Bedford/St. Martin's for their interest in this project, for their intuition about the shape it might take, and for their alert editorial guidance. I would also like to thank Erica Appel, Shuli Traub, Peter Jacoby, Nina Gantcheva, Andrew Flynn, and my permissions editor, the efficient Fred T. Courtright of the Permissions Company. I was helped in assembling material by my assistant Kristin Lambert. Finally, I want to express my warmest gratitude to Sylvan Barnet, who first suggested I write such a book, who had faith in its completion, and who has selflessly read, as a friend, every word in all editions. His detailed comments have been invaluable, and his patient counsel, in the ups and downs of revision, was appreciated more than he will ever know, or than I can ever say.

Brief Contents

Contents

Part III
Anthology *369*

Appendices 653

Chronological Contents

About Poets and Poetry

Poets possess two talents: one is imagination, the other is a mastery of language. Many people, writers and nonwriters alike, see the world imaginatively: to accompany such people to a party or an exhibition or a play is to see the event more keenly and more vividly than one might have done alone. The world takes on more color; things are seen from a new slant; events are freshly interpreted and highlighted; a vivacity of response is summoned up. With one sort of imaginative person, everything is seen more darkly: the guests at the party seem trivial, grotesque; the exhibition is tragic; the play is an emblem of despair. In the company of an imaginative person of a different sort, we see the world, as the cliché has it, through rose-colored glasses: people seem better, the world kinder, the cause for optimism stronger. In short, imaginative people have the gift of making others see the world as they see it. And as the poet Wallace Stevens put it, "Things seen are things as seen."

While many imaginative people are content to let their sense of the world, conveyed through conversation, vanish as they speak, writers feel compelled to set down their perceptions in writing. Writers often see the imagination, as Stevens saw it, as a "third planet." Just as a given scene looks one way in sunlight, another way in moonlight, so it looks yet a third way in the light of the imagination. "There's a certain slant of light," says Emily Dickinson; "In this blue light, I can take you there," promises Jorie Graham in "San Sepolcro." That is the implicit invitation offered by all writers: that you will see things in a new light, the light of their construction of the world.

We read imaginative works — whether epic, fiction, drama, or poetry — in order to gain a wider sense of the real. Our hunger to know the world, born with us and eager in childhood, finds one of its chief satisfactions in learning about the responses of others. Of course we are pleased to learn that others share our views, but we are also keenly interested to find out that others see the real differently from us. This is partly a matter of temperament (say, mournful versus humorous), partly a matter of experience (male versus female, young versus old), partly an accidental matter of what happens in a writer's historical epoch (war versus peace). Some forms of literature (we can call them the social genres) such as epic, fiction, and drama, make us look at the wide panorama of a social group — a nation, a village, a family. Though all of the social genres used to be written in verse (Milton, Chaucer, Shakespeare), nowadays the social world is usually observed through prose. We know one America through the eyes of Herman Melville, another through Edith Wharton, yet another through Ralph Ellison. Each of them induces us to live for a while in the light of a fresh imagining of the United States. And in addition to an imaginative view of America, each of these writers has a mastery of language — Melville's encyclopedic and torrential language of whaling, Wharton's fastidious language of social difference, and Ellison's brooding and intense intellectual language of the "invisible man."

But besides the narrative and dramatic social genres, there exists the large body of poetry we call lyric. Lyric is the genre of private life: it is what we say to ourselves when we are alone. There may be an addressee in lyric (God, or a beloved), but the addressee is always absent. (The dramatic monologue, a form Browning made famous, has a silent addressee on stage, but this is the exception to the rule of the absent addressee.) In a way, imagination is at its most unfettered in lyric because the writer need not give a recognizable portrait of society, as the novelist or dramatist must. Because the lyric represents a moment of inner meditation, it is relatively short, and always exists in a particular place — "here" — and a particular time — "now." It may speak about the there and then, but it speaks about them from the here and now. It lets us into the innermost chamber of another person's mind, and makes us privy to what he or she would say in complete secrecy and safety, with none to overhear.

The diary is the nearest prose equivalent to the lyric, but a diary is seen by a reader as the words of another person, whereas a lyric is meant to be spoken by its reader as if the reader were the one uttering the words. A lyric poem is a script for performance by its reader. It is, then, the most intimate of genres, constructing a twinship between writer and reader. And it is the most universal of genres, because it presumes that the reader resembles the writer enough to step into the writer's shoes and speak the lines the writer has written as though they were the reader's own:

> Two roads diverged in a yellow wood,
> And sorry I could not travel both
> And be one traveler, long I stood
> And looked down one as far as I could
> To where it bent in the undergrowth.
>
> — ROBERT FROST,
> "The Road Not Taken"

To read these lines is to be transformed into the hesitating speaker. We do not listen to him; we become him.

Sometimes, of course, the speaker is more narrowly specified, as a certain type of person or even as an individual. Yet even when there is a clear disparity of personal character — as when I, a twenty-first-century white American woman, am reading Blake's lyric spoken by a little black boy in eighteenth-century England — the lyric poet expects that I will put myself into the subject-position of the little black boy, and make the boy's words my own. Though some theorists have suggested that we "overhear" the speaker of lyric (making lyric into a kind of monodrama of which we are the audience), it is more often true that I do not become a disinterested spectator overhearing the lyric speaker: rather, the words of the speaker become my own words. This imaginative transformation of self is what is offered to us by the lyric.

Because lyric is a short form (unlike the epic or the verse-tale), it must be more concise than narrative or drama. Every word has to count. So does every gap. In fact, lyric depends on gaps, and depends even more on the reader to fill in the gaps. It is suggestive rather than exhaustive. As the poet W. B. Yeats said in a 1925 letter, referring to *Hamlet* (but perhaps with his own writing of lyric in mind), "Tell a little & he is Hamlet; tell all & he is nothing. Nothing has life except the incomplete." In the following pages, suggestions are made on how to go about exploring a lyric, in order to fill in its gaps and make the most of its hints, so that the course of its emotions can be understood in their full subtlety.

Even though lyric sometimes makes greater demands on us than do the more explicit genres, a poem always (if it is successful) attracts us enough to make us willing to bear with it while we try to understand it better. A poem, said T. S. Eliot, can communicate while it is still imperfectly understood. It can communicate because it exhibits a mastery of language, in addition to an imaginative sense of the world. We are drawn in by words used in unusual and compelling ways — ways that appeal to the senses of sight and hearing and bodily tension, as well as to the mind. We are also drawn in by the architecture of the poem — the manner in which its parts are arranged, so as to make a structure that reflects emotional intensity. We are drawn in by its volatility and its surprising resources of strategy. And finally, we are drawn in because every poem enters into a continuing conversation with its culture — querying it, amplifying it, rebelling against it, subverting it, aestheticizing it, enhancing it. Robert Frost, in "The Gift Outright," says that when the English came to the American continent, they found a land "still unstoried, artless, unenhanced." Our present anthropological awareness means that no twenty-first-century poet could think of the America of the Puritans as "unstoried" or "artless": the various and widespread Native American cultures had already covered the American continent with stories and with arts. The aim of every artist, then and now, is to contribute those stories, that art, and enhancement that will endow both place and time with significance.

Lyric has recently undergone, in the United States, many significant changes. Twenty-first-century America is a far more heterogeneous country than pre–twenty-first-century England, and contemporary American lyric naturally reflects its own culture and epoch. The availability of translations means that an American poet is now almost as likely to be influenced by a Polish or South American poet — Czeslaw Milosz or Pablo Neruda — as by an English or American poet. Lyric speakers are more ready to define themselves sexually, ethnically, or racially; yet lyric still hopes for the reader's willingness to place himself or herself in the writer's subject-position. Because the dominant influence on a medium is always the medium itself as it has existed through time, the dominant influence on English-language verse is still English as it has been used by preceding poets. That is why one is unlikely to read contemporary poetry well without having read the English poetry from which it descends. The selections here are all in English (lyric poetry being notoriously untranslatable) and are divided between poems that have stood up well over time and other, more recent poems, which, while they may reflect some long-continuing concerns in American life (racism, war, religious faith), also take on new modes in both content (Adrienne Rich's feminism, W. S. Merwin's ecological concern) and style (the reticence of Elizabeth Bishop, the dream-idiom of John Berryman, the "snapshots" of Robert Lowell).

Like all arts, lyric is meant to give pleasure — imaginative, linguistic, intellectual, and moral. If one hasn't enjoyed a poem and been moved by it, one hasn't really experienced it as an artwork. There are moments in life when one poem suits and another doesn't. The poems in this book will not invariably please everybody, because each of us brings a unique

life-experience, and a different expectation of art, to the page. Nonetheless, many of these poems have won and kept readers because in them
readers have found the most moving revelation of all — that of their own
inner life, enacted in words adequate to both sorrow and joy. The rule of
thumb for the encounter with any art is to dwell on what moves you or
gives you pleasure, and skip over, for the time being, what leaves you
cold. But if you remember that someone, somewhere, has been fiercely
attracted by each of these poems, you may be willing to give the ones
you first neglect a second chance. Often, a door that has been shut can
open marvelously at the second knock.

I

AN INTRODUCTION TO POETRY

The Sick Rose

O Rose thou art sick
The invisible worm
That flies in the night
In the howling storm

The Poem as Life

Poems have their origins in life, especially in the formal or informal ceremonies that occur at crucial moments or phases in a single private life — birth, adolescence, marriage, death — or at public moments when we collectively commemorate a war, a religious feast, a holiday. Equally, poems show life lived in a spatial environment, whether immediate (one's house, one's region) or cosmic (the world, the galaxy); they also show seasonal or ritual moments of time. The first questions to ask of any poem are *What piece of life, private or public, is it concerned with?* and *Where and when is this life being lived?*

Of course, cliché haunts all the well-known and well-worn occasions of life. In the occasions of private life shown us by greeting cards or popular magazines, babies are "lovable," brides are "beautiful," fiftieth wedding anniversaries are "happy"; in the public life, cliché tells us that young men should fight in war, that cities are thriving communities, and that Americans should take pride in their country's history. We are also accustomed to clichés of time and space, often hearing, for example, that the springtime of life leads only to the narrow space of the grave. As we trace some of these central aspects of life through poems, the first thing to notice is how the poet manages to avoid cliché — how he or she brings originality to the moment. We look in this chapter at a sample of several poems, the first group representing events in private life, the second group chiefly taking up moments in public life, and the third group expressing some place in space or some moment in the natural seasons of time. In Chapter 2 we will look again at the same poems, to see how they are not only representations of life but also works of art.

The Private Life

"Write a poem about a birth," says the culture to the poet; and what the poet writes (speaking in the person of a newborn baby) may shock the reader:

WILLIAM BLAKE (1757 – 1827)
Infant Sorrow

My mother groaned, my father wept —
Into the dangerous world I leapt,
Helpless, naked, piping loud,   *like*
Like a fiend hid in a cloud.   *demon*
                                     spawn

Struggling in my father's hands,
Striving against my swaddling bands,
Bound and weary, I thought best
To sulk upon my mother's breast.

A different interpretation of the moment

Precisely because our culture does not usually say that a baby resembles "a fiend hid in a cloud," we find the poem arresting. It makes us stop and think. Now let us look at the next phase of life, childhood.

The child's first day of school is an event marked by conventional behavior (new clothes, an apple for the teacher, says the cliché). Louise Glück has written a poem about how a mother feels seeing her child go off into the power of a new authority, who may or may not be kind to the child:

LOUISE GLÜCK (b. 1943)
The School Children

The children go forward with their little satchels.
And all morning the mothers have labored
to gather the late apples, red and gold,
like words of another language.

And on the other shore
are those who wait behind great desks
to receive these offerings.

G is hymn kind of menacing appearance

How orderly they are — the nails
on which the children hang
their overcoats of blue or yellow wool.

And the teachers shall instruct them in silence
and the mothers shall scour the orchards for a way out,
drawing to themselves the gray limbs of the fruit trees
bearing so little ammunition.

The new clothes and the apples for the teacher are here, but they have been made strangely sinister. Once again, the reader is made to stop and think. What is so disturbing about this poem?

Next, the child comes to the apparently quiet period between infancy and puberty, a period psychologists call "latency" because sexuality seems dormant. At this time, intense same-sex friendships form; the child is never seen without his or her "best friend," so much so that Eddie and Bill become a single noun: "Have you seen EddieandBill?" But gradually hormones change Eddie and Bill into adolescents, and the pagan god of sex (whom E. E. Cummings here identifies with goat-footed Pan, the god of all) makes his appearance. We know that in heterosexual development the twosomes "eddieandbill" and "bettyandisbel," so inseparable, will soon, with real anguish and yet with painful anticipation of sexual joy, split up, leave their childish games, and re-form into the new twosomes "eddieandbetty" and "billandisbel":

E. E. CUMMINGS (1894 – 1962)
in Just-

in Just-
spring   when the world is mud-
luscious the little
lame balloonman

whistles   far   and wee

and eddieandbill come
running from marbles and
piracies and it's
spring

when the world is puddle-wonderful

the queer
old balloonman whistles
far   and   wee
and bettyandisbel come dancing

from hop-scotch and jump-rope and

it's
spring
and
    the

       goat-footed

balloonMan   whistles
far *Healing*
and *their*
wee *innocence*

The reader senses something threatening and seductive in the balloon-man, and knows that this is not merely a simple poem about spring hop-scotch and jump-rope. Also, the typographic arrangement is puzzling. What is Cummings up to?

In Robert Hayden's "Those Winter Sundays," we see an adult man (whom we identify with Hayden himself) remembering winter Sunday mornings when he would have to go to church. With painful recognition, he recalls the actions of his father on those mornings: he would get up before the rest of the family and get the furnace (its fire banked for the night) going again. Only then, when the house was warm, would he call his son, who would rise and dress without ever thanking his father for making the rooms warm or for polishing his "good shoes" for church. The poem ends in adult self-reproach for the boy's indifference to his father's actions.

ROBERT HAYDEN (1913 – 1980)
Those Winter Sundays

Sundays too my father got up early
and put his clothes on in the blueblack cold,
then with cracked hands that ached
from labor in the weekday weather made
banked fires blaze. No one ever thanked him.

I'd wake and hear the cold splintering, breaking.
When the rooms were warm, he'd call,
and slowly I would rise and dress,
fearing the chronic angers of that house,

Speaking indifferently to him,
who had driven out the cold

and polished my good shoes as well.
What did I know, what did I know
of love's austere and lonely offices?

As adolescents take their first step into adult emotional relations, they learn what it is to be troubled in love, even forsaken. This is a love poem by Walt Whitman to a male lover who has deserted him, but it soon turns into a poem for everyone who has been deserted:

WALT WHITMAN (1819 – 1892)
Hours Continuing Long

Hours continuing long, sore and heavy hearted,
Hours of the dusk, when I withdraw to a lonesome and
    unfrequented spot, seating myself, leaning my face in my
    hands;
Hours sleepless, deep in the night, when I go forth, speeding
    swiftly the country roads, or through the city streets, or
    pacing miles and miles, stifling plaintive cries;
Hours discouraged, distracted — for the one I cannot content
    myself without, soon I saw him content himself without me;
Hours when I am forgotten (O weeks and months are passing, but
    I believe I am never to forget!)
Sullen and suffering hours! (I am ashamed — but it is useless — I
    am what I am);
Hours of my torment — I wonder if other men ever have the
    like, out of the like feelings?
Is there even one other like me — distracted — his friend, his
    lover, lost to him?
Is he too as I am now? Does he still rise in the morning, dejected,
    thinking who is lost to him? and at night, awaking, think
    who is lost?
Does he too harbor his friendship silent and endless? harbor his
    anguish and passion?
Does some stray reminder, or the casual mention of a name, bring
    the fit back upon him, taciturn and deprest?
Does he see himself reflected in me? In these hours, does he see
    the face of his hours reflected?

The phases of life succeed one another, and we could go on to give examples of poems about parenting, maturity, loss, and old age. Poems, in short, trace the general and special phases of life down to its end in death, and, in religious poems, even to an afterlife. Each of these phases can provoke many different responses — joy, bitterness, bravery, stoicism. Here, for instance, is a twentieth-century poem about the last phase of autumnal life by a writer who, to his grief, sees that all his youthful hopes and imaginings have become old, dilapidated, and sullied. Yet, he feels, he would have missed something had he not had to encounter this final bleakness and to muster the effort of will that it calls from him — to find a new fortitude, a new self-knowledge.

WALLACE STEVENS (1879 – 1955)
The Plain Sense of Things

After the leaves have fallen, we return
To a plain sense of things. It is as if
We had come to an end of the imagination,
Inanimate in an inert savoir.

It is difficult even to choose the adjective
For this blank cold, this sadness without cause.
The great structure has become a minor house.
No turban walks across the lessened floors.

The greenhouse never so badly needed paint.
The chimney is fifty years old and slants to one side.
A fantastic effort has failed, a repetition
In a repetitiousness of men and flies.

Yet the absence of the imagination had
Itself to be imagined. The great pond,
The plain sense of it, without reflections, leaves,
Mud, water like dirty glass, expressing silence

Of a sort, silence of a rat come out to see,
The great pond and its waste of the lilies, all this
Had to be imagined as an inevitable knowledge,
Required, as a necessity requires.

This poem of a late phase of life shows the poet feeling cold, sad, inert — and yet rising to the challenge of seeing this phase truly, as a necessary part of experience. Although many of the feelings of loss that Stevens expresses are conventional in descriptions of old age, he succeeds in making them fresh.

These poems of the private life are all meant to be said by anyone, by everyone. We will come later, in a chapter about place and history, to poems that are more personally specific than these — poems that could be said only by a person belonging to a particular subgroup in society.

The Public Life

Some public poems commemorate communal celebration — Thanksgiving or the Fourth of July or Christmas. (What can a poet do to write a new kind of Christmas poem? Well, he can stage his poem a day early and write "The Night before Christmas," as Clement Moore did.) Public poems often concern crucial single public events. Here is a poem joining two events in the history of American blacks — the blowing-up of an Alabama church in which four young black girls were killed and an imagined episode in the slave trade at the time of the American Revolution (the phrase "middle passage" refers to the route that slave ships once took from Africa to the South):

MICHAEL S. HARPER   (b. 1938)
American History

For John Callahan
Those four black girls blown up
in that Alabama church
remind me of five hundred
middle passage blacks,
in a net, under water
in Charleston harbor
so *redcoats* wouldn't find them.
Can't find what you can't see
can you?

"History" rarely ends with a question mark, but Harper's cynical question replicates the cynicism of the slave dealers.

Other public poems are written about the state of common life, shared by some population in a certain time and place. We might tend to think of such poems as written about violent wrongs such as genocide or slavery, but Charles Simic's "Old Couple" is about the plight of a hidden group of victims — the urban poor in old age, for whom all possible scenarios — eviction, murder, illness, death from malnutrition — are equally frightening:

CHARLES SIMIC (b. 1938)

Old Couple

They're waiting to be murdered,
Or evicted. Soon
They expect to have nothing to eat.
As far as I know, they never go out.

A vicious pain's coming, they think.
It will start in the head
And spread down to the bowels.
They'll be carried off on stretchers, howling.

In the meantime, they watch the street
From their fifth floor window.
It has rained, and now it looks
Like it's going to snow a little.

I see him get up to lower the shades.
If their window stays dark,
I know that his hand has reached hers
Just as she was about to turn on the lights.

Who is the watcher here? Does he share the life of the old couple, and if so, how?

Of course, the private life and the public life are not separate issues, and there are many poems in which the two are mirror images of each other. In Robert Lowell's "Skunk Hour," the decline of the inhabitants of the Maine town where the speaker lives mirrors his own decline into voyeurism and madness. Besides the public life and the private life, "Skunk Hour" invokes the life of nature, which has a sturdy strength (pictured in the dauntless invading "mother skunk with her column of kittens") lacking in the public and private spheres:

ROBERT LOWELL (1917 – 1977)

Skunk Hour

For Elizabeth Bishop

Nautilus Island's hermit
heiress still lives through winter in her Spartan cottage;
her sheep still graze above the sea.
Her son's a bishop. Her farmer

is first selectman in our village;
she's in her dotage.

Thirsting for
the hierarchic privacy
of Queen Victoria's century,
she buys up all
the eyesores facing her shore,
and lets them fall.

The season's ill —
we've lost our summer millionaire,
who seemed to leap from an L. L. Bean
catalogue. His nine-knot yawl
was auctioned off to lobstermen.
A red fox stain covers Blue Hill.

And now our fairy
decorator brightens his shop for fall;
his fishnet's filled with orange cork,
orange, his cobbler's bench and awl;
there is no money in his work,
he'd rather marry.

One dark night,
my Tudor Ford climbed the hill's skull;
I watched for love-cars. Lights turned down,
they lay together, hull to hull,
where the graveyard shelves on the town. . . .
My mind's not right.

A car radio bleats,
"Love, O careless Love. . . ." I hear
my ill-spirit sob in each blood cell,
as if my hand were at its throat. . . .
I myself am hell;
nobody's here —

only skunks, that search
in the moonlight for a bite to eat.
They march on their soles up Main Street:
white stripes, moonstruck eyes' red fire
under the chalk-dry and spar spire
of the Trinitarian Church.

I stand on top
of our back steps and breathe the rich air —
a mother skunk with her column of kittens swills the garbage pail.
She jabs her wedge-head in a cup
of sour cream, drops her ostrich tail,
and will not scare.

What relations are implied here between the town's public life and the speaker's private life, between his private life and the life of nature?

Nature and Time

The poem-as-life notices, besides the inevitable themes of public and private life, two other great intertwined subjects — nature (the earth, the sun, the moon, the stars, animals, plants) and time, with its seasons and months. Because nature and time are such ancient resources for poetry, perhaps the hardest achievement is to write an original poem about, say, spring. An anonymous thirteenth-century poet began our spring poetry as he heard the cuckoo (the herald of spring) and saw all of nature come to life. At that time, there was only one word, "sumer," for the new season after winter; the word "spring" was a later invention.

ANONYMOUS

The Cuckoo Song

Sumer is icumen in,	
Lhude° sing, cuccu!	*loud*
Groweth sed and bloweth med°	*meadow*
And springth the wude nu.	
Sing, cuccu!	
Awe° bleteth after lomb,	*ewe*
Lhouth° after calve cu,°	*loweth / cow*
Bulluc sterteth,° bucke verteth° —	*leaps / breaks wind*
Murie sing, cuccu!	
Cuccu, cuccu.	
Wel singes thu, cuccu.	
Ne swik° thu never nu!	*stop*

The spring songs of the Middle Ages generated a whole series of seasonal poems.

A contemporary poet, Dave Smith, writes his spring poem in an auto junkyard, using a pun on the word "spring" to make new sap rise even in rusty steel:

DAVE SMITH (b. 1942)
The Spring Poem

> *Every poet should write a Spring poem.*
> — LOUISE GLÜCK

Yes, but we must be sure of verities
such as proper heat and adequate form.
That's what poets are for, is my theory.
This then is a Spring poem. A car warms
its rusting hulk in a meadow; weeds slog
up its flanks in martial weather. April
or late March is our month. There is a fog
of spunky mildew and sweaty tufts spill
from the damp rump of a back seat. A spring
thrusts one gleaming tip out, a brilliant tooth
uncoiling from Winter's tension, a ring
of insects along, working out the Truth.
Each year this car, melting around that spring,
hears nails trench from boards and every squeak sing.

We feel that the rusting car warms into new life partly because it has been
used by courting couples who have lent their presence to the phrases
Smith uses for the back seat — its "damp rump," its "spunky mildew and
sweaty tufts." When even a metal spring puts out new shoots, when even
nails spring free from the boards they have been hammered into, we know
that spring is irresistible.

The seasons have become a constant resource for poets describing
stages of human life, so that in reading poems as life we can't fail to think
of Keats's sonnet on the human seasons, which sets out the great analogy
between nature and ourselves:

JOHN KEATS (1795 – 1821)
The Human Seasons

Four seasons fill the measure of the year;
    There are four seasons in the mind of man.
He has his lusty Spring, when fancy clear
    Takes in all beauty with an easy span.
He has his Summer, when luxuriously
    Spring's honeyed cud of youthful thought he loves
To ruminate, and by such dreaming nigh
    His nearest unto heaven. Quiet coves
His soul has in its Autumn, when his wings
    He furleth close; contented so to look

On mists in idleness — to let fair things
　　Pass by unheeded as a threshold brook.
He has his Winter too of pale misfeature,
Or else he would forego his mortal nature.

A poet can choose any one of the "human seasons" and find its counter-part in the natural world.

When poets describe Time, they tend to employ many of the im-ages of passing time that have entered cultural memory — such motifs as the waves of the sea, the progress of the sun from dawn to dusk, the fall of great men, the tragedy of early death, Time the Grim Reaper, and so on. Here, using such time-honored resources, is Shakespeare on Time. In his first model of how we imagine Time, the moments of our life are seen as waves of the sea, all alike; in his second model, the moments of our life are like the dramatic rise and eclipse of a sun, or the rise and fall of a tragic hero; and in his third model, we scarcely have time to live before Death scythes us down.

WILLIAM SHAKESPEARE (1564 – 1616)
Sonnet 60

Like as the waves make toward the pebbled shore,
So do our minutes hasten to their end,　*contemplation of mortality*
Each changing place with that which goes before,
In sequent° toil all forwards do contend.　Time goes　*repetitive*
Nativity,° once in the main° of light,　one way　*birth / sea*
Crawls to maturity, wherewith being crowned,　Birth to death
Crooked eclipses 'gainst his glory fight,
And Time that gave doth now his gift confound.
Time doth transfix the flourish° set on youth,　*beauty*
And delves the parallels° in beauty's brow,　*furrows*
Feeds on the rarities of nature's truth,
And nothing stands but for his scythe to mow.　Death the Grim Reaper
　　And yet to times in hope my verse shall stand,　his poems will
　　Praising thy worth, despite his cruel hand.　stand the test
　　　　　　　　　　　　　　　　　　time　　　　　　of time

What does Shakespeare set against Time in the final couplet?

In Brief: The Poem as Life

The first thing to notice about *any* poem is what piece of life (a dis-appointment in love, the death of a parent, an absence from a friend, a crisis of personal confidence, a moment of fear) the poem is about. Lyric poems spring from moments of disequilibrium: something has happened to disturb the status quo. Hope has come to rebuke despair; love has come to thaw coldness; envy has come to upset happiness; shame has come to interfere with self-esteem. If you can't find the piece of life that the poem is about, read the poem again, speaking it aloud in your own voice. It helps to ask, "Under what circumstances would I find myself saying these words?" The poem is *written for you to say. You* are the speaker of every lyric poem you read. That is what a lyric poem is: it is a speech made for you to utter. (We will come later to poems spoken to a silent listener by a defined character — not you, but, for instance, a madman or a Renaissance duke — poems that we call dramatic monologues.)

Once you have made a plausible hypothesis about what piece of life the poem is about, you can go on to see how the poem, though *about* life, is *not* life. This is the subject of our next chapter, which returns to these poems.

Reading Other Poems

Think about the following poems as utterances coming out of a particular life situation. Try to make deductions from each one.

- ◆ What has recently happened to the speaker?
- ◆ What aspect of his or her life has the speaker been thinking about? Is this a private life situation (a family death, for instance) or a public situation (a religious massacre, a war memorial)?
- ◆ What stage of life has the speaker reached?
- ◆ How much does the speaker tell you about his or her feelings?

You might ask, too, whether these are the feelings and the remarks you might expect to find expressed in this situation (comparing them with what people might normally say or feel).

- ◆ How do Sir Thomas Wyatt's feelings change as he reacts to having been jilted?
- ◆ What feelings arise in Ben Jonson when his beloved first son dies?
- ◆ Do John Milton's remarks about revenge surprise you?
- ◆ What does John Keats most regret when he thinks he will die while he is still young (as he did)?
- ◆ Why do you suppose Emily Dickinson represented herself as a boy in the poem about coming across a snake? Can you describe the feeling at the close of Dickinson's poem in different words?

"Those Winter Sundays" (see page 6) and "Theme for English B" (see page 19) are by black writers: one takes up the tension between a black student and his white teacher in a freshman English class; the other doesn't mention race at all.

- ◆ When do you think a life situation might lead to the mention of race, and when not?
- ◆ Jonson's poem expresses the feelings of a father for his son; can you compare it to Robert Hayden's poem expressing the feelings of a son for his father?
- ◆ Are Dylan Thomas's words the usual ones addressed by a son to a dying father?
- ◆ How do these compare with the feelings expressed by Sylvia Plath when she thinks about her relation to her father? And with Rita Dove's recollection of her childhood evenings with her father in "Flash Cards"?

Both Milton and Yusef Komunyakaa look at large social issues: in Milton's case, the massacre of a large number of Protestant "heretics" by Catholic forces in northern Italy; in Komunyakaa's case, the residue of the Vietnam War as represented by the Vietnam War Memorial in Washington.

- ◆ In what way do the tones adopted by these two poets differ?
- ◆ How do you think a poet decides how "loudly" to speak when he or she speaks of public issues?

Literature can be sharply critical of the life it represents. In *Homecoming,* Julia Alvarez describes attending, as a seventeen-year-old college student, a South American wedding reception where the bride is Alvarez's cousin and the groom a man from Minnesota. What aspects of the reception does the poet emphasize as she presents the life led by her relatives? Can you isolate the main faults, as she sees them, of the society she now analyzes, much later, with the eyes of an outsider?

SIR THOMAS WYATT (1503 – 1542)
They Flee from Me

flee

They flee from me, that sometime did me seek,
With naked foot stalking in my chamber.

I have seen them, gentle, tame, and meek,
That now are wild, and do not remember
That sometime they put themselves in danger
To take bread at my hand; and now they range,
Busily seeking with a continual change.

Thankèd be Fortune it hath been otherwise,
Twenty times better; but once in special,
In thin array, after a pleasant guise,
When her loose gown from her shoulders did fall,
And she me caught in her arms long and small,°   *slender*
Therewithal sweetly did me kiss
And softly said, "Dear heart, how like you this?"

It was no dream, I lay broad waking.
But all is turned, thorough my gentleness,
Into a strange fashion of forsaking;
And I have leave to go, of her goodness,
And she also to use newfangleness.
But since that I so kindely am servèd,
I fain would know what she hath deservèd.

BEN JONSON (1572 – 1637)
On My First Son

Farewell, thou child of my right hand,[1] and joy;
My sin was too much hope of thee, loved boy:
Seven years thou wert lent to me, and I thee pay,
Exacted by thy fate, on the just day.
O could I lose all father now! for why
Will man lament the state he should envy,
To have so soon 'scaped world's and flesh's rage,
And, if no other misery, yet age?
Rest in soft peace, and asked, say, "Here doth lie
Ben Jonson his best piece of poetry."
For whose sake henceforth all his vows be such
As what he loves may never like too much.

---

[1] A literal translation of the Hebrew "Benjamin," the boy's name. Jonson's son was born in 1596 and died of the plague in 1603.

JOHN MILTON (1608 – 1674)
On the Late Massacre in Piedmont[1]

Avenge, O Lord, thy slaughtered saints, whose bones
    Lie scattered on the Alpine mountains cold,
    Even them who kept thy truth so pure of old
    When all our fathers worshiped stocks° and stones,   *idols*
Forget not: in thy book record their groans
    Who were thy sheep and in their ancient fold
    Slain by the bloody Piemontese that rolled
    Mother with infant down the rocks. Their moans
The vales redoubled to the hills, and they
    To Heaven. Their martyred blood and ashes sow
    O'er all th' Italian fields where still doth sway
The triple tyrant,[2] that from these may grow
    A hundredfold, who having learnt thy way
    Early may fly the Babylonian woe.[3]

JOHN KEATS (1795 – 1821)
When I have fears that I may cease to be

When I have fears that I may cease to be
    Before my pen has gleaned my teeming brain,
Before high-pilèd books, in charact'ry,°   *written letters*
    Hold like rich garners the full-ripened grain;
When I behold, upon the night's starred face,
    Huge cloudy symbols of a high romance,
And think that I may never live to trace
    Their shadows, with the magic hand of chance;
And when I feel, fair creature of an hour,
    That I shall never look upon thee more,
Never have relish in the faery power
    Of unreflecting love! — then on the shore
Of the wide world I stand alone, and think
Till Love and Fame to nothingness do sink.

---

[1]The Vaudois, or Waldenses, a Protestant people living in the northwestern part of Italy, were subjected in 1655 to a bloody persecution because they refused to accept Catholicism.
[2]The pope, as claiming authority on earth and in heaven and hell.
[3]Protestants frequently identified the Roman Catholic church with Babylon.

EMILY DICKINSON (1830 – 1886)

A narrow Fellow in the Grass

A narrow Fellow in the Grass
Occasionally rides –
You may have met Him – did you not
His notice sudden is –

The Grass divides as with a Comb –
A spotted shaft is seen –
And then it closes at your feet
And opens further on –

He likes a Boggy Acre
A Floor too cool for Corn –
Yet when a Boy, and Barefoot –
I more than once at Noon

Have passed, I thought, a Whip lash
Unbraiding in the Sun
When stooping to secure it
It wrinkled, and was gone –

Several of Nature's People
I know, and they know me –
I feel for them a transport
Of cordiality –

But never met this Fellow
Attended, or alone
Without a tighter breathing
And Zero at the Bone –

LANGSTON HUGHES (1902 – 1967)

Theme for English B

The instructor said,

> *Go home and write*
> *a page tonight.*
> *And let that page come out of you —*
> *Then, it will be true.*

I wonder if it's that simple?
I am twenty-two, colored, born in Winston-Salem.
I went to school there, then Durham, then here
to this college on the hill above Harlem.

I am the only colored student in my class.
The steps from the hill lead down into Harlem,
through a park, then I cross St. Nicholas,
Eighth Avenue, Seventh, and I come to the Y,
the Harlem Branch Y, where I take the elevator
up to my room, sit down, and write this page:

It's not easy to know what is true for you or me
at twenty-two, my age. But I guess I'm what
I feel and see and hear, Harlem, I hear you:
hear you, hear me — we two — you, me, talk on this page.
(I hear New York, too.) Me — who?
Well, I like to eat, sleep, drink, and be in love.
I like to work, read, learn, and understand life.
I like a pipe for a Christmas present,
or records — Bessie,[1] bop, or Bach.
I guess being colored doesn't make me *not* like
the same things other folks like who are other races.
So will my page be colored that I write?
Being me, it will not be white.
But it will be
a part of you, instructor.
You are white —
yet a part of me, as I am a part of you.
That's American.
Sometimes perhaps you don't want to be a part of me.
Nor do I often want to be a part of you.
But we are, that's true!
As I learn from you,
I guess you learn from me —
although you're older — and white —
and somewhat more free.

This is my page for English B.

DYLAN THOMAS (1914 – 1953)

Do Not Go Gentle into That Good Night

Do not go gentle into that good night,
Old age should burn and rave at close of day;
Rage, rage against the dying of the light.

---

[1]Bessie Smith (1898?–1937), African American blues singer.

Though wise men at their end know dark is right,
Because their words had forked no lightning they
Do not go gentle into that good night.

Good men, the last wave by, crying how bright
Their frail deeds might have danced in a green bay,
Rage, rage against the dying of the light.

Wild men who caught and sang the sun in flight,
And learn, too late, they grieved it on its way,
Do not go gentle into that good night.

Grave men, near death, who see with blinding sight
Blind eyes could blaze like meteors and be gay,
Rage, rage against the dying of the light.

*scenario
is made
clear*

And you, my father, there on the sad height,
Curse, bless, me now with your fierce tears, I pray.
Do not go gentle into that good night.
Rage, rage against the dying of the light.

Sylvia Plath (1932 – 1963)
Daddy

You do not do, you do not do
Any more, black shoe
In which I have lived like a foot
For thirty years, poor and white,
Barely daring to breathe or Achoo.   5

Daddy, I have had to kill you.
You died before I had time —
Marble-heavy, a bag full of God,
Ghastly statue with one gray toe[1]
Big as a Frisco seal   10

And a head in the freakish Atlantic
Where it pours bean green over blue
In the waters off beautiful Nauset.
I used to pray to recover you.
Ach, du.[2]   15

---

[1]Otto Plath's diabetes caused a gangrenous toe, which led to the septicemia that killed him.

[2]German: "Ah, you." The second-person familiar form (*du*) is used for intimates.

In the German tongue, in the Polish town
Scraped flat by the roller
Of wars, wars, wars.
But the name of the town is common.
My Polack[3] friend   20

Says there are a dozen or two.
So I never could tell where you
Put your foot, your root,
I never could talk to you.
The tongue stuck in my jaw.   25

It stuck in a barb wire snare.
Ich, ich, ich, ich,[4]
I could hardly speak.
I thought every German was you.
And the language obscene   30

An engine, an engine
Chuffing me off like a Jew.
A Jew to Dachau, Auschwitz, Belsen.[5]
I began to talk like a Jew.
I think I may well be a Jew.   35

The snows of the Tyrol,[6] the clear beer of Vienna[7]
Are not very pure or true.
With my gypsy ancestress and my weird luck
And my Taroc pack and my Taroc pack[8]
I may be a bit of a Jew.   40

I have always been scared of *you,*
With your Luftwaffe,[9] your gobbledygoo.
And your neat moustache
And your Aryan[10] eye, bright blue.
Panzer-man, panzer-man,[11] O You —   45

---

[3]Derogatory slang for "Polish."

[4]German: "I, I, I, I."

[5]Nazi concentration camps.

[6]Alpine region of Austria.

[7]Capital of Austria. Plath's mother was of Austrian descent; Austria was annexed by the Nazis.

[8]Pack of cards used in fortune-telling.

[9]The Nazi air force.

[10]Word used by Nazis to characterize those of "pure" or unadulterated German stock.

[11]Man resembling a German armored tank.

Not God but a swastika[12]
So black no sky could squeak through.
Every woman adores a Fascist,
The boot in the face, the brute
Brute heart of a brute like you.   50

You stand at the blackboard, daddy,[13]
In the picture I have of you,
A cleft in your chin instead of your foot
But no less a devil for that, no not
Any less the black man who   55

Bit my pretty red heart in two.
I was ten when they buried you.
At twenty I tried to die
And get back, back, back to you.
I thought even the bones would do.   60

But they pulled me out of the sack,
And they stuck me together with glue.
And then I knew what to do.
I made a model of you,
A man in black with a Meinkampf[14] look   65

And a love of the rack and the screw.[15]
And I said I do, I do.
So daddy, I'm finally through.
The black telephone's off at the root,
The voices just can't worm through.   70

If I've killed one man, I've killed two —
The vampire who said he was you
And drank my blood for a year,
Seven years, if you want to know.
Daddy, you can lie back now.   75

There's a stake in your fat black heart[16]
And the villagers never liked you.
They are dancing and stamping on you.

---

[12]Symbol of the Nazi party.

[13]Otto Plath was a professor of entomology at Boston University.

[14]German: "My struggle," the title of Hitler's manifesto.

[15]Rack, screw: instruments of torture.

[16]Traditionally, a vampire was buried at a crossroads with a stake through his heart.

They always *knew* it was you.
Daddy, daddy, you bastard, I'm through.   80

RITA DOVE (b. 1952)
Flash Cards

In math I was the whiz kid, keeper
of oranges and apples. *What you don't understand,*
master, my father said; the faster
I answered, the faster they came.

I could see one bud on the teacher's geranium,
one clear bee sputtering at the wet pane.
The tulip trees always dragged after heavy rain
so I tucked my head as my boots slapped home.

My father put up his feet after work
and relaxed with a highball and *The Life of Lincoln.*
After supper we drilled and I climbed the dark

before sleep, before a thin voice hissed
numbers as I spun on a wheel. I had to guess.
Ten, I kept saying, *I'm only ten.*

YUSEF KOMUNYAKAA (b. 1947)
Facing It

My black face fades,
hiding inside the black granite.
I said I wouldn't,
dammit: No tears.
I'm stone. I'm flesh.
My clouded reflection eyes me
like a bird of prey, the profile of night
slanted against morning. I turn
this way — the stone lets me go.
I turn that way — I'm inside
the Vietnam Veterans Memorial
again, depending on the light
to make a difference.
I go down the 58,022 names,
half-expecting to find
my own in letters like smoke.

I touch the name Andrew Johnson;
I see the booby trap's white flash.
Names shimmer on a woman's blouse
but when she walks away
the names stay on the wall.
Brushstrokes flash, a red bird's
wings cutting across my stare.
The sky. A plane in the sky.
A white vet's image floats
closer to me, then his pale eyes
look through mine. I'm a window.
He's lost his right arm
inside the stone. In the black mirror
a woman's trying to erase names:
No, she's brushing a boy's hair.

JULIA ALVAREZ (b. 1950)

Homecoming

When my cousin Carmen married, the guards
at her father's *finca*° took the guests' bracelets   *ranch*
and wedding rings and put them in an armored truck
for safekeeping while wealthy, dark-skinned men,
their plump, white women and spoiled children   5
bathed in a river whose bottom had been cleaned
for the occasion. She was Tío's° only daughter;   *Uncle's*
and he wanted to show her husband's family,
a bewildered group of sunburnt Minnesotans,
that she was valued. He sat me at their table   10
to show off my English, and when he danced with me,
fondling my shoulder blades beneath my bridesmaid's gown
as if they were breasts, he found me skinny
but pretty at seventeen, and clever.
Come back from that cold place, Vermont, he said,   15
all this is yours! Over his shoulder
a dozen workmen hauled in blocks of ice
to keep the champagne lukewarm and stole
glances at the wedding cake, a dollhouse duplicate
of the family rancho, the shutters marzipan,   20
the cobbles almonds. A maiden aunt housekept,
touching up whipped cream roses with a syringe
of eggwhites, rescuing the groom when the heat

melted his chocolate shoes into the frosting.
On too much rum Tío led me across the dance floor,   25
dusted with talcum for easy gliding, a smell
of babies underfoot. He twirled me often,
excited by my pleas of dizziness, teasing me
that my merengue° had lost its Caribbean.   *a dance*
Above us, Chinese lanterns strung between posts   30
came on and one snapped off and rose
into a purple postcard sky.
A grandmother cried: *The children all grow up too fast.*
The Minnesotans finally broke loose and danced a Charleston
and were pronounced good gringos° with latino hearts.   *non-*
The little sister, freckled with a week of beach,   *Hispanics*
her hair as blonde as movie stars', was asked
by maids if they could touch her hair or skin,
and she backed off, until it was explained to her,
they meant no harm. *This is all yours,*   40
Tío whispered, pressing himself into my dress.
The workmen costumed in their workclothes danced
a workman's jig. The maids went by with trays
of wedding bells and matchbooks monogrammed
with Dick's and Carmen's names. It would be years   45
before I took the courses that would change my mind
in schools paid for by sugar from the fields around us,
years before I could begin to comprehend
how one does not see the maids when they pass by
with trays of deviled eggs arranged in daisy wheels.   50
— It was too late, or early, to be wise —
The sun was coming up beyond the amber waves
of cane, the roosters crowed, the band struck up
Las Mañanitas, a morning serenade. I had a vision
that I blamed on the champagne: 55
the fields around us were burning. At last
a yawning bride and groom got up and cut
the wedding cake, but everyone was full
of drink and eggs, roast pig, and rice and beans.
Except the maids and workmen,   60
sitting on stoops behind the sugar house,
ate with their fingers from their open palms
windows, shutters, walls, pillars, doors,
made from the cane they had cut in the fields.

2

The Poem as Arranged Life

Analytic Shape

The preceding chapter, "The Poem as Life," suggested that poems originate in crucial moments of private life (for instance, marriage) or public life (for instance, a revolutionary era), and that they are set in recognizable places (in a junkyard, for example) or times (in spring). But to speak of the poem "as life" is not to say that it is simply a transcription of what has occurred. Life itself is a continuation of successive moments in one stream. Art interrupts the stream and constructs one segment or level of the stream for processing. In a single act, it describes, analyzes, and confers form on that segment. The form it confers by its ways of organizing the poem makes visible the contour of that life-moment as the poet perceives it. The poet discovers the emotional import of that life-moment by subjecting it to analysis; the analysis then determines how the moment is described, and the invented organizational form that replicates it. These are remarks that will become clear when we look at particular poems, so let us go back to our poems-as-life to see how they are *arranged* life — that is, in what way they are formal constructions of life. What organizational patterns have the poets chosen?

The Private Life

Blake's baby, first of all. For Blake, every moment in life could be seen in either of two ways — innocently or with experience. The innocent way of seeing a baby is what we might call both a cliché and a truth: a baby *is* beautiful, guileless, smiling, appealing, the joy of its mother's days. In an earlier poem, "Infant Joy," Blake shows us what the innocent mother, in her fantasy, would like the baby to say to her as he tells her how to name him (stanza 1), and what she would then say to him (stanza 2):

WILLIAM BLAKE (1757 – 1827)

Infant Joy

"I have no name,
I am but two days old."
"What shall I call thee?"
"I happy am,
Joy is my name."
"Sweet joy befall thee!"

"Pretty joy!
Sweet joy but two days old,
Sweet joy I call thee;
Thou dost smile,
I sing the while —
Sweet joy befall thee!"

But a baby is also the bundle of tension that will generate its future sorrows, as Blake asserts in "Infant Sorrow," the companion-poem to "Infant Joy." If you think back, he suggests, to how awful it was to be a baby when you were one, then you will see infancy from the point of view of "experience" rather than the maternal doting "innocence." You will remember how dangerous the world seemed to you when you were small, how helpless you felt, how little power you had over your environment and your belongings, how often you cried in frustration, how fiendish your unsatisfied shrieks must have seemed to your parents, how you must have longed to wrest personal control of your physical self from your parents' attentions. This remarkable sympathetic description of *babyhood from the point of view of the rebellious and unhappy baby* was Blake's originating insight; he then had to arrange his intuition of the baby's rage into an analytic and poetic shape.

WILLIAM BLAKE (1757 – 1827)
Infant Sorrow

My mother groaned, my father wept —
Into the dangerous world I leapt,   *physical*
Helpless, naked, piping loud,
Like a fiend hid in a cloud.

Struggling in my father's hands,
Striving against my swaddling bands,
Bound and weary, I thought best   *mental*
To sulk upon my mother's breast.

Blake analyzes the baby into two aspects, its physical body and its mental operations; he gives a stanza to each aspect. The main verb of the first stanza is the physical word "leapt"; the main verb of the second stanza is the mental word "thought." First the baby leaps into the world; then he thinks about his condition and decides what attitude to take toward it (he finally decides to sulk, after fruitlessly struggling and striving).

If the *division into the physical and the mental* is the most basic analytic move of the poem (causing it to divide itself into two stanzas), what other shapes does Blake confer on his piece of life? We notice that the baby's mother and father are present in each of the stanzas: by repeating the shape "parents-baby, parents-baby," Blake shows us that the baby does not exist alone but lives always in dependency on his parents. First, they preside at his birth, while his mother groans in labor and his father weeps in sympathy. Next, they literally enclose him, as they occupy the first and last line of the second stanza; the baby is held in his father's hands in the first line and supported on his mother's breast in the last. This *environmental* "parents-baby, parents-baby" shape is superimposed on the first shape ("baby-body, baby-mind") that we perceived. Just as the first shape made concrete — physically represented — Blake's analytic separation of the baby into body and mind, the second shape shows Blake's perception of the baby's total physical and moral impotence. He must continue to live (stanza 2) in the power of his parents who gave him existence (stanza 1), and it will be a long time before he will be old enough to have the independence he furiously craves.

Blake confers a third analytic shape on the poem with all the adjectives that the baby uses about himself: "helpless," "naked," "piping," "like a fiend hid," "struggling," "striving," "bound," and "weary." These are all realistic except "like a fiend hid." The realistic adjectives tell us how much any infant already knows about his intolerable condition; but the adjectival comparison, "[I am] like a fiend hid in a cloud," tells us that the baby can summon up a very strange analogy. We conclude (as would Blake, a Christian), that the baby has come into this life from a previous supernatural existence where he knew angels and devils. The baby (to his dismay) realizes that in this horrible new struggling embodied state he is more like the fiends he remembers than like the angels he resembled in heaven. The adjectival division of the baby's *self-awareness* into an *"earthly"* one (conscious of being naked, struggling, etc.) and a *"supernatural"* one (recalling fiends — and presumably their counterpart angels — known to his former life) reflects the baby's rage and self-division.

The fourth analytic shape Blake confers on his picture of the baby's state is a grammatical one — a contrast between present participial adjectives and non-"ing" adjectives. We see in this shape Blake's *contrast between doing and feeling* — between the baby's participial adjectives of action ("piping," "struggling," "striving") and his other adjectives of feeling ("helpless," "naked," "like a fiend," "bound," "weary"). The present participles show us what the baby can *do* (he can pipe, he can struggle, he can strive); the other adjectives tell us how he *feels* — his sufferings and his self-estimation as a fiend. We can understand his struggling and striving; but the unusual word "piping" tells us that in Blake's view the baby is not screaming or shrieking — he is making a song. "Piping" is a musical word, and it represents the beginning of language (or at least vocal expression) in the baby. He is full of sorrow, but he is also expressing his sorrow vocally.

There are other verbal effects we could mention: for instance, the fact that the baby is shown actively "leaping" into the world, rather than passively "being born"; that the successively weaker participial line-beginnings — "Struggling," "Striving," "Bound" — enact (act out, give us in miniature) the baby's eventual resignation into his sulky state; that the little couplets (pairs of rhyming lines) demonstrate Blake's decision to use the simplest sort of rhyme for the baby's speech; that the space between the stanzas represents the transition from being born to living. But as we look back on the task the poet set himself — "Find a shape for saying how life seems to the baby as he's born and just afterward" — we see that the poem has had to find several shapes for just that. To the extent that the poem exhibits analytic shapes, it has been removed from the stream of undifferentiated moments of existence and brought into the formal world of art. A poem that at first looks like a description ("Helpless, naked, piping loud, / Like a fiend hid in a cloud") is in fact an analysis of aspects of the baby's condition, arranged in ways (such as division into physical and mental, parents in each stanza, recall of heavenly preexistence, a contrast between acting and feeling) that show how the baby perceives life.

To sum up: by "analytic shape" I mean any meaningful patterning in the poem that "acts out" one of the insights the poet has had about the experience treated by the poem. It is as though in this poem Blake, with a poet's instinct, thought, "How shall I show that the baby is a mind as well as a body?" and decided, "I'll make a two-stanza poem, with the main *verb* in the first stanza a body-word, and the main *verb* in the second stanza a mind-word" (Shape 1). Then he thought, "How will I show the baby's dependence on its parents?" and decided, "I'll put the *nouns* 'mother' and 'father' in each stanza to show that the baby is always dependent on his parents" (Shape 2). Then, "How will I show the baby's previous supernatural life? By having him, amid all his *realistic* self-adjectives, include one *supernatural* adjectival comparison alluding to that previous life" (Shape 3). Then, "How can I show what the baby is feeling as well as what the baby is doing? I'll give him *present-participial adjectives* of doing *and non-'ing' adjectives* of feeling" (Shape 4). These decisions organize the poem, giving it structures that are dynamic ones, constantly overlapping and interlocking, making up the overall organization of the poem.

Of course, such patterns occur in lightning-quick ways to the trained mind of the poet. A composer does not say, "I think this is the place for a diminished seventh," or "Perhaps it would be effective to follow eighth-note triplets with a dotted quarter note." No, the composer "hears the music" and writes it down; it is only later that analysts demonstrate the patterns that make the music seem intended, not chaotic. A poet, too, "hears the poem," writes it down, and then further refines its visible patterns. Naturally, when a given pattern precedes the composition of the poem ("I want to write a sonnet"), much will be dictated by the preexistent formal requirements; but even then, the swift internal processes of composition organize the temporal, spatial, grammatical, and syntactic shapes of the poem more by instinct than by conscious plan. One could say that artists are people who think naturally in highly patterned ways.

As this summary shows, it is up to the reader to notice patterns such as those Blake uses. "How is it that the main action of the baby is a body-action in stanza 1 and a mind-action in stanza 2? What does this tell me about the baby's condition?" Or, "How is it that among all these realistic adjectives suiting the baby's state I find this one weird one — 'like a fiend hid in a cloud'? How does the newborn baby know about fiends hiding in clouds? What does this tell me about the baby's mind?"

A pattern shows that the poet has analyzed, and then replicated in language, some aspect of the content of the poem. We can therefore call a pattern an analytic shape. (In well-written poems, most of the larger perceived patterns will be analytically meaningful.) Much is explained to us about the baby by the patterns we have seen. The *main-verb pattern* tells us that the baby is composed of mind and body, which do separate things. The *noun-repeat pattern* ("mother," "father") tells us of the baby's dependency. The *realistic/supernatural adjectival pattern* of contrast tells us of the baby's memory of a past state. The *present-participial adjectives/other adjectives pattern* shows us the baby doing and the baby feeling. These few patterns remind us that there can be shapes of:

1. simple meaning-contrast (the antonyms "leapt" and "thought");

2. word-repetition ("mother," "father");

3. series, whether similar or broken ("like a fiend" breaks the realistic series and therefore stands out);

4. grammatical contrast (here, present-participial adjectives versus other adjectives, showing us actions versus feelings).

To discern the patterns in any poem, you may have to notice, then, such things as contrasts of meaning, repetitions of words, items in series, and grammatical emphases. Then, having seen such patterns, you can begin to ask yourself if they show you something about the situation in the poem that makes sense of the experience depicted.

We can ask, now, how does Louise Glück give formal shape to the first day of school?

As we've seen, Glück takes her cast of characters and their props from our conventional picture of the first day of school: there are children with their new primary-color clothes ("overcoats of blue or yellow wool"), their first book-bags or lunch-boxes ("their little satchels"), and their apples (from their family's orchard) for the teachers. The teachers "wait behind . . . desks." The mothers are left behind as the children "go forward" to school. So far, so ordinary. No one would be surprised to be told these details about the first day of school. But Glück gives us more, and more sinister, details:

LOUISE GLÜCK (b. 1943)
The School Children

The children go forward with their little satchels.
And all morning the mothers have labored
to gather the late apples, red and gold,
like words of another language.

And on the other shore
are those who wait behind great desks
to receive these offerings.

How orderly they are — the nails
on which the children hang
their overcoats of blue or yellow wool.

And the teachers shall instruct them in silence
and the mothers shall scour the orchards for a way out,
drawing to themselves the gray limbs of the fruit trees
bearing so little ammunition.

We perceive poetic shape mostly through *oddness*. There are several oddnesses here. The apples are said to be "like words of another language." The school is said to be "on the other shore" of some unspecified body of water. The teachers' (ordinary) desks are said to be "great" desks — and the teachers wait, like gods, to receive "offerings." The only detail given about the school itself is that it has an orderly row of nails serving as coat hooks. The limbs of the fruit trees in the orchards which the mothers "scour" for "a way out" are "gray," and the apples are seen, at the end of the poem, as "ammunition." These are the oddnesses any account of the shapes of the poem would have to make sense of. And we could see this fourteen-line poem as a variant form of sonnet.

We also perceive shape through the *division into stanzas* — here, four of them, with their appropriate dramatis personae, or cast of characters. Stanza 1 is for the *children,* the *mothers,* and the *apples;* stanza 2 is for the *teachers* and the *apples;* stanza 3 is for the *nails;* and stanza 4 is for the *teachers* (doing one thing at school) and the *mothers* (doing another thing in the orchards with apples). Why is this the way the characters come on the stage? Why do the nails have a stanza to themselves? Why isn't the word "apples" mentioned in the last stanza?

We perceive shape through *series:* the apples, which were "words of another language" in stanza 1, and "these offerings" in stanza 2, are "ammunition" in stanza 4. The apples are the only image that changes, and they become more pathetic as the poem goes on.

At this point, we can say that the first basic shape that the poem confers on the opening of school is a *spatial* one. There is a terrible and dangerous separation of teacher-territory from mother-territory: they lie on opposite shores of a watery divide. The two regions speak different languages, and the apples are the only words in the teacher-language that can bridge the gap. The two regions are also in conflict; but the teachers have nails and the mothers have only apples — as propitiatory offerings, as ammunition against the teachers' power. The mothers' desperate work ("all morning the mothers have labored"; "the mothers shall scour the orchards") to protect the children is bound to fail — they have "so little ammunition" from the already-withering fruit trees (next year's apples will be of no use, since the children will be wholly socialized into their public school-selves by then). The day will come when the children will have to go to school without an apple to offer to those mysterious strangers, the teachers, who speak another language, who wait behind their monumental "great desks." What will happen then?

The *spatial* shape of the great divide into two territories is matched by the *temporal* shape of the poem. By "temporal shape" I mean what happens to the poem as it progresses in time. Here, as the poem advances from stanza 1 to stanza 2 to stanza 3, the gaze of the narrator narrows from the home group (mothers and children) to the people behind the "great desks" to the sinister single objects "orderly . . . nails." Then the gaze of the narrator broadens again, to the children firmly in the power of the teacher (who will quell their native language and reduce them to the silence and orderliness of socialization) and the mothers, on the other shore, who will wildly seek a way, by scouring the orchards for apples (which they now think of solely as "ammunition") to fight the trap that is closing on their children.

These two axes, Space and Time, are often used to organize poems. In Glück's poem, the first represents the analysis of the life-event into different regions (home and school), and the second represents the analysis of the life-event into successive temporal stages (here, from the child's point of view — leaving home, seeing the teacher behind the "great desk," divesting yourself of your new coat and leaving an effigy of yourself hanging on a nail, and being "instructed in silence" by the teacher). The last stanza of the poem, unlike all the rest (which are written in the present tense) is written in the future tense: the teachers "shall instruct" the children; the mothers "shall scour" the orchards. This is a prophetic future tense (otherwise the phrases would read "will instruct" and "will scour"). The future tense represents a prediction from the main present-tense account in the poem, but it is a logical conjecture from the very first words, "The children go forward."

The purpose of Glück's two main shapes, one of space and one of time, is to make the transition from home to school sinister. We imagine primary-school children walking to a school close by, but we learn (in the shape of the two regions) that the school is on "another shore." We imagine a cordial relation between home and school, but the temporal plot shows us an alienation between them ("another language") so that the mothers must try propitiation ("offerings") and then open conflict ("ammunition") to save the children. These two sinister shapes of widening space and future loss "act out," most of all, the mothers' sense that their children are far off, in the power of alien beings, in danger, and essentially without hope of rescue. This reinterpretation of the conventionally cheerful view of the first day of school forces us to rethink our previous notion: Is not the first day of school really more like Glück's idea of it than like the conventionally happy version? The artist's distrust of group "order" and "silence" lies behind this critique of early education.

The shape that E. E. Cummings puts on life is simpler. He separates the two sexes, and shows us what age they are by their games (marbles and piracies for the boys, hop-scotch and jump-rope for the girls). He makes the children same-sex conjoined twins, so to speak — eddieandbill and bettyandisbel. He troubles their same-sex play by an apparently insignificant figure of pleasure, a balloonman:

E. E. CUMMINGS (1894 – 1962)
in Just-

in Just-
spring   when the world is mud-
luscious the little
lame balloonman

whistles   far   and wee

and eddieandbill come
running from marbles and
piracies and it's
spring

when the world is puddle-wonderful

the queer
old balloonman whistles
far   and   wee
and bettyandisbel come dancing

from hop-scotch and jump-rope and

it's
spring
and
     the

          goat-footed

```
balloonMan        whistles
far
and
wee
```

The balloonman enters three times with his seductive whistle. We are left to imagine its ultimate sexual effect on the preadolescent children — but the effect is not in doubt because he draws the couples away from their same-sex childhood play, forecasting their regrouping into sexual couples. In the triple appearance of the balloonman, we find him characterized by different adjectives — "little lame," "queer old," and "goat-footed." He also acquires an honorific capital "M" in his last appearance, where we see the goat-feet which proclaim him a nature-spirit, even a god — therefore he is a balloonMan. (In ancient Greece the god of nature was the goat-footed Pan.) We call the phrase repeating the return of the balloonman a *refrain:*

> The little lame balloonman whistles far and wee
> The queer old balloonman whistles far and wee
> The goat-footed balloonMan whistles far and wee

We notice that other things in the poem also come round thrice:

> in Just- / spring   when the world is mud- / luscious
> it's / spring / when the world is puddle-wonderful
> it's / spring

We can now see that the "plot" of the poem is:

1. Spring, balloonman, boys together;
2. Spring, balloonman, girls together;
3. Spring, balloonMan, —— ?

When we ask ourselves: "What does Cummings imply about the completion of the poem? What is the missing plot element?" we answer: "girl with boy, boy with girl."

To his conjoined-twin trick, and his triple balloonman refrain, and his triple appearance of spring, and the "missing" sexual conclusion to his plot, Cummings adds yet another element of shape — his typographic arrangement of these things. The "horizontal" whistling — "whistles far   and wee" — looks as though it is happening within the space we move in. But the "vertical" whistle —

> whistles
>
> far
> and
> wee

makes it seem as though the balloonman is gradually, like a Pied Piper, receding in space, taking the newly sexual couples off with him. Typographically speaking, too, the important word "spring" always comes first in the lines in which it appears.

There is an odd stop, inserted at the line-break, between the adjectives characterizing the balloonman at first: "little — [Is he lame? Yes, maybe] / lame balloonman"; "queer — [Does he walk that way because he's old, not lame? Yes, maybe] / old balloonman." And then the puzzle is resolved: he's not lame; he's not old; he walks oddly because he is "goat-footed." And there's no more hesitation: he's a god — he's the balloonMan.

If we were talking about the life-moment Cummings has selected, we would say it is the spring of life — the moment when childhood ends, same-sex friendships break up, adolescents hear the alluring call of sexuality, and sexual couples first form. That is a summary of the poem, but it has not explained the shapes Cummings has invented to act out the life-moment. Only an examination of form — in Cummings, typographic as well as verbal form — shows us how the poem *enacts* (represents by several formal shapes) the moment it has chosen, and makes us see the *processes* of that moment, how it gradually unfolds in time, with both pathos and joy.

ROBERT HAYDEN (1913 – 1980)
Those Winter Sundays

Sundays too my father got up early
and put his clothes on in the blueblack cold,
then with cracked hands that ached
from labor in the weekday weather made
banked fires blaze. No one ever thanked him.

I'd wake and hear the cold splintering, breaking.
When the rooms were warm, he'd call,
and slowly I would rise and dress,
fearing the chronic angers of that house,

Speaking indifferently to him,
who had driven out the cold
and polished my good shoes as well.

What did I know, what did I know
of love's austere and lonely offices?

Hayden structures his poem in three stanzas: 5 lines, 4 lines, 5 lines. Not exactly equal, but close enough to make us look for a three-part structure of thought. Looking again, we see that the first stanza is about the father, the second stanza about the son, and the third stanza (in its first three lines) about the spoken interaction between father and son. There is a two-line coda, which at first we merely note.

What can we say about the way Hayden presents his father? The most important word in the first line is the unobtrusive "too": we have to say it as Hayden wants us to, as a contrastive to what we would expect, if we think of Sunday as a day of rest. "Sundays *too* my father got up early." We see from this that on every weekday the father had to get up early to go to work; Sunday is the one day he could have slept longer. The house is blue with cold, but since it is before dawn, Hayden says that the cold is "blueblack." Next we find out that the father is a menial laborer who works out of doors, whose skin is cracked from the winter weather, and whose hands ache from the week's exertions. As Hayden's recollections accumulate, he comes to the reason why his father roused himself each day in the dark: it was to put new coal in the furnace and make its heat rise up and "blaze." "Sundays too" means that the father's dawn rising on the weekdays is continued on Sunday. Over and over, week after week, Hayden's father did this.

After this narrative (told in the habitual past — the tense other languages call the imperfect, or continuing past), we have the first comment by the speaker: "No one ever thanked him." The "ever" matches "Sundays": Sunday after Sunday went by, with everyone in the house benefiting from the father's sacrifice in getting up in the pre-dawn darkness and warming the house while the others were sleeping. Not on any one of those Sundays did anyone — wife or child — ever say a word of appreciation. This is stated as a fact of late recognition; it was not until the son was an adult that he realized someone should have uttered a word of thanks. This comment makes us think: "Did I ever thank my mother for driving me to hockey practice at 5 a.m. day after day?" "Did I ever thank my father for taking a second job to pay my tuition?" Do children ever thank parents? Should they? The moral question of the poem is thus set: Was I an ungrateful son? And if so, why was I?

The second stanza "belongs" to the son. We notice a change in tense: this time the imperfect appears in its full form. "I [would] wake and hear . . . he [would] call . . . I would rise and dress." This formulation emphasizes the habitual nature of the interaction: on "those winter

Sundays," father and son would act out the same ritual: the son would stay in bed while the house was warming up; then, at his father's call, he would rise. Then a more sinister aspect of the habitual relation appears: at every rising, the son was "fearing the chronic angers of that house." Every word here counts. A permanent and daily sense of fear has been instilled in the son by the angers (presumably of the parents); like the child's fear, the angers are "chronic" — a word that implies a constantly recurring disease.

The third stanza (with its deliberate initial capital, in the middle of a sentence) shows us the result of the house's atmosphere of tension, its outbreaks of anger. The son has already distanced himself from his father's quarrels, simply waiting to get older and leave "that" house. He speaks "indifferently" to the hero who had "driven out the cold," made it splinter and break. But there is another side to the father, a gentler one: he has polished his son's shoes — the "good" shoes that he wears only on Sundays, to church — "as well." Nothing constrained the father to add this kindness; the son could have polished his own shoes. It is the "extra" measure in the testimony of the shoes that, in retrospect, breaks the son's heart. He does not need to say, "I never thanked him": we know that already.

With that — the polishing of the shoes — the narrative proper of the poem ends. The son makes his final comment on his relation to his father, matching the earlier one. Like the first comment — "No one ever thanked him" — the closing reflection is one of self-reproach, mitigated only by the son's youth at the time. Since then, he has realized what love is, and what sacrifices it makes. That they are done silently does not make them less acts of love. "What did I know, what did I know / of love's austere and lonely offices?" The two adjectives reveal more of the father's nature. He was lonely in the house where the only tones taken toward him were those of anger or indifference. And he was austere in the performance of love's "offices": he spoke no words of reproach, did not break his own taciturnity to utter words of love.

As we look back on the arrangement Hayden has given to his poem, we notice the clear division of stanzas already mentioned: father in past [comment]; son in past; father and son in past [comment]. But we also notice the continuous past voiced in two "pastnesses" — the simple past "concealing" the habitual nature implied by "too"; the evidently habitual past voiced in the successive uses of "would." These are followed by the pluperfect: the father "had driven out" the cold and "[had] polished my good shoes as well." When did he do this? While the house was warming up, when he could have been having breakfast. Instead of serving his own needs, we can imagine him seeing his son's scuffed shoes,

getting out shoe polish and a rag, applying the polish, and then, after letting it dry, buffing the shoes to a shine. Only then did he awaken his son.

One of the ways of making the story in a poem seem "real" is to
establish several panels of time. If we reconstruct the panels of time here,
this is how they look:

Conditions existing *before* the poem begins:

a. Working-class father, working at outside menial work six days a week

b. Angers in the house that explode frequently

c. Son living in habitual fear

Panels of time *in* the poem:

1. The father gets up early;

2. He gets the furnace going again, and puts in new coal;

3. He polishes his son's shoes;

4. Once the house is warm, he calls his son;

5. The son gets up slowly, afraid (as always) of anger in the house,
   speaking indifferently to his father, even while noting that his father
   had polished his shoes.

6. Adult son, recollecting "those winter Sundays" in "that house"
   (distancing himself by the pointing adjectives "those" and "that"),
   repents never having thanked his father, while letting us know that
   no one else in the house did either.

7. Adult son, in a second moment of self-reproach, sees his father's
   lonely and tacit way of expressing love.

Once we see these panels of time, the son's whole past with his father
is made explicit, and we become aware of how much Hayden has compressed into his fourteen lines. And once we see that there are fourteen
lines, we suspect that Hayden is writing a variation on the sonnet: 5-4-5
instead of 4-4-4-2 (Shakespeare). He keeps an echo of the Shakespearean
closing couplet by ending his poem with a two-line summary.

What is the music governing this poem? We notice first the pre-
eminence of hard *c* sounds: "Clothes, black, cold, cracked, ached,
banked, thanked." Then "cold, breaking, call, chronic." The repeated
harsh *c* is unmistakably an echo of the anger in the house, but when we
arrive at the last stanza, there is one last echo ("cold") and then the hard
sound disappears. The last line abandons the unforgiving *c*'s and sub-
sides into quiet *s*'s ("austere offices") and liquid *l*'s: ("love's . . . lonely
offices") — sounds reflecting the subsiding of the son's past hostility into
forgiveness and reconciliation with the dead father. Hayden also binds his

poem together by words that repeat the same sounds, as "thanked" echoes "banked," as "breaking" echoes "wake," as "fearing" and "speaking" echo "hear." He also binds the poem together through the predominance of emphatic downbeats ("SUN-days TOO my FAther GOT up EARly"), which continue throughout the poem until the subsidence into quiet iambs at the end: "of LOVE's ausTE-RE and LONEly OFfiCes."

Robert Hayden was black; would the poem be different if he had revealed that autobiographical information? Consider why he might have omitted it. (In the long run, as Hayden became well-known, the poem would bear that information implicitly; perhaps he thought that his biography would suffice to place the poem in a racial context as well as a working-class one.) Yet it is also a frequent strategy of lyric to de-specify its protagonist: we might know from certain poems that Yeats was old, but not that he was Irish; or that he was Irish, but not old. A lyric cannot bear the social information native to the novel; its compression leads it to the essential rather than the adventitious. In other poems, Hayden takes up explicitly the historical experience of American blacks; in short, he gives us the information necessary to each poem.

From the parents' house, the youth issues into the world, and into sexuality. We have said that Whitman's "Hours Continuing Long" is a poem of forsaken love; its first line tells us that its special subject is how *long* the hours seem to the one forsaken. How does the poem act out the length of the hours?

WALT WHITMAN (1819 – 1892)
Hours Continuing Long

Hours continuing long, sore and heavy hearted,
Hours of the dusk, when I withdraw to a lonesome and
    unfrequented spot, seating myself, leaning my face in my
    hands;
Hours sleepless, deep in the night, when I go forth, speeding
    swiftly the country roads, or through the city streets, or
    pacing miles and miles, stifling plaintive cries;
Hours discouraged, distracted — for the one I cannot content
    myself without, soon I saw him content himself without me;
Hours when I am forgotten (O weeks and months are passing, but
    I believe I am never to forget!)
Sullen and suffering hours! (I am ashamed — but it is useless — I
    am what I am);
Hours of my torment — I wonder if other men ever have the
    like, out of the like feelings?

Is there even one other like me — distracted — his friend, his
   lover, lost to him?
Is he too as I am now? Does he still rise in the morning, dejected,
      thinking who is lost to him? and at night, awaking, think
      who is lost?
Does he too harbor his friendship silent and endless? harbor his
      anguish and passion?
Does some stray reminder, or the casual mention of a name, bring
      the fit back upon him, taciturn and deprest?
Does he see himself reflected in me? In these hours, does he see
      the face of his hours reflected?

Certainly the successive long weary lines beginning with the word
"Hours" — there are six of these, five in a row, then an interruption
("Sullen and suffering hours!"), then another one — act out the theme
of the poem. We will have to account for the interruption, but for the
moment we can say that the first seven lines of the poem make us see and
feel, by a series of statements exhaustedly resembling one another, the
inertia of the weary hours.

Then the poem makes its major change of shape, turning from one
grammatical form (*statements*) to a different one (*questions*). We see now
that it is basically a *two-part* poem, the parts distinguished by this central
grammatical turn. Do the two parts differ in anything besides grammatical form? Part I is solely about the speaker; but Part II wonders whether
there are "other men" like the speaker, or even "one other like me."

Before the poem began, there was of course "one other like" the
speaker — his lover. The speaker was one of two; now he is alone; he would
like to be one of two again. The usual hope might be to find another lover,
but that is a path that this poem does not, cannot, take, since the speaker is
still too much in love to imagine finding a new lover. No — the speaker
will imagine that there is another person as dejected as he is himself, a
brother in suffering, who will be his twin in endurance. This is a replace-
ment strategy: the lost lover is "replaced" by the imagined twin-in-grief.

What causes this evolution in the poem? Can we explain what motivates the transition from solitary grief to the imagining of a fellow sufferer?
It may come from a wish to replace the lost lover; but the poem suggests another motivation, too. Let us look at the two-line central turning-point of
the poem, beginning with the line that does not open with "Hours" and
continuing into the line where statements turn to questions:

Sullen and suffering hours! (I am ashamed — but it is useless — I
   am what I am);

> Hours of my torment — I wonder if other men ever have the
>   like, out of the like feelings?

We can see that the first movement out of the self toward society is one of unexplained shame: "If others could see me, they would rebuke me; and yes, I am ashamed — but it is useless — I am what I am." We do not know, and will never know, whether the poet is ashamed of his homosexuality (he later suppressed this poem from his collection *Leaves of Grass*) or of his sullen dejection (Whitman strongly wished to appear a positive poet of democratic strength). Eventually the poet surmises that some group of men might not recoil from him, because they themselves have had similar feelings. At least there may be one such man — and the poem then does a reprise in the third person ("Does he too harbor his friendship silent and endless?") of what the speaker had previously said of himself in the first person ("I withdraw to a lonesome and unfrequented spot," etc.).

This shape — doing something once, then doing it again differently — is one we have already seen in Cummings's poem, where we saw spring come three times and heard the balloonman whistle three times. Here, love is expressed in the first person, via statements, and then in the third person, via questions; this shape tells us that what seemed at first shamefully personal may perhaps be shared by others, perhaps by everyone. It is like hearing a melody twice, the first time in the major key, the second time in the minor. Art thrives on such variations.

Stevens's poem consists of five quatrains. Although the lines are somewhat irregular in length, they keep returning to a pentameter base. The orderliness of the poem — the fact that its stanzas are all of the same length, and that its lines keep reverting to the pentameter norm — suggests that this is not a wayward or willful poem, but rather a sober and steadfast one.

WALLACE STEVENS (1879 – 1955)
The Plain Sense of Things

After the leaves have fallen, we return
To a plain sense of things. It is as if
We had come to an end of the imagination,
Inanimate in an inert savoir.

It is difficult even to choose the adjective
For this blank cold, this sadness without cause.
The great structure has become a minor house.
No turban walks across the lessened floors.

The greenhouse never so badly needed paint.
The chimney is fifty years old and slants to one side.
A fantastic effort has failed, a repetition
In a repetitiousness of men and flies.

Yet the absence of the imagination had
Itself to be imagined. The great pond,
The plain sense of it, without reflections, leaves,
Mud, water like dirty glass, expressing silence

Of a sort, silence of a rat come out to see,
The great pond and its waste of the lilies, all this
Had to be imagined as an inevitable knowledge,
Required, as a necessity requires.

As we scan the poem for pattern, we notice that its language is sometimes abstract and at other times concrete. We might try writing out the poem again, in two columns, one for the speaker's generalizing statements and the other for his specific examples.

The Plain Sense of Things

Abstract	**Concrete**
	After the leaves have fallen, we return / To
a plain sense of things. It is as if /	
We had come to an end of the imagination, /	
Inanimate in an inert savoir. /	
It is difficult even to choose the adjective /	For this blank cold,
this sadness without cause. /	
	The great structure has become a minor house. /
	No turban walks across the lessened floors. /
	The greenhouse never so badly needed paint. /
	The chimney is fifty years old and slants to one side. /

A fantastic effort has failed, a
    repetition /
In a repetitiousness of men
    and flies. /
Yet the absence of the
    imagination
had / Itself to be imagined.
The plain sense of it,
    without reflections,

silence / Of a sort,
silence

Had to be imagined
    as an inevitable
    knowledge, /
Required, as a necessity
    requires.

The great pond, /

leaves, / Mud, water like
    dirty glass, expressing

of a rat come out to see, /
The great pond and its waste
    of the lilies, all this /

It is clear that the back-and-forth pattern between concrete visualization and abstract contemplation in "The Plain Sense of Things" mimics the way that a reflective mind tends to see a concrete piece of evidence and then to express it in intellectual ways. In analyzing such a poem, it's often useful first to re-create the visual side (and only later to consider the thoughts paralleling it). Here, reading down the right-hand column, we see that it is late autumn (the leaves have all fallen) and that it is cold. We are in the presence of what was once, in the past, a "great structure," but which has now declined to "a minor house." It is uninhabited (though once, the speaker knows, an exotic turban-wearing person inhabited it), and the floors, deprived of that former presence, seem "lessened." There is a greenhouse (the mark of a rich estate), but it is badly weathered and cries out for paint. The chimney of the house (once warmed by its inner fire) is now a half-century old, so old that it has lost its true uprightness and slants forlornly to one side. The great pond (another mark of a rich estate), which, in spring and summer, was filled with beautiful reflections, now has a surface "like dirty glass," obscured by mud and fallen leaves. Because nothing "looks back at" the speaker from the surface of the great pond, he feels a silence of a sort: the visible world is not returning his gaze, is not speaking to him.

It is at this point that we are startled. Into this inanimate scene of decline, there intrudes a bright-eyed animate presence: that of "a rat come out to see." Something in the world *is* gazing back at the speaker; someone, like him, is inspecting the scene. But the rat is not reflecting on the past grandeur of the surroundings. It has just come out to see what there is to see now, today.

The speaker reverts to the scene, taking his last look — remarking with sadness the "waste of the lilies" of the great pond, all of them now dead. Still, he has perceived, in his companion the rat, another manner of looking: merely, without mournful nostalgia, to "come out to see."

What thoughts, then, have been prompted by the sight of the great estate in decline? If we look down the left-hand column, we see that the formulation of the title — the plain sense of things (implying certainty) — has been lessened in stanza 1 to a plain sense of things — a sense that hasn't yet become specific. We suspect from the title that the specificity is to come — and, sure enough, it does arrive, in the the of stanza 4 — "the plain sense of it." We notice that this progression in certainty has a parallel: whereas in the first stanza the speaker (speaking in the plural of human generalization) says that we have come to an end of the imagination, in the fourth stanza, he speaks of the absence of the imagination. Something, then, happens between the opening of the poem and stanza 4, by which the speaker has come from a and an to the and the. By stanza 4 the speaker has come to new and specific forms of knowledge: he knows what the plain sense of things is, and he knows what the absence of the imagination is.

How do the other thoughts of the speaker connect with this most basic one? To find yourself "in-animate in an in-ert savoir" is to be next to dead ("inanimate" means without *anima*, Latin for "spirit"; and "inert" means without *ars*, Latin for "art"). The inability of language to move off the rails of repeated sound suggests, here, the stultifying absence of new stimuli: "an end of the im-ag-in-ation, / In-an-im-ate in an in-ert savoir." The proof of the inertness of the imagination is its inability to offer up any adjectives except the uncommunicative "blank" and "without cause," signs of absence lacking positive specificity.

The next abstract summing-up emphasizes the speaker's strenuous earlier strivings after hope and achievement: they were "a fantastic effort," but one that is now seen to be a failure — carrying out the repeated human pattern of mortality and bodily corruption. (Flies are the accompaniment of corpses in literature as in life.)

It is at this point in our inventory of the column of abstract thoughts that the grieving sighs of the poem come to a surprising halt. The speaker pulls himself up by his bootstraps both with his resolved

"Yet" and with his verb of necessity — "<u>had</u> to be imagined," twice stated (in stanzas 4 and 5). The second time the verb appears, it has a complement: "Had to be imagined as an inevitable knowledge." We see that the speaker's earlier words of deadness — "inanimate," "inert" — have now been transmuted into a word of necessity — "inevitable" — that which cannot be escaped (from Latin, *evitare,* "to shun").

The first shape that we have noticed, then, is this oscillatory one of the mind moving from spectacle (the ruined estate) to thought (summing-up), back to spectacle again, and so on. A second shape that we have seen is that of sadness countered by resolve ("And yet"). If that second shape had been perfectly observed, no sadness would have occurred after the moment of resolve: the graph of the poem would show a grieving slide down, and then a recovery to a resolute steady-state of stoic fortitude. But that is not what we see. Stevens allows three further moments of sadness after the brave resolve: these are enunciated in three phrases. "Without reflections" recalls the time when the pond allowed images of the world; "water like dirty glass" recalls, by its contrastive adjective, when the water was like clear glass; and "the great pond and its waste of the lilies" recalls, by its noun of decline, the earlier time when the lilies were in bloom. Stevens allows us to see, here, the believable momentary "backsliding" of a mind into sadness even after it has resolved to grieve no longer; and yet he also shows us how that mind pulls itself up again with its reiterated "had to be imagined." We might call this shape that of argument and counterargument: sadness against resolve, resolve against sadness.

A third shape (besides the oscillatory one between thought and spectacle and the "backsliding" one of argument between resolve and grief) is one of persistent repetition. In part, we are alerted to the presence of this shape by the almost instant repetition of the title (with a slight variation) in line 2: just after hearing "The Plain Sense of Things" we hear "a plain sense of things." Repetition is always the sign of the mind scrutinizing what it has just said and either confirming or changing its phrasing as it judges it. A list of the moments of semantic repetition would go as follows:

The Plain Sense of Things
a plain sense of things
the plain sense of it

this blank cold
this sadness without cause

the great structure
the great pond
the great pond and its waste of the lilies

a repetition
in a repetitiousness of men and flies

an end of the imagination
the absence of the imagination

had itself to be imagined
had to be imagined

after the leaves have fallen
leaves

silence of a sort
silence of a rat come out to see

required
as a necessity requires

Anyone reading the poem aloud will recognize that this patterning of insistent semantic repetition (remarkable in a short poem) is backed by persistent phonetic repetition (which we have already seen in "inanimate in an inert savoir" and which often reappears, for example, in the *f*'s of "a fantastic effort has failed"). Depending on one's view of the poem, one could find various explanations of this "repetition-shape": among other functions, it certainly reinforces the idea that what has happened — the decline of the estate, the aging of the speaker, the failure of the speaker's hopes — is "a repetition in a repetitiousness." We would not believe that statement had not some pattern in the poem borne it out.

We can see another repetition-shape, this time syntactic, in the instancing of specific details of decline. These are all presented in short declarative sentences: the structure, the turban, the greenhouse, the chimney. Each sentence has the same basic shape: subject-predicate (although Stevens is careful to allow for some variation). And each sentence is of the same length — one end-stopped line:

The great structure has become a minor house.
No turban walks across the lessened floors.

The greenhouse never so badly needed paint.
The chimney is fifty years old and slants to one side.

The detail that escapes this one-line declarative shape is the pond. We could have had a sentence, comparable to the others, that said, "The great pond is obscured with leaves and mud." However, the treatment of the great pond "breaks the shape" into which the other elements were ostentatiously and repetitively fitted. The pond is more complex than a greenhouse that needs paint or a chimney that slants. When the speaker turns his gaze to the pond, a spate of descriptive phrases, of a very mixed sort, pours from his lips:

the great pond,

the plain sense of it,

without reflections,

leaves,

mud,

water like dirty glass,

expressing silence (of a sort)

silence (of a rat come out to see)

the great pond and its waste of the lilies — all this . . .

Depending on your view of the entire poem, you might find many different things to say about this passage. The former inarguable inventory of decay, absence, effacement, and decline — "structure . . . turban . . . greenhouse . . . chimney" — and the summing-up of that inventory in the absolute certainty of "a fantastic effort has failed" — differ in tone and mood from the passage on the pond, which is both more heart-stricken and more "confused," as it mixes the abstract and the concrete, sight with hearing, the inanimate with the animate, the nonrepetitive with the repetitive, all turning on the pun on the word "reflections" — which means both "thoughts" and "images."

We now perceive that the rigid shapes that we have so far come across — discursive oscillation between abstract and concrete; emotional argument (sadness) versus counterargument (resolve); and repetitiveness on the semantic, syntactic, and phonetic planes — exist only to be broken in the climactic ingathering of the pond. The speaker is acquiring his new way of seeing — seeing as the rat sees. He "backslides" in saying that the pond is "without reflections" and "like dirty glass" and that it displays "its waste of the lilies," but he mixes with this nostalgia the "plain sense" of the pond: leaves; mud; silence. His "confusion" is shown by his desertion of his earlier formula — doling out one end-stopped line to each detail — for his inventory of decay. Now sentiment overspills the line-ends and mixes up categories:

> The great pond,
> The plain sense of it, without reflections, leaves,
> Mud, water like dirty glass, expressing silence
>
> Of a sort, silence of a rat come out to see,
> The great pond and its waste of the lilies, all this . . .

The "orderly" proportion of sentiment to line returns at the end of the poem in "Required, as a necessity requires" — but even this is not a syntactically complete sentence in itself, as the inventory lines about the greenhouse and the chimney are.

Another shape comes into view when we see how the complex passage on the pond is bracketed, firmly, between the two appearances of "had to be imagined":

> Yet the absence of the imagination
> had / Itself to be imagined.
> The great pond . . .
> The great pond . . .
> Had to be imagined.

This is the shape of imprisonment. There is no way to keep the pond purely in nostalgia; necessity grips it in its talons. Necessity "requires": the word comes from the Latin *re* + *quaerere*, "to ask again." "Required, as a necessity requires": Stevens has his poem act out the "again" of the Latin prefix *re*.

Finally, we might notice one more fleeting semantic shape of the poem — the substitution of the word "knowledge" in stanza 5 for the word "savoir" in stanza 1. "Savoir" (French: "to know how") has come into English in the phrase "savoir-faire," which means "to know how to manage in a social situation." An "inert savoir" tells us that the speaker's practical knowledge has lapsed into a paralysis, an inertia, approaching the condition of death ("inanimate"). By the end of the poem, the speaker has been resurrected from his collapse; by resolving to open his imagination to what the absence of the imagination might mean in his life, he has acquired a new "inevitable" knowledge, proper to, and necessary in, old age. By opening his eyes to death, he can see not only decline from his former estate (literal and metaphorical) but the nature of his present state. He realizes that this, however painful, is an improvement over denial. He also sees the comedy in inventing an inquisitive rat as his mentor in a better, more objective, seeing.

The presence of several patterns operating within one poem is what gives us the sense of complexity that we feel in reading "The Plain Sense of Things." We feel the rigidity of the aging mind making its sad inventory and deducing its conclusive thoughts; we also feel the emotional fortitude in the pattern that counters nostalgia with resolve; we feel the exertion of the will as the mind strives to find the slight (but crucial) difference between "a" plain sense (general) and "the" plain sense (particular) of its condition; we feel the further exertion of the stoic mind in deciding that it will offer its "Yet": "Yet the absence of the imagination had / Itself to be imagined." And we sense the cascade of feeling generating the waterfall of phrases about the "great pond" — a symbol of that youthful mind that once was full of image–reflections, that believed it could mirror the world in art, that had confidence in the erotic beauty of its lilies. Finally, we feel not only the iron brackets of necessity surrounding the new view of the pond but also the poet's sense that necessity will ask of him, again and again as he ages, that he revise his sense of the world. It will also force him to take on the posture, not of a mourner, but of a curious spectator, imitating his companion the rat.

You can absorb a good deal of Stevens's feelings about the bleakness and fortitude of age just by reading "The Plain Sense of Things" and by being emotionally receptive to its statements and its symbols. But if you are curious about how Stevens makes the poem "work," and why the poem is memorable, you will have to seek out its patterns and inquire how they act on your own imagination to render vivid the complex feelings encoded in the poem.

The Public Life

As we turn from the private to the public life, we come to this very brief poem by Michael S. Harper — which nonetheless has the comprehensive title "American History." It consists of two parts. The first is a personal statement ("Those . . . girls . . . remind me of five hundred . . . blacks"), and the second is the sardonic quip following it, spoken by someone who seems to be giving us a knowing wink: "Can't find what you can't see / can you?"

MICHAEL S. HARPER (b. 1938)

American History

For John Callahan [handwritten: close friend of Ralph Ellison (Invisible Man)]

Those four black girls blown up
in that Alabama church
remind me of five hundred
middle passage blacks,
in a net, under water
in Charleston harbor
so *redcoats* wouldn't find them.
Can't find what you can't see [handwritten: line break, increases intensity]
can you? [handwritten: very hopeless, Mr Punch]

[handwritten in left margin: rhyme caused outrage]

The "invisibility" of blacks in American culture has been a persistent theme of black authors; Ralph Ellison called his famous autobiographical novel *Invisible Man*. A few blacks more or less, in racist contexts, would scarcely be noticed. The furor caused by the death of four young black girls when a bomb exploded in a black church was one of the signs of the rising civil rights movement; yet those who placed the bomb didn't care how many blacks they killed. Harper's anecdote of American ship-captains drowning slaves so they would not be stolen, as items of value, by British troops suggests the perennial "invisibility" of blacks throughout American history, from the very beginning. The wry quip at the end of the poem makes even more horrible the "success" of hiding — by murder — the valuable slaves to keep them from the redcoats.

By calling his poem "American History" Harper suggests that the episodes he recounts represent, better than textbooks bearing that name, the real narrative of American events. The real American history remains to be written, the poem implies. So we must see, between these two markers — the invisibility of drowned blacks in the Revolution, the invisibility of bombed blacks in the twentieth century — a whole silent procession of comparable incidents, decade by decade, from the seventeenth century till today. In this way, by evoking the shape "normally" belonging to the title "American History" (a long textbook full of patriotic self-glorification), Harper makes us see his little shape as one that could be extended into a very big one.

We come to another marginalized group in public life, Charles Simic's aged poor:

CHARLES SIMIC (b. 1938)

Old Couple

They're waiting to be murdered,
Or evicted. Soon   ,
They expect to have nothing to eat.
As far as I know, they never go out.

A vicious pain's coming, they think.
It will start in the head
And spread down to the bowels.
They'll be carried off on stretchers, howling.

In the meantime, they watch the street
From their fifth floor window.
It has rained, and now it looks
Like it's going to snow a little.

I see him get up to lower the shades.
If their window stays dark,
I know that his hand has reached hers
Just as she was about to turn on the lights.

If we quickly sum up the subject of each of the four stanzas of Simic's
"Old Couple," we might come up with something like this:

1. Three possible futures for the old couple — murdered, evicted,
   starved;
2. Another possible future — terminal illness;
3. The present interim before one of these horrors happens;
4. The suppositions of the speaker watching them.

A quick summary of this sort at least shows that the horrors die
down, by stanza 3, to the brief and fragile peace of the interim moment
at the end; this decline in horror is one overall shape of the poem. But it
leaves out the presence of the person watching the old couple. It is this
person who speaks the poem, and we identify him, since this is not a dramatic monologue, with the author of the poem. He knows, in stanza 1,
what the old people are thinking. He comments on their behavior ("As
far as I know, they never go out"). He watches them compulsively ("I see
him get up to lower the shades"). He even invents what they do when he
cannot observe them ("I know that his hand has reached hers").

If the shape of the old people's lives is a downhill dread of contin-ual terror, what is the shape of the watcher's life? The poet asks us to imagine the passing days of a watcher in a nearby building. At some point in the past, he noticed the old couple across the way; perhaps at that point they were still going out for walks or to the store. That seems to have stopped. But when they were still visible in the neighborhood, the watcher noted their mutual devotion, which causes him now to imagine the old man reaching for his wife's hand. The watcher is so conscious of the few things the old couple can look at that he has reduced his own consciousness to the tenuousness of theirs: "It has rained, and now it looks / Like it's going to snow a little" — an observation of no real im-portance, except to people who have nothing else but the weather to observe (but it also suggests worsening weather, one more threat). The old couple have become so real to the watcher that he has absorbed their terrors into his own mind. He knows that one of these days he will either see them taken out on stretchers, howling in pain, or see their pos-sessions on the sidewalk as they are evicted with no place to go, or he will hear that they have been murdered, or that someone has found them dead of malnutrition in their apartment. There are simply no other pos-sible futures to imagine for them; the watcher knows this.

As soon as we see the watcher/speaker as the principal conscious-ness in the poem, we read the work as a protest-poem against the condi-tions of modern urban life. The neglect by society of its most helpless members means that anyone in a modern city becomes necessarily a watcher of cases like this. Nobody can be free of horror and guilt, as the probable future seeps from the victims to their neighbors.

The two interlocking shapes — the heading-for-disaster life-shape of the old couple, the ongoing and speculative life-shape of the watcher — make up the figure of the poem. Spatially, we are given two rooms — the implied room of the watcher, the room of the old couple across the street; temporally, we are presented with the several envisaged plots of the old couple meeting their end, each plot as terrifying as the other. The plots exhaust all possibilities. The old couple have no one to rescue them — they will end in a public hospital ward for the indigent, in a shelter for the homeless, out on the street after being evicted, in the morgue after being murdered, or in their bed, starved.

Many poems have two or more interlocking shapes. We have seen such shapes in "Infant Sorrow" (the baby as mind and body; the baby as dependent on parents; the baby as part human, part supernatural; the baby as a doing creature and a feeling creature), and again in "Old Couple" (the successive shapes of the couple's envisaged horrifying futures; the watcher's steady-state speculative shape). When several overlapping and interlocking shapes are present at once in a poem, it becomes potentially more interesting — because it is more complex, as life is — than poems that have only one shape. The ideal poem would have a temporal shape, a spatial shape, a rhythmic shape, a phonetic shape, a grammatical shape, a syntactic shape, and so on — each one beautifully worked out, each one graphically presenting in formal terms an aspect of the emotional and intellectual import of the poem. One way we distinguish more accomplished poems from less accomplished ones is the control of the artist over a number of shapes at once. Other things being equal, the more shapes that are being evoked, the more pleasure one derives from the poem because more of its inner life has been thought through, analyzed, and made visible in form by its creator.

The manuscript drafts of Robert Lowell's "Skunk Hour" show that it originally began in the way that a traditional lyric might — "One dark night," etc. The present stanza 5 was the beginning of the poem:

ROBERT LOWELL (1917 – 1977)
Skunk Hour

For Elizabeth Bishop

Nautilus Island's hermit
heiress still lives through winter in her Spartan cottage;
her sheep still graze above the sea.
Her son's a bishop. Her farmer
is first selectman in our village;
she's in her dotage.

Thirsting for
the hierarchic privacy
of Queen Victoria's century,
she buys up all
the eyesores facing her shore,
and lets them fall.

The season's ill —
we've lost our summer millionaire,
who seemed to leap from an L. L. Bean
catalogue. His nine-knot yawl
was auctioned off to lobstermen.
A red fox stain covers Blue Hill.

And now our fairy
decorator brightens his shop for fall;
his fishnet's filled with orange cork,

[handwritten: confessional poet]

orange, his cobbler's bench and awl;
there is no money in his work,
he'd rather marry.

One dark night,
my Tudor Ford climbed the hill's skull;
I watched for love-cars. Lights turned down,
they lay together, hull to hull,
where the graveyard shelves on the town. . . .
My mind's not right. *[handwritten: Internal conflict]*

A car radio bleats,
"Love, O careless Love. . . ." I hear
my ill-spirit sob in each blood cell, *[handwritten: violent, emotionally volatile]*
as if my hand were at its throat. . . .
I myself am hell; *[handwritten: ill-spirit's throat — suicidal]*
nobody's here —

only skunks, that search
in the moonlight for a bite to eat.
They march on their soles up Main Street;
white stripes, moonstruck eyes' red fire
under the chalk-dry and spar spire *[handwritten: Finds some compulsory]*
of the Trinitarian Church.

I stand on top
of our back steps and breathe the rich air —
[handwritten: is that a] a mother skunk with her column of kittens swills the garbage pail.
[handwritten: poet] She jabs her wedge-head in a cup
of sour cream, drops her ostrich tail,
and will not scare.

Lowell brackets his "lyric center" — stanzas 5 and 6 — with a set of "characters" fore and a set of animals aft. This three-part shape is instantly visible:

1. Grotesque inhabitants of my Maine town;
2. Myself;
3. A mother skunk and her kittens taking over the town.

Each of the three parts has an inner shape of its own. In the first part, the native "hermit heiress" owns two stanzas, while the lesser summer millionaire and "fairy decorator," transients both, own only one stanza each. (The manuscript suggests that all of these are figures for the poet himself. Whereas the final version says "There is no money in his work, / he'd rather marry" about the "fairy decorator," in the draft the poet says this about himself: "There is no money in this work, / I'd rather marry.") Lowell inherited his house in Castine, Maine, from his aunt who lived there, but he only went there summers, like the "summer millionaire." No longer living in one of the roles proper to his Brahmin lineage — hermit, or bishop, or landowner — the speaker has declined into the unvirile role of an artist, comparable to that of the man whom the town contemptuously terms the "fairy decorator."

After presenting these disguised figures for himself in the first part of the poem, the speaker shows us himself in the second part as a voyeur, aware of his own madness as he spies on lovers in cars. The gradually intensifying shape of this middle part is one of mortified self-watching: "My Tudor Ford climbed the hill's skull," not "I drove up the hill." And it is one of psychological self-judging: "My mind's not right." And it is one of medical self-diagnosis: "I hear / my ill-spirit sob in each blood cell." Finally, it is one of ethical self-damnation: "I myself am hell." After the disengaged tone of detached social commentary that dominates the first part of the poem, describing Castine, these damning first-person sentences chill the blood.

Then come the skunks. Nature takes over from the decadent culture of Castine. The skunks invade the town. The mother is the general; her offspring are her military "column." We are watching the barbarians (disciplined, vital, fiery-eyed) take over Rome (declining, degenerate, chalk-dry). The vivid verbs used of the skunks energize the exhaustions and distresses of the poem: the skunks *search,* and *march;* the mother skunk *swills* the garbage pail, *jabs* her head into the cup, *drops* her tail, *will not* scare. The speaker is (almost) glad to resign his inherited world to the skunks; certainly he is in no shape to govern it, or even to live in it, any more. It is a poem of total abdication from rule by the originally ruling, now depleted, Brahmin class. It was Lowell's revenge on his own heritage, which he always regarded with mixed admiration and contempt. And it shows his heritage gradually disappearing back into nature, as all cultures eventually do.

Nature and Time

Almost the whole appeal of the little medieval spring song we saw as our first example of nature poetry comes from its rhythm. Here I have marked the "silent *e's*," which were pronounced ("uh") in the Middle Ages, so that the original rhythm can be heard:

ANONYMOUS
The Cuckoo Song

Sumer is icumen in,
        Lhudè sing, cuccu!
Groweth sed and bloweth med
        And springth the wudè nu.
            Sing, cuccu!

Awè bleteth after lomb,
        Lhouth after calvè cu,
Bulluc sterteth, buckè verteth —
        Murie sing, cuccu!
            Cuccu, cuccu.
        Wel singès thu, cuccu.
        Ne swik thu never nu!

At first, as we expect in a simple ballad quatrain (a four-line stanza with alternating four-beat and three-beat lines), a four-beat line ("SUmer IS iCUMen IN") is here followed by a three-beat line ("LHUde SING, cuCU!") and another four-beat line is followed by a three-beat line, all of them about the renewing of vegetation. But to our surprise an unexpected three-beat echo-line is added as a fifth line — "Sing, cuccu!"

Then the poem starts up again. Naturally, we expect another 4 / 3 / 4 / 3 pattern, and we find it, yet this second quatrain is not about vegetation but about the renewing of animal life (ewe and lamb, cow and calf, bullock and buck). We might even expect another echo-line, and we receive it — "Cuccu, cuccu." But this is followed by another surprise — two more three-beat lines, a little congratulation to the harbinger of spring: "Wel singes thu, cuccu. / Ne swik thu never nu!" The lilt of the whole makes us recognize it as a song, even though we find it in printed form.

Besides its rhythmic shape, then, this little two-stanza poem has exhibited a logical shape, separating the vegetative springing of seed and meadow and wood (stanza 1) from the animal springing of bullocks (stanza 2), and it has also made a pleasing alternation between description ("Sumer is icumen in") and direct address ("Sing, cuccu!"). It has even displayed another shape: in both stanzas some verbs precede their nouns ("Groweth sed," "Lhouth after calve cu") and some do not ("Sumer is icumen in," "Bulluc sterteth"). These changes make for unpredictability, and therefore pleasure, since we derive pleasure in poems, just as in life, not only from pattern but from the interruption of pattern. If everything were unpredictable we would have chaos, but what we usually find in a good poem is the unpredictable within an overarching purposiveness.

Dave Smith's poem on spring uses one of the oldest European lyric forms, that of the sonnet. Smith's sonnet is a hybrid one, with a Shakespearean rhyming *ababcdcd* octave and a Petrarchan sestet, *efefee*:

DAVE SMITH (b. 1942)
The Spring Poem

> [Every poet should write a Spring poem.]
> — LOUISE GLÜCK

Yes, but we must be sure of verities A
such as proper heat and adequate form. B
That's what poets are for, is my theory. A
This then is a Spring poem. A car warms B
its rusting hulk in a meadow; weeds slog C
up its flanks in martial weather [April D
or late March is our month.] There is a fog C
of spunky mildew and sweaty tufts spill D
from the damp rump of a back seat. A spring E
thrusts one gleaming tip out, a brilliant tooth F
uncoiling from Winter's tension, a ring E
of insects along, working out the Truth. F
Each year this car, melting around that spring, G
hears nails trench from boards and every squeak sing. G

Although Smith, in homage to Shakespeare's spring sonnets ("From you have I been absent in the spring," etc.), has given his spring sonnet a Shakespearean octave, he has not divided his sonnet neatly, in terms of thought-units, into three quatrains and a couplet, as Shakespeare usually did. Instead, Smith's poem begins as a reply to the remark by Louise Glück, couching its reply in stern theoretical language about proper and adequate verities. It then announces its own existence: "This then is a Spring poem."

The rest of the poem is description: an actual present-tense description of the rusting car, followed (in the closing couplet) by a habitual-present-tense description of what happens "each year," reassuring us that the previous present-tense process has happened before and happens, in fact, every year. But there is one odd moment in the description of weeds, fog, mildew, tufts, back-seat spring, nails, and boards. It is the phrase about the insects who gather on the metal spring: they are "working out the Truth." The word "truth" is the Anglo-Saxon form of the Latinate word "verity" (used earlier in line 1 in the plural, "verities"), so we know that the insects are experiencing "proper heat and adequate form" and are stand-ins for the poet seeking his verities. As the metal tooth of the spring uncoils, so the weeds and the rest of nature are uncoiling from winter tension, and the poet has to follow along that uncoiling motion, tracing the path of truth as the insects trace the new path afforded them by the newly sprung spring.

From the end of line 4 through line 12, each line spills over into the next one as the scene uncoils before us. Nothing is end-stopped, everything is growing and expanding. (Poems usually indicate a pause at the end of a line either by a break in thought or by the use of a comma, a period, or some other mark of punctuation; when lines "run over," we are to infer an ongoing rush of thought or feeling.) The last two lines of Smith's poem, though, because they tell us what happens "every year" instead of what is happening "now," are a neat couplet; they represent not discovery but summary. Smith has given us first the theory of the spring poem, then the spring poem in action, and finally the spring poem in habitual summary, showing us his three responses to Glück's demand — "I know the theory, I know the thing itself, and I know it happens every year." He also shows us that he is aware Shakespeare did it first, while refusing, as a Modernist, to follow the Renaissance neatness of the four Shakespearean separate thought-units, one for each quatrain, one for the couplet.

Keats's sonnet on the human seasons is written in imitation of Shakespeare, meaning that it has four quatrains and a couplet. Spring happens in quatrain 1, summer in 2, autumn in 3, and winter in the couplet; we can see Keats's orderly arrangement at work. Since not only this procession of the four seasons but also its analogy to human life (from spring-youth to winter-old age) are all predictable once the subject is decided upon, how will Keats make his (known in advance) process aesthetically interesting?

JOHN KEATS (1795 – 1821)
The Human Seasons

Four seasons fill the measure of the year;
    Four seasons are there in the mind of man.
He hath his lusty spring, when fancy clear
    Takes in all beauty with an easy span:
He hath his summer, when luxuriously
    He chews the honied cud of fair spring thoughts,

Till, in his soul dissolv'd, they come to be
    Part of himself. He hath his autumn ports
And havens of repose, when his tired wings
    Are folded up, and he content to look
On mists in idleness: to let fair things
    Pass by unheeded as a threshold brook.
He hath his winter too of pale misfeature,
Or else he would forego his mortal nature.

First of all, Keats doesn't speak of the seasons of the human *body* — doesn't say, "Man has his spring of youth, his summer of maturity, his autumn of decline, and his winter of death." That cliché was too well known. He decides to put the seasons inside man's *mind*. Does the mind, like the body, have seasons? And if so, what are they like (since the mind, in the ordinary sense, does not grow old)? Briefly put, what Keats says is that in youth the mind finds an easy pleasure in spanning the whole world, absorbing everything beautiful. In mental summer, man reconsiders the "fair . . . thoughts" of his spring, redigesting them till they dissolve in his soul and become totally internalized, part of himself. During his mental autumn, he rests, folds his wings, and doesn't try to see everything — he is "content to look / On mists in idleness." At this stage, he allows fair things to "pass by unheeded," as a cottager might fail to notice the brook that flows by beyond his threshold. What does the man look on in winter? Not "all beauty," not "fair things," not even "mists" — rather, he looks on "pale misfeature." Why must he look on the diseased and the deformed? Because otherwise, he would "forego his mortal nature." He would forget that he too must grow pale and die, if he looked only on the beautiful or the misty.

This is a brief summary of a complex poem, but it is enough to show the rapid progress of the Keatsian seasonal sketches — the winged fancy of spring, the cud chewing of summer during the pondering of beauty in the soul, the ports and havens for man's autumn migration, the folding of his tired wings among the mists of uncertainty, the threshold brook passing by unheeded outside the house of (as Keats called himself) the "spiritual cottager." Keats's poems often lead us along by a succession of such descriptions. Without the unexpectedness of all these lightly drawn images, the procession of the seasons might be too predictable. And Keats lets each of the first three seasons slip into the next almost imperceptibly, imitating the way of nature. Only winter is unmistakably set apart in the couplet, as misfeature replaces feature.

In Chapter 1, we looked at Shakespeare's three models of life in Sonnet 60: the steady-state model of successive waves in which each moment of life resembles its predecessor and its successor; the rise-and-eclipse-of-the-sun model that sketches a catastrophic view of life; and the third, worst, model, in which we do not even have time to grow before we are scythed down. This structure in itself would have seemed sufficient to many poets. In fact, it would have seemed too much. Often, poems offer only one model of whatever they are discussing. But Shakespeare found it irresistible, very often, to let each of his quatrains set up a model *different* from those set up by the others. The intellectual tension thereby generated — "Is life a steady-state procession? Or a single long climb and fall? Or nothing but successive and premature annihilations?" — involves the reader strongly in the progress of the poem:

WILLIAM SHAKESPEARE (1564 – 1616)
Sonnet 60

Like as the waves make toward the pebbled shore,
So do our minutes hasten to their end,
Each changing place with that which goes before,
In sequent toil all forwards do contend.
Nativity, once in the main of light,
Crawls to maturity, wherewith being crowned,
Crooked eclipses 'gainst his glory fight,
And Time that gave doth now his gift confound.
Time doth transfix the flourish set on youth,
And delves the parallels in beauty's brow,
Feeds on the rarities of nature's truth,
And nothing stands but for his scythe to mow.
    And yet to times in hope my verse shall stand,
    Praising thy worth, despite his cruel hand.

Each of Shakespeare's three models of Time is a mini-poem in itself. The first model displays itself in balanced ceremonious full uninterrupted lines, like successive waves, making its analogy calmly, as a sermon might:

Metaphor (in simile-form) $\longrightarrow$ Like as the waves . . . shore,

Literal truth $\longrightarrow$ So do our minutes . . . end,

Elaboration $\longrightarrow$ Each changing . . . before,

                            In sequent toil . . . contend.

The next model is far more troubled, and its pace is charted by its governing words in *cr*: *"crawls," "crowned," "crooked."*

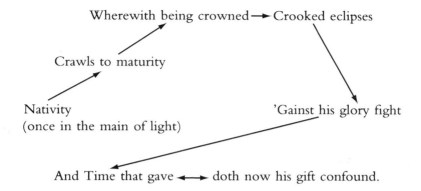

We see nativity crawl up to crowning, then crookedness fight it to death. Time gives on the left, takes away on the right. This is what we think of as the tragic model embedded in those of Shakespeare's plays that show the rise and fall of a character like Macbeth or Othello. It is completely different from Shakespeare's steady-state model in quatrain 1.

Shakespeare's third model consists neither of steady-state waves nor of rising and eclipsed sun. It shows us a drastic speed-up in the rate of extinction. It took three lines for the sun to be extinguished; now the deaths occur at the rate of one per line for two lines, and then several per line:

> Time doth transfix the flourish set on youth,
> And delves the parallels in beauty's brow,
> Feeds on the rarities of nature's truth,
> And nothing stands but for his scythe to mow.

These destructions take place with appalling rapidity, but, what is worse, the way they are related by the syntax of the clauses puts death before lived life. Transfixing precedes flourishing, wrinkles (delved "parallels") precede the appearance of the beautiful brow, devouring precedes the growing of the rare items in nature's garden. Finally, life itself is seen to exist for scything, and for that alone: "*Nothing* stands but *for* his scythe to mow." The poet Gerard Manley Hopkins was later to say bitterly, remembering this line, that man was born *for* death: "It is the blight man was *born for.*"

Shakespeare's three mini-poems, three incompatible models of life, have now been sketched in his sonnet. They are all about Time, and how nothing stands. The couplet, in revenge, shifts from "Time" to "times," and makes them "times in hope" — that is, the envisaged future. The couplet also shifts from "nothing stands" to something standing. In future times ("times in hope"), when the organic world has died, the inorganic world of art, which the scythe cannot mow down, will stand:

> And yet to *times* in hope my verse shall *stand,*
> Praising thy worth, despite his cruel hand.

This boast might seem to vanquish Time, if the poem did not end with the hand of Time itself, characterized by an adjective — "cruel" — which opens with the same *cr-* of doom that we remember from the tragic series "crawls," "crowned," "crooked." "Cruel" comes from the Latin *cruor,* "blood" — and Time's bloody hand is set over against the "hand," or handwriting, that creates verse praising worth. It is something of a standoff — but even that is a victory for the rarities of art's truth. After the three competing models of natural life, each more destructive than the last, Shakespeare has closed his sonnet with a model of the endurance — not forever, but at least to "times in hope" — of his verse.

This second look at our original poems suggests that one can't fully understand a poem until one sees the various shapes into which meaning has been arranged. We have seen steady-state shapes, and shapes of increase and decrease; shapes of contrast and alternation; shapes of series, both internally consistent and inconsistent; shapes of pointed metrical emphasis, of space and time. There is no lack of shapes for poets to imitate — every human action conducted over time offers such a shape, of success or failure, of stasis or catastrophe, of contest or conciliation. The dynamism of such shapes gives dynamism to poetry.

In Brief: The Poem as Arranged Life

We have seen, by taking a second look at the poems introduced in Chapter 1, how each of these poems is not only an utterance springing from a life-situation, but also a construction, an arrangement. The elements that can enter into the arranging of a poem are very various. The author can be arranging a sound-pattern while arranging a list of parallel elements, and also, simultaneously, advancing the plot through a series of changes in tense or mood. Or the author can be setting up a stanza form at the same time as a logical form: the stanza form may tell us that the poem is a ballad, while the construction may tell us that the poem is built on a logical contrast between "then" and "now." A poem may say "the same thing" three times ("I am growing old"), but each time may use a different model for aging and thus convey a different emphasis. Tones of voice can be varied, from protest to resignation, while another element is held constant (say, the tense of the verbs). By learning to look at each level of organization — phonetic, grammatical, syntactic, psychological, temporal, spatial, and so on — you learn to see the work the author is doing to make the poem both interesting on many levels and coherent in its arrangements. We will be looking at all of these levels in greater detail in subsequent chapters.

Reading Other Poems

The following poems have strong and visible structures. Think first about the life-situation out of which each emerges, and then begin to explore the way in which the life-situation has been imagined and arranged. "Lord Randal," for instance, is structured by the stages of its narrative, as is George Herbert's "Love."

♦ Does each of these poems begin at the outset of its narrative, or do some begin in the middle?

Given that every plot has a beginning and an end, the writer has the most free play in composing the middle. At the beginning of Herbert's poem, the sinful soul has arrived, after death, at the gate of heaven; at the end of the poem, the soul sits down and participates in the heavenly banquet.

♦ What happens in the middle?

♦ How many stages are there between beginning and end?

John Donne's poem doesn't reach the beginning of its story about a husband's departure on a journey — "I must go" — until it has traversed a long comparison of the way virtuous men die and the way virtuous spouses part. How does Donne end his plot?

Shakespeare, Robert Herrick, and Robert Frost, on the other hand, use contrastive structures to explore two different states: Shakespeare contrasts depression and elation; Herrick presents a woman clothed and the same woman naked; Frost contrasts the life lived and the life unlived. Rather than contrast, Walt Whitman uses analogy: he explains his own actions through those of a spider.

♦ How does the structure of each of these poems reinforce the contrast or the comparison?

◆ What is the imaginative spin put on each poem by the images chosen?

Thomas Hardy's poem about the collision of an iceberg and the *Titanic* begins in the present, with the sunken ship.

◆ Where does it end?

◆ Where else could it have begun or ended?

The most tightly structured of all these poems is probably "Tichborne's Elegy." Each of its three stanzas is constructed on roughly the same plan, but with variations.

◆ Can you describe the basic plan and specify how it varies in each stanza?

◆ Try rearranging the stanzas. Would it be the same poem if you interchanged stanzas 1 and 3?

◆ Can you see how the tenses change in the poem?

In her "footnote" to a report on torture issued by Amnesty International, Margaret Atwood has had to decide how to structure the chief elements of her poem: persons who are tortured and their torturers; a torture chamber; and a witness ("the man who works here"). If you draw a map of the poem, in what section is the scene of torture located? Where does Atwood put the torture chamber? What element is used to close the poem? Whose emotions does the poem follow closely? Where does this graph of emotions begin and end? Why?

Marilyn Nelson chooses an unexpected arrangement for a poem about animals at the zoo when she puts her poem into the form of a sonnet (fourteen five-beat lines, consisting of two quatrains and two tercets, with fairly regular rhymes). Look to see what animals inhabit the first quatrain, the second, the third, the couplet. Which animals are most specifically represented? Which have had names given to them? Nelson's choice of form is partly explained by her quotation from a sonnet by the German poet Rainer Maria Rilke concerning Orpheus, the legendary Thracian poet; according to Greek mythology, when Orpheus sang, animals listened and trees danced.

ANONYMOUS
Lord Randal

1

"O where ha' you been, Lord Randal, my son?
And where ha' you been, my handsome young man?"

"I ha' been at the greenwood; mother, mak my bed soon,
For I'm wearied wi' huntin', and fain wad lie down."

2

"And wha met ye there, Lord Randal, my son?
And wha met you there, my handsome young man?"
"O I met wi' my true-love; mother, mak my bed soon,
For I'm wearied wi' huntin', and fain wad lie down."

3

"And what did she give you, Lord Randal, my son?
And what did she give you, my handsome young man?"
"Eels fried in a pan; mother, mak my bed soon,
For I'm wearied wi' huntin', and fain wad lie down."

4

"And wha gat your leavin's, Lord Randal, my son?
And wha gat your leavin's, my handsome young man?"
"My hawks and my hounds; mother, mak my bed soon,
For I'm wearied wi' huntin', and fain wad lie down."

5

"And what becam of them, Lord Randal, my son?
And what becam of them, my handsome young man?"
"They stretched their legs out and died; mother, mak my bed
    soon,
For I'm wearied wi' huntin', and fain wad lie down."

6

"O I fear you are poisoned, Lord Randal, my son!
I fear you are poisoned, my handsome young man!"
"O yes, I am poisoned; mother, mak my bed soon,
For I'm sick at the heart, and I fain wad lie down."

7

"What d' ye leave to your mother, Lord Randal, my son?
What d' ye leave to your mother, my handsome young man?"
"Four and twenty milk kye;° mother, mak my bed soon,   *cattle*
For I'm sick at the heart, and I fain wad lie down."

8

"What d' ye leave to your sister, Lord Randal, my son?
What d' ye leave to your sister, my handsome young man?"
"My gold and my silver; mother, mak my bed soon,
For I'm sick at the heart, and I fain wad lie down."

9

"What d' ye leave to your brother, Lord Randal, my son?
What d' ye leave to your brother, my handsome young man?"
"My houses and my lands; mother, mak my bed soon,
For I'm sick at the heart, and I fain wad lie down."

10

"What d' ye leave to your true-love, Lord Randal, my son?
What d' ye leave to your true-love, my handsome young man?"
"I leave her hell and fire; mother, mak my bed soon,
For I'm sick at the heart, and I fain wad lie down."

WILLIAM SHAKESPEARE (1564 – 1616)
Sonnet 29

When in disgrace° with fortune and men's eyes,   *disfavor*
I all alone beweep my outcast state,
And trouble deaf heaven with my bootless° cries,   *futile*
And look upon myself and curse my fate,
Wishing me like to one more rich in hope,
Featured like him, like him with friends possessed,
Desiring this man's art, and that man's scope,
With what I most enjoy contented least;
Yet in these thoughts myself almost despising,
Haply I think on thee, and then my state
(Like to the lark at break of day arising
From sullen earth) sings hymns at heaven's gate,
      For thy sweet love remembered such wealth brings
      That then I scorn to change my state with kings.

CHIDIOCK TICHBORNE (d. 1586)
Tichborne's Elegy

Written with his own hand in the Tower before his execution

My prime of youth is but a frost of cares,
My feast of joy is but a dish of pain,
My crop of corn is but a field of tares,
And all my good is but vain hope of gain;
The day is past, and yet I saw no sun,
And now I live, and now my life is done.

My tale was heard and yet it was not told,
My fruit is fallen and yet my leaves are green,
My youth is spent and yet I am not old,
I saw the world and yet I was not seen;
My thread is cut and yet it is not spun,
And now I live, and now my life is done.

I sought my death and found it in my womb,
I looked for life and saw it was a shade,
I trod the earth and knew it was my tomb,
And now I die, and now I was but made;
My glass° is full, and now my glass is run,   *hourglass*
And now I live, and now my life is done.

JOHN DONNE (1572 – 1631)
A Valediction: Forbidding Mourning

1   As virtuous men pass mildly away,
        And whisper to their souls to go,
    Whilst some of their sad friends do say
        The breath goes now, and some say, No;

2   So let us melt, and make no noise,
        No tear-floods, nor sigh-tempests move,
    'Twere profanation of our joys
        To tell the laity our love.

3   Moving of th' earth brings harms and fears,
        Men reckon what it did and meant;
    But trepidation of the spheres,
        Though greater far, is innocent.

4   Dull sublunary° lovers' love   *earthly*
        (Whose soul is sense) cannot admit
    Absence, because it doth remove
        Those things which elemented it.

5   But we by a love so much refined
        That our selves know not what it is,
    Inter-assurèd of the mind,
        Care less, eyes, lips, and hands to miss.

6   Our two souls therefore, which are one,
        Though I must go, endure not yet

[Handwritten annotations: "farewell", "men speaking to soul", "Beging with death", "very peaceful", "analogy to come", "Not sure if he's actually dead or not?", "state change, no fuss", "Irreverant", "disrespect", "show no emotion when they part - don't make a scene", "Parting is like death?", "Earthquakes?", "can't explain what's happening", "Geographical, cosmological", "Material, need physical relationship", "connected", "Don't miss physical aspects as much as their actual connection"]

A breach, but an expansion,
    Like gold to airy thinness beat.

If they be two, they are two so
    As stiff twin compasses are two;
Thy soul, the fixed foot, makes no show
    To move, but doth, if th' other do.

And though it in the center sit,
    Yet when the other far doth roam,
It leans and hearkens after it,
    And grows erect, as that comes home.

Such wilt thou be to me, who must
    Like th' other foot, obliquely run;
Thy firmness makes my circle just,
    And makes me end where I begun.

[handwritten marginalia: "Reassurance"; "Don't seperate exactly, but just get farther away from each other"; "the wife"; "↳ moves w/ the other leg"; "Compasses used for map drawing"; "will return"]

ROBERT HERRICK (1591 – 1674)

Upon Julia's Clothes

Whenas in silks my Julia goes,
Then, then, methinks, how sweetly flows
That liquefaction of her clothes.

Next, when I cast mine eyes, and see
That brave vibration each way free,
O, how that glittering taketh me!

GEORGE HERBERT (1593 – 1633)

Love (III)

Love bade me welcome: yet my soul drew back,
    Guilty of dust and sin.
But quick-eyed Love, observing me grow slack
    From my first entrance in,
Drew nearer to me, sweetly questioning
    If I lacked anything.

"A guest," I answered, "worthy to be here":
    Love said, "You shall be he."
"I, the unkind, ungrateful? Ah, my dear,
    I cannot look on thee."

Love took my hand, and smiling did reply,
>   "Who made the eyes but I?"

"Truth, Lord; but I have marred them; let my shame
>   Go where it doth deserve."
"And know you not," says Love, "who bore the blame?"
>   "My dear, then I will serve."
"You must sit down," says Love, "and taste my meat."
>   So I did sit and eat.

WALT WHITMAN (1819 – 1892)
A Noiseless Patient Spider

A noiseless patient spider,
I mark'd where on a little promontory it stood isolated,
Mark'd how to explore the vacant vast surrounding,
It launch'd forth filament, filament, filament, out of itself,
Ever unreeling them, ever tirelessly speeding them.

And you O my soul where you stand,
Surrounded, detached, in measureless oceans of space,
Ceaselessly musing, venturing, throwing, seeking the spheres to
>   connect them,
Till the bridge you will need be form'd, till the ductile anchor
>   hold,
Till the gossamer thread you fling catch somewhere, O my soul.

THOMAS HARDY (1840 – 1928)
The Convergence of the Twain

Lines on the loss of the Titanic

>   *1*

>   In a solitude of the sea
>   Deep from human vanity,
And the Pride of Life that planned her, stilly couches she.

>   *2*

>   Steel chambers, late the pyres
>   Of her salamandrine fires,
Cold currents thrid,° and turn to rhythmic tidal lyres.   *thread*

3

Over the mirrors meant
To glass the opulent
The sea-worm crawls — grotesque, slimed, dumb, indifferent.

4

Jewels in joy designed
To ravish the sensuous mind
Lie lightless, all their sparkles bleared and black and blind.

5

Dim moon-eyed fishes near
Gaze at the gilded gear
And query: "What does this vaingloriousness down here?"

6

Well: while was fashioning
This creature of cleaving wing,
The Immanent Will that stirs and urges everything

7

Prepared a sinister mate
For her — so gaily great —
A Shape of Ice, for the time far and dissociate.

8

And as the smart ship grew
In stature, grace, and hue,
In shadowy silent distance grew the Iceberg too.

9

Alien they seemed to be:
No mortal eye could see
The intimate welding of their later history,

10

Or sign that they were bent
By paths coincident
On being anon twin halves of one august event,

11

Till the Spinner of the Years
Said "Now!" And each one hears,
And consummation comes, and jars two hemispheres.

Robert Frost (1874 – 1963)
The Road Not Taken

Two roads diverged in a yellow wood,
And sorry I could not travel both
And be one traveler, long I stood
And looked down one as far as I could
To where it bent in the undergrowth;

Then took the other, as just as fair,
And having perhaps the better claim,
Because it was grassy and wanted wear;
Though as for that, the passing there
Had worn them really about the same,

And both that morning equally lay
In leaves no step had trodden black.
Oh, I kept the first for another day!
Yet knowing how way leads on to way,
I doubted if I should ever come back.

I shall be telling this with a sigh
Somewhere ages and ages hence:
Two roads diverged in a wood, and I —
I took the one less traveled by,
And that has made all the difference.

Margaret Atwood (b. 1939)
Footnote to the Amnesty Report on Torture

The torture chamber is not like anything
you would have expected.
No opera set or sexy chains and
leather–goods from the glossy
porno magazines, no thirties horror   5
dungeon with gauzy cobwebs; nor is it
the bare cold-lighted
chrome space of the future
we think we fear.
More like one of the seedier   10
British Railways stations, with scratched green
walls and spilled tea,

crumpled papers, and a stooped man
who is always cleaning the floor.

It stinks, though; like a hospital,   15
of antiseptics and sickness,
and, on some days, blood
which smells the same anywhere,
here or at the butcher's.

The man who works here   20
is losing his sense of smell.
He's glad to have this job, because
there are few others.
He isn't a torturer, he only
cleans the floor: 25
every morning the same vomit,
the same shed teeth, the same
piss and liquid shit, the same panic.

Some have courage, others
don't; those who do what he thinks of   30
as the real work, and who are
bored, since minor bureaucrats
are always bored, tell them
it doesn't matter, who
will ever know they were brave, they might   35
as well talk now
and get it over.

Some have nothing to say, which also
doesn't matter. Their
warped bodies too, with the torn   40
fingers and ragged tongues, are thrown
over the spiked iron fence onto
the Consul's lawn, along with
the bodies of children
burned to make their mothers talk.   45

The man who cleans the floors
is glad it isn't him.
It will be if he ever says
what he knows. He works long hours,
submits to the searches, eats   50
a meal he brings from home, which tastes
of old blood and the sawdust

he cleans the floor with. His wife
is pleased he brings her money
for the food, has been told   55
not to ask questions.

As he sweeps, he tries
not to listen; he tries
to make himself into a wall,
a thick wall, a wall   60
soft and without echoes. He thinks
of nothing but the walk back
to his hot shed of a house,
of the door
opening and his children   65
with their unmarked skin and flawless eyes
running to meet him.

He is afraid of
what he might do
if he were told to,   70
he is afraid of the door,

he is afraid, not
of the door but of the door
opening; sometimes, no matter
how hard he tries,   75
his children are not there.

MARILYN NELSON (b. 1946)
Live Jazz, Franklin Park Zoo

> *Kubie sobbed when a nearby jazz band stopped playing.*
> — *CHRISTIAN SCIENCE MONITOR*, 8/27/96

A tree grew. Oh, remembering gorillas!
O *Orpheus singt!*[1] Oh, Africa in the ear!
The recluse, Vip, came out. Gigi sat still
and wide-eyed, black face pressed against the bars.

---

[1] From Rainer Maria Rilke's *Sonnets to Orpheus*.

Kubie lay on his back, as he usually does,
vacantly staring. Then he turned over, hairy chin
on one huge leather palm; with his other hand
he scratched his head, contemplatively picked his nose.

The zebras' ears twirled. Behind their fancy fences,
the silenced animals listened to something new.
Suddenly their calls, even the lion's roar,

shrank in their hearts, as they knew something more.
And where there had been, at most, a nest of boughs
to receive it, music built a cathedral in their senses.

3

Poems as Pleasure

Every artwork exists to evoke pleasures that are easier to feel than to describe. Music, for instance, gives rhythmic pleasure and melodic pleasure and harmonic pleasure, in different proportions in different pieces. Some paintings afford the pleasure of recognizable representation; some (purely abstract or nonobjective) do not. Sketches in black-and-white and sketches in color both give pleasure, but of different kinds. We can say in general that all artworks appeal to our (apparently inborn) love of patterning, whether the rhythmic and melodic patterning we hear in music, or the visual patterning we see in a painting or a quilt, or the patterning of volume that we see in architecture, from a cathedral to a cottage. Pattern and rhythm are very closely connected, so closely that people talk of the rhythm of repetition in the successive vaults of a church nave, or the rhythm of repeated curves in a painting.

Since the base of all organic life is repetition (repeated motion in growth and form), and since human life, by its heartbeat and breathing, is innately rhythmic, we can suppose that there is a biological basis for our recognition of, and apparently instinctive pleasure in, repetition. Besides our almost unconscious biological patterns of breathing and sleeping, we enjoy simple repetitive patterned body motions — rocking a baby, swimming, riding a bicycle. Babies learn by patterned repetition, and the pleasure of learning and recognizing new and old patterns is probably the source of our deepest pleasure in art. Most of the true and wise things said in artworks have also been said (in less-patterned and un-rhythmic ways) in philosophy and letters and newspaper editorials and conversation, where they also may strike us as true and wise, but not as art. In distinguishing literary artworks from other verbal pieces of truth or wisdom, we tend to be moved by the more intense patterning of the artwork.

The excess of patterning, beyond what is necessary to convey paraphrasable meaning, gives the work what we sometimes call "literariness." Just as a painting can use its elements of pattern — line (bold or delicate), color (moody or cheerful), and visual allusions (such as posing a figure in a gesture known to us from Greek sculpture) — to "say" more than merely "Here is a young woman naked," or "Here is a house in a field," so poems too convey their effects through their manner as much as through their matter. In using pattern in excess of what is strictly necessary for prose meaning, the poet reveals an intent to make art as well as to represent being. The representational urge of most poets is very strong, and every serious poet has something serious to say. Yet though a poet such as Yeats often says "the same thing" in his essays, letters, and speeches — works that we would not tend to call art — as he has said in a poem, we feel a great difference in the manner of the saying. What, then, are the pleasures we find in poems that we cannot find in a prose paraphrase of the same poem or in an essay advocating the same ideas?

Rhythm

The first and most elementary pleasure in all poetry is rhythm. Poetry is far more visibly rhythmic than most prose, and its rhythms are recurrent. Even in free verse, where lines are of unpredictably different lengths and may not rhyme, we often hear the same rhythms recurring. T. S. Eliot's character J. Alfred Prufrock, for instance, both wants to encounter experience (especially sexual experience) and wants to run away from it. His "theme rhythm," as a fellow teacher once pointed out to me, is a little initial skip (˘˘´) in which *two* unstressed syllables are followed by one stressed syllable: "Let us GO." But the little excited skip can't be kept up — each time Prufrock uses it, it dies out into the "ordinary" rhythm of one unstressed syllable followed by one stressed syllable (˘´). "Let us GO, then, YOU and I." And the subsequent lines continue to begin with a skip and die out into a walk, off and on, throughout the poem, right down to the line that is the third from the end, which is the last time we hear the skip:

We have LINGered in the chambers of the sea
By sea-girls wreathed in seaweed red and brown
Till human voices wake us, and we drown.

Good free verse always matches its rhythms to the emotional content of
its utterance — in Prufrock's words, "As if a magic lantern threw the
nerves in patterns on a screen."

But free verse, though it is a major form in contemporary poetry, is
a relatively recent invention. Most poetry in most languages, historically
speaking, has had a regular rhythm (though much of it has not had
rhyme). English verse began in Anglo-Saxon poetry with no rhyme but a
strong four-beat rhythm, and that four-beat rhythm is still very natural to
us. In Anglo-Saxon poetic rules, at least three of the four stressed words in
a line had to begin with the same consonant-sound ("cat" and "king,"
even though they begin with different consonants, begin with the same
consonant-sound). A modern poet writing in four-beat lines reminds us,
by his matching stressed consonant-sounds and words (see those italicized
below) that he knows the old forms. Here is the beginning of Wallace
Stevens's "A Postcard from the Volcano," in which the dead (like the dead
buried in Pompeii by the eruption of Mount Vesuvius) speak to the generations following them who are excavating their buried city:

> Children picking up our bones
> Will *never know* that these *were once*
> As quick° as foxes on the hill;   *fast, alive*
>
> And that in autumn, when the grapes
> Made *sharp* air *sharper* by their smell
> These had a *being, breathing* frost;
>
> And least *will* guess that *with* our bones
> We *left much more, left what* still is
> The *look* of things, *left what we* felt
>
> At *what we* saw.

After the conquest of England by the French in 1066, Anglo-
Saxon forms of poetry gave way to newer forms that counted by syllables instead of solely by stress. Gradually, a stable set of possible English
rhythms evolved and were given names borrowed from Greek meters
(iambic, trochaic, and so on; see appendix "On Prosody" in this volume).
A number of rhymed stanza-forms (such as the sonnet and the villanelle)
were adapted from European models. Poets can always invent new
rhythms and new stanza-forms (as Gerard Manley Hopkins did in the

second half of the nineteenth century, and as the free-verse poets did in the twentieth century). They can also revive or adapt older forms (Wallace Stevens, for instance, made the pentameter three-line stanza of Dante his favorite form, though he did not use Dante's rhymes). The more you read, the more you tend to notice the rhythms poets write in, and how the stanzas rhyme.

Rhythm itself is a distinct pleasure. Here are some samples of things people have liked:

Nursery rhythms, strong and emphatic:

> Ding, dong, bell,
> Pussy's in the well.
> Who threw her in?
> Little Johnny Thin.
> Who pulled her out?
> Little Tommy Stout.

The insistent hypnotic rhythms (ONE-two-three-four) of Edgar Allan Poe's four-beat lines in "The Raven":

> Once upon a midnight dreary, while I pondered weak and weary,
> Over many a quaint and curious volume of forgotten lore,
> As I nodded, nearly napping, suddenly I heard a tapping,
> As of someone gently rapping, rapping at my chamber door.

The excited and syncopated five-beat rhythms of Hopkins's "The Starlight Night":

> Look at the stars! look, look up at the skies!
>   O look at all the fire-folk sitting in the air!
>   The bright boroughs, the circle-citadels there!
> Down in dim woods the diamond-delves! the elves'-eyes!

The complex four-beat rhythms of Algernon Charles Swinburne's "When the Hounds of Spring," where dactyls (ONE-two-three) and trochees (ONE-two) predominate:

> And PAN by NOON and BACCHus by NIGHT,
>   FLEETer of FOOT than the FLEET-foot KID,
> FOLLows with DANCing and FILLS with deLIGHT
>   The MAEnad AND the BASSarid;°   *Bacchus's devotees*

And SOFT as LIPS that LAUGH and HIDE,
The LAUGHing LEAVES of the TREES diVIDE,
And SCREEN from SEEing and LEAVE in SIGHT
    The GOD purSUing, the MAIDen HID.

When rhythms become too insistent, they seem like parodies of themselves. For "Hiawatha," Henry Wadsworth Longfellow picked up the four-beat trochaic rhythm (ONE-two) of the Scandinavian epics, but because it is not, in its unrhymed form, a native narrative rhythm in English, it becomes tedious, as in this description of Hiawatha making a picture of the earth:

For the earth he drew a straight line,
For the sky a bow above it;
White the space between for day-time,
Filled with little stars for night-time;
On the left a point for sunrise,
On the right a point for sunset,
On the top a point for noon-tide.

Such a repetitive rhythm was bound to give rise to parodies. George A. Strong's runs, in part:

Of the skin he made him mittens,
Made them with the fur side inside,
Made them with the skin side outside.

Most English verse is made up of rhythms less insistent than those I have been illustrating. The usual English rhythms are one-TWO (iambic) or ONE-two (trochaic), and the usual English line has three or four or five stresses. In most verse, the pleasures of rhythm come from the tension between the basic metrical scheme of the line (one-TWO, one-TWO, one-TWO, one-TWO, one-TWO, as if you were to say, five times, "Untie, untie, untie, untie, untie") and the actual spoken intonation of the line. The underlying scheme of *all* of Shakespeare's dramatic poetry is "Untie untie untie untie untie," but what we actually find is an enormously flexible spoken line:

Tomorrow, and tomorrow, and tomorrow,
Creeps in this petty pace from day to day,
To the last syllable of recorded time.

We hear the undersong of the *metrical scheme* as a child might mechanically recite it, as if to a metronome:

> ToMORRow, AND toMORRow, AND toMORRow,
> Creeps IN this PETTy PACE from DAY to DAY,
> To THE last SYLLable OF reCORDed TIME.

And we also sense the oversong of the *natural intonation of the words* as they would be ordinarily spoken:

> ToMORRow, and toMORRow, and toMORRow,
> CREEPS IN this PETTy PACE from DAY to DAY,
> To the LAST SYLLable of reCORDed TIME.

A good actor makes an amalgam of metrical scheme and natural intonation, so that the audience hears a *rhythm* that keeps both the undersong of five beats and the oversong of urgent speech. One of the hardest things to do in poetry is to write hundreds of lines obeying the same *scheme* (as Milton does with his unrhymed five-beat lines in *Paradise Lost*) while varying the *rhythm,* so that the reader's ear does not tire. Of course, composers do the same. Every measure of a musical piece in 4/4 time has four beats to the measure, but not every measure is composed of four quarter-notes. There are eighth-notes, sixteenth-notes, half-notes, whole notes, held notes, notes with trills on them, and so on.

Knowing the musical weight, so to speak, of every possible syllable in the language is the gift of great poets. Some syllables are heavy, some light; some long, some short; some open, some closed; some nasal, some mellow; some sharp, some sweet. Keats, in his poem "If by dull rhymes," advises himself and other poets to care at least as much for syllabic wealth as King Midas cared for his gold, and not to repeat lifeless and worn-out strategies:

> Let us inspect the lyre, and weigh the stress
> Of every chord, and see what may be gained
> By ear industrious, and attention meet;
> Misers of sound and syllable, no less
> Than Midas of his coinage, let us be
> Jealous of dead leaves in the bay wreath crown.

Rhythms should be recurrent but not boring, hearable but not predictable.

Rhyme

We seem to be born liking sounds that match. Children make up games with simple counting rhymes. "One, two, button my shoe" still lives, though no one wears high-button shoes any more. Rhyme makes for conclusiveness and the sense of an ending. Once you accept the principle of rhyme, you can do many various things with it.

Rhythmically speaking, the simplest rhymes are monosyllables — *day, say*. You get a different effect from disyllables — *reason, treason*. The effect often becomes comic once you get trisyllables — *temptation, relation*. You can combine words having different numbers of syllables — *lover, discover*.

Graphically speaking, the simplest rhymes are those that are spelled the same — *day, say*. You get a different effect, even with monosyllables, when they are spelled differently — *day, weigh*. When you have three monosyllables, all with different spelling, the sense of poetic invention is even stronger — *day, weigh, fey*. Though amateur poets tend to rhyme monosyllables spelled the same way, poets interested in technical invention tend to investigate all the possibilities of more complicated polysyllabic and differently spelled rhyming words.

Grammatically speaking, the simplest rhymes are those in which both words are the same part of speech — say, two verbs (*weigh, neigh*) or two nouns (*cat, hat*). As soon as you have two words that are matched by rhyme but that don't match in other ways — say, a noun and a verb (*day, weigh*) — you feel a slight shock of difference.

Semantically speaking, the most satisfactory rhymes are ones in which the two rhyming words have some meaning-relation to each other. The meaning-relation may be one of sameness (*high/sky*) or difference (*island/highland*).

Some poets care a great deal more about making their rhymes meaningful than others do. Comic poets especially like to make points by ridiculous rhymes: here is Lord Byron on the young Don Juan's classical education, which Juan's mother (Donna Inez) must countenance but which she finds shocking. We can imagine how Byron amused himself rhyming "goddesses," "bodices," and "Odysseys":

> His classic studies made a little puzzle,
>> Because of filthy loves of gods and goddesses,
> Who in the earlier ages raised a bustle,
>> But never put on pantaloons or bodices;
> His reverend tutors had at times a tussle,
>> And for their Aeneids, Iliads, and Odysseys,

Were forced to make an odd sort of apology,
For Donna Inez dreaded the Mythology.

To make end-rhymes, one must have at least two lines, explaining why Keats thought of a kiss as a rhyme (and perhaps of a rhyme as a kiss of language). Arranging lines (usually rhyming lines, but not necessarily so) in a perceptible shape makes a stanza. One of the well-known stanza forms in English is a stanza of six five-beat lines rhyming *ababcc*. That is, the first and third lines rhyme on one sound — here designated *a;* the second and fourth lines rhyme on a different sound, *b;* and the fifth and sixth lines rhyme on yet another sound, *c*. Though this can be used in a long poem (it is in fact called the "*Venus and Adonis* stanza" because Shakespeare used it in his narrative poem of that name), it is also used by Ben Jonson in his one-stanza satiric poem on a lustful glutton allegorically named "Gut":

BEN JONSON (1572 – 1637)
On Gut

Gut eats all day and lechers all the night;
So all his meat he tasteth over twice;
And, striving so to double his delight,
He makes himself a thoroughfare of vice.
Thus in his belly can he change a sin:
Lust it comes out, that gluttony went in.

Most poems written in stanza-form, unlike "On Gut," consist of more than one stanza. Stanzas have names (see the appendix "On Prosody"), and poems using the same stanza forms belong to a recognizable family. Yeats may use a stanza-form associated with Geoffrey Chaucer; Keats may use the sonnet-form we associate with Shakespeare. As we read the later poet, we are reminded of the earlier one (and as we read the earlier one, we sometimes think forward to how a later poet will write in this stanza-form). Poets make certain stanza-forms their own. Dante wrote the whole of the *Divine Comedy* in three-line pentameter stanzas with interlaced rhyme, and ever since, anyone writing in this form or one of its modern adaptations — from Percy Bysshe Shelley in the nineteenth century through Wallace Stevens and Seamus Heaney in the twentieth century — evokes Dante.

Some stanzaic forms undergo interesting changes over time. Early narrative ballads were written in a stanza rhyming *abcb,* meaning that only the second and fourth lines rhymed. Usually the first line had four beats, the second three, the third four, and the fourth three (which we represent as 4/3/4/3). The early ballads were primarily stories in verse: the important feature in them was a plot of love, mystery, or adventure that moved incrementally on, often to disaster. Characterization and emotional reaction and description were kept to a minimum. Here is a representative ballad stanza, clearly interested in setting up a story:

> There lived a wife at Usher's Well,
>> And a wealthy wife was she;
> She had three stout and stalwart sons,
>> And sent them o'er the sea.

In the nineteenth century, William Wordsworth, though he was still interested in telling stories, was more concerned with the inner states and emotional responses accompanying events than in the events themselves. He invented what he called "lyrical ballads"; they were still written in the ballad stanza, and were allied to storytelling, but their emphasis was "lyrical" — that is, emotional and private rather than factual and plot-governed. Here is the ending of one of Wordsworth's lyrical ballads:

> She lived unknown, and few could know
>> When Lucy ceased to be;
> But she is in her grave, and, oh,
>> The difference to me!

Both "The Wife of Usher's Well" and Wordsworth's poem have the same stanzaic arrangement — four beats, three beats, four beats, three beats — with the second and fourth lines rhyming (and in Wordsworth's poem the first and third lines rhyming as well). Whenever we see this 4/3/4/3 rhyming stanza turn up, we are reminded that it goes back to our earliest folk poetry. When later poets want to write in an archaic way, they often use this stanza or a variant on it (see Samuel Taylor Coleridge's "Rime of the Ancient Mariner" and Keats's "La Belle Dame sans Merci").

The ballad stanza is four lines long, and so is called a quatrain, as are all stanzas of four lines. But there are other kinds of rhymes that a quatrain can use besides *abcb* or *abab*. It can use *aabb,* as in "Infant Sorrow":

> My mother groaned, my father wept —
> Into the dangerous world I leapt,
> Helpless, naked, piping loud,
> Like a fiend hid in a cloud.

Or a quatrain can rhyme *abba,* a form that Alfred, Lord Tennyson used in his long elegy "In Memoriam":

> Ring out, wild bells, to the wild sky,
> > The flying cloud, the frosty light:
> > The year is dying in the night;
> Ring out, wild bells, and let him die.

Several different variables combine to make stanzas: the length of the stanza (here, in our examples, four lines); the stress-length of the individual lines (4/3/4/3 in the ballads, 4/4/4/4 in Blake's and Tennyson's poems); the arrangement of the rhymes (whether *abab, aabb,* or *abba*); and the combination of stressed and unstressed syllables. Poets experiment with all these variables to make the different kinds of stanzas named below (which are described at fuller length in the appendix "On Prosody"):

Two lines: *couplet*

Three lines: *tercet*

Four lines: *quatrain*

Five lines: *cinquain*

Six lines: *sixain* or *sestet*

Seven lines: *rime royal* (rhyming *ababbcc*)

Eight lines: *ottava rima* (rhyming *abababcc*)

Nine lines: *Spenserian stanza* (rhyming *ababbcbcc*)

Fourteen lines: *sonnet*

By and large, the longer stanzas listed above are written in five-beat widths. But almost any combination of width (number of beats per line) and length (number of lines) and rhyme has been tried by someone. The important thing is to notice what the poet has been up to in the way of metrical form — rhymes, line-width, and stanza-shape — and to recall, if you can, other poems that have the same stanzaic shape as the one you are reading. One of the pleasures offered by poetry is a technical cousinship among poems, recognizable if you are used to registering the stanzaic shapes they take.

Structure

The structures of a poem are the intellectual or logical shapes into which its thoughts are dynamically organized. Any overarching structure can have many substructures. We saw, in "Infant Sorrow," a general structure in which the first stanza shows us the physical baby, the second the baby as thinker. Within that general structure we saw others — the presence of the parents in each stanza, the decline from *struggling* to *striving* to *bound,* and so on. Perhaps the greatest pleasure given by poetry is the sense that dynamic structure and thought are so intimately connected that each gives coherence to the other. We sometimes express this by saying that the structure of the poem *enacts* (acts out, dramatizes) by way of a dynamic evolution of form what the poem *says* by way of assertion.

How does one come to perceive the structure by which the poem conveys its assertions? As we saw in Chapter 2, it takes something like X-ray vision, by which you look for patterns. Patterns occur at many levels in poetry, just as they do in the physical universe: one can look for patterns in subatomic behavior, in atomic behavior, in molecular behavior, and so on, all the way up to the patterns of the planets and the stars. If you think of a poem as a small universe, you can begin looking at the smallest patterns (the binding-together of certain words by rhyme or by similar initial sounds) or at the largest patterns (the number of sentences and their relations to each other as a dynamic pattern of thinking). One level of investigation may not yield much: the poem you are looking at may not rhyme, and there may be only a relatively small number of alliterating words (words beginning with the same consonant-sound). At this point, you would probably give up looking for interesting sound-patterns, and move on to sentence-relations. Or, on another level, the poem may not have many descriptive phrases representing people or a landscape — it may be mostly statement (say, of philosophical truths). At this point, you would stop looking for a pattern of descriptive images, and perhaps move on to patterns of diction. Or, on another level, that of plot, nothing much may seem to happen. Do not be discouraged; if the energy of the poem is not in plot, it may be in its grammatical play; if it is not in grammatical play, it may be in images; if it is not in images, it may be in rhythm.

What, for instance, could we find to say about this poem, called simply "Poem," by William Carlos Williams?

WILLIAM CARLOS WILLIAMS (1883 – 1963)

Poem

As the cat
climbed over
the top of

the jamcloset
first the right
forefoot

carefully
then the hind
stepped down

into the pit of
the empty
flowerpot

There certainly isn't much that is philosophical or intellectual here. In fact, if the four stanzas were written out as the one sentence they are, it wouldn't seem like a poem at all: "As the cat climbed over the top of the jamcloset, first the right forefoot, carefully, then the hind, stepped down into the pit of the empty flowerpot." And the "plot" — a cat finding its way — is an ordinary event seen every day. A good strategy in examining a poem is always to see why the poet wrote out its sentences in the way he or she did. Williams divided his sentence into four stanzas, each of three lines. How did he decide where to break his sentence, and why did he group the twelve pieces three-by-three? If we reread the poem asking the questions that the pause after each line encourages us to ask, we can see the meaning of Williams's line-breaks:

As the cat	*did what?*
climbed over	*over what?*
the top of	*of what?*
the jamcloset	*how?*
first the right	*paw? rear leg?*
forefoot	*then? (a mistaken question; it turns out Williams wanted me to ask "how?")*
carefully	*then what?*
then the hind	*did what?*
stepped down	*where?*
into the pit of	*oops! of what?*
the empty	*what has a "pit" anyhow?*
flowerpot	*not what you expected, kittycat!*

Well, this more or less shows me why Williams put his unsteady little pauses where he did. But why did he group his lines three by three? This action inserts three "major pauses" at certain points to punctuate the "minor pauses" at the end of each line. The first major pause comes when the cat stops before the descent into unknown regions (which it cannot see) from the top of the jamcloset. The second comes after the right forefoot has found (hurrah!) a place to poise. The third comes after the hind leg successfully (whee!) moves to follow the forefoot. Then comes the farcical end, when the poor cat finds itself trapped inside a deep flower-pot instead of safe on a flat surface.

Williams's lines consist, sometimes, of only a single word — "fore-foot," "carefully," "flowerpot." Each line represents a cat-step, so these are particularly fraught steps. Some lines have two words — these are steps of medium difficulty. We end up feeling that the lines of *three* or even *four* words — "As the cat," "the top of," "first the right," "into the pit of," are almost carefree, almost lilting.

As for Williams's stanzas, they are all adverbial, ornaments attached to the central main verb, "stepped." There is the "as" stanza, the "first" stanza, the "then" stanza, and the "into" stanza. They are all equal in length, as though the cat had made four neat forays into what it hoped would be stability, but what it found was captivity. Clearly the initial confident tenta-tiveness and the ultimate bewildering failure of the cat delighted Williams as a little emblem of human venturing. Whenever a poet calls a poem "Poem" it means that the story told in the poem resembles the making of poetry itself. Like the cat, the poet ventures out into the hazards of thin air, places a "foot" (a metrical foot, no doubt) on a possible landing, tries another foot after it, and may find farce instead of success.

It would be of no use to go to this poem looking for harmonious melody, or philosophical assertion, or nature description, or rhyme, or song-rhythm, or historical insight, or Freudian dreamwork, or gender problems. Each poem leads you to the questions it makes sense to ask it. It makes sense to ask this poem about its twelve lines and its four stanzas and its three white spaces and its line-breaks; it makes sense to ask what the cat expected and what the cat found; it makes sense to ask why the poet gave this humble anecdote the honorific name "Poem." It makes sense, too, to ask what the poet who writes such a poem understands poetry to be — to which we might answer that it is the imaginative perception of the ordi-nary; and the comic perception of hazards-and-landings; and the emblem-atic perception of how an animal's small ventures might be like ours.

Let us look for a moment at a very different sort of poem alto-gether, "We Real Cool," by Gwendolyn Brooks:

GWENDOLYN BROOKS (1917 – 2000)
We Real Cool

> *The Pool Players.*
> *Seven at the Golden Shovel.*

We real cool. We
Left school. We

> Lurk late. We
> Strike straight. We
>
> Sing sin. We
> Thin gin. We
>
> Jazz June. We
> Die soon.

"We" is a strong unit through gin, strikes and sin — until "we" is missing at the end of the line.

The first thing that strikes anyone reading this poem is that its sentences are arranged "wrong." It "should" read,

> We real cool.
> We left school.
>
> We lurk late.
> We strike straight.

And so on. The second thing that strikes the ear is that most of the poem is spoken in the present tense, but two things break that pattern — the past tense in "We *left* school" and the implied future tense — or is it? — in the "We die soon" that ends the poem.

The subtitle of the poem tells us who is speaking — seven pool players at the Golden Shovel pool room. The first line of the poem — "We real cool" instead of "We're real cool" — tells us the pool players are black, as they omit the verb "to be." Why are the poem's rhymes displaced to the "wrong" place in the lines, and why do its tenses change? How do these practices of the poet enact something about the seven pool players? And how, we might add, are we to explain that all their sentences consist of three words? And why do their sentences have so many internal binding sounds — "lurk late," "strike straight," "sing sin," "thin gin," "jazz June"? All the answers to such questions must be conjectural, but the analyst's aim is to make the conjectural answers as plausible as possible, so that they "account for" those patterns in which the composing poet, and the responsive reader, take pleasure.

In answering the questions that the poem makes us ask, we notice that instead of a "rhyme" at the end of each line, the insistent "We" appears down the right margin. "We" is the real word binding these seven adolescents together — they are a group giving each other solidarity. We get so used to seeing "We" at the end of every line — one, two, three, four, five, six, seven — that when we "miss" it at the end of line 8 we know that its absence is a sign of the imminent death of the group. The poverty-stricken sentences — after all, the first complete sentences made by babies consist of two or three words, "Me want that," "I go bed" — are a sign that indeed these young men have "left school" and its more complex possibilities of language. Nonetheless, their syntactically simple sentences are full of a feel for language — if they had stayed in school, they might have produced, among them, a poet or two. They like groups of words that sound "jazzy," and they like singing and playing games — all inclinations characteristic of poets. The trouble is the gin and the sin and the gambling and the school leaving and the lurking into late hours.

It makes sense to ask this poem questions about its rhymes, its syntax, its tenses, its word placement, in order to know who these "cool" adolescents are, how the poet enacts their solidarity, their gifts, their appetites, and their mistakes. It makes sense, once one knows that this is a poem about young black dropouts, to ask what the poet's feelings about them are — "young, talented with words, doomed." It makes sense to ask this poem about its wit (these young men make their every word count — their three-word sentences have three full beats). It makes sense, too, to ask it about racial questions (the white world is entirely absent — why?). It makes sense to put the poem in a genre — the genre of elegy, especially the subgroup of elegies that mourn people who died much too young. This is an elegy with no visible offer of consolation — there is no better purpose served by the deaths of the young men, no envisaged heaven for them to go to after their death, no legacy they leave behind them of children begotten or accomplishments completed. It makes sense, as well, to ask to whom the young men are speaking. To us? To themselves? Highly literate readers may recall a "we" elegy spoken by the small band of Spartan soldiers who died in 480 B.C., at Thermopylae, an elegy that is perhaps the classical ancestor of this poem:

> Go tell the Spartans, thou who passest by,
> That here, obedient to their laws, we lie.

We can then see the poem not simply as an elegy by Gwendolyn Brooks for these young men, but as their self-epitaph, which could be inscribed on their grave: "We / Die soon." The apparent future tense of the last line then becomes a generalized present tense about the fate of all such adolescents: "We — people like us — always die soon."

The important thing is to be accustomed to looking, in any poem, at several levels — the sound, the rhythms and rhymes, the grammar, the images, the sentences, the plot, the assertions, the allusions, the self-contradictions. Somewhere the energy of the poem awaits you. The moment you see the main and subordinate patterns, you smile, and it "all makes sense."

Images

Though people sometimes refer to "images" in poems, a word is not the same thing as a picture. Words refer; images represent. When poets use nouns or phrases referring to something that an artist could represent by graphic means (a painting or sketch), they use them either for descriptive purposes or as illustrative examples. The images can be either literally pictorial ("This is the forest primeval") or figurative, as when Wordsworth says of a young woman that she is "A violet by a mossy stone, / Half hidden from the eye." Shakespeare's three images in Sonnet 60 for time's action (ocean waves; a sun that rises and is eclipsed; a repeated destructive attack by a spear, a spade, a maw, a scythe) give three illustrative ways of thinking about life: life is a steady state in which each moment, wavelike, resembles the next; or, life is a glowing rise followed by a catastrophic blackout; or, life is experienced as a continuous and premature and universal execution. These are not compatible images, and the poem makes us see each later image obliterating the former model(s).

Images, in fact, serve in poems as a shorthand for argument. It is quicker to show than to tell. It is a rule of thumb in poems that when a second, different, image follows a first, the second one is somehow importantly supplementing, or indeed correcting or supplanting, the first, because of some perceived inadequacy in the first image (otherwise, the poem would not have needed the second). So, when William Blake wanders through London despairing at the evils of modern life, he first mentions, as a major evil that comes to mind, "the mind-forg'd manacles" of false beliefs. But he does not stop there. He replaces the manacles with the institution that imposes them, and that permits the exploitation of the poor and the powerless — the Church. Yet the Church is not the worst evil: after all, to lose one's life is worse than to be manacled in mind or to be poor, and so Blake goes on to indict the monarchy, which sends its sons off to be killed. Yet even that image of evil does not suffice. He must supplement Church and Palace with one more, the worst — the corruption of the sexual life which, by prostitution and syphilis, blinds the newborn infant in the cradle. Blake's images rise, supplementing and even replacing one another, to the fatal last word in the last line:

WILLIAM BLAKE (1757 – 1827)
London

I wander thro' each charter'd street,
Near where the charter'd Thames does flow,

And mark in every face I meet
Marks of weakness, marks of woe.

In every cry of every man,
In every Infant's cry of fear,
In every voice, in every ban,
The mind-forg'd manacles I hear.

How the Chimney-sweeper's cry
Every black'ning Church appalls;
And the hapless Soldier's sigh
Runs in blood down Palace walls.

But most thro' midnight streets I hear
How the youthful Harlot's curse
Blasts the new-born Infant's tear,
And blights with plagues the Marriage hearse.

It is necessary to see the climactic order of Blake's images ("But *most* . . . I hear") in order to set them in relation to each other. Every image needs to be related to others in the same poem, but in an imaginative, not a mechanical, way. You need to enter the mind of the speaker, make yourself into the speaker, and ask yourself how you are connecting things in your ongoing expression.

Argument

A poem often looks as though it is making an argument. But "real" arguments are made in prose (theological tracts argue about God, philosophical books argue ethics or metaphysics, political papers argue politics). Arguments in poems are miniature imitations of "real" arguments, and are often designed to show the moves in the argumentative game rather than to make a full argument in order to persuade a "real-life" person. The debates in poems are often sophisticated games, as when a "shepherd" (really a courtier in pastoral disguise) tries to persuade a "nymph" (an aristocratic young woman playing at being a rustic shepherdess) to love him. She counters with a mini-sermon on the transience of all earthly love, relenting at the end to wish things were otherwise:

CHRISTOPHER MARLOWE (1564 – 1593)
The Passionate Shepherd to His Love

Come live with me and be my love,
And we will all the pleasures prove°   *experience*

That valleys, groves, hills, and fields,
Woods, or steepy mountain yields.

And we will sit upon the rocks,
Seeing the shepherds feed their flocks,
By shallow rivers to whose falls
Melodious birds sing madrigals.

And I will make thee beds of roses
And a thousand fragrant posies,
A cap of flowers, and a kirtle
Embroidered all with leaves of myrtle;

A gown made of the finest wool
Which from our pretty lambs we pull;
Fair linèd slippers for the cold,
With buckles of the purest gold;

A belt of straw and ivy buds,
With coral clasps and amber studs:
And if these pleasures may thee move,
Come live with me, and be my love.

The shepherd swains shall dance and sing
For thy delight each May morning:
If these delights thy mind may move,
Then live with me and be my love.

SIR WALTER RALEGH (1554 – 1618)
The Nymph's Reply to the Shepherd

If all the world and love were young,
And truth in every shepherd's tongue,
These pretty pleasures might me move
To live with thee and be thy love.

Time drives the flocks from field to fold
When rivers rage and rocks grow cold,
And Philomel° becometh dumb;   *the nightingale*
The rest complains of cares to come.

The flowers do fade, and wanton fields
To wayward winter reckoning yields;
A honey tongue, a heart of gall,
Is fancy's spring, but sorrow's fall.

Thy gowns, thy shoes, thy beds of roses,
Thy cap, thy kirtle, and thy posies
Soon break, soon wither, soon forgotten —
In folly ripe, in reason rotten.

Thy belt of straw and ivy buds,
Thy coral clasps and amber studs,
All these in me no means can move
To come to thee and be thy love.

But could youth last and love still breed,
Had joys no date° nor age no need,   *end*
Then these delights my mind might move
To live with thee and be thy love.

There exist within poetic tradition debates between body and soul, between gardeners and mowers, between God and man, between the owl and the nightingale, between the flower and the leaf, between a philosopher and a poet. Such debates usually raise perennial questions — hedonism versus asceticism, night versus day, the mirthful man versus the pensive man, the active life versus the contemplative life, and so on. Partly *because* such questions cannot be settled, the pleasure in a poem of argument lies in seeing what strategic moves, and what new speakers, can be invented for such perennial arguments.

Poignancy

We often say a poem is "moving." What makes a poem moving? Normally, it is the relation between the situation implied in the poem (say, a lover at a girl's window) and the utterance of the poem (plaintive, or witty, or ecstatic).

Often, the situation in a poem changes as the poem develops, and the utterance changes along with the new event or the new perception. We never expect, for instance, that anyone we love will be taken from us, however logically we may "know" that death comes to everyone. Somehow we "repress" (as we now say) our knowledge that those we love most are themselves mortal. Wordsworth's speaker in a famous poem says that his mind (he calls it his "spirit") "slumbered" when it exempted his beloved from the threat of mortality. In the first stanza of the poem, the insidious word "seemed" hints at the forthcoming catastrophe:

WILLIAM WORDSWORTH (1770 – 1850)
A slumber did my spirit seal

A slumber did my spirit seal;
    I had no human fears: *out of touch with the world*
She seemed a thing that could not feel
    The touch of earthly years. *Almost angelic, cannot age*

A white space intervenes between stanza 1 and stanza 2. When we begin stanza 2, we see that the girl has died between the two stanzas — that the white space represents her death. The first stanza was delusion; the second is reality:

like in death No motion has she now, no force;
    She neither hears nor sees; *sciency language*
Rolled round in earth's diurnal course,
    With rocks, and stones, and trees. *Adds signs of life*

What is poignant here is, first of all, the speaker's total suppression of the narrative of her death. He does not say, "But then she sickened and she died" — it is too painful for him to say that bald sentence. He makes her still the subject of his second sentence, as she was the subject of the last part of his first sentence: "She seemed . . . Has she now . . . ; She neither hears nor sees." But the sentence of stanza 2 is all negation in its predicates: Motion? No. Force? No. Hears? No. Sees? No. We then realize, looking back, that there was a comparable negation in stanza 1: Can feel earthly years? No. But that was preceded by the verb "seemed." Now, it proves untrue. She *can* feel the touch of earthly years, so much so that the word the speaker lightly used of her in stanza 1 — "thing" — turns out to be the accurate word. She is now a thing, as rocks and stones and trees are things, and she is as inertly rolled round, day and night, by the planet's motion as those other "things" are.

If the poignancy is partly in the speaker's mistake, and partly in his unwitting use of the word "thing," it lies also, in stanza 2, in his stern truthfulness. He speaks in strictly inorganic physical terms: motion, force, diurnal course, rocks, stones. He has mentioned hearing and seeing, organic functions, only to deny them. Nonetheless, he ultimately relents: in placing his beloved not only with rocks and stones and planetary motion, but also — and lastly — with organic and living trees, he gives her a posthumous association with life. The poem would be very different — and almost inhuman — if the last line read, "With granite, stones, and rocks." The poignancy of any poem comes with the struggle between uttering truth and honoring the undertow of strong feeling.

Wisdom

Poems descend in part from wisdom literature — prayers, spells, riddles, epigrams, proverbs, aphorisms. "What oft was thought but ne'er so well expressed" (Alexander Pope) is one description of poetry, and we respond (especially when we are young) to what poetry can tell us about human experience. Countless adolescents have memorized lines such as "How do I love thee? Let me count the ways" (Elizabeth Barrett Browning). Poetry is the most concise form of literature, and it has perfected techniques for rapid and deft exposition (partly by the shorthand arguments of imagery). Many people read poetry chiefly for the wisdom they find there, scarcely knowing that the wisdom seems wiser for having been expressed so memorably. There is a psychological wisdom in lyric: one of its functions is to give us a believable representation of what Matthew Arnold called "the dialogue of the mind with itself." When we see a credible representation of grief, or rebellion, or delusion, we feel the assuaging assent that comes from a ratification of something we have felt but have not previously seen represented. "Strength came where weakness was not known to be," as Wordsworth says of a similar experience. It is important to everyone to find his or her own experience mirrored back; some find this mirroring chiefly in novels, others in poetry, depending on personal taste. The dazzling variety of voices in lyric, each available to any reader as a vicarious voice in which to speak, lets us move through many experiences comparable to our own. Often we find (as we are being John Donne — "Sweetest love, I do not go / For weariness of thee" — or Elizabeth Bishop — "I caught a tremendous fish" —) that the exhilaration of having a new voice and new insight reverberates back into our "real" experiences of a comparable sort.

A New Language

Each major artist creates in a distinctive way. Though early Beethoven can sound like Mozart, or early Mozart like Haydn, in their maturity they end up sounding different from the predecessors whom they imitated in youth. We can walk into a museum and say, "That's a Van Gogh," or "That's a Picasso," because each major painter has a distinctive way of representing and coloring the world. It is the same with poets: we can tell (after a while) Tennyson from William Butler Yeats, and Milton from Edmund Spenser, and Adrienne Rich from Anne Sexton, even though in many cases there are resemblances in subject matter. It is not subject matter that distinguishes artists, it is treatment. There are hundreds of portraits of distinguished-looking men, but anyone who has spent some time in museums can tell a Velásquez from a Hals, and either from a Cézanne.

A distinctive style is created in part by the artist and in part by the epoch in which the artist works. One can tell a Renaissance painting from a nineteenth-century painting, a piece of anonymous fifteenth-century music from a piece of anonymous seventeenth-century music. (I will say more about this in the chapter "History and Regionality.") Within what any given epoch permits, many styles are possible (as one can tell from looking at twentieth-century American painting or poetry). Wordsworth said that the poet must create the taste by which he is enjoyed; that is, the poet trains the audience to like a new sort of art. The training takes time, and each new poet you read is training you to like a new personal shorthand of images and a systematically original language. If a poet does not appeal to you now, look again at the work in ten years, and you may like it then. Acculturation is fast in some cases, slow in others. But if many people have found a poet's language memorable, you may some day find it memorable, too. Each person's taste hovers at a different evolutionary moment. A person brought up on Christian prayer comes to Christian religious poetry with great ease; someone who has never heard a Christian prayer or hymn may take a long time to get used to George Herbert or Christina Rossetti. An ecologist may not be put off by the scientific vocabulary in the poems of A. R. Ammons or Amy Clampitt; someone who has never heard of the Cambrian shield or pheromones may be more apprehensive. The rule of thumb is to let the poem work on you over time.

Finding Yourself

The strangest experience in reading poetry, as in writing it, is to find yourself in it, to be yourself in it. We sometimes speak of this as finding a "favorite poet." This is a poet whose writing is so close to your own way of seeing and thinking that there seems no barrier at all between you and the poet. Such a poet is a powerful reflecting mirror of your own sensibility and creativity. In that poet's work, you find yourself "more truly and more strange" (as Wallace Stevens put it in "Tea at the Palaz of Hoon"). Sometimes poets are mirrors for a whole generation, and become bestsellers on that account — as T. S. Eliot and Robert Frost and Adrienne Rich and Allen Ginsberg have been in the United States in the twentieth century. Other American poets, just as good, remain known to relatively few readers (who nonetheless claim them as intensely as the country at large claims the bestsellers). Samuel Johnson said (in his "Preface to Shakespeare") that it was only after a century had passed, and the topical interest of a piece of literature had died down, that one could tell whether it would last. Luckily, you do not have to worry about the potential durability of works in which you find a voice and a reflecting mirror; that question will take care of itself. The important thing is to feel companioned, as you go through life, by a host of poems that speak to your experience. And, in the long run, the poems you first read because you wanted to find out about love or death you will read again because of the living quality of the voice that speaks in them, that quality we call "style."

In Brief: Poems as Pleasure

No single poem offers all the pleasures of poetry. As you read, you will sometimes be caught up in the lilt of a rhythm, sometimes intrigued by plot; at other times you may be struck by an insight, moved by the poignancy of tone, or puzzled and pleased by a subversive and unexpected move by the text. The important thing is to be ready for whatever the poem offers, and to take it on its own terms, not requiring philosophical discourse from a song, or simplicity from a knotted problem-poem. The single best way to gain pleasure from a poem is to read it aloud; if you let the poem take you on its journey, you will know intuitively where it has led you. The next pleasure is to find words for what you felt and thought on that journey; and the next is to find what aspects of the poem — structure, images, argument — generated those feelings and those thoughts. Chapter 4 will suggest some ways by which you can describe the various aspects of poems from which these pleasures arise.

Reading Other Poems

All the following poems combine representation and strong patterning. Both Theodore Roethke and William Carlos Williams declare by their titles that they will employ strong rhythmic patterning.

◆ Can you graph the rhythms their lines enact?

Some poets can create strong patterns in very brief poems. William Blake's "The Sick Rose" consists (if one were to consider it clinically) of six lines of diagnosis followed by two of prognosis (or forecast of the course of the rose's disease).

◆ Do the rhymes in any way suggest the plot?

Gerard Manley Hopkins's "sonnet" of reduced proportions — a six-line "octave" followed by a four-and-a-half-line "sestet" — is divided into two ways of talking about "dappled" beauty — beauty that is spotted, variegated, multiple.

◆ What is the pattern of discussion in the first part of the poem, offered in words like "skies," "trout," "trades"? And in the second, offered in words like "all things," "whatever is fickle," and so on?

Rhythms can differ greatly, from the lilt of "My Papa's Waltz" to the hypnotic repetitive rhythms of D. H. Lawrence's "Snake" to the long-breathed lines of Derek Walcott's "The Season of Phantasmal Peace." Read each of these aloud to hear the difference in yourself as you become the person speaking the poem.

◆ How much can you say about the tones of voice of the speaker as they issue from you?

Sometimes a structural pattern can be borrowed, as we saw in this chapter with the passionate shepherd's invitation and the nymph's reply (in which she borrows the shepherd's stanza-form and vocabulary). The anterior structure generating a poem is sometimes well known in the poet's culture; sonneteers, for instance, were accustomed to praise their lady's beauties one by one. To understand Shakespeare's mocking reply to such a practice, you need to imagine that he has just read a poem beginning "My mistress' eyes shine brightly like the sun; / Coral is not more red than her lips' red, / She walks on air, she does not tread the ground," and so on. "I don't know about *your* mistress," says Shakespeare, "but *mine* has no such powers. *My* mistress' eyes are nothing *like* the sun."

◆ How precisely can you deduce from Shakespeare's reply the anterior claims of praise that he is mocking?

Description in lyric often proceeds by successive images, piled up in a montage of evidence. Consider Robert Frost's two poems about the apple harvest: the first, "After Apple-Picking," offers "realistic" images of the overwhelming harvest followed by a succession of dream-images, only to return, in the third section of the poem, to realistic images again. By contrast to this flood of images about the anxiety of trying to pluck all possible apples, "Unharvested" presents only a single image — a ring of fallen apples on the ground below a tree that was not harvested — but this image is investigated for all it can yield. And in its fourteen lines this sonnet-variant makes a pattern consistent with the circle of unharvested apples.

◆ What is the symbolic suggestion of apple picking?
◆ What different effects does Frost pursue for the image constellation of apple harvesting?

Both Robert Herrick's "To the Virgins, to Make Much of Time" and Thomas Hardy's "The Darkling Thrush" are poems giving moral advice, in the form of argument against an implied other moral position. Should virgins hasten to marry or not? At the end of the old century, should one despair or not?

- ◆ What means of persuasion does each author find to make the message seem not only wise but also moving?
- ◆ Rephrase the advice in a prose proposition. Does it lose its poignancy?

If you were asked by a friend to describe Blake's style in "The Sick Rose," can you think of three or four adjectives you might use for an answer?

Finally, can you see the patterning-by-pronouns ("I" versus "he") in Elizabeth Alexander's poem about a summer love affair? How does it change from stanza to stanza?

WILLIAM SHAKESPEARE (1564 – 1616)
Sonnet 130

My mistress' eyes are nothing like the sun; A
Coral is far more red than her lips' red; B
If snow be white, why then her breasts are dun; A
If hairs be wires, black wires grow on her head. B
I have seen roses damasked,° red and white, C   *variegated*
But no such roses see I in her cheeks, D
And in some perfumes is there more delight C
Than in the breath that from my mistress reeks. D
I love to hear her speak, yet well I know E
That music hath a far more pleasing sound; F
I grant I never saw a goddess go;° E   *walk*
My mistress when she walks treads on the ground. F
    And yet by heaven I think my love as rare G
    As any she belied with false compare. G

ROBERT HERRICK (1591 – 1674)
To the Virgins, to Make Much of Time

Gather ye rosebuds while ye may,
    Old time is still a-flying;
And this same flower that smiles today
    Tomorrow will be dying.

The glorious lamp of heaven, the sun,
   The higher he's a-getting,
The sooner will his race be run,
   And nearer he's to setting.

That age is best which is the first,
   When youth and blood are warmer;
But being spent, the worse, and worst
   Times still succeed the former.

Then be not coy, but use your time,
   And, while ye may, go marry;
For, having lost but once your prime,
   You may forever tarry.

WILLIAM BLAKE (1757 – 1827)
The Sick Rose

O Rose, thou art sick!
The invisible worm
That flies in the night,
In the howling storm,

Has found out thy bed
Of crimson joy:
And his dark secret love
Does thy life destroy.

GERARD MANLEY HOPKINS (1844 – 1889)
Pied Beauty

Glory be to God for dappled things —
   For skies of couple-colour as a brinded cow;
      For rose-moles all in stipple upon trout that swim;
Fresh-firecoal chestnut-falls; finches' wings;
   Landscape plotted and pieced — fold, fallow, and plough;
      And áll trádes, their gear and tackle and trim.
All things counter, original, spare, strange;
   Whatever is fickle, freckled (who knows how?)
      With swift, slow; sweet, sour; adazzle, dim;
He fathers-forth whose beauty is past change:
         Praise him.

THOMAS HARDY (1840 – 1928)

The Darkling Thrush

I leant upon a coppice gate
    When Frost was spectre-gray,
And Winter's dregs made desolate
    The weakening eye of day.
The tangled bine-stems° scored the sky   *wood-bine*
    Like strings of broken lyres,
And all mankind that haunted nigh
    Had sought their household fires.

The land's sharp features seemed to be
    The Century's corpse outleant,
His crypt the cloudy canopy,
    The wind his death-lament.
The ancient pulse of germ and birth
    Was shrunken hard and dry,
And every spirit upon earth
    Seemed fervourless as I.

At once a voice arose among
    The bleak twigs overhead
In a full-hearted evensong
    Of joy illimited;
An aged thrush, frail, gaunt, and small,
    In blast-beruffled plume,
Had chosen thus to fling his soul
    Upon the growing gloom.

So little cause for carolings
    Of such ecstatic sound
Was written on terrestrial things
    Afar or nigh around,
That I could think there trembled through
    His happy good-night air
Some blessed Hope, whereof he knew
    And I was unaware.

ROBERT FROST (1874 – 1963)

After Apple-Picking

My long two-pointed ladder's sticking through a tree
Toward heaven still,

And there's a barrel that I didn't fill
Beside it, and there may be two or three
Apples I didn't pick upon some bough.
But I am done with apple-picking now.
Essence of winter sleep is on the night,
The scent of apples: I am drowsing off.
I cannot rub the strangeness from my sight
I got from looking through a pane of glass
I skimmed this morning from the drinking trough
And held against the world of hoary grass.
It melted, and I let it fall and break.
But I was well
Upon my way to sleep before it fell,
And I could tell
What form my dreaming was about to take.
Magnified apples appear and disappear,
Stem end and blossom end,
And every fleck of russet showing clear.
My instep arch not only keeps the ache,
It keeps the pressure of a ladder-round.
I feel the ladder sway as the boughs bend.
And I keep hearing from the cellar bin
The rumbling sound
Of load on load of apples coming in.
For I have had too much
Of apple-picking: I am overtired
Of the great harvest I myself desired.
There were ten thousand thousand fruit to touch,
Cherish in hand, lift down, and not let fall.
For all
That struck the earth,
No matter if not bruised or spiked with stubble,
Went surely to the cider-apple heap
As of no worth.
One can see what will trouble
This sleep of mine, whatever sleep it is.
Were he not gone,
The woodchuck could say whether it's like his
Long sleep, as I describe its coming on,
Or just some human sleep.

Unharvested

A scent of ripeness from over a wall.
And come to leave the routine road
And look for what had made me stall,
There sure enough was an apple tree
That had eased itself of its summer load,
And of all but its trivial foliage free,
Now breathed as light as a lady's fan.
For there there had been an apple fall
As complete as the apple had given man.
The ground was one circle of solid red.

May something go always unharvested!
May much stay out of our stated plan,
Apples or something forgotten and left,
So smelling their sweetness would be no theft.

D. H. LAWRENCE (1885 – 1930)
Snake

A snake came to my water-trough
On a hot, hot day, and I in pyjamas for the heat,
To drink there.

In the deep, strange-scented shade of the great dark carob-tree
I came down the steps with my pitcher   5
And must wait, must stand and wait, for there he was at the trough
    before me.

He reached down from a fissure in the earth-wall in the gloom
And trailed his yellow-brown slackness soft-bellied down, over the
    edge of the stone trough
And rested his throat upon the stone bottom,
And where the water had dripped from the tap, in a
    small clearness,   10
He sipped with his straight mouth,
Softly drank through his straight gums, into his slack
    long body,
Silently.

Someone was before me at my water-trough,
And I, like a second comer, waiting.   15

He lifted his head from his drinking, as cattle do,
And looked at me vaguely, as drinking cattle do,
And flickered his two-forked tongue from his lips, and mused a
    moment,
And stooped and drank a little more,
Being earth-brown, earth-golden from the burning bowels of
    the earth   20
On the day of Sicilian July, with Etna° smoking.   *the volcano*

The voice of my education said to me
He must be killed,
For in Sicily the black, black snakes are innocent, the gold are
    venomous.

And voices in me said, If you were a man   25
You would take a stick and break him now, and finish him off.

But must I confess how I liked him,
How glad I was he had come like a guest in quiet, to drink at
    my water-trough
And depart peaceful, pacified, and thankless,
Into the burning bowels of this earth?   30

Was it cowardice, that I dared not kill him?
Was it perversity, that I longed to talk to him?
Was it humility, to feel so honoured?
I felt so honoured.

And yet those voices: 35
If you were not afraid, you would kill him!

And truly I was afraid, I was most afraid,
But even so, honoured still more
That he should seek my hospitality
From out the dark door of the secret earth.   40

He drank enough
And lifted his head, dreamily, as one who has drunken,
And flickered his tongue like a forked night on the air, so black;
Seeming to lick his lips,
And looked around like a god, unseeing, into the air,   45
And slowly turned his head,
And slowly, very slowly, as if thrice adream,

Proceeded to draw his slow length curving round
And climb again the broken bank of my wall-face.

And as he put his head into that dreadful hole,   50
And as he slowly drew up, snake-easing his shoulders, and entered
    farther,
A sort of horror, a sort of protest against his withdrawing into that
    horrid black hole,
Deliberately going into the blackness, and slowly drawing himself
    after,
Overcame me now his back was turned.

I looked round, I put down my pitcher,   55
I picked up a clumsy log
And threw it at the water-trough with a clatter.

I think it did not hit him,
But suddenly that part of him that was left behind convulsed
    in undignified haste,
Writhed like lightning, and was gone   60
Into the black hole, the earth-lipped fissure in the wall-front,
At which, in the intense still noon, I stared with fascination.

And immediately I regretted it.
I thought how paltry, how vulgar, what a mean act!
I despised myself and the voices of my accursed human
    education.   65

And I thought of the albatross,[1]
And I wished he would come back, my snake.

For he seemed to me again like a king,
Like a king in exile, uncrowned in the underworld,
Now due to be crowned again.   70

And so, I missed my chance with one of the lords
Of life.
And I have something to expiate;
A pettiness.

---

[1]Albatross: the bird shot and killed by the Seaman in Coleridge's "The Rime of the
Ancient Mariner."

WILLIAM CARLOS WILLIAMS (1883 – 1963)
The Dance

In Breughel's[1] great picture, The Kermess,
the dancers go round, they go round and
around, the squeal and the blare and the
tweedle of bagpipes, a bugle and fiddles
tipping their bellies (round as the thick-
sided glasses whose wash they impound)
their hips and their bellies off balance
to turn them. Kicking and rolling about
the Fair Grounds, swinging their butts, those
shanks must be sound to bear up under such
rollicking measures, prance as they dance
in Breughel's great picture, The Kermess.

THEODORE ROETHKE (1908 – 1963)
My Papa's Waltz

The whiskey on your breath
Could make a small boy dizzy;
But I hung on like death:
Such waltzing was not easy.

We romped until the pans
Slid from the kitchen shelf;
My mother's countenance
Could not unfrown itself.

The hand that held my wrist
Was battered on one knuckle;
At every step you missed
My right ear scraped a buckle.

You beat time on my head
With a palm caked hard by dirt,
Then waltzed me off to bed
Still clinging to your shirt.

---

[1]Pieter Brueghel (also spelled Breughel) the Elder (1521?–1569) was a Flemish
painter famed for his pictures of peasant life, such as that of an open-air festival, or
"Kermess."

4

Describing Poems

There are many ways of describing poems. As new sorts of poems are invented, as cross-fertilizing among cultures takes place, we need to come up with new descriptions. But it is useful to know some of the ways in which critics have described poems in the past, and to learn a handy set of methods for exploring a poem to find things worth describing in it. This chapter is a quick look at some techniques you can use to describe a poem you have read.

The large category "poetry" has often been divided into subcategories. We are concerned here not with the longer genres, epic poetry and dramatic poetry, but with the smaller kinds of relatively short poetry. Here are some of them. (A longer list can be found in the appendix "On Lyric Subgenres.")

Poetic Kinds

Narrative versus Lyric; Narrative in Lyric

We tend to distinguish *narrative* poems from *lyric* poems. A *narrative* poem (for instance, a ballad) tells a story — for example, about the murder of Lord Randal, or (as in the case of "Frankie and Johnny") about the revenge a woman took on her unfaithful lover. A *lyric,* on the other hand, may contain the germ of a story — say, a man's regret that a love affair is ending — but the poem dwells less on the plot than on the man's feelings (despair, grief, resentment, and so on). Wordsworth put the two kinds together and called some of his short poems "lyrical ballads" — meaning poems that, although they imply or even tell a story, make the characters' feelings more important than the plot. Narrative and lyric sometimes overlap, because most narrative poems include feeling and reflection as well as plot, and most lyric poems have an implied plot of sorts.

Lyric poems in which there is a distinct narrative interest often show changes in tense: "Once I *did* this but now I *can* no longer *do* it, and in the future I *will* never *do* it again." (Poems that are primarily lyric meditations on a single subject are often phrased in the present tense alone: "The expense of spirit in a waste of shame / Is lust in action.") To see the way tenses organize the narrative plot of a poem, let's look at a poem by Adrienne Rich, spoken by a woman who has emerged from the exhaustions of motherhood and is thinking that she will at last have a private life again. She retraces her own birth and ambitious adolescence, then shows her inner deprivation as her life (once she became a mother) was handed over to others in what sometimes seemed to her a form of slavery; she concludes with her present anticipation of a new — but aging — self. I have put the MAIN VERBS in uppercase so as to emphasize the tense changes; the *present participles* (which help make presentness) in italic; and the **past participles** (which help make pastness) in boldface:

Adrienne Rich (b. 1929)
Necessities of Life

Piece by piece I SEEM	*present*
to re-enter the world: I first BEGAN	*past*
a small, **fixed** dot, still SEE	*present*
that old myself, a dark-blue thumbtack	
pushed into the scene,	
a hard little head *protruding*	
from the pointillist's buzz and bloom,	
After a time the dot	
BEGINS to ooze. Certain heats	*present*
MELT it. Now I WAS hurriedly	*present/past*
BLURRING into ranges	
of **burnt** red, *burning* green,	
whole biographies SWAM up and	
SWALLOWED me like Jonah.	*past*

Jonah! I WAS Wittgenstein,   *past*
Mary Wollstonecraft, the soul

of Louis Jouvet, dead
in a **blown-up** photograph.

Till, **wolfed** almost to shreds,
I LEARNED to make myself   *past*

unappetizing. Scaly as a dry bulb
thrown into a cellar

I USED myself, LET nothing use me.   *past*
Like *being* on a private dole,

sometimes more like *kneading* bricks in Egypt.
What life WAS then, WAS mine,   *past*

now and again TO LAY   *infinitive*
one hand on a warm brick

and TOUCH the sun's ghost   *infinitive*
with economical joy,

now and again TO NAME   *infinitive*
over the bare necessities.

So much for those days. Soon
practice MAY MAKE me middling-perfect, I'LL   *modal future*

DARE inhabit the world   *future*
trenchant in motion as an eel, solid

as a cabbage-head. I HAVE invitations: *present*
a curl of mist STEAMS upward   *present*

from a field, visible as my breath,
houses along a road STAND waiting   *present*

like old women *knitting,* breathless
TO TELL their tales.   *infinitive*

One can see the *narrative* here unfolding in the verbs and verbals (tensed verbs, infinitives, present and past participles), and can watch the past becoming momentarily present in memory (in present participles like "protruding" and "kneading"). The future becomes tenseless, and thereby infinitely extendable, by means of an infinitive ("breathless / to tell their tales"). It is always useful to look for the narrative in all poems, and to decide how much of the poem is narrative versus how much "stays the same" as it meditates for a while without changing its stance.

Some poems are almost purely *meditative*. Here is the contemporary poet Philip Larkin on estrangement between two people who have been lovers for a long time. You will notice that "nothing happens," that the speaker is still in the same predicament at the end as at the beginning. The whole poem, except for the general statement of the first line, takes place in the present tense, as many meditations do:

PHILIP LARKIN (1922 – 1985)
Talking in Bed

Talking in bed ought to be easiest,
Lying together there goes back so far,
An emblem of two people being honest.

Yet more and more time passes silently.
Outside, the wind's incomplete unrest
Builds and disperses clouds about the sky,

And dark towns heap up on the horizon.
None of this cares for us. Nothing shows why
At this unique distance from isolation

It becomes still more difficult to find
Words at once true and kind,
Or not untrue and not unkind.

The *narrative* here — concerning the way talk becomes harder and harder as lovers gradually grow apart — is less important than the *meditation* on this problem conducted by the poet, as he says many things about it: that intimate talk should be easy, that he and his companion have a common past, that bed used to be the place where honesty had a chance, that the outside restless and menacing world is no help, and that there is no explanation for the increasing difficulty summed up in the last two lines. Here, the successive items reflected on in the meditation are the focus of interest, converging on the final redefinition of the problem in the last two lines. A meditative poem asks you to notice all its successive "takes" on the subject being considered.

In short, look for the *plot* in narrative lyrics where the tenses change, and look for *successive "takes"* on a subject in meditative lyrics.

Classifying Lyric Poems

Lyric poems themselves are generally classified in three ways: by *content*, by *speech act*, and by *outer form*.

Content: We could classify the poems by Rich and Larkin according to their *content,* calling Rich's an *autobiography* and Larkin's a *love-poem.*

Speech act: Or we could classify the two poems according to their *speech acts,* calling Rich's a *confessional narration* and Larkin's a *meditation* on estrangement.

Outer form: Or we could classify the poems according to their *outer form,* describing Rich's as a *poem in unrhymed couplets* and Larkin's as a *poem in rhymed tercets.*

Each of these classifications requires that we investigate the poem for something different — for what its content is, what sort of speech acts it is engaging in, and what outer form it displays.

Content Genres

Here are some of the most frequent kinds (or *genres,* the French word for "kinds") of lyric poems identified by *content:*

The love poem

The aubade (a dawn poem in which one of the lovers, usually, is waked by the sun and speaks)

The nocturne (a night scene)

The pastoral (a poem spoken by a shepherd; loosely, a poem in the countryside)

The elegy (a poem mourning a death)

The epithalamion (a poem celebrating a wedding)

The prayer

The autobiography

The flower poem

The sea poem

The travel poem

The birthday poem

There are enough poems of all the above sorts so that any poet writing a travel poem is bound to remember other travel poems, and so on. The poet expects the reader, often, to know how such poems usually go (a travel poem, for instance, normally reaches a destination). The poet then often "changes the rules," and violates the very expectations that the poem has set up. The seventeenth-century poet George Herbert, for instance, in a poem called "Pilgrimage," leads us by his title to expect that he will find a destination, but all he finds is "a lake of brackish waters" instead of a place of spiritual healing. Flower poems, to give another example, usually praise the flower, but William Blake writes of a "sunflower, weary of time" and makes us wonder about the weariness of the flower. The dawn poem is usually spoken by one lover to the other, as in *Romeo and Juliet;* John Donne makes his dawn poem unusual by addressing the sun: "Busy old fool, unruly sun!" In every case, a poet writing with a known content will want to do something new and interesting with that content. The more poems you have read, the more pleasure you will get from reading a new poem, since you will be alert to the new thing the poet is doing. It is the "new twist," as well as the old thing done very well in a new way, that gives the pleasure.

The first poet to invent a kind sets a problem: What do lovers say when the sun comes up and interrupts their lovemaking? Every subsequent poet finds a new solution to the problem. No one solution is better, in theory, than any other; and a rich poetic problem is one that keeps on generating new solutions.

Emily Dickinson, for instance, wrote a prayer-poem describing a heart praying to an invisible power. The success of the poem depends on our having a sense that the usual prayer is addressed to God, has a reverential tone, and asks for some hoped-for good: only if we know these normal conditions will we see Dickinson's blasphemy. Dickinson tells us in the first stanza that *someone* is being addressed by the Heart, but it is not until the second stanza that that person addressed is described as an "inquisitor," a torturer. And the hoped-for good asked for by the Heart changes as the poem goes on, giving the poem its dynamic shape or inner form, as the praying Heart changes from someone demanding pleasure to an abject prisoner craving from God "the privilege to die":

EMILY DICKINSON (1830 – 1886)
The Heart asks Pleasure – first –

The Heart asks Pleasure – first –
And then – Excuse from Pain –
And then – those little Anodynes°   *painkillers*
That deaden suffering –

And then – to go to sleep –
And then – if it should be
The will of its Inquisitor
The privilege to die –

This two-stanza description of a prayer is organized as a list of goods asked for. Its dynamic shape can be indicated as a long chain of petitions, all of them the direct objects of the verb "asks":

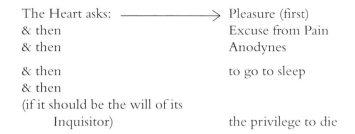

Why does Dickinson divide this single list into two stanzas? What makes stanza 2 worth separating from stanza 1? As soon as we ask this question we realize that we don't know, in stanza 1, whom the Heart is addressing with its prayer. If we translate Dickinson's narrative into the Heart's direct pleas, the young Heart says: "I want Pleasure." Pleasure never comes; that prayer goes unanswered. "Well, then, I want to have no more Pain," says the Heart, still believing that its unknown Addressee in heaven would prefer to bestow pleasure or at least painlessness on the petitioner. But the pain goes on, unabated. "Well, then, please give me some drugs to lessen the suffering," asks the Heart. Throughout the first stanza the Heart still wants to maintain consciousness, even if it should be consciousness dulled by a sedative. Throughout the first stanza the Heart still believes in the potential benevolence of the Person listening to these demands.

But no anodynes are forthcoming, and the Heart foresees that its life will be one of unrelieved suffering. "At least let me sleep," prays the Heart, now willing to forgo consciousness. But that prayer goes unanswered, too; nights of insomniac suffering succeed days full of undeadened pain. It is at this point that the Heart redefines the person addressed. This person on high is clearly totally nonbenevolent, having denied the Heart any morsel of pleasure, having even denied a letup in pain, refusing to give painkilling medicines, withholding even the relief from pain given by sleep. What can we call such a torturer? Dickinson reaches to the Renaissance image of a church-licensed torturer, an Inquisitor. The Inquisitor has total power; the tortured Heart, none. Once you recognize that the person in charge of your destiny is a torturer and that you are totally in his power, nothing is left for you but to be abject, to cringe, to say, "Oh Inquisitor, if it be thy will, grant me the privilege of dying." It is to this suicidal point that the Heart comes at the end of her prayer, when she is willing (as she was not in the first stanza) to forgo consciousness entirely. She now clearly perceives (as she did not in the first stanza) that she is in the hands not of a benevolent God but of a relentlessly cruel one. At last we see why Dickinson divided her list of petitions in two.

The petitionary form described in this poem is that of a Christian prayer. A poem describing a "standard" Christian prayer might say:

The soul asks peace of mind,
And then for virtue's power,
And then for hope and charity
In every evil hour;

And then for faith in grief,
And then — if it should be
The will of its Creator-God —
His face at death to see.

A "conventional" prayer-poem of this sort is the "ghost-model" behind Dickinson's blasphemous rewriting of the genre. Dickinson expects her reader to react strongly to her departure from the conventional ways of talking to God. All poets expect readers to know (from ordinary social behavior) what sort of content would normally appear in the usual prayer, or the usual wedding song, or the conventional funeral speech, and to measure the poem's departures in content from the norm.

Speech Acts

When we classify poems by their speech acts, we draw attention to their *manner* of expression more than to their content. I can apologize for any number of things — my tardiness, or my mistakes, or my clothing — but in each of these cases my speech act (whatever its content) is an *apology.* Similarly, I can protest about time, or death, or love — but in every case, my speech act is a *protest.* Since the language of most poems can be thought of as a series of utterances by a speaker, the poet expects you to track the person's successive speech acts, just as you might do in life when you might say, "First, she *criticized* me, then she *apologized,* then she *explained* why she was upset, and finally she *asked* if we could still be friends." A poem's speech acts need to be followed and identified in just this way: "The speaker *declares* his love, and then *vows* that he will always be faithful, while *protesting* the indifference of his beloved and *reproaching* her for it." Here are a few speech acts that often organize poems (a longer list is provided in the appendix "On Speech Acts"):

Apology

Apostrophe (a direct second-person address to another, usually of higher rank)

Declaration

Boast

Command

Interrogation

Exclamation

Description

Hypothesis

Rebuttal

Narration

Prayer

Debate or dialogue

Reproach

We have seen a *narration* of autobiography in Rich's poem "Necessities of Life," a *narration* of prayer in Dickinson's "The Heart asks Pleasure – first –." A poem whose *speech act* was prayer would be, unlike the Dickinson poem, addressed directly to God, like George Herbert's "Discipline," which begins,

> Throw away thy rod,
> Throw away thy wrath,
>   O my God,
> Take the gentle path.

Or the speech act of a poem can be a *command*. Commands are normally given by people; one way of being original in a command-poem would be to have the commands given by something that normally doesn't talk. This is what Carl Sandburg does in his poem "Grass," where the grass speaks. This poem surveys the sites of famous battles during the Napoleonic Wars, the Civil War, and the First World War:

CARL SANDBURG (1878 – 1967)
Grass

Pile the bodies high at Austerlitz and Waterloo.
Shovel them under and let me work —
    I am the grass; I cover all.

And pile them high at Gettysburg
And pile them high at Ypres and Verdun.
Shovel them under and let me work.
Two years, ten years, and passengers ask the conductor:

> What place is this?
> Where are we now?
>
> I am the grass.
> Let me work.

This poem contains other speech acts besides its repeated *commands* ("pile," "shovel them under," "let me work"). It also contains a repeated *self-definition* ("I am the grass") and a piece of *narration* "Two years . . . and passengers ask . . . what place is this?" If we were mapping this poem by the grass's speech acts, numbering the commands in sequence (1, 2, and so on), it would read:

> *Command* 1a ("pile")
> *Commands* 2a and 3a ("shovel them under," "let me work")
> > *Self-definition* 1a ("I am the grass")
>
> *Command* 1b ("and pile")
> *Command* 1c ("and pile")
> *Commands* 2b and 3b ("shovel them under" and "let me work")
> *Narration* ("passengers ask")
>
> > (Inserted *question* by passengers: "What . . . ?")
> > (Inserted *question* by passengers: "Where . . . ?")
>
> > *Self-definition* 1b ("I am the grass")
> > *Command* 3c ("let me work")

When we "map" a poem by its speech acts, we are often enabled to see its skeletal structure and to describe it precisely, saying, "This is a poem of repeated *commands* by the grass. The grass *defines itself* by its work of covering-over the dead of all battles, important in their day but soon forgotten, as the *questions* asked by later passers-by, *narrated* by the grass, reveal." This is a far more exact way of describing a poem than to mention only its theme, saying, "This poem is about the way in which past battles are soon forgotten." In noting the way the poet has made this thematic cliché memorable — by having the grass be the speaker, and by giving it relatively few and repeated speech acts to use — one sees the poem not merely as a statement about war but as a constructed piece of art. Since the language of most poems can be thought of as a series of utterances by a speaker, the poet expects the reader to track and identify the speech acts, just as we do in life. Here, the repetitiveness of form is used to emphasize the sameness of all wars, as burial follows burial repeatedly.

Outer Form

A poem can also be classified according to various aspects of its *outer form,* having to do with meter, rhyme, and stanza-form. (The appendix "On Prosody" describes these aspects more fully.) With respect to prosody, here are a few examples of kinds of naming.

Line-Width

Some form-names have to do with the *width* of the poetic *line.* A pentameter poem is a poem in lines *five* beats *wide:*

> When I / see BIRCH / es BEND / to LEFT / and RIGHT . . .
> I LIKE / to THINK / some BOY'S / been SWING / ing THEM.

A trimeter poem is a poem in lines *three* beats *wide:*

> It is TIME / that I MADE / my WILL;
> I CHOOSE / upSTAND / ing MEN.

The single most important thing to remember in deciding how many beats a line has is that you cannot ascertain this in isolation. You need to look at the lines surrounding it, and, if it occurs in a poem with stanzas, at matching lines in other stanzas. The reason you need surrounding or matching lines is that many lines, taken by themselves, could be read in different ways. Take the line from Hamlet's famous soliloquy "To be or not to be: that is the question." You could read this line, taken by itself, in two different ways:

> To BE or NOT to be: THAT is the QUESTion.   (*4 beats*)
> To BE or NOT to BE: THAT is the QUESTion.   (*5 beats*)

We decide that the line is meant to have five beats because the lines surrounding it in Hamlet's speech mostly seem to fall into place if we read them with five beats:

> To DIE, to SLEEP; to SLEEP, perCHANCE to DREAM,   (*5*)
> And IN that SLEEP of DEATH what DREAMS may COME   (*5*)
> When WE have SHUFFled OFF this MORtal COIL   (*5*)
> Must GIVE us PAUSE.

This gives us the evidence we need to decide that we should read our dubious line as "To BE or NOT to BE: THAT is the QUESTion," with five beats.

Similarly, the line with which William Butler Yeats begins his poem "Easter 1916" is "I have met them at close of day." Taken by itself, we could read this line perfectly reasonably as having four beats ("I HAVE met THEM at CLOSE of DAY") if it were followed by another four-beat line, as in this piece of doggerel:

> I have met them at close of day,   *(4)*
> But they have never greeted me,   *(4)*
> And though I now am old and gray,   *(4)*
> I think that we cannot agree.   *(4)*

In point of fact, though, Yeats's line is followed by a long series of lines that all have three beats each, which makes us read it, too, with a three-beat rhythm — "I have MET them at CLOSE of DAY":

> I have MET them at CLOSE of DAY   *(3)*
> COMing with VIVid FAces,   *(3)*
> From COUNTer or DESK among GREY   *(3)*
> EIGHTeenth-CENtury HOUSes.   *(3)*

The rule of thumb, then, is always to look at lines *in groups* when you are deciding how many beats they have. Find another stanza in the poem matching the one you are dubious about, and see if its pattern is clearer. (All similar stanzas in a poem have the same arrangement of beats.) The best way to "hear" the beats of a poem is to read it aloud, and to notice the natural stresses of the sentences as you read, deciding, in dubious cases, how to read the line by comparing it with others.

Rhythm

Some form-names have to do with the *rhythm* of the line. Rhythms are either *rising* (one-TWO, one-TWO would be an example) or *falling* (ONE-two-three, ONE-two-three would be an example). Shakespeare's blank verse has a two-syllable rising rhythmic unit represented as one-TWO, ˘´. Five of these building units make up the Shakespearean line — *five* beats *wide,* in a *rising* rhythm: ˘´˘´˘´˘´˘´; "To DIE, to SLEEP; to SLEEP, perCHANCE to DREAM." *Falling* rhythm is much heavier than rising rhythm, and is often used to imitate marching, hoofbeats, or some form of raw power, as in Blake's poem on the TYger that goes ONE-two, ONE-two: "TYger, TYger, BURNing BRIGHT / IN the FORests OF the NIGHT."

Poem-Length

Some form-names have to do with the *length* of the *whole poem:* Wallace Stevens's "Sunday Morning" is a poem in eight *cantos,* in which each *canto* (a single long stanza) has fifteen lines. The name *sonnet* normally means that the poem in question has fourteen lines.

Combinatorial Form-Names

Some form-names have to do with the width *and* rhythm *and* length *and* rhymes of the *whole poem:* a "Shakespearean sonnet" is a poem with lines *five* beats *wide* in a two-syllable *rising* rhythm; it is *fourteen* lines long, and the lines rhyme *abab cdcd efef gg* (making three quatrains in alternate rhyme and a rhyming couplet).

These qualities of form are explained systematically in the appendix "On Prosody." They need to be observed routinely, in the case of every poem you read. Once you have described its *content* (a spring poem, an elegy) and its successive *speech acts* (a narration, a plea), look at the *outer form.* How many lines does the whole poem have? How many stanzas? Are they all the same shape? How wide is the line? Where do the rhymes come? What is the overall rhythm? It helps to jot down what you observe in the margin next to the poem on the page ("Elegy; lament, protest, consolation; fifteen alternately rhymed pentameter quatrains in rising rhythm"). That way you have a handle on the poem the next time you look at it.

Inner Structural Form

Besides its *outer form* ("This is a poem in quatrains in falling rhythm rhyming *aabb*" — a description of Blake's "Tyger"), every poem has *internal structural form.* This is its dynamic shape, which derives from the curve traced by the emotions of the poem as they change over its duration. That emotional curve is plotted by connecting two, three, or more points of the poem, a rise from depression to hope to joy, for instance — or a decline from triumph through doubt to despair. Very few poems represent an unchanging steady state of the same emotion all through.

Some poems are two-part (*binary*) poems, like William Wordsworth's "A slumber did my spirit seal" (which we saw changing from illusion to stern knowledge), or like Dickinson's "The Heart asks Pleasure – first –" (which we saw changing its conception of God from benevolence to cruelty). Another fundamentally binary form is the debate poem, where A speaks, then B challenges A, then A replies to B, back and forth.

There are also many three-part (*ternary*) poems, which often take on the internal structure of beginning, modulation, end (a song-form preserved in lyric). For an example of three-part form, see W. B. Yeats's "Crazy Jane Talks with the Bishop."

Internal forms are infinitely variable, since they represent emotional response, always volatile. One well-known internal structure is that of the "surprise" ending, where the last few lines reverse everything that has gone before. George Herbert's poem "The Collar" is full of rebellion against God, until the very end:

> But as I raved, and grew more fierce and wild
> > At every word,
> Methoughts I heard one calling, *Child!*
> > And I replied, *My Lord.*

In investigating the internal structure of a poem, one should try to divide it into parts along its "fault lines." Where does the logic of the argument seem to break? Where does the poem change from first person to second person? Where does the major change in tense or speech act take place? Here are some of the ingredients of internal structural form that will help you to explore a poem.

Sentences

Poems are, on the whole, made of sentences, and sentences are an important internal structuring principle of poems. For instance, there will often be a procession of short sentences, and then one very long sentence, or vice versa. The poet means us to notice how many sentences there are in a poem, and how they relate to one another. There may be a generalizing sentence ("How do I love thee? Let me count the ways") followed by many particulars; or many small instances leading up to more important ones, as in Robert Herrick's summary of his poetic subjects, ending at the hope of salvation:

ROBERT HERRICK (1591 – 1674)
The Argument of His Book

I sing of brooks, of blossoms, birds, and bowers,
Of April, May, of June, and July flowers.
I sing of Maypoles, hock carts, wassails, wakes,
Of bridegrooms, brides, and of their bridal cakes.
I write of youth, of love, and have access
By these to sing of cleanly wantonness.
I sing of dews, of rains, and, piece by piece,
Of balm, of oil, of spice, and ambergris.
I sing of times trans-shifting, and I write
How roses first came red and lilies white.
I write of groves, of twilights, and I sing
The court of Mab° and of the fairy king.   *queen of the fairies*
I write of hell; I sing (and ever shall)
Of heaven, and hope to have it after all.

You can often discover a lot about a poem by copying out its successive sentences in prose, putting each one under its predecessor. You can then ask yourself how they resemble one another, and how they differ, and why.

Person

Sentences are written either in the first person (*I/me* in the singular, *we/us* in the plural); the second person (*you* — archaic forms are *thou* in the nominative singular, *thee* in the objective singular, and *ye* in the plural); or the third person (*he/him, she/her,* and *it* in the singular; *they/ them* in the plural). A *change of person* as a poem goes along is a significant structuring device. A change to the second person, addressing a person ("you") in the poem who hasn't appeared before, usually raises the temperature of a poem, as when Wordsworth, after a long monologue in "Tintern Abbey," turns to his sister, saying, "For thou art with me here upon the banks / Of this fair river," and we learn for the first time that he is not alone. An elegy often begins by trying to keep the dead person "alive" by directly addressing him or her, and may then subside into the third person, speaking no longer of "you" but of "the body," as Robert Lowell does in his elegy for his mother, "Sailing Home from Rapallo." He is bringing his mother's body from Italy (where she had died) home to New England, and we gradually see Charlotte Lowell turn from being a "you" to being "the corpse":

> **Your** nurse could only speak Italian,
> but after twenty minutes I could imagine **your** final week,
> and tears ran down my cheeks. . . .
>
> When I embarked from Italy with **my mother's body**,
> the whole shoreline of the *Golfo di Genova°*   Gulf of Genoa
> was breaking into fiery flower.
>
> . . . . .
>
> **Mother** traveled first-class in the hold.
>
> . . . . .
>
> In the grandiloquent lettering on **Mother's** coffin,
> *Lowell* had been misspelled LOVEL.
> **The corpse**
> was wrapped like *panettone* in Italian tinfoil.

Person reveals the poet's relation to the world. Is the poet in the world of "you" or "we" — other persons — or in a solitary world inhabited only by the "I" of the poem? Or a world with no addressees, full of "its" and "thems"?

Agency

Every sentence has a subject; the subject is the agent of the verb. Many poems have one subject ("I") for every sentence: in them, agency never changes. Others have a single *change in agency:* see, for instance, Randall Jarrell's "The Death of the Ball Turret Gunner," in which the subject of all the main verbs is "I" until the last line, when, because the ball turret gunner has been killed, the "I" vanishes and "they" take over. The "I" who acted becomes the "me" who is acted on. Here is the complete poem:

RANDALL JARRELL (1914 – 1965)
The Death of the Ball Turret Gunner

From my mother's sleep I fell into the State,
And I hunched in its belly till my wet fur froze.
Six miles from earth, loosed from its dream of life,
I woke to black flak and the nightmare fighters.
When I died *they* washed *me* out of the turret with a hose.

Some poems have a different subject for every sentence — these make the reader take on several different perspectives at once. See, for instance, Lowell's "Skunk Hour," where in the first stanza alone there are four different subjects that govern verbs:

Nautilus Island's hermit
heiress still lives through winter in her Spartan cottage;
her *sheep* still graze above the sea.
Her *son*'s a bishop. Her *farmer*
is first selectman in our village;
she's in her dotage.

Heiress, sheep, son, farmer: all govern verbs ("lives," "graze," "is," "is"). These agents are all linked in an elaborate system of center and satellites. The *hermit heiress* has *her* cottage, *her* sheep, *her* son, and *her* farmer (unfortunately, there is also *her* dotage, which she is in). The heiress still in some sense owns her sheep, her son, and her farmer (they are all *hers*); but because they are all given independent existence as agents in the poem, we know they are no longer hers, really. They are separate from her, separate subjects; and the only things that are really hers now are her cottage and her dotage; only these two rhyming nouns, among "her" possessions, are not independent agents governing a verb. *By tracing agency through a poem we can tell who is ruling it as it goes along.* In "Skunk Hour," the various inhabitants of the seaside town at first "own" the poem; then the disturbed speaker "owns" the poem while he carries out his voyeuristic acts; but finally it is the mother skunk with her column of kittens who "owns" the poem and the town, as in the last stanza the troubled speaker yields agency to the skunk:

> I **stand** on top
> of our back steps and **breathe** the rich air —
> a *mother skunk* with her column of kittens *swills* the garbage pail.
> *She jabs* her wedge-head in a cup
> of sour cream, *drops* her ostrich tail,
> and *will not scare.*

It is important to know who "owns," by agency, each part of every poem.

Tenses

Sentences are written in tenses, and tenses are also an important internal structuring aspect of the poem, making it move in time (as we saw in Adrienne Rich's "Necessities of Life") from past to present to future. *Tense-changes* ask to be noticed. Sometimes, even often, they are the main point of the poem. As we saw earlier, in Wordsworth's "A slumber did my spirit seal," the first stanza is in the past tense, the second in the present tense. The first stanza stands for delusion ("seemed"); the second stanza for reality; and the white gap between the two tenses represents the death of the beloved. Here are the tensed verbs:

WILLIAM WORDSWORTH (1770 – 1850)
A slumber did my spirit seal

> A slumber *did* my spirit *seal;*
>   I *had* no human fears;
> She *seemed* a thing that *could not feel*
>   The touch of earthly years.
>
> No motion *has* she now, no force;
>   She neither *hears* nor *sees;*
> Rolled round in earth's diurnal course,
>   With rocks, and stones, and trees.

The main structuring agent of the poem is the *tense-change,* bracketing the invisible (infinite, untensed) white-space moment of the girl's death.

Images, or Sensual Words

"We thought in images," said Robert Lowell in a poem to his friend and fellow poet John Berryman. Though words in poetry can only refer and not really picture, a linkage of references in the same category of sense-perceivable words — say, many words about the moon, such as "bright," "beams," "round," "white," and so on — tend to create the impression of the object to which they all refer. Linked words (referring especially to the senses of sight and hearing) help to structure many poems. These words can be all of one sort (a collection of names of different flowers, for instance, in Milton's "Lycidas") or they can be of different sorts: that is, a series of specific nouns like "flood," "earthquake," "fire," and "shipwreck" can all help to construct the single abstract category "catastrophe." There are systematic ways in which the concrete words that some refer to as "images" may be assembled, too: they may be arranged in *parallel,* or in *contrast,* or in a ranked *hierarchy.* See how Sylvia Plath arranges her images in "Metaphors":

SYLVIA PLATH (1932 – 1963)
Metaphors

I'm a riddle in nine syllables,
An elephant, a ponderous house,
A melon strolling on two tendrils.
O red fruit, ivory, fine timbers!
This loaf's big with its yeasty rising.
Money's new-minted in this fat purse.
I'm a means, a stage, a cow in calf.
I've eaten a bag of green apples,
Boarded the train there's no getting off.

In this poem, Plath runs through many *parallel images* to express her feelings about being pregnant. The first is her ignorance of what her baby will be (boy? girl? placid? temperamental? tall? short?) at the end of nine months: it is a "riddle." Next, she emphasizes (via the elephant) the weight she has gained and (via the house) the difficulty of movement. Next, she emphasizes (via the melon) her new shape and how fragile her legs feel (like tendrils) supporting her abdomen. From the melon, she generalizes to the newborn baby as a "red fruit" — then generalizes further to its precious potential as "ivory" and "fine timbers." The dynamism of the progress of pregnancy is pointed to in the organic "yeasty rising" of bread; but then the dynamism (given its value) is made inorganic, as money is "new-minted" (but with a return to her weight in the referral to herself as a "fat" purse).

The next set of metaphors, however, departs from what we could reasonably call "images." "I'm a means, a stage." These *abstractions* — a means to an end, a stage in a process — show the poet generalizing beyond the dynamic images (bread rising, money being newly minted) to dynamism itself, a dynamism that reaches to a foreseen conclusion.

Immediately the poet returns to *images*. She is a pregnant cow (another reference to her unwieldy size) who has "eaten a bag of green apples" (thought to provoke labor in cows); and she is a helpless and fearful passenger, unable to leave the rushing forward motion of the train that will take her to her unknown destination.

You might ask yourself both why the poet passes from images to abstractions, and equally why she does not end in abstractions but returns to images for closure. Does it seem dehumanizing for the author to call herself a means? a stage? Each of Plath's images has a part-to-whole relation to the theme of the poem. Taken all together, they give the poem its emotional resonance. Which parts are cheerful? Which are triumphant? Which are apprehensive? How would the poem be different if it ended with the elephant? the money? the cow? the stage? Why does Plath end, do you think, with the train?

Exploring a Poem

What follows is a series of things to note when you run through a poem to see what its parts are and how they fit together. Let us use this list on a sonnet by John Keats, called "On First Looking into Chapman's Homer." There are a few things we have to know to understand the references in the poem: Keats did not know Greek, and so he first read Homer's *Odyssey* in the Renaissance translation by George Chapman; Apollo is the Greek god of poetry; Keats believed (mistakenly) that it was the Spanish conquistador Cortez who, in exploring Panama ("Darien"), discovered the Pacific Ocean (in reality it was Balboa, but the historical error doesn't matter for the imaginative purposes of the poem). Keats tells us what it is like, even for a reader as experienced in poetry as he, to come across Homer's Odyssean epic (from which he draws his opening travel imagery) for the first time:

JOHN KEATS (1795 – 1821)
On First Looking into Chapman's Homer

Much have I travell'd in the realms of gold,
    And many goodly states and kingdoms seen;
    Round many western islands have I been
Which bards in fealty° to Apollo hold.   *allegiance*

Oft of one wide expanse had I been told
    That deep-brow'd Homer ruled as his demesne;°   *domain*
    Yet did I never breathe its pure serene°   *atmosphere*
Till I heard Chapman speak out loud and bold:
Then felt I like some watcher of the skies
    When a new planet swims into his ken;°   *view*
Or like stout Cortez when with eagle eyes
    He star'd at the Pacific — and all his men
Look'd at each other with a wild surmise —
    Silent, upon a peak in Darien.

How do we go about exploring such a poem? Let us try a series of steps.

1. Meaning

This is the usual sort of information-retrieval reading that we do with any passage of prose or verse. We come up with a summary of greater or lesser length giving the import of the passage as we make sense of it. Here, we might arrive at something like "The speaker says that he had traveled through a lot of golden terrain — had read a lot of poems — and people had told him about the Homeric domain, but he had never breathed its air till he heard Chapman speak out. Then he felt like an astronomer discovering a new planet; or like the explorer who discovered the Pacific, whose men, astonished by his gaze, guessed at his discovery." This sort of meaning-paraphrase is necessary, but less useful in poetry than in prose. In many poems there is rather little in the way of plot or character or message or "information" in the ordinary sense, and that little can be quickly sketched (perhaps initially, especially in the case of a complex poem, by the teacher to the class). Hoping to learn things about the poem that are more interesting than simply "what it says" in prose, we try to construct its

2. Antecedent Scenario ("Backstory")

What has been happening *before* the poem starts? What has disturbed the status quo and set the poem in motion? Here, we know what has happened: the speaker has picked up Homer (in Chapman's translation) for the first time, and has had a revelatory experience. But the antecedent scenario is not always given to us so clearly. If it is not evident right away, one moves on hopefully to

3. A Division into Structural Parts

Because small units are more easily handled than big ones, and because the process of a poem, even one as short as a sonnet, can't be

addressed all at once with a single global question like "W
here?" we divide the poem into pieces. One way of dividing u.
up is to notice that it falls, by its rhymes, into two large parts: "I ne.
knew Homer till I read Chapman" (*abbaabba*) and "Then I felt like this"
(*cdcdcd*). The first part takes up the first eight lines, connected by the two
rhyme-sounds represented by -*old* (rhyme *a*) and -*een* (rhyme *b*); and the
second part takes up the last six lines, connected by a new set of rhyme-
sounds, represented by -*ies* (rhyme *c*) and -*en* (rhyme *d*). There are other
ways, besides this 8:6 division, to divide this poem into parts, as we shall
see, but let us work first within this 8:6 division-by-rhyme. In order to
suggest a meaningful relation of the parts, it is useful to look at

4. The Climax

In Keats's sonnet, the climax seems to come when Cortez stares at
the Pacific — the high point of the poem. What is special about this
experience? Why does it replace the image of the astronomer discovering a new planet? In lyric poems, the various parts tend to cluster around
a moment of special significance — which its attendant parts lead up to,
lead away from, help to clarify, and so on. The climax usually manifests
itself by such things as greater intensity of tone, an especially significant
metaphor, a change in rhythm, or a change in person. Having located the
climax, one can now move back to

5. The Other Parts

About each part, it is useful to ask how it *differs* from the other
parts. What is distinctive in it by contrast to the other members of the
poem? Does something shift gears? Does the tense change? Does the
predominant grammatical form change? (For example, does the poem
stop emphasizing nouns and start emphasizing participles?) Is a new
person addressed? Have we left a general overlook for certain particulars? Here, we notice that the first four lines talk in *general* about states,
kingdoms, and islands. The next four lines talk about *one* special "wide
expanse," the one ruled by Homer. The next part says, "I felt like an
astronomer discovering a new planet." And the last part produces a new
comparison: "I felt like an explorer discovering a new ocean, accompanied by his companions." Some questions immediately arise: Why
doesn't the poem end after the poet says, "I felt as though I had discovered a new planet"? Why does he feel he needs a *second* comparison?
And why, in the second comparison, does he need not only a single
discoverer comparable to the astronomer, but a discoverer *accompanied
by a group of companions* ("all his men")? Once these four parts (general

realms; Homer's expanse; solo astronomer / planet; Cortez and men / Pacific Ocean) have been isolated, one can move on to the game called

6. Find the Skeleton

What is the dynamic curve of emotion on which the whole poem is arranged? "I am much travelled, and have visited [presumably by ship] many islands; however, I had never visited the Homer-expanse till I heard Chapman; then I breathed the air of the Homer-expanse, and it was like finding" — like finding what? The first stab at comparison ("like finding a new planet") isn't quite right — you can't walk on a planet and explore it and get to know it the way you get to know islands and states. Well, what would be a better comparison? And the speaker realizes that whereas other poets seem feudal lords of a given piece of earth — a state, a kingdom, an island — Homer is different *not just in degree but in kind*. He is, all by himself, an *ocean*. A new ocean, unlike a planet, is something on one's own plane that one can actually explore; yet it is something so big that it must contain many new islands and realms within it. When we understand this, we can identify the curve of astonishment in the poem when the Homer-*expanse* (a carefully chosen word that doesn't give away too much) turns out to be not just another piece of land, and not some faraway uninhabitable body in the sky, but a whole unexplorable ocean, hitherto unguessed at. The tone has changed from one of ripe experience ("Much have I travell'd") to one of ignorance (the speaker has never breathed the air of the vast Homeric expanse, though others had, and had told him about it), to the revelation of the "wild surmise" — we have found not just another bounded terrain, but an unsuspected ocean! This curve of emotion, rising from an almost complacent sense of experience to an astonished recognition, is the emotional skeleton of the poem. We can then ask about

7. Games the Poet Plays with the Skeleton

If "On First Looking into Chapman's Homer," by its content, is a then/now poem ("I used not to know Homer / Now I do"), what is the event bridging the then and the now? It is reading Homer in Chapman's translation. "Reading" is not an "event" in the usual sense: most then/now poems (like "A slumber did my spirit seal") are about some more tangible event (a death, an absence, a catastrophe). Keats plays a game, then, with the then/now poem in making its fulcrum an experience of reading. By saying that reading, too, is an Event, Keats makes the then/now poem new.

If this is a riddle-poem (and it is: "What is Homer-land like?"), how is the riddle prepared? It is prepared by a series of alternatives: "I have seen realms, states, kingdoms, islands." Some "expanse" is ruled by Homer, but I have not seen it yet. Will it be a realm? a state? a kingdom? another island? The first "answer" to the riddle is, "None of the above; Homer-land is a *new planet!*" But that is the wrong answer (one can't travel to and explore a new planet, and the speaker *is* exploring Homer), so the poem tries again to answer the riddle, and this time does it correctly: "None of the above; Homer-expanse is a *new ocean!*" The poet has played a game with our sense of the poem as a riddle by answering not in the category we anticipated from his former travels (a piece of land) but in an unexpected one (ocean), thus making the riddle-poem new.

Keats plays another game with the ignorance/discovery skeleton by making his poem a hero-poem. He makes the reward at the end of the emotional curve — the discovery of the new ocean — not a solitary experience (like that of the "watcher of the skies" seeing the planet), but a communal one. We normally think of reading as an uneventful private act. Why did Keats make it heroic? Furthermore, why did he show the heroic discovery being made not by a single explorer but by a company of explorers? Cortez is not alone on the isthmus of Panama, but is accompanied by "all his men / Look[ing] at each other with a wild surmise." When one discovers the Homeric "expanse" one reads alone, but one becomes thereby a member of a company of people who have discovered Homer — those people who had "oft . . . told" the speaker about Homer. A feat like Homer's writing the *Odyssey* is as heroic as the exploits of Achilles: mastery of such an intellectual discovery is itself a form of heroic exploration. Such a cultural discovery, Keats implies by the presence of Cortez's men, is collective, not private. Keats thought of himself as a poet among poets; a reader of Homer among readers of Homer; an explorer among explorers. And in this way he made the hero-poem both newly intellectual and newly communal and democratic.

Having seen the genre games that the poet plays with his skeleton — as a then/now poem, a riddle-poem, a hero-poem — one can go on to ask about

8. Language

Of course, we have been looking at language all along, but now we can do it more consciously. How many *sentences* does the poem have? (Two.) Where does the break between sentences come? (After line 4.) This gives us, as I promised earlier, a new division into parts: not the 8:6 of the then/now structure, but the 4:10 of the knowledge/discovery structure, which locates for us the moment in which traveled complacency turns to longing for Homeric acquaintance. *Poems often have several overlapping internal structures.* It is one of the signs of a complex poem that its rhymes may be dividing the poem one way, its theme another way, its action from inception through climax another way, its grammar another way, its sentences yet another way. Each of these divisions has something to tell us about the emotional dynamic of the poem.

What *parts of speech* predominate in the poem? (For a further explanation of these, see the appendix "On Grammar.") In Keats's sonnet, the chain of *nouns* of space — "realms," "states," "kingdoms," "islands," "expanse," "demesne," "planet," "Pacific" — stands out as one unifying link.

What other *words*, regardless of whether they are different parts of speech, make a *chain of significant relation?* You might notice how words of seeing and watching — "seen," "watcher," "ken," "eagle eyes," "star'd," "look'd at" — connect the parts of the poem as do the nouns of space.

What *contexts* are expressed in the diction? (We notice traveling, sailing, exploring, astronomical observation, feudal loyalty, and so on.)

Is the *diction* modern or ancient? (Keats uses archaic words like "realms of gold," "goodly," "bards," "fealty," "demesne," "pure serene," and "ken," which help us sense how long Homer has been alive in our culture.) A close look at language always leads to

9. Tone

The calm beginning, in the voice of ripe experience ("Much have I travell'd") mounts to the excitement of the "wild surmise," which then suddenly is confirmed by the breathless "silent" of the last line, and by the image of the "peak," corresponding to this heightened moment. Reading a poem aloud as if it were your own utterance makes you able to distinguish the various *tones of voice* it exhibits, and to name them. At this point, we can turn to

10. Agency and Speech Acts

Who has agency in this poem? We notice that the main verbs are all governed by the "I" who speaks the poem: "I have travelled . . . and seen . . . [and] have been . . . [and] had been told . . . yet [never] did I breathe . . . I heard . . . Then felt I." But we notice that in the subordinate clauses a great many other subagencies are present. Bards hold islands, Homer rules an expanse, Chapman speaks out, the new planet swims into ken, Cortez stares at the Pacific, and his men look with wild surmise at each other. It is by the interpenetration of the rather colorless main verbs denoting the sedentary activity of reading, and the other more public or active actions of the other agents, that Keats draws his new acquaintance with the *Odyssey* into large realms of cultural activity. The speech act of this poem is a single long *narration* of the speaker's more remote and recent pasts. The unusual thing about the speech act (narration) and agency (a single main agent) is that they stop so soon: the last narrative verb by the agent is "Then felt I" in line 9. After that, the attention of the poem never comes back to the speaker, but instead expands out to the most exalted sorts of cultural discovery — that of an astronomer, that of explorers.

11. Roads Not Taken

What are the *roads not taken* in the poem? The sonnet might have ended with the comparison of the self to an astronomer. Would this have been as satisfactory? Or the expanse ruled over by Homer might have been shown as a new continent rather than as a new ocean. Would this have been equally revealing? Or the poem might have been written in the third person instead of the first person:

> Many have travelled in the realms of gold,
>> And they have goodly states and kingdoms seen;
>> Round many western islands have they been
> Which bards in fealty to Apollo hold.

Is this as dramatic as the first person? Or the poem might have *begun* with the reading of Chapman's Homer, instead of leading up to it:

> I once heard Chapman speak out loud and bold;
>> He told me of a wide expanse unseen,
> (Better than other states and realms of gold)
>> That deep-brow'd Homer ruled as his demesne.
> Then felt I like stout Cortez on his peak,
>> When with his eagle eyes he saw the sea. . . .

We can see how presenting the climax in line 5, as in this rewriting, creates a very different structural shape from the 4:10 knowledge/discovery structure building up to the Pacific. It is useful to think of plausible *roads not taken* by a poem, because they help to identify the roads that *were* taken. With a clear idea of the function of each piece of the poem within the whole, and of the dynamic curve of emotion governing the order in which the pieces appear, we can then pass on to

12. Genre, Form, and Rhythm

What is the *content* genre of the poem? A dramatic change between then and now; a poem about reading; a poem about a hero; a poem about collective experience. (It can be compared to other poems about newness, about reading, about heroes, about collectivity.)

What is the *speech act* genre of the poem? A *narration in the first person* of a significant event marking one life-period off from another; and an *asking-a-riddle:* "What is reading Homer like?" (It can be compared to other first-person narrations and to other riddle-poems.)

What is the *formal* genre of the poem? A sonnet (using the usual five-beat rising-rhythm line found in sonnets) rhyming *abbaabba cdcdcd.* (It can be compared to other sonnets rhyming the same way.) About form, we always need to ask how it has been made vivid; see below for remarks on Keats's rhythm. We can then move on to the last issue, which is always

13. The Imagination

What has the poet's *imagination invented* that is striking, or memorable, or beautiful? We can tell, from the metaphors of sailing, that before writing his poem Keats had been reading Homer's *Odyssey,* and had been thinking about what Odysseus had discovered as he sailed from realm to realm, from island to island. Wanting to describe his own first reading of Homer, Keats imaginatively borrows from the very book he has been reading, using the image of travel, saying that reading poetry in general is like voyaging from Shakespeare-land to Milton-kingdom to Spenser-state, but that reading Homer is not like finding just another piece of land to visit: it is like finding a new planet, or, even better, a whole unexpected new ocean to sail in. Keats *imagined* these large analogies — sailing, astronomical observation, discovering an ocean — for the act of reading in general, and for reading Homer in particular; they enliven the sonnet. What makes the poem touching is the imagined change from the complacency of the well-traveled speaker to the astonishment of the discoverer of Homer, and the poet's realization that in reading Homer he has joined a company of others who have also discovered the Homeric ocean, sharing his "wild surmise." It is characteristic of Keats to see poetry as a collective act: he said in a letter, "I think I shall be among the English poets after my death," not "I think I shall be famous after my death."

But the imagination is not invested in themes and images alone. The imagination of a poet has to extend to the rhythm of the poem as well. What the imagination has invented here that is *rhythmically* memorable is the change from the stately first ten lines — because even the astronomer doesn't have to do anything but look through his telescope — to the strenuous broken rhythms of the heroic last four lines, with their four sharply differentiated parts:

1. Or like stout Cortez when with eagle eyes he star'd at the Pacific —
2. And all his men look'd at each other with a wild surmise —

3. Silent,

4. Upon a peak in Darien.

The intent, piercing stare of "stout Cortez"; the amazed mutual conjecture of his men; the sudden, short, transfixed silence of the whole group; the summit of foreign experience on which the action takes place — each of these four facts is given its own rhythmically irregular phrase, so different from the undisturbed and measured pentameter narration in "Then felt I like some watcher of the skies / When a new planet swims into his ken." A poem needs *imaginative rhythms* as well as *imaginative transformation* of content.

You will, of course, read most poems without investigating them in this detailed way for their inner processes. But as soon as you want to know *how a poem works*, as well as what it says, and *why it is poignant or compelling*, you will find yourself beginning to study it, using methods like the ones sketched here. Soon, it becomes almost second nature for you to notice sentences, tense-changes, speech acts, tonal variants, changes of agency, rhythms, rhymes, and other ingredients of internal and outer structure. Just as an archaeologist studies ruins, while the rest of us simply walk through Pompeii not understanding much of what we see, a student of poetry becomes more than simply a reader. You become more like a conductor who studies the musical score before conducting the piece in performance.

You can experience a poem with great pleasure as a general reader; or you can also learn how to explore it, to gain the more experienced pleasure that a student of architecture feels inside a Renaissance palace, or that an engineer feels looking at the San Francisco Bay Bridge. In every case, study adds to what you are able to perceive. Poems — because they are short and written in your own mother tongue — are very rewarding things to study as well as to read, to learn by heart as well as to study. They keep you company in life.

Exploring a poem under the broad headings given above will almost always lead you to a deeper understanding of the poem as a work of art, constructed in a dense and satisfying and surprising way. Though we almost always respond first to the quickly sensed "message" of a poem, the *reason* for our response (even if we do not at first know this) is the *arrangement* of the message (on many intersecting planes) into a striking and moving form. To give a poem its due as a work of art, we need to be able to see it as an *arranged* message. Looking through the poem thoroughly helps us realize the kind of work the poet puts into constructing this urgent expression of life as it is seen, sensed, and reflected on. Even the simplest of short poems will show imagination and architectural construction.

In Brief: Describing Poems

When you are looking for useful ways to describe a poem, this checklist of questions can guide your exploration:

1. *Meaning:* Can you paraphrase in prose the general outline of the poem?

2. *Antecedent scenario:* What has been happening before the poem begins? What has provoked the speaker into utterance? How has a previous equilibrium been unsettled? What is the speaker upset about?

3. *Division into parts:* How many are there? Where do the breaks come?

4. *The climax:* How do the other parts fall into place around it?

5. *The other parts:* What makes you divide the poem into these parts? Are there changes in person? In agency? In tense? In parts of speech?

6. *Find the skeleton:* What is the emotional curve on which the whole poem is strung? (It helps to draw a shape — a crescendo, perhaps, or an hourglass shape, or a sharp ascent followed by a steep decline — so you'll know how the poem looks to you as a whole.)

7. *Games with the skeleton:* How is this emotional curve made new?

8. *Language:* What are the contexts of diction, chains of significant relation, parts of speech emphasized, tenses, and so on?

9. *Tone:* Can you name the pieces of the emotional curve — the changes in tone you can hear in the speaker's voice as the poem goes along?

10. *Agency and its speech acts:* Who is the main agent in the poem, and does the main agent change as the poem progresses? See what the main speech act of the agent is, and whether that changes. Notice oddities about agency and speech acts.

11. *Roads not taken:* Can you imagine the poem written in a different person or tense, with the parts rearranged, or with an additional stanza or one stanza left out? Why might the poet have wanted *these* pieces in *this* order?

12. *Genres:* What are they by content, speech act, and outer form?

13. *The imagination:* What has it invented that is new, striking, memorable — in content, in genre, in analogies, in rhythm, in a speaker?

Reading Other Poems

If you were to give a genre-name by *content* to each of the poems below, you could begin, "Shakespeare: lust-poem"; "Herbert: prayer-poem"; "Marvell: solitude-poem," and go on through the list down to "Alexie: decline-poem." If you were to give a genre-name by *form* to each one, you could begin, "Shakespeare: sonnet"; "Herbert: shaped poem"; "Marvell: poem in 8-line couplet-stanzas"; down to "Alexie: poem in tercets," and so on. If you were to group them according to person, you could say, "Shakespeare: third person"; "Herbert: third person and first person"; "Marvell: third person and first person," and so forth. If you were to name them by principal speech act, you could say, "Shakespeare: definition"; "Herbert: apostrophe"; "Marvell: description"; down to "Alexie: narration." Try making such a list, and see how each question — content? form? person? speech act? — gives you a different purchase on the poem. You can expand that purchase by expanding the number of questions you put to the poem. For instance, where is the climax? Does the poem have a happy ending? From what position — participant, observer, judge — does the speaker operate? The following are merely some sample questions.

- ◆ What is the emotional curve traced by Shakespeare in his speaker's feelings about lust? By Ezra Pound in the young wife's feelings? Can you see how the tones of voice change with the feelings?

- ◆ How many different emotional responses to the fact of his blindness does Milton express? Can you suggest why Bradstreet's poem begins and ends in "we," while the middle uses other pronouns?

Consider how the poet's imagination has worked on the material.

- ◆ As Jorie Graham sees Piero della Francesca's painting of the young but majestic standing Virgin, pregnant and unbuttoning her dress before she goes into labor, how does the poet's imagination respond to the painting?

- ◆ As Mark Strand imagines courtship, how does he make it comic?

- ◆ As Heaney imagines that the anxiety of writing is like confronting police at a border checkpoint, how does he make that confrontation vivid?

- ◆ As Sherman Alexie imagines the decline of life on an Indian reservation, through what example does he convey it?

In longer poems like "Ode to a Nightingale," "Dover Beach," and "Mending Wall," the more scannings you make the more you see. You can begin anywhere that interests you. Anything you notice helps to build up your picture of the poem's world. In "Dover Beach" you might notice how one setting — on the English coast — leads to another — the Aegean Sea, and how one topic — love — leads to another — the ebbing of religious faith. These large structural blocks make you perceive how the poem is composed, and enable you to look at the micro-structures within each part. You can even begin your scanning at the end of the poem: when you look at the close of "Ode to a Nightingale" and see that it ends with two unresolved questions, you are more prepared for its inner vexations. Be patient with your scannings: each new run-through reveals more of the strategy of the poem, and enables you to describe the energies of the poem better.

WILLIAM SHAKESPEARE (1564 – 1616)
Sonnet 129

Th'expense of spirit in a waste of shame
Is lust in action, and till action, lust
Is perjured, murderous, bloody, full of blame,
Savage, extreme, rude, cruel, not to trust;
Enjoyed no sooner but despisèd straight,
Past reason hunted, and no sooner had,
Past reason hated as a swallowed bait,
On purpose laid to make the taker mad:
Mad in pursuit and in possession so,
Had, having, and in quest to have, extreme;
A bliss in proof,° and proved, a very woe,   *in the experience*
Before, a joy proposed, behind, a dream.
    All this the world well knows; yet none knows well
    To shun the heaven that leads men to this hell.

GEORGE HERBERT (1593 – 1633)
Easter Wings

    Lord, who createdst man in wealth and store,
      Though foolishly he lost the same,
        Decaying more and more
          Till he became
           Most poor:
           With thee

O let me rise
As larks, harmoniously,
And sing this day thy victories:
Then shall the fall further the flight in me.

My tender age in sorrow did begin;
And still with sicknesses and shame
Thou didst so punish sin,
That I became
Most thin.
With thee
Let me combine,
And feel this day thy victory;
For, if I imp[1] my wing on thine,
Affliction shall advance the flight in me.

ANDREW MARVELL (1621 – 1678)
The Garden

How vainly men themselves amaze
To win the palm, the oak, or bays,[1]
And their incessant labors see
Crowned from some single herb, or tree,
Whose short and narrow-vergèd shade   5
Does prudently their toils upbraid;
While all flowers and all trees do close
To weave the garlands of repose!

Fair Quiet, have I found thee here,
And Innocence, thy sister dear?   10
Mistaken long, I sought you then
In busy companies of men.
Your sacred plants, if here below,
Only among the plants will grow;
Society is all but rude   15
To this delicious solitude.

No white nor red was ever seen
So amorous as this lovely green.
Fond lovers, cruel as their flame,

---

[1]To graft feathers on a damaged wing so as to improve powers of flight. (A term from falconry.)

[1]Awards for military, civic, or poetic achievement.

Cut in these trees their mistress' name: 20
Little, alas, they know or heed
How far these beauties hers exceed!
Fair trees, wheresoe'er your barks I wound,
No name shall but your own be found.

    When we have run our passion's heat,   25
Love hither makes his best retreat.
The gods, that mortal beauty chase,
Still in a tree did end their race:
Apollo hunted Daphne so,
Only that she might laurel grow;   30
And Pan did after Syrinx speed,
Not as a nymph, but for a reed.[2]

    What wondrous life is this I lead!
Ripe apples drop about my head;
The luscious clusters of the vine   35
Upon my mouth do crush their wine;
The nectarine and curious peach
Into my hands themselves do reach;
Stumbling on melons, as I pass,
Insnared with flowers, I fall on grass.   40

    Meanwhile the mind, from pleasure less,° *from lesser pleasure*
Withdraws into its happiness;
The mind, that ocean where each kind
Does straight its own resemblance find;[3]
Yet it creates, transcending these,   45
Far other worlds and other seas,
Annihilating all that's made
To a green thought in a green shade.

    Here at the fountain's sliding foot,
Or at some fruit tree's mossy root,   50
Casting the body's vest aside,
My soul into the boughs does glide:
There, like a bird, it sits and sings,
Then whets and combs its silver wings,

---

[2]Daphne, to escape Apollo, turned into a laurel tree. Syrinx, to escape Pan, turned into a reed. Marvell implies that Apollo and Pan desired these transformations.

[3]Alluding to the popular notion that the flora and fauna of the land have their parallels in the sea.

And, till prepared for longer flight,   55
Waves in its plumes the various light.

    Such was that happy garden-state,
While man there walked without a mate:
After a place so pure and sweet,
What other help could yet be meet!   60
But 'twas beyond a mortal's share
To wander solitary there:
Two paradises 'twere in one
To live in paradise alone.

    How well the skillful gardener drew   65
Of flowers and herbs this dial new,
Where, from above, the milder sun
Does through a fragrant zodiac run;
And as it works, th' industrious bee
Computes its time as well as we!   70
How could such sweet and wholesome hours
Be reckoned but with herbs and flowers?

JOHN MILTON (1608 – 1674)
When I Consider How My Light Is Spent

When I consider how my light is spent
    Ere half my days in this dark world and wide,
    And that one talent which is death to hide
    Lodged with me useless, though my soul more bent
To serve therewith my Maker, and present
    My true account, lest he returning chide;
    "Doth God exact day-labor, light denied?"
    I fondly ask; but Patience to prevent
That murmur, soon replies, "God doth not need
    Either man's work or his own gifts; who best
    Bear his mild yoke, they serve him best. His state
Is kingly. Thousands at his bidding speed
    And post o'er land and ocean without rest:
    They also serve who only stand and wait."

ANNE BRADSTREET (c. 1612 – 1672)
To My Dear and Loving Husband

If ever two were one, then surely we.
If ever man were loved by wife, then thee;

If ever wife was happy in a man,
Compare with me ye women if you can.
I prize thy love more than whole mines of gold,
Or all the riches that the East doth hold.
My love is such that rivers cannot quench,
Nor ought but love from thee give recompense.
Thy love is such I can no way repay;
The heavens reward thee manifold, I pray.
Then while we live, in love let's so persever,
That when we live no more we may live ever.

JOHN KEATS (1795 – 1821)
Ode to a Nightingale

1

My heart aches, and a drowsy numbness pains
    My sense, as though of hemlock[1] I had drunk,
Or emptied some dull opiate to the drains
    One minute past, and Lethe-wards[2] had sunk:
'Tis not through envy of thy happy lot,
    But being too happy in thine happiness —
        That thou, light-wingèd Dryad of the trees,
          In some melodious plot
Of beechen green, and shadows numberless,
    Singest of summer in full-throated ease.

2

O, for a draught of vintage! that hath been
    Cooled a long age in the deep-delvèd earth,
Tasting of Flora° and the country green,   *goddess of flowers*
    Dance, and Provençal song,[3] and sunburnt mirth!
O for a beaker full of the warm South,
    Full of the true, the blushful Hippocrene,[4]
        With beaded bubbles winking at the brim,
          And purple-stainèd mouth;
That I might drink, and leave the world unseen,
    And with thee fade away into the forest dim:

---

[1]A plant that produces a powerful sedative, and from which it is also possible to produce a poison.

[2]Souls waiting in Hades to be reborn drink the waters of Lethe in order to forget their past existence.

[3]Provence was the home of the medieval troubadours.

[4]A fountain near Mount Helicon in Greece; its water induced poetic inspiration.

3

Fade far away, dissolve, and quite forget
    What thou among the leaves hast never known,
The weariness, the fever, and the fret
    Here, where men sit and hear each other groan;
Where palsy shakes a few, sad, last gray hairs,
      Where youth grows pale, and specter-thin, and dies,
        Where but to think is to be full of sorrow
         And leaden-eyed despairs,
    Where Beauty cannot keep her lustrous eyes,
      Or new Love pine at them beyond tomorrow.

4

Away! away! for I will fly to thee,
    Not charioted by Bacchus and his pards,[5]
But on the viewless° wings of Poesy,   *invisible*
    Though the dull brain perplexes and retards:
Already with thee! tender is the night,
    And haply the Queen-Moon is on her throne,
      Clustered around by all her starry Fays;°   *fairies*
        But here there is no light,
    Save what from heaven is with the breezes blown
      Through verdurous glooms and winding
        mossy ways.

5

I cannot see what flowers are at my feet,
    Nor what soft incense hangs upon the boughs,
But, in embalmèd° darkness, guess each sweet   *perfumed*
    Wherewith the seasonable month endows
The grass, the thicket, and the fruit tree wild;
    White hawthorn, and the pastoral eglantine;
      Fast fading violets covered up in leaves;
        And mid-May's eldest child,
    The coming musk-rose, full of dewy wine,
      The murmurous haunt of flies on summer eves.

6

Darkling° I listen; and for many a time   *in the dark*
    I have been half in love with easeful Death,

---

[5]Bacchus is the Greek god of wine, often represented in a chariot drawn by leopards ("pards").

Called him soft names in many a musèd rhyme,
    To take into the air my quiet breath;
Now more than ever seems it rich to die,
    To cease upon the midnight with no pain,
      While thou art pouring forth thy soul abroad
        In such an ecstasy!
Still wouldst thou sing, and I have ears in vain —
    To thy high requiem become a sod.

7

Thou wast not born for death, immortal Bird!
    No hungry generations tread thee down;
The voice I hear this passing night was heard
    In ancient days by emperor and clown:
Perhaps the selfsame song that found a path
    Through the sad heart of Ruth,[6] when, sick for home,
      She stood in tears amid the alien corn;
        The same that ofttimes hath
Charmed magic casements, opening on the foam
    Of perilous seas, in faery lands forlorn.

8

Forlorn! the very word is like a bell
    To toll me back from thee to my sole self!
Adieu! the fancy cannot cheat so well
    As she is famed to do, deceiving elf.
Adieu! adieu! thy plaintive anthem fades
    Past the near meadows, over the still stream,
      Up the hill side; and now 'tis buried deep
        In the next valley-glades:
Was it a vision, or a waking dream?
    Fled is that music: — Do I wake or sleep?

Matthew Arnold (1822 – 1888)

Dover Beach

The sea is calm tonight.
The tide is full, the moon lies fair
Upon the straits; on the French coast the light

---

[6] In the Old Testament Book of Ruth, Ruth was a faithful widow who followed her mother-in-law to a foreign land; there, as she was gleaning in a field, she was glimpsed by the master Boaz, who then married her.

Gleams and is gone; the cliffs of England stand,
Glimmering and vast, out in the tranquil bay.
Come to the window, sweet is the night-air!
Only, from the long line of spray
Where the sea meets the moon-blanched land,
Listen! you hear the grating roar
Of pebbles which the waves draw back, and fling,
At their return, up the high strand,
Begin, and cease, and then again begin,
With tremulous cadence slow, and bring
The eternal note of sadness in.

Sophocles long ago
Heard it on the Aegean, and it brought
Into his mind the turbid ebb and flow
Of human misery; we
Find also in the sound a thought,
Hearing it by this distant northern sea.

The Sea of Faith
Was once, too, at the full, and round earth's shore
Lay like the folds of a bright girdle furled.
But now I only hear
Its melancholy, long, withdrawing roar,
Retreating, to the breath
Of the night-wind, down the vast edges drear
And naked shingles of the world.

Ah, love, let us be true
To one another! for the world, which seems
To lie before us like a land of dreams,
So various, so beautiful, so new,
Hath really neither joy, nor love, nor light,
Nor certitude, nor peace, nor help for pain;
And we are here as on a darkling plain
Swept with confused alarms of struggle and flight,
Where ignorant armies clash by night.

ROBERT FROST (1874 – 1963)
Mending Wall

Something there is that doesn't love a wall,
That sends the frozen-ground-swell under it,
And spills the upper boulders in the sun;

And makes gaps even two can pass abreast.
The work of hunters is another thing:
I have come after them and made repair
Where they have left not one stone on a stone,
But they would have the rabbit out of hiding,
To please the yelping dogs. The gaps I mean,
No one has seen them made or heard them made,
But at spring mending-time we find them there.
I let my neighbor know beyond the hill;
And on a day we meet to walk the line
And set the wall between us once again.
We keep the wall between us as we go.
To each the boulders that have fallen to each.
And some are loaves and some so nearly balls
We have to use a spell to make them balance:
"Stay where you are until our backs are turned!"
We wear our fingers rough with handling them.
Oh, just another kind of outdoor game,
One on a side. It comes to little more:
There where it is we do not need the wall:
He is all pine and I am apple orchard.
My apple trees will never get across
And eat the cones under his pines, I tell him.
He only says, "Good fences make good neighbors."
Spring is the mischief in me, and I wonder
If I could put a notion in his head:
"*Why* do they make good neighbors? Isn't it
Where there are cows? But here there are no cows.
Before I built a wall I'd ask to know
What I was walling in or walling out,
And to whom I was like to give offense.
Something there is that doesn't love a wall,
That wants it down." I could say "Elves" to him,
But it's not elves exactly, and I'd rather
He said it for himself. I see him there
Bringing a stone grasped firmly by the top
In each hand, like an old-stone savage armed.
He moves in darkness as it seems to me,
Not of woods only and the shade of trees.
He will not go behind his father's saying,
And he likes having thought of it so well
He says again, "Good fences make good neighbors."

EZRA POUND (1885 – 1972)
The River-Merchant's Wife: A Letter[1]

While my hair was still cut straight across my forehead
I played about the front gate, pulling flowers.
You came by on bamboo stilts, playing horse,
You walked about my seat, playing with blue plums.
And we went on living in the village of Chokan:
Two small people, without dislike or suspicion.

At fourteen I married My Lord you.
I never laughed, being bashful.
Lowering my head, I looked at the wall.
Called to, a thousand times, I never looked back.

At fifteen I stopped scowling,
I desired my dust to be mingled with yours
Forever and forever and forever.
Why should I climb the look out?

At sixteen you departed,
You went into far Ku-to-yen, by the river of swirling eddies,
And you have been gone five months.
The monkeys make sorrowful noise overhead.

You dragged your feet when you went out.
By the gate now, the moss is grown, the different mosses,
Too deep to clear them away!
The leaves fall early this autumn, in wind.
The paired butterflies are already yellow with August
Over the grass in the West garden;
They hurt me. I grow older.
If you are coming down through the narrows of the river Kiang,
Please let me know beforehand,
And I will come out to meet you
      As far as Cho-fu-Sa.

MARK STRAND (b. 1934)
Courtship

There is a girl you like so you tell her
your penis is big, but that you cannot get yourself

---

[1]Adapted from the Chinese of Li Po (700?–762). Ernest Fenellosa (1853–1908), an American orientalist and collector, made the translation from which Pound worked.

to use it. Its demands are ridiculous, you say,
even self-defeating, but to be honored somehow,
briefly, inconspicuously in the dark.

When she closes her eyes in horror,
you take it all back. You tell her you're almost
a girl yourself and can understand why she is shocked.
When she is about to walk away, you tell her
you have no penis, that you don't

know what got into you. You get on your knees.
She suddenly bends down to kiss your shoulder and you know
you're on the right track. You tell her you want
to bear children and that is why you seem confused.
You wrinkle your brow and curse the day you were born.

She tries to calm you, but you lose control.
You reach for her panties and beg forgiveness as you do.
She squirms and you howl like a wolf. Your craving
seems monumental. You know you will have her.
Taken by storm, she is the girl you will marry.

SEAMUS HEANEY (b. 1939)
From the Frontier of Writing

The tightness and the nilness round that space
when the car stops in the road, the troops inspect
its make and number and, as one bends his face

towards your window, you catch sight of more
on a hill beyond, eyeing with intent
down cradled guns that hold you under cover

and everything is pure interrogation
until a rifle motions and you move
with guarded unconcerned acceleration —

a little emptier, a little spent
as always by that quiver in the self,
subjugated, yes, and obedient.

So you drive on to the frontier of writing
where it happens again. The guns on tripods;
the sergeant with his on-off mike repeating

data about you, waiting for the squawk
of clearance: the marksman training down
out of the sun upon you like a hawk.

And suddenly you're through, arraigned yet freed,
as if you'd passed from behind a waterfall
on the black current of a tarmac road

past armour-plated vehicles, out between
the posted soldiers flowing and receding
like tree shadows into the polished windscreen.

JORIE GRAHAM (b. 1950)
San Sepolcro[1]

In this blue light
        I can take you there,
snow having made me
        a world of bone
seen through to. This
        is my house,

my section of Etruscan
        wall, my neighbor's
lemontrees, and, just below
        the lower church,
the airplane factory.
        A rooster

crows all day from mist
        outside the walls.
There's milk on the air,
        ice on the oily
lemonskins. How clean
        the mind is,

holy grave. It is this girl
        by Piero
della Francesca,[2] unbuttoning
        her blue dress,
her mantle of weather,
        to go into

labor. Come, we can go in.
        It is before

---

[1]A town in Italy whose name translates to "holy grave."
[2]Piero della Francesca (1420?–1492), Italian painter, whose fresco of the pregnant
Virgin Mary, *La Madonna del Parto*, is described in the poem.

the birth of god. No-one
      has risen yet
to the museums, to the assembly
      line — bodies

and wings — to the open air
      market. This is
what the living do: go in.
      It's a long way.
And the dress keeps opening
      from eternity

to privacy, quickening.
      Inside, at the heart,
is tragedy, the present moment
      forever stillborn,
but going in, each breath
      is a button

coming undone, something terribly
      nimble-fingered
finding all of the stops.

SHERMAN ALEXIE (b. 1966)

Evolution

Buffalo Bill opens a pawn shop on the reservation
right across the border from the liquor store
and he stays open 24 hours a day, 7 days a week

and the Indians come running in with jewelry
television sets, a VCR, a full-length beaded buckskin outfit
it took Inez Muse 12 years to finish. Buffalo Bill

takes everything the Indians have to offer, keeps it
all catalogued and filed in a storage room. The Indians
pawn their hands, saving the thumbs for last, they pawn

their skeletons, falling endlessly from the skin
and when the last Indian has pawned everything
but his heart, Buffalo Bill takes that for twenty bucks

closes up the pawn shop, paints a new sign over the old
calls his venture THE MUSEUM OF NATIVE AMERICAN
      CULTURES
charges the Indians five bucks a head to enter.

5

The Play of Language

Language is the principal raw material out of which poets construct their experiments (rhythmic patterns are the other chief raw materials). By the single word "language" we mean many things:

Sound Units

The sound units of a poem are its syllables. The word "enemy" has three successive sounds, *en-eh-mee*. Readers are conscious of a sound effect when they hear two end-words rhyme; but poets are conscious of *all* the sounds in their lines, just as they are of the rhythms of a line. Poets "bind" words together in a line by having them share sounds, whether consonants (*alliteration,* as in "*broken bread*") or vowels (*assonance,* as in "*when . . . sessions*"). This makes the words sound as if they "belong" together by natural affinity. Note how Shakespeare uses the vowel sounds *eh* and *uh* and the consonant sounds *n, t, th,* and *s* in this line from Sonnet 20: "When to the sessions of sweet silent thought . . ." Good poets tend to bind together words that have an important meaning-connection, as Robert Frost does in this line from "Birches": "When I see *b*irches *b*end to left and right . . ." and as Sylvia Plath does in these lines from "Ariel":

> Sta*sis* in dar*kness.*
> Then the *substanceless b*lue
> *P*our of tor and *distances . . .*

Word Roots

These are the pieces of words that come from words in earlier languages, often Greek, Latin, or Anglo-Saxon. Poets usually are aware of the roots of the words they use. Many of these roots are preceded by prefixes, which also retain their original meanings. These prefixes sometimes change their spelling to "blend" with the root that follows:

re- ("again"): return, revolve, repair, represent, etc.

ex- ("out of"): explain, expire, exhale, etc.

pre- ("in front of"): precede, prefer, preclude, etc.

com- (*cum,* "with"): compare, commemorate, connote, colloquium, etc.

de- ("away from"): delete, defer, delay, defend, etc.

in- ("not"): inexplicable, innocent, immiscible, etc.

We have two main streams of language in English: our basic short words generally come from Anglo-Saxon, and our more complicated words from Latin (often through French). In the past, English was closer to Latin and French than it is today (during the Renaissance, for example, educated people usually knew several languages), and poets drew on that closeness. In Sonnet 15, Shakespeare wrote:

> When I *consider* everything that grows
> Holds in perfection but a little moment,
> That this huge stage presenteth naught but shows
> Whereon the *stars* in secret influence comment;
> When I *perceive* that men as plants increase,
> Cheerèd and checked even by the selfsame sky,
>
> . . . . .
>
> Then the *conceit* of this in*con*stant stay
> Sets *you* most rich in *you*th before my sight . . .

Here, he expected his readers to know that "consider" comes from a root (which we also find, for instance, in the word "sidereal") meaning "stars" — a word that appears in line 4. He also expected them to notice that the word "consider" is composed of two parts, con- and -sider, and that the next "I"-verb ("perceive") is followed by a noun ("conceit") which combines the con- of "consider" with the -ceive of "perceive." Perhaps he also expected at least some of his readers to see how the *con*- of "consider" and "conceit" is repeated in "in*con*stant" (and that the word "you" is contained in "youth").

We now live in an age when most readers are not schooled in Latin and therefore are less likely to recognize the Latin implications in English words. Still, we can easily find this information, especially for a word that seems unusually important in a poem, by consulting a dictionary.

Words

The meaning of a word in a poem is determined less by its dictionary definition (a single word like "stage" or "store" can have many definitions in a comprehensive dictionary) than by the words around it. Every word in a poem enters into relation with the other words in that poem. These relations can be of several kinds:

1. *thematic* (or meaning) relation — as we would connect "stars" and "sky" in the quotation above;

2. *phonemic* relation — as we would connect "stage," "stars," "secret," "selfsame," "sky," and "stay" in the quotation above by their initial *s*'s and *st*'s;

3. *grammatical* relation — as "cheerèd" and "checked" (already linked *phonemically* by their sounds, and *thematically* by their being antonyms of each other) are both verbal adjectives modifying "men";

4. *syntactic* relation — as "When I consider" and "When I perceive" introduce dependent clauses in "I," both modifying the main clause, "Then the conceit . . . sets you."

Each word, then, exists in several "constellations" of relation, all of which the reader needs to notice in order to see the overlapping structures of language in the poem.

Sentences

When we think about a poem, it's useful to write out its sentences in ordinary prose order, and then see what has been done to them in verse. For each sentence, it's indispensable to identify the grammatical *subject* — the person, place, or thing in charge of the verb, so to speak — and the *predicate* — the verb telling what the grammatical subject is or does (present tense), was or did (past tense), or will be or will do (future tense). In the course of a poem, *subjects* can change (the poet can say, "*I* love you" and then say "*You* love me"), *predicates* can change (the poet can say, "I *love* you" and then, "I *hate* you"), and *tenses* can change (the poet can say, "I *love* you now," and later say, "But I *will* not *love* you tomorrow"). By tracking these changes of subject, predicate, and tense you can see the dynamic of the poem: where and with whom it began, what's happening to it, where it's going, and where it ends up.

The more complex the poem, the more necessary this tracking is, if you're to get a firm sense of who is doing (or saying) what when, in each part. But even a "simple" poem repays attention of this sort. In Robert Frost's "Stopping by Woods on a Snowy Evening," the grammatical *subject* alone changes from "I" to "house" to "he" (the owner) to "horse" to "he" (the horse) to "sound" to "woods" to "I."

ROBERT FROST (1874 – 1963)
Stopping by Woods on a Snowy Evening

Whose woods these are *I* think *I* know.
His *house* is in the village, though;
He will not see me stopping here
To watch his woods fill up with snow.

My little *horse* must think it queer
To stop without a farmhouse near
Between the woods and frozen lake
The darkest evening of the year.

He gives his harness bells a shake
To ask if there is some mistake.
The only other *sound*'s the sweep
Of easy wind and downy flake.

The *woods* are lovely, dark and deep
But *I* have promises to keep,
And miles to go before *I* sleep,
And miles to go before *I* sleep.

One can imagine a version of this poem (I apologize for its crudeness) in which the subject never changes, and is "I" throughout:

I know these woods, their owner too,
I feel in watching them some fear,
I sense my little horse's rue,
Pausing without a farmhouse near.

I hear his harness bells now shake
In wonder at my strange mistake.

I hear the sound of falling snow,
All easy wind and downy flake.

I love the woods so dark and deep,
But I have promises to keep,
And miles to go before I sleep,
And miles to go before I sleep.

Why does Frost, do you think, give a *subject*-position not only to himself but also to the owner of the woods and to his horse? And why does he also give it to inanimate things (the woods that fill up with snow, the sound of the wind)? The short answer is that everything in a poem that has subject-position is "alive" and can "do things": the owner of the woods is alive enough to see (but won't) the trespasser; the little horse is alive enough to query his master's odd behavior; the woods are alive enough to be "lovely, dark and deep"; and the silence in the snowy woods is deep enough to make the sound "of easy wind and downy flake" come alive, too. The whole world of the poem, in short, is animate and animated. This is far more interesting, at least in Frost's view of nature, than to make the speaker the only live person in the scene.

Sentences are, grammatically speaking, made up of words that function in different ways. Some words can function in several different ways: for instance, the word "stage" can be either a *noun* ("Have you built the *stage* yet?") or a *verb* ("Will they *stage* a Shakespeare play this season?"). The poet intends you to notice how each word *functions*, as well as what it *means*.

There are conventional names in grammar for words in their functions. You probably remember the basic names of most of the "parts of speech" (as they are called); if not, you might want to turn to the appendix "On Grammar" to refresh your memory.

In clarifying the *function* of each word in a poem, you can see the parade of main statements (nouns plus verbs) making up the logical skeleton of the poem, and you can distinguish these main clauses from the poet's ornamental or explanatory additions. Ask yourself, about each *main* piece of the skeleton, "What would be lost if I deleted this statement?" (What would be lost if we left out the little horse's query in "Stopping by Woods," for instance?) Then ask yourself what purpose is served by the pieces *outside* the noun-verb skeleton — explanations, additions, and ornaments. Sometimes, as in Dickinson's "The Heart asks," the "add-ons" to the main skeleton are of crucial importance. Here is the poem with its add-ons printed in italics:

EMILY DICKINSON (1830 – 1886)
The Heart asks Pleasure – first –

The Heart asks Pleasure – *first* –
And *then* – Excuse *from Pain* –
And *then* – *those little* Anodynes
That deaden suffering –

And *then* – to go to sleep –
And *then* – *if it should be*
The will of its Inquisitor
The privilege to die –

Think what the bare skeleton would be: "The heart asks pleasure and excuse and anodynes and to go to sleep and the privilege to die." It is the adjectives and adverbs that punctuate the poem into its successive phases of torture.

Implication

Because poems are short, they depend more on implication than longer works, such as novels, do. A novel has time and leisure to spell things out; a poem compresses the maximum into each word. Because a poem can only suggest, not expatiate, it requires *you* to supply the concrete instances for each of its suggestions. At the end of his late poem "The Tower," William Butler Yeats draws an escalating list of the ills of old age, gradually arriving at the worst of all. He fears, he says,

> . . . the wreck of body,
> Slow decay of blood,
> Testy delirium
> Or dull decrepitude,
> Or what worse evil come —
> The death of friends, or death
> Of every brilliant eye
> That made a catch in the breath.

A lyric poet like Yeats expects *you to think concretely* as he speaks abstractly, since his words are to be yours. What do you mean when you tell me that you fear in yourself "the wreck of body"? Perhaps paralysis, perhaps a wasting disease — it doesn't matter, but you *must* (in reading the line to yourself or speaking it aloud) have *something* actively in mind that corresponds in *your* mind to Yeats's words. "Slow decay of blood": perhaps, remembering Yeats's use of "blood" elsewhere, you will connect this phrase with the cooling of the hot blood of passion. "Testy delirium": you may think of brain damage from strokes, or incoherence from fever. "Dull decrepitude": you may think of senility. For "the death of friends," you might think of the friend you would miss the most. Then you arrive at the strange periphrasis (indirect way of speaking) marking the climax: What, Yeats makes us ask, is worse than bodily aging, worse than mental decay, worse than the death of friends? What is this "death / Of every brilliant eye / That made a catch in the breath"? The "death / Of every brilliant eye" is an indirect way of speaking of the death of a beautiful and beloved face — the worst event of all, the disappearance of the one face in the world that was everything to you. Perhaps, Yeats implies with "every," there were several such faces in his long life.

This process of paying attention to words, their functions, their logical arrangements in sentences, and their implications is what we really mean by "close" reading. It means spelling out, in your *own* mind — since the words of a poem are given to you to say *as if they were your own* — what the generalizing phrases of the poem mean *in your own case* as you extend their implications to yourself. Only then can you speak the words of the poem with conviction.

Lyric always generalizes. It is a blueprint of life, not a detailed transcription of it (as a novel can seem to be). Lyric, as Elizabeth Bishop said, is a map, not a photograph. Lyric is an algebraic equation, giving you x and y (decay, decrepitude, delirium) and asking you to fill in the poet's equation with your own "real numbers." A lyric asks you to be its co-creator, as you supply your own inner particulars for its generalizations.

Implication can be present in rhythm as well as in words. In Chapter 4, for instance, we saw the excited broken rhythms succeeding, in the close, the stately opening rhythms in Keats's "On First Looking into Chapman's Homer." In every case, you can discover implication by asking "Why?" Why is Yeats's list given in this order? Why do Keats's rhythms change at the end? Why isn't Keats's first metaphor (an astronomer discovering a new planet) good enough, so that he has to progress to a better metaphor (the discovery of the Pacific Ocean by an explorer and his men)? As Samuel Taylor Coleridge said, "Poetry is the best words in the best order." Your task, as a student of poetry, is to form hypotheses about why the poet arranged *these* words in *this* order till the poem seemed a satisfying whole. Your reflections on these matters will bring you into the heart of the poem, will give you intenser pleasure, and will make the poem an increasingly satisfying whole to you.

The Ordering of Language

Because poetry is a temporal art, it has to unfold sequentially, one piece after another. First I say *x,* then *y,* then *z.* But the *logical* relations among *x, y,* and *z* may not be additive or sequential ones. *X, y,* and *z* may instead be radii of the same circle, as in George Herbert's sonnet "Prayer," where the successive definitions all relate radially to the one subject:

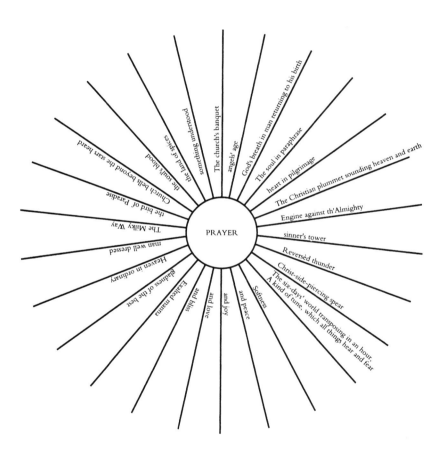

GEORGE HERBERT (1593 – 1633)

Prayer (I)

Prayer, the church's banquet, angels' age,
    God's breath in man returning to his birth,
      The soul in paraphrase, heart in pilgrimage,
The Christian plummet sounding heaven and earth;

Engine against th'Almighty, sinner's tower,
    Reversèd thunder, Christ-side-piercing spear,
    The six-days' world transposing in an hour,
A kind of tune, which all things hear and fear:

Softness, and peace, and joy, and love, and bliss,
    Exalted manna, gladness of the best,
    Heaven in ordinary, man well dressed,
The Milky Way, the bird of Paradise,
    Church bells beyond the stars heard, the soul's blood,
    The land of spices; something understood.

This list of all the things that prayer is might best be represented as radii of a circle: Herbert's order is one of radial amplification of one concept, prayer. But does the poem, in addition to its *radial* order, have a *temporal* order? That is, does something "happen" to the concept of prayer as the poem progresses? Most readers will be aware that thinking of prayer as "reversèd thunder" is not the same in feeling-tone as thinking of it as "softness, and peace, and joy, and love, and bliss." You may want to track the changes in mind of the speaker as the poem progresses, as the speaker exchanges one metaphor for another — only to give up entirely on metaphor at the end. In short, a poem can have more than one "shape" — here, it has both a static radial shape and a dynamic temporal unfolding.

Frequently the ordering of a poem's language offers a gradual clarification of meaning. At first, in Sonnet 66, Shakespeare's speaker sees only a procession of terrible miscarriages of justice in the world:

WILLIAM SHAKESPEARE (1564 – 1616)
Sonnet 66

Tired with all these, for restful death I cry:
As to behold desert a beggar born,
And needy nothing trimmed in jollity,
And purest faith unhappily forsworn,
And gilded honour shamefully misplaced,
And maiden virtue rudely strumpeted,
And right perfection wrongfully disgraced, . . .

At this point, most readers (especially those who have been imaginatively "filling in" the implications of Shakespeare's categories with their own current examples of the same vices) will begin to see that these actions have no agents. Who reduced the deserving ("desert") to beggary? Who misplaced honor, bestowing it on the unworthy instead of the worthy?

Who has seduced the maiden? As the procession of wrongs continues in the poem, the speaker's vision becomes clarified: he can see now not only the victims but their victimizers accompanying them:

> And strength *by limping sway* disablèd,
> And art made tongue-tied *by authority,*
> And *folly, doctor-like,* controlling skill, . . .

The procession is now advancing two-by-two, instead of one-by-one; for instance, "strength" is hampered by "limping sway" (incompetent authority). Then, the two-by-two procession is interrupted by an anomalous solo figure:

> And simple truth miscalled simplicity.

Who can this be but the poem itself (in the person of its author)? Its "simple truth" is called, wrongly, "simplicity" ("political naïveté," in modern terms) by its detractors. Finally, we come, at the end, to the chief authority figure, who in a liturgical or court procession would be the Bishop or King. Here we see the chief agent of all the miscarriages of justice, leading his ultimate allegorical victim:

> And captive good attending captain ill.

Captain Ill is a secularized form of Satan, "the prince of this world." Just as the speaker of Shakespeare's sonnet sees more clearly as the procession winds on, so do we, until the author of all evil is revealed. This leaves the speaker with no hope of amelioration. Because Ill is Captain, and Good is always Captive in his power, there is no visible justice in this world. And so the speaker, though he is still longing for death, decides against it, not out of hope but out of protectiveness for his beloved:

> Tired with all these, from these would I be gone,
> Save that to die, I leave my love alone.

"Alone" is a terrible word in the evil world of this sonnet. In danger of being alone, strumpeted, tongue-tied, disgraced, disabled — who, in these circumstances, could abandon his beloved?

We can see the "shape" of this poem in several ways:

1. As a long procession bracketed by the speaker's two declarations of exhaustion;

2. More precisely, we can see the procession itself subdivided into three main parts: one-by-one, two-by-two, and a final archetype (a generalizing personification) of Good in captivity to Ill;

3. Or we can see a single shape (disillusion and exhaustion) for the first thirteen lines, "redeemed" by line 14, which reveals that the speaker has one value, love, as yet uncorrupted by the world.

The more ways we see the governing linguistic order of the poem, the more human complexity we can perceive within it.

The ordering of experience in shapes of radial or logical clarification — clarification by hierarchy, clarification by a comparison of then to now, clarification by here versus there, or clarification by rise-and-decline (to name only four common "shapes") — is what gives poetry its aura of mastery. Even when its "content" is tragic — as in Dickinson's list of the heart's requests, or Shakespeare's procession of injustice — the fact that the list has been ordered into an understood set or a hierarchy reassures us that the mind can understand what the heart cannot endure, and that the imagination can find a linguistic shape for the structures of reality, even for those that are most tragic.

There is no linguistic ingredient too small to attract the poet's interest. Wallace Stevens makes poems that turn on the difference between the definite and indefinite article ("the" versus "a"); Yeats constructs a poem ("In Memory of Eva Gore-Booth and Con Markiewicz") that turns on a movement from "I" to "you" to "we" as a sign of reconciliation of enemies. Shakespeare can build a whole sonnet ("Th'expense of spirit in a waste of shame," Sonnet 129) on a contrast between nouns and adjectives (nouns give essence, we are reminded; adjectives give qualities). The play of language is the chief cause for the aesthetic success of any poem. Without play at many levels of language, from phonemes to logical structures, a poem is merely prose with line-breaks added.

Let's look at a sample poem, Michael Drayton's "Since there's no help," to try to bring to bear on it what this chapter has said about examining the language of a poem very closely at several levels — its sound-units, its etymological roots, its sentences with their words functioning as parts of speech, its subjects and predicates, tenses and moods, its imaginative play of language, and its processes of implication. The poem is spoken by a young man whose beloved, we infer, has just declared that their love affair is over:

MICHAEL DRAYTON (1564 – 1631)
Since there's no help

Since there's no help, come let us kiss and part;
Nay, I have done, you get no more of me,
And I am glad, yea glad with all my heart
That thus so cleanly I myself can free;
Shake hands forever, cancel all our vows,

> And when we meet at any time again,
> Be it not seen in either of our brows
> That we one jot of former love retain.
> Now at the last gasp of love's latest breath,
> When, his pulse failing, passion speechless lies,
> When faith is kneeling by his bed of death,
> And innocence is closing up his eyes;
> Now if thou wouldst, when all have given him over,
> From death to life thou mightst him yet recover.

Here are the main independent clauses of the first sentence of the poem, which occupies the octave, or first eight lines, of the sonnet. The clauses are here written out as statements, with the **pronouns** in boldface and the *predicates* italicized:

> Come *let* **us** *kiss* and *part*
> **I** *have done*
> **You** *get* no more of **me**
> **I** *am* glad
> [*let* **us**] *shake* hands
> [*let* **us**] *cancel* vows
> *be* **it** not *seen*

The first sentence, then, moves through several verbs in the hortatory mood — "let us kiss and part," "let us shake hands," "let us cancel all our vows," "[let] it not be seen" — interspersed with verbs in the indicative mood, one in the past tense ("I have done") and two in the future tense ("you [will] get no more of me" and "when we [shall] meet at any [future] time"). The pronouns change from **us** to **I** to **you** to **me** to **I** to **us** to **it**. All of these changes are indexes of the speaker's troubled state, as he darts from mood to mood, from tense to tense, and from subject position to object position. Although many of the dependent clauses add information ("Since there's no help," "that thus so cleanly I myself can free," "that we one jot of former love retain"), yet the skeleton above of the main clauses makes the import of the sentence clear.

The case is very different when we come to the second sentence, which takes up the last six lines (the sestet) of the sonnet. It has only one main clause: "**Thou** *mightst* him yet *recover*." All the other clauses are strung from this one. "Thou mightst him recover" — when?

> Now at the last gasp of love's latest breath
> [Now] when passion speechless lies

> [Now] when faith is kneeling by his bed
> [Now] when innocence is closing up his eyes
> Now when all have given him over

All of these adverbial clauses "lead up" like the steps of a staircase to the main clause, giving the sestet its long suspense. In this way the relatively straightforward march of main clauses in the octave changes dramatically once we meet the long delay of the main clause in the sestet.

When we look at the kind of words these two sentences are composed of, we notice that with a few exceptions — "cancel" and "retain" — most of the words of the octave are those short brisk words we tend to associate with our Anglo-Saxon linguistic heritage — "help," "come," "kiss," "get," "glad," "heart," "clean," and so on. When we come to the sestet, the number of Latin- or Romance-derived words rises — "pulse," "fail," "passion," "faith," "innocence," "close," "recover." Even if readers do not recognize the roots of all these words, they will sense how the more ceremonious sestet departs from the brisk colloquial nature of the words in the octave, not only because of the rise of Latin-derived words but also because of the suspended syntax.

It is clear that the speaker speaks about himself *in the first person* ("I") in the octave: "Nay, I have done, you get no more of me." But in the sestet, we see a change in language: instead of speaking directly about himself, the speaker speaks in the *third person* of someone called "Passion" who is lying on his "bed of death," whose "pulse [is] failing," who is emitting the last gasp of love's breath. This dying person is attended by two mourners: Faith is kneeling by his deathbed, and Innocence is closing the eyes of the dying man. This little third-person tableau is a way of avoiding first-person speech (otherwise, by the principle of inertia, the speaker would have continued as he began). The change to the third person makes us ask, "What would this closing tableau have been like if it, like the octave, had been put in the first person?"

> Now, at the last gasp of my loving breath,
> My passion has no words to say to thee,
> I seem to lose the faith I had, and death
> Of love is death of innocence in me.
> Now if thou wouldst, when I have given love over,
> From death to life thou mightst me yet recover.

We can see that it's more dignified to ask the woman to rescue "Passion" than to say, "Please, even at this last gasp of passion, rescue *me*."

Because the octave has been phrased in the *hortatory* ("let us") and *indicative* ("I am glad") moods, we especially notice, when we come to the sestet, that it turns for its main clause to the *conditional* mood: "Now *if* thou *wouldst* . . . / thou *mightst* him yet recover." This holds out a grain of hope — if she *would* do this, she *might* bring him back to life. This is "politer" than saying, in the imperative, "Do this, and he will be cured." It is a plea, not a command.

After the relatively plain octave, in which the words are linked by the concept of saying farewell and canceling vows, we come to two conspicuous sets of linked words in the sestet. One is a set of abstract nouns — Love, Passion, Faith, and Innocence. They are the actors in the little tableau. The other set of words is medical and funereal — "gasp," "breath," "pulse failing," "speechless," "bed of death," "closing . . . eyes," "life," "recover." Normally, it is human beings who are in the situation where here we find Passion — dying among mourners. Drayton brings together in the sestet two incompatible sets of linked words — one abstract, one medically concrete — and constructs his surprising little third-person tableau with them to show us how the lover feels: he is not *really* dying physically, but emotionally "a deathbed scene" is the best description for what is happening to his passion — and he hopes that externalizing his inward feelings in this theatrical tableau may persuade his beloved to have pity on him.

We see from the closing tableau, and the plea with which it ends, that the speaker put on his original bluster ("Nay, I have done, you get no more of me, / And I am glad, yea glad") to hide the real dismay and despair that his closing tableau reveals.

These are only some of the moves we could make in beginning to study the language of this poem, and to ask the questions it provokes: "Why the change in person between octave and sestet?" "Why the introduction of the little tableau?" "Why is the sestet so ceremoniously written after the colloquial language of the octave?" "Why is the main clause of the sestet in the conditional mood?" "Why is the main clause of the sestet so long suspended adverbially before we get to it?"

Of course, we eventually have to move on from the use of language to the wider purposes of the poem — Drayton's conception of passion, and its relation to love, faith, and innocence, and his apt psychological observation of the defenses put up by the jilted lover, before the lover breaks down into his final abject plea. But that is material for a longer study, in which we might compare this poem to others written by Drayton, and get a better idea of his general poetic procedures. In each case, though, the first place to begin is with the play of language. In it, we find the imagination at work.

In Brief: The Play of Language

Since the language of lyric is condensed, every word carries weight, and all aspects of grammar and syntax (parts of speech, speech acts, even word roots) are full of significance. Poets are people steeped in language: "For many years," said Emily Dickinson, "my lexicon was my only companion." It is helpful to look at each sentence by itself, and at its chief agent, and at what the agent does. What are the interesting or unusual words in the sentence? What speech acts are taking place? What is implied in the "white space" between sentences or stanzas? Is the organization linear (start-to-finish), radial (a cluster of phrases around a center), or recursive (doubling back on itself)? Does the language change from concrete to abstract, or vice versa? Language gives you the *manner* of the poem, as well as its matter.

Reading Other Poems

There is no poem that does not play with language. As the following poems demonstrate, some are more overt about it, some less so. Language is both spoken and written, and the poet thinks about both aspects: how the poem sounds, how it looks on the page.

Not everything written can be spoken: see E. E. Cummings's poem on the way the grasshopper rearranges his limbs while leaping.

◆ If you trace the stages of the grasshopper's motions, how does Cummings mimic them?

Track the gestures implicit in the language of the Duke as he talks to the envoy arranging the new marriage. See how inconspicuously Robert Browning uses rhyme, and how the Duke's syntax shapes his powerful ongoing sentences. In the case of Wallace Stevens's two-room poem, ask what you see in the first room, the kitchen, versus what you see in the second room, the bedroom, and how language is invented to match the reality in each room.

Repetition of language is one of the weapons in the armory of poetry, and certain verse-forms entail the "foregrounding" of one or two lines by repetition.

◆ What are the repeated lines in Elizabeth Bishop's villanelle "One Art"? Can you describe the effect on the reader of having them recur so often? To how many things are these lines applied?

In free verse, too, repetition makes us aware of patterning. The word "deer," appearing for the first time in the title of Joy Harjo's "Song for the Deer and Myself to Return On," serves as the linch-pin of the lines that follow, as it is four times repeated. At first the speaker is alone; eventually she is part of a compound subject ("the deer and I"). By this time, the deer have been humanized: they "wonder," they "are trying to figure out a song." Because of this patterning emphasizing the deer, and because they are gradually brought into the human world of the speaker, we may be surprised when the deer disappear from the last two lines of the poem. Can you suggest why that happens?

The play of language is deeply felt when a poem has to convey changes over time.

◆ Can you see the time specified in each of Keats's stanzas in his autumn ode? What sort of language predominates in each stanza (for example, the infinitives in stanza 1)? What sort of noises end the poem?

◆ Can you compare the language used to guide the reader through the time sequence in Keats to the language that guides mentions of time in Yeats's poem about the swans? What sort of language does Yeats use about himself, in contrast to the language he uses about the swans?

Both John Donne's "Holy Sonnet 14" and H. D.'s "Oread" are poems structured by commands.

◆ Who is being commanded? Can they be commanded?

◆ What kind of language appears in the commands?

◆ Can the commands be obeyed?

◆ Do some commands in the poem differ from others?

◆ Imagine each poem rewritten as a narrative rather than as a command: Can you then see the poet's attraction to this syntactic form?

Henry Reed's poem "Naming of Parts" is structured by repetition and by puns: What are their expressive functions?

Sometimes the play of language is structured on the relation of one metaphor to another (as Donne shifts from calling himself a usurped town to calling himself a betrothed woman, with consequences for the diction of the poem). At other times, the play of language depends on the relation of one language to another (as Lorna Dee Cervantes asserts the perpetual presence, in her mind, of both Spanish and English).

◆ What is your reaction to this mixed diction? (There is an old tradition of mixed diction in English poetry, beginning with poems written partly in English and partly in Latin.)

JOHN DONNE (1572 – 1631)
Holy Sonnet 14

Batter my heart, three-personed God; for You
As yet but knock, breathe, shine, and seek to mend;
That I may rise and stand, o'erthrow me, and bend
Your force to break, blow, burn, and make me new.
I, like an usurped town, to another due,
Labor to admit You, but O, to no end;
Reason, Your viceroy in me, me should defend,
But is captivèd, and proves weak or untrue.
Yet dearly I love You, and would be lovèd fain,
But am betrothed unto Your enemy.
Divorce me, untie or break that knot again;
Take me to You, imprison me, for I,
Except You enthrall me, never shall be free,
Nor ever chaste, except You ravish me.

JOHN KEATS (1795 – 1821)
To Autumn

1

Season of mists and mellow fruitfulness,
    Close bosom-friend of the maturing sun;
  Conspiring with him how to load and bless
    With fruit the vines that round the thatch-eaves run;
  To bend with apples the mossed cottage-trees,
    And fill all fruit with ripeness to the core;
      To swell the gourd, and plump the hazel shells
  With a sweet kernel; to set budding more,
And still more, later flowers for the bees,
Until they think warm days will never cease,
    For Summer has o'er-brimmed their clammy cells.

2

Who hath not seen thee oft amid thy store?
  Sometimes whoever seeks abroad may find
Thee sitting careless on a granary floor,
  Thy hair soft-lifted by the winnowing wind;

Or on a half-reaped furrow sound asleep,
 Drowsed with the fume of poppies, while thy hook
  Spares the next swath and all its twinèd flowers:
And sometimes like a gleaner thou dost keep
  Steady thy laden head across a brook;
  Or by a cider-press, with patient look,
   Thou watchest the last oozings hours by hours.

3

Where are the songs of Spring? Aye, where are they?
  Think not of them, thou hast thy music too —
While barrèd clouds bloom the soft-dying day,
  And touch the stubble-plains with rosy hue;
Then in a wailful choir the small gnats mourn
  Among the river sallows,° borne aloft   *low-growing willows*
   Or sinking as the light wind lives or dies;
And full-grown lambs loud bleat from hilly bourn;
  Hedge crickets sing; and now with treble soft
  The redbreast whistles from a garden-croft;[1]
   And gathering swallows twitter in the skies.

ROBERT BROWNING (1812 – 1889)
My Last Duchess

Ferrara

That's my last duchess painted on the wall,
Looking as if she were alive. I call
That piece a wonder, now: Frà Pandolf's hands
Worked busily a day, and there she stands.
Will't please you sit and look at her? I said   5
"Frà Pandolf" by design, for never read
Strangers like you that pictured countenance,
The depth and passion of its earnest glance,
But to myself they turned (since none puts by
The curtain I have drawn for you, but I)   10
And seemed as they would ask me, if they durst,
How such a glance came there; so, not the first
Are you to turn and ask thus. Sir, 'twas not
Her husband's presence only, called that spot

---

[1]Small field at the edge of a property, often leased to another proprietor.

Of joy into the Duchess' cheek: perhaps 15
Frà Pandolf chanced to say "Her mantle laps
Over my lady's wrist too much," or "Paint
Must never hope to reproduce the faint
Half-flush that dies along her throat": such stuff
Was courtesy, she thought, and cause enough 20
For calling up that spot of joy. She had
A heart — how shall I say? — too soon made glad,
Too easily impressed; she liked whate'er
She looked on, and her looks went everywhere.
Sir, 'twas all one! My favor at her breast, 25
The dropping of the daylight in the West,
The bough of cherries some officious fool
Broke in the orchard for her, the white mule
She rode with round the terrace — all and each
Would draw from her alike the approving speech, 30
Or blush, at least. She thanked men — good! but thanked
Somehow — I know not how — as if she ranked
My gift of a nine-hundred-years-old name
With anybody's gift. Who'd stoop to blame
This sort of trifling? Even had you skill 35
In speech — which I have not — to make your will
Quite clear to such an one, and say, "Just this
Or that in you disgusts me; here you miss,
Or there exceed the mark" — and if she let
Herself be lessoned so, nor plainly set 40
Her wits to yours, forsooth, and made excuse,
— E'en then would be some stooping; and I choose
Never to stoop. Oh sir, she smiled, no doubt,
Whene'er I passed her; but who passed without
Much the same smile? This grew; I gave commands; 45
Then all smiles stopped together. There she stands
As if alive. Will't please you rise? We'll meet
The company below, then. I repeat,
The Count your master's known munificence
Is ample warrant that no just pretense 50
Of mine for dowry will be disallowed;
Though his fair daughter's self, as I avowed
At starting, is my object. Nay, we'll go
Together down, sir. Notice Neptune, though,
Taming a sea-horse, thought a rarity, 55
Which Claus of Innsbruck cast in bronze for me!

HENRY REED (1914 – 1986)

Naming of Parts

Today we have naming of parts. Yesterday,
We had daily cleaning. And tomorrow morning,
We shall have what to do after firing. But today,
Today we have naming of parts. Japonica
Glistens like coral in all of the neighboring gardens,
     And today we have naming of parts.

This is the lower sling swivel. And this
Is the upper sling swivel, whose use you will see,
When you are given your slings. And this is the piling swivel,
Which in your case you have not got. The branches
Hold in the gardens their silent, eloquent gestures,
     Which in our case we have not got.

This is the safety-catch, which is always released
With an easy flick of the thumb. And please do not let me
See anyone using his finger. You can do it quite easy
If you have any strength in your thumb. The blossoms
Are fragile and motionless, never letting anyone see
     Any of them using their finger.

And this you can see is the bolt. The purpose of this
Is to open the breech, as you see. We can slide it
Rapidly backwards and forwards: we call this
Easing the spring. And rapidly backwards and forwards
The early bees are assaulting and fumbling the flowers:
     They call it easing the Spring.

They call it easing the Spring: it is perfectly easy
If you have any strength in your thumb: like the bolt,
And the breech, and the cocking-piece, and the point of balance,
Which in our case we have not got; and the almond-blossom
Silent in all of the gardens and the bees going backwards and
       forwards,
     For today we have naming of parts.

WILLIAM BUTLER YEATS (1865 – 1939)

The Wild Swans at Coole

The trees are in their autumn beauty,
The woodland paths are dry,

Under the October twilight the water
Mirrors a still sky;
Upon the brimming water among the stones
Are nine-and-fifty swans.

The nineteenth autumn has come upon me
Since I first made my count;
I saw, before I had well finished,
All suddenly mount
And scatter wheeling in great broken rings
Upon their clamorous wings.

I have looked upon those brilliant creatures,
And now my heart is sore.
All's changed since I, hearing at twilight,
The first time on this shore,
The bell-beat of their wings above my head,
Trod with a lighter tread.

Unwearied still, lover by lover,
They paddle in the cold
Companionable streams or climb the air;
Their hearts have not grown old;
Passion or conquest, wander where they will,
Attend upon them still.

But now they drift on the still water,
Mysterious, beautiful;
Among what rushes will they build,
By what lake's edge or pool
Delight men's eyes when I awake some day
To find they have flown away?

WALLACE STEVENS (1879 – 1955)
The Emperor of Ice-Cream

Call the roller of big cigars,
The muscular one, and bid him whip
In kitchen cups concupiscent curds.
Let the wenches dawdle in such dress
As they are used to wear, and let the boys
Bring flowers in last month's newspapers.
Let be be finale of seem.
The only emperor is the emperor of ice-cream.

Take from the dresser of deal,
Lacking the three glass knobs, that sheet
On which she embroidered fantails once
And spread it so as to cover her face.
If her horny feet protrude, they come
To show how cold she is, and dumb.
Let the lamp affix its beam.
The only emperor is the emperor of ice-cream.

H. D. (1886 – 1961)
Oread [1]

Whirl up, sea —
whirl your pointed pines,
splash your great pines
on our rocks,
hurl your green over us,
cover us with your pools of fir.

E. E. CUMMINGS (1894 – 1962)
r-p-o-p-h-e-s-s-a-g-r

                         r-p-o-p-h-e-s-s-a-g-r
              who
a)s w(e loo)k
upnowgath
        PPEGORHRASS
                              eringint(o–
aThe):l
        eA
           !p:
S   a
              (r
rIvInG   .gRrEaPsPhOs)
                                        to
rea(be)rran(com)gi(e)ngly
,grasshopper;

---

[1] A nymph of the mountains and hills.

ELIZABETH BISHOP (1911 – 1979)
One Art

The art of losing isn't hard to master;
so many things seem filled with the intent
to be lost that their loss is no disaster.

Lose something every day. Accept the fluster
of lost door keys, the hour badly spent.
The art of losing isn't hard to master.

Then practice losing farther, losing faster:
places, and names, and where it was you meant
to travel. None of these will bring disaster.

I lost my mother's watch. And look! my last, or
next-to-last, of three loved houses went.
The art of losing isn't hard to master.

I lost two cities, lovely ones. And, vaster,
some realms I owned, two rivers, a continent.
I miss them, but it wasn't a disaster.

— Even losing you (the joking voice, a gesture
I love) I shan't have lied. It's evident
the art of losing's not too hard to master
though it may look like (*Write* it!) like disaster.

JOY HARJO (b. 1951)
Song for the Deer and Myself to Return On

This morning when I looked out the roof window
before dawn and a few stars were still caught
in the fragile weft of ebony night
I was overwhelmed. I sang the song Louis taught me:
a song to call the deer in Creek, when hunting,
and I am certainly hunting something as magic as deer
in this city far from the hammock of my mother's belly.
It works, of course, and deer came into this room
and wondered at finding themselves
in a house near downtown Denver.
Now the deer and I are trying to figure out a song
to get them back, to get all of us back,

because if it works I'm going with them.
And it's too early to call Louis
and nearly too late to go home.

LORNA DEE CERVANTES (b. 1954)
Poema para los Californios Muertos[1]

> *Once a refuge for Mexican Californios . . .*
> — PLAQUE OUTSIDE A RESTAURANT
> IN LOS ALTOS, CALIFORNIA, 1974

These older towns die
into stretches of freeway.
The high scaffolding cuts a clean cesarean[2]
across belly valleys and fertile dust.
What a bastard child, this city
lost in the soft
llorando de las madres.[3]
Californios moan like husbands of the raped,
husbands de la tierra,
tierra la madre.[4]

I run my fingers
across this brass plaque.
Its cold stirs in me a memory
of silver buckles and spent bullets,
of embroidered shawls and dark rebozos.[5]
Yo recuerdo los antepasados muertos.
Los recuerdo en la sangre,
la sangre fértil.[6]

What refuge did you find here,
ancient Californios?
Now at this restaurant nothing remains

---

[1]Poem for the dead Californios. (*Californios* — original inhabitants when California was still Mexico.)

[2]A cesarean is a surgical incision of the walls of the abdomen and uterus for delivery of offspring.

[3]Crying of the mothers.

[4]Of the land, the mother earth.

[5]A rebozo is a long shawl worn by Mexican women.

[6]I remember the dead ancestors. I remember them in my blood, my fertile blood.

but this old oak and an ill-placed plaque.
Is it true that you still live here
in the shadows of these white, high-class houses?
Soy la hija pobrecita
pero puedo maldecir estas fantasmas blancas.
Las fantasmas tuyas deben aquí quedarse,
solas las tuyas.[7]

In this place I see nothing but strangers.
On the shelves there are bitter antiques,
yanqui remnants
y estos no de los Californios.[8]
A blue jay shrieks
above the pungent odor of crushed
eucalyptus and the pure scent
of rage.

---

[7] I am only your poor daughter, but I can curse these white ghosts. Only your ghosts should remain here, only yours.

[8] And these not of the Californios.

6

Constructing a Self

[handwritten annotation: For Credibility]
[handwritten list:]
- *Multiple aspects → a past*
- *Change of discourse*
- *Giving location in space + time*
- *knowledge (testimony)*
- *Motivations*
- *Typicality – Generalizability*

If you are a poet wanting to create, on paper, a self into whose shoes a reader will be willing to step, a self whose voice a reader will willingly take on, you have probably only a short space (maybe 150 words) in which to give your lyric speaker credibility. You must create a personality provoked into speech; tones of voice tracking both provocation and response; and enough variability of expression to make for fictive robustness. How to do it?

Multiple Aspects

[handwritten annotation: antecedent scenario]

The single most successful way is to give your speaker not only a present but a past, and often not just a yesterday, but the day before that, and the year before that, and five years before that. (See Wordsworth's "Lines Composed a Few Miles above Tintern Abbey" for a stunning lengthy version of this process.) You invite your reader to "turn into" the speaker, uttering the sentences of the poem; you construct a whole temporal self available to be inhabited, a believable "thickly described" life to be entered. Here is Shakespeare's Sonnet 30, "When to the sessions of sweet silent thought," in which a speaker with a multiphased past comes alive:

William Shakespeare (1564 – 1616)
Sonnet 30

When to the sessions of sweet silent thought
I summon up remembrance of things past,
I sigh the lack of many a thing I sought,
And with old woes new wail my dear time's waste;
Then can I drown an eye (unused to flow)
For precious friends hid in death's dateless night,
And weep afresh love's long since canceled woe,
And moan th'expense of many a vanished sight.
Then can I grieve at grievances foregone,
And heavily from woe to woe tell o'er
The sad account of fore-bemoanèd moan,
Which I new pay as if not paid before.
    But if the while I think on thee (dear friend)
    All losses are restored and sorrows end.

The speaker (whose initial "when" means "whenever") is referring to a series of habitual actions. This in itself gives the speaker a continuous life stretching from the past to the present; he often has sessions of silent thought when he voluntarily summons past things to mind. In fact, when he does this, he finds himself in tears — an unusual event for him: "Then can I drown an eye, *unused to flow*."

We're now in a better position to reconstruct the speaker's multi-phased life. Let's call the time when he as yet did not have a friend T_1, the next phase T_2, and so on:

T_1: He doesn't yet have friends A, B, C.

T_2: He makes friends with A, B, C.

T_3: He enjoys the friendship over time.

T_4: Friends A, B, C die.

T_5: He weeps at the moment of their death.

T_6: Grief turns to stoicism; his tears stop.

T_7: He spends a long time without weeping; his tears are "unused to flow."

T_8: He often summons up, voluntarily, the old grief so that he can "drown" again in tears for his dead friends.

This pattern recurs throughout the poem, as, for instance: he "weep[s] *afresh* love's *long since canceled* woe." He was without love; then had it; then lost it, and wept in woe; that woe was (apparently) canceled, and he was dry-eyed for a long time; now he can weep afresh for that woe. In fact, this process, many times safely and even luxuriously repeated, now suddenly awakens such grief in the speaker that he pays his debt of grief anew: "I new pay," he says, "*as if not paid before.*" This is a frightening experience. He thought he could summon up at will old griefs, and almost enjoy renewing them in "sessions of *sweet* silent thought." Yet suddenly the session is no longer sweet but painfully acute — grief recurs as if for the first time. It is this acute grief that pitches the speaker into looking for consolation in his present state; at least he has a friend now, friend Z:

> But if the while I think on thee (dear friend)
> All losses are restored and sorrows end.

This discovery of present joy stabilizes the character of the speaker at one point in his multiphased life. But the overall effect of the sonnet is to make us know the speaker as someone who has undergone many psychological phases — joy, grief, stoicism, loss, renewed grief — over time, and this confers on him a "reality" of prolonged existence that we take on as we speak his words.

Change of Discourse

Another way, if you are a poet, to give your speaker credibility is to let her change discourses in midstream. In "Diving into the Wreck," Adrienne Rich lets her practical, well-equipped speaker drift into hypnotic reverie once she's under water:

> I put on
> the body-armor of black rubber
> the absurd flippers
> the grave and awkward mask. . . .
>
> I go down.
> My flippers cripple me,
> I crawl like an insect down the ladder. . . .
>
> This is the place.
> And I am here, the mermaid whose dark hair
> streams black, the merman in his armored body.
> We circle silently
> about the wreck

we dive into the hold.
I am she: I am he

whose drowned face sleeps with open eyes
whose breasts still bear the stress. . . .

By the end, after this entrance to incantatory and androgynous language, the personality of the speaker seems to have more than one facet. The more facets — practical, mystical, baffled, exalted — the "thicker" the description.

Space and Time

Yet another way of giving historical believability to your speaker is, in the course of your poem, to relocate him or her in space and time. In "Mid-Term Break," the Irish poet Seamus Heaney (pronounced "Shāmus Hēney") writes about his return home from boarding school for the funeral of his four-year-old brother, killed by a car. ("College" in the first line refers to a boarding school.)

SEAMUS HEANEY (b. 1939)
Mid-Term Break

I sat all morning in the college sick bay
Counting bells knelling classes to a close.
At two o'clock our neighbors drove me home.

In the porch I met my father crying —
He had always taken funerals in his stride —
And Big Jim Evans saying it was a hard blow.

The baby cooed and laughed and rocked the pram
When I came in, and I was embarrassed
By old men standing up to shake my hand

And tell me they were "sorry for my trouble."
Whispers informed strangers I was the eldest,
Away at school, as my mother held my hand

In hers and coughed out angry tearless sighs.
At ten o'clock the ambulance arrived
With the corpse, stanched and bandaged by the nurses.

Next morning I went up into the room. Snowdrops
And candles soothed the bedside; I saw him
For the first time in six weeks. Paler now,

Wearing a poppy bruise on his left temple,
He lay in the four foot box as in his cot.
No gaudy scars, the bumper knocked him clear.

A four foot box, a foot for every year.

We first see the speaker in the morning at his boarding school, after he has been notified of his brother's death; next we see him being driven home; next he is on the porch at home; next inside the house; next, present at evening when the body is brought from the hospital by an ambulance; next, the following morning, upstairs seeing the body of his brother laid out on the bed; next, seeing his brother in the coffin before the funeral. The living presence of the speaker over two days, in several places, makes him seem a "real person," into whose believable narrative we can enter. We track the changes in space and time by a series of markers in the poem:

Space	*Time*
in the college sick bay	all morning
home	two o'clock
in the porch	
I came in	
	whispers . . . as my mother
	held my hand
the ambulance arrived	at ten o'clock
up into the room . . . bedside	next morning
the four foot box	

Poets expect you to "track," even if unconsciously, such relocations of the speaker in space and time, as you "become" the person who goes from school to the porch, from the porch to the room inside, from the downstairs to the upstairs, and who, in the end, however reluctantly, takes up a mourner's position next to the coffin.

Testimony

Speakers also can be made credible by their intimate knowledge of a given historical time and place and its inhabitants. We feel this in E. E. Cummings's speaker who satirizes "the Cambridge ladies who live in furnished souls" and mocks their taste for Henry Wadsworth Longfellow. Walt Whitman speaks as a witness to the events recounted in "Song of

Myself ": "I am the man; I suffered; I was there;" and his Civil War poems offer vivid, almost cinematically detailed accounts of real events in "A March in the Night Hard Press'd" or "Cavalry Crossing a Ford." Even in a poem of symbolic experience, such as Samuel Taylor Coleridge's "Rime of the Ancient Mariner," the mariner tells so many particular details of his supernatural experiences, along with many natural ones, that we are drawn to find both halves of his tale reliable.

Motivations

How does the poet lead us to understand the selves that are so sketchily created on the page, in whose voices we find ourselves speaking? We tend, as the poem goes on, to fill in its gaps, and to think that Shakespeare's speaker weeping afresh has a whole "real life" in between his reported bouts of grief, stoicism, and renewed weeping. We assume that Coleridge's Ancient Mariner is being truthful about how he passes, like night, from land to land retelling his tale, and that he had a life before he shot the albatross. We also invent plausible reasons for the fact that a speaker who has formerly spoken of his estrangement from his beloved ("Since there's no help, come let us kiss and part") can say, only thirteen lines later, that his beloved could resuscitate love "from death to life." By postulating reasonable motivations, justifications, and conclusions in the gaps between words or lines, we ascribe to the speaker a "realness" that literature is designed to offer in order to persuade us of its insights about experience.

Typicality

Yet another aspect of credibility in a lyric speaker comes from typicality, a powerful resource of lyric. Anyone can put himself or herself into the unstipulated place and indefinite time of Shakespeare's speaker summoning up remembrance of things past. Even when the place and subject are specific (as they are in "the Cambridge ladies"), anyone, male or female, who lived in Cambridge might be the speaker of the poem. Even when the event is wholly personal, as in "Mid-Term Break," the emotions of the stunned adolescent recalled by the speaker are those that any adolescent in such a situation would probably experience. To create such a representative set of reactions, Heaney, like many lyric poets, deletes many particular autobiographical details (the presence of his siblings, the specific religious ceremonies surrounding a home wake in Ireland such as the recitation of the rosary) in order to make the experience related in the poem typical, rather than narrowly personal.

A lyric, then, wants us to be its speaker. We are not to *listen to* the speaker, but to *make ourselves into* the speaker. We speak the words of the poem as though we were their first utterers. The speaker's past is our past; his motivations are ours, his emotions ours, his excuses ours, his predictions ours. A poem is a set of instructions for voicing; listened to carefully, it tells us how to say its sentences — regretfully, apprehensively, bitterly, elatedly. We call these ways of voicing the *tones* of the poem. They are sufficiently typical that any reader can utter them.

Tone as Marker of Selfhood

Though poetry has become a written art, it has never lost its roots in speech. And since the first thing a poem asks of you is to read it aloud as though you were saying *it as your own words,* you must sound angry if "you" are angry, sad if "you" are sad. The poem itself tells you how to sound. Every lyric is uttered in response to a situation that has disturbed some former equilibrium: "you" have been told someone no longer loves you ("Since there's no help"), or that your brother has been killed in an accident ("Mid-Term Break"), or that "We don't like modern poetry" (the "Cambridge ladies," says Cummings, "believe in Christ and Longfellow, both dead"). Robert Frost went so far as to say, "Everything written is as good as it is dramatic. . . . [A poem is] heard as sung or spoken by a person in a scene — in character, in a setting." Because you cannot know the whole situation of the speaker till you have read the whole poem, you often are not sure what set of intonations to give the poem as you *first* read it aloud. But as you get to know it better, it begins to speak itself believably in your mind, and its speaker's character and emotions, mediated through the tones of utterance, become yours.

Take, for example, the first stanza of Emily Dickinson's poem, spoken above the many graves of her Dickinson ancestors in the cemetery of Amherst, Massachusetts:

Safe in their Alabaster Chambers –
Untouched by Morning
And untouched by Noon –

> Sleep the meek members of the Resurrection –
> Rafter of satin
> And Roof of stone.

Is it good or bad for the dead to be "safe" in their mausoleums or graves? Is it good or bad to be "untouched" by morning and noon? Is it desirable to be ensconced under satin rafters and a roof of stone? In what tone are you to say these lines?

As you get to know the poem, you may decide that Dickinson thought it was certainly a deprivation to exist insensible to both morning and noon; that she is judging the dead as timid ("meek") people who always wanted to be "safe": now, indeed, and ironically, they are. When you learn that Dickinson rewrote the poem to remove the implication of resurrection — substituting "lie" for "sleep" in line 4 — you may decide that she thought her dead ancestors had been cheated by their credulous belief in an afterlife to which they would awaken. And however fine it may be to have satin rafters in your coffin, those rafters exist, after all, under that claustrophobic mausoleum-roof "of stone." Your tone might well then become ironic as you read the words "safe" and "untouched," seeing those words as the poet's gibe at the conventional timidity of her ancestors' lives.

In telling someone else how you see this poem, you probably would have to say, "I hear Dickinson being critical of the dead, with a dismissive and almost contemptuous tone in her description of them as 'safe' and 'untouched.'" And in speaking the poem aloud, you, as the speaker of these sentiments, would make your own voice take on that dismissive tone. In this way, every poem suggests to its readers the tones with which they might give voice to it; and conversely, the tones you feel to be present, as you get to know the poem well, give you clues to the perceptions and emotions of the self, constructed in the poem, that generates those tones.

Here, for instance, is a short poem in which an adult, who knows suffering well, comes upon a young girl who is crying because the leaves are falling from the trees in the wood called "Goldengrove." The adult thinks her grief trivial and childish, and rebukes her for wasting her tears on trees, prophesying that life soon enough will give her more serious things to cry about. But she continues nevertheless to cry, asking *why* the leaves have to fall. The poem turns on the adult's response to the child's *"Why?"* I've marked, next to the lines, the tones of voice they suggest. (In the third line from the end, "ghost guessed" means, approximately, "your spirit intuited.")

GERARD MANLEY HOPKINS (1844 – 1889)
Spring and Fall

To a Young Child

Márgarét, áre you gríeving	*bantering disbelief*
Over Goldengrove unleaving?	
Leáves, líke the things of mán, you	*patronizing reproach*
With your fresh thoughts care for, can you?	
Áh, ás the héart grows ólder	*chilly prophecy of rational future*
It will come to such sights colder	
By and by, nor spare a sigh	
Though worlds of wanwood leafmeal lie;	*regret*
And yet you *will* weep and know why.	*impatience*
Now no matter, child, the name:	*insight, surprised*
Sórrow's spríngs áre the sáme.	*recognition and admission*
Nor mouth had, no nor mind, expressed	
What héart héard of, ghóst guéssed;	*self-reproach*
It ís the blíght mán was bórn for,	*universal despair*
It is Margaret you mourn for.	*grief*

By the end, the speaker is ashamed at rebuking Margaret's tears, and sees that adult grief and child grief are one; both lament the consequences of the fall of man — the temporality and mortality of all things. In "tracking the tones" of such a poem, readers can differ over the exact name of each tone, but every reader will hear changes of tone over the length of the poem. Uttering this poem, you must at first be the superior and patronizing adult; then, as you come to acknowledge your own shortsightedness, you feel the heavy weight of human destiny — that we are all born for blight, and that our tears, even when they seem to be shed for falling leaves, are in reality shed for our implicit recognition of our own fate. As you perceive the tones and say the words of this adult speaker, his selfhood — in his original pride of superior knowledge and his subsequent willingness to be ashamed of himself — becomes potentially credible.

The speaker's change in view has to be persuasively "put over" by your own voice as you speak (even if only mentally) the words, or the poem will lack its striking effect of self-rebuke and final shared grief. However, lyric poems are usually *inner meditations,* not dramatic or declaimed speeches; one can't be an orator or an actor in speaking a lyric aloud. One has to be a self, musing aloud over inner responses, not someone addressing an audience, or even someone speaking aloud in solitude like an actor delivering a soliloquy. Even when there is an auditor (here, Margaret), the lyric represents the *inner* speech or meditation of its utterer, and must sound inward and reflective rather than outer-directed and rhetorical. As William Butler Yeats said, "Out of the quarrel with others, we make rhetoric; out of the quarrel with ourselves, poetry." All the tones of a poem are the tones of an inward, not an outward, quarrel; the credible self in the lyric is the private divided self of the inner life. Even in a dramatic monologue (which is publicly addressed to another person, as Robert Browning's Duke addresses the ambassador), it is important to perceive the revelation of the inner life of the speaker by the poem. The Duke reveals himself to be jealous and homicidal, even though he may not be aware how much of himself is visible in his outwardly smooth and aristocratic speech. To see a dramatic monologue as simultaneously a self-protective public speech and an unconsciously self-revealing document is to read it as dramatic lyric demands, doubly.

Imagination

The selves constructed in poems needn't have original ideas (in fact, few of them do), but they must have imagination — and the imagination of the reader of the poem must somehow (by art) be drawn into the imagination of the speaker. The word "imagination" covers almost anything unusual and nonfactual in the way the self conveys thought. Often something said "imaginatively" is logically absurd, as in this couplet from William Blake's "Auguries of Innocence":

> If the Sun and Moon should doubt,
> They'd immediately go out.

This is an imaginative way of saying that life lives on faith, and that skepticism is corrosive to radiant living. Here is another example, this time from W. H. Auden's ballad "As I Walked Out One Evening":

> The glacier knocks in the cupboard,
>   The desert sighs in the bed,
> And the crack in the teacup opens
>   A lane to the land of the dead.

Such imaginativeness in the poetic self asks you to free-associate: even in the cupboard of the food supply, a coming Ice Age is making itself heard; even in the midst of lovemaking, aridity appears; a small flaw in a cup suggests the great Flaw in life, that we are not immortal.

Why — as the question is often put — do the poets (or their constructed poetic selves) say what they mean in "other" words? No poet would agree with putting the question this way. Poets tell us that in poems they say *exactly* what they mean in words chosen precisely to mean what they (the words) say. "Bed-desert-sigh" is an *exact* transcription, in Auden's speaker's mind, of what he felt in bed; "crack-lane-death," he thinks when he takes that teacup out of the cupboard; and even though he may close the door of the cupboard, a freezing-hidden-thing, the rigor mortis of the human relations in the house, makes its knocking heard behind the silent wood.

John Ashbery, in "Self-Portrait in a Convex Mirror," calls the surface of a poem its "visible core." The emotional core of Auden's poem, which we infer from the appearance on its surface of the glacier and the desert, is the inner feeling of dread that Auden's speaker feels even in the midst of the "safest" surroundings — his kitchen, his bed. And the dread seems to be lodged not in him but in his very cups and cupboards; *they* seem uneasy, disturbed, flawed. Psychologists call this reaction "projection" — when we "project" our inner emotion upon the world so that outside things seem uncanny or threatening. It would *not* be accurate, in this case, for the poet to say, "I feel dread and aridity" — that would be a generalizing summary, not a transcription of how concretely he feels a threat in every object at home. And poets wish to give accurate transcripts of feeling, as well as accurate transcripts of the structures of reality.

"How would I be feeling if I said *exactly this*?" is the question readers must ask as they read the words about the doubting sun uttered by the self that Blake constructs. And the answer is something like, "I'd be feeling that if the sun suddenly went out, it would be like my starting to doubt my belief in God — everything would go black." The animism by which the sun and moon become doubters like us, or by which a desert can sigh in a bed, is part of imagination's capacity to make the whole world alive. A credible self in poetry is one who can make us feel as he or she does. The poet shows; the poet does not simply tell. The poet transmits things "on the pulses," as Keats said; the senses are reproduced in words.

Words like "dread," "suspicion," "skepticism," and "faith" are words from the discourses of psychology and theology, rather than words from the senses or feelings. The senses and the feelings are poetry's stock-in-trade; words like "cup" and "desert," "sun" and "moon," never age in the way intellectual discourse does.

It is easy to describe, when reading striking excerpts like the ones from Blake and Auden, how the poet is using language "imaginatively" and

creating a "flesh-and-blood self." But what about poems that seem factu-
ally written, without the odd personal deflections of language that characterize an idiosyncratic self? Here is a passage from Tennyson's "Mariana"
that may seem largely like straightforward natural description, a passage
transcribed by a camera rather than uttered by a defined self:

> About a stone-cast from the wall
>   A sluice with blacken'd waters slept,
> And o'er it many, round and small,
>   The cluster'd marish-mosses crept.
> Hard by a poplar shook alway,
>   All silver-green with gnarlèd bark:
>   For leagues no other tree did mark
> The level waste, the rounding gray.

There are in the stanza two relatively inconspicuous metaphors: the
sluice *sleeps,* the mosses *creep.* Sleeping waters and creeping vegetation are
not in themselves notably imaginative. Everything else — the wall, the
sluice-channel, the round small marsh-grasses, the single shaking silver-
green poplar with its gnarled bark, the level waste of land meeting the
rounding gray of the horizon — seems factual, transcribed, uninfected by
imagination. Of course the passage is highly decorative in terms of
sound, but where is the imagination, or the imagining self?

It is only when we see the whole of "Mariana" — which contains
seven of these stanzas — that we realize what the imagination is con-
tributing to the poem. Tennyson is representing in "Mariana" the stream
of consciousness of a girl waiting, with increasing hopelessness, for her
lover to come. Because she has nothing else to occupy her mind, she
notes, minutely and exhaustedly, every item in her surroundings, every
small change of atmosphere during the long hours as they pass. It is in the
accumulation of seven stanzas' worth of mounting ennui, apprehension,
and loathing that we see Tennyson's imagination at work creating the
imagination of Mariana. He gives each stanza its own peculiar atmosphere. We have already seen the unpromising "blacken'd waters" and
"level waste" outside; here is a stanza in which Mariana perceives the
inside atmosphere, as the day wears on without the arrival of her lover:

> All day within the dreary house
>   The doors upon their hinges creak'd;
> The blue fly sung in the pane; the mouse
>   Behind the moldering wainscot shriek'd.

The buzz of the fly, the shriek of the mouse, the creak of the hinges —
by these details we understand the hope within hopelessness with which
Mariana listens for the slightest sound of an arrival, and is rewarded only
by these tiny interruptions of the deathly silence.

Where a poem offers such "facts" as the blackened waters or the
creaking hinges, they are always facts seen through the lens of a particular
feeling, which has been imagined by the poet, and ascribed to the imagination of the speaker. It is the *successive* feelings enacted by the poem that
will lead you to see how the imagination is at work, even in the most "factual" lines. There is not a very great distance between Tennyson's "factual"
mouse squeaking behind the wainscot and Auden's glacier knocking in the
cupboard. Both of them serve chiefly as transcripts of the believable feelings of the constructed self rather than as a record of actual things.

Another way poets often show imagination operating in their fictive selves is to take a conventional timeline — birth, youth, maturity, old
age, death (for example), or spring, summer, autumn, winter — and place
the poem in a spot on the timeline that no one else has used. Dickinson
(remembering Tennyson's "Mariana" where "the blue fly sung in the
pane") inserts her (posthumous) speaker, who is recalling her own death,
into the timeline of life at its very last gasp, the moment when she actually died. It is imaginative to employ a speaker speaking posthumously,
but that had been done before — for instance, by George Herbert in
"Love (III)." Dickinson's speaker takes the old tradition of "holy dying"
and revises it blasphemously:

EMILY DICKINSON (1830 – 1886)
I heard a Fly buzz – when I died –

I heard a Fly buzz – when I died –
The Stillness in the Room
Was like the Stillness in the Air –
Between the Heaves of Storm –

The Eyes around – had wrung them dry –
And Breaths were gathering firm
For that last Onset – when the King
Be witnessed – in the Room –

I willed my Keepsakes – Signed away
What portion of me be
Assignable – and then it was
There interposed a Fly –

With Blue – uncertain stumbling Buzz –
Between the light and me –
And then the Windows failed – and then
I could not see to see –

Dickinson is perfectly aware that the death of a Christian ought to take place when God, the "King," comes to take the soul to heaven, and she shows the mourners waiting precisely for "that last Onset." But instead of Christ's "Today shalt thou be with me in Paradise," the speaker reports a "Blue – uncertain stumbling Buzz," and dies. In inventing this sacrilegious rendering of the conventional "happy death" of the Christian believer, Dickinson has found a way for imagination to re-represent death, this time in wholly bodily and nihilistic form. Dickinson in this instance has inserted her fictive (and credibly blasphemous) self into the human timeline at the very last second.

Other poets, using the seasonal timeline, will also make their fictive selves speak from a new place. Wallace Stevens does not say, "At the beginning of spring" (a cliché), but rather, "At the earliest ending of winter" ("Not Ideas About the Thing But the Thing Itself"); he does not say, "The leaves have all fallen" (a cliché for autumn), but rather, "The last leaf that was going to fall had fallen" ("An Ordinary Evening in New Haven"). The poet can likewise choose an unusual moment in a timeline by referring to the hours of the day: "There's a certain Slant of light," says Dickinson — the first time in literature that a writer has alluded to the light on late winter afternoons. These imaginative perceptions make a poetic self arresting, as well as believable.

Another strategy of the poetic imagination is to insert into a genre — say, the sonnet — where the reader might expect a conventional topic (love or death), a new topic, such as prayer (Herbert) or the massacre of "heretics" (Milton) or a car junkyard (Dave Smith). This "turn" of the speaker surprises the reader and refreshes the genre; the expectations of the sonnet form become roomier, deeper, riskier. Or the imagination can borrow a form from another literature and write a poem in that form in English, as Edward FitzGerald borrowed the Persian Rubáiyát and Allen Ginsberg borrowed the sutra (a Buddhist treatise form) in his "Sunflower Sutra." Or a poet's imagination can flout the moral expectations of society: Thomas Hardy's "ruined maid" is quite happy in her new circumstances — "'One's pretty lively when ruined,' said she."

An imaginative self can range freely through space and time, and can ask startling questions like, "What if this present were the world's last night?" (Donne). It can draw unusual comparisons, as when the birches bent by the weight of vanished snow seem to Frost "like girls on hands and knees that throw their hair / Before them over their heads to dry in the sun." It matters less *how* the imaginative self renews feeling — through a surreal phrase like Auden's "glacier . . . in the cupboard," through an old image like Pan revived as Cummings's balloonMan, through a genre-violation like Milton's sonnet of "slaughtered saints," or through blasphemy, as when Dickinson substitutes a fly for Christ in the death-room — than *that* it renews feeling through a reconceiving of familiar circumstance.

The real appeal of the imagination, when it appears in a poetic speaker, is that one never knows what it will do next. Tonight the Last Judgment? Doubt eclipsing the sun and the moon? A speaker addressing us from beyond the grave? For every self you meet speaking in poetry, the first question — and the last question — to ask is: "Where in these words do I see the imagination at work?" Without imagination, the noblest idea is empty of *poetic* interest, and the most heartfelt confession merely a twice-told tale. With imagination, the world is made new, and seen sharply, clearly, at an angle. We go to poetry, as to fiction, for the shock of the newly seen. "Things seen," says Stevens, "are things as seen." It is in the "as" of a credible speaker that the imagination lives.

Persona

There are many ways to refer to the self who speaks a poem. Some-times, in obviously autobiographical lyrics, we simply use the name of the author: "Keats writes about reading Homer for the first time." In this sort of shorthand, we mean, by the word "Keats," "the author as he lets us see himself in the speaker of this poem, in his fictive poetic self." The author's fictive self overlaps with, but is not identical to, his "real" self, because a poem obeys many laws (of form, of structure, of language) that may deflect it from factual accuracy.

Robert Lowell begins his poem "Bright Day in Boston" with the phrase, "Joy of standing up my dentist." In fact (as he later said) he *had* kept his dentist appointment, and only after it was over had he taken the walk recorded in the poem. But — as he also said — the felt impulse to skip the dentist, which in life he had *not* obeyed, made a "truer" emotional beginning to the poem. We can say, then, that "Lowell" stood up his dentist, while Lowell did not. It is often easiest, once one has made clear that one means the author rather than the person, to say "Keats" or "Lowell" in referring to the speaker of a poem.

But there are poems where the speaker is clearly not the author: Yeats, for instance, writes several poems in the voice of an old woman whom he calls "Crazy Jane." It is customary, in such cases, to refer to the speaker of the poem as a "persona" adopted by Yeats. The word "persona" comes from the Latin verb *personare* — "to *speak through* a mask." Only when the speaker is wearing a mask — that is, cannot possibly be seen as the actual author because of a difference of age, or sex, or national origin — does it make sense to speak of a "persona." Otherwise it is preferable to refer simply to "the speaker."

Why would a poet adopt a persona? Why does an educated, prosperous poet want to take on the voice of a poor old woman of the roads? What is there that the poet wants to express that he can utter only in Crazy Jane's voice? These are the questions that anyone writing on Yeats's late poetry must ask. Here is the most famous of Crazy Jane's poems. In it, Jane encounters the Bishop, who once (as we know from another poem in the sequence) was a priest in the parish where Jane and her lover, Jack, lived; he banned Jack from the parish, supposedly for religious reasons. Now, in old age, Crazy Jane and the Bishop once again exchange words:

WILLIAM BUTLER YEATS (1865 – 1939)
Crazy Jane Talks with the Bishop

I met the Bishop on the road
And much said he and I.
"Those breasts are flat and fallen now,
Those veins must soon be dry;
Live in a heavenly mansion,
Not in some foul sty."

"Fair and foul are near of kin,
And fair needs foul," I cried.
"My friends are gone, but that's a truth
Nor grave nor bed denied,
Learned in bodily lowliness
And in the heart's pride.

"A woman can be proud and stiff
When on love intent;
But Love has pitched his mansion in
The place of excrement;
For nothing can be sole or whole
That has not been rent."

We can deduce, from the Bishop's opening remarks about the state of Crazy Jane's breasts — that they are "flat and fallen now" — that he had improperly noticed their unflat and unfallen shape in the past, and that when he banished Jack it was because of jealousy rather than piety. After the first stanza, the rest of the poem is Jane's. We notice that she can say things that a philosophical poet like Yeats might feel called upon, if he spoke in his own voice, to qualify further ("fair needs foul," for instance); but Crazy Jane, as the voice of peasant wisdom (speaking, we should notice, in an adaptation of an old folk ballad), does not need to be philosophically subtle. And although her final assertion — that "Love has pitched his mansion in / The place of excrement" — is based on a dry Augustinian remark ("We are born between urine and feces"), she can phrase that observation more passionately because it is her own female body that is in question; to the Bishop's stable "heavenly mansion" she opposes the nomadic "mansion" of Love, a tent pitched in "the place of excrement."

Crazy Jane says things, in short, that Yeats as a philosophically educated person, and as a man, could not say in his own person. That is the usefulness of adopting a persona. Well brought-up girls, in Dickinson's day, were not allowed to roam the fields barefoot; and so, when Dickinson wants to show the terror of encountering a snake underfoot, she has a boy speak her poem. When you see an obvious persona speaking a poem (as in so many of Browning's "dramatic monologues"), ask yourself what the persona is being used to express that the poet could not believably convey in a contemporary "real-life" voice. Poets often take on the voice of someone long dead: black poets like Robert Hayden and Rita Dove have written in the voices of slaves, to give vicarious utterance to those who were historically denied literacy and consequently expression in writing. William Blake did the same when he spoke in the persona of a "little black boy," showing the boy already corrupted by Christian teaching:

My mother bore me in the southern wild,
And I am black, but O! my soul is white;
White as an angel is the English child:
But I am black as if bereav'd of light.

The assumption of the persona of a black child by a white poet, or of a female persona by a male poet, has been criticized by those who believe that only a black can speak of the black experience, only a woman of a woman's experience. Many have retorted that the very function of the imagination is to enable us to imagine the Other, and that only by such leaps of the imagination across the gaps of gender, race, and age can poetry induce its readers to practice that enabling fellow-feeling. Readers who might not have reflected on class issues, or issues of religious tyranny, or issues of the place of the sexual in the spiritual, can be brought, by Crazy Jane's encounter with the Bishop, to think of these issues afresh. It does not matter who wrote the lyric, if the self presented in the lyric is a credible one invested with imaginative power. Because every speaker of a lyric is a constructed speaker, made "alive" by the imagination, and delineated in the play of language, a poem asks that as you step into the shoes of the speaker, you notice how language has been arranged to make that act possible.

In Brief: Constructing a Self

As you read a poem, ask yourself questions about the speaker constructed within the poem. Where is he or she in time and space? Over how long a period? With what motivations? How typical? Speaking in what tones of voice? Imagining life how? Resembling the author or different from the author? The more you can deduce about the speaker, the better you understand the poem. If you think about what has been happening to the speaker *before* the poem begins (if that is implied by the poem), you will understand the speaker better.

Reading Other Poems

The constituents of selfhood that are being emphasized in any one poem can be seen from both content and form.

- What kind of a self do you feel you have if you find a tree to be a close relative, as Walt Whitman's speaker does?
- What kind of a self do you feel you have if you speak meditatively and slowly, as Whitman's fictive self does?

    You can ask these questions of each of the poems that follow.

- What kind of a self do you feel you have if you call yourself "Nobody," as Emily Dickinson's speaker does?
- You might expect that Thomas Hardy's "ruined maid" would feel herself to be a nobody (and so she might, in another poet's hands). But she feels herself quite a somebody. Why? Does the rhythm of Hardy's poem reinforce or contradict the attitude taken by the fictive speaker toward the prostitute?
- What kind of a self usually utters a "love song"? Do you find that kind of a self in T. S. Eliot's poem? How does Prufrock's prophecy of his self in old age ("Do I dare to eat a peach? / I shall wear white

flannel trousers, and walk upon the beach") help to construct your idea of his present self?

♦ The free-verse rhythms in which Prufrock speaks betray his personality, too. How?

♦ Eliot gradually assembles traits of Prufrock (beginning with his name) so that we understand him better and better as the poem proceeds. Can you characterize these traits?

The self of the speaker can sometimes only be deduced from what he or she says in observing another.

♦ John Dryden's little song "Sylvia the Fair" enables you to deduce the speaker's attitude toward sexuality. How would you characterize it?

When we come to more explicitly social identities (often imposed by others rather than self-chosen), we arrive at speakers who must construct an identity in part from pregiven materials (as Countee Cullen and Carl Phillips do).

♦ How does Cullen's speaker confront this problem in "Heritage"?

♦ How are the contrasting positions imagined in this "dialogue of the mind with itself"?

♦ Can you speculate why Cullen gave his speaker the strong rhythmic form seen here (technically known as trochaic tetrameter rhyming couplets), rather than constructing the self of his speaker in, say, meditative blank verse, often used for such poems of internal debate (as, say, in Shakespeare's soliloquies)?

♦ How do Cullen's methods of defining himself vis-à-vis Africa compare with those of Phillips? To what extent is the speaker of each poet a type rather than a unique individual?

Because a self is often constructed, whether in a novel or a poem, around a decisive moment of crisis or choice, we can find the selfhood crystallizing around a single episode. William Butler Yeats's airman is an Irishman in the British army, defending England though he has never lived there, participating in a war in which his own country (Ireland) was neutral. Alone in his airplane, he sees his life clearly, and a young indeterminate self suddenly crystallizes.

♦ In what rhythms does he speak? Are they uncertain and wavering, or strong and emphatic?

♦ How, both negatively and positively, does he delineate his newly discovered self?

On the other hand, sometimes a self is constructed as much by social conditions as by a moment of decision.

◆ How did Elsie (in real life, William Carlos Williams's household help) end up the way she did?

◆ Williams imagines a group of social causes that cooperate to keep many Elsies from having a rewarding and independent life: each of them has contributed to the kind of self Elsie now is. Can you connect these causes to her self as it is described?

◆ Can you construct a plausible picture of the speaker's self from his personal and social feelings about Elsie?

In contrast to the self chosen in a moment, there is the self assumed to be stable: Anne Sexton's speaker assumes she belongs to a typical category of persons ("Her Kind"), and Charles Wright, though he writes many self-portraits, confers a temporary stability on the speaker of each one.

◆ How do Sexton and Wright assemble a stable speaking self through images?

JOHN DRYDEN (1631 – 1700)
Sylvia the Fair

1

SYLVIA the fair, in the bloom of fifteen,
Felt an innocent warmth as she lay on the green;
She had heard of a pleasure, and something she guess'd
By the towzing, and tumbling, and touching her breast.
She saw the men eager, but was at a loss,
What they meant by their sighing, and kissing so close;
     By their praying and whining,
       And clasping and twining,
       And panting and wishing,
       And sighing and kissing,
     And sighing and kissing so close.

2

"Ah!" she cried, "ah! for a languishing maid,
In a country of Christians, to die without aid!
Not a Whig, or a Tory, or Trimmer[1] at least,
Or a Protestant parson, or Catholic priest,

---

[1]A trimmer is one who inclines to either of two opposing political parties, as interest dictates.

To instruct a young virgin, that is at a loss,
What they meant by their sighing, and kissing so close!
      By their praying and whining,
       And clasping and twining,
       And panting and wishing,
       And sighing and kissing,
    And sighing and kissing so close."

3

Cupid, in shape of a swain, did appear,
He saw the sad wound, and in pity drew near;
Then show'd her his arrow, and bid her not fear,
For the pain was no more than a maiden may bear.
When the balm was infus'd, she was not at a loss,
What they meant by their sighing and kissing so close;
      By their praying and whining,
       And clasping and twining,
       And panting and wishing,
       And sighing and kissing,
    And sighing and kissing so close.

WALT WHITMAN (1819 – 1892)

I Saw in Louisiana a Live-Oak Growing

I saw in Louisiana a live-oak growing,
All alone stood it and the moss hung down from the branches,
Without any companion it grew there uttering joyous leaves of
    dark green,
And its look, rude, unbending, lusty, made me think of myself,
But I wonder'd how it could utter joyous leaves standing alone
    there without its friend near, for I knew I could not,
And I broke off a twig with a certain number of leaves upon it, and
    twined around it a little moss,
And brought it away, and have placed it in sight in my room,
It is not needed to remind me as of my own dear friends,
(For I believe lately I think of little else than of them,)
Yet it remains to me a curious token, it makes me think of manly
    love;
For all that, and though the live-oak glistens there in Louisiana
    solitary in a wide flat space,
Uttering joyous leaves all its life without a friend a lover near,
I know very well I could not.

EMILY DICKINSON (1830 – 1886)
I'm Nobody! Who are you?

I'm Nobody! Who are you?
Are you – Nobody – Too?
Then there's a pair of us!
Don't tell! they'd advertise – you know!

How dreary – to be – Somebody!
How public – like a Frog –
To tell one's name – the livelong June –
To an admiring Bog!

WILLIAM BUTLER YEATS (1865 – 1939)
An Irish Airman Foresees His Death

I know that I shall meet my fate
Somewhere among the clouds above;
Those that I fight I do not hate,
Those that I guard I do not love;
My country is Kiltartan Cross,
My countrymen Kiltartan's poor,
No likely end could bring them loss
Or leave them happier than before.
Nor law, nor duty bade me fight,
Nor public men, nor cheering crowds,
A lonely impulse of delight
Drove to this tumult in the clouds;
I balanced all, brought all to mind,
The years to come seemed waste of breath,
A waste of breath the years behind
In balance with this life, this death.

THOMAS HARDY (1840 – 1928)
The Ruined Maid

"O 'Melia, my dear, this does everything crown!
Who could have supposed I should meet you in Town?
And whence such fair garments, such prosperi-ty?"
"O didn't you know I'd been ruined?" said she.

"You left us in tatters, without shoes or socks,
Tired of digging potatoes, and spudding up docks;
And now you've gay bracelets and bright feathers three!"
"Yes: that's how we dress when we're ruined," said she.

"At home in the barton° you said 'thee' and 'thou,'   *farm*
And 'thik oon,' and 'theäs oon,' and 't'other'; but now
Your talking quite fits 'ee for high compa-ny!"
"Some polish is gained with one's ruin," said she.

"Your hands were like paws then, your face blue and bleak
But now I'm bewitched by your delicate cheek,
And your little gloves fit as on any la-dy!"
"We never do work when we're ruined," said she.

"You used to call home-life a hag-ridden dream,
And you'd sigh, and you'd sock; but at present you seem
To know not of megrims° or melancho-ly!"   *low spirits*
"True. One's pretty lively when ruined," said she.

"I wish I had feathers, a fine sweeping gown,
And a delicate face, and could strut about Town!"
"My dear — a raw country girl, such as you be,
Cannot quite expect that. You ain't ruined," said she.

T. S. ELIOT (1888 – 1965)
The Love Song of J. Alfred Prufrock

> *S'io credessi che mia risposta fosse*
> *A persona che mai tornasse al mondo,*
> *Questa fiamma staria senza più scosse.*
>
> *Ma perciocche giammai di questo fondo*
> *Non tornò vivo alcun, s' i'odo il vero,*
> *Senza tema d'infamia ti rispondo.*[1]

Let us go then, you and I,
When the evening is spread out against the sky
Like a patient etherised upon a table;
Let us go, through certain half-deserted streets,
The muttering retreats   5
Of restless nights in one-night cheap hotels
And sawdust restaurants with oyster-shells:
Streets that follow like a tedious argument
Of insidious intent
To lead you to an overwhelming question . . .   10

---

[1]From Dante's *Inferno,* Canto 27, lines 61–66. Guido da Montefeltro speaks, after Dante questions him: "If I thought that my reply were to be to someone who would ever return to the world, this flame would be still, without further motion. But since no one has ever returned alive from this depth, if what I hear is true, I answer you without fear of shame."

Oh, do not ask, "What is it?"
Let us go and make our visit.

    In the room the women come and go
Talking of Michelangelo.

    The yellow fog that rubs its back upon the window-panes, 15
The yellow smoke that rubs its muzzle on the window-panes,
Licked its tongue into the corners of the evening,
Lingered upon the pools that stand in drains,
Let fall upon its back the soot that falls from chimneys,
Slipped by the terrace, made a sudden leap,   20
And seeing that it was a soft October night,
Curled once about the house, and fell asleep.

    And indeed there will be time
For the yellow smoke that slides along the street,
Rubbing its back upon the window-panes;   25
There will be time, there will be time
To prepare a face to meet the faces that you meet;
There will be time to murder and create,
And time for all the works and days[2] of hands
That lift and drop a question on your plate;   30
Time for you and time for me,
And time yet for a hundred indecisions,
And for a hundred visions and revisions,
Before the taking of a toast and tea.

    In the room the women come and go   35
Talking of Michelangelo.

    And indeed there will be time
To wonder, "Do I dare?" and, "Do I dare?"
Time to turn back and descend the stair,
With a bald spot in the middle of my hair —   40
[They will say: "How his hair is growing thin!"]
My morning coat, my collar mounting firmly to the chin,
My necktie rich and modest, but asserted by a simple pin —
[They will say: "But how his arms and legs are thin!"]
Do I dare   45
Disturb the universe?
In a minute there is time
For decisions and revisions which a minute will reverse.

---

[2]The Greek poet Hesiod (eighth century B.C.) wrote *Works and Days,* a poem
about country life.

For I have known them all already, known them all:
Have known the evenings, mornings, afternoons,   50
I have measured out my life with coffee spoons;
I know the voices dying with a dying fall
Beneath the music from a farther room.
     So how should I presume?

     And I have known the eyes already, known them all —   55
The eyes that fix you in a formulated phrase,
And when I am formulated, sprawling on a pin,
When I am pinned and wriggling on the wall,
Then how should I begin
To spit out all the butt-ends of my days and ways?   60
     And how should I presume?

     And I have known the arms already, known them all —
Arms that are braceleted and white and bare
[But in the lamplight, downed with light brown hair!]
Is it perfume from a dress   65
That makes me so digress?
Arms that lie along a table, or wrap about a shawl.
     And should I then presume?
     And how should I begin?

    . . . . .

Shall I say, I have gone at dusk through narrow streets   70
And watched the smoke that rises from the pipes
Of lonely men in shirt-sleeves, leaning out of windows? . . .

     I should have been a pair of ragged claws
Scuttling across the floors of silent seas.

    . . . . .

And the afternoon, the evening, sleeps so peacefully!   75
Smoothed by long fingers,
Asleep . . . tired . . . or it malingers,
Stretched on the floor, here beside you and me.
Should I, after tea and cakes and ices,
Have the strength to force the moment to its crisis?   80
But though I have wept and fasted, wept and prayed,
Though I have seen my head [grown slightly bald] brought in
    upon a platter,[3]

---

[3]The head of John the Baptist was delivered on a platter to Salome (Matthew 14: 1–11).

I am no prophet — and here's no great matter;
I have seen the moment of my greatness flicker,
And I have seen the eternal Footman hold my coat, and snicker,   85
And in short, I was afraid.

    And would it have been worth it, after all,
After the cups, the marmalade, the tea,
Among the porcelain, among some talk of you and me,
Would it have been worth while,   90
To have bitten off the matter with a smile,
To have squeezed the universe into a ball
To roll it toward some overwhelming question,
To say: "I am Lazarus,[4] come from the dead,
Come back to tell you all, I shall tell you all" —   95
If one, settling a pillow by her head,
    Should say: "That is not what I meant at all.
    That is not it, at all."

    And would it have been worth it, after all,
Would it have been worth while,   100
After the sunsets and the dooryards and the sprinkled streets,
After the novels, after the teacups, after the skirts that trail along
    the floor —
And this, and so much more? —
It is impossible to say just what I mean!
But as if a magic lantern threw the nerves in patterns
    on a screen: 105
Would it have been worth while
If one, settling a pillow or throwing off a shawl,
And turning toward the window, should say:
    "That is not it at all,
    That is not what I meant, at all."   110

       · · · · ·

No! I am not Prince Hamlet, nor was meant to be;
Am an attendant lord, one that will do
To swell a progress,° start a scene or two,   *royal procession*
Advise the prince; no doubt, an easy tool,
Deferential, glad to be of use,   115
Politic, cautious, and meticulous;

---

[4]Lazarus was raised from the dead by Jesus (John 11:1–44).

Full of high sentence,° but a bit obtuse;   *sententiousness*
At times, indeed, almost ridiculous —
Almost, at times, the Fool.

    I grow old . . . I grow old . . .   120
I shall wear the bottoms of my trousers rolled.

    Shall I part my hair behind? Do I dare to eat a peach?
I shall wear white flannel trousers, and walk upon the beach.
I have heard the mermaids singing, each to each.

    I do not think that they will sing to me.   125

    I have seen them riding seaward on the waves
Combing the white hair of the waves blown back
When the wind blows the water white and black.

    We have lingered in the chambers of the sea
By sea-girls wreathed with seaweed red and brown   130
Till human voices wake us, and we drown.

WILLIAM CARLOS WILLIAMS (1883 – 1963)
To Elsie

The pure products of America
go crazy —
mountain folk from Kentucky

or the ribbed north end of
Jersey   5
with its isolate lakes and

valleys, its deaf-mutes, thieves
old names
and promiscuity between

devil-may-care men who have taken   10
to railroading
out of sheer lust of adventure —

and young slatterns, bathed
in filth
from Monday to Saturday   15

to be tricked out that night
with gauds°   *jewelry*
from imaginations which have no

peasant traditions to give them
character
but flutter and flaunt
20

sheer rags — succumbing without
emotion
save numbed terror

under some hedge of choke-cherry
or viburnum —
which they cannot express —
25

Unless it be that marriage
perhaps
with a dash of Indian blood
30

will throw up a girl so desolate
so hemmed round
with disease or murder

that she'll be rescued by an
agent —
reared by the state and
35

sent out at fifteen to work in
some hard-pressed
house in the suburbs —

some doctor's family, some Elsie —
voluptuous water
expressing with broken
40

brain the truth about us —
her great
ungainly hips and flopping breasts
45

addressed to cheap
jewelry
and rich young men with fine eyes

as if the earth under our feet
were
an excrement of some sky
50

and we degraded prisoners
destined
to hunger until we eat filth

while the imagination strains 55
after deer
going by fields of goldenrod in

the stifling heat of September
Somehow
it seems to destroy us 60

It is only in isolate flecks that
something
is given off

No one
to witness 65
and adjust, no one to drive the car

COUNTEE CULLEN (1903 – 1946)
Heritage

For Harold Jackman

What is Africa to me:
Copper sun or scarlet sea,
Jungle star or jungle track,
Strong bronzed men, or regal black
Women from whose loins I sprang 5
When the birds of Eden sang?
One three centuries removed
From the scenes his fathers loved,
Spicy grove, cinnamon tree,
What is Africa to me? 10

So I lie, who all day long
Want no sound except the song
Sung by wild barbaric birds
Goading massive jungle herds,
Juggernauts of flesh that pass 15
Trampling tall defiant grass
Where young forest lovers lie,
Plighting troth beneath the sky.
So I lie, who always hear,
Though I cram against my ear 20
Both my thumbs, and keep them there,
Great drums throbbing through the air.
So I lie, whose fount of pride,
Dear distress, and joy allied,

Is my somber flesh and skin,   25
With the dark blood dammed within
Like great pulsing tides of wine
That, I fear, must burst the fine
Channels of the chafing net
Where they surge and foam and fret.   30
Africa? A book one thumbs
Listlessly, till slumber comes.
Unremembered are her bats
Circling through the night, her cats
Crouching in the river reeds,   35
Stalking gentle flesh that feeds
By the river brink; no more
Does the bugle-throated roar
Cry that monarch claws have leapt
From the scabbards where they slept.   40
Silver snakes that once a year
Doff the lovely coats you wear,
Seek no covert in your fear
Lest a mortal eye should see;
What's your nakedness to me?   45
Here no leprous flowers rear
Fierce corollas in the air;
Here no bodies sleek and wet,
Dripping mingled rain and sweat,
Tread the savage measures of   50
Jungle boys and girls in love.
What is last year's snow to me,
Last year's anything? The tree
Budding yearly must forget
How its past arose or set —   55
Bough and blossom, flower, fruit,
Even what shy bird with mute
Wonder at her travail there,
Meekly labored in its hair.
One three centuries removed   60
From the scenes his fathers loved,
Spicy grove, cinnamon tree,
What is Africa to me?

So I lie, who find no peace
Night or day, no slight release   65

From the unremittent beat
Made by cruel padded feet
Walking through my body's street.
Up and down they go, and back,
Treading out a jungle track.   70
So I lie, who never quite
Safely sleep from rain at night —
I can never rest at all
When the rain begins to fall;
Like a soul gone mad with pain   75
I must match its weird refrain;
Ever must I twist and squirm,
Writhing like a baited worm,
While its primal measures drip
Through my body, crying, "Strip!   80
Doff this new exuberance.
Come and dance the Lover's Dance!"
In an old remembered way
Rain works on me night and day.

Quaint, outlandish heathen gods   85
Black men fashion out of rods,
Clay, and brittle bits of stone,
In a likeness like their own,
My conversion came high-priced;
I belong to Jesus Christ,   90
Preacher of Humility;
Heathen gods are naught to me.

Father, Son, and Holy Ghost,
So I make an idle boast;
Jesus of the twice-turned cheek,   95
Lamb of God, although I speak
With my mouth thus, in my heart
Do I play a double part.
Ever at Thy glowing altar
Must my heart grow sick and falter,   100
Wishing He I served were black,
Thinking then it would not lack
Precedent of pain to guide it,
Let who would or might deride it;
Surely then this flesh would know   105
Yours had borne a kindred woe.

Lord, I fashion dark gods, too,
Daring even to give You
Dark despairing features where,
Crowned with dark rebellious hair,   110
Patience wavers just so much as
Mortal grief compels, while touches
Quick and hot, of anger, rise
To smitten cheek and weary eyes.
Lord, forgive me if my need   115
Sometimes shapes a human creed.
All day long and all night through,
One thing only must I do:
Quench my pride and cool my blood,
Lest I perish in the flood,   120
Lest a hidden ember set
Timber that I thought was wet
Burning like the dryest flax,
Melting like the merest wax,
Lest the grave restore its dead.   125
Not yet has my heart or head
In the least way realized
They and I are civilized.

ANNE SEXTON (1928 – 1974)
Her Kind

I have gone out, a possessed witch,
haunting the black air, braver at night;
dreaming evil, I have done my hitch
over the plain houses, light by light:
lonely thing, twelve-fingered,[1] out of mind.
A woman like that is not a woman, quite.
I have been her kind.

I have found the warm caves in the woods,
filled them with skillets, carvings, shelves,
closets, silks, innumerable goods;
fixed the suppers for the worms and the elves:
whining, rearranging the disaligned.
A woman like that is misunderstood.
I have been her kind.

---

[1]Witches were thought to have six fingers on each hand.

I have ridden in your cart, driver,
waved my nude arms at villages going by,
learning the last bright routes, survivor
where your flames still bite my thigh
and my ribs crack where your wheels wind.[2]
A woman like that is not ashamed to die.
I have been her kind.

CHARLES WRIGHT (b. 1935)
Self-Portrait

Someday they'll find me out, and my lavish hands,
Full moon at my back, fog groping the gone horizon, the edge
Of the continent scored in yellow, expectant lights,
White shoulders of surf, a wolf-colored sand,
The ashes and bits of char that will clear my name.

Till then, I'll hum to myself and settle the whereabouts.
Jade plants and oleander float in a shine.
The leaves of the pepper tree turn green.
My features are sketched with black ink in a slow drag through the
        sky,
Waiting to be filled in.

Hand that lifted me once, lift me again,
Sort me and flesh me out, fix my eyes.
From the mulch and the undergrowth, protect me and pass me on.
From my own words and my certainties,
From the rose and the easy cheek, deliver me, pass me on.

CARL PHILLIPS (b. 1959)
Africa Says

Before you arrive, forget
the landscape the novels are filled with,
the dull retro-colonial glamour
of the British Sudan, Tunis's babble,
the Fat Man, Fez, the avenue that is Khartoum.
Forget the three words you know of
this continent: *baraka, baksheesh,*
assassin, words like chipped knives thrust

---

[2]In the seventeenth century, women thought to be witches were often tortured on the wheel (which stretched the victim's body till the bones broke), then burned at the stake.

into an isolation of sand and night.
These will get you only so far.

In the dreams of the first night,
Africa may seem just another body to
sleep with, a place where you can lay
your own broken equipment to rest.
You have leisure to wonder at her being
a woman, at your being disappointed
with this. You come around to asking
what became of her other four fingers,
how she operates on six alone.
You wipe the sweat from
your chest with her withered hand, raised
and two-fingered; observe, as she sleeps,
how that hand casts the perfect
jackal on a wall whose color
is the same as that of the country

itself, a dark, unpalatable thing who
uses a bulbed twig to paint her lids
in three parallel zones that meet and
kiss one another. She smells of henna or
attar, or rises steeped in musk that in other
women does not stray from between the legs.
She says she has no desire to return
with you. Don't be surprised if
she takes nothing you offer, and moves
on bare feet away from you, or if
you wake feeling close to something,
the gauze damp and loose at your face.

And should you choose to leave, know better
than to give the city a farewell sweep of
the eye. To the pith-helmeted mosques, the slim
and purposeless boulevardiers, the running
sores at the breasts of the women who beg
beside stalled trains, you were never here.
For this reason, you may decide to stay put,
thinking you have left nothing finished.
You may have an urge
to make each move count.
You may have learned nothing at all.

7

Poetry and Social Identity

poetic speaker!

The identity of the lyric speaker (by contrast to the speaker of satire or of dramatic monologue, for instance) has historically been "open-ended," meaning that the words of the speaker could be spoken by any reader within the culture. In the past, in literate cultures, both Western and Eastern, education was preliminary to the (male) professions; and writers, who usually came from the group of those so educated, directed their writings to people who belonged to the same group and possessed the same culture. As we look at the lyrics being produced today, especially in the United States, we can see a marked change in the conception of the lyric speaker. The speaker often is not "neutral" but is given a defined nationality, race, class, sex, or sexual preference, so that we may say, "This is a poem spoken by an African American," or "The speaker is a mother who addresses her sister," or "This is a gay love poem spoken by one man to another," or "This is a poem spoken in Hispanic dialect."

The choice of identity in a poem is up to the writer, for whom identity is never simple. All writers know that besides the forms of identity listed above (which can be combined into such a mixture as "African American middle-class gay male") there are other important identity components such as religion, generation (elder or younger), family roles, social roles, and so on. There is a riddle-game called "Who are you?" to test how people primarily identify themselves: answers by the same

213

person could vary from "I'm a Marine" to "I'm Eric's father" to "I'm a Catholic" to "I'm a Chicano" to "I'm Joan's husband" to "I'm the suspect" — all sayable by the very same person, depending on the situation and the context. When you read a poem with a clearly identified speaker, you need to ask yourself which *one or more* of his or her inevitably many identities the writer is invoking.

The poet Adrienne Rich, for instance, has poems entitled "A Marriage in the 'Sixties," "Sisters," "At the Jewish New Year," "Twenty-One Love Poems," "Mother-in-Law," "Heroines," and "Grandmothers," in which she presents herself, successively, as a wife, a sister, a perplexed Jew, a woman writing love poems to a woman, a lesbian daughter-in-law, an investigator of class privilege, and a granddaughter. These are identities belonging to Rich insofar as she is an individual; in other poems Rich adopts a collective identity ("we" or "you"), which makes the speaker representative of a class, such as "women" or "poets." Here are two of Rich's identity-poems. Can we say why the identities the poet chooses are relevant to the poems? The first poem is a dialogue between the mother-in-law (who speaks aloud, in italics) and the daughter-in-law (who silently replies when her mother-in-law says, "Tell me something"):

[handwritten annotation: · Multiplicity of Identities that can be explored.]

ADRIENNE RICH (b. 1929)

Mother-in-Law

Tell me something
>   you say
> Not: What are you working on now, is there anyone special,
> how is the job
> do you mind coming back to an empty house   5
> what do you do on Sundays
Tell me something . . .
>   Some secret
> we both know and have never spoken?
> Some sentence that could flood with light   10
> your life, mine?
Tell me what daughters tell their mothers
everywhere in the world, and I and only I
even have to ask. . . .
Tell me something.   15
>   Lately, I hear it: Tell me something true,
> daughter-in-law, before we part,
> tell me something true before I die

And time was when I tried.
You married my son, and so   20
strange as you are, you're my daughter
Tell me. . . .
    I've been trying to tell you, mother-in-law
    that I think I'm breaking in two
    and half of me doesn't even want to love   25
    I can polish this table to satin because I don't care
    I am trying to tell you, I envy
    the people in mental hospitals their freedom
    and I can't live on placebos
    or Valium, like you   30

A cut lemon scours the smell of fish away
You'll feel better when the children are in school
    I would try to tell you, mother-in-law
    but my anger takes fire from yours and in the oven
    the meal bursts into flames   35
Daughter-in-law, before we part
tell me something true
    I polished the table, mother-in-law
    and scrubbed the knives with half a lemon
    the way you showed me to do   40
    I wish I could tell you —
               Tell me!
They think I'm weak and hold
things back from me. I agreed to this years ago.
Daughter-in-law, strange as you are,   45
tell me something true

tell me something
           Your son is dead
    ten years, I am a lesbian,
    my children are themselves.   50
    Mother-in-law, before we part
    shall we try again? Strange as I am,
    strange as you are? What do mothers
    ask their own daughters, everywhere in the world?
    Is there a question?   55
           Ask me something.

If we sort out the speaker's multiple identities as she reveals them to
us here, we find out that she is a daughter-in-law, a member of a younger

generation addressing a member of the older generation, a person with a job, a person living alone, a mother, a widow, and a lesbian. We also are given a glimpse into her past, when she was the mother of young children not yet in school, a young woman taking lessons from her mother-in-law on how to polish a table and how to remove a fish smell from knives by rubbing them with a lemon, a young woman with a dangerously submerged anger. This double exposure — older identity superimposed on younger identity — is a familiar technique in lyric poetry, serving as it does to point up changes in identity over time. But the constant in the poem is the mother-in-law, saying now as she said then, *"Tell me something,"* while the daughter-in-law answers now, as she did not then, "Ask me something." In her youth, the daughter-in-law was afraid to tell the truth because what she would have said ("I think I'm breaking in two") was too frightening to articulate even to herself. Now she is prepared to try to create a bridge of honest speaking between herself and her mother-in-law: "Your son is dead / ten years, I am a lesbian." But it is not enough to speak the truth; she wants an answering gesture from her mother-in-law, wants her to show some interest in her daughter-in-law's life — "What are you working on now?" "Is there anyone special?" "How is the job?" — almost anything. You will notice that in this poem Rich is *not* mobilizing identities ("I am a poet"; "I am half-Jewish") that she will use for other poems. Why not? In what way is each of the identities she *does* bring out here useful to the poem? A good rule of thumb is that in a poem where you see multiple identities, past as well as present, each of them is in some way necessary to make the poem work.

The relation between son and father (from the point of view of the son) has been frequently explored in literature. Rich broadens the topic of relation between the generations into daughter-in-law and mother-in-law — a relation not often explored, if ever, in lyric. And though the relation to one's mother-in-law has been made the subject of frequent jokes, Rich shows it as one that entails well-meaning gestures on both sides (the mother-in-law giving household advice, the daughter-in-law cooking a meal for the mother-in-law) but in which no truth-telling is possible, until, late in the day, the speaker senses that a desire for truth hovers in the mother-in-law's question, so that it becomes "Tell me something true, / . . . before we part." The brutal answer — "Your son is dead / ten years, I am a lesbian, / my children are themselves" — surprises us. It is of course a clearing of the ground, as though the speaker demands that these facts be accepted before any further truths are possible. The tenuous relational links between the two women — "You married my son; we are both women; your children are my grandchildren" — are all true, but they are not the whole truth. "Your son is dead; I am a lesbian and you are not; the children are no longer children or grandchildren but adults" — these are the facts that must be accepted, says the daughter-in-law, before any further intimacy is possible. The hopeful end of the poem — "Ask me something" — is a request for that further intimacy, on a new basis, in the few years left.

The junctures at which mother-in-law and daughter-in-law meet are of course the son/husband, grandchildren, common-sex junctures. Being a daughter-in-law is an identity negotiated around these junctures. What happens when the people enabling the junctures disappear? With the son dead, and the children grown, does the daughter-in-law identity have any reality left? Is only an estranged generational relation present — older heterosexual woman, younger lesbian woman? Or can a new identity bond — a mother-daughter one — be formed? "What do mothers / ask their own daughters, everywhere in the world? / Is there a question? // Ask me something."

By investigating a particular facet of identity — here, the unexplored one (in literature) of daughter-in-law-hood — the poet renews and deepens identity itself. At the same time, no poem was ever made viable by its topic alone. What does Rich do to stylize the identity juncture she wants to explore? And what do her chosen stylizations tell us about experience?

First of all, as I have said, Rich creates a double exposure of her young self and her older self; this tells us that although there is a separation between Rich as angry young mother and Rich as older lesbian living alone, the later self has not forgotten or obliterated her younger self — there is a continuity of the ego over time. Another principal tactic is Rich's use of a repeated refrain of double address ("Mother-in-law," "Daughter-in-law" — names people don't usually use in address); she borrows this repeated double address from a famous ballad, "Edward, Edward":

> "Why does your brand° so drop with blood,   *sword*
>   Edward, Edward?
> Why does your brand so drop with blood,
>   And why so sad gang ye,° O?"   *go you*
> "O, I have killed my hawk so good,
>   Mother, mother:
> O, I have killed my hawk so good,
>   And I had no more but he, O."

Yet another stylization is the repetition of request ("Tell me something," "Ask me something"). Fourteen times "tell" occurs, three times "ask." If we graphed the poem, it would be a series of spirals coming back, again and again, to those two points — "Tell me," "Ask me." This stylized recurrence represents the wish of the two women to stay in touch in spite of the disappearance of the former links between them. The poem is written in good faith, hoping that one will ask so that the other can tell.

It is not enough, therefore, to point out in what identity or identities a poem is written. We need to see how that identity, conferred by biology or by society, may be subjected to critique by the imagination (as it is here), and how it is stylized into poetry.

Here, by contrast, is one of Rich's poems in which the identity of the speaker is *not* very strongly particularized. The speaker, however, offers a new collective identity to a group of people addressed as "Prospective Immigrants." Presumably the speaker is someone who immigrated some time ago, and who speaks from the other side of the door that the new group may or may not choose to pass through:

ADRIENNE RICH (b. 1929)
Prospective Immigrants Please Note

Either you will
go through this door
or you will not go through.

If you go through
there is always the risk
of remembering your name.

Things look at you doubly
and you must look back
and let them happen.

If you do not go through
it is possible
to live worthily

to maintain your attitudes
to hold your position
to die bravely

but much will blind you,
much will evade you,
at what cost who knows?

The door itself
makes no promises.
It is only a door.

To go through the door is to join a group of which the speaker is presumably one member. In this poem, Rich does not speak as a mother, a wife, a widow, a daughter-in-law, a Jew, a poet, a lesbian, or even as a woman. Her identity is "Immigrant," "One Who Has Gone through the Door." This is a slightly more particularized identity than "person" or "self" or "soul" (our names for the speaker of the normative generalized lyric of the past), but it is not very much more specific.

What can we deduce from the poem about the collective identity of those who immigrate to this new land? That it is painful to remember your old name here; that there is a double consciousness here, and an acquiescence in event; that you will see more clearly; that you will confront much. What can we deduce about those who choose not to go through the door? That they can retain their old names; that it is not ignoble to choose to stay where they are (they can live worthily, maintain their attitudes, hold on to their position, even die bravely). But they will be to some degree blind, to some degree unconscious, to some degree penalized.

This poem clearly draws on actual experiences of immigrants to the United States, who often lost their own names at Ellis Island when the Inspectors of Immigration affixed new ones to them. Immigrants to America found strange new things to look at and strange new events to undergo; they learned to live with the double consciousness of the hyphenated American. And the poem draws on the experience of those who stayed home in Europe, Asia, Africa, and Latin America and chose not to emigrate — who held on to what they knew, and paid the price of never finding a New World.

Yet we feel that this is a poem not about physical immigration but about spiritual immigration. The "prospective immigrants" do not have to cross oceans or wait at Ellis Island or undergo quarantine; they have only to open a nameless door. Once through the door, they cannot go back. Clearly, however, the speaker is glad of his/her own past decision to join the immigrant group; the poem is, after all, an invitation to new vision and an abjuring of blindness. This poem is an example of an ancient literary genre: the immemorial promise of a better spiritual life.

How does Rich stylize her warning to prospective immigrants about joining the immigrant community? She does it by making her poem fork into the two possible decisions — to go through the door, or not:

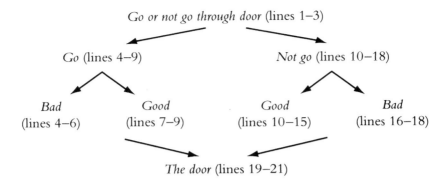

At the end, Rich brings us back to the very door where we began, waiting for us to make our choice. Because entry to a more complex level of inner life is a choice open to all, Rich's speaker is neither gendered nor identified in any other way — nor are her co-immigrants or the prospective immigrants. In writing about an author who has, over the course of a career, spoken in many different identities, you will want to decide which identity is (or which identities are) operative in any given poem, and why.

An author who encounters an identity already preconstructed for him or her by society ("You are a woman"; "You are Boston Irish"; "You are a black male") is inevitably made conscious of identity questions by encountering the stereotypes attached by society to certain identities. Langston Hughes, writing not only about himself but about the wider Harlem community, shows particular awareness not only of race identity in itself, as society constructs it, but of alternative identities within the same group, constructed by the group about itself. Sometimes, as in the poem "Dream Variations," he writes about himself as black:

> Rest at pale evening . . .
> A tall, slim tree . . .
> Night coming tenderly
>   Black like me.

But sometimes, as in "Cross," he is a speaker of mixed race:

> My old man died in a fine big house.
> My ma died in a shack.
> I wonder where I'm gonna die,
> Being neither white nor black?

Sometimes, as in "I, Too," he is declaredly American, as well as black:

> I, too, sing America.
>
> I am the darker brother.

Sometimes, as in "Afro-American Fragment," he is African American:

> Subdued and time-lost
> Are the drums — and yet
> Through some vast mist of race
> There comes this song
> I do not understand,
> This song of atavistic land,
> Of bitter yearnings lost
> Without a place —
> So long,
> So far away
> Is Africa's
> Dark face.

And sometimes he is identified not by color, but only by his exceptional intelligence — which perhaps in childhood isolated him, even more than his color, as a social "monster." The North, as Hughes points out in other poems, does not lynch blacks as the South did — but the North finds victims it wants to kill spiritually, among them children distinguished by exceptional talent or intelligence:

LANGSTON HUGHES (1902 – 1967)
Genius Child

> This is a song for the genius child.
> Sing it softly, for the song is wild.
> Sing it softly as ever you can —
> Lest the song get out of hand.
>
> *Nobody loves a genius child.*
>
> Can you love an eagle,
> Tame or wild?
>
> Wild or tame,
> Can you love a monster
> Of frightening name?
>
> *Nobody loves a genius child.*
>
> *Kill him* — and let his soul run wild!

How does Hughes bring imagination to the theme of the marginalized "genius child"? And how does he stylize his poem? He suggests that even to mention the genius child is dangerous — any song about him is "wild" and likely to "get out of hand." The tribe will recognize the song as something outside their culture, and will persecute the song and the singer as well as the genius child. But then the imagination of the poet does a 180-degree turn. He understands the feelings of the tribe. Could any of us love another species, a monster? And that is how the genius child appears to people. The refrain is absolute: nobody, absolutely nobody loves the child — and we are to believe that "nobody" includes the genius child's parents, his siblings, his teachers, his peers. The surprising and horrifying solution — a "lynching" to set the pariah free — is the most unsparing in all of Hughes's work. Culture no longer has any room for a wild soul; it is a kindness to put it to death.

Hughes was himself a genius at the assuming of different identities within the black community, male and female, upright and delinquent, upper-class and lower-class, educated and uneducated. Here he is in one of the poems written in "black English":

LANGSTON HUGHES (1902 – 1967)
Me and the Mule

My old mule,
He's got a grin on his face.
He's been a mule so long
He's forgot about his race.

I'm that old mule —
Black — and don't give a damn!
You got to take me
Like I am.

A poem like this makes us think about the mule's "race" — half horse, half donkey. The gradual consolidation of the mule's "identity" consoles his owner, who makes the half-humorous, half-serious analogy with himself: live long enough and you become just yourself, not someone's notion of you. "You" says the black speaker to his white audience, "got to take me / Like I am." "You got to" — the whites have no choice, because this black knows himself so well he yields none of his individual autonomy to white society. Hughes stylizes his poem by giving us the mule's "success" first to "guarantee" his speaker's eventual triumph. By the end, the speaker's grin matches the one he imagines on the mule.

Our identities are constructed, according to the modern paradox, by others. We are taught to see ourselves first as our parents see us ("Sally's the one who's good at sports"), next as our peers see us ("You're black!" "You're just a girl!"), next as society as a whole sees us ("Statistics show that a high percentage of scientists are males"), and even as literature conceives us ("What are little girls made of? Sugar and spice and everything nice"). It is against these disabling conceptions from outside that inner authenticity makes its struggle. And the disabling conceptions — say, of race — do not have to come from "outside" the group itself. One of Hughes's most stinging poems embodies the mortified hatred of "upper-class" blacks for "lower-class" ones:

LANGSTON HUGHES (1902 – 1967)
High to Low

God knows
We have our troubles, too —
One trouble is you:
you talk too loud,
cuss too loud,
look too black,
don't get anywhere,
and sometimes it seems
you don't even care.
The way you send your kids to school
stockings down,
(not Ethical Culture)
the way you shout out loud in church,
(not St. Phillips)
and the way you lounge on doorsteps
just as if you were down South,
(not at 409)
the way you clown —
the way, in other words,
you let me down —
me, trying to uphold the race
and you —
well, you can see,
we have our problems,
too, with you.

· Fighting the defining of your identity from outside forces

The blacks who are looked down on by the Ethical Culture / St. Phillips set (the names are those of a fashionable school and church) are already having pejorative identities ("too loud," "too black," "don't even care") constructed for them by their very own fellow blacks. Add these to the identities constructed for them by the surrounding whites, and the construction of an authentic self has two strikes against it before it can begin. Even the notion of what an "authentic self" might be is modeled by cultural expectations into which we are born.

Poetry is one of the great means in which one identity reaches out to another, tries to explain itself to another, brings up images to clarify itself (Rich's meal bursting into flames in the oven, Hughes's grinning and ornery mule), finds a diction that speaks its mind, and finds a stylized form to enact its appeal. There is a danger that a reader will take the identity in a lyric as more simple than it is, and will mentally invoke a stereotype of the female speaker or the black speaker or the gay speaker or the Catholic speaker. But good poems are thoroughly considered constructions; and in order for the poem to be interesting, the author must critique or reinvent the social stereotype. A lyric to keep in mind when reading identity-poems is Seamus Heaney's "Terminus," a poem announcing that a poet's identity is always at least a double one, because any poet worthy of the name has "second thoughts." Heaney, a Northern Irish poet, grew up on a farm but within sight of industry, in a rural place where people still used horses to draw wagons but took the train to go to the city. One "terminus" or border of the farm was the "march drain" — the creek marking the border ("march") between two parishes. Heaney, as a child, lived also along divides in the world of words — on the borderline between his parents' secular proverbs and their Biblical stories — both equally stimulating to the nascent poet's mind. And he lived between the present (Northern Ireland governed by England) and the better past (before the Irish earls, defeated by the British, fled to France in 1798, ending Irish independence). "Is it any wonder," the poet asks, given all these influences on my identity, that "when I thought / I would have second thoughts?" Any reflective poet has "second thoughts" about both inherited and acquired "identities," and it is those "second thoughts," and their origins, that Heaney so well identifies:

Seamus Heaney (b. 1939)
Terminus

I

When I hoked° there, I would find   *fished*
An acorn and a rusted bolt.

If I lifted my eyes, a factory chimney
And a dormant mountain.

If I listened, an engine shunting
And a trotting horse.

Is it any wonder when I thought
I would have second thoughts?

II

When they spoke of the prudent squirrel's hoard
It shone like gifts at a nativity.

When they spoke of the mammon of iniquity
The coins in my pockets reddened like stove-lids.

I was the march drain and the march drain's banks
Suffering the limit of each claim.

III

Two buckets were easier carried than one.
I grew up in between.

My left hand placed the standard iron weight.
My right tilted a last grain on the balance.

Baronies, parishes met where I was born.
When I stood on the central stepping stone

I was the last earl on horseback in midstream
Still parleying, in earshot of his peers.

—generalizability

Though a poem like Heaney's particularizes much about his identity (Irish, rural, Catholic, modern), it still does not specify idiosyncrasies that would point him out as a single individual. Even Rich's self-identification as lesbian widow, mother of children, daughter-in-law, could fit many people.

The most extreme reach of the "identity poem" is a poem that specifies its speaker so completely that he or she becomes entirely unique. No one but Frank O'Hara could speak the poem entitled "The Day Lady Died," a poem showing O'Hara's humdrum day suddenly brought to a stunned halt as he sees a newspaper headline announcing the death of the famous jazz singer Billie Holiday. The poem goes, in part:

It is 12:20 in New York a Friday
three days after Bastille day, yes
it is 1959 and I go get a shoeshine
because I will get off the 4:19 in Easthampton
at 7:15 and then go straight to dinner . . .
and in the GOLDEN GRIFFIN I get a little Verlaine
for Patsy with drawings by Bonnard . . .

and for Mike I just stroll into the PARK LANE
Liquor Store and ask for a bottle of Strega and
then I go back where I came from to 6th Avenue
and the tobacconist in the Ziegfeld Theatre and
casually ask for a carton of Gauloises and a carton
of Picayunes, and a NEW YORK POST with her face on it.

Nobody but Frank O'Hara is doing just these things in this order on this specified date, buying presents for specified friends named Patsy and Mike. In such a poem, not only are time and space fully specified, but personal identity is unmistakably that of only one person. The construction of a speaker in such a poem is as far as possible from the normative lyric construction of a "universal" or "representative" speaker, like the one in an anonymous English love song who says (as almost anyone in the world might say), "Love me little, love me long, / Is the burden of my song":

Constant love is moderate ever,
And it will through life persever;
Give me that, with true endeavor
        I will it restore.

Why would the lyric poet sometimes want to construct a specified speaker instead of a universal one? Perhaps as modern life has grown more heterogeneous, it seems harder to some poets to speak for everyone. In England, before the turn of the century, there was a relatively small educated class confined to one island nation possessing only two universities. In such a country, with such an audience, the lyric poet could address his cultivated audience as though his speech and theirs were one. The poet in contemporary America, with its diversity of types and interests, may feel it only reasonable to speak more narrowly — not always, but sometimes. The uniqueness of each person is one modern article of faith — and by making himself unique, O'Hara suggests that each person lives a common shared event differently. Many people, on that day in New York, saw the headline about Billie Holiday's death: but, says the poet, your moment and mine were different. Let me tell you how it was for me; that will make you think how it was for you. The appeal to representativeness is still present, but it is an appeal to sameness-in-difference. Every lyric, no matter how socially specified, assumes that it speaks a language its readers can understand — even if in their own different terms.

In Brief: Poetry and Social Identity

Remembering Rich, remembering Hughes, remembering Heaney, remembering O'Hara, ask yourself, with respect to any identity-poem, "Between what borders, left and right, does this poem flow? What does it see when it looks up? or down? or around? Which words shine with morality? Which redden with shame? How does it see the past? the present? In what communities does it station itself? Against what others does it contend? To what degree does it specify its own uniqueness?" The rich contribution of identity formation to poetry, especially in the twentieth century, both criticizes and renews our inherited sense of the lyric speaker, reminding us that if we stand in the shoes of the poem, we do so not only in general ways but also in our own individualized way.

Reading Other Poems

Besides an idiosyncratic and unique personal identity, all of us have social identity, arising from groups to which we belong or are consigned. As you read the following poems, consider what portion of social identity each speaker claims as his or her own, or ascribes to his characters. Robert Southwell's speaker, for instance, has a vision identifying him as a Christian believer; Thomas Nashe's speaker is a victim of the plague for whom the whole world has narrowed into one great mortuary. We may know only one identifying trait of the speaker from the *thematic* content of the poem. (We may know other traits from the speaker's tone, the images used, and so on.)

- ◆ By contrast, how many personal identifying traits can you find in Anne Bradstreet's poem?
- ◆ What difference does it make in the effect of a poem to have the self of its speaker so narrowly specified?

Would you rather read a poem that you can speak without feeling that a particular person uttered it — a poem that can be uttered by almost anyone, because its feelings are so general, and its speaker so apparently universal? Or would you rather feel that the poem is introducing you to the life and speech of a unique individual? (Neither one of these is better than the other; but we all have varying aesthetic responses, and you may prefer one to the other; reflect on why you do.)

- If you are not a Christian, how are you able to read Southwell's poem with imaginative sympathy?

- Explore your own answers to such questions, which are profound ones and affect all art. Can a non-Christian respond to a painting of the nativity of Jesus?

- Can a white person respond to Rita Dove's portrait of her widowed grandmother's first participation in an "integrated" social occasion?

- Is the drama of a poem spoken by a socially specified individual (Edward Lear describing himself as others might see him, Gerard Manley Hopkins speaking as a Catholic priest) different from that of a poem spoken by an abstract speaker?

- Sylvia Plath's "applicant" gets her identity from her envisaged social role. What is that role? Does it allow for any personal individuality? Can you compare Plath's view of the individuality allowed within marriage to Anne Bradstreet's view? (You do not have to choose: one purpose of reading poetry is to let you see the world through many different lenses.)

- William Blake's persona, the little black boy, is a type rather than a person; but though we imagine ourselves in his shoes, speaking his words so full of pathos, are we not also objective observers, realizing the extent to which he is parroting what he has been taught (souls are white, angels are white, and so on)?

- What is the use, to Blake, of the persona of the little black boy, when the poet could equally well have written a poem protesting slavery in his own adult voice?

- Why do you think he had the little black boy speak in "heroic quatrains" — broad pentameter alternately rhyming quatrains — usually used for a philosophic or noble subject?

Poems exploring social identity must often face the fact that not all members of the social group share the same attitudes.

- In David Mura's poem about the internment of Japanese Americans during World War II, what are the attitudes dramatized? In what does the conflict consist?

- In Sheila Ortiz Taylor's "The Way Back," the brother's choices offend both family members and neighbors. In what ways do the social identities of both brother and sister differ from the group identities around them?

ROBERT SOUTHWELL (1561 – 1595)
The Burning Babe

As I in hoary winter's night stood shivering in the snow,
Surprised I was with sudden heat which made my heart to glow;
And lifting up a fearful eye to view what fire was near,
A pretty babe all burning bright did in the air appear;
Who, scorchèd with excessive heat, such floods of tears did shed
As though his floods should quench his flames which with his
      tears were fed.
"Alas," quoth he, "but newly born in fiery heats I fry,
Yet none approach to warm their hearts or feel my fire but I!
My faultless breast the furnace is, the fuel wounding thorns,
Love is the fire, and sighs the smoke, the ashes shame and scorns;
The fuel justice layeth on, and mercy blows the coals,
The metal in this furnace wrought are men's defilèd souls,
For which, as now on fire I am to work them to their good,
So will I melt into a bath to wash them in my blood."
With this he vanished out of sight and swiftly shrunk away,
And straight I callèd unto mind that it was Christmas day.

THOMAS NASHE (1567 – ?1601)
A Litany in Time of Plague

Adieu, farewell, earth's bliss;
This world uncertain is;
Fond are life's lustful joys;
Death proves them all but toys;
None from his darts can fly;
I am sick, I must die.
      Lord, have mercy on us!

Rich men, trust not in wealth,
Gold cannot buy you health;
Physic himself must fade.
All things to end are made,
The plague full swift goes by;
I am sick, I must die.
      Lord, have mercy on us!

Beauty is but a flower
Which wrinkles will devour;
Brightness falls from the air;
Queens have died young and fair;

Dust hath closed Helen's eye.
I am sick, I must die.
    Lord, have mercy on us!

Strength stoops unto the grave,
Worms feed on Hector brave;
Swords may not fight with fate,
Earth still holds ope her gate.
"Come, come!" the bells do cry.
I am sick, I must die.
    Lord, have mercy on us.

Wit with his wantonness
Tasteth death's bitterness;
Hell's executioner
Hath no ears for to hear
What vain art can reply.
I am sick, I must die.
    Lord, have mercy on us.

Haste, therefore, each degree,
To welcome destiny;
Heaven is our heritage,
Earth but a player's stage;
Mount we unto the sky.
I am sick, I must die.
    Lord, have mercy on us.

ANNE BRADSTREET (c. 1612 – 1672)

A Letter to Her Husband, Absent upon Public Employment

My head, my heart, mine eyes, my life, nay, more,
My joy, my magazine° of earthly store,   *storehouse*
If two be one, as surely thou and I,
How stayest thou there, whilst I at Ipswich lie?
So many steps, head from the heart to sever,
If but a neck, soon should we be together.
I, like the Earth this season, mourn in black,
My Sun is gone so far in's zodiac,
Whom whilst I 'joyed, nor storms, nor frost I felt,
His warmth such frigid colds did cause to melt.
My chillèd limbs now numbèd lie forlorn;
Return; return, sweet Sol, from Capricorn;
In this dead time, alas, what can I more

Than view those fruits which through thy heat I bore?
Which sweet contentment yield me for a space,
True living pictures of their father's face.
O strange effect! now thou art southward gone,
I weary grow the tedious day so long;
But when thou northward to me shalt return,
I wish my Sun may never set, but burn
Within the Cancer of my glowing breast,
The welcome house of him my dearest guest.
Where ever, ever stay, and go not thence,
Till nature's sad decree shall call thee hence;
Flesh of thy flesh, bone of thy bone,
I here, thou there, yet both but one.

WILLIAM BLAKE (1757 – 1827)

The Little Black Boy

My mother bore me in the southern wild,
And I am black, but O! my soul is white;
White as an angel is the English child:
But I am black as if bereav'd of light.

My mother taught me underneath a tree,
And sitting down before the heat of day,
She took me on her lap and kissèd me,
And pointing to the east, began to say:

"Look on the rising sun: there God does live,
And gives his light, and gives his heat away;
And flowers and trees and beasts and men receive
Comfort in morning, joy in the noon day.

"And we are put on earth a little space,
That we may learn to bear the beams of love,
And these black bodies and this sun-burnt face
Is but a cloud, and like a shady grove.

"For when our souls have learn'd the heat to bear,
The cloud will vanish; we shall hear his voice,
Saying: 'Come out from the grove, my love & care,
And round my golden tent like lambs rejoice.'"

Thus did my mother say, and kissèd me;
And thus I say to little English boy:
When I from black and he from white cloud free,
And round the tent of God like lambs we joy,

I'll shade him from the heat till he can bear
To lean in joy upon our father's knee;
And then I'll stand and stroke his silver hair,
And be like him, and he will then love me.

EDWARD LEAR (1812 – 1888)
How Pleasant to Know Mr. Lear

How pleasant to know Mr. Lear!
    Who has written such volumes of stuff!
Some think him ill-tempered and queer,
    But a few think him pleasant enough.

His mind is concrete and fastidious,
    His nose is remarkably big;
His visage is more or less hideous,
    His beard it resembles a wig.

He has ears, and two eyes, and ten fingers,
    Leastways if you reckon two thumbs;
Long ago he was one of the singers,
    But now he is one of the dumbs.

He sits in a beautiful parlor,
    With hundreds of books on the wall;
He drinks a great deal of Marsala,
    But never gets tipsy at all.

He has many friends, laymen and clerical;
    Old Foss is the name of his cat;
His body is perfectly spherical,
    He weareth a runcible hat.

When he walks in a waterproof white,
    The children run after him so!
Calling out, "He's come out in his night-
    Gown, that crazy old Englishman, oh!"

He weeps by the side of the ocean,
    He weeps on the top of the hill;
He purchases pancakes and lotion,
    And chocolate shrimps from the mill.

He reads but he cannot speak Spanish,
    He cannot abide ginger-beer:
Ere the days of his pilgrimage vanish,
    How pleasant to know Mr. Lear!

GERARD MANLEY HOPKINS (1844 – 1889)
Felix Randal

Felix Randal the farrier,° O is he dead then?   *blacksmith*
    my duty all ended,
Who have watched his mould of man, big-boned and
    hardy-handsome
Pining, pining, till time when reason rambled in it and some
Fatal four disorders, fleshed there, all contended?

Sickness broke him. Impatient, he cursed at first, but mended
Being anointed° and all; though a heavenlier   *in last rites*
    heart began some
Months earlier, since I had our sweet reprieve
    and ransom°   *Holy Communion*
Tendered to him. Ah well, God rest him all road ever he offended!

This seeing the sick endears them to us, us too it endears.
My tongue had taught thee comfort, touch had quenched
    thy tears,
Thy tears that touched my heart, child, Felix, poor Felix Randal;

How far from then forethought of, all thy more boisterous years,
When thou at the random° grim forge, powerful   *ramshackle*
    amidst peers,
Didst fettle° for the great grey drayhorse his bright   *shape*
    and battering sandal!

SYLVIA PLATH (1932 – 1963)
The Applicant

First, are you our sort of a person?
Do you wear
A glass eye, false teeth or a crutch,
A brace or a hook,
Rubber breasts or a rubber crotch,

Stitches to show something's missing? No, no? Then
How can we give you a thing?
Stop crying.
Open your hand.
Empty? Empty. Here is a hand

To fill it and willing
To bring teacups and roll away headaches
And do whatever you tell it.

15 Will you marry it?
It is guaranteed

To thumb shut your eyes at the end
And dissolve of sorrow.
We make new stock from the salt.
I notice you are stark naked.
20 How about this suit —

Black and stiff, but not a bad fit.
Will you marry it?
It is waterproof, shatterproof, proof
Against fire and bombs through the roof.
25 Believe me, they'll bury you in it.

Now your head, excuse me, is empty.
I have the ticket for that.
Come here, sweetie, out of the closet.
Well, what do you think of *that?*
30 Naked as paper to start

But in twenty-five years she'll be silver,
In fifty, gold.
A living doll, everywhere you look.
It can sew, it can cook,
35 It can talk, talk, talk.

It works, there is nothing wrong with it.
You have a hole, it's a poultice.
You have an eye, it's an image.
My boy, it's your last resort.
Will you marry it, marry it, marry it.

DAVID MURA (b. 1952)
An Argument: On 1942

For My Mother

Near Rose's Chop Suey and Jinosuke's grocery,
the temple where incense hovered and inspired
dense evening chants (prayers for Buddha's mercy,
colorless and deep), that day he was fired . . .

— No, no, no, she tells me. Why bring it back?
The camps are over. (Also overly dramatic.)
Forget *shoyu*°-stained *furoshiki,*°   soy sauce / scarf
        mochi° on a stick: rice cakes
You're like a terrier, David, gnawing a bone, an old, old trick . . .

Mostly we were bored. Women cooked and sewed,
men played blackjack, dug gardens, a *benjo.*°   *toilet*
Who noticed barbed wire, guards in the towers?
We were children, hunting stones, birds, wild flowers.

Yes, Mother hid tins of *utskemono*° and eel   *pickles*
beneath the bed. And when the last was peeled,
clamped tight her lips, growing thinner and thinner.
But cancer not the camps made her throat blacker

. . . And she didn't die then . . . after the war, in St. Paul,
you weren't even born. Oh I know, I know, it's all
part of your job, your way, but why can't you glean
how far we've come, how much I can't recall —

David, it was so long ago — how useless it seems . . .

RITA DOVE (b. 1952)
Wingfoot Lake

(Independence Day, 1964)

On her 36th birthday, Thomas° had shown her   *Beulah's dead*
her first swimming pool. It had been   *husband*
his favorite color, exactly — just
so much of it, the swimmers' white arms jutting
into the chevrons of high society.
She had rolled up her window
and told him to drive on, fast.

Now this *act of mercy:* four daughters
dragging her to their husbands' company picnic,
white families on one side and them
on the other, unpacking the same
squeeze bottles of Heinz, the same
waxy beef patties and Salem potato chip bags.
So he was dead for the first time
on Fourth of July — ten years ago

had been harder, waiting for something to happen,
and ten years before that, the girls
like young horses eyeing the track.
Last August she stood alone for hours
in front of the T.V. set
as a crow's wing moved slowly through
the white streets of government.
That brave swimming

scared her, like Joanna saying
Mother, we're Afro-Americans now!
What did she know about Africa?
Were there lakes like this one
with a rowboat pushed under the pier?
Or Thomas' Great Mississippi
with its sullen silks? (There was
the Nile but the Nile belonged

to God.) Where she came from
was the past, 12 miles into town
where nobody had locked their back door,
and Goodyear hadn't begun to dream of a park
under the company symbol, a white foot
sprouting two small wings.

SHEILA ORTIZ TAYLOR (b. 1939)
The Way Back

for Uncle Jim

They stand in this Christmas snapshot
poised like adagio dancers
facing each other
their arms draped around
their matching bones   5
brother and sister
while behind them
out of focus
the family
spins   10

Around these two
youngest of thirteen
held now for eternity
in this moment before their
twin feet slide them out   15
in a celestial tango
a silence gathers

We see their handsome faces
Indian bones in glinting cheeks
their raven hair, gray-streaked   20
their eyes as deep and dark as wells
holding a history of careless loss
land, lovers, mothers, maps

The way back is a land
more innocent than this   25
He joined the navy
She married a judge
They both baked bread in institutional ovens
He wrote long letters home
and sent his mother silk pillows   30
embroidered with military targets

He baked bread while
his eight brothers lost fingers
toes, knees, elbows
He could almost hear the bullets   35
thud into dough
and the sound made him rise
growing from uniform to uniform
until they had to declare peace

Home again   40
he folded away his whites
kissed his sisters
and told his brothers
he was going to become
a hairdresser   45
news that made their wounds ache
more than seemed possible
Finally he followed them to work at Lockheed
learned to drill holes in himself
discovered insomnia   50
married a beautician named Molly
whose hair he dyed green every Christmas

He loved all holidays
Life needed themes
spelled out in sparkles, sprinkles   55
cutouts, paste-ups
but most of all
in costume.

Halloweens found brother and sister
on their knees   60
before bolts of cloth
and wimpling tissue
pins in their mouths

blue chalk on their hands
for years   65
artists of the self

You can see it here
in this snapshot
white polyester pants belling out

around white cowboy boots   70
red western shirts
tailored close to the rib
Indian silver at the waist
twins in spirit
if not by birth   75
holding each other
in a light embrace
their grace
not lost

And yet   80
the way back is a land
more innocent than this
The time came round
when neighbors
preferring razor blades to invention   85
would not let their children
trick or treat
where a grown man
put costumes on.

That Christmas night   90
very late
he backed his throbbing
Continental
into the dark garage
that shut down tight behind him   95
crawled into the backseat
bearing a bottle of champagne
one glass
a photograph

8

History and Regionality

Poetry is always interested in time and space. Sometimes these can be very generally expressed, as we saw in "A slumber did my spirit seal." Time in this poem means simply past versus present; space encloses first two individuals, then the whole planet:

WILLIAM WORDSWORTH (1770 – 1850)
A slumber did my spirit seal

A slumber did my spirit seal;
    I had no human fears:
She seemed a thing that could not feel
    The touch of earthly years.

No motion has she now, no force;
    She neither hears nor sees;
Rolled round in earth's diurnal course,
    With rocks, and stones, and trees.

But poetry is not only interested in such large general uses of space and time. It is also interested in time specified — in history. Especially for nations emerging from colonial status — America after the Revolution, Ireland after 1916 — history needs to be made freshly significant, newly sacred. Important events need to be memorialized (as "The Star-Spangled

Banner" commemorates the battle of Fort McHenry; as William Butler Yeats's "Easter 1916" meditates on Ireland's Easter Rising). Important heroes and heroines need to be immortalized (as John Greenleaf Whittier's "Barbara Frietchie" salutes a semilegendary heroine of the Civil War; as Yeats's "A Rose Tree" salutes Padraic Pearse, executed for his part in the Easter Rising). And poetry about history is not only celebratory. Problematic aspects of history have to be investigated (as Herman Melville queries war enthusiasm in "The March into Virginia" during the Civil War; as Adrienne Rich decries the 1953 execution of Ethel Rosenberg in "For Ethel Rosenberg"; as Seamus Heaney scrutinizes the violent conflicts in Northern Ireland in "North").

History

Immediate challenges arise for a lyric poet who is writing a poem about (or within or against) history. In the first place, written history is a narrative genre, and the history of a complex event (the American Revolution, the Civil War in England leading to the execution of Charles I, the Easter Rising) is not only narratively complicated, but always politically disputed. The English narrate the American Revolution from a point of view (that of the losing side) very different from the celebratory view taken in American history books. Propaganda always exists on both sides of any historical question, as on both sides of any disputed ethical question. It is up to the poet to see beyond the simplifications of propaganda (always unfair to the intricacy of any disputed event) and to present the crises of history in a way that does not diminish their ambiguity and their painfulness.

How does the poet incorporate history within the miniature dimensions of the lyric? There are several central techniques:

1. Focusing on a problem rather than on incidents;

2. Finding an emblematic scene or scenes;

3. Finding a symbolic or mythological equivalent for a historical episode;

4. Seeing the human inside of the event as corresponding to the historical outside;

5. Finding an epigrammatic summation;

6. Adopting a prophetic or philosophic view larger than that of a mere eyewitness.

Let us see how these techniques come into play in Melville's Civil War poem, "The March into Virginia," written in fear and dismay after the Union forces were twice routed by the Confederate army in the first and second battles of Manassas (sometimes called the first and second battles of Bull Run). The Union army — composed of young, patriotic, impulsive, untried recruits — marched gaily into battle, only to suffer carnage. The few who survived had to march into battle once again, knowing, this time, the horrors ahead. Was their original innocence of any value? Can naive ignorance be of ultimate political use? Melville begins his consideration by reflecting on this problem: he admits how little we would undertake if we knew beforehand the "lets and bars" — obstacles and hindrances — that we would encounter:

> Did all the lets and bars appear
>   To every just or larger end,
> Whence should come the trust and cheer?
>   Youth must its ignorant impulse lend —
> Age finds place in the rear.
>   All wars are boyish, and are fought by boys,
> The champions and enthusiasts of the state:
>   Turbid ardours and vain joys
>   Not barrenly abate —
>   Stimulants to the power mature,
>   Preparatives of fate.

Having stated the paradox that enthusiasm for war is both ignorant ("All wars are boyish, and are fought by boys") and useful (the boys' "vain joys" and patriotic ardor bring forth the fruit of mature power, through which one can hope for the reinstatement of the Union), Melville can go on to set the scene of the boys' heedless march into Virginia:

> Who here forecasteth the event?
> What heart but spurns at precedent
> And warnings of the wise,
> Contemned foreclosures of surprise?
> The banners play, the bugles call,
> The air is blue and prodigal.
>   No berrying party, pleasure-wooed,
> No picnic party in the May,
> Ever went less loth than they
>   Into that leafy neighbourhood.

After this naturalistic scene painting, Melville breaks into a foreboding symbolic discourse of myth. The intoxicated glee of the boys, comparable to that of the devotees of the wine god Bacchus, will lead them into being sacrificed. They resemble, in fact, the Hebrew children sacrificed to the idol Moloch:

> In Bacchic glee they file toward Fate,
> Moloch's uninitiate;
> Expectancy, and glad surmise
> Of battle's unknown mysteries.

From his prophetic and mythological distance, Melville then returns, in close focus, to a last snapshot of the emotional state of the naive boys as they "file toward Fate":

> All they feel is this: 'tis glory,
> A rapture sharp, though transitory,
> Yet lasting in belaureled story.
> So they gaily go to fight,
> Chatting left and laughing right.

At this point, the speaker of the poem, who had begun philosophically and had continued scenically, becomes once again a prophet, foreseeing the end of these boys, some dead, some surviving the shame of defeat to fight, a year later, the battle of second Manassas:

> But some who this blithe mood present,
>> As on in lightsome files they fare,
> Shall die experienced ere three days are spent —
>> Perish, enlightened by the volleyed glare;
> Or shame survive, and, like to adamant,
>> The throe of Second Manassas share.

We can now see that Melville epitomizes the war for us by showing us three stages in an emblematic young soldier's experience: his initial gaiety and desire for fame and glory, his "enlightenment" in the volleyed glare as he learns, perishing, what war is; or, for one who survives the shame of defeat, a third stage, beyond mere "enlightenment," in which the soldier becomes "like to adamant" in his stony and steeled knowledge of degradation, violence, and death. By his philosophic problematizing of ignorance and courage, by his visual scenes of carefree young soldiers, by his penetration of their emotional attitudes, by his shorthand references to the mythic Bacchus and Moloch to represent poles of blithe ignorance and pitiless extinction, by his schematizing the experience of war in three stages, and by his final prophecy — that the boys "shall die experienced" or shall share "the throe of Second Manassas" — Melville puts a year of the Civil War, and the problems it raised for him, into the short confines of lyric.

Not all of these techniques appear in every historical poem, but the poet always needs some of these strategies to make history pliable to lyric. Though Melville intermittently takes a philosophic position above the scene of battle, it is clear from his inner snapshots of the recruits' feelings that he sympathizes with the Union side, hoping that the youthful Union forces' "turbid ardours" will be useful to the country in stimulating its ultimate Fate.

In some history poems, the poet is immediately engaged, writing from within a particular moment, representing himself or herself as a historically specified person, of specified political or historical allegiance, and (as we will see) of specified geographic origin. This tradition in American verse begins with *Leaves of Grass,* in which the author named himself and his home: "Walt Whitman, a kosmos, of Manhattan the son," and specified even his age, "I, now thirty-seven years old in perfect health begin." However, we notice that even this socially specified self also identifies himself as "a kosmos," that is, a representative universe. The lyric poet, even when engaged in social self-specification, intends representativeness as well. This is the case in Robert Lowell's unrhymed sonnet about the March on the Pentagon in 1967 protesting the Vietnam War. Lowell took part in the March (vividly described later by Norman Mailer in *The Armies of the Night*), as the protesters went, several abreast, toward the Pentagon — only to be routed by the Army:

ROBERT LOWELL (1917 – 1977)
The March 1

For Dwight Macdonald

Under the too white marmoreal Lincoln Memorial,
the too tall marmoreal Washington Obelisk,
gazing into the too long reflecting pool,
the reddish trees, the withering autumn sky,
the remorseless, amplified harangues for peace —
lovely to lock arms, to march absurdly locked
(unlocking to keep my wet glasses from slipping)
to see the cigarette match quaking in my fingers,
then to step off like green Union Army recruits
for the first Bull Run, sped by photographers,

the notables, the girls . . . fear, glory, chaos, rout . . .
our green army staggered out on the miles-long green fields,
met by the other army, the Martian, the ape, the hero,
his new-fangled rifle, his green new steel helmet.

It is clear that Lowell is remembering Melville's poem about the "green Union Army recruits / for the first Bull Run" as he writes of his own first foray into battle. But he is a middle-aged man, feeling absurd in the fraternal political gesture of locked arms, hating (as only a poet could) the awful propaganda slogans of the March being relentlessly boomed out over his head by the marchers' public address system. Nor does the poet feel akin to the ideology affirmed by the state architecture of Washington: its marble monuments inspired by Rome ("marmoreal") and Egypt ("obelisk"), its supersized conception of itself (which he sees as too white, too tall, too long). He is no hero — his glasses keep slipping, his hands quake with fear. The poem is scenic with a vengeance for its first eight lines, but the scenes are always infused with the poet's attitude toward what they show. Just when we wonder whether anything philosophic, epigrammatic, prophetic, or emblematic might come along to sum up and give point to Lowell's procession of scenes, we meet just what we have been expecting — first the allusion to Melville as an epigrammatic summing up of ignorance about to be turned into experience, then an emblematic series of nouns ("fear, glory, chaos, rout") summing up the stages of both political protest and armed war. The poem returns, at the end, to a scenic mode, this time a scene not of a march but of a confrontation, as the "green army" of the protesters is met by the real Army in tactical gear. We see three "green's" in succession: the green (inexperienced) protesters, the "miles-long" ideologically too-big green (grass) fields of the Washington Mall, and the literal green metal of the Army soldier's helmet. This "irrational" repetition of "green" in several different contexts makes the closing scene feel epigrammatic, "tied together," "final."

And the closing scene, unlike the literal scenes preceding it, has elements of the surreal. What does it seem like when you find yourself, as an American protester, being confronted inimically by your own American Army, composed of green recruits like yourself? And how do you feel about the Army now? You have a confused set of impressions as you see your first soldier in riot gear: "He looks like a Martian, something out of science fiction; no, with his hulking posture he looks more like an ape; but wait, this is *our* Army, he's a hero; odd, he seems to have a new-fangled kind of rifle, not the kind I remember from newsreels; he's the archetypal warrior, archaic, helmeted, like the warriors of Troy, only his helmet is new, and it is made of steel, not bronze." Some such latent content is contained within the last two lines, a content more "intellectual" than the scenes with which the poem opened, and therefore able to satisfy our desire that the poet "make something" — if only by revealing how confusing it is to be opposing your own American Army — of his experience. Though Lowell's poem is about a specific historical event, and represents the poet himself not only in his physical being (his fear, his glasses) but also in his political taking of sides, it is a representative poem, too, about the confused emotions Lowell feels in protesting the actions of his own government — a set of emotions anyone might feel.

A simpler "propaganda" poem written by a participant in the March would probably not have shown a sweating and awkward protagonist with his glasses slipping down his nose; it would certainly not have called the peace messages "the *remorseless,* amplified *harangues* for peace"; and it would not have seen the Army soldier as *both* ape and hero. It is Lowell's accuracy, both to his own motives for marching (the critique of America's imperial ambitions) and to his own sense of absurdity (including his mixed reactions to the Army soldier) that makes the poem humanly believable.

Even the simplest "history" poem usually has scene, epigram, feeling, and "philosophic" comment. Here is Langston Hughes's little song-and-echo poem, "World War II":

LANGSTON HUGHES (1902 – 1967)
World War II

What a grand time was the war!
    Oh, my, my!
What a grand time was the war!
    My, my, my!
In wartime we had fun,
Sorry that old war is done!
What a grand time was the war,
    My, my!

Echo:
    Did
    Somebody
    Die?

Here, Hughes is not writing as a socially specified singular self — as a black poet or as "Langston Hughes," a man of a certain age living in a certain city; rather, he writes a public chorus for the late 1940s, and counterpoints the chorus with a single satiric and epigrammatic echo. Hughes can sympathize with the chorus of voices praising wartime: following the catastrophe of the 1929 Depression and its long dreary aftermath of stinted lives, the plentiful jobs (in defense, in war work, in communications and services) brought about by the war effort rejuvenated many a poor family. The chorus has not a single dissenting voice, as all join in for the refrain, "Oh, my, my!" Who utters the haunting echo? Is it the philosophic poet? Is it a forgotten Gold Star mother? Is it the voice of history? Whoever it is, each of its words is significant. The chorus's words all run together horizontally — "In wartime we had fun." But the Echo's voice runs vertically:

> *Did*
> *Somebody*
> *Die?*

This is the way oracles speak: every word with a line to itself, every word capitalized, every word in italics. These are sacred words, whereas the words of the chorus are profane words. By such simple means Hughes shows us two comments on history, both "correct," but irreconcilable.

One of the problems in reading history poems is that one has to know something about history, and about the import of historical events within a given culture. Someone who knew nothing about the Civil War, or the March on Washington, or about the economic boom brought by World War II, would have difficulty taking in the attitudes and implications of these poems by Melville, Lowell, and Hughes. To this extent, lyric poets writing history poems have to depend on the shared knowledge of a common culture — and American readers wishing to understand an English poem about, say, the English Civil War have to learn, perhaps, many things that an English reader would have learned in school and that the poet took for granted in composing the poem. It is up to the poet to give the reader as much information as possible in the poem, but there is a limit to what can be conveyed in a short space. The generalized lyric usually has a longer shelf-life than the historically specified lyric because it does not make such particular demands on the reader. Yet nothing matches the vivid scenic, topical, and philosophic intensity of the best history poems, especially as they are first encountered by the audience to whom their topic is an urgent and contemporary one.

"Revisionary" history poems aim to turn the received view of a given historical circumstance upside down. War was treated heroically by classical literature, and the quotation from the Roman poet Horace, "Dulce et decorum est pro patria mori" ("It is sweet and fitting to die for one's country"), had been taken as the epitome of the proper attitude for young men going off to war. The introduction of such inhuman fighting methods as poison gas in World War I made a revisionary view of war almost inevitable, and the most famous poem of that war, dismantling armed struggle as a noble act, was composed by the English poet Wilfred Owen, who died in the war in 1918. You will see that in spite of the revisionary aims of the poem, it uses the familiar strategies of scenic presentation, crucial event, emotional insight, a mythic interlude (here, a recurrent dream), and epigrammatic summation (via Horace). It is spoken not by someone removed at a philosophic distance, but by one of the soldiers undergoing a gas attack:

WILFRED OWEN (1893 – 1918)
Dulce et Decorum Est

Bent double, like old beggars under sacks,
Knock-kneed, coughing like hags, we cursed through sludge,
Till on the haunting flares we turned our backs
And towards our distant rest began to trudge.
Men marched asleep. Many had lost their boots
But limped on, blood-shod. All went lame; all blind;
Drunk with fatigue; deaf even to the hoots
Of tired, outstripped Five-Nines° that dropped behind.   *gas shells*

Gas! GAS! Quick, boys! — An ecstasy of fumbling,
Fitting the clumsy helmets just in time;
But someone still was yelling out and stumbling
And flound'ring like a man in fire or lime . . .
Dim, through the misty panes and thick green light,
As under a green sea, I saw him drowning.

In all my dreams, before my helpless sight,
He plunges at me, guttering, choking, drowning.

If in some smothering dreams you too could pace
Behind the wagon that we flung him in,
And watch the white eyes writhing in his face,
His hanging face, like a devil's sick of sin;
If you could hear, at every jolt, the blood
Come gargling from the froth-corrupted lungs,
Obscene as cancer, bitter as the cud
Of vile, incurable sores on innocent tongues, —

My friend, you would not tell with such high zest
To children ardent for some desperate glory,
The old Lie: Dulce et decorum est
Pro patria mori.

Owen chooses as a form for his poem the alternately rhyming iambic pentameter four-line stanza known as the "heroic quatrain" because it was used for noble narratives. The irony of attaching its heroic lineage to the squalor and tragedy of gas warfare must have appealed to the revisionary poet. "Dulce et Decorum Est" reads at first like a realistic, unshaped report. Owen jams his quatrains together to obscure the regularity of his form (one can read the poem without realizing, at first, that it is written in rhyming quatrains). However, his report is "broken" by the shortest passage — the two-line recurrent dream about the dying gassed man — which is marked off from the rest of the poem not only by its brevity and its dream-based present tense, but also by its repetition of an identical rhyme-word: "drowning" rhymes with "drowning."

Regionality

When the generalized space of lyric — the vague spatial context, say, of "A slumber did my spirit seal" — gives way to a particular climate, geography, and scenery, we say that we have a regional poem. Wordsworth's poetry has made the Lake District of northern England a place of tourism and literary pilgrimage; Hopkins made the scenery of North Wales enter English poetry; Longfellow, Whittier, Frost, and Lowell became famous for their poems of New England; Robinson Jeffers immortalized Big Sur on the California coast; and Elizabeth Bishop, though American by birth, wrote many memorable poems about the landscapes of Brazil. These are only a few relatively recent examples. In older countries, descriptive poems (and landscape paintings) blanket the whole landscape: there is scarcely a town in Italy that has not been represented by a painter or a poet of classical or modern times.

The power of imagination to clothe a landscape in powerful allusive images is nowhere better seen than in Robert Lowell's "The Quaker Graveyard in Nantucket." This is a powerful, violent, and tumultuous poem, boiling up from the page as it follows the poet's meditations as he looks at the graveyard in Nantucket where the Quaker whalers buried their dead. Yet when one goes and looks at that very graveyard, it is simply a placid green slope, for the most part unmarked by headstones. It is Lowell's poem that has transformed that placid and uninformative space into a powerful container of ocean combers, whaling ships, wounded whales, harpoons, dead bodies, and fearful prayers. To visit the graveyard before, and then after, reading Lowell's poem is to see how regional poetry clothes the land in reminiscence, intimations of history, and imaginative power. The same is true of Longfellow's poem "The Jewish Cemetery in Newport." One might easily pass by an old cemetery with graves inscribed in Hebrew letters; but after reading Longfellow's meditation on the early Jewish settlers, now vanished into "the long, mysterious Exodus of death," one sees the cemetery with different eyes.

Though European colonizers thought the New World bare of culture, Native Americans had already consecrated certain lands and mountains as sacred, and had composed poetry about them. This first acculturation of space in the United States has been in great part lost, with many of the Indian languages and their oral literatures fallen into extinction. But an imaginative claim to American territory is now being repeated by Native American poets such as Sherman Alexie, who recalls, in his poem "On the Amtrak from Boston to New York City," a well-meaning woman whose ideas of American history, American landscape, and American literature start with the Revolutionary period and end with Thoreau:

SHERMAN ALEXIE (b. 1966)
On the Amtrak from Boston to New York City

The white woman across the aisle from me says, "Look,
look at all the history, that house
on the hill there is over two hundred years old,"
as she points out the window past me

into what she has been taught. I have learned
little more about American history during my few days
back East than what I expected and far less
of what we should all know of the tribal stories

whose architecture is 15,000 years older
than the corners of the house that sits
museumed on the hill. "Walden Pond,"
the woman on the train asks, "Did you see Walden Pond?"

and I don't have a cruel enough heart to break
her own by telling her there are five Walden Ponds
on my little reservation out West
and at least a hundred more surrounding Spokane,

the city I pretend to call my home. "Listen,"
I could have told her. "I don't give a shit
about Walden. I know the Indians were living stories
around that pond before Walden's grandparents were born

and before his grandparents' grandparents were born.
I'm tired of hearing about Don-fucking-Henley[1] saving it, too,
because that's redundant. If Don Henley's brothers and sisters
and mothers and fathers hadn't come here in the first place

then nothing would need to be saved."
But I didn't say a word to the woman about Walden
Pond because she smiled so much and seemed delighted
that I thought to bring her an orange juice

back from the food car. I respect elders
of every color. All I really did was eat
my tasteless sandwich, drink my Diet Pepsi
and nod my head whenever the woman pointed out

another little piece of her country's history
while I, as all Indians have done
since this war began, made plans
for what I would do and say the next time

somebody from the enemy thought I was one of their own.

The first English colonists, as Robert Frost says in "The Gift Out-right," felt estranged in America because their own culture was English. They lived on land they had conquered, but they were still "unpossessed" by it. It was not until they (we) broke the tie to England, Frost argues, that we could give ourselves to the land "vaguely realizing west-ward, / But still unstoried, artless, unenhanced." It was the hope of writ-ers to give that land stories, art, enhancement. By writing narrative poems such as "The Wreck of the Hesperus" (about a wreck off the New England shore), "Evangeline" (about the exile of the Acadians), and Hiawatha (about Indians of New England), Longfellow hoped to give to the unstoried land the aura of legend. But Longfellow also wrote New England regional lyrics without narrative aim, like his famous poem about the coastal waters, "The Tide Rises, the Tide Falls":

The tide rises, the tide falls,
The twilight darkens, the curlew calls;

---

[1]Don Henley: a popular musician who organized benefit concerts to save Walden Pond from real estate developers.

> Along the sea-sands damp and brown
> The traveller hastens toward the town,
>   And the tide rises, the tide falls.

Is this a poem that a poet who had grown up in Tulsa would write? Probably not; and in sensing that a child of the desert or the prairie would find rhythms not in the tides but perhaps in the winds, would write not about the wreck of the Hesperus but about the devastation caused by a tornado, we begin to see how the poetry of a large country like the United States (or Russia, or China) necessarily begins to have a large component of regional difference.

But the "regional" poet can also be one whose sense of a place is sharpened by coming to that landscape late in life. Elizabeth Bishop's poems of Brazil, such as "Questions of Travel," convey the mixed sense of estrangement combined with wonder and amazement that is felt by one to whom the tropics were a late revelation:

> There are too many waterfalls here; the crowded streams
> hurry too rapidly down to the sea,
> and the pressure of so many clouds on the mountaintops
> makes them spill over the sides in soft slow-motion,
> turning to waterfalls under our very eyes. . . .
>
> Should we have stayed at home and thought of here? . . .
>
> But surely it would have been a pity
> not to have seen the trees along this road,
> really exaggerated in their beauty,
> not to have seen them gesturing
> like noble pantomimists, robed in pink. . . .

The poet never describes landscape without entering it kinesthetically, feeling the motion of the crowded streams, humanizing the trees into noble pantomimists. Landscape in poetry is always *projected outward from the writing self,* which has, before the composition of the poem, absorbed it and colored it with the personality of the writer. It is not "London" that we see in William Blake's "London," which begins, "I wander through each charter'd street," but rather London-as-interpreted-by-Blake. Similarly, it is not "London" that we see in Wordsworth's "Composed upon Westminster Bridge," but rather "London-as-interpreted-by-Wordsworth" or "Wordsworth-turned-into-London." Because Wordsworth loved tranquil and sublime scenery, the bustle of daytime London repelled him; yet he found a way to discover "his"

London, a London that could resemble him and his way of being. It was the London of dawn, when the air was free of smoke and the Thames was free of barges and the streets free of noise, when the architectural features of the city seemed almost like items in a natural landscape:

WILLIAM WORDSWORTH (1770 – 1850)
Composed upon Westminster Bridge, September 3, 1802

Earth hath not anything to show more fair:
Dull would he be of soul who could pass by
A sight so touching in its majesty:
This City now doth, like a garment, wear
The beauty of the morning; silent, bare,
Ships, towers, domes, theatres, and temples lie
Open unto the fields, and to the sky;
All bright and glittering in the smokeless air.
Never did sun more beautifully steep
In his first splendour, valley, rock, or hill;
Ne'er saw I, never felt, a calm so deep!
The river glideth at his own sweet will:
Dear God! the very houses seem asleep;
And all that mighty heart is lying still!

Just as the "history poem" must have a problem, and scenes to illustrate it, and a point of view from which to consider it, and a summing-up of insight somewhere in its close, so the "geography poem" must have a problem — and scenes, and a point of view, and a "solution," if only temporary, to the problem. That is, description is never "merely description." Wordsworth's powerful visual sense, repelled by daytime London, is nonetheless forced to concede aesthetic beauty to dawn London — is forced even to concede that the sight of man's most ambitious creative product — a city — is no less impressive than the sight of nature: "Never did sun more beautifully steep . . . valley, rock, or hill." As the list "valley, rock, or hill" is compared to the list "Ships, towers, domes, theatres, and temples," it is clear that the City wins. Nature has "majesty," of course, but its majesty is not "touching" as the majesty of the human city, a human product, is. Yet the beauty of the morning is only a temporary "garment" that the City briefly wears; and the tension between the satisfying, because unchanging, beauty of the valley or hill and the temporary, but touching, majesty of the City gives the poem its oscillations of feeling as the poet wrestles with his own taste, and concedes worth to the fallen majesty of the human over the serene majesty of his beloved nature.

In Brief: History and Regionality

In thinking about history poems, the main thing to remember is that there is always a tension between the copiousness of history and the brevity of lyric. To see how a structure as brief as lyric can present, speculate on, and judge history is to see a form straining against its own limits. When it succeeds, it strikes us as a triumph of style over difficulty. It is also useful to remember that the history poem has been a genre chiefly undertaken, until recently, by men, since they were the group admitted to warfare, political rights, and historical decision making. As women increasingly take on political responsibility, history will be "owned" by women as much as by men, and "poems on affairs of state" will be written by men and women alike. The notable public poems written in the last several years by such poets as Adrienne Rich, Amy Clampitt, and Jorie Graham (on such topics as the atomic bomb, the Vietnam War Memorial, and the B-52 bombers on perpetual alert) show the increasing intervention of women's poetry in political life.

When you encounter a poem of geography or regionality, ask yourself how it embodies a problem and how landscape has been "lyricized" — that is, made a bearer of human feeling. Usually there will be at least two points of view in the poem (as in Bishop's mixed feelings about Brazil, and Wordsworth's mixed feelings about London). These points of view represent an emotional, and even a moral, quarrel within the poet. As Marianne Moore says in "The Steeple-Jack," speaking of a New England town in a storm, "It is a privilege to see so / much confusion." And that is indubitably true. At the same time, her protagonist "sees boats // at sea progress white and rigid as if in / a groove" and likes that "elegance of which / the source is not bravado." Should the modern American poem throw itself open to the privilege of confusion, or should it have a formal elegance not defensive but self-generated? Moore wants — and attains — both; she is famous for her profusion of detail and her unobtrusive elegance of formulation. Her New England town is herself, and she becomes its displays, whether dynamic or rigid. It is always the author that the landscape reveals to us; and the landscape of lyric is always revelatory because the author is within it, projecting it from its preliminary reconstitution in the imagination.

Reading Other Poems

Ask yourself what the time-axis and the space-axis are for each of the poems that follow.

◆ Does the poem take place over time, and if so, how many episodes does it show? (You can trace, through "Tintern Abbey," Wordsworth's entire development to adulthood, from his "glad animal movements" as a child to his political disillusion to his present restoration.)

◆ Does the poem bring in several different spaces? (Look at "Tintern Abbey" and see whether it all takes place outdoors.)

◆ Some poems, like W. S. Merwin's "The Asians Dying" (about the Vietnam War), treat only one episode of time. How is that episode made significant?

◆ Does the poem refer, as Robert Hayden's does, to a time in the historical past? If so, what does that epoch mean to the speaker?

◆ Why would a nineteenth-century man such as Keats write a poem about ancient Greece?

◆ If the poem treats a contemporary episode (as Yeats treats the 1916 Irish insurrection), how is the chaos of history ordered into the brief space of a lyric?

◆ Does the poem move from space to space as it goes along, or does it remain in one place?

◆ How big is the space delineated in the poem? (That is, would Stevens's "Anecdote" be a different poem if it lacked the words "wilderness" or "Tennessee"?)

◆ If the poem treats imagined spaces (as Coleridge does in the fantastic visions of "Kubla Khan"), how are those spaces laid out and demarcated?

Derek Walcott writes the relatively new genre, the airplane poem: he takes off from Love Field, Dallas, and contemplates the state of the nation from an enormous height (a height no one could see from earlier than the twentieth century).

◆ What advantages (and disadvantages) come from writing at such a spatial distance?

◆ Does his adaptation of Dante's *terza rima* suggest a (perhaps hellish) expanse to be gazed at?

Jorie Graham contemplates a barbed-wire-enclosed field full of B-52 bombers on perpetual alert, kept running always in case they must respond instantly to an enemy threat. Her field of vision then takes in two more episodes — one of a marriage, one of the murder of the first poet, Orpheus.

◆ Can you link these three episodes, one in public space, one in private space, one in mythological space?

Lowell's "For the Union Dead," too, takes place in several spaces, and also over several times, stretching from the Revolutionary War to the poet's current America of forced school integration and New England decline (symbolized by the destruction of the Boston Common to make an underground garage for the cars that have invaded the city).

◆ Can you track Lowell's spaces and times, and suggest some reasons why the poem does not proceed chronologically in time or in some ordered spatial way?

Simon Ortiz's poem, too, is ordered by both space and time, as are many quest-poems.

◆ What are its temporal and spatial coordinates?

◆ What is the object of its quest?

Robert Hayden's poem enacts itself in a time and place tersely announced by its title. What do the two parts of the poem tell us about "night" and "Mississippi"?

The new narratives inserted by immigrants constitute important modifications of ideas of "Americanness" and of "history." Gary Soto's "History" is a reflection on the anonymity of immigrants, on the numerous untold stories behind their migration, their sorrows, and their joys. By giving the grand name "History" to his poem about one inconspicuous woman, Soto asks us to reflect on the sort of events we unreflectively call "history."

◆ Is his account chronological? If not, why not, do you think?

Silvia Curbelo, too, emphasizes the hidden history behind migration, as her Cuban "boat-person" encodes his past life in music.

◆ What three episodes from his previous life does music summon up for the *balsero*?

For Dionisio Martínez, growing up in a house where the first language is not English makes the child realize that an entire history precedes the family's arrival in an English-speaking country. That history is deduced only from fragmented conversations and angers.

◆ How does Martínez intertwine space, time, and language in "History as a Second Language"?

Samuel Taylor Coleridge (1772 – 1834)
Kubla Khan[1]

Or a Vision in a Dream. A Fragment
In Xanadu did Kubla Khan
A stately pleasure dome decree:
Where Alph, the sacred river, ran
Through caverns measureless to man
    Down to a sunless sea.   5
So twice five miles of fertile ground
With walls and towers were girdled round:
And there were gardens bright with sinuous rills,
Where blossomed many an incense-bearing tree;
And there were forests ancient as the hills,   10
Enfolding sunny spots of greenery.

But oh! that deep romantic chasm which slanted
Down the green hill athwart a cedarn cover!
A savage place! as holy and enchanted
As e'er beneath a waning moon was haunted   15
By woman wailing for her demon lover!
And from this chasm, with ceaseless turmoil seething,
As if this earth in fast thick pants were breathing,
A mighty fountain momently was forced:
Amid whose swift half-intermitted burst   20
Huge fragments vaulted like rebounding hail,
Or chaffy grain beneath the thresher's flail:
And 'mid these dancing rocks at once and ever
It flung up momently the sacred river.
Five miles meandering with a mazy motion   25
Through wood and dale the sacred river ran,
Then reached the caverns measureless to man,
And sank in tumult to a lifeless ocean:
And 'mid this tumult Kubla heard from far
Ancestral voices prophesying war!   30

---

[1]Ruler of the Mongol dynasty in thirteenth-century China. Coleridge has invented the topography and place names in the poem.

The shadow of the dome of pleasure
Floated midway on the waves;
Where was heard the mingled measure
From the fountain and the caves.
It was a miracle of rare device,   35
A sunny pleasure dome with caves of ice!

A damsel with a dulcimer
In a vision once I saw:
It was an Abyssinian maid,
And on her dulcimer she played,   40
Singing of Mount Abora.
Could I revive within me
Her symphony and song,
To such a deep delight 'twould win me,
That with music loud and long,   45
I would build that dome in air,
That sunny dome! those caves of ice!
And all who heard should see them there,
And all should cry, Beware! Beware!
His flashing eyes, his floating hair!   50
Weave a circle round him thrice,
And close your eyes with holy dread,
For he on honey-dew hath fed,
And drunk the milk of Paradise.

WILLIAM WORDSWORTH (1770 – 1850)
*Lines Composed a Few Miles above Tintern Abbey on
Revisiting the Banks of the Wye During a Tour*

July 13, 1798

Five years have passed; five summers, with the length
Of five long winters! and again I hear
These waters, rolling from their mountain-springs
With a soft inland murmur. Once again
Do I behold these steep and lofty cliffs,   5
That on a wild secluded scene impress
Thoughts of more deep seclusion; and connect
The landscape with the quiet of the sky.
The day is come when I again repose
Here, under this dark sycamore, and view   10
These plots of cottage ground, these orchard tufts,

Which at this season, with their unripe fruits,
Are clad in one green hue, and lose themselves
'Mid groves and copses. Once again I see
These hedgerows, hardly hedgerows, little lines   15
Of sportive wood run wild; these pastoral farms,
Green to the very door; and wreaths of smoke
Sent up, in silence, from among the trees!
With some uncertain notice, as might seem
Of vagrant dwellers in the houseless woods,   20
Or of some Hermit's cave, where by his fire
The Hermit sits alone.

                              These beauteous forms,
Through a long absence, have not been to me
As is a landscape to a blind man's eye;   25
But oft, in lonely rooms, and 'mid the din
Of towns and cities, I have owed to them,
In hours of weariness, sensations sweet,
Felt in the blood, and felt along the heart;
And passing even into my purer mind,   30
With tranquil restoration — feelings too
Of unremembered pleasure; such, perhaps,
As have no slight or trivial influence
On that best portion of a good man's life,
His little, nameless, unremembered, acts   35
Of kindness and of love. Nor less, I trust,
To them I may have owed another gift,
Of aspect more sublime; that blessed mood,
In which the burthen of the mystery,
In which the heavy and the weary weight   40
Of all this unintelligible world,
Is lightened — that serene and blessed mood,
In which the affections gently lead us on —
Until, the breath of this corporeal frame
And even the motion of our human blood   45
Almost suspended, we are laid asleep
In body, and become a living soul;
While with an eye made quiet by the power
Of harmony, and the deep power of joy,
We see into the life of things.   50

                              If this
Be but a vain belief, yet, oh! how oft —

In darkness and amid the many shapes
Of joyless daylight; when the fretful stir
Unprofitable, and the fever of the world,   55
Have hung upon the beatings of my heart —
How oft, in spirit, have I turned to thee,
O sylvan Wye! thou wanderer through the woods,
How often has my spirit turned to thee!

      And now, with gleams of half-extinguished thought,   60
With many recognitions dim and faint,
And somewhat of a sad perplexity,
The picture of the mind revives again;
While here I stand, not only with the sense
Of present pleasure, but with pleasing thoughts   65
That in this moment there is life and food
For future years. And so I dare to hope,
Though changed, no doubt, from what I was when first
I came among these hills; when like a roe
I bounded o'er the mountains, by the sides   70
Of the deep rivers, and the lonely streams,
Wherever nature led — more like a man
Flying from something that he dreads than one
Who sought the thing he loved. For nature then
(The coarser pleasures of my boyish days,   75
And their glad animal movements all gone by)
To me was all in all. — I cannot paint
What then I was. The sounding cataract
Haunted me like a passion; the tall rock,
The mountain, and the deep and gloomy wood,   80
Their colors and their forms, were then to me
An appetite; a feeling and a love,
That had no need of a remoter charm,
By thought supplied, nor any interest
Unborrowed from the eye. — That time is past,   85
And all its aching joys are now no more,
And all its dizzy raptures. Not for this
Faint I, nor mourn nor murmur; other gifts
Have followed; for such loss, I would believe,
Abundant recompense. For I have learned   90
To look on nature, not as in the hour
Of thoughtless youth; but hearing oftentimes
The still, sad music of humanity,

Nor harsh nor grating, though of ample power
To chasten and subdue. And I have felt   95
A presence that disturbs me with the joy
Of elevated thoughts; a sense sublime
Of something far more deeply interfused,
Whose dwelling is the light of setting suns,
And the round ocean and the living air,   100
And the blue sky, and in the mind of man:
A motion and a spirit, that impels
All thinking things, all objects of all thought,
And rolls through all things. Therefore am I still
A lover of the meadows and the woods,   105
And mountains; and of all that we behold
From this green earth; of all the mighty world
Of eye, and ear — both what they half create,
And what perceive; well pleased to recognize
In nature and the language of the sense   110
The anchor of my purest thoughts, the nurse,
The guide, the guardian of my heart, and soul
Of all my moral being.

           Nor perchance,
If I were not thus taught, should I the more   115
Suffer my genial spirits to decay:
For thou art with me here upon the banks
Of this fair river; thou my dearest Friend,[1]
My dear, dear Friend; and in thy voice I catch
The language of my former heart, and read   120
My former pleasures in the shooting lights
Of thy wild eyes. Oh! yet a little while
May I behold in thee what I was once,
My dear, dear Sister! and this prayer I make,
Knowing that Nature never did betray   125
The heart that loved her; 'tis her privilege,
Through all the years of this our life, to lead
From joy to joy: for she can so inform
The mind that is within us, so impress
With quietness and beauty, and so feed   130
With lofty thoughts, that neither evil tongues,

---

[1]He is referring to his sister, Dorothy Wordsworth (1771–1855), writer and diarist.

Rash judgments, nor the sneers of selfish men,
Nor greetings where no kindness is, nor all
The dreary intercourse of daily life,
Shall e'er prevail against us, or disturb   135
Our cheerful faith, that all which we behold
Is full of blessings. Therefore let the moon
Shine on thee in thy solitary walk;
And let the misty mountain winds be free
To blow against thee: and, in after years,   140
When these wild ecstasies shall be matured
Into a sober pleasure; when thy mind
Shall be a mansion for all lovely forms,
Thy memory be as a dwelling place
For all sweet sounds and harmonies; oh! then,   145
If solitude, or fear, or pain, or grief
Should be thy portion, with what healing thoughts
Of tender joy wilt thou remember me,
And these my exhortations! Nor, perchance —
If I should be where I no more can hear   150
Thy voice, nor catch from thy wild eyes these gleams
Of past existence — wilt thou then forget
That on the banks of this delightful stream
We stood together; and that I, so long
A worshipper of Nature, hither came   155
Unwearied in that service; rather say
With warmer love — oh! with far deeper zeal
Of holier love. Nor wilt thou then forget,
That after many wanderings, many years
Of absence, these steep woods and lofty cliffs,   160
And this green pastoral landscape, were to me
More dear, both for themselves and for thy sake!

JOHN KEATS (1795 – 1821)
Ode on a Grecian Urn

1

Thou still unravished bride of quietness,
    Thou foster child of silence and slow time,
Sylvan historian, who canst thus express
    A flowery tale more sweetly than our rhyme:
What leaf-fringed legend haunts about thy shape

Of deities or mortals, or of both,
        In Tempe or the dales of Arcady?[1]
    What men or gods are these? What maidens loath?
What mad pursuit? What struggle to escape?
        What pipes and timbrels? What wild ecstasy?

2

Heard melodies are sweet, but those unheard
        Are sweeter; therefore, ye soft pipes, play on;
Not to the sensual ear, but, more endeared,
        Pipe to the spirit ditties of no tone:
Fair youth, beneath the trees, thou canst not leave
        Thy song, nor ever can those trees be bare;
            Bold Lover, never, never canst thou kiss,
Though winning near the goal — yet, do not grieve;
        She cannot fade, though thou hast not thy bliss,
            Forever wilt thou love, and she be fair!

3

Ah, happy, happy boughs! that cannot shed
        Your leaves, nor ever bid the Spring adieu;
And, happy melodist, unwearièd,
        Forever piping songs forever new;
More happy love! more happy, happy love!
        Forever warm and still to be enjoyed,
            Forever panting, and forever young;
All breathing human passion far above,
        That leaves a heart high-sorrowful and cloyed,
            A burning forehead, and a parching tongue.

4

Who are these coming to the sacrifice?
        To what green altar, O mysterious priest,
Lead'st thou that heifer lowing at the skies,
        And all her silken flanks with garlands dressed?
What little town by river or sea shore,
        Or mountain-built with peaceful citadel,
            Is emptied of this folk, this pious morn?
And, little town, thy streets forevermore
        Will silent be; and not a soul to tell
            Why thou art desolate, can e'er return.

---

[1] Traditional pastoral landscapes.

5

O Attic shape! Fair attitude! with brede°   *embroidery*
 Of marble men and maidens overwrought,
With forest branches and the trodden weed;
  Thou, silent form, dost tease us out of thought
As doth eternity: Cold Pastoral!
  When old age shall this generation waste,
   Thou shalt remain, in midst of other woe
Than ours, a friend to man, to whom thou say'st,
  "*Beauty is truth, truth beauty,* — that is all
   Ye know on earth, and all ye need to know."

WILLIAM BUTLER YEATS (1865 – 1939)
Easter 1916[1]

I have met them at close of day
Coming with vivid faces
From counter or desk among grey
Eighteenth-century houses.
I have passed with a nod of the head   5
Or polite meaningless words,
Or have lingered awhile and said
Polite meaningless words,
And thought before I had done
Of a mocking tale or a gibe   10
To please a companion
Around the fire at the club,
Being certain that they and I
But lived where motley is worn:
All changed, changed utterly: 15
A terrible beauty is born.

That woman's days were spent
In ignorant good-will,
Her nights in argument
Until her voice grew shrill.   20
What voice more sweet than hers
When, young and beautiful,

---

[1]The title refers to the Easter Rebellion against the British on April 24, 1916. Republicans seized buildings and a park in the center of Dublin. They were killed or captured by April 29 and the leaders were executed in May.

She rode to harriers?[2]
This man had kept a school
And rode our wingèd horse;[3]　　　　　　　　25
This other his helper and friend[4]
Was coming into his force;
He might have won fame in the end,
So sensitive his nature seemed,
So daring and sweet his thought.　　　　　　　30
This other man I had dreamed
A drunken, vainglorious lout.[5]
He had done most bitter wrong
To some who are near my heart,
Yet I number him in the song;　　　　　　　35
He, too, has resigned his part
In the casual comedy;
He, too, has been changed in his turn,
Transformed utterly:
A terrible beauty is born.　　　　　　　40

Hearts with one purpose alone
Through summer and winter seem
Enchanted to a stone
To trouble the living stream.
The horse that comes from the road,　　　　　　　45
The rider, the birds that range
From cloud to tumbling cloud,
Minute by minute they change;
A shadow of cloud on the stream
Changes minute by minute;　　　　　　　50
A horse-hoof slides on the brim,
And a horse plashes within it;
The long-legged moor-hens dive,
And hens to moor-cocks call;

---

[2]Yeats's friend, Countess Markiewicz, née Constance Gore-Booth (1868–1927), was involved in the rebellion. Because she was a woman, she was not executed, and is therefore omitted from the final roll call.

[3]Patrick Pearse (1879–1916), the founder of St. Enda's School for Boys at Rathfarnham near Dublin, was one of the leaders of the rebellion. He was also a poet. (The winged horse is Pegasus, a symbol of poetic inspiration.)

[4]Thomas MacDonagh (1878–1916), poet and dramatist.

[5]Major Thomas MacBride had been married to Maud Gonne, whom Yeats loved; they had divorced.

Minute by minute they live: 55
The stone's in the midst of all.

Too long a sacrifice
Can make a stone of the heart.
O when may it suffice?
That is Heaven's part, our part   60
To murmur name upon name,
As a mother names her child
When sleep at last has come
On limbs that had run wild.
What is it but nightfall?   65
No, no, not night but death;
Was it needless death after all?
For England may keep faith
For all that is done and said.[6]
We know their dream; enough   70
To know they dreamed and are dead;
And what if excess of love
Bewildered them till they died?
I write it out in a verse —
MacDonagh and MacBride   75
And Connolly and Pearse
Now and in time to be,
Wherever green is worn,
Are changed, changed utterly:
A terrible beauty is born.   80

WALLACE STEVENS (1879 – 1955)
Anecdote of the Jar

I placed a jar in Tennessee,
And round it was, upon a hill.
It made the slovenly wilderness
Surround that hill.

The wilderness rose up to it,
And sprawled around, no longer wild.
The jar was round upon the ground
And tall and of a port in air.

---

[6]England had promised Home Rule for Ireland.

It took dominion everywhere.
The jar was gray and bare.
It did not give of bird or bush,
Like nothing else in Tennessee.

Robert Lowell (1917 – 1977)

For the Union Dead[1]

> *"Relinquunt Omnia Servare Rem Publicam."*[2]

The old South Boston Aquarium stands
in a Sahara of snow now. Its broken windows are boarded.
The bronze weathervane cod[3] has lost half its scales.
The airy tanks are dry.

Once my nose crawled like a snail on the glass;   5
my hand tingled
to burst the bubbles
drifting from the noses of the cowed, compliant fish.

My hand draws back. I often sigh still
for the dark downward and vegetating kingdom   10
of the fish and reptile. One morning last March,
I pressed against the new barbed and galvanized

fence on the Boston Common.[4] Behind their cage,
yellow dinosaur steamshovels were grunting
as they cropped up tons of mush and grass   15
to gouge their underworld garage.[5]

Parking spaces luxuriate like civic
sandpiles in the heart of Boston.
A girdle of orange, Puritan-pumpkin colored girders
braces the tingling Statehouse,   20

---

[1]Soldiers who died fighting for the North in the Civil War. The poem is written about a bronze bas-relief opposite the Massachusetts State House on Beacon Street, in Boston; the monument, by Augustus St. Gaudens (1848–1897), commemorates Colonel Robert Gould Shaw (1837–1863), who commanded the first all–African American regiment in the North and who was killed while leading an attack on Fort Wagner in South Carolina. The monument represents Shaw on horseback flanked by African American foot soldiers.

[2]Lowell has changed the inscription on the monument from the singular to the plural, so that it reads: "They leave everything behind to serve the Republic."

[3]Codfish, the symbol of Boston.

[4]Park facing the State House.

[5]The construction of the garage beneath the Common was attended by graft and corruption.

shaking over the excavations, as it faces Colonel Shaw
and his bell-cheeked Negro infantry
on St. Gaudens' shaking Civil War relief,
propped by a plank splint against the garage's earthquake.

Two months after marching through Boston, 25
half the regiment was dead;
at the dedication,
William James[6] could almost hear the bronze Negroes breathe.

Their monument sticks like a fishbone
in the city's throat. 30
Its Colonel is as lean
as a compass-needle.

He has an angry wrenlike vigilance,
a greyhound's gentle tautness;
he seems to wince at pleasure, 35
and suffocate for privacy.

He is out of bounds now. He rejoices in man's lovely,
peculiar power to choose life and die —
when he leads his black soldiers to death,
he cannot bend his back. 40

On a thousand small town New England greens,
the old white churches hold their air
of sparse, sincere rebellion; frayed flags
quilt the graveyards of the Grand Army of the Republic.

The stone statues of the abstract Union Soldier 45
grow slimmer and younger each year —
wasp-waisted, they doze over muskets
and muse through their sideburns . . .

Shaw's father wanted no monument
except the ditch, 50
where his son's body was thrown
and lost with his "niggers."[7]

The ditch is nearer.
There are no statues for the last war here;

---

[6]Philosopher and psychologist (1842–1910).

[7]Shaw's father could have had his son's body brought home (officers had that privilege, while infantry were buried where they fell), but he refused, knowing his son's affection for his men.

on Boylston Street, a commercial photograph   55
shows Hiroshima boiling

over a Mosler Safe, the "Rock of Ages"
that survived the blast. Space is nearer.
When I crouch to my television set,
the drained faces of Negro school-children[8] rise like balloons.   60

Colonel Shaw
is riding on his bubble,
he waits
for the blessèd break.

The Aquarium is gone. Everywhere,   65
giant finned cars nose forward like fish;
a savage servility
slides by on grease.

Robert Hayden (1913 – 1980)
Night, Death, Mississippi

I

A quavering cry. Screech-owl?
Or one of them?
The old man in his reek
and gauntness laughs —

One of them, I bet —
and turns out the kitchen lamp,
limping to the porch to listen
in the windowless night.

Be there with Boy and the rest
if I was well again.
Time was. Time was.
White robes like moonlight

In the sweetgum dark.
Unbucked that one then
and him squealing bloody Jesus
as we cut it off.

---

[8]Schools in the South were being forcibly desegregated in 1960.

Time was. A cry?
A cry all right.
He hawks and spits,
fevered as by groinfire.

Have us a bottle,
Boy and me —
he's earned him a bottle —
when he gets home.

II

Then we beat them, he said,
beat them till our arms was tired
and the big old chains
messy and red.

O Jesus burning on the lily cross

Christ, it was better
than hunting bear
which don't know why
you want him dead.

O night, rawhead and bloodybones night

You kids fetch Paw
some water now so's he
can wash that blood
off him, she said.

O night betrayed by darkness not its own

W. S. MERWIN (b. 1927)

The Asians Dying

When the forests have been destroyed their darkness remains
The ash the great walker follows the possessors
Forever
Nothing they will come to is real
Nor for long
Over the watercourses
Like ducks in the time of the ducks
The ghosts of the villages trail in the sky
Making a new twilight

Rain falls into the open eyes of the dead
Again again with its pointless sound
When the moon finds them they are the color of everything
The nights disappear like bruises but nothing is healed
The dead go away like bruises
The blood vanishes into the poisoned farmlands

Pain the horizon
Remains
Overhead the seasons rock
They are paper bells
Calling to nothing living

The possessors move everywhere under Death their star
Like columns of smoke they advance into the shadows
Like thin flames with no light
They with no past
And fire their only future

Derek Walcott (b. 1930)

The Gulf

For Jack and Barbara Harrison

I

The airport coffee tastes less of America.
Sour, unshaven, dreading the exertion
of tightening, racked nerves fuelled with liquor,

some smoky, resinous bourbon,
the body, buckling at its casket hole,
a roar like last night's blast racing its engines,

watches the fumes of the exhausted soul
as the trans-Texas jet, screeching, begins
its flight and friends diminish. So, to be aware

of the divine union the soul detaches
itself from created things. "We're in the air,"
the Texan near me grins. All things: these matches

from LBJ's[1] campaign hotel, this rose
given me at dawn in Austin by a child,
this book of fables by Borges,[2] its prose

---

[1] Lyndon Baines Johnson (1908–1975), thirty-sixth president of the United States.
[2] Jorge Luis Borges (1899–1986), Argentine writer.

a stalking, moonlit tiger. What was willed
on innocent, sun-streaked Dallas, the beast's claw
curled round that hairspring rifle[3] is revealed

on every page as lunacy or feral law;
circling that wound we leave Love Field.
Fondled, these objects conjure hotels,

quarrels, new friendships, brown limbs
nakedly moulded as these autumn hills
memory penetrates as the jet climbs

the new clouds over Texas; their home means
an island suburb, forest, mountain water;
they are the simple properties for scenes

whose joy exhausts like grief, scenes where we learn,
exchanging the least gifts, this rose, this napkin,
that those we love are objects we return,

that this lens on the desert's wrinkled skin
has priced our flesh, all that we love in pawn
to that brass ball, that the gifts, multiplying,

clutter and choke the heart, and that I shall
watch love reclaim its things as I lie dying.
My very flesh and blood! Each seems a petal

shrivelling from its core. I watch them burn,
by the nerves' flare I catch their skeletal
candour! Best never to be born,

the great dead cry. Their works shine on our shelves,
by twilight tour their gilded gravestone spines,
and read until the lamplit page revolves

to a white stasis whose detachment shines
like a propeller's rainbowed radiance.
Circling like us; no comfort for their loves!

---

[3]Reference to the assassination of President John F. Kennedy in Dallas on November 22, 1963.

II

The cold glass darkens. Elizabeth wrote once
that we make glass the image of our pain;
I watch clouds boil past the cold, sweating pane

above the Gulf. All styles yearn to be plain
as life. The face of the loved object under glass
is plainer still. Yet, somehow, at this height,

above this cauldron boiling with its wars,
our old earth, breaking to familiar light,
that cloud-bound mummy with self-healing scars

peeled of her cerements again looks new;
some cratered valley heals itself with sage,
through that grey, fading massacre a blue

lighthearted creek flutes of some siege
to the amnesia of drumming water.
Their cause is crystalline: the divine union

of these detached, divided states, whose slaughter
darkens each summer now, as one by one,
the smoke of bursting ghettos clouds the glass

down every coast where filling station signs
proclaim the Gulf, an air, heavy with gas,
sickens the state, from Newark to New Orleans.

III

Yet the South felt like home. Wrought balconies,
the sluggish river with its tidal drawl,
the tropic air charged with the extremities

of patience, a heat heavy with oil,
canebrakes, that legendary jazz. But fear
thickened my voice, that strange, familiar soil

prickled and barbed the texture of my hair,
my status as a secondary soul.
The Gulf, your gulf, is daily widening,

each blood-red rose warns of that coming night
when there's no rock cleft to go hidin' in
and all the rocks catch fire, when that black might,

their stalking, moonless panthers turn from Him
whose voice they can no more believe, when the black X's
mark their passover with slain seraphim.

IV

The Gulf shines, dull as lead. The coast of Texas
glints like a metal rim. I have no home
as long as summer bubbling to its head

boils for that day when in the Lord God's name
the coals of fire are heaped upon the head
of all whose gospel is the whip and flame,

age after age, the uninstructing dead.

SIMON J. ORTIZ (b. 1941)
Bend in the River

Flicker flies by.
His ochre wing
is tied to prayer sticks.
Pray for mountains,
the cold strong shelter.

Sun helps me to see
where Arkansas River
ripples over pebbles.
Glacial stone moves slowly;
it will take a while.

A sandbank cuts sharply
down to a poplar log
buried in damp sand.
Shadow lengths tell me
it is afternoon.

There are tracks
at river's edge, raccoon,
coyote, deer, crow,
and now my own.

My sight follows
the river upstream
until it bends.
Beyond the bend
is more river
and, soon, the mountains.
We shall arrive,
to see, soon.

JORIE GRAHAM (b. 1950)
What the End Is For

Grand Forks, North Dakota

A boy just like you took me out to see them,
    the five hundred B-52's on alert on the runway,
fully loaded fully manned pointed in all the directions,
    running every minute
of every day.   5
    They sound like a sickness of the inner ear,

where the heard foams up into the noise of listening,
    where the listening arrives without being extinguished.
The huge hum soaks up into the dusk.
    The minutes spring open. Six is too many.   10
From where we watch,
    from where even watching is an anachronism,

from the 23rd of March from an open meadow,
    the concertina wire in its double helix
designed to tighten round a body if it turns   15
    is the last path the sun can find to take out,
each barb flaring gold like a braille being read,
    then off with its knowledge and the sun
is gone. . . .

That's when the lights on all the extremities, like an outline   20
        like a dress,
    become loud in the story,
and a dark I have not seen before
    sinks in to hold them one
by one.   25
    Strange plot made to hold so many inexhaustible
screams.
    Have you ever heard in a crowd mutterings of
blame

that will not modulate that will not rise?   30
    He tells me, your stand-in, they *stair-step* up.
He touches me to have me look more deeply
    in
to where for just a moment longer
    color still lives: 35
the belly white so that it looks like sky, the top

some kind of brown, some soil — How does it look
from up there now
    this meadow we lie on our bellies in, this field Iconography
tells me stands for sadness   40
    because the wind can move through it uninterrupted?
What is it the wind
    would have wanted to find and didn't

leafing down through this endless admiration unbroken
    because we're too low for it   45
to find us?
    Are you still there for me now in that dark
we stood in for hours
    letting it sweep as far as it could down over us
unwilling to move, irreconcilable? What *he*   50
    wants to tell me,

his whisper more like a scream
    over this eternity of engines never not running,
is everything: how the crews assigned to each plane
    for a week at a time, the seven boys, must live   55
inseparable,
    how they stay together for life,
how the wings are given a life of
    seven feet of play,

how they drop practice bombs called *shapes* over Nevada,   60
    how the measures for counterattack in air
have changed and we
    now forego firepower for jamming, for the throwing
of false signals. The meadow, the meadow hums, love, with
        the planes,   65
    as if every last blade of grass were wholly possessed

by this practice, wholly prepared. The last time I saw you,
    we stood facing each other as dusk came on.
I leaned against the refrigerator, you leaned against the door.
    The picture window behind you was slowly extinguished,   70
the tree went out, the two birdfeeders, the metal braces on them.
    The light itself took a long time,

bits in puddles stuck like the useless
    splinters of memory, the chips
of history, hopes, laws handed down. *Here, hold these* he says,   75
    these grasses these

torn pods, he says, smiling over the noise another noise, *take these*
    he says, my hands wrong for
the purpose, here,
    not–visible–from–the–sky, prepare yourself with these, boy   80
        and
bouquet of
    thistleweed and wort and william and
timothy. We stood there. Your face went out a long time
    before the rest of it. Can't see you anymore I said. *Nor I,*   85
you, whatever you still were
    replied.
When I asked you to hold me you refused.
    When I asked you to cross the six feet of room to hold me

you refused. Until I   90
    couldn't rise out of the patience either any longer
to make us
    take possession.
Until we were what we must have wanted to be:
    shapes the shapelessness was taking back.   95
Why should I lean out?
    Why should I move?
When the Maenads tear Orpheus limb from limb,
    they throw his head

out into the river.[1]   100
    Unbodied it sings
all the way downstream, all the way to the single ocean,
    head floating in current downriver singing,
until the sound of the cataracts grows,
    until the sound of the open ocean grows and the voice.   105

GARY SOTO (b. 1952)
History

Grandma lit the stove.
Morning sunlight
Lengthened in spears
Across the linoleum floor.

---

[1]Orpheus was torn to pieces by Maenads, savage female followers of Dionysus, god
of drunkenness and revelry. Orpheus's severed head, floating down the Thracian river,
Hebrus, reached the island of Lesbos, the home of lyric poetry, where it was buried.

Wrapped in a shawl,   5
Her eyes small
With sleep,
She sliced *papas*,°   *potatoes*
Pounded chiles
With a stone   10
Brought from Guadalajara.

                        After
Grandpa left for work,
She hosed down
The walk her sons paved   15
And in the shade
Of a chinaberry,
Unearthed her
Secret cigar box
Of bright coins   20
And bills, counted them
In English,
Then in Spanish,
And buried them elsewhere.
Later, back   25
From the market,
Where no one saw her,
She pulled out
Pepper and beet, spines
Of asparagus   30
From her blouse,
Tiny chocolates
From under a paisley bandana,
And smiled.

That was the fifties   35
And Grandma in her fifties,
A face streaked
From cutting grapes
And boxing plums.
I remember her insides   40
Were washed of tapeworm,
Her arms swelled into knobs
Of small growths —
Her second son
Dropped from a ladder   45

And was dust.
And yet I do not know
The sorrows
That sent her praying
In the dark of a closet,   50
The tear that fell
At night
When she touched loose skin
Of belly and breasts.
I do not know why   55
Her face shines.
Or what goes beyond this shine,
Only the stories
That pulled her
From Taxco° to San Joaquin,   *a town and county in southern*   60
Delano to Westside,   *Mexico*
The places
In which we all begin.

SILVIA CURBELO (b. 1955)
Balsero[1] *Singing*

When he opens his mouth
he is drifting, he is
in the air, and the child

he's remembering leans out
of some dark window
in his head. The sunlight

is incidental, falling
all around him like a word
or a wing. In another dream

he is dancing in a cottage by the sea
and music is a language he has just
learned to speak, the cool *yes*

of her throat. The sky goes on
for days with its one cloud waving,
the song lifting him like a sail.

---

[1]Refugee from Cuba in a raft, or *balsa*.

The real boat is lost
at sea, one voice nailed
to the planks of history, salt

on the tongue of thirty years.
A window empties
its small cargo —

an eyelash, grief. Each new breath
is a harbor, then a wave
closes over it

like a book.

DIONISIO MARTÍNEZ (b. 1956)
History as a Second Language

I grew up hearing the essence
of conversations in the next room.
My father and his friends conspired
in the next room. The new regime
succeeded in spite of their plot.
The next room is usually dark. People
whisper in it. You hear only so much.
Just enough if you know what to listen for.
I thought I heard a murder in the next
room. It was the radio. I thought
I heard a murder long after the radio
had been thrown against the wall and smashed
to bits. It was a whore at the end of
a long day. Families like mine
always managed to have a whore or two
as "good" friends. It made us look
less rich, less whatever being rich meant.
In those days things became
the meanings we gave them and not the other
way around, not like today. The next room
meant the room next door. If you looked
hard enough, you could see through the wall.
The specifics of a conversation
were not necessary to understand a plot
or a confession; the blurred
view through the wall was enough

to know more or less how the whores
earned their pay, how a government
might have failed, how a single threat
would keep a family together through war
and sabotage. The room next door
made us what we became with time in exile:
failed lovers, experts in the mechanics
of things we never learned to name.

9

Attitudes, Values, Judgments

You're under no obligation to like all the remarks or attitudes you come across in art. Past artists reflect the prejudices and beliefs of their time, just as our twenty-first-century writers will reveal, to later readers, the (frequently unconscious) presumptions and beliefs of our era. It is notoriously hard to believe that morally we are much superior to our ancestors. Social attitudes may progress in one or another area (we in America no longer recommend public hangings or beheadings), but we are sure to seem as backward and ignorant to our descendants as even our recent ancestors seem to us.

Nor are artists necessarily morally better than others in their private or public actions. Genius does not guarantee moral probity in the ordinary activities of life. What, then, are the moral obligations of artists insofar as they are artists? (As people, they exist under the same moral imperatives as anyone else, and are conditioned by their cultures in their interpretation of those imperatives.) How — to put our question another way — can artists betray their artistic principles?

They can betray themselves as artists, and their art itself, by saying what society wants to hear, rather than what seems true; by papering over the actual with the agreeable or the socially enjoined; by falling into the comfortable habits of the past instead of reinventing their medium. If, however, the artist has the talent to work the medium accurately — to reveal in stylized language the structure of reality as it is delivered by perception, emotion, and thought — without being cowed by convention or audience response, there is a chance that the artwork will succeed.

This does not mean that a work has to be composed entirely freely, with no external conditions laid upon it. On the contrary. Many commissioned artworks have been spectacularly successful — Michelangelo's paintings in the Sistine Chapel, Bach's cantatas for Sunday services, Milton's "Lycidas," written for an anthology of verse compiled in honor of a college acquaintance who was drowned. In fact, nothing is more stimulating to some artists than a patron's saying, "I'd like you to make a painting in a semicircular shape to fit that space over the door; and I'd like it to represent Apollo; and you may have exactly four ounces of gold leaf to decorate it with." Poetry is less often commissioned than music, sculpture, or painting, yet William Blake represents his *Songs of Innocence* as "commissioned" by a child-Muse:

> Piping down the valleys wild
> Piping songs of pleasant glee
> On a cloud I saw a child,
> And he laughing said to me,
>
> "Pipe a song about a Lamb";
> So I piped with merry cheer.
> "Piper, pipe that song again" —
> So I piped, he wept to hear.

And Shakespeare's sonnets seem to have begun as a commissioned sequence urging an aristocratic young man to marry and beget an heir.

A poem sometimes seeks out its own commissions, so to speak, by casting itself as a letter replying to a request or a question. Gerard Manley Hopkins's friend and fellow poet Robert Bridges asks Hopkins, in a letter, why he has sent him no poems lately. In response, Hopkins sends a verse-letter in the form of a sonnet ("To R.B.") explaining that inspiration has forsaken him:

> Sweet fire, the sire of muse, my soul needs this;
> I want the one rapture of an inspiration.
> Oh then if in my lagging lines you miss
> The roll, the rise, the carol, the creation,
> My winter world, that scarcely breathes that bliss,
> Now yields you, with some sighs, our explanation.

We may suppose that this poem might never have been written without the pressure of Bridges's "commissioning" question. It is always useful, in considering the attitudes of a poem, to ask what has occasioned it. Has an anterior question, reproach, or command brought it into being? If we do not ask this question, we are likely to mistake the poem's attitudes, values, and tone.

Consider the following example:

WILLIAM SHAKESPEARE (1564 – 1616)
Sonnet 76

Why is my verse so barren of new pride?
So far from variation or quick change?
Why with the time do I not glance aside
To new-found methods and to compounds strange?
Why write I still all one, ever the same,
And keep invention in a noted weed,°   *well-known garment*
That every word doth almost tell my name,
Showing their birth, and where they did proceed?
O know, sweet love, I always write of you,
And you and love are still my argument;
So all my best is dressing old words new,
Spending again what is already spent:
     For as the sun is daily new and old,
     So is my love, still telling what is told.

Shakespeare's Sonnet 76 has usually been read as a self-interrogation in which Shakespeare laments the barrenness and sameness of his poems. Improbably enough, according to this reading, Shakespeare thought ill of his own work, accusing himself of a boring similarity in all his poems:

Why is my verse so barren of new pride?
So far from variation or quick change?
Why with the time do I not glance aside
To new-found methods and to compounds strange?
Why write I still all one, ever the same,
And keep invention in a noted weed,
That every word doth almost tell my name,
Showing their birth and where they did proceed?

If this were all we had of the poem, we might indeed think Shakespeare is reproaching himself. But the next part of the sonnet shows that this is an "answer-poem," replying to an implied question previously asked by Shakespeare's young patron: "Why do you bring me nothing but sonnets, old-fashioned poems?" Shakespeare replies, "O know, sweet love, I always write of you":

> And you and love are still my argument;
> So all my best is dressing old words new,
> Spending again what is already spent:
>> For as the sun is daily new and old,
>> So is my love, still telling what is told.

Armed with this knowledge of implied question and answer, we can now better imagine the "antecedent scenario" of the poem. The fashionable young man, who has by now received many sonnets from Shakespeare, is surprised that his poet keeps writing in this old-fashioned form, already in existence for over two hundred years. Other poets have gone on to new things. Why can't his poet write a satire, or a picturesque narrative, or a debate-poem? "Why," asks the up-to-date young man of the poet, "are you always writing the same old sonnets, all the same sort, so that everyone who sees them says, 'Oh, of course, another piece by Shakespeare'?" And he continues, "How about doing something new next time?" Shakespeare, only too conscious of the young man's ignorant and trendy dismissal of his incomparable poems, gives the soft answer that turns away wrath, repeating and quoting the young man's reproach, but finding nonetheless a way to defend himself. We can now reconstruct the poem as it should be read: not as Shakespeare's reproach to himself but as his reproof of the young man:

> *Why* [you ask] is my verse so barren of "new pride"?
> So far from "variation" or "quick change"?
> *Why* with the time do I not glance aside
> To "new-found methods" and to "compounds strange"?
> *Why* write I still "all one," "ever the same,"
> And keep invention in a "noted weed,"
> That every word doth almost "tell my name,"
> Showing their birth and where they did proceed?
> O know, sweet love, I always write of you,
> And you and love are still my argument;
> So all my best is dressing old words new,
> Spending again what is already spent:
>> For as the sun is daily new and old,
>> So is my love, still telling what is told.

This deft but gentle rebuke reminds the young man, at the close, that nobody looks up at the sky at dawn and says, "The sun again! How boring and repetitive!" There are things so precious — the sun and love being among them — that we never have enough of them. And poetry, after all, never has new *words* — all the words are already present in the language. The only thing *any* poet can do is "dress [that is, arrange] old words new," re-spending the words that poetic predecessors have already spent.

Our view of the attitudes expressed by the speaker in this sonnet depends very much on whether we see it as *self-reproach* or as a *rebuke to the young man*. This reminds us that before we can evaluate the attitudes and values expressed in a poem we must try to be as accurate as possible in describing them. These are delicate questions; and the sophistication of poems (and of the people who write them) warns us against too hasty a judgment. One has to understand a poem well before judging it. (And really understanding the implications of a poem usually depends on having read many other poems by that poet.)

Evaluation depends on where you stand with respect to the things described in a poem. Until fairly recently, the poems that Langston Hughes wrote about Harlem — representing such realities as sexual intercourse before marriage, marital infidelity, children born out of wedlock, prostitution and pimping, and the strife between Jewish landlords and black tenants — were simply not represented in general anthologies of American poetry or anthologies of poetry by blacks. Much of Hughes's subject matter seemed indecent to whites and blacks alike; and black anthologists wanted to print poems that were "a credit to the race." Hughes's veracity — his refusal to betray the structure of reality as he saw it for something more acceptable — is today much admired, but was in his lifetime often criticized. Judges were judging not his art — represented in his striking sequences on Harlem and his adaptation of jazz rhythms — but what they saw as his failure to condemn immorality, on the one hand, and his washing dirty social linen in public, on the other.

It is not desirable to let a difference in values blind us to the imaginative mastery of language and form in such poets as the atheist Robinson Jeffers (whose nihilism was much criticized) or the social realists Langston Hughes and Allen Ginsberg. The nineteenth-century anthologists who censored Charles Baudelaire's depiction of lesbianism are replaced in our day by those who censor Ginsberg's depiction of homosexuality. The accurate representation of reality is, for the artist, the highest morality. It is immoral to conceal the way human beings live, or what human beings think. The tension between allowing an artist free expression and, for instance, shielding the sensibilities of the young is a real one; and most societies have worked out a gradual scale according to which the young can be exposed to art of increasing moral complexity.

However, in countries with active political or religious censorship, where free expression is not permitted at all, artists perform marvelous end-runs around forbidden topics. During the Cold War years, ingenious Eastern European poets in Russia, Poland, Hungary, and other Iron Curtain countries constructed allegorical poems which were seemingly "harmless" but which everyone could read as a coded critique of the regime. Even under censorship, art will find a way to be free — though sometimes the artist may suffer imprisonment and death.

It is impossible not to notice the attitudes and values expressed in a poem. In fact, they are often the first thing we do notice. Yet a criticism of attitudes and values alone does not come to grips with what a poet really has to offer, which is a personal sense of the world, an idiosyncratic temperament, a unique imagination, and a new linguistic lens through which readers may see the world afresh.

How, then, are we to evaluate the success of a poem if we cannot base our judgment on its attitudes and values? Robert Lowell, in the poem "Epilogue," printed last in his final book, *Day by Day,* suggests one way. Despairing of his unrhymed modern "snapshots" of reality, he asks why he can't make something as beautiful as the radiant interiors painted by the seventeenth-century Dutch artist Jan Vermeer. He is thinking particularly of one painting, which shows a girl reading a letter; Lowell imagines her "yearning" for its absent writer. She stands by a casement window from which light steals across the wall behind her, illuminating the map on the wall (which is, in Vermeer and elsewhere, a figure for the abstraction of art). Here is the poem:

Robert Lowell (1917 – 1977)

Epilogue

Those blessèd structures, plot and rhyme —
why are they no help to me now
I want to make
something imagined, not recalled?
I hear the noise of my own voice:
The painter's vision is not a lens,
it trembles to caress the light.
But sometimes everything I write

with the threadbare art of my eye
seems a snapshot
lurid, rapid, garish, grouped,
heightened from life,
yet paralyzed by fact.
All's misalliance.
Yet why not say what happened?
Pray for the grace of accuracy
Vermeer gave to the sun's illumination
stealing like the tide across a map
to his girl solid with yearning.
We are poor passing facts,
warned by that to give
each figure in the photograph
his living name.

At its middle, the poem collapses in despair: "All's misalliance." But then the poet gets a second wind: What is wrong with describing his life truthfully as he sees it? "Yet why not say what happened?" He resolves his poem by realizing that though his "snapshot[s]" may not look superficially like Vermeer's paintings, he and Vermeer have in common the artist's truest motive — accuracy of representation. The artist can vow accuracy, but he or she must pray for the other ingredient in successful art — grace. "Pray for *the grace of accuracy,*" the poet tells himself. One part of his function as a poet is a duty to set down contemporary facts of life before they disappear; but he can only hope and pray that by the grace of aesthetic power he can give to the people of his century (who will otherwise be anonymous numbers in a census, "poor passing facts") their "living name." That living name is conferred only by the *grace* of art — its aesthetic power that often seems bestowed from the outside, like religious "grace." By the end of the poem, the poet can stop referring to his work by the ugly and clipped word "snapshot," and can speak of it as "writing with light" — a "photo-graph." He, like Vermeer, will also become a writer with light if he can attain "the grace of accuracy."

This poem suggests that we must judge any poem we read as a representation of its author's perception of reality; but we must also judge it as an experiment in its medium, according to its portion of "grace" — what Hopkins called "the roll, the rise, the carol, the creation."

If, in one direction, we judge poetry, it is also true that in another direction the poem judges us. It looks at us with a steady gaze and dares us to judge ourselves by its revelations. "The poet judges, not as the judge judges but as the sun falling around a helpless thing," said Walt Whitman.

To observe and convey reality is itself a judgment on reality, even if the poem makes no explicit judgment on the reality conveyed.

Rita Dove, a contemporary African American poet, writes about the "poetic justice" of art in a poem about a painting she saw in Germany by a modern painter, Christian Schad. He had painted, in the twenties, in Berlin, a portrait of two circus "freaks": one of them was a man with a bone disease that caused his shoulder bones to protrude like wings. He was billed as "Agosta the Winged Man." The other "freak" was a perfectly normal black woman who, billed as "Rasha, the Black Dove," was displayed as an exotic jungle creature, dancing entwined with a boa constrictor. The black Rita Dove, seeing "the Black Dove" — who, but for an accident of time, could have been herself — depicts Schad, the painter, planning the double portrait he is about to begin, attempting to decide where its power will lie. Is it in the mercilessness of his unsparing view of his subjects? No,

> The canvas,
> not his eye, was merciless. . . .
>
> Schad would place him°   *Agosta*
> on a throne, a white sheet tucked
> over his loins, the black suit jacket
> thrown off like a cloak.
> Agosta had told him
>   of the medical students
> at the Charité,°   *a hospital*
> that chill arena
>
>   where he perched on
> a cot, his torso
> exposed, its crests and fins
> a colony of birds, trying
> to get out . . .
>   and the students,
> lumps caught
> in their throats, taking notes.
>
> Ah, Rasha's
>   foot on the stair.
> She moved slowly, as if she carried
> the snake around her body
> always. . . .

> Agosta in
> classical drapery, then,
> and Rasha at his feet.
> Without passion. Not
> the canvas
> > but their gaze,
> > so calm,
> was merciless.

Is it the painter's eye, seeing the social marginalization of his subjects (one black, one deformed) that is merciless in its accuracy? Or is it the canvas, demanding how paint shall be used, and how the picture will be composed, that is merciless? Schad decides that neither of these is true. It is neither his eye nor the canvas that is merciless, but the gaze of his two subjects, saying, "Here we are. This is how we were seen, in Berlin, in 1929." The gaze is merciless because it is, like the portrait which depicts it, "without passion." The painting is not propaganda; it is not "social protest art"; it is simply an accurate transcription (with the "grace" of its compositional arrangements with which Schad has taken such care) of "Reality, Berlin, 1929." Nothing more than this is necessary; but how hard it is to ensure that the eye and the canvas and the gaze maintain this accuracy of perception — without exaggeration, without deletion.

There have been other suggestions by poets on how to make and judge art, each understandable within its culture and its century. The religious poet George Herbert thought that if one wrote for God alone, one would write well: "If I please him, I write fine and wittie." Similarly, Milton said, in "Lycidas," that the poet should look for true fame only from the "pure eyes / And perfect witness of all-judging Jove." These reflections suggest that the poets did not find the immediate judgment of contemporaries a reliable measure for any poet.

We, too, can be warned by such remarks that poems that last for a long time tend to satisfy many criteria of success, and to interest many generations of future writers. It is, in the last analysis, chiefly by the admiration of other writers that writers become "canonized." In one strand of the canonical male line (male because until recently it was chiefly males who were educated in complex uses of language) Spenser admires Chaucer, Milton admires Spenser, Wordsworth admires Milton, Keats admires Wordsworth, Tennyson admires Keats, Eliot admires Tennyson, Auden admires Eliot, Merrill admires Auden, and so it has gone. It is no accident that almost every contemporary woman poet in America, from Adrienne Rich through Jorie Graham to Lucie Brock-Broido, has written a poem to or about Emily Dickinson, or that Dickinson herself wrote a poem about her favorite woman poet, Elizabeth Barrett Browning, or that Elizabeth Bishop wrote a poem to Marianne Moore, creating a comparable ongoing line of female "canonization." It is also true that canonization crosses gender lines: T. S. Eliot and Wallace Stevens and William Carlos Williams and A. R. Ammons admired the poetry of Marianne Moore; Hopkins admired Christina Rossetti; Dickinson admired Emerson; and Moore admired La Fontaine. It is the admiration of poets for each other's accomplishments in the medium of language that keeps poetry alive; and poets keep poetry honest in their fine-tuned admiration of any writing that is not only "accurate with respect to the structures of reality" but also full of "the grace of accuracy," giving the "poor passing facts" of every era their "living name."

In Brief: Attitudes, Values, Judgments

If we keep the honorific name "poetry" to mean "verse that succeeds in achieving lasting interest over time," we are still uncertain of the amount of "poetry" being produced by our own century. There is a great deal of verse being written, all of it, of course, of documentary interest to sociologists or anthropologists or cultural critics. For such scholars, the overt message, or representation of life in a poem, means more than the skill with which that message or representation has been arranged. We all read for message and picture, but readers with a strong commitment to poetry as an art require in it those new symbolic structures, invented by talented artists of every age, that both affront and refresh. An experienced reader of poetry is soon bored by the already known and the clichéd; but the previously unheard, the previously unknown, arranged in a form true to a temperament, and transmitting a shock of pleasure — this makes for the renewal of both life and art. It is this capacity of poetry to rewrite the old that we value in it, that we search out in it, and that we judge it by.

Reading Other Poems

Each of the following poems expresses a strong moral attitude: that is, at least two sets of opposing values are presented, and the poet (through a sympathetic or unsympathetic speaker) comes out in favor of one set. This entails describing, or at least implying, the contrasting set of values that the poet repudiates.

◆ In each poem, trace the way the repudiated value is presented — whether in Phillis Wheatley's advocacy of Christianity over paganism, or John Milton's corrupt bishops, or Rita Dove's dictator, or Walt Whitman's astronomer, or William Butler Yeats's imperial rulers, or Louise Glück's speaker's sexual partner.

◆ Does the poet imply that the reader already agrees with his or her preferred value?

Sometimes the poet's preference may be surprising (see Jonson, Lovelace, Whitman, and Glück). The woman poet has to examine the clichés of women's advancement. In these cases, when the poet cannot count on the agreement of the reader, what sort of persuasive means does he or she employ?

Sometimes a poem that seems to express values admired by the poet's contemporaries can later be subject to question. Robert Frost was invited to read his 1942 sonnet "The Gift Outright" at the inauguration of President John F. Kennedy.

◆ What are the patriotic values expressed in the sonnet?

◆ How might they be viewed now by a Native American reader? How do you respond when you read both "with the grain" of the poem and also "against the grain"?

It is a useful exercise to read strongly moral poems from the poet's view and also from a different viewpoint.

◆ What might Lucasta have said back to the man going off to war; or Ben Jonson's addressee back to the poet; or an astronomer back to Whitman?

◆ How might the recipient of Elizabeth Barrett Browning's love-sonnet have felt? (Would you want to be loved "with the passion put to use" of abandoned religious belief?)

◆ What would a believer in original sin make of Ginsberg's "Sunflower Sutra," with its belief in original innocence?

◆ How might the man accused in Heidy Steidlmayer's "Knife-Sharpener's Song" respond to her account of his infidelity?

Dove, though she opposes the slave-holding and slave-murdering Dominican dictator Rafael Trujillo, lets him speak and articulate his motives in order that her reader may get inside his mind. Though finally, in reading these poems, you may come to sympathize with the poet's view, it is useful to position yourself, at least temporarily, on both sides of the question being debated. That way you sharpen your sense of the attitudes being expressed, the values being contested, and the judgments being made.

John Milton (1608 – 1674)
Lycidas

> *In this monody[1] the author bewails a learned friend, unfortunately drowned in his passage from Chester on the Irish seas, 1637. And by occasion foretells the ruin of our corrupted clergy, then in their height.*

Yet once more, O ye laurels, and once more
Ye myrtles brown, with ivy never sere,
I come to pluck your berries harsh and crude,
And with forced fingers rude,
Shatter your leaves before the mellowing year.   5
Bitter constraint, and sad occasion dear,
Compels me to disturb your season due;
For Lycidas is dead, dead ere his prime,
Young Lycidas, and hath not left his peer.
Who would not sing for Lycidas? He knew   10
Himself to sing, and build the lofty rhyme.
He must not float upon his watery bier
Unwept, and welter to the parching wind,
Without the meed of some melodious tear.
    Begin then, sisters of the sacred well°   *muses*   15
That from beneath the seat of Jove doth spring,
Begin, and somewhat loudly sweep the string.
Hence with denial vain, and coy excuse;
So may some gentle Muse°   *poet*
With lucky words favor my destined urn,   20
And as he passes turn,
And bid fair peace be to my sable shroud.
For we were nursed upon the selfsame hill,
Fed the same flock, by fountain, shade, and rill.
    Together both, ere the high lawns appeared   25
Under the opening eyelids of the morn,
We drove afield, and both together heard
What time the grayfly winds her sultry horn,

---

[1]A dirge sung by a single voice.

Battening our flocks with the fresh dews of night,
Oft till the star that rose at evening bright   30
Toward Heaven's descent had sloped his westering wheel.
Meanwhile the rural ditties were not mute,
Tempered to th' oaten flute,
Rough satyrs danced, and fauns with cloven heel
From the glad sound would not be absent long,   35
And old Damoetas² loved to hear our song.
     But O the heavy change, now thou art gone,
Now thou art gone, and never must return!
Thee, shepherd, thee the woods and desert caves,
With wild thyme and the gadding vine o'ergrown,   40
And all their echoes mourn.
The willows and the hazel copses green
Shall now no more be seen,
Fanning their joyous leaves to thy soft lays.
As killing as the canker° to the rose,   *cankerworm*   45
Or taint-worm to the weanling herds that graze,
Or frost to flowers that their gay wardrobe wear,
When first the white thorn blows;°   *blossoms*
Such, Lycidas, thy loss to shepherd's ear.
     Where were ye, nymphs, when the remorseless deep   50
Closed o'er the head of your loved Lycidas?
For neither were ye playing on the steep,
Where your old Bards, the famous Druids lie,
Nor on the shaggy top of Mona high,
Nor yet where Deva spreads her wizard stream:³   55
Ay me! I fondly dream —
Had ye been there — for what could that have done?
What could the Muse⁴ herself that Orpheus bore,
The Muse herself, for her inchanting son
Whom universal Nature did lament,   60
When by the rout that made the hideous roar,
His gory visage down the stream was sent,

---

²A conventional name from pastoral poetry, possibly referring to a Cambridge tutor.

³Mona is the Roman name for the Isle of Anglesey, off the Welsh coast. Deva is the river Dee, which flows into the Irish Sea. Its changes were said to foretell good or ill for England and Wales.

⁴Calliope, the muse of epic poetry. Her son, Orpheus, was slain by Thracian women, and his head cast into the river Hebrus.

Down the swift Hebrus to the Lesbian shore?
    Alas! What boots° it with uncessant care   *profits*
To tend the homely slighted shepherd's trade,   65
And strictly meditate the thankless Muse?
Were it not better done as others use,
To sport with Amaryllis in the shade,
Or with the tangles of Neaera's hair?[5]
Fame is the spur that the clear spirit doth raise   70
(That last infirmity of noble mind)
To scorn delights, and live laborious days;
But the fair guerdon° when we hope to find,   *reward*
And think to burst out into sudden blaze,
Comes the blind Fury[6] with th' abhorrèd shears,   75
And slits the thin spun life. "But not the praise,"
Phoebus° replied, and touched my trembling   *Apollo, god of*
    ears;   *poetic inspiration*
"Fame is no plant that grows on mortal soil,
Nor in the glistering foil
Set off to th' world, nor in broad rumor lies,   80
But lives and spreads aloft by those pure eyes,
And perfect witness of all-judging Jove;
As he pronounces lastly on each deed,
Of so much fame in Heaven expect thy meed."
    O fountain Arethuse,[7] and thou honored flood,   85
Smooth-sliding Mincius crowned with vocal reeds,
That strain I heard was of a higher mood.
But now my oat° proceeds,   *oaten-pipe song*
And listens to the herald of the sea°   *Triton*
That came in Neptune's plea.   90
He asked the waves, and asked the felon winds,
"What hard mishap hath doomed this gentle swain?"
And questioned every gust of rugged wings
That blows from off each beakèd promontory;
They knew not of his story,   95
And sage Hippotades° their answer brings,   *god of winds*
That not a blast was from his dungeon strayed,
The air was calm, and on the level brine,

---

[5]Amaryllis and Neaera: conventional names for shepherdesses.

[6]Atropos, not one of the Furies, but the Fate who cuts the thread of life.

[7]Arethusa was a nymph pursued by Alpheus. She fled under the sea to Sicily, where she came up as a fountain.

Sleek Panope° with all her sisters played. *sea nymph*
It was that fatal and perfidious bark 100
Built in th' eclipse, and rigged with curses dark,
That sunk so low that sacred head of thine.
    Next Camus,[8] reverend sire, went footing slow,
His mantle hairy, and his bonnet sedge,
Inwrought with figures dim, and on the edge 105
Like to that sanguine flower inscribed with woe.[9]
"Ah! who hath reft," quoth he, "my dearest pledge?"
Last came and last did go
The pilot of the Galilean lake,° *Saint Peter*
Two massy keys he bore of metals twain 110
(The golden opes, the iron shuts amain).
He shook his mitered locks, and stern bespake:
"How well could I have spared for thee, young swain,
Enow of such as for their bellies' sake,
Creep and intrude, and climb into the fold! 115
Of other care they little reckoning make,
Than how to scramble at the shearers' feast,
And shove away the worthy bidden guest.
Blind mouths! That scarce themselves know how to hold
A sheep-hook, or have learned aught else the least 120
That to the faithful herdsman's art belongs!
What recks it them? What need they? They are sped;
And when they list, their lean and flashy songs
Grate on their scrannel° pipes of wretched straw. *meager*
The hungry sheep look up, and are not fed, 125
But swoln with wind, and the rank mist they draw,
Rot inwardly, and foul contagion spread,
Besides what the grim wolf with privy paw
Daily devours apace, and nothing said.
But that two-handed engine at the door 130
Stands ready to smite once, and smite no more."[10]
    Return, Alpheus,° the dread voice is past, *(see note 7)*
That shrunk thy streams; return, Sicilian muse,
And call the vales, and bid them hither cast
Their bells and flowerets of a thousand hues. 135

---

[8]God of the river Cam, representing Cambridge University.

[9]The hyacinth, supposedly marked with the Greek cry of lamentation, "aiai."

[10]Milton has in mind some instrument of retribution that will punish the corrupt clergy.

Ye valleys low where the mild whispers use,
Of shades and wanton winds, and gushing brooks,
On whose fresh lap the swart star[11] sparely looks,
Throw hither all your quaint enameled eyes,
That on the green turf suck the honeyed showers,   140
And purple all the ground with vernal flowers.
Bring the rathe° primrose that forsaken dies,   *early*
The tufted crow-toe, and pale jessamine,
The white pink, and the pansy freaked° with jet, *dappled*
The glowing violet,   145
The musk-rose, and the well attired woodbine.
With cowslips wan that hang the pensive head,
And every flower that sad embroidery wears:
Bid amaranthus all his beauty shed,
And daffadillies fill their cups with tears,   150
To strew the laureate hearse where Lycid lies.
For so to interpose a little ease,
Let our frail thoughts dally with false surmise.
Ay me! Whilst thee the shores and sounding seas
Wash far away, where'er thy bones are hurled,   155
Whether beyond the stormy Hebrides,
Where thou perhaps under the whelming tide
Visit'st the bottom of the monstrous world;
Or whether thou, to our moist vows denied,
Sleep'st by the fable of Bellerus old,   160
Where the great vision of the guarded mount
Looks toward Namancos and Bayona's hold;[12]
Look homeward angel now, and melt with ruth:
And, O ye dolphins, waft the hapless youth.
   Weep no more, woeful shepherds, weep no more, 165
For Lycidas your sorrow is not dead,
Sunk though he be beneath the watery floor,
So sinks the day-star° in the ocean bed,   *sun*
And yet anon repairs his drooping head,
And tricks° his beams, and with new-spangled ore, *dresses* 170
Flames in the forehead of the morning sky:

---

[11]Sirius, the Dog Star, associated with the hot days of late summer.
[12]Bellerus is a giant said to be buried at Land's End in Cornwall. St. Michael's Mount is also in Cornwall. The angel looks toward Namancos and Bayona on the Spanish coast.

So Lycidas sunk low, but mounted high,
Through the dear might of him that walked the waves,
Where other groves, and other streams along,
With nectar pure his oozy locks he laves,   175
And hears the unexpressive° nuptial song,   *inexpressible*
In the blest kingdoms meek of joy and love.
There entertain him all the saints above,
In solemn troops and sweet societies
That sing, and singing in their glory move,   180
And wipe the tears forever from his eyes.
Now, Lycidas, the shepherds weep no more;
Henceforth thou art the genius° of the shore,   *protective deity*
In thy large recompense, and shalt be good
To all that wander in that perilous flood.   185
        Thus sang the uncouth swain to th' oaks and rills,
While the still morn went out with sandals gray;
He touched the tender stops of various quills,
With eager thought warbling his Doric° lay: *rustic*
And now the sun had stretched out all the hills,   190
And now was dropped into the western bay;
At last he rose, and twitched his mantle blue:
Tomorrow to fresh woods, and pastures new.

BEN JONSON (1572 – 1637)
Still to Be Neat

Still to be neat, still to be dressed,
As you were going to a feast;
Still to be powdered, still perfumed;
Lady, it is to be presumed,
Though art's hid causes are not found,
All is not sweet, all is not sound.

Give me a look, give me a face
That makes simplicity a grace;
Robes loosely flowing, hair as free;
Such sweet neglect more taketh me
Then all th' adulteries of art.
They strike mine eyes, but not my heart.

RICHARD LOVELACE (1618 – 1657)
To Lucasta, Going to the Wars

Tell me not, sweet, I am unkind
That from the nunnery
Of thy chaste breast and quiet mind,
To war and arms I fly.

True, a new mistress now I chase,
The first foe in the field;
And with a stronger faith embrace
A sword, a horse, a shield.

Yet this inconstancy is such
As you too shall adore;
I could not love thee, dear, so much,
Loved I not honor more.

PHILLIS WHEATLEY (1753 – 1784)
On Being Brought from Africa to America

'Twas mercy brought me from my pagan land,
Taught my benighted soul to understand
That there's a God, that there's a Savior too:
Once I redemption neither sought nor knew.
Some view our sable race with scornful eye,
"Their color is a diabolic die.°"   *dye*
Remember, Christians, Negros, black as Cain,
May be refined, and join th' angelic train.

ELIZABETH BARRETT BROWNING (1806 – 1861)
How Do I Love Thee?

How do I love thee? Let me count the ways.
I love thee to the depth and breadth and height
My soul can reach, when feeling out of sight
For the ends of Being and ideal Grace.
I love thee to the level of everyday's
Most quiet need, by sun and candle-light.
I love thee freely, as men strive for Right;
I love thee purely, as they turn from Praise.
I love thee with the passion put to use

In my old griefs, and with my childhood's faith.
I love thee with a love I seemed to lose
With my lost saints — I love thee with the breath,
Smiles, tears, of all my life! — and, if God choose,
I shall but love thee better after death.

WALT WHITMAN (1819 – 1892)
When I Heard the Learn'd Astronomer

When I heard the learn'd astronomer,
When the proofs, the figures, were ranged in columns before me,
When I was shown the charts and diagrams, to add, divide, and
    measure them,
When I sitting heard the astronomer where he lectured with
    much applause in the lecture-room,
How soon unaccountable I became tired and sick,
Till rising and gliding out I wander'd off by myself,
In the mystical moist night-air, and from time to time,
Look'd up in perfect silence at the stars.

WILLIAM BUTLER YEATS (1865 – 1939)
Meru[1]

Civilisation is hooped together, brought
Under a rule, under the semblance of peace
By manifold illusion; but man's life is thought,
And he, despite his terror, cannot cease
Ravening through century after century,
Ravening, raging, and uprooting that he may come
Into the desolation of reality:
Egypt and Greece, good-bye, and good-bye, Rome!
Hermits upon Mount Meru or Everest,
Caverned in night under the drifted snow,
Or where that snow and winter's dreadful blast
Beat down upon their naked bodies, know
That day brings round the night, that before dawn
His glory and his monuments are gone.

---

[1]In Hindu mythology, Meru is a sacred mountain at the center of the world. It is
the home of Vishnu, the god who preserves humanity.

ROBERT FROST (1874 – 1963)

The Gift Outright

The land was ours before we were the land's.
She was our land more than a hundred years
Before we were her people. She was ours
In Massachusetts, in Virginia,
But we were England's, still colonials,
Possessing what we still were unpossessed by,
Possessed by what we now no more possessed.
Something we were withholding made us weak
Until we found it was ourselves
We were withholding from our land of living,
And forthwith found salvation in surrender.
Such as we were we gave ourselves outright
(The deed of gift was many deeds of war)
To the land vaguely realizing westward,
But still unstoried, artless, unenhanced,
Such as she was, such as she would become.

ALLEN GINSBERG (1926 – 1997)

Sunflower Sutra[1]

I walked on the banks of the tincan banana dock and sat down
    under the huge shade of a Southern Pacific locomotive to
    look at the sunset over the box house hills and cry.
Jack Kerouac[2] sat beside me on a busted rusty iron pole,
    companion, we thought the same thoughts of the soul,   5
    bleak and blue and sad-eyed, surrounded by the gnarled
    steel roots of trees of machinery.
The oily water on the river mirrored the red sky, sun sank on top
    of final Frisco peaks, no fish in that stream, no hermit in
    those mounts, just ourselves rheumy-eyed and hungover   10
    like old bums on the riverbank, tired and wily.
Look at the Sunflower, he said, there was a dead gray shadow
    against the sky, big as a man, sitting dry on top of a pile of
    ancient sawdust —

---

[1]Buddhist religious text.
[2]Jack Kerouac (1922–1969), friend of Ginsberg's and author of *On the Road* and other autobiographical novels.

— I rushed up enchanted — it was my first sunflower,   15
    memories of Blake[3] — my visions — Harlem
and Hells of the Eastern rivers, bridges, clanking Joes Greasy
    Sandwiches, dead baby carriages, black treadless tires
    forgotten and unretreaded, the poem of the riverbank,
    condoms & pots, steel knives, nothing stainless, only the   20
    dank muck and the razor sharp artifacts passing into the
    past —
and the gray Sunflower poised against the sunset, crackly bleak
    and dusty with the smut and smog and smoke of olden
    locomotives in its eye —   25
corolla of bleary spikes pushed down and broken like a battered
    crown, seeds fallen out of its face, soon-to-be-toothless
    mouth of sunny air, sunrays obliterated on its hairy head like
    a dried wire spiderweb,
leaves stuck out like arms out of the stem, gestures from the   30
    sawdust root, broke pieces of plaster fallen out of the black
    twigs, a dead fly in its ear,
Unholy battered old thing you were, my sunflower O my soul, I
    loved you then!
The grime was no man's grime but death and human   35
    locomotives,
all that dress of dust, that veil of darkened railroad skin, that smog
    of cheek, that eyelid of black mis'ry, that sooty hand or
    phallus or protuberance of artificial worse-than-dirt —
    industrial — modern — all that civilization spotting your   40
    crazy golden crown —
and those blear thoughts of death and dusty loveless eyes and ends
    and withered roots below, in the home-pile of sand and
    sawdust, rubber dollar bills, skin of machinery, the guts and
    innards of the weeping coughing car, the empty lonely   45
    tincans with their rusty tongues alack, what more could I
    name, the smoked ashes of some cock cigar, the cunts of
    wheelbarrows and the milky breasts of cars, wornout asses
    out of chairs & sphincters of dynamos — all these
entangled in your mummied roots — and you there standing   50
    before me in the sunset, all your glory in your form!
A perfect beauty of a sunflower! a perfect excellent lovely
    sunflower existence! a sweet natural eye to the new hip

---

[3]William Blake (1757–1827), English poet and author of "Ah! Sun-flower."
Ginsberg in 1948 had had a vision in which he heard Blake's voice reciting his poems.

moon, woke up alive and excited grasping in the sunset
   shadow sunrise golden monthly breeze!   55
How many flies buzzed round you innocent of your grime, while
   you cursed the heavens of the railroad and your flower soul?
Poor dead flower? when did you forget you were a flower? when
   did you look at your skin and decide you were an impotent
   dirty old locomotive? the ghost of a locomotive? the   60
   specter and shade of a once powerful mad American
   locomotive?
You were never no locomotive, Sunflower, you were a sunflower!
And you Locomotive, you are a locomotive, forget me not!
So I grabbed up the skeleton thick sunflower and stuck it at my 65
   side like a scepter,
and deliver my sermon to my soul, and Jack's soul too, and anyone
   who'll listen,
— We're not our skin of grime, we're not our dread bleak dusty
   imageless locomotive, we're all beautiful golden sun-   70
   flowers inside, we're blessed by our own seed & golden hairy
   naked accomplishment-bodies growing into mad black
   formal sunflowers in the sunset, spied on by our eyes under
   the shadow of the mad locomotive riverbank sunset Frisco
   hilly tincan evening sitdown vision.   75

LOUISE GLÜCK (b. 1943)
Mock Orange

It is not the moon, I tell you.
It is these flowers
lighting the yard.

I hate them.
I hate them as I hate sex,
the man's mouth
sealing my mouth, the man's
paralyzing body —

and the cry that always escapes,
the low, humiliating
premise of union —

In my mind tonight
I hear the question and pursuing answer
fused in one sound

that mounts and mounts and then
is split into the old selves,
the tired antagonisms. Do you see?
We were made fools of.
And the scent of mock orange
drifts through the window.

How can I rest?
How can I be content
when there is still
that odor in the world?

RITA DOVE (b. 1952)
Parsley[1]

1. *The Cane Fields*

There is a parrot imitating spring
in the palace, its feathers parsley green.
Out of the swamp the cane appears

to haunt us, and we cut it down. El General
searches for a word; he is all the world   5
there is. Like a parrot imitating spring,

we lie down screaming as rain punches through
and we come up green. We cannot speak an R —
out of the swamp, the cane appears

and then the mountain we call in whispers *Katalina*.[2]   10
The children gnaw their teeth to arrowheads.
There is a parrot imitating spring.

El General has found his word: *perejil*.
Who says it, lives. He laughs, teeth shining
out of the swamp. The cane appears   15

in our dreams, lashed by wind and streaming.
And we lie down. For every drop of blood
there is a parrot imitating spring.
Out of the swamp the cane appears.

---

[1]Dove's note: "*Parsley:* On October 2, 1937, Rafael Trujillo (1891–1961), dictator of the Dominican Republic, ordered 20,000 blacks killed because they could not roll the letter *r* in *perejil*, the Spanish word for parsley."

[2]Properly "Katarina."

2. The Palace

The word the general's chosen is parsley.   20
It is fall, when thoughts turn
to love and death; the general thinks
of his mother, how she died in the fall
and he planted her walking cane at the grave
and it flowered, each spring stolidly forming   25
four-star blossoms. The general

pulls on his boots, he stomps to
her room in the palace, the one without
curtains, the one with a parrot
in a brass ring. As he paces he wonders   30
Who can I kill today. And for a moment
the little knot of screams
is still. The parrot, who has traveled

all the way from Australia in an ivory
cage, is, coy as a widow, practising   35
spring. Ever since the morning
his mother collapsed in the kitchen
while baking skull-shaped candies
for the Day of the Dead,[3] the general
has hated sweets. He orders pastries   40
brought up for the bird; they arrive

dusted with sugar on a bed of lace.
The knot in his throat starts to twitch;
he sees his boots the first day in battle
splashed with mud and urine   45
as a soldier falls at his feet amazed —
how stupid he looked! — at the sound
of artillery. *I never thought it would sing*
the soldier said, and died. Now

the general sees the fields of sugar   50
cane, lashed by rain and streaming.
He sees his mother's smile, the teeth
gnawed to arrowheads. He hears
the Haitians sing without R's
as they swing the great machetes: 55
Katalina, they sing, *Katalina,*

---

[3]November 1, the Feast of All Souls.

mi madle, mi amol en muelte.[4] God knows
his mother was no stupid woman; she
could roll an R like a queen. Even
a parrot can roll an R! In the bare room   60
the bright feathers arch in a parody
of greenery, as the last pale crumbs
disappear under the blackened tongue. Someone

calls out his name in a voice
so like his mother's, a startled tear   65
splashes the tip of his right boot.
My mother, my love in death.
The general remembers the tiny green sprigs
men of his village wore in their capes
to honor the birth of a son. He will   70
order many, this time, to be killed

for a single, beautiful word.

HEIDY STEIDLMAYER (b. 1969)
Knife-Sharpener's Song

I said no word of her to him,
nor he of her to me, *oh yes.*

We sharpened down the sliding

hour the knives wooled thick
with rust, *oh yes*; the days grew

small and wider, stripping

words down to their edge —
cutthroat, flashy, without a flaw,

what he did to me, *oh yes.*

Turn by turn, those knives of hers
shone quietly aware, *oh yes,*

not I but she would be the one

he carefully undressed —
but he said no word of her to me

nor I to him of us, *oh yes.*

---

[4]"My mother, my love in death." In the Spanish, the *r*'s have been changed to *l*'s to simulate the Haitians' inability to roll their *r*'s.

10

Poets on Poetry

Poetry as Imagination

Poets have often described — sometimes to themselves, sometimes to others, through letters, essays, or poems — what they believe the art of poetry to be. Poets have the advantage of their hands-on experience of trying to make a poem "come out right" in language — of having to intuit its rhythms, choose its symbols, develop its structures, invent its strategies, map its evolving feelings. But poets also know that something precedes their writing words on a page or chanting lines into the air. The usual name for that something-that-precedes is "imagination" or "conceiving" or, in the past, "fancy," or "invention." In *A Midsummer Night's Dream,* Shakespeare's Theseus begins by describing the poet's imagining eye, and follows that with the poet's capable pen:

> The poet's eye, in a fine frenzy rolling,
> Doth glance from heaven to earth, from earth to heaven;
> And as imagination bodies forth
> The forms of things unknown, the poet's pen
> Turns them to shapes, and gives to airy nothing
> A local habitation and a name.

The poet's conceiving is an inchoate and shadowy process, a contour forming itself in the mind, but often escaping before it can be caught:

"Poetry is a pheasant disappearing into the brush," says Wallace Stevens, in his "Adagia": the poem is the image the brightly feathered bird leaves behind. Percy Bysshe Shelley writes, in *A Defence of Poetry,* that "the mind in creation is as a fading coal which some invisible influence . . . awakens to transitory brightness . . . ; but when composition begins, inspiration is already on the decline, and the most glorious poetry that has ever been communicated to the world is probably a feeble shadow of the original conception of the poet." Like Stevens, Shelley emphasizes the gap between the initial imaginative radiance (the feathered pheasant, the burning coal) and its residue in words. When a poem succeeds, it is because the poet has gradually found for the orig- inal contour a visible and audible form in rhythmic lines and inspired words. Emily Dickinson describes, in "Shall I take thee," the poet's successive attempts to select the right word for the original strong but invisible feeling from among all the words presenting themselves for her inspection:

> Shall I take thee, the Poet said
> To the propounded word?
> Be stationed with the Candidates
> Till I have finer tried —

In spite of all her testing and refining, Dickinson admits that she cannot find the right word by trying; it arrives by itself unexpectedly, like an angelic messenger. Will alone is not enough to make a poem: "Not unto nomination / The Cherubim reveal."

Art's Fictions, Truth's Claims

Since the aim of this book is to acquaint you with lyric poetry, we should examine what poets have said about lyric. When the felt, invisible contour takes on visible form, what claim does this form — the poem that we read or hear — have on us? From Plato on, listeners have been suspi- cious of the speech that is art, because it seems to purvey as truth what is in fact fiction. In "Because I could not stop for Death," Emily Dickinson, to convey her realization of the horror of death, invents a story of a gentle- man coming in a carriage to lead her to her grave. Art-speech presents a fiction that seems nonetheless to make defiant truth-claims: "The Imagi- nation," said Keats (in a letter of November 22, 1817), "may be compared to Adam's dream — he awoke and found it truth." Should we trust or distrust fictive creation? We have been trained by our schooling and by newspapers to read for factual information-retrieval, but that purpose is insufficient for poetry. What, then, are we reading for?

Philip Sidney offers, in his *Defence of Poesie,* the best defense of creative fiction in poetry, saying, "The poet nothing lieth, for he nothing affirmeth." Poetry, in this view, is a proffered hypothesis, a way of saying, "Suppose you look at it this way." Shelley, in his *Defence,* says of poets, "Their language is vitally metaphorical; that is, it marks the before unapprehended relations of things." Blake, for instance, brings together in "London" the "before unapprehended relations" among the poor, the church, the military, and the court, seeing

> How the Chimney-sweeper's cry
> Every blackning Church appalls;
> And the hapless Soldier's sigh
> Runs in blood down Palace walls.

It is through the vitality of its hitherto-unapprehended metaphors — such as the sigh of blood, here — that poetry exerts its imaginative claim on us. Shelley is careful to claim that the language of poets is *vitally* metaphorical because ordinary language, of course, is full of metaphors — trite and tired ones. The truth of metaphor, as used by poets, lies in its being the most exact and precise description in words of an inner state of affairs. If poetry is the history of feeling, as Wordsworth said in his "Preface to *Lyrical Ballads,*" it is also, in his words, "the science of feeling." Every science asserts the precision of its results; so does poetry. We ask of every poem, as it offers its hypothesis to our eye and ear, whether it has rendered with exactness the sequence of feelings it embodies.

Poetry as Song

Although textbooks sometimes define poetry as the form of speech that contains metaphors, similes, hyperbole, allusion, and so on, in fact all these figures of speech are to be found in any common political speech or newspaper editorial. Other books define lyric poetry as the most compressed form of language — as if they have never seen a political slogan ("I like Ike") or heard a commercial jingle. Poetry (long and short, epic and lyric) is only one of the many human forms employing original imagination and striking language (novels, plays, and proverbs are others; so, often, are advertising and cartoons). If neither its use of figures of speech nor its compression of language differentiates lyric poetry from other literary genres, what is its distinctive character?

There have been many answers to this question, but they all include elements of musicality — a flexible rhythm, a volatility of tone. For Wordsworth in "The Solitary Reaper," poetry is intrinsically song, an instance of memorable harmony. Even though the reaper's language and subject matter are unintelligible to the poet, he bears her music in his heart long after his departure:

> Whate'er the theme, the Maiden sang
> As if her song could have no ending;
> I saw her singing at her work,
> And o'er the sickle bending; —
> I listened, motionless and still;
> And, as I mounted up the hill,
> The music in my heart I bore,
> Long after it was heard no more.

The singing woman, but now in exotic form, with power beyond the human, appears in Coleridge's "Kubla Khan":

> A damsel with a dulcimer
> In a vision once I saw:
> It was an Abyssinian maid,
> And on her dulcimer she played,
> Singing of Mount Abora.
>
> (37 – 41)

The poet yearns to revive within himself her "symphony and song" (but not her subject matter, a mountain he has never seen). And in a twentieth-century version of the singing woman, Wallace Stevens, in "The Idea of Order at Key West," compares the meaningless noise of the sea uttered by its *genius loci,* the spirit of the place, to the more sublime human creation of articulate song by a woman walking on a beach:

> She sang beyond the genius of the sea.
> The water never formed to mind or voice,
>
> . . . . .
>
> [But] what she sang was uttered word by word.

If poetry is song — a song that can even be unintelligible, too far away to be heard accurately, or remote in its concerns — then the subject matter of lyric is less important than its harmony, and musical invention is the supreme test of the poet. It is certain that without a compelling rhythm, no poem can survive.

Poetry as Words

Besides requiring imagination and an intuitive rhythm, lyric poetry requires words. Like Stevens, Emily Dickinson insists, in "The Brain − is wider than the Sky − ," that the most God-like power of the brain is to turn sound into syllables, meaninglessness into language. God makes sound, but only the poet can make syllables. The whole creation can indeed fit, with its sights and sounds, inside any human brain, but when the poet brings the noise of the world into the meaningful syllables of language, she becomes a creator rivalling God:

> The Brain is just the weight of God −
> For − Heft them − Pound for Pound −
> And they will differ − if they do −
> As Syllable from Sound −

By this test, the best syllable-maker becomes supreme among poets. However, this focus on the smallest building block of language, the phoneme or syllable, is not always a poet's focus when deciding the kind of construction that most distinguishes the poet. When we say "Shakespeare" we mean the whole body of his work, not a single poem. A huge thought-edifice — the achievement of a lifetime devoted to imagination, reflection, and language — is what Stevens praises, in "To an Old Philosopher in Rome," as the accomplishment of the philosopher-poet George Santayana who, at the moment of death, stops and beholds what he has made:

> Total grandeur of a total edifice,
> Chosen by an inquisitor of structures
> For himself. He stops upon this threshold,
> As if the design of all his words takes form
> And frame from thinking and is realized.

The quality of the poet's total *oeuvre* is always a part of our literary evaluation of that poet.

Poetry as an Evolving Structure

The metaphor of "a total edifice" suggests something permanent and static. Although it is true that a poem becomes an object once it is fixed in language, it is also true that when a poem is revived by being read, it takes on its original fluid and cascading form, evolving from one level to another, changing its appearance as it goes. Robert Frost, in "The Figure a Poem Makes," said of the poem that it "begins in delight, it inclines to the impulse, it assumes direction with the first line laid down, it runs a course of lucky events, and ends in a clarification of life — not necessarily a great clarification, such as sects and cults are founded on, but . . . a momentary stay against confusion." Sylvia Plath, focusing — like Frost — on the ever-changing evolution of the poem, imagined it as a stream of tears flowing over a skull and coming to rest in a pool where "fixed stars govern a life" ("Words"). In this way she renders both the poem's inner current of activity and its eventual subsidence into permanent form.

Syllable or stream? Edifice or song? Fading coal or fixed species? Efforts to characterize lyric continue to change over time while remaining revealing in each instance. The most profound recent image of the poem may be the ecological one of A. R. Ammons who, in "Easter Morning," sees a poem as "ripples round the brook's ripplestone." For Ammons, the stone represents the poem's central imaginative or ethical concern: from it, ripples spread out to the environment in ever-widening amplification of its shape. Founding a magazine, Ezra Pound used for its title a metaphor for the poem — a vortex. A vortex, too, has a circular form, but for Pound the poem deepens rather than widens, descending closer and closer to its original feeling or conception and (as it evolves toward its ultimate destination) narrows further and further to its final point of concentrated energy. Poets rarely characterize poems in terms of linear plot: that vectored form belongs principally to prose (dramatic, expository, narrative). A poem does not "get anywhere": it occupies itself with making more profound its apprehension of its originating concern.

Yeats says in a late letter (January 4, 1939) that "man can embody the truth but he cannot know it": only when the abstraction of thought has found a perceptual "body" can it claim authenticity. That body, in the case of the lyric, can often assume a spherical form: Ammons called one of his long poems "Sphere: The Form of a Motion." The elements of the poem, like those of an atom, are always in motion around its nucleus of feeling, and the motion demonstrates its own kinetic energy. Like Ammons, Stevens sees the fundamental shape of a poem as an orb in "A Primitive Like an Orb"; "It is / As if the central poem became the world, / And the world the central poem," so that in the end, the lesser poems compose themselves into a greater one:

Not merely into a whole, but a poem of
The whole, the essential compact of the parts,
The roundness that pulls tight the final ring[.]

The preceding images of poetry are consoling ones, ranging from its individual seraphic syllables to its "total grandeur" as a life-work; they are images of song, of harmony, of metaphorical insight, of inspiration, of the achievement of a spherical or vortical energy. Concepts are always in dispute, but a painting or poem simply is. It establishes an irrefutable presence. "You can refute [the philosopher] Hegel, but not the Saint or the Song of Sixpence," said Yeats, in the letter of 1939 quoted above.

Poetry as a Destructive Force

But there are other views of poetry voiced by its poets, more sinister or threatening ones. A lyric poet such as Plath, alienated to some degree from society not only by a rare gift but also by a necessary urge to truthful utterance, fears her own drive, as her words become the galloping hoof-beats that will carry her into danger (as they do in "Words" and "Ariel"). "The blood-jet is poetry," Plath said in "Kindness"; "[t]here is no stopping it." The poet's gift can be a burden, even a curse; the poet can become a *poète maudit* (an "accursèd poet," one who lives outside society) when asserting moral positions condemned by family and friends. And the poem can frequently feel oppressive to the poet who conceives it: "Poetry is a destructive force," says Stevens (in the lyric by that name), describing the poem as a beast lodged in his heart: "A lion, an ox in his breast." Suddenly the image reverses itself: "He is like a man / In the body of a violent beast." The devastations of emotion are felt as the poem reveals, even while it may resist, its shames or its passions. Dickinson, too, felt the dangers of words, representing herself as "Vesuvius at home" ("Volcanoes be in Sicily"). The volcano is secretive, but his "projects pink" will one day erupt:

The reticent volcano keeps
His never-slumbering plan;
Confided are his projects pink
To no precarious man.

The lethal molten core of the volcano resembles the imaginative turmoil in the creative mind; it is Shelley's fiery coal magnified beyond measure.

The Idea of Lyric

Poets present the idea of lyric from many different angles, depending on the work at hand. In "The Figure a Poem Makes," Frost bluntly defines a poem emotionally: "No tears in the writer, no tears in the reader." Stevens urges, in his "Adagia," a necessary tether of art to life: "Reality is only the base. But it is the base." After a series of negative definitions ("My God, a verse is not a crown, / No point of honour, or gay suit," and so on), George Herbert finds, in "The Quidditie," that poetry is the means by which he comes closest to God: "But it is that which while I use / I am with Thee, and most take all." John Berryman, in his *Dream Songs,* views poetry as the place where the Id is free to express itself in ways disapproved of by the ordinary world. Some poets expressly emphasize (as Berryman does in his title) the song-like or playful nature of poetry; others place more weight on its intellectual power. Wordsworth's most famous passage on the intellectual power of words (*The Prelude* V, 597–607) praises their creation of a "transparent veil" of words through which we can see — in an imaginatively transfigured way — all of Nature, including its invisible winds, its Platonic Forms, and its material substances:

> Visionary power
> Attends the motions of the viewless winds,
> Embodied in the mystery of words:
> There, darkness makes abode, and all the host
> Of shadowy things work endless changes, — there,
> As in a mansion like their proper home,
> Even forms and substances are circumfused
> By that transparent veil with light divine,
> And, through the turnings intricate of verse,
> Present themselves as objects recognised,
> In flashes, and with glory not their own.

Wordsworth rightly declares that by means of language the elements of nature present themselves as "objects *recognized*." Art does not conceal the elements of reality; it makes them visible.

Why Poetry at All?

Some poets, in spite of their commitment to art, nonetheless wittily confess its annoyances. Marianne Moore begins her poem called "Poetry," "I, too, dislike it." Art exhibits contrivance and willed arrangements;

Moore, a poet who delighted in observation, is asking implicitly, "Why isn't the eye enough?" What is it in the human mind that calls out for a rendition in language of what we have already seen and noted? Wordsworth would answer that the "light divine" of words alchemically alters nature into intelligibility by a language that connects heart and world; and James Merrill, in "Processional," also asserts the alchemical function of language, as

> . . . in three lucky strokes of word golf LEAD
> Once again turns (LOAD, GOAD) to GOLD.

Lyric can be for the poet (and for readers who recognize this use) a precious refuge for secrets that cannot be spoken aloud, and an intimate form of communication. Dickinson, in an unsent poem, "I shall not murmur," closes by saying to her friend "Katie" that she cannot reveal her (unspecified) secret to the people she loves on earth:

> Divulging it would rest my Heart
> But it would ravage theirs –
> Why, Katie, Treason has a Voice
> But mine – dispels – in Tears.

The intimacy of such a poem is closely related to the intimacy of the "familiar" letter (so called because it is a letter to a friend or family member, in contrast to a business letter or other formal letter). In fact, Dickinson's most famous definition of her own poetry declares it to be a letter:

> This is my letter to the World
> That never wrote to Me –

It turns out that by "the World" Dickinson means her fellow Americans of the future, to whom she tells Nature's news. Through my letter, says Dickinson,

> [Nature's] Message is committed
> To Hands I cannot see –
> For love of Her – Sweet – countrymen –
> Judge tenderly – of Me

As we turn Dickinson's page, ours are the "Hands [she could] not see," and it is to our judgment that she submits herself.

Poetry over Time

Definitions of poetry vary not only by metaphor (a spherical shape, ripples round a ripplestone, a letter to the world) but also with historical circumstances. It was not until after the industrial revolution that a poet could say, as William Carlos Williams did in *The Wedge,* that a poem is a "small (or large) machine made of words" — or, as Auden put it in *The Dyer's Hand,* "a verbal contraption." We see a poem anew when we conceive of it as having gears, belts, a motor, or levers; we understand through Williams's startling metaphor that each word of the poem has to be a functional part, that it has to raise or lower a piston, ignite a spark, create a mixture of gases, activate a brake. The dynamic notion of a machine carrying out multiple functions differs roundly from the notion of a poem as a mirror held up to nature (Shakespeare). In a draft preface to his poems, Wilfred Owen, writing during World War I, declared a new locus for poetry: "The poetry is in the pity." In our time, poets might see the poem as a code (comparable to the German Enigma code that English cryptologists broke in World War II). A contemporary poet influenced by the idea of genetic information might define a poem as a set of chromosomes containing all the instructions necessary for the reconstruction of the whole organism in the reader's mind. We can expect history to continue to offer new definitions of poetry, re-imagining both its moral center and its strategic techniques.

Older definitions of poetry, by poets strongly influenced by the concept of prophecy and sacred scripture, have given way in the modern world to a new humility and to efforts at objective, even scientific, statement. "No ideas but in things," cries Williams in "A Sort of a Song," recommending an eye on the object in preference to a Platonic eye turned skyward. But even in the realm of things, the poet struggles to escape the reins of convention. The difficulty of modern poetry comes into being, as the great Romanian poet Paul Celan insisted, in the service of communication. He mentions (in his "Meridian" speech) what the reader is likely to come across in contemporary writing: "difficulties of vocabulary, the faster flow of syntax or a more awakened sense of ellipsis [what is left out]." He continues: "This obscurity, if it is not congenital, has been bestowed on poetry by strangeness and distance (perhaps of its own making) and for the sake of an encounter."[1] As Stevens also thought, the poem "must resist the intelligence / Almost successfully" so as to evoke in the reader the sense of an encounter with a person as yet unknown, an encounter demanding attention, concentration, and sympathy.

---

[1]Paul Celan, in his *Collected Prose,* trans. Rosmarie Waldrop (Riverdale-on-Hudson, NY: Sheep Meadow Press, 1986).

The poetry of the past — "tradition" — is modified, as Eliot said in his essay "Tradition and the Individual Talent," by the "individual talent" of the new poet: when a new poem makes its way into public acceptance, its presence makes every other poem in the collective assemblage of poetry adjust slightly, giving birth to new ideas of what poetry is and does. Poets themselves are always adjusting in this way to their changing circumstances: Keats referred in a letter (October 27, 1818) to the "chameleon" poet, ever sensitive to the varying background colors of his time and place. But no matter what its era, a poem can never become memorable if it does not possess what T. S. Eliot, in his essay on Milton, called "the auditory imagination." In remembering Eliot's remark, the contemporary poet Seamus Heaney says:

> I presume Eliot was thinking here about the cultural depth charges latent in certain words and rhythms, that binding secret between words in poetry that delights not just the ear but the whole backward and abysm of mind and body; thinking of the energies beating in and between words that the poet brings into half-deliberate play; thinking of the relationship between the word as pure vocable, as articulate noise, and the word as etymological occurrence, as symptom of human history, memory and attachments.[2]

Those energies "beating in and between words" in contemporary poetry have sought many ways to manifest themselves, some of them disturbing. In her essay "Some Notes on Silence" (1984), Jorie Graham describes the results when a modern poet confronts the unknown:

> The syntax begins to buckle and bend back and break . . . In the poets that go that way, twisted syntax, breaks against smooth sequence or sense, line breaks of queer kinds, white spaces, interruptions, dashes, overpunctuation, delays, clotted rich diction, obscurity, disorder, ellipses, sentence fragments, digressive strategies — every modulation in certainty — are all tools for storming the walls.

The heartening thing for bewildered readers is that all poetry becomes simpler over time: today's college sophomores read Hopkins's sonnets or Eliot's "The Waste Land" or Moore's bestiary poems more easily than the readers who first experienced these difficult works, because commentaries and teachers have smoothed the path that once seemed so arduous. Poetry, as Eliot once said when speaking of Dante, can communicate when it is only imperfectly understood. The auditory imagination

---

[2]Seamus Heaney, *Finders Keepers: Selected Prose 1971–2001* (New York: Farrar, Straus and Giroux, 2002), 81.

convinces the ear, feelings are aroused almost unknowingly, and the terrain is already half won even before the intellect begins to pose its questions.

The Poet's Audience

To whom is lyric poetry speaking? It has been felt (especially by groups lacking knowledge of the culture from which a poem emerged) that poetry is a coterie possession, appealing only to an elite. Such an idea was forcefully disclaimed by Wordsworth in his "Preface to *Lyrical Ballads*" (a group of poems published jointly by Wordsworth and Coleridge). There, Wordsworth posed the central question (using, as was then common, the word "man" to mean "person"):

> What is a Poet? To whom does he address himself? And what language is to be expected from him? — He is a man speaking to men: a man, it is true, endowed with . . . a more comprehensive soul than [is] supposed to be common among mankind. . . . The knowledge both of the Poet and the Man of science is pleasure; [but] the Man of science seeks truth as a remote and unknown benefactor . . . [while] the Poet, singing a song in which all human beings join with him, rejoices in the presence of truth as our visible friend and hourly companion.

Wordsworth claims that all persons in his audience have felt the emotions treated by his poems — but have lacked the flexibility of language to express them adequately. He continues, "Among the qualities [previously] enumerated as principally conducing to form a Poet, is implied nothing different in kind from other men, but only in degree." It was for that reason that Wordsworth could consider his brother John "a silent poet," and could trust his sister Dorothy's impressions of an incident as firmly as he trusted his own. Emerson, too, declared in his essay "The Poet" that "The poet is representative. He stands among partial men for the complete man, and apprises us not of his wealth but of the commonwealth."

Although most poets would endorse Wordsworth's claim that the subject matter of poetry is the wide range of emotions felt by human beings, and although many poets conveying those emotions in memorable language were received with enthusiasm by the public (and still are), other poets (such as Hopkins and Dickinson) were not fully recognized until decades after their own deaths. And it is equally true that many poets very popular in their own day have sunk into oblivion. Current taste is not always a reliable index to the judgment of posterity. Yet poets depend intimately on recognition by their hearers: "To have great poets," said Whitman in the preface to *Leaves of Grass,* "there must be great audiences too." With a superb confidence, Dickinson wrote (in a letter), "If Fame belongs to me, I cannot escape her." The audience, gradually reshaped by culture — a culture in part formed by the poet — arrives at a place where Whitman is no longer thought "disgraceful" (as Emily Dickinson believed) or "a scoundrel" (as Hopkins had heard) but rather one of the major poets of his era. A faith that audiences are ultimately available (if at the moment invisible) strengthens poets: "I think," said the young and frail Keats, "that I shall be among the English Poets after my death" (letter of October 14, 1818). He was right. Elizabeth Barrett Browning, in her novel-in-verse *Aurora Leigh,* summed up the relation of the poet to renown:

> What the poet writes,
> He writes: mankind accepts it, if it suits,
> And that's success: if not, the poem's passed
> From hand to hand, and yet from hand to hand,
> Until the unborn snatch it, crying out
> In pity on their fathers' being so dull,
> And that's success too.

Poetry and Style

Poets (like composers, like painters and sculptors, like choreographers and all other artists) love form, because, like any other technique (such as playing the flute or playing tennis) when mastered it releases the self into free activity. Young poets learn form by imitation: before he was "Berryman" the young John Berryman imitated Shakespeare, Hopkins, Yeats, and Auden. By writing in all these styles, he accumulated in youth a repertoire of linguistic and symbolic possibility that in maturity enabled him to invent the unique language of his "dream songs." But, depending on the vicissitudes of history, the sort of form that appeals to one poet may appear indefensible to another: Milton vigorously rejected rhyme in favor of blank verse for *Paradise Lost;* later, however, John Keats, revolting against Milton's Christian severity, said of Milton, "Life to him would be death to me" (letter of September 17–27, 1819). Milton had dismissed classical mythology and pursued a Latinate diction; Keats loved "the beautiful mythology of Greece" and said "English ought to be kept up" (letter of September 21, 1819). Seamus Heaney, after writing a broad English pentameter for some time in his youth, found that he wanted a thinner, "Northern" music, and for a time adopted short lines. Some poets rhyme, others do not; some like a conspicuous rhythm, while others prefer more subtle effects. In reading poems, as in looking at paintings or listening to music, you have to be willing, for a while, to assent to the artist's style, to see the angle of vision embodied by that style; then you can decide, if you wish, not to like it (or at least, not at the moment). Hopkins said, in a memorable judgment, that Browning was like a man getting up to speak with his mouth full of bread and cheese. You, too, have a right to have an opinion of a poet's style. But make it a provisional one; your taste may well change over time.

The true argument for form of any sort is that it gives joy. Forms and styles are infinitely variable: any one of them causes instant happiness when it succeeds. Nobody can read E. E. Cummings's little joke on the pliability of form (in a grasshopper's motions) without feeling an exhilaration as the grasshopper's name is rearranged until, when he stops, it becomes fixed in its iconic form as "grasshopper." To borrow and adapt an older form can be exhilarating: Shelley and Yeats and Heaney take up Dante's *terza rima* (formed of interwoven rhyming tercets), and modify it to fit their own language and possibilities of rhyme. Poets (from classical times on) have liked to make a poem into a graphic shape — as Herbert constructed his poem "Easter Wings" so that it looks on the page like two sets of wings, or as Apollinaire wrote a drooping mouse's tail. In short, in all languages, poets have experimented with the kinds of play that their language will accommodate. Sometimes the play is light, sometimes serious. To Frost, in "Two Tramps in Mud Time," poetry was ultimately "play with mortal stakes."

All poems, in all styles, desire communication with a reader. Paul Celan said, on receiving a prize:

> A poem, being an instance of language, hence essentially dialogue, may be a letter in a bottle thrown out to sea with the — not always strong — hope that it may somehow wash up somewhere, perhaps on a shoreline of the heart.[3]

The letter from the heart of the poet, made buoyant by the bottle of form, is sent off, in hope, to an unknown shoreline. Only the watcher by that shoreline decides which bottle to retrieve, and whether to read the letter within. When the letter is read responsively, the poem — and the emotions of its vanished author — are revived, and the longed-for circuit of dialogue is complete.

---

[3]Paul Celan, "Speech on the Occasion of Receiving the Literature Prize of the Free Hanseatic City of Bremen," in his *Collected Prose,* trans. Rosmarie Waldrop (Riverdale-on-Hudson, NY: Sheep Meadow Press, 1986), 34.

II

WRITING ABOUT POETRY

11

Writing about Poems

Basic Principles

In writing about a poem, the most important thing to remember is that a poem is not an essay or a "message," it is a thing imagined, an artwork like a piece of music or a painting or a dance. Your first task is to see how the theme of the work is being imagined: how the literal statement of the poet's feeling has been transformed. After that, you can experience the poem as you hear a piece of music or see a dance, as something unfolding itself in **time**, with a beginning, middle, and end. Or, you can see it from afar in the way you see a painting (or from above as you might see a terrain from an airplane) — as a **space** full of things and "colors" set in relation to each other. Both of these ways of seeing are indispensable.

Considered as pieces extending themselves over time, poems have a "plot" — not so much one of events as one of feelings. A poem might begin in despair and rise toward hope; or might begin in hope and end in despair. A good question to begin with, when reading a poem as a series of events in time, is how the place you find yourself in at the end is different from the place you found yourself in at the beginning. If you take stock of Z, where you end up, and A, where you began, you are likely to be able to plot the B, F, O, and W that lie between.

And considered as a space where parts are arranged in relation to each other, poems have a configuration, just as paintings do: the poet may contrast one part to another (as painters put light against shade), or set one part above another in a hierarchy, or may create an imbalance by which twelve lines are "outweighed" by a closing couplet. A good question to begin with, when reading a poem as a spatial arrangement, is what parts it falls into and how they relate to each other in size, feeling-tone, and language.

A Brief Example

Let us take a brief lyric by Robert Herrick as an example of how we might approach a poem. We must of course read it whole before saying anything, since we can't really estimate the beginning until we have seen the end. And reading it whole means thinking about the title as well:

ROBERT HERRICK (1591 – 1674)
Divination by a Daffodil

When a daffodil I see
Hanging down his head towards me,
Guess I may what I must be:
First, I shall decline my head;
Secondly, I shall be dead;
Lastly, safely burièd.

We can say, at first reading, that the poet compares himself, in his mortality, to a transient natural object. This is not a new idea. What has Herrick done to turn it into a poem? How has he newly imagined this theme?

He has, first of all, made the commonplace act of seeing a flower into an act of "divination." In classical times, priests "divined" the future by examining the entrails of a sacrificed animal. Herrick transfers this bloody act to something light and beautiful and glancing when he chooses, as his **symbolic object**, the daffodil (with its characteristic drooping head). Second, Herrick doesn't begin with the comparison of his fate to that of the daffodil — he might have said, "When a daffodil I spy, / I know that I, like it, shall die." Instead, he divides his poem into **two parts**: he reserves the comparison to the second half of the **single-sentence** poem, leaving us to guess, as we read the first half, what he might be going to divine from his daffodil.

When you note the general metrical scheme of this poem[1] — "**strong** weak / **strong** weak / **strong** weak / **strong**" — you can see that the author wanted the first word of the line to bear emphasis, but not really for the purposes of the first half (which could equally well have read "weak **strong** / weak **strong**," etc.: "A daffodil appears to me; / His head is hanging down, and we / Can guess from that what we must be"). The real purpose of the meter is clear when we arrive at the second half of the poem: it is to give weight to "*First* . . . / *Secondly* . . . / *Lastly*," which ring with inexorable emphasis in summoning up the last stages of life: illness, death, and burial. When you examine the **rhyme** (**aaabbb**) you see that it possesses the same inevitability in the second half: the relatively uninteresting rhymes of the first half (**see, me, be**) are supplanted by the death-knell of **head, dead, burièd**.

Once you have studied the **symbolic imagination**, the **words**, the **syntax of the sentences**,[2] the poem's **division into parts**, and the **rhyme and rhythm**,[3] you are prepared to make a sketch of the "drama" of the poem — that is, to see its <u>beginning</u>, <u>middle</u>, and <u>end</u> as elements in an unfolding of human emotion. Someone is speaking the words of the poem, and that someone is now you; lyrics are designed as scripts for performance (not by an actor; by the reader). Speak the poem as if it were you who had been compelled into speech by something that had upset your equilibrium — otherwise you would have had no reason to break into words. Then try to imagine the "backstory" behind your utterance. What was happening to you before the poem began that makes you speak in this way? This is where you must use your imagination. Presumably Herrick has often seen daffodils, but something has recently happened — a sense of aging or of approaching death — that makes this daffodil into an emblem he uses to divine his future. Interestingly, though Herrick was a clergyman, he makes no mention in this poem of an afterlife, choosing to see himself in purely material terms, as another living being on a par with an unremarkable flower. On the other hand, his method in the poem — divining a message from a natural object — is very much a religious method (as his title suggests), by which man reads messages from God in the works of God's creation. Seventeenth-century poetry is full of such "messages" drawn from natural things and events.

---

[1] For more on meter, see the appendix "On Prosody," pages 653–68.

[2] For more on words and sentences, see Chapter 5, "The Play of Language," pages 155–57.

[3] For more on rhyme and rhythm, see pages 78–86 in Chapter 3, "Poems as Pleasure," and pages 656–68 in the appendix "On Prosody."

To sum up: Herrick has made his theme — man's mortality — into a poem by imagining that one can divine one's fate from a flower; by arranging a perfect spatial symmetry (three lines each) to flower and man; and by letting us hear, after the inoffensive first three lines, the heavy tread of his own death announcement.

A Longer Example

When you have seen one way of treating a flower, it puts other ways — especially those from other centuries — into sharper relief. Suppose that, having seen Herrick's poem on daffodils, you now turn to study a poem on daffodils by William Wordsworth, "I Wandered Lonely as a Cloud."

WILLIAM WORDSWORTH (1770 – 1850)
I Wandered Lonely as a Cloud

I wandered lonely as a cloud
That floats on high o'er vales and hills,
When all at once I saw a crowd,
A host, of golden daffodils;
Beside the lake, beneath the trees,
Fluttering and dancing in the breeze.

Continuous as the stars that shine
And twinkle on the milky way,
They stretched in never-ending line
Along the margin of a bay:
Ten thousand saw I at a glance,
Tossing their heads in sprightly dance.

The waves beside them danced; but they
Outdid the sparkling waves in glee;
A poet could not but be gay,
In such a jocund company;
I gazed — and gazed — but little thought
What wealth the show to me had brought:

For oft, when on my couch I lie
In vacant or in pensive mood,
They flash upon that inward eye
Which is the bliss of solitude;
And then my heart with pleasure fills,
And dances with the daffodils.

After you have spent some time studying the poem (and have noticed that all its lines have four beats), your notebook might look like this:

I wandered lonely as a cloud	a	Speaker <u>lonely</u>; why is he like a cloud?	4
That floats on high o'er vales and hills,	b	Natural scene stretched out, hills and valleys	4
When all at once I saw a crowd,	a	<u>crowd</u>: word generally used of people	4
A host, of golden daffodils;	b	<u>host</u>: armies, but here flowers	4
Beside the lake, beneath the trees,	c	Closer focus than vales and hills	4
Fluttering and dancing in the breeze.	c	Can flowers <u>dance</u>? aren't they rooted?	4

Continuous as the stars that shine
And twinkle on the milky way,
They stretched in never-ending line
Along the margin of a bay:

Ten thousand saw I at a glance,

Tossing their heads in sprightly dance.

Much further focus — up to stars
Difference between <u>shine</u> and <u>twinkle</u>?
Exaggeration, "never-ending" like stars
First "beside" the lake; now entire margin
Exaggeration again; and <u>saw</u> becomes <u>a</u> glance
Daffodils = people, having "heads" they "toss"

The waves beside them danced; but they
Outdid the sparkling waves in glee;
A poet could not but be gay,
In such a jocund company;
I gazed — and gazed — but little thought
What wealth the show to me had brought:

Waves now like people too, dancing
Flowers have feelings: <u>glee</u>
Wasn't he *lonely* when he started?
<u>company</u>; he's not alone anymore
<u>saw</u> > <u>glance</u> > <u>gazed and gazed</u>
<u>golden</u> (l.4) = <u>wealth</u>; <u>show</u>, not <u>company</u> now

For oft, when on my couch I lie

In vacant or in pensive mood,
They flash upon that inward eye
Which is the bliss of solitude;
And then my heart with pleasure fills,

And dances with the daffodils.

<u>oft</u>: past anecdote over, now present tense
Difference between <u>vacant</u> and <u>pensive</u>?
<u>flash</u>; not <u>dance</u> or <u>flutter</u> or <u>toss</u>: why?
<u>solitude</u>: different from first <u>lonely</u>?
Earlier, <u>eye</u> (outward and inward); now <u>heart</u>?
Same rhyme-sound as in stanza 1

Everyone's first notebook jottings are somewhat idiosyncratic. If you decide to think first about **words**, several in the poem would send you to a dictionary to check out etymologies and different connotations. Poets — since words are their stock-in-trade — always have a very specific sense of the aura around each word. Here are some roots and meanings relevant to this poem, taken from the *American Heritage Dictionary*:

lonely: derived from alone

crowd (Old English *crudan,* to hasten): generally used of the common people

host (Latin *hostis,* army, enemy)

daffodil: from asphodel (Greek *asphodelos*), a yellow flower

shine (Old English *scinan,* to shine): beam, emit light, reflect light, gleam, glisten

twinkle (Old English *twinklian,* to twinkle): to flicker, glimmer, sparkle

glance (Middle English *glansen,* to strike obliquely): to direct the gaze briefly

sprightly (Latin *spiritus,* spirit): buoyant, animated, full of life, with briskness, gaily

glee (Middle English *gle,* entertainment): jubilant gaiety, joy

gay (French *gai*): exuberant, merry, bright

jocund (Latin *jucundus,* delighted, <*juvare,* to delight): cheerful, merry

gaze (Middle English *gasen,* to gaze): prolonged and studied looking, often indicative of wonder, fascination, awe, or admiration

vacant (Latin *vacare,* to be empty): expressionless, blank, not filled with activity

pensive (Latin *pensare,* to think, <*pendere,* to weigh): engaged in deep, often melancholy thoughtfulness

flash (Middle English *flashen,* to splash): to burst forth into or as if into flame; to appear or occur suddenly; *flash* refers to a sudden and brilliant but short-lived outburst of light

bliss (Old English *bliss*): extreme happiness, joy, the ecstasy of salvation, spiritual joy

solitude (Latin *solus,* alone): the state of being alone or remote from others; isolation

We can notice — without yet doing much with the fact — that there are "families" of words evident here, just as there were in the Herrick poem:

◆ *glee, gay,* and *jocund* (a family of being happy, in terms of both meaning and — in the case of the first two — alliteration);

◆ *glance, glee, gay, gaze* (words connected by alliteration, joining looking and happiness);

◆ *saw, glance, gaze* (a family of looking);

◆ *float, flutter, dance, shine, twinkle, toss, flash, fill* (a family of verbs of motion)

Something will have to be said about these families, which help to organize the poem. And something should be said about the balance between words coming from the German side of English (Anglo-Saxon) and words coming from the Latin-French side. Wordsworth seems to be balancing Latinate words (*jocund, vacant, pensive, solitude*) with Germanic words (*glee, bliss, shine, twinkle*).

So much for words. What about **sentences**? The first sentence is the first stanza. The second sentence is the second stanza. What do we expect next? That the third sentence will be the third stanza. But that is not what happens: the third and fourth stanzas together make up the third sentence, and the "hinge" that joins the third and fourth stanzas is the couplet, "I gazed — and gazed — but little thought / What wealth the show to me had brought." This couplet leads into the exemplification of the "wealth" in stanza 4. The third sentence is twice as long as the other two (and therefore bears twice the weight).

We have our preliminary findings about words and sentences. What about **rhyme** and **rhythm**? The stanzas rhyme **ababcc**: that is, there is a quatrain followed by a couplet — a rhyme-scheme that implies: "I have something to say (my quatrain), and then I have something to add (my couplet)." There are 4 beats per line, and the basic meter is: weak **strong**, weak **strong**, weak **strong**, weak **strong**. We can see that this meter is more or less kept in the first five lines of the poem, but that in line 6, to emphasize the unexpected motion of the flowers, Wordsworth changes the first two syllables to read "**strong** weak": "Fluttering." A careful reader will see that for his concluding rhyme ("fills / daffodils") Wordsworth has reused one of the rhyme-sounds from his first stanza ("hills / daffodils"), giving us a strong sense of the end coming back to the beginning.

We've now done a fair amount of looking at the poem in terms of **words**, **sentences**, **rhyme** and **rhythm**. Now, suppose we look at the poem **temporally**, to see what changes we can observe in it as it goes along? Let us look at **A**, where the speaker is when the poem opens: he is alone, feeling *lonely,* feeling as unconnected to the world as a cloud is when floating high above the earth. Let us look at **Z**, where the speaker is when the poem ends; he is still alone, but he is no longer lonely; now he feels *the bliss of solitude.* What has made the difference? By the end, he has had, often, involuntary experiences of delight; alone in his room, he has perhaps been thinking of nothing, or reflecting in a slightly melancholy way about life, when suddenly, unasked, the daffodils flash into his mind so vividly that he sees them with his "inward eye." The experience makes that empty container, his heart, fill with pleasure, recapturing his previous pleasure on that apparently forgotten day.

Because the speaker in this poem doesn't differentiate himself (by gender, occupation, or age) from the author, we can refer to him as "Wordsworth," while remembering that he is a fictive creation, who speaks in verse — as the real Wordsworth, in real life, would not have done. We must ask how the poet has succeeded in conveying the earlier pleasure of his speaker so that we are convinced that the daffodils have indeed lasted intensely in his mind, without any conscious effort on his part. If we have seen **A** and **Z**, we now have to decide what goes on between lines 1–2 (**A**) and lines 19–24 (**Z**). All the verbs of motion, all the verbs of seeing, all the verbs of delight (those "families" of words we saw earlier) help to explain how we move from **A** to **Z**.

Now let us look at the poem **spatially**, "from above," so to speak, as if we were looking at a map spread out at our feet. We notice that there are three descriptions of the daffodils, three "glances" at the same phenomenon. The first glance ("I saw") shows us the daffodils as **many** (*a crowd, a host*), **in a landscape** (*lake, trees*), and **in motion** (*fluttering, dancing*). The second glance ("at a glance") shows us the daffodils as **many** (*stars . . . on the milky way, ten thousand*), **in a landscape** (*margin of a bay*), and **in motion** (*tossing their heads in sprightly dance*). The third glance ("I gazed — and gazed") shows us the daffodils as **many** (*company*), **in a landscape** (*waves beside them*), and **in motion** (*outdid the sparkling waves in glee*). We would draw distinctions about these three descriptions if we were considering them **temporally** (the distinction between seeing, glancing, and gazing, for instance), but in considering them **spatially**, as three versions of "the same thing," we notice that the important things about the daffodils (reiterated by the speaker each time he looks at them) is that they are <u>not alone</u> since there are many of them; that they feel <u>at home in nature</u>, beside the lake and beneath the trees and on the margin of a bay next to the waves; that they are not gloomily rigid but in joyous <u>motion</u> responsive to the waves and the breeze. We would not be so sure <u>why</u> the daffodils were so important to Wordsworth unless he had shown us, three times, the very same qualities in them. What may seem repetition in a poem is often intensification.

Again, as we look at the poem **spatially**, we notice that it is divided into two parts: outdoors (stanzas 1–3) and indoors (stanza 4). The outdoor part, phrased in the past tense, tells of one particular day when the poet saw the daffodils; the indoor part, phrased in what we call the habitual present tense (representing something that happens often), removes the daffodils from a physical scene (in nature) to a virtual scene (in the mind). Wordsworth makes explicit, at the end, the connection between what the eye has seen, glanced at, and finally gazed at (imprinting the scene firmly) and what the heart feels. Just as Herrick uses his second stanza to alter the perspective from the daffodils to human beings ("we"), so Wordsworth uses his last stanza to bring the daffodils indoors: in each case, something has changed so that we recognize that the poem has been brought to closure.

We haven't yet said how Wordsworth makes credible the interaction between the speaker and the flowers that made the scene so important. If we look at **the subjects of the sentences** in our spatial overview, we see that **the speaker** governs the first sentence ("**I** wandered lonely") and the daffodils are the objects of his observation ("I saw a crowd, a host, of golden daffodils"). But **the daffodils** govern the first part of the second sentence: ("**They** stretched"), while **the speaker** governs the second part ("ten thousand saw **I**"). **The daffodils**, along with the waves, govern the first part of the third sentence ("The waves . . . danced; but **they** outdid the sparkling waves"), while **the speaker** governs the second part ("**A poet** could not but be gay . . . **I** gazed — and gazed"). Finally, in the last stanza's continuation of the third sentence, **the daffodils** govern the first main clause ("**They** flash") while **the speaker** governs the second ("**my heart** with pleasure fills"). What we see, then, is an antiphonal structure of alternation (A; B / A; B) in which the poet and the daffodils engage in a "syntactic dialogue," as first one predominates, then the other. We "believe in" the speaker's interaction with the daffodils because the poem shows it happening. As Herrick paralleled daffodils with human beings, so Wordsworth shows them interacting.

Finally, we might notice that Wordsworth has put the word *dance,* in one or another of its variants, in each stanza. *Dancing; dance; danced; dances.* And we notice that the word *dance* alliterates with the word *daffodils,* making them "belong" together phonetically.

Getting It Down on Paper

Now, suppose you are to write a paper about how Wordsworth's poem "works." Remember that your readers probably will not have the poem at hand. When you are discussing a poem as brief as "Daffodils" (or any poem that is but a page or so in length), it is a courtesy to your readers to reproduce it early in your paper. Nonetheless, as you discuss the poem, you are still responsible for "tucking in" any information your readers need in order to understand what you are talking about. You don't want them to be flipping back and forth between your analysis and the poem.

Indeed, you should always write as if your readers cannot see the poem (as will be the case with longer poems you discuss, anyway), being careful to explain how the poem looks on the page — its stanzas, its rhymes. And you have the responsibility, as the speaker's surrogate, of explaining to your readers why the daffodils that day had the power over you that they did (even if you only realized it later). And you have the responsibility, as the poet's surrogate, of explaining how you set up your artifact in order to make it not only clear but beautiful.

Begin with a Question

A good way to begin a paper on a poem is to put before your reader some of the questions that occurred to you as you were studying the poem:

> Wordsworth writes a poem about the importance, to him, of a day in which he came upon a bed of daffodils next to a lake and watched them as they seemed to dance because of the breeze passing through them. Why would a bed of flowers become of lasting importance? What was it about them that later impelled the poet into speech? Does he seem to write the poem immediately after seeing them — was it the beauty of the sight that made him want to record it? Or was the poem written much later — and if so, what was it, at that later time, that made him write about the daffodils he had seen perhaps months before?

A paper that begins with your genuine questions about a poem draws your reader into the subject in a way that a set of conclusions would not. Besides, the reader is not yet ready to hear your conclusions: conclusions are interesting only after the questions to which they are the answers have been first made compelling to the reader. It is not a good idea, then, to start your paper by saying:

> Memory was important to Wordsworth. Often, experiences were more significant to him a long time after they had happened, and that is why he wrote a poem about daffodils he had seen long before.

Such a beginning, in addition to being a bit solemn, takes all the suspense out of the poem. One of the effects of the poem — and you are responsible for evoking those effects in your reader — is to make you wonder why the poet is emphasizing three times something so common in England as an extended bed of daffodils.

In evoking the effects of the poem, you might say:

> The speaker is concerned to set himself before us as someone lonely, disconnected from the human world, until he comes upon the daffodils. How do they seem to him when he first *sees* them? He is impressed first by their sheer number, next by the way they fit into the landscape, and third by their motion. Although this motion is really imparted to them by the breeze, the speaker prefers to think of them as engaging in both involuntary (*fluttering*) and voluntary (*dancing*) actions. Strange as it may seem, we learn nothing more, basically, about the daffodils when the speaker sees them again (at a *glance*) in stanza 2, and again (with a double *gaze*) in stanza 3: they are many, they are an intimate part of the landscape, and they dance. Why is it that these three qualities of the daffodils so strike the speaker, and what do we learn from the slight difference in the poem's representations of them as it returns to them for a second and a third time?

This makes your reader

- notice the three repetitions;
- notice what they have in common;
- wonder what distinguishes them from each other; and
- see how they emphasize the power of this scene to move the speaker.

As you go on, you can ask further questions. Are we surprised, after seeing this scene three times, that the poem suddenly goes on fast-forward, to a future experience (often repeated) of the daffodils, this time in virtual vision rather than real vision? How does the poet connect this anomalous last stanza to his three previous visions of the daffodils? And so on. The more questions you ask, the more interested your reader will be to see what answers you will provide.

Present Your Case

You may be thinking at this point, "How do I work in the facts about the **rhyme** and **meter**?" It is useless just to name the rhyme and meter; nobody learns anything from a sentence that says, "The poem, in iambic tetrameter, rhymes **ababcc**." Such a sentence is true, but uninformative. It is, of course, easier to talk about rhyme and meter (see pages 653–59) once you have acquired a sense of how set forms are used over time by different poets; but anyone can see that blank verse ("Of man's first disobedience, and the fruit / Of that immortal tree whose mortal taste / Brought death into the world, and all our woe") sounds very different, in its solemnity, from the dance-meter of "And then my heart with pleasure fills, / And dances with the daffodils." So somewhere along the way — when you are empha-sizing the repetition of the word *dance,* perhaps — you might add that Wordsworth has very naturally written the poem in a meter — iambic tetrameter — that suggests lightness, the same meter that Milton used for his poem on happiness, *L'Allegro*: "But come thou goddess fair and free, / In heaven yclept Euphrosyne." As for the rhyme, you can point out that in a poem that keeps coming back to the same scene, the appearance of a refrain in the recurrent couplets is appropriate. Imagine the last stanza if it had no break into quatrain and couplet, if it rhymed **ababab**:

> For oft, when on my couch I lie
> In vacant or in pensive mood,
> They flash upon that inward eye
> Which is the bliss of solitude;
> And then I feel the pleasure nigh
> Of daffodils on which I brood.

When the stanza is not broken in two, marked off by rhyme as a quatrain plus a couplet, one doesn't feel the sense of afterthought, of add-on, so important to the poem, which is itself all about the "add-on" of subse-quent mental reference to earlier physical experience — Wordsworth's great theme. In brief, insert your reflections on rhyme and meter where they best fit with your discussion of the poem's theme and manner, just as, in considering Herrick's poem, you might mention the effect of the strong first syllables when you are treating the speaker's conviction of his coming death.

Draw Your Conclusions

At the end of your paper, after integrating all you've noticed about the words, sentences, and rhyme and rhythm of the poem; after working out how to describe the poem's emotional evolution in time and the pat-terns you see in it from a spatial overview, posing questions for your reader all the way, you are entitled to tell the reader your conclusions. You might say:

> Wordsworth must convince his reader of the continuing importance, to him, of a single experience — his coming across a bed of daffodils. The poem, it turns out, is not only about seeing daffodils; it is about the "bliss" and wonder of memory — the fact that our memory unconsciously stores phenomena to which we have deeply responded and can make those phenomena "flash" into view long afterward, when we are unoccupied and alone.
>
> In his first loneliness, the speaker — a person alienated from the earth as much as a high-floating cloud would be, a wanderer who lacks company, a destination, and delight — comes upon the beautiful daffodils and is struck by the contrast between his state and theirs because <u>they</u> are at home in nature, they <u>do</u> have company, and they seem content to respond in sheer delight to the breeze that sets them in motion, so as even to "outdo" the dancing waves beside them. Lost in their sheer number and extent, in their beauty, naturalness, and freedom, the poet — expressing their happiness in a "dance-rhythm" of iambic tetrameter — is unable to tear himself away (as we see from his repeating the original scene twice more, each time with small but significant differences).
>
> The poet's perception alternates between his own agency and that of the daffodils: he sees, they act, he sees, they act, he gazes, and we begin to understand what it means to impress a scene on the mind by constant internal dialogue with it. All the time, the little stanza, which is composed of a basic statement and then an afterthought, acts out the way the mind frames a notion, and then adds to it, decoratively or reminiscently.
>
> The poet turns both to simple Anglo-Saxon words (*shine, twinkle, glee, flash*) with their familiar commonness, and to less familiar Latinate words (*continuous, jocund, vacant, pensive*), with their overtones of learning, to suggest that the flowers bring out all the parts of his sensibility, from childlike perception to literary response. By the end, the poet has found not only "company" in the "never-ending line" of daffodils, but nourishment for the future: his outward eye, brought into company and into nature and into delight, has, unbeknownst to him, stored up the daffodils as nurture for the "inward eye" that now makes solitude not "lonely" but "bliss[ful]."

No one paper can say everything about even a short poem. "I Wandered Lonely as a Cloud" can be set into larger frames: among other Wordsworth poems; among other daffodil poems; among other loneliness poems or nature poems; among other Romantic poems; among poems in iambic tetrameter; among poems about memory; and so on. Each "frame" shows the poem somewhat differently and gives one a better handle on the special idiosyncrasy of this poem.

Keeping Your Readers in Mind

What you chiefly want readers to feel, if they turn back from your paper to read the poem, is that you haven't left out anything important. A reader might say, reading an imperfect paper, "I would never have known that Wordsworth does the initial scene *three* times!" (This might be the reader's reaction if your discussion had essentially turned this into a poem that has two parts: "Wordsworth saw daffodils and liked them; Wordsworth remembers daffodils later.") Or a reader might say (if you had neglected to talk about vocabulary), "It sounded like such an <u>artless</u> poem in your paper; I never would have guessed that it had Latinate words like *sprightly* and *jocund* and *vacant* and *solitude* in it." Or, "You never said it had such a dance-like rhythm!" Or, "I had no idea that it was organized by 'see; glance; gaze' or that there was all that alliteration linking all those 'g' words together — *golden, glance, glee, gay, gazed, gazed* — or that there was *dance* in every stanza." Or, "But how could you have left out the difference between *lonely* at the beginning and *the bliss of solitude* at the end? It really sums up the whole difference between the poet's mood before he sees the daffodils and after!" A good paper leaves the readers, when they come back to the poem, feeling, "Oh, yes! And yes! Of course!" It makes readers see aspects of the poem they may not have noticed themselves, in their more cursory reading of the poem, but now see clearly because you have showed them those things.

A Note on Writing about Unrhymed Poems

The examples we saw above, "Divination by a Daffodil" and "I Wandered Lonely as a Cloud," are poems in rhymed stanzas. Since the beginning of the twentieth century many poets have been writing in what is called "free verse," that is, lines of irregular length that do not rhyme according to a fixed pattern and may not rhyme at all. Nonetheless, such poems *are* patterned — by repetition of rhythms, parallel syntactic patterns, metaphorical alliances, recurrent tones, alliteration, and so on. They usually fall into parts (two, three, or four), just as rhymed stanzaic poems do. One can imagine a poem parallel to "I Wandered Lonely as a Cloud" written in free verse, but it would still have to have the built-in pattern of a single outdoor experience in the past matched by a later blissful habitual indoor experience; by the pattern of the outward eye versus the inward eye; by the pattern of loneliness followed by "company"; by the pattern of a scene repeated to intensify its effect; and so on. The principal thing to remember is that all well-written verbal art is based on pattern-repetition, structural organization, and memorable language: these are as readily identified in free verse as in metered verse.

Organizing Your Paper

You do *not* have to "go through" the poem inch by inch, line by line. "In the first line the author says. . . . In the second line the author adds. . . . In line three, the poet goes on to observe . . . ," etc. Your reader would die of boredom. There is nothing wrong with starting a paper — as a means of posing some of your initial questions, perhaps — by looking at the ending.

> Wordsworth ends his poem with the speaker enjoying "the bliss of solitude" — the very same speaker who complained, at the beginning, that he was "wandering," with no company, "as lonely as a cloud," alienated from both man and nature. How did this melancholy person translate himself into a state of bliss?

Or your paper can begin in the middle of the poem:

> "I Wandered Lonely as a Cloud" is a poem divided between a single day in the past and many days in the present — the past day when the speaker "saw a crowd / A host, of golden daffodils" and the present days when the daffodils "flash upon [his] inward eye." The hinge between these two parts of the poem comes at the end of the third stanza:
>
> > I gazed — and gazed — but little thought
> > What wealth the show to me had brought:

What is that "wealth"? and how did the common spectacle of "golden" daffodils become transmuted into a different sort of gold, the "wealth" of involuntary memory?

Or your paper can begin with a feature of the poem:

> We might expect that a poem beginning "I wandered" would keep to this format throughout, with the speaker as the subject of all the verbs: "I saw," "I gazed," "I thought," and so on. But we notice that Wordsworth's poem on the daffodils offers a peculiar grammatical alternation between the poet as agent and the flowers as agent: it is almost as if they are engaging in a dialogue. The poet notices; then the flowers do something; then the poet notices; then the flowers do something else; then the poet notices yet again. Wordsworth is teaching us, so to speak, how to look so that the scenes we see can have lasting meaning for us. We need to be willing to receive the impress of the phenomena around us; but we also need to *see*, to <u>glance</u>, to **gaze** — and **GAZE**, with increasing intensity. And this is not necessarily a solemn process: in every stanza of the poem, some thing or person "dances" in this dialogue of the eye with nature.

In short, your paper can begin anywhere, as long as it is well organized and somehow includes all the main features of the poem.

A Note on Well-Ordered Paragraphs

One of the chief features of a well-organized paper is the internal arrangement of its paragraphs. A well-ordered paragraph has a point of view, and a subject that does not change markedly as the paragraph evolves. Here is an example of a badly organized paragraph, in which every sentence jumps to a different grammatical subject:

> Wordsworth is writing about seeing a bed of daffodils. The speaker has been wandering in a lonely mood, but then he glimpses the flowers. The 6-line stanza is written with a rhyming couplet at the end, in which we see the daffodils "fluttering and dancing in the breeze." Nature is for the poet a source of refreshment and solace. Often the Romantic poets found a recourse in nature that they could not find in urban life. Metaphors from nature are important to the Romantics; this is seen in Wordsworth's comparison of his loneliness to that of a cloud. The daffodils represent to Wordsworth the happiness and company to be found in nature.

The grammatical subjects of the successive sentences of this paragraph are *Wordsworth, the speaker, the stanza, Nature, the Romantic poets, metaphors,* and *daffodils.* A reader feels seasick as the paragraph lurches from focus to focus. The writer should choose one focus: the paragraph should be about Wordsworth, the composer of the poem; or about the speaker who utters the poem; about the scene in the poem (daffodils); about the technique of the poem (the stanzas, sentence-forms, rhymes); about Romantic poets and their relation to nature; or about metaphors in the poem.

A new paragraph is the place to change the focus. After a paragraph on Wordsworth as poet, it might be fine to have a paragraph about the speaker, followed by a paragraph about the metaphors in the poem — providing logical transitions are found to get from one topic to the next. For instance, if you had opened with a brief summary of the plot of the poem, telling about the speaker's loneliness and his seeing the daffodils first with his outward eye and then with his inward eye, you could bring that paragraph to a close by saying, "Yet behind this speaker, with his interest in the psychology of memory-imprinting, we find Wordsworth the author, who is constructing this speaker, and these stanzas, and these metaphors." Then you could have a paragraph about the author and how he has arranged the poem scenically, rhythmically, metaphorically, and so on.

Ideally, in a well-organized paper, you ought to be able to delete, from each paragraph, the follow-up sentences supporting the topic sentence, and be left with a "skeleton" consisting of nothing but the topic sentences for each paragraph. That skeleton would make sense by itself, would proceed logically, and would contain all the main points of your paper. Some writers like to do a sentence-outline of this sort after taking notes on the poem and seeing what the notes add up to in general terms. Then all they have to do is to fill in the evidence supporting the topic sentence for each paragraph. This is a sturdy and logical way of ordering a paper. In rereading and revising your paper, you might try typing out what you consider the topic sentence of each paragraph and seeing how well those sentences hang together as a logical sequence. Often you discover that something you have noticed late, and written down late, really belongs somewhere earlier in the paper, or that an earlier sentence properly should be brought down into the conclusion.

Checking Your Work

Three serious defects can mar a paper on a poem. One such defect is having made the poem boring to your reader. Ask yourself why it was important to the poet to write this poem, and then you will make it urgent to your reader, too. Another defect is to have misrepresented the poem, so that the reader will say, "Well, I never understood from your paper that the speaker was *lonely* when he came across the daffodils!" And perhaps the worst defect is to have treated the poem as though it is simply a message, rather than an artifact — something arranged by a writer to be beautiful, patterned, coordinated, musical, and memorable. To avoid these defects, read your paper over, saying to yourself:

- ◆ Have I made my reader see the urgency of the poem?
- ◆ Have I noticed all the important points about words, sentences, rhyme and rhythm, emotional curve over time, spatial patterning, and memorable language?
- ◆ Have I treated this as an artwork and not merely as a statement?

By the time you finish your paper, if you have done your work well, you will almost know the poem by heart, because you will have seen how it fits together. Your reader should see that, too.

It is important that your paper offer no typographical or grammatical obstructions to your reader:

- ◆ Messiness is an obstruction;
- ◆ Misspelling is an obstruction;
- ◆ Misquotation of your text is an obstruction;
- ◆ Mistakes in grammar and syntax are obstructions.

The paper has obligations to the poem: it should be almost as beautiful as the poem is, almost as interesting as the poem is, almost as memorable as the poem is.

There may be a part of the poem that you simply can't fit into your overview. If so, admit it and go on. Sometimes just writing about your difficulty solves it, and in going back, you see how the stanza fits in or why that metaphor was used. But even if you don't see how to solve your difficulty, you can leave it as a problem for your reader; there's nothing readers like better than being asked to think about an enigma that you have left open for their reflection.

12

Studying Groups of Poems

Sometimes you will want to assemble a group of poems by a single author in order to write in depth about that author's practice. The best way to do this is to find a group of poems about a single theme or a group of poems concerning a single problem. To illustrate this process, we reprint, first, four poems written by Walt Whitman (1819–1892) about Abraham Lincoln after Lincoln was assassinated, with some information found in books about the assassination; and second, a number of poems by Emily Dickinson that consider the problem of how we mark off and describe events as they take place in time.

Walt Whitman: Poems on Lincoln

What are some of the ways Whitman might choose to write about his murdered president? Lincoln was shot by the Confederate sympathizer John Wilkes Booth, one of a group of conspirators, on Good Friday, April 14, 1865, shortly before the end of the Civil War. The assassination was dramatic: Lincoln was shot in his box at the theater, in full sight of his wife and the audience; he died several hours later. It was decided that he would be buried in Illinois, his home state, rather than in Washington. After a funeral service in Washington, a ceremonial train, decked in black and bearing the coffin, would traverse the states in a long trajectory across the East before arriving at Springfield. At every stop that the train made, buildings were draped in black, and ceremonies included the tolling of bells, music, services, sermons, and processions, with long lines of citizens waiting to pass by the body lying in state. The body of Lincoln's young son William, who had died a few years earlier, was disinterred and brought on the train to be reburied in the tomb that would hold the president's coffin. The conspirators were brought to justice and hanged. How much of this information, you might ask yourself, will Whitman use?

Some of the sermons preached, and poems written, on Lincoln's death spoke of him as a "martyr," drawing an analogy with Christ's death on Good Friday. Others compared Lincoln (whose Emancipation Proclamation freed the slaves) to Moses, who led the Hebrews out from their slavery in Egypt to the promised land in Canaan. You might wonder, knowing these facts, whether Whitman uses any such Judeo-Christian analogies in his poems, and you store this question away.

Only two of Whitman's four poems are dated: the first ("Hush'd Be the Camps To-day") was written on May 4, 1865, shortly after Lincoln's death; and the last, "This Dust Was Once the Man," was published in 1871. The two middle poems — "O Captain! My Captain!" and "When Lilacs Last in the Dooryard Bloom'd" — were composed sometime in 1865 or 1866.

"Hush'd Be the Camps To-day" is a poem spoken not in Whitman's own voice but in the collective voice of the soldiers for whom Lincoln was the commander-in-chief. It consists of a series of quasi-military orders, beginning with the command that a silence be maintained in the camps during Lincoln's funeral service in Washington: "Hush'd be the camps to-day." Because Whitman thought that Lincoln would be buried in Washington, he closes the poem as the soldiers imagine the "invaulting" of the body:

Hush'd Be the Camps To-day

Hush'd be the camps to-day,
And soldiers let us drape our war-worn weapons,
And each with musing soul retire to celebrate,
Our dear commander's death.

No more for him life's stormy conflicts,
Nor victory, nor defeat — no more time's dark events,
Charging like ceaseless clouds across the sky.

But sing poet in our name,
Sing of the love we bore him — because you, dweller in
　　　camps, know it truly.

As they invault the coffin there,
Sing — as they close the doors of earth upon him — one verse,
For the heavy hearts of soldiers.

It has been conjectured that Whitman's second-written poem of these four may have been "O Captain! My Captain!" since it is the one replying to the soldiers' collective wish — in "Hush'd Be the Camps" — that the poet compose and sing a song in *their* voice. Because a young recruit speaks the poem, Whitman composes it in a ballad-measure of the sort that was popular in folk-poetry of his day. Lincoln is here not the commander-in-chief of the army but rather the captain of the ship of state, killed just before the victorious ship is about to make harbor.

O Captain! My Captain!

O Captain! my Captain! our fearful trip is done,
The ship has weather'd every rack, the prize we sought is won,
The port is near, the bells I hear, the people all exulting,
While follow eyes the steady keel, the vessel grim and daring:
    But O heart! heart! heart!
     O the bleeding drops of red,
      Where on the deck my Captain lies,
       Fallen cold and dead.

O Captain! my Captain! rise up and hear the bells;
Rise up — for you the flag is flung — for you the bugle trills,
For you bouquets and ribbon'd wreaths — for you the shores
    a-crowding,
For you they call, the swaying mass, their eager faces turning;
    Here Captain! dear father!
     This arm beneath your head!
      It is some dream that on the deck,
       You've fallen cold and dead.

My Captain does not answer, his lips are pale and still,
My father does not feel my arm, he has no pulse nor will,
The ship is anchor'd safe and sound, its voyage closed and done,
From fearful trip the victor ship comes in with object won;
    Exult O shores, and ring O bells!
     But I with mournful tread,
      Walk the deck my Captain lies,
       Fallen cold and dead.

Whitman, understandably, must have wished to write an elegy for
Lincoln in his own voice and his own verse-measure. The elegy he composes, in which he speaks in the first person as himself, is his longest
poem about Lincoln and the one that has become a classic of American
literature; for this reason, you might want to spend most of the space in
your paper on "When Lilacs Last in the Dooryard Bloom'd":

When Lilacs Last in the Dooryard Bloom'd

1

When lilacs last in the dooryard bloom'd,
And the great star early droop'd in the western sky in the night,
I mourn'd, and yet shall mourn with ever-returning spring.

Ever-returning spring, trinity sure to me you bring,
Lilac blooming perennial and drooping star in the west,   5
And thought of him I love.

2

O powerful western fallen star!
O shades of night — O moody, tearful night!
O great star disappear'd — O the black murk that hides the star!
O cruel hands that hold me powerless — O helpless soul   10
    of me!
O harsh surrounding cloud that will not free my soul.

3

In the dooryard fronting an old farm-house near the white-wash'd
    palings,
Stands the lilac-bush tall-growing with heart-shaped leaves of rich
    green,
With many a pointed blossom rising delicate, with the perfume
    strong I love,
With every leaf a miracle — and from this bush in the   15
    dooryard,
With delicate-color'd blossoms and heart-shaped leaves of rich
    green,
A sprig with its flower I break.

4

In the swamp in secluded recesses,
A shy and hidden bird is warbling a song.

Solitary the thrush, 20
The hermit withdrawn to himself, avoiding the settlements,
Sings by himself a song.

Song of the bleeding throat,
Death's outlet song of life — (for well dear brother I know,
If thou wast not granted to sing thou would'st surely die.) 25

5

Over the breast of the spring, the land, amid cities,
Amid lanes and through old woods, where lately the violets
    peep'd from the ground, spotting the gray debris,
Amid the grass in the fields each side of the lanes, passing the
    endless grass,
Passing the yellow-spear'd wheat, every grain from its shroud in
    the dark-brown fields uprisen,
Passing the apple-tree blows of white and pink in the orchards, 30
Carrying a corpse to where it shall rest in the grave,
Night and day journeys a coffin.

6

Coffin that passes through lanes and streets,[1]
Through day and night with the great cloud darkening the land,
With the pomp of the inloop'd flags with the cities draped in 35
    black,
With the show of the States themselves as of crape-veil'd women
    standing,
With processions long and winding and the flambeaus of the
    night,
With the countless torches lit, with the silent sea of faces and the
    unbared heads,
With the waiting depot, the arriving coffin, and the sombre faces,
With dirges through the night, with the thousand voices rising 40
    strong and solemn,
With all the mournful voices of the dirges pour'd around the
    coffin,
The dim-lit churches and the shuddering organs — where amid
    these you journey,

---

[1]Lincoln's funeral procession traveled from Washington, D.C., to Springfield, Illinois, stopping along the way so that people could honor the slain president.

With the tolling tolling bells' perpetual clang,
Here, coffin that slowly passes,
I give you my sprig of lilac.   45

7

(Nor for you, for one alone,
Blossoms and branches green to coffins all I bring,
For fresh as the morning, thus would I chant a song for you O
    sane and sacred death.

All over bouquets of roses,
O death, I cover you over with roses and early lilies,   50
But mostly and now the lilac that blooms the first,
Copious I break, I break the sprigs from the bushes,
With loaded arms I come, pouring for you,
For you and the coffins all of you O death.)

8

O western orb sailing the heaven,   55
Now I know what you must have meant as a month since I walk'd,
As I walk'd in silence the transparent shadowy night,
As I saw you had something to tell as you bent to me night after
    night,
As you droop'd from the sky low down as if to my side, (while the
    other stars all look'd on,)
As we wander'd together the solemn night, (for something I   60
    know not what kept me from sleep,)
As the night advanced, and I saw on the rim of the west how full
    you were of woe,
As I stood on the rising ground in the breeze in the cool
    transparent night,
As I watch'd where you pass'd and was lost in the netherward
    black of the night,
As my soul in its trouble dissatisfied sank, as where you sad orb,
Concluded, dropt in the night, and was gone.   65

9

Sing on there in the swamp,
O singer bashful and tender, I hear your notes, I hear your call,
I hear, I come presently, I understand you,
But a moment I linger, for the lustrous star has detain'd me,
The star my departing comrade holds and detains me.   70

10

O how shall I warble myself for the dead one there I loved?
And how shall I deck my song for the large sweet soul that
    has gone?
And what shall my perfume be for the grave of him I love?

Sea-winds blown from east and west,
Blown from the Eastern sea and blown from the Western sea,   75
    till there on the prairies meeting,
These and with these and the breath of my chant,
I'll perfume the grave of him I love.

11

O what shall I hang on the chamber walls?
And what shall the pictures be that I hang on the walls,
To adorn the burial-house of him I love?   80

Pictures of growing spring and farms and homes,
With the Fourth-month eve at sundown, and the gray smoke
    lucid and bright,
With floods of the yellow gold of the gorgeous, indolent, sinking
    sun, burning, expanding the air,
With the fresh sweet herbage under foot, and the pale green leaves
    of the trees prolific,
In the distance the flowing glaze, the breast of the river, with a   85
    wind-dapple here and there,
With ranging hills on the banks, with many a line against the sky,
    and shadows,
And the city at hand with dwellings so dense, and stacks of
    chimneys,
And all the scenes of life and the workshops, and the workmen
    homeward returning.

12

Lo, body and soul — this land,
My own Manhattan with spires, and the sparkling and   90
    hurrying tides, and the ships,
The varied and ample land, the South and the North in the light,
    Ohio's shores and flashing Missouri,
And ever the far-spreading prairies cover'd with grass and corn.

Lo, the most excellent sun so calm and haughty,
The violet and purple morn with just-felt breezes,

The gentle soft-born measureless light,   95
The miracle spreading bathing all, the fulfill'd noon,
The coming eve delicious, the welcome night and the stars,
Over my cities shining all, enveloping man and land.

13

Sing on, sing on you gray-brown bird,
Sing from the swamps, the recesses, pour your chant from   100
    the bushes,
Limitless out of the dusk, out of the cedars and pines.

Sing on dearest brother, warble your reedy song,
Loud human song, with voice of uttermost woe.

O liquid and free and tender!
O wild and loose to my soul — O wondrous singer!   105
You only I hear — yet the star holds me, (but will soon depart,)
Yet the lilac with mastering odor holds me.

14

Now while I sat in the day and look'd forth,
In the close of the day with its light and the fields of spring, and
    the farmers preparing their crops,
In the large unconscious scenery of my land with its lakes and   110
    forests,
In the heavenly aerial beauty, (after the perturb'd winds and the
    storms,)
Under the arching heavens of the afternoon swift passing, and the
    voices of children and women,
The many-moving sea-tides, and I saw the ships how they sail'd,
And the summer approaching with richness, and the fields all busy
    with labor,
And the infinite separate houses, how they all went on, each   115
    with its meals and minutia of daily usages,
And the streets how their throbbings throbb'd, and the cities
    pent — lo, then and there,
Falling upon them all and among them all, enveloping me with
    the rest,
Appear'd the cloud, appear'd the long black trail,
And I knew death, its thought, and the sacred knowledge of
    death.

Then with the knowledge of death as walking one side of me,   120

And the thought of death close-walking the other side of me,
And I in the middle as with companions, and as holding the hands
    of companions,
I fled forth to the hiding receiving night that talks not,
Down to the shores of the water, the path by the swamp in
    the dimness,
To the solemn shadowy cedars and ghostly pines so still.   125

And the singer so shy to the rest receiv'd me,
The gray-brown bird I know receiv'd us comrades three,
And he sang the carol of death, and a verse for him I love.

From deep secluded recesses,
From the fragrant cedars and the ghostly pines so still,   130
Came the carol of the bird.

And the charm of the carol rapt me,
As I held as if by their hands my comrades in the night,
And the voice of my spirit tallied the song of the bird.

Come lovely and soothing death,   135
Undulate round the world, serenely arriving, arriving,
In the day, in the night, to all, to each,
Sooner or later delicate death.

Prais'd be the fathomless universe,
For life and joy, and for objects and knowledge curious,   140
And for love, sweet love — but praise! praise! praise!
For the sure-enwinding arms of cool-enfolding death.

Dark mother always gliding near with soft feet,
Have none chanted for thee a chant of fullest welcome?
Then I chant it for thee, I glorify thee above all,   145
I bring thee a song that when thou must indeed come, come
    unfalteringly.

Approach strong deliveress,
When it is so, when thou hast taken them I joyously sing the dead,
Lost in the loving floating ocean of thee,
Laved in the flood of thy bliss O death.   150

From me to thee glad serenades,
Dances for thee I propose saluting thee, adornments and feastings
    for thee,
And the sights of the open landscape and the high-spread sky are fitting,
And life and the fields, and the huge and thoughtful night.

The night in silence under many a star, 155
The ocean shore and the husky whispering wave whose voice I know,
And the soul turning to thee O vast and well-veil'd death,
And the body gratefully nestling close to thee.

Over the tree-tops I float thee a song,
Over the rising and sinking waves, over the myriad fields and the 160
*   prairies wide,*
Over the dense-pack'd cities all and the teeming wharves and ways,
I float this carol with joy, with joy to thee O death.

15

To the tally of my soul,
Loud and strong kept up the gray-brown bird,
With pure deliberate notes spreading filling the night. 165

Loud in the pines and cedars dim,
Clear in the freshness moist and the swamp-perfume,
And I with my comrades there in the night.

While my sight that was bound in my eyes unclosed,
As to long panoramas of visions. 170

And I saw askant the armies,
I saw as in noiseless dreams hundreds of battle-flags,
Borne through the smoke of the battles and pierc'd with missiles I
    saw them,
And carried hither and yon through the smoke, and torn and
    bloody,
And at last but a few shreds left on the staffs, 175
    (and all in silence,)
And the staffs all splinter'd and broken.

I saw battle-corpses, myriads of them,
And the white skeletons of young men, I saw them,
I saw the debris and debris of all the slain soldiers of the war,
But I saw they were not as was thought, 180
They themselves were fully at rest, they suffer'd not,
The living remain'd and suffer'd, the mother suffer'd,
And the wife and the child and the musing comrade suffer'd,
And the armies that remain'd suffer'd.

16

Passing the visions, passing the night, 185
Passing, unloosing the hold of my comrades' hands,

Passing the song of the hermit bird and the tallying song of my
    soul,
Victorious song, death's outlet song, yet varying ever-altering
    song,
As low and wailing, yet clear the notes, rising and falling, flooding
    the night,
Sadly sinking and fainting, as warning and warning, and yet   190
    again bursting with joy,
Covering the earth and filling the spread of the heaven,
As that powerful psalm in the night I heard from recesses,
Passing, I leave thee lilac with heart-shaped leaves,
I leave thee there in the door-yard, blooming, returning with
    spring.

I cease from my song for thee,   195
From my gaze on thee in the west, fronting the west,
    communing with thee,
O comrade lustrous with silver face in the night.

Yet each to keep and all, retrievements out of the night,
The song, the wondrous chant of the gray-brown bird,
And the tallying chant, the echo arous'd in my soul,   200
With the lustrous and drooping star with the countenance full
    of woe,
With the holders holding my hand nearing the call of the bird,
Comrades mine and I in the midst, and their memory ever to
    keep, for the dead I loved so well,
For the sweetest, wisest soul of all my days and lands —
    and this for his dear sake,
Lilac and star and bird twined with the chant of my soul,   205
There in the fragrant pines and the cedars dusk and dim.

Finally, in 1871, Whitman writes an epitaph for Lincoln. An epitaph (from Greek *epi,* "upon," and *tophos,* "tomb") has to be short
enough to be inscribed on a tombstone, and it has to be written in an
impersonal way. No "voice," as such, speaks this poem unless it is the
voice of History, pronouncing finally on Lincoln, not as man — his
body is now dust — but as historical personage: "This Dust Was Once
the Man":

This Dust Was Once the Man

This dust was once the man,
Gentle, plain, just and resolute, under whose cautious hand,

Against the foulest crime in history known in any land or age,
Was saved the Union of these States.

Suppose you have gathered these four poems together as the products of Whitman's need to celebrate, memorialize, elegize, and even write
an epitaph for Lincoln. You might separate them first into two groups: the
three poems in which Whitman does *not* speak in his own voice, and
"Lilacs," in which he does.

- ◆ In "Hush'd Be the Camps To-day," what sort of voice appears in the
  collective wishes of the soldiers?
- ◆ What can they do to mourn Lincoln?
- ◆ What is the one thing they need someone else to do for them?
- ◆ How do they imagine the moment when that is done?
- ◆ Why, do you think, did Whitman want to write a poem in the voice
  of the soldiers?

Then you might ask:

- ◆ What sort of voice and verse-measure do we hear coming from the
  young naval recruit whose captain has just been shot?
- ◆ In what sort of rhythms does he speak?
- ◆ What emotion does he chiefly express?
- ◆ How does he express his relation to the fallen captain?
- ◆ How does the allegorical metaphor of the ship of state play out in
  the poem?
- ◆ Of what use is that metaphor to Whitman in writing the poem?
- ◆ What changes occur in the young sailor's speech in the last stanza?
- ◆ For what sort of audience is the ballad-like stanza of this poem
  intended?

Then you might consider the epitaph "This Dust Was Once the Man":

- ◆ In what voice does History speak?
- ◆ What sort of vocabulary does History use, by comparison with the
  vocabulary of the soldiers in "Hush'd Be the Camps To-day" or that
  of the young recruit in "O Captain! My Captain!"?
- ◆ What sort of syntax does History employ?
- ◆ Why does History use the passive verb-form ("the Union was
  saved") instead of the active form ("he saved the Union")?
- ◆ Who saved the Union?

◆ What adjectives does History use of Lincoln, and is there any significance to their order?

◆ If the poetic that underlies "O Captain! My Captain!" is that of popular ballad verse, what are the characteristics of epitaph-writing that underlie "This Dust"?

You have seen what it occurred to Whitman to say in the voice of soldiers who have just received the news of the death of their commander-in-chief; in the voice of a youthful sailor holding the dead body of his slain captain; and in the voice of History, impersonally summarizing Lincoln's high achievements in ending slavery and preserving the Union. Now you are better prepared to see what Whitman says in his own voice.

But first, you might stand off a bit from all the poems to consider what they add up to as poetry of the Civil War and of assassination. In these poems, do you see battles? Do you see the Emancipation Proclamation? Do you see the assassination? Do you see the punishment of the conspirators? Do you see slaves? members of Congress? generals? members of the Confederacy? And you might see what the poems add up to in elegizing Lincoln the private man. Do we see his wife? his living children? his dead son William, about to be buried with him? It is by selection from all available material that the writer makes his emphasis clear.

As you study "Lilacs," before writing about it, you will want to look at it section by section, since it is such a long poem. A good way of thinking about any poem is to write it out in your own handwriting, thinking of yourself as a poet composing the lines, and asking, "Why have I said this?" "Why have I followed this section with the next section?" "Why have I changed my focus?" and so on. But "Lilacs" is too long for this procedure, and for a poem of this length the best strategy for seeing it clearly is to write a one-sentence summary of each section, noticing the manner as well as the matter of the section. Your summaries of the first few sections of "Lilacs" might look like this:

1. Lilac, star, and thought as trinity of mourning: star "droops," lilac is a perennial. Spring perennial too.

2. Star disappears; speaker held helpless in harsh dark cloud. O, O, O, O, O, O, O, O — eight of them!

3. Lilac bush — 5-line description leading up in line 17 to the action: "A sprig . . . I break."

4. Thrush: Talks to thrush ("dear brother"); singing prevents dying.

5. Like lilac stanza — long lead-in ("passing . . . passing . . . carrying") to action: "journeys a coffin."

By the time you get to later stanzas, you will have noticed that Whitman not only talks to the thrush, he also talks to the coffin (stanza 6), to death (stanza 7), to the star (stanza 8), and to the thrush again (stanza 9); and you will see that these addressees represent different planes of existence: the material (the coffin), the abstract (death), the celestial (the star), the animal (the thrush). You will also notice that having once addressed all of these symbolic beings, the poet turns back to put questions to himself in stanzas 10–11 and to act as a displayer of the American landscape (stanza 12), before returning to address the thrush a second time in stanza 13.

By amassing one-sentence descriptions in this way, you'll have begun to see the ways Whitman manages his poem — by exclamations, by direct address, by ranging to different planes of experience, and so on. Soon these will gather together to give you several talking points for your paper.

In writing about a long poem such as this, you will find certain sections that you want to concentrate on and others that you will want to treat more lightly. This choice depends on what your main point concerning "Lilacs" is. If you want to talk about the poet's direct addresses to other beings, you might choose stanzas 4 and 13, in which he addresses the thrush, and then explain why he ceases to address the thrush in the second person but rather talks about the bird in the third person from line 126 on ("The singer so shy to the rest receiv'd me"). You might notice that this does not happen right away with the lilac or the star: in line 193 the speaker says, addressing the lilac directly, "Passing, I leave thee lilac," and in line 195 he says to the star, "I cease from my song for thee." Eventually all three symbols are spoken of in the third person: "Lilac and star and bird twined with the chant of my soul" (line 205).

If, on the other hand, your main point about "Lilacs" is how private a poem it is by comparison to the more public poems of the camps, the young sailor, and the epitaph, you might want to concentrate on the word "love" as it appears throughout this poem. Or if you want to emphasize its meditation on death — excluded from the other three poems — you would want to concentrate on the very long stanza 14, containing Whitman's "translation" of the song of the bird, "Come lovely and soothing death."

If (to take another example) you are interested in how Whitman, while abjuring Christian symbols of martyrdom, resurrection, afterlife in heaven, and so on, renews the imagination of death from other sources, you would want to concentrate on stanza 11 (where Whitman draws on the Egyptian practice of painting the insides of tombs with scenes from daily life) and stanzas 14–15 (where Whitman draws on the Greek conception of an underworld haunted by shades, which he transfers to the swamp).

By writing out a brief summary of each section of the long poem, you will easily be able to assemble possible points of comparison and contrast with the other poems and to have a quick reference for finding the parts of the long poem that you want to cite.

What can we learn from comparisons of this sort among poems by the same author that have a theme in common? We learn, first, that no theme determines the form a poem takes — that the death of Lincoln can be looked at in many different ways, from many points of view — singular, collective, public, private, allegorical, and so on. Once the writer has chosen the point of view for a poem ("I think I'll have it be a young sailor mourning the captain of the ship of state") there is still the verse-form to be decided on; and then how many stanzas; and then how the opening and closing might work; and then what the emotional range of the poem will be. Each decision helps determine the ultimate shape of the poem.

Such a set of comparisons also induces us to make evaluative judgments. Most readers have thought "Lilacs" the best of these poems. This is a chance for you to ask yourself whether you agree, and if so why; or if not, why not? Perhaps readers prefer private mourning to public epitaphs; is this a fair preference? Or perhaps readers like the clear "trinity" of symbols — lilac and star and bird — in "Lilacs." Do you? Or perhaps readers feel that a longer poem can include more of the many feelings prompted by Lincoln's death. Do you?

We can also, by comparing poems in the same broad genre (these are all elegies for Lincoln), see the capacity of a single genre to contain many subgenres — here, the elegy voiced by a group ("Hush'd Be the Camps To-day"); the elegy voiced by a "naive" speaker (here, the young sailor); the impersonal elegy voiced by "History" ("This Dust"); and the elegy voiced by the poet in his own speech. You can carry this knowledge to the next elegiac poem you read; it will sharpen your sense of the idiosyncrasy of that poem.

Finally, by comparing poems, we find out something about ourselves in relation to Whitman: that we like best the Whitman of a collective voice, or the Whitman of historical severity, or the Whitman of panorama, or the Whitman of folk-ballad, or the Whitman of intimacy of address, or the Whitman of long unrolling sentences, or the Whitman of the renewal of imagination from Egyptian and Greek sources. As we sort out our own responses, we are discovering where our taste and judgment lead us; but also, as we read a number of poems, we are broadening our own sense of what poetry can do. Robert Frost has a relevant comment about reading a poem in the light of other poems. In a short essay first published in the *New York Times Book Review* (March 31, 1954), he said:

> A poem is best read in the light of all the other poems ever written. We read A the better to read B (we have to start somewhere; we may get very little out of A). We read B the better to read C, C the better to read D, D the better to go back and get something more out of A. Progress is not the aim, but circulation. The thing is to get among the poems where they hold each other apart in their places as the stars do.

Emily Dickinson: Poems on Time

Let us suppose you have been asked to write a paper on a selection of poems by Emily Dickinson (1830–1886) that concern a similar theme. You are to suggest what the poems have in common, how they differ from each other, what qualities of human psychological response they are interested in, and with what variety of poetic means Dickinson conceptualizes and stylizes their subject matter.

Here, a selection of eight poems has been made for you, all of them concerned with events in time, each of them structuring time in its own way. Dickinson investigates in these poems how she experiences time and how one might express different senses of time when composing narratives in verse. After reading the poems below, and the brief questions following them, you might decide which three poems you will focus on for your paper, choosing those that most attract you by the emotions conveyed by the strategies Dickinson finds to arrange her plot-events, and by the language that she presses into service for each poem.

1

The most naive experience of time, one that we all have, is a linear one with a beginning and end separated by a set of markers. It could be the year from January to December divided by months, or the day from dawn to midnight divided by hours, or (projected on space) the journey from Boston to New York punctuated by the stops made by the train.

Dickinson sets out this equable and predictable idea of time in her poem about watching the local train: "I like to see it lap the Miles":

I like to see it lap the Miles —

I like to see it lap the Miles —
And lick the Valleys up —

And stop to feed itself at Tanks –
And then – prodigious step

Around a Pile of Mountains –
And supercilious peer
In Shanties – by the sides of Roads –
And then a Quarry pare

To fit its sides
And crawl between
Complaining all the while
In horrid – hooting stanza –
Then chase itself down Hill –

And neigh like Boanerges –[1]
Then – prompter than a Star
Stop – docile and omnipotent
At its own stable door –

◆ How do you think Dickinson decided on the train's stops?

◆ Does anything untoward happen to the train? If not, why not?

◆ Where does the train end up?

◆ What sort of human experience of time (exciting? placid? even? irregular? inconsistent? routine?) does the poem enact?

◆ How does Dickinson suggest her feelings when watching the progress of the train?

◆ Does life ever unroll over time in the way the story of the train does?

2

In a poem more sinister than "I like to see it lap the Miles," Dickinson again represents linear time by the stops made by a conveyance. This is her tale of a carriage ride with Death: "Because I could not stop for Death."

Because I could not stop for Death –

Because I could not stop for Death –
He kindly stopped for me –
The Carriage held but just Ourselves –
And Immortality.

---

[1]Boanerges, or "Sons of Thunder," an epithet applied by Jesus to the disciples James and John, sons of Zebedee (Mark 3:17). It was metaphorically applied to a thunderous preacher.

We slowly drove – He knew no haste
And I had put away
My labor and my leisure too,
For His Civility –

We passed the School, where Children strove
At Recess – in the Ring –
We passed the Fields of Gazing Grain –
We passed the Setting Sun –

Or rather – He passed Us –
The Dews drew quivering and Chill –
For only Gossamer, my Gown –
My Tippet° – only Tulle –   *shawl*

We paused before a House that seemed
A Swelling of the Ground –
The Roof was scarcely visible –
The Cornice – in the Ground –

Since then – 'tis Centuries – and yet
Feels shorter than the Day
I first surmised the Horses' Heads
Were toward Eternity –

◆ What are the stops here? Does the poem begin when the journey begins? Does the poem end when the journey ends? If not, why not?

◆ Does the journey end where it began, as the train's journey did?

◆ Dickinson here reflects on how memory can change the perception of time: What was the longest internal "day" of Dickinson's life? Why?

◆ The poet says, "Since then – 'tis Centuries": is it, really? If not, what does this line convey?

◆ The poem uses as its end-brackets two words that negate time: "Immortality" and "Eternity." How does the dictionary distinguish between them? Which is more appealing?

◆ The poet has imagined Death as a courteous gentleman who, neglected by the speaker, comes calling to remind her of his existence. Can you imagine other ways of imagining this event in one's existence?

3

Linear time can be divided by subjective criteria, too, as life modulates from one state to another. In "The Heart asks Pleasure – first,"

Dickinson creates a main clause – "The Heart asks" – and follows it by a series of requests by the heart, of which the first is "pleasure." These requests are joined by the repeated phrase "And then," emphasizing the inexorable links of this temporal sequence.

The Heart asks Pleasure – first –

The Heart asks Pleasure – first –
And then – Excuse from Pain –
And then – those little Anodynes
That deaden suffering –

And then – to go to sleep –
And then – if it should be
The will of its Inquisitor
The privilege to die –

- At what approximate point in life does this narrative begin?
- What is the first criterion of change noticed by the heart?
- At what point does the narrative end? Or does it end at all?
- The "pieces" of time segmented here are of the same syntactic length until the last one arrives. Why does the syntax "spread out" at this point?
- What does one learn from the last segment that one had not known before?
- Who is in control of the segmentation of time felt by the speaker? What motivates the torturer? Why is he given the name by which he is called? Why has he not been named sooner?
- Are these "stops" on the journey of life universal and predictable, according to Dickinson?
- How would the import of the poem change if it were spoken in the first person — if the first line said, "My Heart asks Pleasure – first"?

4

So far, time has been shown as a linear structure, with a beginning followed by a series of stops. The stops separating beginning and end in this journey can be familiar and predictable (as with the course of the train), both familiar and unfamiliar (as with the ride in Death's carriage), or they can be markers gradually intensifying in emotional effect (as in "The Heart asks"). Do we ever structure time in ways that disrupt this linear pattern of a beginning, followed by intermediate stops, approaching an end? Can temporal patterning disappear altogether?

When Dickinson's self is cleft in two by suffering ("I felt a Cleaving in my Mind"), time no longer seems to resemble itself.

I felt a Cleaving in my Mind

I felt a Cleaving in my Mind –
As if my Brain had split –
I tried to match it – Seam by Seam –
But could not make them fit –

The thought behind, I strove to join
Unto the thought before –
But Sequence ravelled out of Sound –
Like Balls – upon a Floor –

There are two manuscripts (one a partial one, of the second stanza only) for "I felt a Cleaving in my Mind." The manuscript of the complete poem shows a variant for lines 7–8, in which "Sequence ravelled out of reach, / Like balls upon a floor." The simile of balls of yarn that unravel as they fall to the floor and roll out of reach is a domestic one. How does the reading chosen by Dickinson's editor, "Sequence ravelled out of Sound" — with its implied metaphor of a musical sequence that disappears into inaudibility — change your sense of the speaker's feeling?

The Dust behind I strove to join
Unto the Disk before –
But Sequence ravelled out of Sound
Like Balls upon a Floor –

The manuscript that contains only the second stanza substitutes, for the relatively literal lines 5–6 ("The thought behind, I strove to join / Unto the thought before"), the following metaphorical lines: "The Dust behind I strove to join / Unto the Disk before." Can one make a mental "sequence" that would link a smooth, solid, and perfect "disk" to an atomized and formless "dust"? What has happened to thought, according to this metaphor? How does an incapacity for sequential thinking affect one's sense of time?

5

In the linear plot of crisis that structures "I felt a Cleaving in my Mind" time also is cleft in two — into "before" and "after" the crisis. (In

Dickinson the arranging of time around a single event makes for either binary poems ["The Soul selects her own Society − / Then − shuts the Door"] or for three-part series reducing life to beginning, middle, and end ["Born − Bridalled − Shrouded"]). If this is what happens to one's sense of time when a single crisis has occurred, how is that sense of time affected when crisis is multiplied? Dickinson considers the horrifying recurrence of catastrophe in "The first Day's Night had come": you will see in this poem the same conclusion-in-aftermath that was present in "Because I could not stop for Death":

The first Day's Night had come −

The first Day's Night had come −
And grateful that a thing
So terrible − had been endured −
I told my Soul to sing −

She said her strings were snapt −
Her Bow − to atoms blown −
And so to mend her − gave me work
Until another Morn −

And then − a Day as huge
As Yesterdays in pairs,
Unrolled its horror in my face −
Until it blocked my eyes −

My Brain − begun to laugh −
I mumbled − like a fool −
And tho' 'tis Years ago − that Day −
My Brain keeps giggling − still.

And Something's odd − within −
That person that I was −
And this One − do not feel the same −
Could it be Madness − this?

◆ How does Dickinson indicate the comparative magnitude of the second catastrophe?

◆ How does the recurrence of catastrophe affect the brain of the speaker?

◆ Analyze the contribution of each of the verbs in the second-to-last stanza: "laugh," "mumble," and "giggle." What sense of time does the speaker now experience, do you think?

6

"After great pain, a formal feeling comes" begins when the crisis is already over. Dickinson has nothing to say about the time before the crisis, nor does she specify the nature or temporal extent of the crisis itself: we know it only from its result, "great pain."

After great pain, a formal feeling comes

After great pain, a formal feeling comes –
The Nerves sit ceremonious, like Tombs –
The stiff Heart questions 'was it He, that bore,'
And 'Yesterday, or Centuries before'?

The Feet, mechanical, go round –
A Wooden way
Of Ground, or Air, or Ought –
Regardless grown,
A Quartz contentment, like a stone –

This is the Hour of Lead –
Remembered, if outlived,
As Freezing persons, recollect the Snow –
First – Chill – then Stupor – then the letting go –

◆ What does the first stanza tell us about the speaker's sense of time?

◆ Do the speaker's feet advance in their motion? How do you know?

◆ In the last stanza, time is given weight: "This is the Hour of Lead." Can you extrapolate from this metaphor to others like it? "This is the day of ___"? "This is the noon of ___"? Can a time of "lead" advance?

◆ A second "story" — about freezing in the snow — is told in the last three lines of the poem. Is this a linearly narrated story? How does it end? How does it resemble the first story?

◆ What is the point of adding this second story to the first one?

◆ How does the speaker's experience of time "after great pain" differ from that in "I like to see it lap the Miles" or "The Heart asks Pleasure – first"?

7

In the poem "There's a certain Slant of light," Dickinson begins with a "stopped frame" of the light itself, defining it. It is only in the last stanza that she shows us the beginning-point of the light: "When it comes."

There's a certain Slant of light

There's a certain Slant of light,
Winter Afternoons –
That oppresses, like the Heft
Of Cathedral Tunes –

Heavenly Hurt, it gives us –
We can find no scar,
But internal difference,
Where the Meanings, are –

None may teach it – Any –
'Tis the Seal Despair –
An imperial affliction
Sent us of the Air –

When it comes, the Landscape listens –
Shadows – hold their breath –
When it goes, 'tis like the Distance
On the look of Death –

If Dickinson had unfolded the progress of the light in linear fashion (in the manner of the train making its journey), she would have made a different poem, one (with apologies to Dickinson) like this:

When a Shaft – of Light – comes
Slanting through the Trees
On a Winter afternoon
Weighing on our Eyes –

Then we feel, within our Brain –
A Cathedral Tune –
As the steady Shadows lean –
Darker – into Dim –

Then Light fading – fainter still –
Tells us of Despair –
As the Landscape vanishes
In the somber Air –

Till the ones who held their Breath,
Watching ebbing Light –
Still afflicted – perish – with it –
At the fall of Night –

Consider how Dickinson changes our perception of time by "crowding" the light's coming and going, beginning and end, into the last quatrain. What does this make us feel about the light that we would not feel if its appearance were "played out" as it is in the linear version that has been made up here to contrast with the original?

8

Finally, here is a poem in which Dickinson herself reflects on how time is affected by pain: "Pain – expands the Time . . . / Pain contracts – the Time" she writes paradoxically:

Pain – expands the Time

Pain – expands the Time –
Ages coil within
The minute Circumference
Of a single Brain –

Pain contracts – the Time –
Occupied with Shot
Gamuts of Eternities
Are as they were not –

- ◆ Dickinson could have written two separate poems — one on how pain expands time and another on how pain contracts time. What is gained, do you think, by putting mutually contradictory perceptions into a single poem?
- ◆ Is there any such thing as "sequence" in this poem?
- ◆ We see here again Dickinson's use of the word "eternity" in connection with time. We met it before in "Because I could not stop for Death," but there it appeared in the singular. What is the effect here of making it plural?
- ◆ Can you explain the sort of pain that expands time and compare it with the sort of pain that contracts time? It may help to reflect that this poem (with its "shot," or bullet) was probably written in 1864, during the Civil War.

Writing Your Paper

After you have read and reflected on these eight poems about time, in order to write your paper you will want to select a few (say, three) to concentrate on (while reserving the right to make brief reference to some or all of the others as you compose your essay). Always choose to write on the poems that stir you most, those you are drawn to explore in more detail.

One reader might want to treat Dickinson's whimsy as she invents the stops for her train — and the remnant of that whimsy as she imagines the carriage ride with Death — with an ironic remnant of the whimsy in her mention, in "The Heart asks Pleasure" of "those little Anodynes / That deaden suffering."

Another might be drawn to Dickinson's radical use of metaphor, centering on the strange and unworldly metaphors Dickinson uses to describe the stopping of time in "After great pain" (what is "A Quartz contentment, like a stone")? Grouped around "After great pain" might be the other strange metaphors in "Pain – expands the Time": what are "Gamuts of Eternities"?

Yet another reader might be drawn to Dickinson's relentlessness when writing of time and could investigate aspects like the following:

- How episodes in time are linked (e.g., by the grim "and then's" of "The Heart asks");

- What happens when relentlessness has to walk in a circle (in "After great pain");

- What the result is when crisis is piled on crisis, and the second "and then" is bigger ("AND THEN") than the first (as in "The first Day's Night had come").

No matter which three poems you choose to concentrate on, you should make a list in two columns, grouping the aspects of your poems:

What Is Literal	*What Is Imagined*
Things in Common: Matter	*Things Different: Matter*
Things in Common: Style	*Things Different: Style*

Under *What Is Literal* put whatever basic psychological life-experience the poem conveys. For "After great pain," you might write, "Aftermath of emotional devastation: no sensations or feelings; time confused; time stands still; environment unclear; self rigid." Under *What Is Imagined* you might write, for the same poem, "Nerves like tombs in a cemetery; heart 'stiff' as in *rigor mortis;* 'yesterday' indistinguishable from 'centuries before'; feet on wooden circular track: ground? air?; self — crystalline or stony, which?" Inquiry into figurative language reveals, in each case, an originating emotion that has found its way into language.

Under *Things in Common: Matter* you could list ideas about the sense of time — its beginning, its end, and its interior episodes — that link your three poems together. Your poems might have in common their sense of a crisis marking time into Before and After, for instance; their sense that time has stopped altogether; or their contrast of time with eternity. Under *Things in Common: Style* you might put the fact that all three of your poems have three stanzas; that all three display an iron sequence of inseparably linked events; that they all begin with the first event in a sequence; that they all end in aftermath rather than with the final episode; or that they share syntactic forms. Don't be concerned if only two of your poems show such resemblances: you can always use the third to show differences.

Under *Things Different: Matter* put whatever ideas differentiate your three poems from each other: they may all exhibit different emotional responses to time, or they may treat time as natural in one instance, as unreal in another. Under *Things Different: Style* put any structural and stylistic differences: your poems may begin at the end of their linear sequence; they may not give a true ending to the sequence at all; one may use chiefly verbs, another, nouns; one may be all one sentence, another, composed of several sentences; or one may arrange items in climactic order, another, not.

Decide on an order of treatment of your poems: perhaps shortest to longest, most ordinary to most imaginative, or least paradoxical to most paradoxical. Your reader wants to feel that you are setting out, in some logical order, your ideas about Dickinson's poetic strategies for dealing with the felt experience of time.

Before beginning to write, think about your own feelings about time. Have you ever felt time stand still? Have you ever felt that one year went by much faster than another? Have you ever felt time drag? Have your feelings about time been influenced by the loss of people through death? Has time ever seemed to become more intense, day by day or year by year? Has time ever seemed to go in circles? Has clock-time always seemed real to you? Do the concepts of Eternity and Immortality have meaning for you? It is only by reflecting on your own senses of time that you will be able to make a true connection to Dickinson's experience and to see how each poem stylizes sequence differently so as to be able to render the psychological structure of experience with maximum accuracy.

As you write, remember that a good essay on poetry evokes the atmosphere of a poem (by such words as "leisurely" or "relentless"; "whimsy" or "sublimity"; "sinister" or "light-hearted"; "even" or "irregular"; "intimate" or "public"; "appealing" or "grotesque"). It is not enough to go through the poem and say *what* it says: what you need to show your reader is *how* it says what it says — by what means, with what atmosphere, with what vividness of language, with what turns of syntax, with what temperature in the feelings. Otherwise, if you remain in the realm of paraphrase of ideas, you are not conveying the emotion that propelled the poem into being, that made the poet break her silence.

You must quote the poem, or at least the parts of it you discuss (in the case of a nonprincipal poem), so that the reader can see the evidence for your remarks. It is a good idea to give a brief set of questions at the beginning of your paper, to interest the reader:

> How did Emily Dickinson perceive time? Do her perceptions change with the nature of the experience she is evoking? Can time be sequenced in different ways? Is all time felt as evenly linear, or is it sometimes felt in different ways? When does time stop? How can the structures of our varied experiences of time be enacted with fineness and discrimination in a poem? Some answers to these questions can be found in considering three characteristic poems.

Then you can say, "The first of the three poems, the shortest and most paradoxical, embodies Dickinson's contradictory views of time," and begin with, say, "Pain – expands the Time." After quoting the poem, it is a good idea to give your reader a one-sentence "view" of the chief aspects of the poem: its literal experience, its chief act of imagining, its subject-matter, and its form. These can be given in any order:

> "The Heart asks Pleasure – first" is a one-sentence, two-stanza poem of increasing disillusionment with life, as the heart's requests are ignored with greater and greater cruelty by its hidden "Inquisitor," whose identity is revealed only at the end.

This one-sentence summary gives your reader a thumbnail sketch of how you see the poem and enables your subsequent analysis to fit into a comprehensible overview.

In concluding your paper, now that you have done the analysis of the strategies of the three poems, you can answer some of the questions raised at the beginning:

> Not only does Dickinson expand and contract time, she also alters sequence and in fact stops sequence altogether, as her poems mimic the relativity of time in emotional experience.

Reread your paper to make sure that your logic and your evidence — your evidence will chiefly be quotations supporting your points — are sufficient to persuade your reader that what you say is true. Check that the beginning offers questions to interest the reader and that your conclusion offers answers to the questions raised at the outset. Ask yourself if you have evoked the temperature and feeling-tone of the poems as well as their imaginative and linguistic strategies. Ask yourself if you have shown, in your paper, why Dickinson is considered a gripping poet of intense feeling. If you have done your job well, your reader will come away from your essay not only understanding your three poems in relation to Dickinson's structuring of time, but also wanting to read more of Dickinson's poetry. A good essay whets the appetite of its reader.

III

ANTHOLOGY

SHERMAN ALEXIE (b. 1966)
Reservation Love Song

I can meet you
in Springdale buy you beer
& take you home
in my one-eyed Ford

I can pay your rent
on HUD house get you free
food from the BIA
get your teeth fixed at IHS

I can buy you alcohol
& not drink it all
while you're away I won't fuck
any of your cousins

if I don't get too drunk
I can bring old blankets
to sleep with in winter
they smell like grandmother

hands digging up roots
they have powerful magic
we can sleep good
we can sleep warm

PAULA GUNN ALLEN (1939 – 2008)
Zen Americana

Un is okay.
Un pretentious. Un decided. Un known.
Un ego is where I want to be. How do you open
the door to Un? What does the un place look like,
look alikes?

Un beginning; can I un wake myself, un sleep
motionless in a bright green chair?
Maybe un lamps light the room (the un place).
When I get there, maybe it will be dark, un lit
where it has no occasion to be any way.

(Un celebrated.)
(Un repentant.)
(Un regenerate.)
(Un believed.)

JULIA ALVAREZ (b. 1950)
From *33*

Let's make a modern primer for our kids:[1]
A is for Auschwitz; B for Biafra;
Chile; Dachau; El Salvador; F is
the Falklands; Grenada; Hiroshima
stands for H; Northern Ireland for I;
J is for Jonestown; K for Korea;
L for massacres in Lidice; My Lai;
N, Nicaragua; O, Okinawa;
P is the Persian Gulf and Qatar, Q;
Rwanda; Sarajevo — this year's hell;
T is Treblinka and Uganda U;
Vietnam and Wounded Knee. What's left to spell?
An X to name the countless disappeared
when they are dust in Yemen or Zaire.

A. R. AMMONS (1926 – 2001)
The City Limits

When you consider the radiance, that it does not withhold
itself but pours its abundance without selection into every
nook and cranny not overhung or hidden; when you consider

that birds' bones make no awful noise against the light but
lie low in the light as in a high testimony; when you consider
the radiance, that it will look into the guiltiest

swervings of the weaving heart and bear itself upon them,
not flinching into disguise or darkening; when you consider
the abundance of such resource as illuminates the glow-blue

bodies and gold-skeined wings of flies swarming the dumped
guts of a natural slaughter or the coil of shit and in no
way winces from its storms of generosity; when you consider

---

[1] The sites in the poem are locales of atrocities, wars, coups, massacres, bombings, genocide, etc.

that air or vacuum, snow or shale, squid or wolf, rose or lichen,
each is accepted into as much light as it will take, then
the heart moves roomier, the man stands and looks about, the

leaf does not increase itself above the grass, and the dark
work of the deepest cells is of a tune with May bushes
and fear lit by the breadth of such calmly turns to praise.

Easter Morning

I have a life that did not become,
that turned aside and stopped,
astonished:
I hold it in me like a pregnancy or
as on my lap a child   5
not to grow or grow old but dwell on

it is to his grave I most
frequently return and return
to ask what is wrong, what was
wrong, to see it all by   10
the light of a different necessity
but the grave will not heal
and the child,
stirring, must share my grave
with me, an old man having   15
gotten by on what was left

when I go back to my home country in these
fresh far-away days, it's convenient to visit
everybody, aunts and uncles, those who used to say,
look how he's shooting up, and the   20
trinket aunts who always had a little
something in their pocketbooks, cinnamon bark
or a penny or nickel, and uncles who
were the rumored fathers of cousins
who whispered of them as of great, if   25
troubled, presences, and school
teachers, just about everybody older
(and some younger) collected in one place
waiting, particularly, but not for
me, mother and father there, too, and others   30
close, close as burrowing
under skin, all in the graveyard

assembled, done for, the world they
used to wield, have trouble and joy
in, gone   35

the child in me that could not become
was not ready for others to go,
to go on into change, blessings and
horrors, but stands there by the road
where the mishap occurred, crying out for   40
help, come and fix this or we
can't get by, but the great ones who
were to return, they could not or did
not hear and went on in a flurry and
now, I say in the graveyard, here   45
lies the flurry, now it can't come
back with help or helpful asides, now
we all buy the bitter
incompletions, pick up the knots of
horror, silently raving, and go on   50
crashing into empty ends not
completions, not rondures the fullness
has come into and spent itself from
I stand on the stump
of a child, whether myself   55
or my little brother who died, and
yell as far as I can, I cannot leave this place, for
for me it is the dearest and the worst,
it is life nearest to life which is
life lost: it is my place where   60
I must stand and fail,
calling attention with tears
to the branches not lofting
boughs into space, to the barren
air that holds the world that was my world   65

though the incompletions
(& completions) burn out
standing in the flash high-burn
momentary structure of ash, still it
is a picture-book, letter-perfect   70
Easter morning: I have been for a
walk: the wind is tranquil: the brook
works without flashing in an abundant

tranquility: the birds are lively with
voice: I saw something I had   75
never seen before: two great birds,
maybe eagles, blackwinged, whitenecked
and -headed, came from the south oaring
the great wings steadily; they went
directly over me, high up, and kept on   80
due north: but then one bird,
the one behind, veered a little to the
left and the other bird kept on seeming
not to notice for a minute: the first
began to circle as if looking for   85
something, coasting, resting its wings
on the down side of some of the circles:
the other bird came back and they both
circled, looking perhaps for a draft;
they turned a few more times, possibly   90
rising — at least, clearly resting —
then flew on falling into distance till
they broke across the local bush and
trees: it was a sight of bountiful
majesty and integrity: the having   95
patterns and routes, breaking
from them to explore other patterns or
better ways to routes, and then the
return: a dance sacred as the sap in
the trees, permanent in its descriptions   100
as the ripples round the brook's
ripplestone: fresh as this particular
flood of burn breaking across us now
from the sun.

ANONYMOUS
Sir Patrick Spens[1]

1

The king sits in Dumferling town,
    Drinking the blude-reid° wine: *blood-red*
"O whar will I get guid sailor,
    To sail this ship of mine?"

---

[1]First printed in 1765, the story may be based on a thirteenth-century incident.

2

Up and spak an eldern knicht,
    Sat at the king's richt knee:
"Sir Patrick Spens is the best sailor
    That sails upon the sea."

3

The king has written a braid° letter   *broad*
    And signed it wi' his hand,
And sent it to Sir Patrick Spens,
    Was walking on the sand.

4

The first line that Sir Patrick read,
    A loud lauch° lauchèd he;   *laugh*
The next line that Sir Patrick read,
    The tear blinded his ee.°   *eye*

5

"O wha is this has done this deed,
    This ill deed done to me,
To send me out this time o' the year,
    To sail upon the sea?

6

"Mak haste, mak haste, my mirry men all,
    Our guid ship sails the morn."
"O say na sae,° my master dear,   *so*
    For I fear a deadly storm.

7

"Late, late yestre'en I saw the new moon
    Wi' the auld moon in hir arm,
And I fear, I fear, my dear master,
    That we will come to harm."

8

O our Scots nobles were richt laith°   *loath*
    To weet° their cork-heeled shoon,°   *wet / shoes*
But lang or° a' the play were played   *before*
    Their hats they swam aboon.°   *above*

9

O lang, lang may their ladies sit,
 Wi' their fans into their hand,
Or ere they see Sir Patrick Spens
 Come sailing to the land.

10

O lang, lang may the ladies stand
 Wi' their gold kems° in their hair,   *combs*
Waiting for their ain dear lords,
 For they'll see them na mair.

11

Half o'er, half o'er to Aberdour
 It's fifty fadom deep,
And there lies guid Sir Patrick Spens
 Wi' the Scots lords at his feet.

ANONYMOUS
Western Wind[1]

Western wind, when will thou blow,
 The small rain down can rain?
Christ, if my love were in my arms
 And I in my bed again!

MATTHEW ARNOLD (1822 – 1888)
Shakespeare

Others abide our question. Thou art free.
We ask and ask — thou smilest and art still,
Out-topping knowledge. For the loftiest hill,
Who to the stars uncrowns his majesty,

Planting his stedfast footsteps in the sea,
Making the heaven of heavens his dwelling-place,
Spares but the cloudy border of his base
To the foiled searching of mortality;

And thou, who didst the stars and sunbeams know,
Self-schooled, self-scanned, self-honored, self-secure,
Didst tread on earth unguessed at — better so!

---

[1]A fifteenth-century lyric that survived in an early sixteenth-century manuscript.

All pains the immortal spirit must endure,
All weakness which impairs, all griefs which bow,
Find their sole speech in that victorious brow.

To Marguerite

Yes! in the sea of life enisled,
With echoing straits between us thrown,
Dotting the shoreless watery wild,
We mortal millions live *alone*.
The islands feel the enclasping flow,
And then their endless bounds they know.

But when the moon their hollows lights,
And they are swept by balms of spring,
And in their glens, on starry nights,
The nightingales divinely sing;
And lovely notes, from shore to shore,
Across the sounds and channels pour —

Oh! then a longing like despair
Is to their farthest caverns sent;
For surely once, they feel, we were
Parts of a single continent!
Now round us spreads the watery plain —
Oh might our marges meet again!

Who ordered, that their longing's fire
Should be, as soon as kindled, cooled?
Who renders vain their deep desire? —
A God, a God their severance ruled!
And bade betwixt their shores to be
The unplumbed, salt, estranging sea.

JOHN ASHBERY (b. 1927)
Paradoxes and Oxymorons

This poem is concerned with language on a very plain level.
Look at it talking to you. You look out a window
Or pretend to fidget. You have it but you don't have it.
You miss it, it misses you. You miss each other.

The poem is sad because it wants to be yours, and cannot.
What's a plain level? It is that and other things,

Bringing a system of them into play. Play?
Well, actually, yes, but I consider play to be

A deeper outside thing, a dreamed role-pattern,
As in the division of grace these long August days
Without proof. Open-ended. And before you know
It gets lost in the steam and chatter of typewriters.

It has been played once more. I think you exist only
To tease me into doing it, on your level, and then you aren't there
Or have adopted a different attitude. And the poem
Has set me softly down beside you. The poem is you.

Street Musicians

One died, and the soul was wrenched out
Of the other in life, who, walking the streets
Wrapped in an identity like a coat, sees on and on
The same corners, volumetrics, shadows
Under trees. Farther than anyone was ever
Called, through increasingly suburban airs
And ways, with autumn falling over everything:
The plush leaves the chattels in barrels
Of an obscure family being evicted
Into the way it was, and is. The other beached
Glimpses of what the other was up to:
Revelations at last. So they grew to hate and forget each other.

So I cradle this average violin that knows
Only forgotten showtunes, but argues
The possibility of free declamation anchored
To a dull refrain, the year turning over on itself
In November, with the spaces among the days
More literal, the meat more visible on the bone.
Our question of a place of origin hangs
Like smoke: how we picnicked in pine forests,
In coves with the water always seeping up, and left
Our trash, sperm and excrement everywhere, smeared
On the landscape, to make of us what we could.

MARGARET ATWOOD (b. 1939)
Habitation

Marriage is not
a house or even a tent

it is before that, and colder:

the edge of the forest, the edge
of the desert
the unpainted stairs
at the back where we squat
outside, eating popcorn

the edge of the receding glacier
where painfully and with wonder
at having survived even
this far

we are learning to make fire

This Is a Photograph of Me

It was taken some time ago.
At first it seems to be
a smeared
print: blurred lines and grey flecks
blended with the paper;

then, as you scan
it, you see in the left-hand corner
a thing that is like a branch: part of a tree
(balsam or spruce) emerging
and, to the right, halfway up
what ought to be a gentle
slope, a small frame house.

In the background there is a lake,
and beyond that, some low hills.

(The photograph was taken
the day after I drowned.
I am in the lake, in the center
of the picture, just under the surface.

It is difficult to say where
precisely, or to say
how large or small I am:
the effect of water
on light is a distortion

but if you look long enough,
eventually
you will be able to see me.)

Up

You wake up filled with dread.
There seems no reason for it.
Morning light sifts through the window,
there is birdsong,
you can't get out of bed.

It's something about the crumpled sheets
hanging over the edge like jungle
foliage, the terry slippers gaping
their dark pink mouths for your feet,
the unseen breakfast — some of it
in the refrigerator you do not dare
to open — you will not dare to eat.

What prevents you? The future. The future tense,
immense as outer space.
You could get lost there.
No. Nothing so simple. The past, its density
and drowned events pressing you down,
like sea water, like gelatin
filling your lungs instead of air.

Forget all that and let's get up.
Try moving your arm.
Try moving your head.
Pretend the house is on fire
and you must run or burn.
No, that one's useless.
It's never worked before.

Where is it coming from, this echo,
this huge No that surrounds you,
silent as the folds of the yellow
curtains, mute as the cheerful
Mexican bowl with its cargo
of mummified flowers?
(You chose the colours of the sun,
not the dried neutrals of shadow.
God knows you've tried.)

Now here's a good one:
you're lying on your deathbed.
You have one hour to live.

Who is it, exactly, you have needed
all these years to forgive?

W. H. AUDEN (1907 – 1973)
As I Walked out One Evening

As I walked out one evening,
    Walking down Bristol Street,
The crowds upon the pavement
    Were fields of harvest wheat.

And down by the brimming river 5
    I heard a lover sing
Under an arch of the railway:
    "Love has no ending.

"I'll love you, dear, I'll love you
    Till China and Africa meet, 10
And the river jumps over the mountain
    And the salmon sing in the street,

"I'll love you till the ocean
    Is folded and hung up to dry
And the seven stars go squawking 15
    Like geese about the sky.

"The years shall run like rabbits,
    For in my arms I hold
The Flower of the Ages,
    And the first love of the world." 20

But all the clocks in the city
    Began to whirr and chime:
"O let not Time deceive you,
    You cannot conquer Time.

"In the burrows of the Nightmare 25
    Where Justice naked is,
Time watches from the shadow
    And coughs when you would kiss.

"In headaches and in worry
    Vaguely life leaks away,
And Time will have his fancy 30
    Tomorrow or today.

"Into many a green valley
  Drifts the appalling snow;
Time breaks the threaded dances   35
  And the diver's brilliant bow.

"O plunge your hands in water,
  Plunge them in up to the wrist;
Stare, stare in the basin
  And wonder what you've missed.   40

"The glacier knocks in the cupboard,
  The desert sighs in the bed,
And the crack in the teacup opens
  A lane to the land of the dead.

"Where the beggars raffle the banknotes   45
  And the Giant is enchanting to Jack,
And the Lily-white Boy is a Roarer,
  And Jill goes down on her back.

"O look, look in the mirror,
  O look in your distress;
Life remains a blessing   50
  Although you cannot bless.

"O stand, stand at the window
  As the tears scald and start;
You shall love your crooked neighbor   55
  With your crooked heart."

It was late, late in the evening,
  The lovers they were gone;
The clocks had ceased their chiming,
  And the deep river ran on.   60

Musée des Beaux Arts[1]

About suffering they were never wrong,
The Old Masters: how well they understood
Its human position; how it takes place
While someone else is eating or opening a window or just walking
  dully along;

---

[1]French for "Museum of Fine Arts."

How, when the aged are reverently, passionately waiting
For the miraculous birth, there always must be
Children who did not specially want it to happen, skating
On a pond at the edge of the wood:
They never forgot
That even the dreadful martyrdom must run its course
Anyhow in a corner, some untidy spot
Where the dogs go on with their doggy life and the torturer's
    horse
Scratches its innocent behind on a tree.

In Brueghel's *Icarus,* for instance: how everything turns away
Quite leisurely from the disaster; the ploughman may
Have heard the splash, the forsaken cry,
But for him it was not an important failure; the sun shone
As it had to on the white legs disappearing into the green
Water; and the expensive delicate ship that must have seen
Something amazing, a boy falling out of the sky,
Had somewhere to get to and sailed calmly on.

JOHN BERRYMAN (1914 – 1972)
Dream Song 4

Filling her compact & delicious body
with chicken páprika, she glanced at me
twice.
Fainting with interest, I hungered back
and only the fact of her husband & four other people
kept me from springing on her

or falling at her little feet and crying
"You are the hottest one for years of night
Henry's dazed eyes
have enjoyed, Brilliance." I advanced upon
(despairing) my spumoni. — Sir Bones: is stuffed,
de world, wif feeding girls.

— Black hair, complexion Latin, jeweled eyes
downcast . . . The slob beside her   feasts . . . What wonders is
she sitting on, over there?
The restaurant buzzes. She might as well be on Mars.
Where did it all go wrong? There ought to be a law against Henry.
— Mr. Bones: there is.

Dream Song 45

He stared at ruin. Ruin stared straight back.
He thought they was old friends. He felt on the stair
where her papa found them bare
they became familiar. When the papers were lost
rich with pals' secrets, he thought he had the knack
of ruin. Their paths crossed

and once they crossed in jail; they crossed in bed;
and over an unsigned letter their eyes met,
and in an Asian city
directionless & lurchy at two & three,
or trembling to a telephone's fresh threat,
and when some wired his head

to reach a wrong opinion, 'Epileptic'.
But he noted now that: they were not old friends.
He did not know this one.
This one was a stranger, come to make amends
for all the imposters, and to make it stick.
Henry nodded, un-.

Dream Song 384

The marker slants, flowerless, day's almost done,
I stand above my father's grave with rage,
often, often before
I've made this awful pilgrimage to one
who cannot visit me, who tore his page
out: I come back for more,

I spit upon this dreadful banker's grave
who shot his heart out in a Florida dawn
O ho alas alas
When will indifference come, I moan & rave
I'd like to scrabble till I got right down
away down under the grass

and ax the casket open ha to see
just how he's taking it, which he sought so hard
we'll tear apart
the mouldering grave clothes ha & then Henry
will heft the ax once more, his final card,
and fell it on the start.

FRANK BIDART (b. 1939)

An American in Hollywood

After you were bitten by a wolf and transformed
into a monster who feeds on other human beings

each full moon and who, therefore, in disgust

wants to die, you think *The desire to die is not
feeling suicidal. It abjures mere action. You have*

wanted to die since the moment you were born.

Crazy narratives — that lend what is merely
in you, and therefore soon-to-be-repeated,

the fleeting illusion of logic and cause.

You think *Those alive there, in the glowing rectangle,*°   *the movie screen*
lead our true lives! They have not, as we have been

forced to here, cut off their arms and legs.

There, you dance as well as Fred Astaire,
though here, inexplicably, you cannot.

Sewer. Still black water

above whose mirror
you bend your face. Font.

IF SEE NO END IN IS

What none knows is when, not if.
Now that your life nears its end
when you turn back what you see
is ruin. You think, It is a prison. No,
it is a vast resonating chamber in
which each thing you say or do is

new, but the same. *What none knows is
how to change.* Each plateau you reach, if
single, limited, only itself, in-
cludes traces of all the others, so that in the end
limitation frees you, there is no
end, if you once see what is there to see.

You cannot see what is there to see —
not when she whose love you failed is

standing next to you. Then, as if refusing the knowledge that life unseparated from her is death, as if
again scorning your refusals, she turns away. The end
achieved by the unappeased is burial within.

Familiar spirit, within whose care I grew, within
whose disappointment I twist, may we at last see
by what necessity the double-bind is in the end
the figure for human life, why what we love is
precluded always by something else we love, as if
each no we speak is yes, each yes no.

The prospect is mixed but elsewhere the forecast is no
better. The eyrie where you perch in
exhaustion has food and is out of the wind, if
cold. You feel old, young, old, young: you scan the sea
for movement, though the promise of sex or food is
the prospect that bewildered you to this end.

Something in you believes that it is not the end.
When you wake, sixth grade will start. The finite you know
you fear is infinite: even at eleven, what you love is
what you should not love, which endless bullies intuit unerringly. The future will be different: you cannot see
the end. What none knows is when, not if.

To My Father

I walked into the room.
There were objects in the room. I thought I needed nothing
from them. They began to speak,
but the words were unintelligible, a painful cacophony . . .
Then I realized they were saying
                              the name
of the man who had chosen them, owned them,
ordered, arranged them, their deceased cause,
the secret pattern that made these things order.
I strained to hear: but
the sound remained unintelligible . . .
senselessly getting louder, urgent, deafening.

Hands over my ears, at last I knew
                              they would remain
inarticulate; your name was not in my language.

ELIZABETH BISHOP (1911 – 1979)

At the Fishhouses

Although it is a cold evening,
down by one of the fishhouses
an old man sits netting,
his net, in the gloaming almost invisible,
a dark purple-brown,   5
and his shuttle worn and polished.
The air smells so strong of codfish
it makes one's nose run and one's eyes water.
The five fishhouses have steeply peaked roofs
and narrow, cleated gangplanks slant up   10
to storerooms in the gables
for the wheelbarrows to be pushed up and down on.
All is silver: the heavy surface of the sea,
swelling slowly as if considering spilling over,
is opaque, but the silver of the benches,   15
the lobster pots, and masts, scattered
among the wild jagged rocks,
is of an apparent translucence
like the small old buildings with an emerald moss
growing on their shoreward walls.   20
The big fish tubs are completely lined
with layers of beautiful herring scales
and the wheelbarrows are similarly plastered
with creamy iridescent coats of mail,
with small iridescent flies crawling on them.   25
Up on the little slope behind the houses,
set in the sparse bright sprinkle of grass,
is an ancient wooden capstan,[1]
cracked, with two long bleached handles
and some melancholy stains, like dried blood,   30
where the ironwork has rusted.
The old man accepts a Lucky Strike.
He was a friend of my grandfather.
We talk of the decline in the population
and of codfish and herring   35
while he waits for a herring boat to come in.
There are sequins on his vest and on his thumb.

---

[1]Machine for raising weights by winding cable around a vertical rotating drum.

He has scraped the scales, the principal beauty,
from unnumbered fish with that black old knife,
the blade of which is almost worn away.   40

Down at the water's edge, at the place
where they haul up the boats, up the long ramp
descending into the water, thin silver
tree trunks are laid horizontally
across the gray stones, down and down   45
at intervals of four or five feet.

Cold dark deep and absolutely clear,
element bearable to no mortal,
to fish and to seals . . . One seal particularly
I have seen here evening after evening.   50
He was curious about me. He was interested in music;
like me a believer in total immersion,[2]
so I used to sing him Baptist hymns.
I also sang "A Mighty Fortress Is Our God."[3]
He stood up in the water and regarded me   55
steadily, moving his head a little.
Then he would disappear, then suddenly emerge
almost in the same spot, with a sort of shrug
as if it were against his better judgment.
Cold dark deep and absolutely clear,   60
the clear gray icy water . . . Back, behind us,
the dignified tall firs begin.
Bluish, associating with their shadows,
a million Christmas trees stand
waiting for Christmas. The water seems suspended   65
above the rounded gray and blue-gray stones.
I have seen it over and over, the same sea, the same,
slightly, indifferently swinging above the stones,
icily free above the stones,
above the stones and then the world.   70
If you should dip your hand in,
your wrist would ache immediately,
your bones would begin to ache and your hand would burn
as if the water were a transmutation of fire

---

[2]Form of baptism practiced by some Christian sects.
[3]Hymn of which the original German version was written by Martin Luther
(1483–1546).

that feeds on stones and burns with a dark gray flame. 75
If you tasted it, it would first taste bitter,
then briny, then surely burn your tongue.
It is like what we imagine knowledge to be:
dark, salt, clear, moving, utterly free,
drawn from the cold hard mouth 80
of the world, derived from the rocky breasts
forever, flowing and drawn, and since
our knowledge is historical, flowing, and flown.

Poem

About the size of an old-style dollar bill,
American or Canadian,
mostly the same whites, gray greens, and steel grays
— this little painting (a sketch for a larger one?)
has never earned any money in its life. 5
Useless and free, it has spent seventy years
as a minor family relic
handed along collaterally to owners
who looked at it sometimes, or didn't bother to.

It must be Nova Scotia; only there 10
does one see gabled wooden houses
painted that awful shade of brown.
The other houses, the bits that show, are white.
Elm trees, low hills, a thin church steeple
— that gray-blue wisp — or is it? In the foreground 15
a water meadow with some tiny cows,
two brushstrokes each, but confidently cows;
two minuscule white geese in the blue water,
back-to-back, feeding, and a slanting stick.
Up closer, a wild iris, white and yellow, 20
fresh-squiggled from the tube.
The air is fresh and cold; cold early spring
clear as gray glass; a half inch of blue sky
below the steel-gray storm clouds.
(They were the artist's specialty.) 25
A specklike bird is flying to the left.
Or is it a flyspeck looking like a bird?

Heavens, I recognize the place, I know it!
It's behind — I can almost remember the farmer's name.

His barn backed on that meadow. There it is,   30
titanium white, one dab. The hint of steeple,
filaments of brush-hairs, barely there,
must be the Presbyterian church.
Would that be Miss Gillespie's house?
Those particular geese and cows   35
are naturally before my time.

A sketch done in an hour, "in one breath,"
once taken from a trunk and handed over.
Would you like this? I'll probably never
have room to hang these things again.   40
Your Uncle George, no, mine, my Uncle George,
he'd be your great-uncle, left them all with Mother
when he went back to England.
You know, he was quite famous, an R.A. . . .

I never knew him. We both knew this place,   45
apparently, this literal small backwater,
looked at it long enough to memorize it,
our years apart. How strange. And it's still loved,
or its memory is (it must have changed a lot).
Our visions coincided — "visions" is   50
too serious a word — our looks, two looks:
art "copying from life" and life itself,
life and the memory of it so compressed
they've turned into each other. Which is which?
Life and the memory of it cramped,   55
dim, on a piece of Bristol board,
dim, but how live, how touching in detail
— the little that we get for free,
the little of our earthly trust. Not much.
About the size of our abidance   60
along with theirs: the munching cows,
the iris, crisp and shivering, the water
still standing from spring freshets,
the yet-to-be-dismantled elms, the geese.

Sestina

September rain falls on the house.
In the failing light, the old grandmother
sits in the kitchen with the child

beside the Little Marvel Stove,
reading the jokes from the almanac,
laughing and talking to hide her tears.

She thinks that her equinoctial tears
and the rain that beats on the roof of the house
were both foretold by the almanac,
but only known to a grandmother.
The iron kettle sings on the stove.
She cuts some bread and says to the child,

It's time for tea now; but the child
is watching the teakettle's small hard tears
dance like mad on the hot black stove,
the way the rain must dance on the house.
Tidying up, the old grandmother
hangs up the clever almanac

on its string. Birdlike, the almanac
hovers half open above the child,
hovers above the old grandmother
and her teacup full of dark brown tears.
She shivers and says she thinks the house
feels chilly, and puts more wood in the stove.

It was to be, says the Marvel Stove.
I know what I know, says the almanac.
With crayons the child draws a rigid house
and a winding pathway. Then the child
puts in a man with buttons like tears
and shows it proudly to the grandmother.

But secretly, while the grandmother
busies herself about the stove,
the little moons fall down like tears
from between the pages of the almanac
into the flower bed the child
has carefully placed in the front of the house.

Time to plant tears, says the almanac.
The grandmother sings to the marvelous stove
and the child draws another inscrutable house.

WILLIAM BLAKE (1757 – 1827)
Ah Sun-flower

Ah Sun-flower, weary of time,
Who countest the steps of the Sun,
Seeking after that sweet golden clime
Where the traveller's journey is done:

Where the Youth pined away with desire,
And the pale Virgin shrouded in snow
Arise from their graves and aspire
Where my Sun-flower wishes to go.

The Garden of Love

I went to the Garden of Love,
And saw what I never had seen:
A Chapel was built in the midst,
Where I used to play on the green.

And the gates of this Chapel were shut,
And "Thou shalt not" writ over the door;
So I turn'd to the Garden of Love,
That so many sweet flowers bore,

And I saw it was filled with graves,
And tomb-stones where flowers should be:
And Priests in black gowns were walking their rounds,
And binding with briars my joys & desires.

The Lamb

Little Lamb, who made thee?
Dost thou know who made thee?
Gave thee life & bid thee feed,
By the stream & o'er the mead;
Gave thee clothing of delight,
Softest clothing, wooly, bright;
Gave thee such a tender voice,
Making all the vales rejoice?
Little Lamb, who made thee?
Dost thou know who made thee?

Little Lamb, I'll tell thee,
Little Lamb, I'll tell thee:

He is callèd by thy name,
For he calls himself a Lamb.
He is meek & he is mild,
He became a little child.
I a child, & thou a lamb,
We are callèd by his name.
Little Lamb, God bless thee.
Little Lamb, God bless thee.

The Mental Traveller

I travelled through a land of men,
A land of men and women too,
And heard and saw such dreadful things
As cold earth wanderers never knew.

For there the babe is born in joy   5
That was begotten in dire woe,
Just as we reap in joy the fruit
Which we in bitter tears did sow;[1]

And if the babe is born a boy
He's given to a woman old,   10
Who nails him down upon a rock,
Catches his shrieks in cups of gold.

She binds iron thorns around his head,
She pierces both his hands and feet,
She cuts his heart out at his side   15
To make it feel both cold & heat.

Her fingers number every nerve
Just as a miser counts his gold;
She lives upon his shrieks and cries —
And she grows young as he grows old,   20

Till he becomes a bleeding youth
And she becomes a virgin bright;
Then he rends up his manacles
And binds her down for his delight.

He plants himself in all her nerves   25
Just as a husbandman his mould,

---

[1] *Psalm* cxxvi 5: "They that sow in tears shall reap in joy."

And she becomes his dwelling-place
And garden, fruitful seventyfold.

An aged shadow soon he fades,
Wandering round an earthly cot,°   *cottage*   30
Full fillèd all with gems and gold
Which he by industry had got.

And these are the gems of the human soul:
The rubies and pearls of a lovesick eye,
The countless gold of the aching heart,   35
The martyr's groan, and the lover's sigh.

They are his meat, they are his drink:
He feeds the beggar and the poor
And the wayfaring traveller;
For ever open is his door.   40

His grief is their eternal joy,
They make the roofs and walls to ring —
Till from the fire on the hearth
A little female babe does spring!

And she is all of solid fire   45
And gems and gold, that none his hand
Dares stretch to touch her baby form,
Or wrap her in his swaddling-band.

But she comes to the man she loves,
If young or old, or rich or poor;   50
They soon drive out the agèd host,
A beggar at another's door.

He wanders weeping far away
Until some other take him in;
Oft blind and age-bent, sore distressed,   55
Until he can a maiden win.

And to allay his freezing age
The poor man takes her in his arms:
The cottage fades before his sight,
The garden and its lovely charms;   60

The guests are scattered through the land
(For the eye altering, alters all);
The senses roll themselves in fear,
And the flat earth becomes a ball,

The stars, sun, moon, all shrink away —   65
A desert vast without a bound,
And nothing left to eat or drink
And a dark desert all around.

The honey of her infant lips,
The bread and wine of her sweet smile,   70
The wild game of her roving eye
Does him to infancy beguile.

For as he eats and drinks he grows
Younger and younger every day;
And on the desert wild they both   75
Wander in terror and dismay.

Like the wild stag she flees away;
Her fear plants many a thicket wild,
While he pursues her night & day,
By various arts of love beguiled,   80

By various arts of love and hate,
Till the wide desert planted o'er
With labyrinths of wayward love,
Where roams the lion, wolf and boar,

Till he becomes a wayward babe   85
And she a weeping woman old.
Then many a lover wanders here,
The sun and stars are nearer rolled,

The trees bring forth sweet ecstasy
To all who in the desert roam,   90
Till many a city there is built,
And many a pleasant shepherd's home.

But when they find the frowning babe
Terror strikes through the region wide;
They cry, 'The Babe! the Babe is born!'   95
And flee away on every side.

For who dare touch the frowning form
His arm is withered to its root,
Lions, boars, wolves, all howling flee
And every tree does shed its fruit;   100

And none can touch that frowning form,
Except it be a woman old;

She nails him down upon the rock,
And all is done as I have told.

The Tyger

Tyger! Tyger! burning bright
In the forests of the night,
What immortal hand or eye
Could frame thy fearful symmetry?

In what distant deeps or skies
Burnt the fire of thine eyes?
On what wings dare he aspire?
What the hand, dare seize the fire?

And what shoulder, & what art,
Could twist the sinews of thy heart?
And when thy heart began to beat,
What dread hand? & what dread feet?

What the hammer? what the chain?
In what furnace was thy brain?
What the anvil? what dread grasp
Dare its deadly terrors clasp?

When the stars threw down their spears,
And water'd heaven with their tears,
Did he smile his work to see?
Did he who made the Lamb make thee?

Tyger! Tyger! burning bright
In the forests of the night,
What immortal hand or eye
Dare frame thy fearful symmetry?

RICHARD BLANCO (b. 1968)
Letters for Mamá

For years they came for you:
Awkward size envelopes
Labeled AIR MAIL *(POR AVION)*
Affixed with multiple oversized stamps
Honoring men from another history.
Monthly, you would peel
Through eggshell pages —

White onionskin sheets
That told you the details
Of Kiki's first steps
And your own Mother's death,
The approximate dates
Recorded by postmarks.

[handwritten note: ○ Author's family is in Cuba]

Sometimes there were pictures:
Poor black and white photos
With foreign dimensions
Of children you would point to,
Tell me were my cousins.
I would handle the images,
Look for my resemblance
In an ear, eyebrow or a nose.

[handwritten note: ○ Focus on the letters as a way to connect → everything is mediated or secondhand]

When possible
You would parcel
A few pounds of your absence
Into discreet brown packages
Filled with bubble gum,
Baby clothes, hand-me-downs,
A few yards of taffeta
For your niece's wedding gown,
Which you would later see
Couturiered to her body
In new pictures that would introduce Alfredo,
Her husband, an addition
You would never meet.

Your silent, filed anxieties
Matched the random terrazzo mosaic
Of our porchgarden
Where you sat
Fading into ninety blue miles,
Surrounded by unopened buds of Impatience,
Waiting for the postman,
While gazing at the purgatorial clouds
Swollen with unfallen rain
That would never spew
Through the mouths of coral-faced gods
Into the empty fountains
Of your parched memory.

MICHAEL BLUMENTHAL (b. 1949)
Early Childhood Education

Because I want to educate him early
in the ways of loss, I move my son
like a fugitive from country to country,
language to language, house to house.
Easily as wind, he flutters
over the world's landscapes,
kissing the surfaces, lifting
the splotched graffiti of his toys
from box to box like a traveling salesman.
Strange cities pass, countries
in various stages of transition, currencies
and economies packaged and sold like trips
to exotic places we can never visit. But my son
visits them all, traversing the world
to a postmodern music of cities and countries,
murmuring *Budapest Haifa Quito Cambridge Austin*
under his breath like a *National Geographic,*
time zone to time zone, vineyard to desert.
In the mere seventh year of his life,
he is already a wise man: He moves
through the world like a bodhisattva,°   *Buddhist deity*
a Zen monk, a Hassid,° a politician,   *member of mystical Jewish movement*
kissing the hands of widows and children,
endearing himself to everyone, waving
in a universal tongue as he leaves and arrives:
hello good-bye hello good-bye hello good-bye.

A Marriage

For Margie Smigel and Jon Dopkeen
You are holding up a ceiling
with both arms. It is very heavy,
but you must hold it up, or else
it will fall down on you. Your arms
are tired, terribly tired,
and, as the day goes on, it feels
as if either your arms or the ceiling
will soon collapse.

But then,
unexpectedly,
something wonderful happens:
Someone,
a man or a woman,
walks into the room
and holds their arms up
to the ceiling beside you.

So you finally get
to take down your arms.
You feel the relief of respite,
the blood flowing back
to your fingers and arms.
And when your partner's arms tire,
you hold up your own
to relieve him again.

And it can go on like this
for many years
without the house falling.

Anne Bradstreet (c. 1612 – 1672)
Before the Birth of One of Her Children

All things within this fading world hath end,
Adversity doth still our joys attend;
No ties so strong, no friends so dear and sweet,
But with death's parting blow is sure to meet.
The sentence past is most irrevocable,
A common thing, yet oh, inevitable.
How soon, my Dear, death may my steps attend,
How soon't may be thy lot to lose thy friend,
We both are ignorant, yet love bids me
These farewell lines to recommend to thee,
That when that knot's untied that made us one,
I may seem thine, who is effect am none.
And if I see not half my days that's due,
What nature would, God grant to yours and you;
The many faults that well you know I have
Let be interred in my oblivious grave;
If any worth or virtue were in me,
Let that live freshly in thy memory

And when thou feel'st no grief, as I no harms,
Yet love thy dead, who long lay in thine arms,
And when thy loss shall be repaid with gains
Look to my little babes, my dear remains.
And if thou love thyself, or loved'st me,
These O protect from stepdame's° injury.   *stepmother's*
And if chance to thine eyes shall bring this verse,
With some sad sighs honor my absent hearse;
And kiss this paper for thy love's dear sake,
Who with salt tears this last farewell did take.

LUCIE BROCK-BROIDO (b. 1956)
Carrowmore

All about Carrowmore[1] the lambs
Were blotched blue, belonging.

They were waiting for carnage or
Snuff. This is why they are born

To begin with, to end.
Ruminants do not frighten

At anything — gorge in the soil, butcher
Noise, the mere graze of predators.

All about Carrowmore
The rain quells for three days.

I remember how cold I was, the botched
Job of travelling. And just so.

Wherever I went I came with me.
She buried her bone barrette

In the ground's woolly shaft.
A tear of her hair, an old gift

To the burnt other who went
First. My thick braid, my ornament —

My belonging I
Remember how cold I will be.

---

[1]A location in County Sligo, Ireland, where there is a large prehistoric megalithic cemetery.

Domestic Mysticism

In thrice 10,000 seasons, I will come back to this world
In a white cotton dress. Kingdom of After My Own Heart.
Kingdom of Fragile. Kingdom of Dwarves. When I come home,
Teacups will quiver in their Dresden saucers, pentatonic chimes
Will move in wind. A covey of alley cats will swarm on the side
Porch & perch there, portents with quickened heartbeats
You will feel against your ankles as you pass through.

After the first millennium, we were supposed to die out.
You had your face pressed up against the coarse dyed velvet
Of the curtain, always looking out for your own transmigration:
What colors you would wear, what cut of jewel,
What kind of pageantry, if your legs would be tied
Down, if there would be wandering tribes of minstrels
Following with woodwinds in your wake.

This work of mine, the kind of work which takes no arms to do,
Is least noble of all. It's peopled by Wizards, the Forlorn,
The Awkward, the Blinkers, the Spoon-Fingered, Agnostic Lispers,
Stutterers of Prayer, the Flatulent, the Closet Weepers,
The Charlatans. I am one of those. In January, the month the owls
Nest in, I am a witness & a small thing altogether. The Kingdom
Of Ingratitude. Kingdom of Lies. Kingdom of *How Dare I.*

I go on dropping words like little pink fish eggs, unawares, slightly
Illiterate, often on the mark. Waiting for the clear whoosh
Of fluid to descend & cover them. A train like a silver
Russian love pill for the sick at heart passes by
My bedroom window in the night at the speed of mirage.
In the next millennium, I will be middle aged. I do not do well
In the marrow of things. Kingdom of Trick. Kingdom of Drug.

In a lung-shaped suburb of Virginia, my sister will be childless
Inside the ice storm, forcing the narcissus. We will send
Each other valentines. The radio blowing out
Vaughan Williams on the highway's purple moor.
At nine o'clock, we will put away our sewing to speak
Of lofty things while, in the pantry, little plants will nudge
Their frail tips toward the light we made last century.

When I come home, the dwarves will be long
In their shadows & promiscuous. The alley cats will sneak
Inside, curl about the legs of furniture, close the skins
Inside their eyelids, sleep. Orchids will be intercrossed & sturdy.

The sun will go down as I sit, thin armed, small breasted
In my cotton dress, poked with eyelet stitches, a little lace,
In the queer light left when a room snuffs out.

I draw a bath, enter the water as a god enters water:
Fertile, knowing, kind, surrounded by glass objects
Which could break easily if mishandled or ill-touched.
Everyone knows an unworshipped woman will betray you.
There is always that promise, I like that. Kingdom of Kinesis.
Kingdom of Benevolent. I will betray as a god betrays,
With tenderheartedness. I've got this mystic streak in me.

Self–Deliverance by Lion[1]

To maul is to make a massive loss
Of the history of a body's history.

What will be taken will be the custody
Of soft tissue, and astonishment.

Her hair was a long damp chestnut
River-pelt spilled after an enormous

And important rain. Her body was still sticky
With the lilac repetitions in her cotton dress.

She was found face-up on a cold March morning
By the most menial and tender of the keepers

At the zoo, crewelled with frost marks, cursive
As the dewclaws on a lion's forepaw, massive

And significant. I had hoped for, all that Serengeti°   *African plain in*
Year, a hopelessness of less despair   *Tanzanian game reserve*

Than hope itself. I knew the excellent repair
Of night fell cruel and quickly where

The lions had the mastery of me[2] — aware
Their mastery was by my will, and fair.

---

[1]Poet's note: "The title . . . is adapted from Kay Redfield Jamison's *Night Falls Fast*. In 1995, the body of a thirty-six-year-old transient woman from Little Rock was discovered by a worker at the National Zoo in Washington. She had scaled a barrier, ascended a rough high wall, and crossed a twenty-six-foot moat in order to make her way into the lions' den. Her death by mauling was ruled a suicide."

[2]Poet's note: "From Daniel 6:24; *The lions had the mastery of them / And broke all their bones in pieces*."

EMILY BRONTË (1818 – 1848)
No Coward Soul Is Mine

No coward soul is mine,
No trembler in the world's storm-troubled sphere!
I see Heaven's glories shine,
And Faith shines equal, arming me from Fear.

O God within my breast,
Almighty ever-present Deity!
Life, that in me hast rest
As I, undying Life, have power in thee!

Vain are the thousand creeds
That move men's hearts, unutterably vain;
Worthless as withered weeds,
Or idlest froth, amid the boundless main

To waken doubt in one
Holding so fast by thy infinity,
So surely anchored on
The steadfast rock of Immortality.

With wide-embracing love
Thy spirit animates eternal years,
Pervades and broods above,
Changes, sustains, dissolves, creates and rears.

Though earth and moon were gone,
And suns and universes ceased to be,
And thou were left alone,
Every Existence would exist in thee.

There is not room for Death,
Nor atom that his might could render void
Since thou art Being and Breath,
And what thou art may never be destroyed.

Remembrance

Cold in the earth — and the deep snow piled above thee,
Far, far removed, cold in the dreary grave!
Have I forgot, my only Love, to love thee,
Severed at last by Time's all-severing wave?

Now, when alone, do my thoughts no longer hover
Over the mountains, on that northern shore,

Resting their wings where heath and fern leaves cover
Thy noble heart forever, ever more?

Cold in the earth — and fifteen wild Decembers,
From those brown hills, have melted into spring;
Faithful, indeed, is the spirit that remembers
After such years of change and suffering!

Sweet Love of youth, forgive, if I forget thee,
While the world's tide is bearing me along;
Other desires and other hopes beset me,
Hopes which obscure, but cannot do thee wrong!

No later light has lightened up my heaven,
No second morn has ever shone for me;
All my life's bliss from thy dear life was given,
All my life's bliss is in the grave with thee.

But, when the days of golden dreams had perished,
And even Despair was powerless to destroy,
Then did I learn how existence could be cherished,
Strengthened, and fed without the aid of joy.

Then did I check the tears of useless passion —
Weaned my young soul from yearning after thine;
Sternly denied its burning wish to hasten
Down to that tomb already more than mine.

And, even yet, I dare not let it languish,
Dare not indulge in memory's rapturous pain;
Once drinking deep of that divinest anguish,
How could I seek the empty world again?

GWENDOLYN BROOKS (1917 – 2000)
The Bean Eaters

They eat beans mostly, this old yellow pair.
Dinner is a casual affair.
Plain chipware on a plain and creaking wood,
Tin flatware.

Two who are Mostly Good.
Two who have lived their day,
But keep on putting on their clothes
And putting things away.

And remembering . . .
Remembering, with twinklings and twinges,
As they lean over the beans in their rented back room that is full
    of beads and receipts and dolls and clothes, tobacco crumbs,
    vases and fringes.

Beverly Hills, Chicago

> *"and the people live till they have white hair"*
> — E. M. PRICE

The dry brown coughing beneath their feet,
(Only a while, for the handyman is on his way)
These people walk their golden gardens.
We say ourselves fortunate to be driving by today.

That we may look at them, in their gardens where
The summer ripeness rots. But not raggedly.
Even the leaves fall down in lovelier patterns here.
And the refuse, the refuse is a neat brilliancy.

When they flow sweetly into their houses
With softness and slowness touched by that everlasting gold,
We know what they go to. To tea. But that does not mean
They will throw some little black dots into some water and add
    sugar and the juice of the cheapest lemons that are sold,

While downstairs that woman's vague phonograph bleats, "Knock
    me a kiss."
And the living all to be made again in the sweatingest physical
    manner
Tomorrow. . . . Not that anybody is saying that these people have
    no trouble.
Merely that it is trouble with a gold-flecked beautiful banner.

Nobody is saying that these people do not ultimately cease
    to be. And
Sometimes their passings are even more painful than ours.
It is just that so often they live till their hair is white.
They make excellent corpses, among the expensive flowers. . . .

Nobody is furious. Nobody hates these people.
At least, nobody driving by in this car.

Things, people, lives always look better when you caren away a glimpse af them.

ROBERT BROWNING (1812 – 1889)
"Childe Roland to the Dark Tower Came"[1]

(See Edgar's Song in Lear*)*

1

My first thought was, he lied in every word,
  That hoary cripple, with malicious eye
  Askance to watch the working of his lie
On mine, and mouth scarce able to afford
Suppression of the glee, that pursed and scored
  Its edge, at one more victim gained thereby.

2

What else should he be set for, with his staff?
  What, save to waylay with his lies, ensnare
  All travelers who might find him posted there,
And ask the road? I guessed what skull-like laugh
Would break, what crutch 'gin° write my epitaph   *begin to*
  For pastime in the dusty thoroughfare,

3

If at his counsel I should turn aside
  Into that ominous tract which, all agree,
  Hides the Dark Tower. Yet acquiescingly
I did turn as he pointed: neither pride
Nor hope rekindling at the end descried,
  So much as gladness that some end might be.

4

For, what with my whole world-wide wandering,
  What with my search drawn out through years, my hope
  Dwindled into a ghost not fit to cope
With that obstreperous joy success would bring, —
I hardly tried now to rebuke the spring
  My heart made, finding failure in its scope.

5

As when a sick man very near to death
  Seems dead indeed, and feels begin and end
  The tears, and takes the farewell of each friend,

---

[1]The title is taken from Shakespeare's *King Lear* (III. iv. 173). A "childe" is a medieval term for a youth awaiting knighthood.

And hears one bid the other go, draw breath
Freelier outside, ("since all is o'er," he saith,
    "And the blow fallen no grieving can amend;")

6

While some discuss if near the other graves
    Be room enough for this, and when a day
    Suits best for carrying the corpse away,
With care about the banners, scarves and staves:
And still the man hears all, and only craves
    He may not shame such tender love and stay.

7

Thus, I had so long suffered in this quest,
    Heard failure prophesied so oft, been writ
    So many times among "The Band" — to wit,
The knights who to the Dark Tower's search addressed
Their steps — that just to fail as they, seemed best,
    And all the doubt was now — should I be fit?

8

So, quiet as despair, I turned from him,
    That hateful cripple, out of his highway
    Into the path he pointed. All the day
Had been a dreary one at best, and dim
Was settling to its close, yet shot one grim
    Red leer to see the plain catch its estray.[2]

9

For mark! no sooner was I fairly found
    Pledged to the plain, after a pace or two,
    Than, pausing to throw backward a last view
O'er the safe road, 'twas gone; gray plain all round:
Nothing but plain to the horizon's bound.
    I might go on; naught else remained to do.

10

So, on I went. I think I never saw
    Such starved ignoble nature; nothing throve:
    For flowers — as well expect a cedar grove!

---

[2]Potential victim who has strayed.

But cockle, spurge, according to their law
Might propagate their kind, with none to awe,
    You'd think: a burr had been a treasure trove.

11

No! penury, inertness and grimace,
    In some strange sort, were the land's portion. "See
    Or shut your eyes," said Nature peevishly,
"It nothing skills: I cannot help my case:
'Tis the Last Judgment's fire must cure this place,
    Calcine° its clods and set my prisoners free."   *reduce to ash*

12

If there pushed any ragged thistle-stalk
    Above its mates, the head was chopped; the bents°   *coarse grasses*
    Were jealous else. What made those holes and rents
In the dock's harsh swarth leaves, bruised as to balk
All hope of greenness? 'tis a brute must walk
    Pashing° their life out, with a brute's intents.   *crushing*

13

As for the grass, it grew as scant as hair
    In leprosy; thin dry blades pricked the mud
    Which underneath looked kneaded up with blood.
One stiff blind horse, his every bone a-stare,
Stood stupefied, however he came there:
    Thrust out past service from the devil's stud!

14

Alive? he might be dead for aught I know,
    With that red gaunt colloped° neck a-strain,   *ridged*
    And shut eyes underneath the rusty mane;
Seldom went such grotesqueness with such woe;
I never saw a brute I hated so;
    He must be wicked to deserve such pain.

15

I shut my eyes and turned them on my heart.
    As a man calls for wine before he fights,
    I asked one draught of earlier, happier sights,
Ere fitly I could hope to play my part.
Think first, fight afterwards — the soldier's art:
    One taste of the old time sets all to rights.

16

Not it! I fancied Cuthbert's reddening face
    Beneath its garniture of curly gold,
    Dear fellow, till I almost felt him fold
An arm in mine to fix me to the place,
That way he used. Alas, one night's disgrace!
    Out went my heart's new fire and left it cold.

17

Giles then, the soul of honor — there he stands
    Frank as ten years ago when knighted first.
    What honest man should dare (he said) he durst.
Good — but the scene shifts — faugh! what hangman hands
Pin to his breast a parchment? His own bands
    Read it. Poor traitor, spit upon and curst!

18

Better this present than a past like that;
    Back therefore to my darkening path again!
    No sound, no sight as far as eye could strain.
Will the night send a howlet° or a bat?   *owl*
I asked: when something on the dismal flat
    Came to arrest my thoughts and change their train.

19

A sudden little river crossed my path
    As unexpected as a serpent comes.
    No sluggish tide congenial to the glooms;
This, as it frothed by, might have been a bath
For the fiend's glowing hoof — to see the wrath
    Of its black eddy bespate° with flakes and spumes.   *bespattered*

20

So petty yet so spiteful! All along,
    Low scrubby alders kneeled down over it;
    Drenched willows flung them headlong in a fit
Of mute despair, a suicidal throng:
The river which had done them all the wrong,
    Whate'er that was, rolled by, deterred no whit.

21

Which, while I forded, — good saints, how I feared
    To set my foot upon a dead man's cheek,
    Each step, or feel the spear I thrust to seek

For hollows, tangled in his hair or beard!
— It may have been a water-rat I speared,
    But, ugh! it sounded like a baby's shriek.

22

Glad was I when I reached the other bank.
    Now for a better country. Vain presage!
    Who were the strugglers, what war did they wage,
Whose savage trample thus could pad the dank
Soil to a plash? Toads in a poisoned tank,
    Or wild cats in a red-hot iron cage —

23

The fight must so have seemed in that fell cirque.
    What penned them there, with all the plain to choose?
    No footprint leading to that horrid mews,
None out of it. Mad brewage set to work
Their brains, no doubt, like galley-slaves the Turk
    Pits for his pastime, Christians against Jews.

24

And more than that — a furlong on — why, there!
    What bad use was that engine for, that wheel,
    Or brake, not wheel — that harrow fit to reel
Men's bodies out like silk? with all the air
Of Tophet's° tool, on earth left unaware,   *Hell's*
    Or brought to sharpen its rusty teeth of steel.

25

Then came a bit of stubbed ground, once a wood,
    Next a marsh, it would seem, and now mere earth
    Desperate and done with; (so a fool finds mirth,
Makes a thing and then mars it, till his mood
Changes and off he goes!) within a rood°   *quarter-acre*
    Bog, clay and rubble, sand and stark black dearth.

26

Now blotches rankling, colored gay and grim,
    Now patches where some leanness of the soil's
    Broke into moss or substances like boils;
Then came some palsied oak, a cleft in him
Like a distorted mouth that splits its rim
    Gaping at death, and dies while it recoils.

27

And just as far as ever from the end!
    Nought in the distance but the evening, nought
    To point my footstep further! At the thought,
A great black bird, Apollyon's[3] bosom-friend,
Sailed past, nor beat his wide wing dragon-penned°   *dragon-feathered*
    That brushed my cap — perchance the guide I sought.

28

For, looking up, aware I somehow grew,
    'Spite of the dusk, the plain had given place
    All round to mountains — with such name to grace
Mere ugly heights and heaps now stolen in view.
How thus they had surprised me, — solve it, you!
    How to get from them was no clearer case.

29

Yet half I seemed to recognize some trick
    Of mischief happened to me, God knows when —
    In a bad dream perhaps. Here ended, then,
Progress this way. When, in the very nick
Of giving up, one time more, came a click
    As when a trap shuts — you're inside the den!

30

Burningly it came on me all at once,
    This was the place! those two hills on the right,
    Crouched like two bulls locked horn in horn in fight;
While to the left, a tall scalped mountain . . . Dunce,
Dotard, a-dozing at the very nonce,
    After a life spent training for the sight!

31

What in the midst lay but the Tower itself?
    The round squat turret, blind as the fool's heart,
    Built of brown stone, without a counterpart
In the whole world. The tempest's mocking elf
Points to the shipman thus the unseen shelf
    He strikes on, only when the timbers start.

---

[3]In Revelation 9:11, an angel of the bottomless pit.

32

Not see? because of night perhaps? — why, day
    Came back again for that! before it left,
    The dying sunset kindled through a cleft:
The hills, like giants at a hunting, lay,
Chin upon hand, to see the game at bay, —
    "Now stab and end the creature — to the heft!"

33

Not hear? when noise was everywhere! it tolled
    Increasing like a bell. Names in my ears
    Of all the lost adventurers my peers, —
How such a one was strong, and such was bold,
And such was fortunate, yet each of old
    Lost, lost! one moment knelled the woe of years.

34

There they stood, ranged along the hillsides, met
    To view the last of me, a living frame
    For one more picture! in a sheet of flame
I saw them and I knew them all. And yet
Dauntless the slug-horn[4] to my lips I set,
    And blew. *"Childe Roland to the Dark Tower came."*

ROBERT BURNS (1759 – 1796)

O, Wert Thou in the Cauld Blast

O, wert thou in the cauld blast
    On yonder lea, on yonder lea,
My plaidie to the angry airt,°   *quarter (of the wind)*
    I'd shelter thee, I'd shelter thee.
Or did misfortune's bitter storms
    Around thee blaw, around thee blaw,
Thy bield° should be my bosom,   *shelter*
    To share it a', to share it a'.

Or were I in the wildest waste,
    Sae black and bare, sae black and bare,
The desert were a paradise,
    If thou wert there, if thou wert there.

---

[4]A rough trumpet made from the horn of an ox or cow.

Or were I monarch o' the globe,
    Wi' thee to reign, wi' thee to reign,
The brightest jewel in my crown
    Wad be my queen, wad be my queen.

A Red, Red Rose

O my luve's like a red, red rose,
    That's newly sprung in June;
O my luve's like the melodie
    That's sweetly played in tune.

As fair art thou, my bonnie lass,
    So deep in luve am I;
And I will luve thee still, my dear,
    Till a' the seas gang dry.

Till a' the seas gang dry, my dear,
    And the rocks melt wi' the sun:
O I will luve thee still, my dear,
    While the sands o' life shall run.

And fare thee weel, my only luve,
    And fare thee weel awhile!
And I will come again, my luve,
    Though it were ten thousand mile.

GEORGE GORDON, LORD BYRON (1788 – 1824)
When We Two Parted

When we two parted
    In silence and tears,
Half broken-hearted
    To sever for years,
Pale grew thy cheek and cold,
    Colder thy kiss;
Truly that hour foretold
    Sorrow to this.

The dew of the morning
    Sunk chill on my brow —
It felt like the warning
    Of what I feel now.
Thy vows are all broken,
    And light is thy fame;

I hear thy name spoken,
    And share in its shame.

They name thee before me,
    A knell to mine ear;
A shudder comes o'er me —
    Why wert thou so dear?
They know not I knew thee,
    Who knew thee too well —
Long, long shall I rue thee,
    Too deeply to tell.

In secret we met —
    In silence I grieve,
That thy heart could forget,
    Thy spirit deceive.
If I should meet thee
    After long years,
How should I greet thee? —
    With silence and tears.

LORNA DEE CERVANTES (b. 1954)

Freeway 280

Las casitas[1] near the gray cannery,
nestled amid wild abrazos[2] of climbing roses
and man-high red geraniums
are gone now. The freeway conceals it
all beneath a raised scar.

But under the fake windsounds of the open lanes,
in the abandoned lots below, new grasses sprout,
wild mustard remembers, old gardens
come back stronger than they were,
trees have been left standing in their yards.
Albaricoqueros, cerezos, nogales . . .[3]
Viejitas[4] come here with paper bags to gather greens.
Espinaca, verdolagas, yerbabuena . . . [5]

---

[1] The little houses.
[2] Embraces.
[3] Apricot trees, cherry trees, walnut trees.
[4] Old women.
[5] Spinach, purslane, mint.

I scramble over the wire fence
that would have kept me out.
Once, I wanted out, wanted the rigid lanes
to take me to a place without sun,
without the smell of tomatoes burning
on swing shift in the greasy summer air.

Maybe it's here
en los campos extraños de esta ciudad[6]
where I'll find it, that part of me
mown under
like a corpse
or a loose seed.

VICTORIA CHANG (b. 1970)
$4.99 All You Can Eat Sunday Brunch

[handwritten margin note: •she becomes the things she views a cheap, used, worn]

I am paper mats, plotted with Chinese horoscopes,
snake, dog, cock, table after table of predictable
entertainment. I am wallpaper with raised velvet
flowers, peeling at the seams. I am the crack

of the toilet seat my father cleans with Comet
and a sponge. I am the back booth bandaged

[handwritten margin note: •Speaker is both tied to these things but wishes she wasn't]

with duct tape. I am freshly wrapped egg rolls,
candle glows stacked in a pyramid. I am the cook

arguing with his wife, his face pasted with pork fat.
I am trays of sweet-and-sour pork, fried rice,

fried noodles, egg foo young, over blue flames
that sway like feathers. I am the two-hundred-

pound fathers with untucked shirts. I am my mother
filling trays with food, all tasting the same but wearing

different clothes. I am the bell on the door at two-thirty,
tired from thrashing. I am my father in the back booth

with his calculator, soot rooted in the corner of the keys.
I am my father, mumbling, hunching, punching

keys over and over. I am the minus symbol,
with its turquoise hue, that never disappears.

[6]In the strange fields of this city.

MARILYN CHIN (b. 1955)
Autumn Leaves

My dead piled up, thick, fragrant, on the fire escape.
My mother ordered me again, and again, to sweep it clean.
All that blooms must fall. I learned this not from the Tao,
    but from high school biology.
Oh, the contradictions of having a broom and not a dustpan!
I swept the leaves down, down through the iron grille
and let the dead rain over the Wong family's patio.

And it was Achilles Wong who completed the task.
    We called her:
The-one-who-cleared-away-another-family's-autumn.
She blossomed, tall, benevolent, notwithstanding.

JOHN CLARE (1793 – 1864)
Badger

When midnight comes a host of dogs and men
Go out and track the badger to his den,
And put a sack within the hole, and lie
Till the old grunting badger passes by.
He comes and hears — they let the strongest loose.
The old fox hears the noise and drops the goose.
The poacher shoots and hurries from the cry,
And the old hare half wounded buzzes by.
They get a forkèd stick to bear him down
And clap the dogs and take him to the town,
And bait him all the day with many dogs,
And laugh and shout and fright the scampering hogs.
He runs along and bites at all he meets:
They shout and hollo down the noisy streets.

He turns about to face the loud uproar
And drives the rebels to their very door.
The frequent stone is hurled where'er they go;
When badgers fight, then everyone's a foe.
The dogs are clapped and urged to join the fray;
The badger turns and drives them all away.
Though scarcely half as big, demure and small,
He fights with dogs for hours and beats them all.
The heavy mastiff, savage in the fray,

Lies down and licks his feet and turns away.
The bulldog knows his match and waxes cold,
The badger grins and never leaves his hold.
He drives the crowd and follows at their heels
And bites them through — the drunkard swears and reels.

The frighted women take the boys away,
The blackguard laughs and hurries on the fray.
He tries to reach the woods, an awkward race,
But sticks and cudgels quickly stop the chase.
He turns again and drives the noisy crowd
And beats the many dogs in noises loud.
He drives away and beats them every one,
And then they loose them all and set them on.
He falls as dead and kicked by boys and men,
Then starts and grins and drives the crowd again;
Till kicked and torn and beaten out he lies
And leaves his hold and crackles, groans, and dies.

First Love

I ne'er was struck before that hour
    With love so sudden and so sweet,
Her face it bloomed like a sweet flower
    And stole my heart away complete.
My face turned pale as deadly pale.
    My legs refused to walk away,
And when she looked, what could I ail?
    My life and all seemed turned to clay.

And then my blood rushed to my face
    And took my eyesight quite away,
The trees and bushes round the place
    Seemed midnight at noonday.
I could not see a single thing,
    Words from my eyes did start —
They spoke as chords do from the string,
    And blood burnt round my heart.

Are flowers the winter's choice?
    Is love's bed always snow?
She seemed to hear my silent voice,
    Not love's appeals to know.

I never saw so sweet a face
    As that I stood before.
My heart has left its dwelling-place
    And can return no more.

I Am

I am: yet what I am none cares or knows
    My friends forsake me like a memory lost,
I am the self-consumer of my woes —
    They rise and vanish in oblivious host,
Like shadows in love's frenzied, stifled throes —
And yet I am, and live — like vapors tossed

Into the nothingness of scorn and noise,
    Into the living sea of waking dreams,
Where there is neither sense of life or joys,
    But the vast shipwreck of my life's esteems;
Even the dearest, that I love the best,
Are strange — nay, rather stranger than the rest.

I long for scenes, where man hath never trod,
    A place where woman never smiled or wept —
There to abide with my Creator, God,
    And sleep as I in childhood sweetly slept,
Untroubling, and untroubled where I lie,
The grass below — above the vaulted sky.

LUCILLE CLIFTON (b. 1936)
The Lost Baby Poem

the time i dropped your almost body down
down to meet the waters under the city
and run one with the sewage to the sea
what did i know about waters rushing back
what did i know about drowning
of being drowned

you would have been born into winter
in the year of the disconnected gas
and no car   we would have made the thin
walk over genesee hill into a canada wind
to watch you slip like ice into strangers' hands
you would have fallen naked as snow into winter

if you were here i could tell you these
and some other things

if i am ever less than a mountain
for your definite brothers and sisters
let the rivers pour over my head
let the sea take me for a spiller
of seas   let black men call me stranger
always   for your never named sake

Henri Cole (b. 1956)
Carwash

I love the iridescent tricolor slime
that squirts all over my Honda in random
yet purposeful patterns as I sit in the semi-
dark of the "touch-free" carwash with you.
Listening to the undercarriage blast, I think,
"Love changes and will not be commanded."
I smile at the long flesh-colored tentacles waving
at us like passengers waving good-bye.
Water isn't shaped like a river or ocean;
it mists invisibly against metal and glass.
In the corridor of green unnatural lights
recalling the lunatic asylum, how can I
defend myself against what I want?
Lay your head in my lap. Touch me.

40 Days and 40 Nights

Opening a vein he called my radial,
the phlebotomist introduced himself as Angel.
Since the counseling it had been ten days
of deep inversion — self-recrimination weighed
against regret, those useless emotions.
Now there would be thirty more enduring the notion
of some self-made doom foretold in the palm.

Waiting for blood work with aristocratic calm,
big expectant mothers from Spanish Harlem
appeared cut-out, as if Matisse had conceived them.
Their bright smocks ruffling like plumage before the fan,
they might themselves have been angels, come by land.

Consent and disclosure signed away, liquid gold
of urine glimmering in a plastic cup, threshold
of last doubt crossed, the red fluid was drawn
in a steady hematic ooze from my arm.
"Now, darling, the body doesn't lie," Angel said.
DNA and enzymes and antigens in his head
true as lines in the face in the mirror
on his desk.

       I smiled, pretending to be cheered.
In the way that some become aware of God
when they cease becoming overawed
with themselves, no less than the artist concealed
behind the surface of whatever object or felt
words he builds, so I in my first week
of waiting let the self be displaced by each
day's simplest events, letting them speak
with emblematic voices that might teach me.
They did . . . until I happened on the card
from the clinic, black-framed as a graveyard.
Could the code 12 22 90 have represented
some near time, December 22, 1990, for repentance?
The second week I believed it. The fourth I
rejected it and much else loved, until the eyes
teared those last days and the lab phoned.

Back at the clinic — someone's cheap cologne,
Sunday lamb yet on the tongue, the mind cool as a pitcher
of milk, a woman's knitting needles aflutter,
Angel's hand in mind — I watched the verdict-lips move,
rubbed my arm, which, once pricked, had tingled then bruised.

SAMUEL TAYLOR COLERIDGE (1772 – 1834)
Dejection: An Ode

> *Late, late yestreen I saw the new Moon,*
> *With the old Moon in her arms;*
> *And I fear, I fear, my master dear!*
> *We shall have a deadly storm.*
>   — *BALLAD OF SIR PATRICK SPENCE*

1

Well! If the Bard was weather-wise, who made
    The grand old ballad of Sir Patrick Spence,

This night, so tranquil now, will not go hence
Unroused by winds, that ply a busier trade
Than those which mold yon cloud in lazy flakes,
Or the dull sobbing draft, that moans and rakes
Upon the strings of this Aeolian lute,[1]
        Which better far were mute.
    For lo! the New-moon winter-bright!
    And overspread with phantom light,
    (With swimming phantom light o'erspread
    But rimmed and circled by a silver thread)
I see the old Moon in her lap, foretelling
    The coming-on of rain and squally blast.
And oh! that even now the gust were swelling,
    And the slant night shower driving loud and fast!
Those sounds which oft have raised me, whilst they awed,
    And sent my soul abroad,
Might now perhaps their wonted impulse give,
Might startle this dull pain, and make it move and live!

2

A grief without a pang, void, dark, and drear,
    A stifled, drowsy, unimpassioned grief,
    Which finds no natural outlet, no relief,
       In word, or sigh, or tear —
O Lady! in this wan and heartless mood,
To other thoughts by yonder throstle wooed,
    All this long eve, so balmy and serene,
Have I been gazing on the western sky,
    And its peculiar tint of yellow green:
And still I gaze — and with how blank an eye!
And those thin clouds above, in flakes and bars,
That give away their motion to the stars;
Those stars, that glide behind them or between,
Now sparkling, now bedimmed, but always seen:
Yon crescent Moon, as fixed as if it grew
In its own cloudless, starless lake of blue;
I see them all so excellently fair,
I see, not feel, how beautiful they are!

---

[1]An Aeolian lute or harp is a stringed instrument that produces musical sounds when touched by a current of air.

3

My genial spirits fail;
And what can these avail
To lift the smothering weight from off my breast?
It were a vain endeavor,
Though I should gaze forever
On that green light that lingers in the west:
I may not hope from outward forms to win
The passion and the life, whose fountains are within.

4

O Lady! we receive but what we give,
And in our life alone does Nature live:
Ours is her wedding garment, ours her shroud!
And would we aught behold, of higher worth,
Than that inanimate cold world allowed
To the poor loveless ever-anxious crowd,
Ah! from the soul itself must issue forth
A light, a glory, a fair luminous cloud
Enveloping the Earth —
And from the soul itself must there be sent
A sweet and potent voice, of its own birth,
Of all sweet sounds the life and element!

5

O pure of heart! thou need'st not ask of me
What this strong music in the soul may be!
What, and wherein it doth exist,
This light, this glory, this fair luminous mist,
This beautiful and beauty-making power.
Joy, virtuous Lady! Joy that ne'er was given,
Save to the pure, and in their purest hour,
Life, and Life's effluence, cloud at once and shower,
Joy, Lady! is the spirit and the power,
Which wedding Nature to us gives in dower
A new Earth and new Heaven,
Undreamt of by the sensual and the proud —
Joy is the sweet voice, Joy the luminous cloud —
We in ourselves rejoice!
And thence flows all that charms or ear or sight,
All melodies the echoes of that voice,
All colors a suffusion from that light.

6

There was a time when, though my path was rough,
    This joy within me dallied with distress,
And all misfortunes were but as the stuff
    Whence Fancy made me dreams of happiness:
For hope grew round me, like the twining vine,
And fruits, and foliage, not my own, seemed mine.
But now afflictions bow me down to earth:
Nor care I that they rob me of my mirth;
    But oh! each visitation
Suspends what nature gave me at my birth,
    My shaping spirit of Imagination.

For not to think of what I needs must feel,
    But to be still and patient, all I can;
And haply by abstruse research to steal
    From my own nature all the natural man —
    This was my sole resource, my only plan:
Till that which suits a part infects the whole,
And now is almost grown the habit of my soul.

7

Hence, viper thoughts, that coil around my mind,
    Reality's dark dream!
I turn from you, and listen to the wind,
    Which long has raved unnoticed. What a scream
Of agony by torture lengthened out
That lute sent forth! Thou Wind, that rav'st without,
    Bare crag, or mountain tairn,° or blasted tree,   *pool*
Or pine grove whither woodman never clomb,
Or lonely house, long held the witches' home,
    Methinks were fitter instruments for thee,
Mad Lutanist! who in this month of showers,
Of dark-brown gardens, and of peeping flowers,
Mak'st Devils' yule, with worse than wintry song,
The blossoms, buds, and timorous leaves among.
    Thou Actor, perfect in all tragic sounds!

Thou mighty Poet, e'en to frenzy bold!
    What tell'st thou now about?
      'Tis of the rushing of an host in rout,
  With groans, of trampled men, with smarting wounds —
At once they groan with pain, and shudder with the cold!
But hush! there is a pause of deepest silence!
    And all that noise, as of a rushing crowd,
With groans, and tremulous shudderings — all is over —
  It tells another tale, with sounds less deep and loud!
      A tale of less affright,
      And tempered with delight,
As Otway's[2] self had framed the tender lay —
      'Tis of a little child
      Upon a lonesome wild,
Not far from home, but she hath lost her way:
And now moans low in bitter grief and fear,
And now screams loud, and hopes to make her mother hear.

8

'Tis midnight, but small thoughts have I of sleep:
Full seldom may my friend such vigils keep!
Visit her, gentle Sleep! with wings of healing,
    And may this storm be but a mountain birth,
May all the stars hang bright above her dwelling,
    Silent as though they watched the sleeping Earth!
      With light heart may she rise,
      Gay fancy, cheerful eyes,
  Joy lift her spirit, joy attune her voice;
To her may all things live, from pole to pole,
Their life the eddying of her living soul!
    O simple spirit, guided from above,
Dear Lady! friend devoutest of my choice,
Thus mayest thou ever, evermore rejoice.

---

[2]Thomas Otway (1652–1685), a dramatist whose plays emphasize pathos and sentiment.

The Rime of the Ancient Mariner

In Seven Parts

> *Facile credo, plures esse Naturas invisibiles quam visibiles in*
> *rerum universitate. Sed horum* [sic] *omnium familiam quis*
> *nobis enarrabit? et gradus et cognationes et discrimina et*
> *singulorum munera? Quid agunt? quae loca habitant? Harum*
> *rerum notitiam semper ambivit ingenium humanum, nunquam*
> *attigit. Juvat, interea, non diffiteor, quandoque in animo,*
> *tanquam in tabulà, majoris et melioris mundi imaginem*
> *contemplari: ne mens assuefacta hodiernae vitae minutiis se*
> *contrahat nimis, et tota subsidat in pusillas cogitationes. Sed*
> *veritati interea invigilandum est, modusque servandus, ut certa*
> *ab incertis, diem a nocte, distinguamus.*[1]
>
> — T. BURNET

Part I

An ancient Mariner meeteth three Gallants bidden to a wedding feast, and detaineth one.	It is an ancient Mariner And he stoppeth one of three. — "By thy long gray beard and glittering eye, Now wherefore stopp'st thou me?

The Bridegroom's doors are opened wide,   5
And I am next of kin;
The guests are met, the feast is set:
May'st hear the merry din."

He holds him with his skinny hand,
"There was a ship," quoth he.   10
"Hold off! unhand me, graybeard loon!"
Eftsoons° his hand dropped he.   *immediately*

The Wedding Guest is spellbound by the eye of the old seafaring man, and constrained to hear his tale.

He holds him with his glittering eye —
The Wedding Guest stood still,
And listens like a three years' child: 15
The Mariner hath his will.

The Wedding Guest sat on a stone:
He cannot choose but hear;

---

[1]From Burnet's *Archaeologiae Philosophiae:* "I can easily believe that there are more invisible than visible beings in the universe. But of their families, degrees, connections, distinctions, and functions, who shall tell us? How do they act? Where are they found? About such matters the human mind has always circled without attaining knowledge. Yet I do not doubt that sometimes it is well for the soul to contemplate as in a picture the image of a larger and better world, lest the mind, habituated to the small concerns of daily life, limit itself too much and sink entirely into trivial thinking. But meanwhile we must be on watch for the truth, avoiding extremes, so that we may distinguish certain from uncertain, day from night." Burnet was a seventeenth-century English theologian.

And thus spake on that ancient man,
The bright-eyed Mariner.   20

"The ship was cheered, the harbor cleared,
Merrily did we drop
Below the kirk,° below the hill,   *church*
Below the lighthouse top.

The Mariner tells   The Sun came up upon the left,   25
how the ship   Out of the sea came he!
sailed southward   And he shone bright, and on the right
with a good wind   Went down into the sea.
and fair weather,
till it reached the   Higher and higher every day,
line.   Till over the mast at noon — "   30
The Wedding Guest here beat his breast,
For he heard the loud bassoon.

The Wedding Guest   The bride hath paced into the hall,
heareth the bridal   Red as a rose is she;
music; but the   Nodding their heads before her goes   35
Mariner continueth   The merry minstrelsy.
his tale.

The Wedding Guest he beat his breast,
Yet he cannot choose but hear;
And thus spake on that ancient man,
The bright-eyed Mariner.   40

The ship driven by   "And now the STORM-BLAST came, and he
a storm toward the   Was tyrannous and strong;
South Pole.   He struck with his o'ertaking wings,
And chased us south along.

With sloping masts and dipping prow,   45
As who pursued with yell and blow
Still treads the shadow of his foe,
And forward bends his head,
The ship drove fast, loud roared the blast,
And southward aye we fled.   50

And now there came both mist and snow,
And it grew wondrous cold:
And ice, mast-high, came floating by,
As green as emerald.

The land of ice, and   And through the drifts the snowy clifts°   55   *cliffs*
of fearful sounds   Did send a dismal sheen:
where no living   Nor shapes of men nor beasts we ken —
thing was to be seen.   The ice was all between.

The ice was here, the ice was there,
The ice was all around: 60
It cracked and growled, and roared and howled,
Like noises in a swound!°   *swoon*

Till a great sea bird, At length did cross an Albatross,
called the Albatross,   Thorough the fog it came;
came through the   As if it had been a Christian soul,   65
snowfog and was   We hailed it in God's name.
received with great
joy and hospitality.   It ate the food it ne'er had eat,
                          And round and round it flew.
                          The ice did split with a thunder-fit;
                          The helmsman steered us through!   70

And lo! the Albatross   And a good south wind sprung up behind;
proveth a bird of   The Albatross did follow,
good omen, and   And every day, for food or play,
followeth the ship   Came to the mariners' hollo!
as it returned north-
ward through fog   In mist or cloud, on mast or shroud,   75
and floating ice.   It perched for vespers nine;
                          Whiles all the night, through fog-smoke white,
                          Glimmered the white Moon-shine."

The ancient   "God save thee, ancient Mariner!
Mariner   From the fiends, that plague thee thus! — 80
inhospitably killeth   Why look'st thou so?" — With my crossbow
the pious bird of   I shot the ALBATROSS.
good omen.

Part II

The Sun now rose upon the right:
Out of the sea came he,
Still hid in mist, and on the left   85
Went down into the sea.

And the good south wind still blew behind,
But no sweet bird did follow,
Nor any day for food or play
Came to the mariners' hollo!   90

His shipmates cry   And I had done a hellish thing,
out against the   And it would work 'em woe:
ancient Mariner, for   For all averred, I had killed the bird
killing the bird of   That made the breeze to blow.
good luck.   Ah wretch! said they, the bird to slay, 95
                          That made the breeze to blow!

But when the fog cleared off, they justify the same, and thus make themselves accomplices in the crime.

Nor dim nor red, like God's own head,
The glorious Sun uprist:
Then all averred, I had killed the bird
That brought the fog and mist.   100
'Twas right, said they, such birds to slay,
That bring the fog and mist.

The fair breeze continues; the ship enters the Pacific Ocean, and sails northward, even till it reaches the Line.

The fair breeze blew, the white foam flew,
The furrow followed free;
We were the first that ever burst   105
Into that silent sea.

The ship hath been suddenly becalmed.

Down dropped the breeze, the sails dropped down,
'Twas sad as sad could be;
And we did speak only to break
The silence of the sea!   110

All in a hot and copper sky,
The bloody Sun, at noon,
Right up above the mast did stand,
No bigger than the Moon.

Day after day, day after day,   115
We stuck, nor breath nor motion;
As idle as a painted ship
Upon a painted ocean.

And the Albatross begins to be avenged.

Water, water, everywhere,
And all the boards did shrink;   120
Water, water, everywhere,
Nor any drop to drink.

The very deep did rot: O Christ!
That ever this should be!
Yea, slimy things did crawl with legs   125
Upon the slimy sea.

About, about, in reel and rout
The death-fires danced at night;
The water, like a witch's oils,
Burnt green, and blue and white.   130

And some in dreams assurèd were

A Spirit had followed them; one of the invisible inhabitants of this

Of the Spirit that plagued us so;
Nine fathom deep he had followed us
From the land of mist and snow.

planet, neither departed souls nor angels; concerning whom the learned Jew, Josephus, and the Platonic and Constantinopolitan, Michael Psellus, may be consulted. They are very numerous, there is no climate or element without one or more.

And every tongue, through utter drought,   135
Was withered at the root;
We could not speak, no more than if
We had been choked with soot.

The shipmates, in Ah! well-a-day! what evil looks
their sore distress, Had I from old and young!   140
would fain throw Instead of the cross, the Albatross
the whole guilt on About my neck was hung.
the ancient
Mariner: in sign whereof they hang the dead sea bird round his neck.

Part III

There passed a weary time. Each throat
Was parched, and glazed each eye.
A weary time! a weary time!   145
How glazed each weary eye,
The ancient When looking westward, I beheld
Mariner beholdeth a A something in the sky.
sign in the element
afar off. At first it seemed a little speck,
And then it seemed a mist;   150
It moved and moved, and took at last
A certain shape, I wist.°   *knew*

A speck, a mist, a shape, I wist!
And still it neared and neared:
As if it dodged a water sprite,   155
It plunged and tacked and veered.

At its nearer With throats unslaked, with black lips baked,
approach, it seemeth We could nor laugh nor wail;
him to be a ship; Through utter drought all dumb we stood!
and at a dear ran- I bit my arm, I sucked the blood,   160
som he freeth his And cried, A sail! a sail!
speech from the
bonds of thirst. With throats unslaked, with black lips baked,
Agape they heard me call:
A flash of joy; Gramercy! they for joy did grin,
And all at once their breath drew in,   165
As they were drinking all.

And horror follows. See! see! (I cried) she tacks no more!
For can it be a ship Hither to work us weal;
that comes onward Without a breeze, without a tide,
without wind or She steadies with upright keel!   170
tide?

The western wave was all aflame.
The day was well nigh done!
Almost upon the western wave
Rested the broad bright Sun;
When that strange shape drove suddenly 175
Betwixt us and the Sun.

It seemeth him but the skeleton of a ship.

And straight the Sun was flecked with bars,
(Heaven's Mother send us grace!)
As if through a dungeon grate he peered
With broad and burning face. 180

And its ribs are seen as bars on the face of the setting Sun.

Alas! (thought I, and my heart beat loud)
How fast she nears and nears!
Are those her sails that glance in the Sun,
Like restless gossameres?

The Specter-Woman and her Deathmate, and no other on board the skeleton ship.

Are those her ribs through which the Sun 185
Did peer, as through a grate?
And is that Woman all her crew?
Is that a DEATH? and are there two?
Is DEATH that woman's mate?

Like vessel, like crew!

Her lips were red, *her* looks were free, 190
Her locks were yellow as gold:
Her skin was as white as leprosy,
The Nightmare LIFE-IN-DEATH was she,
Who thicks man's blood with cold.

Death and Life-in-Death have diced for the ship's crew, and she (the latter) winneth the ancient Mariner.

The naked hulk alongside came, 195
And the twain were casting dice;
"The game is done! I've won! I've won!"
Quoth she, and whistles thrice.

No twilight within the courts of the Sun.

The Sun's rim dips; the stars rush out:
At one stride comes the dark; 200
With far-heard whisper, o'er the sea,
Off shot the specter-bark.

At the rising of the Moon,

We listened and looked sideways up!
Fear at my heart, as at a cup,
My lifeblood seemed to sip! 205
The stars were dim, and thick the night,
The steersman's face by his lamp gleamed white;
From the sails the dew did drip —
Till clomb above the eastern bar

The hornèd Moon, with one bright star   210
Within the nether tip.

One after another,

One after one, by the star-dogged Moon,
Too quick for groan or sigh,
Each turned his face with ghastly pang,
And cursed me with his eye.   215

*His shipmates drop
down dead.*

Four times fifty living men,
(And I heard nor sigh nor groan)
With heavy thump, a lifeless lump,
They dropped down one by one.

*But Life-in-Death
begins her work on
the ancient Mariner.*

The souls did from their bodies fly —   220
They fled to bliss or woe!
And every soul, it passed me by,
Like the whizz of my cross-bow!

Part IV

*The Wedding Guest
feareth that a Spirit
is talking to him;*

"I fear thee, ancient Mariner!
I fear thy skinny hand!   225
And thou art long, and lank, and brown,
As is the ribbed sea-sand.

I fear thee and thy glittering eye,
And thy skinny hand, so brown." —

*But the ancient
Mariner assureth
him of his bodily
life, and proceedeth
to relate his horrible
penance.*

Fear not, fear not, thou Wedding Guest!   230
This body dropped not down.

Alone, alone, all, all alone,
Alone on a wide wide sea!
And never a saint took pity on
My soul in agony.   235

*He despiseth the
creatures of the
calm,*

The many men, so beautiful!
And they all dead did lie:
And a thousand thousand slimy things
Lived on; and so did I.

*And envieth that
they should live,
and so many lie
dead.*

I looked upon the rotting sea,   240
And drew my eyes away;
I looked upon the rotting deck,
And there the dead men lay.

I looked to heaven, and tried to pray;
But or ever a prayer had gushed,   245
A wicked whisper came, and made
My heart as dry as dust.

I closed my lids, and kept them close,
And the balls like pulses beat,
For the sky and the sea, and the sea and the sky   250
Lay like a load on my weary eye,
And the dead were at my feet.

But the curse liveth
for him in the eye of
the dead men.

The cold sweat melted from their limbs,
Nor rot nor reek did they:
The look with which they looked on me   255
Had never passed away.

An orphan's curse would drag to hell
A spirit from on high;
But oh! more horrible than that
Is the curse in a dead man's eye!   260
Seven days, seven nights, I saw that curse,
And yet I could not die.

In his loneliness and
fixedness he yearneth
towards the journey-
ing Moon, and the
stars that still so-
journ, yet still move
onward; and every-
where the blue sky
belongs to them, and
is their appointed
rest, and their

The moving Moon went up the sky,
And nowhere did abide:
Softly she was going up,   265
And a star or two beside —

Her beams bemocked the sultry main,
Like April hoar-frost spread;
But where the ship's huge shadow lay,
The charmèd water burnt away   270
A still and awful red.

native country and their own natural homes, which they enter unannounced, as lords that are
certainly expected and yet there is a silent joy at their arrival.

By the light of the
Moon he beholdeth
God's creatures of
the great calm.

Beyond the shadow of the ship,
I watched the water snakes:
They moved in tracks of shining white,
And when they reared, the elfish light   275
Fell off in hoary flakes.

Within the shadow of the ship
I watched their rich attire:
Blue, glossy green, and velvet black,
They coiled and swam; and every track   280
Was a flash of golden fire.

Their beauty and
their happiness.

O happy living things! no tongue
Their beauty might declare:
A spring of love gushed from my heart,

He blesseth them in his heart.	And I blessed them unaware:	285
	Sure my kind saint took pity on me,	
	And I blessed them unaware.	

The spell begins to break.

The self-same moment I could pray;
And from my neck so free
The Albatross fell off, and sank   290
Like lead into the sea.

Part V

Oh sleep! it is a gentle thing,
Beloved from pole to pole!
To Mary Queen the praise be given!
She sent the gentle sleep from Heaven,   295
That slid into my soul.

By grace of the holy Mother, the ancient Mariner is refreshed with rain.

The silly° buckets on the deck,   *lowly*
That had so long remained,
I dreamt that they were filled with dew;
And when I awoke, it rained.   300

My lips were wet, my throat was cold,
My garments all were dank;
Sure I had drunken in my dreams,
And still my body drank.

I moved, and could not feel my limbs: 305
I was so light — almost
I thought that I had died in sleep,
And was a blessèd ghost.

He heareth sounds and seeth strange sights and commotions in the sky and the element.

And soon I heard a roaring wind:
It did not come anear;   310
But with its sound it shook the sails,
That were so thin and sere.

The upper air burst into life!
And a hundred fire-flags sheen,
To and fro they were hurried about!   315
And to and fro, and in and out,
The wan stars danced between.

And the coming wind did roar more loud,
And the sails did sigh like sedge;
And the rain poured down from one black cloud;   320
The Moon was at its edge.

The thick black cloud was cleft, and still
The Moon was at its side:
Like waters shot from some high crag,
The lightning fell with never a jag,   325
A river steep and wide.

The bodies of the   The loud wind never reached the ship,
ship's crew are in-   Yet now the ship moved on!
spirited, and the   Beneath the lightning and the Moon
ship moves on;   The dead men gave a groan.   330

They groaned, they stirred, they all uprose,
Nor spake, nor moved their eyes;
It had been strange, even in a dream,
To have seen those dead men rise.

The helmsman steered, the ship moved on;   335
Yet never a breeze up-blew;
The mariners all 'gan work the ropes,
Where they were wont to do;
They raised their limbs like lifeless tools —
We were a ghastly crew.   340

The body of my brother's son
Stood by me, knee to knee:
The body and I pulled at one rope,
But he said nought to me.

"I fear thee, ancient Mariner!"   345
But not by the souls   Be calm, thou Wedding Guest!
of the men, nor by   'Twas not those souls that fled in pain,
demons of earth or   Which to their corses came again,
middle air, but by a   But a troop of spirits blest:
blessèd troop of
angelic spirits, sent   For when it dawned — they dropped their arms,   350
down by the   And clustered round the mast;
invocation of the   Sweet sounds rose slowly through their mouths,
guardian saint.   And from their bodies passed.

Around, around, flew each sweet sound,
Then darted to the Sun;   355
Slowly the sounds came back again,
Now mixed, now one by one.

Sometimes a-dropping from the sky
I heard the sky-lark sing;
Sometimes all little birds that are,   360

How they seemed to fill the sea and air
With their sweet jargoning!°   *warbling*

And now 'twas like all instruments,
Now like a lonely flute;
And now it is an angel's song,   365
That makes the heavens be mute.

It ceased; yet still the sails made on
A pleasant noise till noon,
A noise like of a hidden brook
In the leafy month of June,   370
That to the sleeping woods all night
Singeth a quiet tune.

Till noon we quietly sailed on,
Yet never a breeze did breathe:
Slowly and smoothly went the ship,   375
Moved onward from beneath.

The lonesome Spirit   Under the keel nine fathom deep,
from the South Pole   From the land of mist and snow,
carries on the ship   The spirit slid: and it was he
as far as the Line,   That made the ship to go.   380
in obedience to the   The sails at noon left off their tune,
angelic troop, but   And the ship stood still also.
still requireth
vengeance.   The Sun, right up above the mast,
                           Had fixed her to the ocean:
                           But in a minute she 'gan stir,   385
                           With a short uneasy motion —
                           Backwards and forwards half her length
                           With a short uneasy motion.

                           Then like a pawing horse let go,
                           She made a sudden bound: 390
                           It flung the blood into my head,
                           And I fell down in a swound.

The Polar Spirit's   How long in that same fit I lay,
fellow demons, the   I have not° to declare;   *am not able*
invisible inhabitants   But ere my living life returned,   395
of the element, take   I heard and in my soul discerned
part in his wrong;   Two voices in the air.
and two of them
relate, one to the   "Is it he?" quoth one, "Is this the man?
other, that penance   By him who died on cross,

long and heavy for the ancient Mariner hath been accorded to the Polar Spirit, who returneth southward.

With his cruel bow he laid full low   400
The harmless Albatross.

The spirit who bideth by himself
In the land of mist and snow,
He loved the bird that loved the man
Who shot him with his bow."   405

The other was a softer voice,
As soft as honey-dew:
Quoth he, "The man hath penance done,
And penance more will do."

Part VI

FIRST VOICE
"But tell me, tell me! speak again,   410
Thy soft response renewing —
What makes that ship drive on so fast?
What is the ocean doing?"

SECOND VOICE
"Still as a slave before his lord,
The ocean hath no blast;   415
His great bright eye most silently
Up to the Moon is cast —

If he may know which way to go;
For she guides him smooth or grim.
See, brother, see! how graciously   420
She looketh down on him."

FIRST VOICE
"But why drives on that ship so fast,
Without or wave or wind?"

The Mariner hath been cast into a trance; for the angelic power causeth the vessel to drive northward faster than human life could endure.

SECOND VOICE
"The air is cut away before,
And closes from behind.   425

Fly, brother, fly! more high, more high!
Or we shall be belated:
For slow and slow that ship will go,
When the Mariner's trance is abated."

*The supernatural
motion is retarded;
the Mariner awakes,
and his penance
begins anew.*

I woke, and we were sailing on   430
As in a gentle weather:
'Twas night, calm night, the moon was high;
The dead men stood together.

All stood together on the deck,
For a charnel-dungeon fitter: 435
All fixed on me their stony eyes,
That in the Moon did glitter.

The pang, the curse, with which they died,
Had never passed away:
I could not draw my eyes from theirs,   440
Nor turn them up to pray.

*The curse is finally
expiated.*

And now this spell was snapped: once more
I viewed the ocean green,
And looked far forth, yet little saw
Of what had else been seen —   445

Like one, that on a lonesome road
Doth walk in fear and dread,
And having once turned round walks on,
And turns no more his head;
Because he knows, a frightful fiend   450
Doth close behind him tread.

But soon there breathed a wind on me,
Nor sound nor motion made:
Its path was not upon the sea,
In ripple or in shade.   455

It raised my hair, it fanned my cheek
Like a meadow-gale of spring —
It mingled strangely with my fears,
Yet it felt like a welcoming.

Swiftly, swiftly flew the ship,   460
Yet she sailed softly too:
Sweetly, sweetly blew the breeze —
On me alone it blew.

*And the ancient
Mariner beholdeth
his native country.*

Oh! dream of joy! is this indeed
The lighthouse top I see?   465
Is this the hill? is this the kirk?
Is this mine own countree?

We drifted o'er the harbor-bar,
And I with sobs did pray —
O let me be awake, my God!   470
Or let me sleep alway.

The harbor bay was clear as glass,
So smoothly it was strewn!
And on the bay the moonlight lay,
And the shadow of the Moon.   475

The rock shone bright, the kirk no less,
That stands above the rock:
The moonlight steeped in silentness
The steady weathercock.

The angelic spirits   And the bay was white with silent light,   480
leave the dead   Till rising from the same,
bodies,   Full many shapes, that shadows were,
                          In crimson colors came.

                          A little distance from the prow
And appear in their   Those crimson shadows were: 485
own forms of light.   I turned my eyes upon the deck —
                          Oh, Christ! what saw I there!

Each corse lay flat, lifeless and flat,
And, by the holy rood!°   *cross of Christ*
A man all light, a seraph°-man,   *angel-like*   490
On every corse there stood.

This seraph-band, each waved his hand:
It was a heavenly sight!
They stood as signals to the land,
Each one a lovely light;   495

This seraph-band, each waved his hand,
No voice did they impart —
No voice; but oh! the silence sank
Like music on my heart.

But soon I heard the dash of oars,   500
I heard the Pilot's cheer;
My head was turned perforce away
And I saw a boat appear.

The Pilot and the Pilot's boy,
I heard them coming fast: 505

Dear Lord in Heaven! it was a joy
The dead men could not blast.

I saw a third — I heard his voice:
It is the Hermit good!
He singeth loud his godly hymns   510
That he makes in the wood.
He'll shrieve my soul, he'll wash away
The Albatross's blood.

Part VII

The Hermit of the   This Hermit good lives in that wood
Wood   Which slopes down to the sea.   515
How loudly his sweet voice he rears!
He loves to talk with marineres
That come from a far countree.

He kneels at morn, and noon, and eve —
He hath a cushion plump: 520
It is the moss that wholly hides
The rotted old oak stump.

The skiff-boat neared: I heard them talk,
"Why, this is strange, I trow!
Where are those lights so many and fair,   525
That signal made but now?"

Approacheth the   "Strange, by my faith!" the Hermit said —
ship with wonder. "And they answered not our cheer!
The planks looked warped! and see those sails,
How thin they are and sere!   530
I never saw aught like to them,
Unless perchance it were

Brown skeletons of leaves that lag
My forest-brook along;
When the ivy tod° is heavy with snow,   *bushy clump*   535
And the owlet whoops to the wolf below,
That eats the she-wolf's young."

"Dear Lord! it hath a fiendish look,"
The Pilot made reply,
"I am a-feared" — "Push on, push on!"   540
Said the Hermit cheerily.

The boat came closer to the ship,
But I nor spake nor stirred;

The boat came close beneath the ship,
And straight a sound was heard. 545

The ship suddenly sinketh.

Under the water it rumbled on,
Still louder and more dread:
It reached the ship, it split the bay;
The ship went down like lead.

The ancient Mariner is saved in the Pilot's boat.

Stunned by that loud and dreadful sound, 550
Which sky and ocean smote,
Like one that hath been seven days drowned
My body lay afloat;
But swift as dreams, myself I found
Within the Pilot's boat. 555

Upon the whirl, where sank the ship,
The boat spun round and round;
And all was still, save that the hill
Was telling of the sound.

I moved my lips — the Pilot shrieked 560
And fell down in a fit;
The holy Hermit raised his eyes,
And prayed where he did sit.

I took the oars: the Pilot's boy,
Who now doth crazy go, 565
Laughed loud and long, and all the while
His eyes went to and fro.
"Ha! ha!" quoth he, "full plain I see,
The Devil knows how to row."

And now, all in my own countree, 570
I stood on the firm land!
The Hermit stepped forth from the boat,
And scarcely he could stand.

The ancient Mariner earnestly entreateth the Hermit to shrieve him; and the penance of life falls on him.

"O shrieve me,° shrieve me, holy man!"   *hear my confession*
The Hermit crossed his brow. 575
"Say quick," quoth he, "I bid thee say —
What manner of man art thou?"

Forthwith this frame of mine was wrenched
With a woeful agony,
Which forced me to begin my tale; 580
And then it left me free.

And ever and anon throughout his future life an agony constraineth him to travel from land to land;

Since then, at an uncertain hour,
That agony returns:
And till my ghastly tale is told,
This heart within me burns.   585

I pass, like night, from land to land;
I have strange power of speech;
That moment that his face I see,
I know the man that must hear me:
To him my tale I teach.   590

What loud uproar bursts from that door!
The wedding guests are there:
But in the garden-bower the bride
And bridemaids singing are:
And hark the little vesper bell,   595
Which biddeth me to prayer!

O Wedding Guest! this soul hath been
Alone on a wide wide sea:
So lonely 'twas, that God himself
Scarce seemèd there to be.   600

O sweeter than the marriage feast,
'Tis sweeter far to me,
To walk together to the kirk
With a goodly company!

To walk together to the kirk,   605
And all together pray,
While each to his great Father bends,
Old men, and babes, and loving friends
And youths and maidens gay!

And to teach, by his own example, love and reverence to all things that God made and loveth.

Farewell, farewell! but this I tell   610
To thee, thou Wedding Guest!
He prayeth well, who loveth well
Both man and bird and beast.

He prayeth best, who loveth best
All things both great and small;   615
For the dear God who loveth us,
He made and loveth all.

The Mariner, whose eye is bright,
Whose beard with age is hoar,

Is gone: and now the Wedding Guest
Turned from the bridegroom's door.

620

He went like one that hath been stunned,
And is of sense forlorn:
A sadder and a wiser man,
He rose the morrow morn.

EDUARDO C. CORRAL (b. 1973)
Monologue of a Vulture's Shadow

I long to return to my master
                 who knew neither fear nor patience.
My master who years ago spiraled
                above a woman
trudging through the desert.
        She raised her face & cursed us:
               Black Torches of Plague, Turd Blossoms.
She lashed out with her hands,
          pinned me to her shoulders.
                  I went slack.
I called for my master.
          I fell across her shoulders like a black shawl.
Now I'm kept on the shelf of an armoire:°   *wardrobe*
              perfumed,
          my edges embroidered with red thread.
She anchors me to her dress with a cameo of a bird
                 clutching prey
as if to remind me of when my master flew close to the desert floor
      & I darkened the arroyos°   *dry riverbeds*
              & the jade geometry of fallen saguaros.°   *cacti*
How could I forget?
        Sometimes my master soared so high
             I ceased to blacken the earth.
What became of me in those moments?
       But the scent of decay always lured my master
            earthward.
     As my master ate, I ate.

William Cowper (1731 – 1800)
The Castaway

Obscurest night involved the sky,
    The Atlantic billows roared,
When such a destined wretch as I,
    Washed headlong from on board,
Of friends, of hope, of all bereft,   5
His floating home forever left.

No braver chief could Albion boast
    Than he with whom he went,[1]
Nor ever ship left Albion's coast,
    With warmer wishes sent.   10
He loved them both, but both in vain,
Nor him beheld, nor her again.

Not long beneath the whelming brine,
    Expert to swim, he lay;
Nor soon he felt his strength decline,   15
    Or courage die away;
But waged with death a lasting strife,
Supported by despair of life.

He shouted; nor his friends had failed
    To check the vessel's course,   20
But so the furious blast prevailed,
    That, pitiless perforce,
They left their outcast mate behind,
And scudded still before the wind.

Some succor yet they could afford;   25
    And, such as storms allow,
The cask, the coop, the floated cord,
    Delayed not to bestow.
But he (they knew) nor ship, nor shore,
Whate'er they gave, should visit more.   30

Nor, cruel as it seemed, could he
    Their haste himself condemn,
Aware that flight, in such a sea,
    Alone could rescue them;

---

[1]Cowper's poem is based on an incident in Richard Walter's *A Voyage Round the World by . . . George Anson* (1748).

Yet bitter felt it still to die   35
Deserted, and his friends so nigh.

He long survives, who lives an hour
    In ocean, self-upheld;
And so long he, with unspent power,
    His destiny repelled;   40
And ever, as the minutes flew,
Entreated help, or cried, "Adieu!"

At length, his transient respite past,
    His comrades, who before
Had heard his voice in every blast,   45
    Could catch the sound no more.
For then, by toil subdued, he drank
The stifling wave, and then he sank.

No poet wept him; but the page
    Of narrative sincere,
That tells his name, his worth, his age,   50
    Is wet with Anson's tear.
And tears by bards or heroes shed
Alike immortalize the dead.

I therefore purpose not, or dream,   55
    Descanting on his fate,
To give the melancholy theme
    A more enduring date:
But misery still delights to trace
Its semblance in another's case.   60

No voice divine the storm allayed,
    No light propitious shone,
When, snatched from all effectual aid,
    We perished, each alone;
But I beneath a rougher sea,   65
And whelmed in deeper gulfs than he.

Epitaph on a Hare

Here lies, whom hound did ne'er pursue,
    Nor swifter greyhound follow,
Whose foot ne'er tainted morning dew,
    Nor ear heard huntsman's hallo',

Old Tiney, surliest of his kind,
    Who, nursed with tender care,

And to domestic bounds confined,
    Was still a wild jack-hare.

Though duly from my hand he took
    His pittance every night,
He did it with a jealous look,
    And, when he could, would bite.

His diet was of wheaten bread,
    And milk, and oats, and straw,
Thistles, or lettuces instead,
    With sand to scour his maw.

On twigs of hawthorn he regaled,
    On pippins' russet peel;
And, when his juicy salads failed,
    Sliced carrot pleased him well.

A Turkey carpet was his lawn,
    Whereon he loved to bound,
To skip and gambol like a fawn,
    And swing his rump around.

His frisking was at evening hours,
    For then he lost his fear;
But most before approaching showers,
    Or when a storm drew near.

Eight years and five round-rolling moons
    He thus saw steal away,
Dozing out all his idle noons,
    And every night at play.

I kept him for his humor's sake,
    For he would oft beguile
My heart of thoughts that made it ache,
    And force me to a smile.

But now, beneath this walnut-shade
    He finds his long, last home,
And waits in snug concealment laid,
    Till gentler Puss shall come.

He, still more agèd, feels the shocks
    From which no care can save,
And, partner once of Tiney's box,
    Must soon partake his grave.

HART CRANE (1899 – 1932)

The Broken Tower

The bell-rope that gathers God at dawn
Dispatches me as though I dropped down the knell
Of a spent day — to wander the cathedral lawn
From pit to crucifix, feet chill on steps from hell.

Have you not heard, have you not seen that corps
Of shadows in the tower, whose shoulders sway
Antiphonal carillons launched before
The stars are caught and hived in the sun's ray?

The bells, I say, the bells break down their tower;
And swing I know not where. Their tongues engrave
Membrane through marrow, my long-scattered score
Of broken intervals . . . And I, their sexton slave!

Oval encyclicals in canyons heaping
The impasse high with choir. Banked voices slain!
Pagodas, campaniles° with reveilles outleaping —   *bell towers*
O terraced echoes prostrate on the plain! . . .

And so it was I entered the broken world
To trace the visionary company of love, its voice
An instant in the wind (I know not whither hurled)
But not for long to hold each desperate choice.

My word I poured. But was it cognate, scored
Of that tribunal monarch of the air
Whose thigh embronzes earth, strikes crystal Word
In wounds pledged once to hope — cleft to despair?

The steep encroachments of my blood left me
No answer (could blood hold such a lofty tower
As flings the question true?) — or is it she
Whose sweet mortality stirs latent power?

And through whose pulse I hear, counting the strokes
My veins recall and add, revived and sure
The angelus of wars my chest evokes:
What I hold healed, original now, and pure . . .

And builds, within, a tower that is not stone
(Not stone can jacket heaven) — but slip
Of pebbles — visible wings of silence sown
In azure circles, widening as they dip

The matrix of the heart, lift down the eye
That shrines the quiet lake and swells a tower . . .
The commodious, tall decorum of that sky
Unseals her earth, and lifts love in its shower.

To Brooklyn Bridge

How many dawns, chill from his rippling rest
The seagull's wings shall dip and pivot him,
Shedding white rings of tumult, building high
Over the chained bay waters Liberty —

Then, with inviolate curve, forsake our eyes
As apparitional as sails that cross
Some page of figures to be filed away;
— Till elevators drop us from our day . . .

I think of cinemas, panoramic sleights
With multitudes bent toward some flashing scene
Never disclosed, but hastened to again,
Foretold to other eyes on the same screen;

And Thee, across the harbor, silver-paced
As though the sun took step of thee, yet left
Some motion ever unspent in thy stride, —
Implicitly thy freedom staying thee!

Out of some subway scuttle, cell or loft
A bedlamite° speeds to thy parapets,   *madman*
Tilting there momently, shrill shirt ballooning,
A jest falls from the speechless caravan.

Down Wall,° from girder into street noon leaks,   *Wall Street*
A rip-tooth of the sky's acetylene;
All afternoon the cloud-flown derricks turn . . .
Thy cables breathe the North Atlantic still.

And obscure as that heaven of the Jews,
Thy guerdon° . . . Accolade thou dost bestow   *reward*
Of anonymity time cannot raise:
Vibrant reprieve and pardon thou dost show.

O harp and altar, of the fury fused,
(How could mere toil align thy choiring strings!)
Terrific threshold of the prophet's pledge,
Prayer of pariah and the lover's cry, —

Again the traffic lights that skim thy swift
Unfractioned idiom, immaculate sigh of stars,
Beading thy path — condense eternity:
And we have seen night lifted in thine arms.

Under thy shadow by the piers I waited;
Only in darkness is thy shadow clear.
The City's fiery parcels all undone,
Already snow submerges an iron year . . .

O Sleepless as the river under thee,
Vaulting the sea, the prairies' dreaming sod,
Unto us lowliest sometime sweep, descend
And of the curveship lend a myth to God.

ROBERT CREELEY (1926 – 2005)
When I think

When I think of where I've come from
or even try to measure as any kind of
distance those places, all the various
people, and all the ways in which I remember them, so that even the skin I
touched or was myself fact of, inside,
could see through like a hole in the wall
or listen to, it must have been, to what
was going on in there, even if I was still
too dumb to know anything — When I think
of the miles and miles of roads, of meals,
of telephone wires even, or even of water
poured out in endless streams down streaks
of black sky or the dirt roads washed clean,
or myriad, salty tears and suddenly it's spring
again, or it was — Even when I think again of
all those I treated so poorly, names, places,
their waiting uselessly for me in the rain and
I never came, was never really there at all,
was moving so confusedly, so fast, so driven
like a car along some empty highway passing,
passing other cars — When I try to think of
things, of what's happened, of what a life is
and was, my life, when I wonder what it meant,
the sad days passing, the continuing, echoing deaths,

all the painful, belligerent news, and the dog still
waiting to be fed, the closeness of you sleeping, voices,
presences, of children, of our own grown children,
the shining, bright sun, the smell of the air just now,
each physical moment, passing, *passing,* it's what
it always is or ever was, just then, just there.

COUNTEE CULLEN (1903 – 1946)

Incident

For Eric Walrond

Once riding in old Baltimore,
    Heart-filled, head-filled with glee,
I saw a Baltimorean
    Keep looking straight at me.

Now I was eight and very small,
    And he was no whit bigger,
And so I smiled, but he poked out
    His tongue, and called me, "Nigger."

I saw the whole of Baltimore
    From May until December;
Of all the things that happened there
    That's all that I remember.

E. E. CUMMINGS (1894 – 1962)

may i feel said he

may i feel said he
(i'll squeal said she
just once said he)
it's fun said she

(may i touch said he
how much said she
a lot said he)
why not said she

(let's go said he
not too far said she
what's too far said he
where you are said she)

may i stay said he
(which way said she
like this said he
if you kiss said she

may i move said he
is it love said she)
if you're willing said he
(but you're killing said she

but it's life said he
but your wife said she
now said he)
ow said she

(tiptop said he
don't stop said she
oh no said he)
go slow said she

(cccome?said he
ummm said she)
you're divine!said he
(you are Mine said she)

"next to of course god america i

"next to of course god america i
love you land of the pilgrims' and so forth oh
say can you see by the dawn's early my
country 'tis of centuries come and go
and are no more what of it we should worry
in every language even deafanddumb
thy sons acclaim your glorious name by gorry
by jingo by gee by gosh by gum
why talk of beauty what could be more beautiful than these heroic happy dead
who rushed like lions to the roaring slaughter
they did not stop to think they died instead
then shall the voice of liberty be mute?"

He spoke.   And drank rapidly a glass of water

EMILY DICKINSON (1830 – 1886)
The Brain – is wider than the Sky –

The Brain – is wider than the Sky –
For – put them side by side –
The one the other will contain
With ease – and You – beside –

The Brain is deeper than the sea –
For – hold them – Blue to Blue –
The one the other will absorb –
As Sponges – Buckets – do –

The Brain is just the weight of God –
For – Heft them – Pound for Pound –
And they will differ – if they do –
As Syllable from Sound –

I like a look of Agony

I like a look of Agony,
Because I know it's true –
Men do not sham Convulsion,
Nor simulate, a Throe –

The Eyes glaze once – and that is Death –
Impossible to feign
The Beads upon the Forehead
By homely Anguish strung.

Much Madness is divinest Sense –

Much Madness is divinest Sense –
To a discerning Eye –
Much Sense – the starkest Madness –
'Tis the Majority
In this, as All, prevail –
Assent – and you are sane –
Demur – you're straightway dangerous –
And handled with a Chain –

Safe in their Alabaster Chambers –

(Version of 1859)
Safe in their Alabaster Chambers –
Untouched by Morning

And untouched by Noon –
Sleep the meek members of the Resurrection –
Rafter of satin
And Roof of stone.

Light laughs the breeze
In her Castle above them –
Babbles the Bee in a stolid Ear,
Pipe the Sweet Birds in ignorant cadence –
Ah, what sagacity perished here!

Safe in their Alabaster Chambers –

(Version of 1861)

Safe in their Alabaster Chambers –
Untouched by Morning –
And untouched by Noon –
Lie the meek members of the Resurrection –
Rafter of Satin – and Roof of Stone!

Grand go the Years – in the Crescent – above them –
Worlds scoop their Arcs –
And Firmaments – row –
Diadems – drop – and Doges[1] – surrender –
Soundless as dots – on a Disc of Snow –

The Soul selects her own Society –

The Soul selects her own Society –
Then – shuts the Door –
To her divine Majority –
Present no more –

Unmoved – she notes the Chariots – pausing –
At her low Gate –
Unmoved – an Emperor be kneeling
Upon her Mat –

I've known her – from an ample nation –
Choose One –
Then – close the Valves of her attention –
Like Stone –

---

[1]Chief magistrates in Venice from the eleventh through the sixteenth centuries.

There's a certain Slant of light

There's a certain Slant of light,
Winter Afternoons –
That oppresses, like the Heft
Of Cathedral Tunes –

Heavenly Hurt, it gives us –
We can find no scar,
But internal difference,
Where the Meanings, are –

None may teach it – Any –
'Tis the Seal Despair –
An imperial affliction
Sent us of the Air –

When it comes, the Landscape listens –
Shadows – hold their breath –
When it goes, 'tis like the Distance
On the look of Death –

Wild Nights – Wild Nights!

Wild Nights – Wild Nights!
Were I with thee
Wild Nights should be
Our luxury!

Futile – the Winds —
To a Heart in port –
Done with the Compass –
Done with the Chart!

Rowing in Eden –
Ah, the Sea!
Might I but moor – Tonight –
In Thee!

John Donne (1572 – 1631)
Breake of day

'Tis true, 'tis day, what though it be?
O wilt thou therefore rise from me?
Why should we rise, because 'tis light?
Did we lie down, because 'twas night?

Love which in spite of darkness brought us hither,
Should in despite of light keep us together.

Light hath no tongue, but is all eye;
If it could speak as well as spy,
This were the worst, that it could say,
That being well, I fain would stay,
And that I lov'd my heart and honor so,
That I would not from him, that had them, go.

Must business thee from hence remove?
Oh, that's the worst disease of love,
The poor, the foul, the false, love can
Admit, but not the busied man.
He which hath business, and makes love, doth do
Such wrong, as when a married man doth woo.

Death, be not proud

Death, be not proud, though some have callèd thee
Mighty and dreadful, for thou art not so;
For those whom thou think'st thou dost overthrow
Die not, poor Death, nor yet canst thou kill me.
From rest and sleep, which but thy pictures be,
Much pleasure; then from thee much more must flow,
And soonest our best men with thee do go,
Rest of their bones, and soul's delivery.
Thou art slave to fate, chance, kings, and desperate men,
And dost with poison, war, and sickness dwell,
And poppy or charms can make us sleep as well
And better than thy stroke; why swell'st thou then?
One short sleep past, we wake eternally,
And death shall be no more; Death, thou shalt die.

The Sun Rising

Busy old fool, unruly sun,
Why dost thou thus,
Through windows and through curtains call on us?
Must to thy motions lovers' seasons run?
Saucy pedantic wretch, go chide
Late school boys and sour prentices,
Go tell court huntsmen that the king will ride,
Call country ants to harvest offices;

Love, all alike, no season knows nor clime,
Nor hours, days, months, which are the rags of time.

        Thy beams, so reverend and strong
        Why shouldst thou think?
I could eclipse and cloud them with a wink,
But that I would not lose her sight so long;
        If her eyes have not blinded thine,
        Look, and tomorrow late tell me,
    Whether both th' Indias of spice and mine
    Be where thou leftst them, or lie here with me.
Ask for those kings whom thou saw'st yesterday,
And thou shalt hear, All here in one bed lay.

        She's all states, and all princes, I,
        Nothing else is.
Princes do but play us; compared to this,
All honor's mimic, all wealth alchemy.
        Thou, sun, art half as happy as we,
        In that the world's contracted thus;
    Thine age asks ease, and since thy duties be
    To warm the world, that's done in warming us.
Shine here to us, and thou art everywhere;
This bed thy center is, these walls, thy sphere.

TIMOTHY DONNELLY (b. 1969)
Reading of Medieval Life, I Wonder Who I Am

Every autumn, Walter, lord of the manor, ruddy
in his cups° among the bundled stooks of wheat,   *drunk*
allowed himself the lustrous pleasure of allowing.
"Peter," he would start, nuzzling the russet
feathers on the head of his extraordinary hawk,   5
"I know you well. You are your master's, equally
cursed and blessed with the voluptuousness
of certain heaven-scented bog-flowers. Its extravagance,
if you will, is matched only by its generosity."
Peter twitched, remembering a swamp rat   10
confused in marshmallows. "Tomorrow, all the hungry
swine my serfs have dieted° on air since March   *fed*
will frisk about the turning labyrinth of oak
that is my private forest. They will feed there. I allow it."

Peter was at home, which was his master's arm;   15
Lord Walter left the field of wheat laid out
for ripening. By morning, word of Walter's
generosity had pierced the daub-and-wattle° walls   *mud and woven twigs*
of all the homes of all his serfs. These too
belonged to Walter, all homes did, and all the sleeping   20
serfs inside them, who were not their own—
although their drowsiness at waking was.
Through mist, the serfs conveyed the swine
to the lord's forest's border and released them there
to feed on fallen acorns; some ascended oaks   25
and shook nuts down into the chaos at the trunks.
Lord Walter would say, "They *clambered*."
He drank of his swine's music from a nearby parapet.°   *battlement*

— I can't be Walter. I lack that confidence. I lack
that sense of intrinsic superiority, and I can't   30
imagine I would ever be at home with holding
claim to another person, much less several thousand.
I can't be Peter, complicit in all that, although
I would like being a bird, just not a raptor, except perhaps
an owl. I can't envision the serfs individually,   35
which is a real failure, one worsened by the fact that,
in this regard, they resemble oaks and swine,
gruesomely tusked in this era. I do see one acorn
in particular, panicked on its stem, and accordingly
I become it, shaken from my branch by a tremendous   40
hand and falling, never not falling — if the falling
stops, it will all be over. The swine will be upon me.

That evening, Walter, his custom since the death
of his beloved Constance, who died delivering
Christopher, the lord's first and only child, who died   45
in turn, it was said, of the selfsame grief
that overtook his father every twilight, rode
upon his sable horse to the cathedral, Peter on his arm.
There, against the gravity of vespers,° Peter   *evening service*
quit his perching on the lord's leather glove   50
and flew in the cathedral, circling. The Adversary,°   *the Devil*
it was said, had claimed both wings, and they —
for the bird's sake — had to be removed, having
carried him higher than the elongated windows

which conveyed the eye to heaven and washed the cathedral's   55
limestone vaults and its innumerable pillars and

the outstretched wings of Peter in thrown moonlight.

RITA DOVE (b. 1952)
Adolescence — II

Although it is night, I sit in the bathroom, waiting.
Sweat prickles behind my knees, the baby-breasts are alert.
Venetian blinds slice up the moon; the tiles quiver in pale strips.

Then they come, the three seal men with eyes as round
As dinner plates and eyelashes like sharpened tines.
They bring the scent of licorice. One sits in the washbowl,

One on the bathtub edge; one leans against the door.
"Can you feel it yet?" they whisper.
I don't know what to say, again. They chuckle,

Patting their sleek bodies with their hands.
"Well, maybe next time." And they rise,
Glittering like pools of ink under moonlight,

And vanish. I clutch at the ragged holes
They leave behind, here at the edge of darkness.
Night rests like a ball of fur on my tongue.

Dusting

Every day a wilderness — no
shade in sight. Beulah
patient among knicknacks,
the solarium a rage
of light, a grainstorm
as her gray cloth brings
dark wood to life.

Under her hand scrolls
and crests gleam
darker still. What
was his name, that
silly boy at the fair with
the rifle booth? And his kiss and

the clear bowl with one bright
fish, rippling
wound!

Not Michael —
something finer. Each dust
stroke a deep breath and
the canary in bloom.
Wavery memory: home
from a dance, the front door
blown open and the parlor
in snow, she rushed
the bowl to the stove, watched
as the locket of ice
dissolved and he
swam free.

That was years before
Father gave her up
with her name, years before
her name grew to mean
Promise, then
Desert-in-Peace.
Long before the shadow and
sun's accomplice, the tree.

Maurice.

PAUL LAURENCE DUNBAR (1872 – 1906)
Harriet Beecher Stowe[1]

She told the story, and the whole world wept
    At wrongs and cruelties it had not known
    But for this fearless woman's voice alone.
    She spoke to consciences that long had slept:
Her message, Freedom's clear reveille, swept
    From heedless hovel to complacent throne.
    Command and prophecy were in the tone
    And from its sheath the sword of justice leapt.
Around two peoples swelled a fiery wave,
    But both came forth transfigured from the flame.

---

[1]Harriet Beecher Stowe (1811–1896) wrote *Uncle Tom's Cabin* (1852), an anti-slavery novel that had an enormous impact on American attitudes toward slavery.

Blest be the hand that dared be strong to save,
    And blest be she who in our weakness came —
    Prophet and priestess! At one stroke she gave
A race to freedom and herself to fame.

Robert Gould Shaw[1]

Why was it that the thunder voice of Fate
    Should call thee, studious, from the classic groves,
    Where calm-eyed Pallas[2] with still footstep roves,
And charge thee seek the turmoil of the state?
What bade thee hear the voice and rise elate,
    Leave home and kindred and thy spicy loaves,
    To lead th' unlettered and despisèd droves
To manhood's home and thunder at the gate?

Far better the slow blaze of Learning's light,
    The cool and quiet of her dearer fane,
Than this hot terror of a hopeless fight,
    This cold endurance of the final pain, —
Since thou and those who with thee died for right
    Have died, the Present teaches, but in vain!

We Wear the Mask

We wear the mask that grins and lies,
It hides our cheeks and shades our eyes —
This debt we pay to human guile;
With torn and bleeding hearts we smile,
And mouth with myriad subtleties.
Why should the world be over-wise,
In counting all our tears and sighs?
Nay, let them only see us, while
    We wear the mask.

We smile, but, O great Christ, our cries
To thee from tortured souls arise.
We sing, but oh the clay is vile
Beneath our feet, and long the mile;
But let the world dream otherwise,
    We wear the mask!

---

[1]Robert Gould Shaw (1837–1863) commanded the first all-Negro regiment in the North. He was killed while leading an attack on Fort Wagner in South Carolina.

[2]Pallas Athena, Greek goddess of wisdom.

ROBERTO DURÁN (b. 1953)
Protest

We the people of color y hueros° too   *light-skinned*
don't have to carry boycott cards
or pin buttons in our skins
consequently we do not protest
we are a protest

T. S. ELIOT (1888 – 1965)
Preludes

I

The winter evening settles down
With smell of steaks in passageways.
Six o'clock.
The burnt-out ends of smoky days.
And now a gusty shower wraps
The grimy scraps
Of withered leaves about your feet
And newspapers from vacant lots;
The showers beat
On broken blinds and chimney-pots,
And at the corner of the street
A lonely cab-horse steams and stamps.
And then the lighting of the lamps.

II

The morning comes to consciousness
Of faint stale smells of beer
From the sawdust-trampled street
With all its muddy feet that press
To early coffee-stands.
With the other masquerades
That time resumes,
One thinks of all the hands
That are raising dingy shades
In a thousand furnished rooms.

III

You tossed a blanket from the bed,
You lay upon your back, and waited;

You dozed, and watched the night revealing
The thousand sordid images
Of which your soul was constituted;
They flickered against the ceiling.
And when all the world came back
And the light crept up between the shutters
And you heard the sparrows in the gutters,
You had such a vision of the street
As the street hardly understands;
Sitting along the bed's edge, where
You curled the papers from your hair,
Or clasped the yellow soles of feet
In the palms of both soiled hands.

IV

His soul stretched tight across the skies
That fade behind a city block,
Or trampled by insistent feet
At four and five and six o'clock;
And short square fingers stuffing pipes,
And evening newspapers, and eyes
Assured of certain certainties,
The conscience of a blackened street
Impatient to assume the world.

I am moved by fancies that are curled
Around these images, and cling:
The notion of some infinitely gentle
Infinitely suffering thing.

Wipe your hand across your mouth, and laugh;
The worlds revolve like ancient women
Gathering fuel in vacant lots.

THOMAS SAYERS ELLIS (b. 1965)
View of the Library of Congress from
Paul Laurence Dunbar High School

for Doris Craig and Michael Olshausen

A white substitute teacher
At an all–black public high school,
He sought me out saying my poems

Showed promise, range, a gift,
And had I ever heard of T. S. Eliot?
No. Then Robert Hayden perhaps?

Hayden, a former colleague,
Had recently died, and the obituary
He handed me had already begun
Its journey home — from the printed page
Back to tree, gray becoming
Yellow, flower, dirt.

No river, we skipped rocks
On the horizon, above Ground Zero,
From the roof of the Gibson Plaza Apartments.
We'd aim, then shout the names
Of the museums, famous monuments,
And government buildings

Where our grandparents, parents,
Aunts, and uncles worked. Dangerous duds.
The bombs we dropped always fell short,
Missing their mark. No one, not even
Carlton Green, who had lived in
As many neighborhoods as me,

Knew in which direction
To launch when I lifted Hayden's
Place of employment —
The Library of Congress —
From the obituary, now folded
In my back pocket, a creased map.

We went home, asked our mothers,
But they didn't know. Richard's came
Close: Somewhere near Congress,
On Capitol Hill, take the 30 bus,
Get off before it reaches Anacostia,
Don't cross the bridge into Southeast.

The next day in school
I looked it up — The National Library
Of the United States in Washington, D.C.,
Founded in 1800, open to all taxpayers
And citizens. *Snap!* My Aunt Doris
Works there, has for years.

[Handwritten margin notes:]
- Born white poets 5
- Imagines the source
- This might mirror his search for the source of his inspiration in a world of white poets 10
- The Library of Congress isn't a hidden building but it's out of bounds for them
- Idea of an entire area (world) that he hasn't accessed 35

[Printed line numbers: 15, 20, 25, 40]

Once, on her day off, she
Took me shopping and bought
The dress shoes of my choice.   45
Loafers. They were dark red,
Almost purple, bruised — the color
Of blood before oxygen reaches it. → nod to a source

I was beginning to think
Like a poet, so in my mind   50
Hayden's dying and my loafers
Were connected, but years apart,
As was Dunbar to other institutions — ° Institutionalized
Ones I could see, ones I could not.   racisms → Can't see
                                         the things that kept
                                         him from "seeing" the
RALPH WALDO EMERSON (1803 – 1882)   Library at Congress

Concord Hymn

Sung at the Completion of the Battle Monument,[1] *July 4, 1837*

By the rude bridge that arched the flood,
    Their flag to April's breeze unfurled,
Here once the embattled farmers stood
    And fired the shot heard round the world.

The foe long since in silence slept;
    Alike the conqueror silent sleeps;
And Time the ruined bridge has swept
    Down the dark stream which seaward creeps.

On this green bank, by this soft stream,
    We set to-day a votive stone;
That memory may their deed redeem,
    When, like our sires, our sons are gone.

Spirit, that made those heroes dare
    To die, and leave their children free,
Bid Time and Nature gently spare
    The shaft we raise to them and thee.

---

[1]Commemorating the battles of Lexington and Concord, April 19, 1775.

LOUISE ERDRICH (b. 1954)

The Strange People

> *The antelope are strange people . . . they are beautiful to look at, and yet they are tricky. We do not trust them. They appear and disappear; they are like shadows on the plains. Because of their great beauty, young men sometimes follow the antelope and are lost forever. Even if those foolish ones find themselves and return, they are never again right in their heads.*
>
> — *PRETTY SHIELD, MEDICINE WOMAN OF THE CROWS*, TRANSCRIBED AND EDITED BY FRANK LINDERMAN (1932)

All night I am the doe, breathing
his name in a frozen field,
the small mist of the word
drifting always before me.

And again he has heard it
and I have gone burning
to meet him, the jacklight
fills my eyes with blue fire;
the heart in my chest
explodes like a hot stone.

Then slung like a sack
in the back of his pickup,
I wipe the death scum
from my mouth, sit up laughing,
and shriek in my speeding grave.

Safely shut in the garage,
when he sharpens his knife
and thinks to have me, like that,
I come toward him,
a lean gray witch,
through the bullets that enter and dissolve.

I sit in his house
drinking coffee till dawn,
and leave as frost reddens on hubcaps,
crawling back into my shadowy body.
All day, asleep in clean grasses,
I dream of the one who could really wound me.

RHINA ESPAILLAT (b. 1932)
Translation

Cousins from home are practicing their English,
picking out what they can, slippery vowels
queasy in their ears, stiff consonants
bristling like Saxon spears too tightly massed
for the leisurely tongues of my home town.

They frame laborious greetings to our neighbors;
try learning names, fail, try again, give up,
hug then and laugh instead, with slow blushes.
Their gestures shed echoes of morning bells,
unfold narrow streets around them like gossip.

They watch us, gleaning with expert kindness
every crumb of good will dropped in our haste
from ritual to ritual; they like the pancakes,
smile at strangers, poke country fingers
between the toes of our city roses.

Their eyes want to know if I think in this
difficult noise, how well I remember
the quiet music our grandmother spoke
in her tin-roofed kitchen, how love can work
in a language without diminutives.

What words in any language but the wind's
could name this land as I've learned it by campfire?
I want to feed them the dusty sweetness
of American roads cleaving huge spaces,
wheatfield clean and smooth as a mother's apron.

I want to tell them the goodness of people
who seldom touch, who bring covered dishes
to the bereaved in embarrassed silence,
who teach me daily that all dialogue
is reverie, is hearsay, is translation.

GUSTAVO PÉREZ FIRMAT (b. 1949)
Turning the Times Tables

> *I am the sum total of my language.*
> — CHARLES SANDERS PEIRCE

¿Y si soy más de uno, Peirce?
¿Y si soy dos,
o tres
o — como diría David —
un millón?
¿En qué momento, en qué participio del mundo
se convierte tu suma en mi resta, Peirce?[1]

I am what is left
after the subtraction of my languages.
I am the division that resists
the multiplication of my languages.
I am the number that won't square,
the figure you can't figure,
the remainder of my languages.

One into two
won't go.
You into tú°   *you (familiar)*
won't go.
Yo° into you   *I*
won't go.
I into yo
won't go.
Nothing into nada°   *nothing*
won't go.

Split the difference.
Split the atom.
Split.
I still won't go.

---

[1]Stanza 1 reads, in translation:

> And if I'm more than one, Peirce?
> And if I'm two,
> or three
> or — as David would say —
> a million?
> At what moment, in what participle of the world
> does your sum turn into my remainder, Peirce?

Some people
just
don't add
up.

MARK FORD (b. 1962)
The Long Man

of Wilmington[1] winces with the dawn; he has just
endured yet another mythical, pointless, starry
vigil. His ankles ache, and the weather looks
irksome and moody; the early traffic whizzes by
regardless, but the news and emblems borne
by each car permeate the soil that sustains
the straggling furze, various grasses, and the odd
towering oak. Across the damp fields a distant
siren pleads for attention; he cannot
move, nor, like a martyr, disprove the lie of the land.

Who was it who established, in the teeth
of so much evidence, the laws of diminishing
returns? I woke up feeling cold and distended,
my feet pointing east, my head in low-hanging
clouds. A stream of curious tags and sayings
flowed like a potion through my veins. I had
the 'look', as some called it, meaning I floated
in an envelope of air that ducked and sheered
between invisible obstacles. The alarmed
senses struggled to respond, then bewailed
the absence of detailed, all-powerful
precedents: I kept picturing someone tracing
a figure on the turf, and wearing this outline
into a path by walking and walking around
the hollow head, immobile limbs, and cavernous torso.

---

[1] A 227-foot-tall figure of a man upright, holding a staff in each hand, carved, probably in the sixteenth century, into the turf of a hill in Wilmington, East Sussex, England, and maintained to the present day.

Robert Frost (1874 – 1963)
Birches

When I see birches bend to left and right
Across the lines of straighter darker trees,
I like to think some boy's been swinging them.
But swinging doesn't bend them down to stay
As ice-storms do. Often you must have seen them   5
Loaded with ice a sunny winter morning
After a rain. They click upon themselves
As the breeze rises, and turn many-colored
As the stir cracks and crazes their enamel.
Soon the sun's warmth makes them shed crystal shells   10
Shattering and avalanching on the snow-crust —
Such heaps of broken glass to sweep away
You'd think the inner dome of heaven had fallen.
They are dragged to the withered bracken by the load,
And they seem not to break; though once they are bowed   15
So low for long, they never right themselves:
You may see their trunks arching in the woods
Years afterwards, trailing their leaves on the ground
Like girls on hands and knees that throw their hair
Before them over their heads to dry in the sun.   20
But I was going to say when Truth broke in
With all her matter-of-fact about the ice-storm
I should prefer to have some boy bend them
As he went out and in to fetch the cows —
Some boy too far from town to learn baseball,   25
Whose only play was what he found himself,
Summer or winter, and could play alone.
One by one he subdued his father's trees
By riding them down over and over again
Until he took the stiffness out of them,   30
And not one but hung limp, not one was left
For him to conquer. He learned all there was
To learn about not launching out too soon
And so not carrying the tree away
Clear to the ground. He always kept his poise   35
To the top branches, climbing carefully
With the same pains you use to fill a cup
Up to the brim, and even above the brim.
Then be flung outward, feet first, with a swish,

Kicking his way down through the air to the ground.   40
So was I once myself a swinger of birches.
And so I dream of going back to be.
It's when I'm weary of considerations,
And life is too much like a pathless wood
Where your face burns and tickles with the cobwebs   45
Broken across it, and one eye is weeping
From a twig's having lashed across it open.
I'd like to get away from earth awhile
And then come back to it and begin over.
May no fate willfully misunderstand me   50
And half grant what I wish and snatch me away
Not to return. Earth's the right place for love:
I don't know where it's likely to go better.
I'd like to go by climbing a birch tree,
And climb black branches up a snow-white trunk   55
Toward heaven, till the tree could bear no more,
But dipped its top and set me down again.
That would be good both going and coming back.
One could do worse than be a swinger of birches.

Design[1]

I found a dimpled spider, fat and white,
On a white heal-all, holding up a moth
Like a white piece of rigid satin cloth —
Assorted characters of death and blight
Mixed ready to begin the morning right,
Like the ingredients of a witches' broth —
A snow-drop spider, a flower like a froth,
And dead wings carried like a paper kite.

What had that flower to do with being white,
The wayside blue and innocent heal-all?
What brought the kindred spider to that height,
Then steered the white moth thither in the night?
What but design of darkness to appall? —
If design govern in a thing so small.

---

[1]The argument from design (order in nature) was often used as a proof for the existence of God.

ALLEN GINSBERG (1926 – 1997)
America

America I've given you all and now I'm nothing.
America two dollars and twentyseven cents January 17, 1956.
I can't stand my own mind.
America when will we end the human war?
Go fuck yourself with your atom bomb.   5
I don't feel good don't bother me.
I won't write my poem till I'm in my right mind.
America when will you be angelic?
When will you take off your clothes?
When will you look at yourself through the grave?   10
When will you be worthy of your million Trotskyites?[1]
America why are your libraries full of tears?
America when will you send your eggs to India?[2]
I'm sick of your insane demands.
When can I go into the supermarket and buy what I need with
my good looks?   15
America after all it is you and I who are perfect not the next world.
Your machinery is too much for me.
You made me want to be a saint.
There must be some other way to settle this argument.
Burroughs is in Tangiers[3] I don't think he'll come back it's
sinister.   20
Are you being sinister or is this some form of practical joke?
I'm trying to come to the point.
I refuse to give up my obsession.
America stop pushing I know what I'm doing.
America the plum blossoms are falling.   25
I haven't read the newspapers for months, everyday somebody
goes on trial for murder.
America I feel sentimental about the Wobblies.[4]
America I used to be a communist when I was a kid I'm not sorry.
I smoke marijuana every chance I get.

---

[1] Communist idealists, followers of Leon Trotsky (1879–1940), the opponent of Stalin.

[2] India was suffering a famine, while America had an agricultural surplus.

[3] William Burroughs (1914–1997), a friend of Ginsberg's and author of the novel *Naked Lunch* (1959), was living in Morocco.

[4] Nickname for members of the Industrial Workers of the World, a union founded in 1905.

I sit in my house for days on end and stare at the roses in the closet.　30
When I go to Chinatown I get drunk and never get laid.
My mind is made up there's going to be trouble.
You should have seen me reading Marx.[5]
My psychoanalyst thinks I'm perfectly right.
I won't say the Lord's Prayer.　35
I have mystical visions and cosmic vibrations.
America I still haven't told you what you did to Uncle Max
　　after he came over from Russia.
I'm addressing you.
Are you going to let your emotional life be run by Time Magazine?
I'm obsessed by Time Magazine.　40
I read it every week.
Its cover stares at me every time I slink past the corner candystore.
I read it in the basement of the Berkeley Public Library.
It's always telling me about responsibility. Businessmen are serious.
　　Movie producers are serious. Everybody's serious but me.
It occurs to me that I am America.　45
I am talking to myself again.
Asia is rising against me.
I haven't got a chinaman's chance.
I'd better consider my national resources.
My national resources consist of two joints of marijuana millions
　　of genitals an unpublishable private literature that goes 1400
　　miles an hour and twentyfive-thousand mental institutions.　50
I say nothing about my prisons nor the millions of underprivileged
　　who live in my flowerpots under the light of five hundred
　　suns.
I have abolished the whorehouses of France, Tangiers is the next
　　to go.
My ambition is to be President despite the fact that I'm a Catholic.
America how can I write a holy litany in your silly mood?
I will continue like Henry Ford my strophes are as individual
　　as his automobiles more so they're all different sexes.
America I will sell you strophes $2500 apiece $500 down on your
　　old strophe
America free Tom Mooney[6]

---

[5]Karl Marx (1818–1883), German political theorist and coauthor, with Friedrich Engels, of *The Communist Manifesto* (1848).

[6]American labor agitator in California, accused of bomb killings and sentenced to death in 1916 but pardoned in 1939.

America save the Spanish Loyalists[7]
America Sacco & Vanzetti[8] must not die
America I am the Scottsboro boys.[9]   60
America when I was seven momma took me to Communist Cell
    meetings they sold us garbanzos[10] a handful per ticket a ticket
    costs a nickel and the speeches were free everybody was
    angelic and sentimental about the workers it was all so sincere
    you have no idea what a good thing the party was in 1935
    Scott Nearing was a grand old man a real mensch Mother
    Bloor made me cry I once saw Israel Amter[11] plain. Every-
    body must have been a spy.
America you don't really want to go to war.
America it's them bad Russians.
Them Russians them Russians and them Chinamen. And them
    Russians.
The Russia wants to eat us alive. The Russia's power mad. She
    wants to take our cars from out our garages.   65
Her wants to grab Chicago. Her needs a Red Readers' Digest.
Her wants our auto plants in Siberia. Him big bureaucracy
    running our fillingstations.
That no good. Ugh. Him make Indians learn read. Him need big
    black niggers. Hah. Her make us all work sixteen hours a
    day Help.
America this is quite serious.
America this is the impression I get from looking in the television
    set.
America is this correct?
I'd better get right down to the job.   70
It's true I don't want to join the Army or turn lathes in precision
    parts factories, I'm nearsighted and psychopathic anyway.
America I'm putting my queer shoulder to the wheel.

---

[7]Those fighting against Franco in the Spanish Civil War.

[8]Nicola Sacco and Bartolomeo Vanzetti were executed in Massachusetts in 1927 for a murder connected with a robbery. Sentiment ran high against them because of their radical beliefs.

[9]The "Scottsboro boys" were nine blacks who were convicted in Alabama of the rape of two white women in 1931. Liberals and radicals believed the conviction to be unproved. Four years later the sentences were reduced in four cases and the charges dropped in five.

[10]Chickpeas.

[11]Scott Nearing (1883–1983), Ella ("Mother") Bloor (1862–1951), and Israel Amter (1881–1954): well-known American Socialists and Communists.

LOUISE GLÜCK (b. 1943)
All Hallows[1]

Even now this landscape is assembling.
The hills darken. The oxen
sleep in their blue yoke,
the fields having been
picked clean, the sheaves
bound evenly and piled at the roadside
among cinquefoil,[2] as the toothed moon rises:

This is the barrenness
of harvest or pestilence.
And the wife leaning out the window
with her hand extended, as in payment,
and the seeds
distinct, gold, calling
Come here
Come here, little one

And the soul creeps out of the tree.

The Balcony

It was a night like this, at the end of summer.

We had rented, I remember, a room with a balcony.
How many days and nights? Five, perhaps — no more.

Even when we weren't touching we were making love.
We stood on our little balcony in the summer night.
And off somewhere, the sounds of human life.

We were the soon to be anointed monarchs,
well disposed to our subjects. Just beneath us,
sounds of a radio playing, an aria we didn't in those years know.

Someone dying of love. Someone from whom time had taken
the only happiness, who was alone now,
impoverished, without beauty.

The rapturous notes of an unendurable grief, of isolation and
      terror,

---

[1]Halloween (short for "All Hallows Eve"), October 31, the evening before All
Saints' Day.
[2]Plant with five-lobed leaves.

the nearly impossible to sustain slow phrases of the ascending
    figures —
they drifted out over the dark water
like an ecstasy.

Such a small mistake. And many years later,
the only thing left of that night, of the hours in that room.

Midsummer

On nights like this we used to swim in the quarry,
the boys making up games requiring them to tear off the girls' clothes
and the girls cooperating, because they had new bodies since
    last summer
and they wanted to exhibit them, the brave ones
leaping off the high rocks — bodies crowding the water.

The nights were humid, still. The stone was cool and wet,
marble for graveyards, for buildings that we never saw,
buildings in cities far away.

On cloudy nights, you were blind. Those nights the rocks were
    dangerous,
but in another way it was all dangerous, that was what we were
    after.
The summer started. Then the boys and girls began to pair off
but always there were a few left at the end — sometimes they'd
    keep watch,
sometimes they'd pretend to go off with each other like the rest,
but what could they do there, in the woods? No one wanted to
    be them.
But they'd show up anyway, as though some night their luck
    would change,
fate would be a different fate.

At the beginning and at the end, though, we were all together.
After the evening chores, after the smaller children were in bed,
then we were free. Nobody said anything, but we knew the nights
    we'd meet
and the nights we wouldn't. Once or twice, at the end of summer,
we could see a baby was going to come out of all that kissing.

And for those two, it was terrible, as terrible as being alone.
The game was over. We'd sit on the rocks smoking cigarettes,
worrying about the ones who weren't there.

And then finally walk home through the fields,
because there was always work the next day.
And the next day, we were kids again, sitting on the front steps in
    the morning,
eating a peach. Just that, but it seemed an honor to have a mouth.
And then going to work, which meant helping out in the fields.
One boy worked for an old lady, building shelves.
The house was very old, maybe built when the mountain was built.

And then the day faded. We were dreaming, waiting for night.
Standing at the front door at twilight, watching the shadows
    lengthen.
And a voice in the kitchen was always complaining about the heat,
wanting the heat to break.

Then the heat broke, the night was clear.
And you thought of the boy or girl you'd be meeting later.
And you thought of walking into the woods and lying down,
practicing all those things you were learning in the water.
And though sometimes you couldn't see the person you were with,
there was no substitute for that person.

The summer night glowed; in the field, fireflies were glinting.
And for those who understood such things, the stars were sending
    messages:
You will leave the village where you were born
and in another country you'll become very rich, very powerful,
but always you will mourn something you left behind, even though
    you can't say what it was,
and eventually you will return to seek it.

ALBERT GOLDBARTH (b. 1948)
The Novel That Asks to Erase Itself

But perhaps that couple sitting in the corner booth
in silence *isn't* working out some bitterness

in what got said, but working on not saying it:
a sturdy and impressive Taj Mahalian construction

that we'll never see, which of course
is the point — as if inventing anti-matter

or zero: something immeasurably important
although beyond our witnessing senses. They might be

the lesson of *Frankenstein,* incarnate
in this neighborhood bar. The genius wasn't

in making the monster; and certainly not
in killing it; but would have been,

invisibly, in not making it to begin with.

Unforeseeables

The authorities imported certain rabbits
to the island, as a remedy for a certain obnoxious weed:
they'd graze it, easily, to a reasonable number.
It's why I thought of Frank and Dorrie and when
their marriage had entered its deep plum moment of melancholia
— none of the usual mood enhancers helped her — and,
at Frank's insistent pleading, she began to see a therapist.
I gave the plan a thumbs-up too. But maybe
you've already guessed: in just a fingersnap or two
of human sexual time, the rabbits overran the countryside,
and rats were imported to check that growth . . . so one year later
officials were offering goat-herders up in the steppes
a bounty of one cent (which was reasonable pay for then
and there) for every rat tail brought to a magistrate.
The lesson: some solutions only add another problem.
Dorrie started to sleep with the therapist.

It's a bit like astrophysics . . . once the answer to the question
is "dark matter," the answer is really another and even
weightier, stickier question. Once the second honeymoon
has used up feeling like the first . . . it's everything else,
all over again — the promises that wear away
at their edges as if from silverfish; the false incriminations —
only now exacerbated by the size of a cruise-ship cabin.
You can see, we're back at the story of Frank and Dorrie.
How could we *not* be? "Plum," I said in section one: the way
the sweetness of the meat inside beseeches us, and the color
of bruise on the outside is appallingly familiar. It's their story;
and it's your story and mine. Once evolution's answer to time
is° the human brain . . . well, here we are, with all of   *becomes*
     our burrs
and webs and unforeseeables. Up in the steppes,
a constable uncovered caves where the locals were busy
breeding rats, *adding* to the population. Of course; a penny a tail.

JORIE GRAHAM (b. 1950)
Of Forced Sightes and Trusty Ferefulness[1]

Stopless wind, here are the columbine seeds I have
collected. What we would do with them is
different. Though both your trick and mine flower blue
and white

with four stem tails and yellow underpetals. Stopless   5
and unessential, half-hiss, half-
lullaby, if I fell in among your laws,
if I fell down into your mind your snow, into the miles

of spirit-drafts you drive, frenetic multitudes,
out from timber to the open ground and back to no   10
avail, if I fell down, warmblooded, ill, into your endless
evenness,

into this race you start them on and will not let them win . . . ?
If I fell in?
What is your law to my law, unhurried hurrying?   15
At my remove from you, today, in your supremest

calculation, re-
adjustment, are these three birds scratching for dead
bark beetles, frozen seeds, too late for being here yet only
        here,
in the stenchfree   20

cold. This is another current, river of rivers, this thrilling
third-act love. Who wouldn't want to stay
behind? They pack the rinds away, the blazing applecores,
the frantic shadow-wings scribbling the fenceposts, window-

panes. Meanwhile you turn, white jury, draft, away,   25
deep justice done.
I don't presume to cross the distances, the clarity,
but what grows in your only open hands? Or is

digressive love,
row after perfect greenhouse row,   30
the garden you're out of for good, wind of the theorems,
of proof, square root of light,

---

[1]Graham's title is quoted from Sir Thomas Wyatt's sonnet beginning: "My galley
charged with forgetfulness."

chaos of truth,
blinder than the mice that wait you out
    in any crack?
This is the best I can do now for prayer — to you,   35
for you — these scraps I throw

my lonely acrobats
that fall
of your accord
right to my windowsill: they pack it away, the grains, the   40

accidents, they pack it deep into the rent
heart of the blue
spruce, skins in with spiky needles. . . . Oh
    hollow
charged with forgetfulness,

through wind, through winter nights, we'll pass,   45
steering with crumbs, with words,
making of every hour
a thought, remembering

by pain and rhyme and arabesques of foraging
the formula for theft   50
under your sky that keeps
sliding away

married to hurry
and grim song.

Soul Says

(Afterword)

To be so held by brittleness, shapeliness.
By meaning. As where I *have to go where you go,*
I *have to touch what you must touch,*
in hunger, in boredom, the spindrift, the ticket . . .
Distilled in you (can you hear me)
the idiom in you, the why —

The flash *of a voice.* The river *glints.*
The mother *opens the tablecloth up into the wind.*
There as the fabric descends — the alphabet of ripenesses,
what is, what could have been.
The bread on the tablecloth. Crickets shrill in the grass.

O pluck my magic garment from me. So.
                                    [lays down his robe]
Lie there, my art —

(This is a form of matter of matter she sang)

(Where the hurry is stopped) (and held) (but not extinguished)
    (no)

(So listen, listen, this will soothe you) (if that is what you want)

Now then, I said, I go to meet that which I liken to
(even though the wave break and drown me in laughter)
the wave breaking, the wave drowning me in laughter —

The Strangers

The hand I placed on you, what if it
didn't exist, where it began, shaking, the declension of
your opening shirt, dusk postponed in each glazed and arctic
button, pale reddish shirt — what if it doesn't
exist — these fingers browsing the cotton surface, swimming in the
                                    steadfast surface —
what if there's no place it can exist
this looking for a place to lie down in,
to make a tiny civilization —
here between the moss and long corridors of afternoon light —
between the exaggerations of the ornamental yews
laying themselves in day's slow caress across the brick apartment
                                    house,
nothing voracious, nothing groping to make a plan find a place,
one of us against a tree now, one of us like a shadow
over water, one of us begging, one of us taking
                    measures,
thinking, rethinking,
between Wednesday and Thursday,
what if it doesn't exist, the place
where this hand lay flat for the first time
against your heart, cotton-denim and flesh
                    between,
to take it forever, first-fruit, from its limb,
tongue-tied, door slamming, cars stalled-out at traffic
                                    light —
is it a muscular place?
is it a cadence this open palm wants?

betrothed to the instant,
swearing allegiance,
a little dialogue between us like footprints,
is it the wingbeat itself it would cross through the
              envelope of flesh
to get, this hand flat on you now, a badge, an x-ray,
homing in, an hypothesis, monosyllabic,
over the supple, gossipy, tin-can heart — unrelenting —
to make you exist —
Whose names does the wind riffle through, trying to see us?
And behind us: these tulips appearing out of nowhere —
the soil opening its thousands of lids. So easy.
A thumb at a time. Whole hands. Grappling back up.
They're flowers because they stop where they do.

THOMAS GRAY (1716 – 1771)
Elegy Written in a Country Churchyard

The curfew tolls the knell of parting day,
    The lowing herd wind slowly o'er the lea,
The plowman homeward plods his weary way,
    And leaves the world to darkness and to me.

Now fades the glimmering landscape on the sight,   5
    And all the air a solemn stillness holds,
Save where the beetle wheels his droning flight,
    And drowsy tinklings lull the distant folds;

Save that from yonder ivy-mantled tower
    The moping owl does to the moon complain   10
Of such, as wandering near her secret bower,
    Molest her ancient solitary reign.

Beneath those rugged elms, that yew tree's shade,
    Where heaves the turf in many a moldering heap,
Each in his narrow cell forever laid,   15
    The rude° forefathers of the hamlet sleep.   *rustic*

The breezy call of incense-breathing morn,
    The swallow twittering from the straw-built shed,
The cock's shrill clarion, or the echoing horn,
    No more shall rouse them from their lowly bed.   20

For them no more the blazing hearth shall burn,
    Or busy housewife ply her evening care;

No children run to lisp their sire's return,
    Or climb his knees the envied kiss to share.

Oft did the harvest to their sickle yield,   25
    Their furrow oft the stubborn glebe° has broke;   *clot of soil*
How jocund did they drive their team afield!
    How bowed the woods beneath their sturdy stroke!

Let not Ambition mock their useful toil,
    Their homely joys, and destiny obscure;   30
Nor Grandeur hear with a disdainful smile
    The short and simple annals of the poor.

The boast of heraldry, the pomp of power,
    And all that beauty, all that wealth e'er gave,
Awaits alike the inevitable hour.   35
    The paths of glory lead but to the grave.

Nor you, ye proud, impute to these the fault,
    If Memory o'er their tomb no trophies raise,
Where through the long-drawn aisle and fretted vault
    The pealing anthem swells the note of praise.   40

Can storied urn or animated bust
    Back to its mansion call the fleeting breath?
Can Honor's voice provoke the silent dust,
    Or Flattery soothe the dull cold ear of Death?

Perhaps in this neglected spot is laid   45
    Some heart once pregnant with celestial fire;
Hands that the rod of empire might have swayed,
    Or waked to ecstasy the living lyre.

But Knowledge to their eyes her ample page
    Rich with the spoils of time did ne'er unroll;   50
Chill Penury repressed their noble rage,
    And froze the genial current of the soul.

Full many a gem of purest ray serene,
    The dark unfathomed caves of ocean bear:
Full many a flower is born to blush unseen,   55
    And waste its sweetness on the desert air.

Some village Hampden,[1] that with dauntless breast
    The little tyrant of his fields withstood;

---

[1]One of the leaders of the opposition to Charles I. He was killed in battle in the English Civil War.

Some mute inglorious Milton here may rest,
    Some Cromwell guiltless of his country's blood.   60

The applause of listening senates to command,
    The threats of pain and ruin to despise,
To scatter plenty o'er a smiling land,
    And read their history in a nation's eyes,

Their lot forbade: nor circumscribed alone   65
    Their growing virtues, but their crimes confined;
Forbade to wade through slaughter to a throne,
    And shut the gates of mercy on mankind,

The struggling pangs of conscious truth to hide,
    To quench the blushes of ingenuous shame,   70
Or heap the shrine of Luxury and Pride
    With incense kindled at the Muse's flame.

Far from the madding crowd's ignoble strife,
    Their sober wishes never learned to stray;
Along the cool sequestered vale of life   75
    They kept the noiseless tenor of their way.

Yet even these bones from insult to protect
    Some frail memorial still erected nigh,
With uncouth rhymes and shapeless sculpture decked,
    Implores the passing tribute of a sigh.   80

Their name, their years, spelt by the unlettered Muse,
    The place of fame and elegy supply:
And many a holy text around she strews,
    That teach the rustic moralist to die.

For who to dumb Forgetfulness a prey,   85
    This pleasing anxious being e'er resigned,
Left the warm precincts of the cheerful day,
    Nor cast one longing lingering look behind?

On some fond breast the parting soul relies,
    Some pious drops the closing eye requires;   90
Even from the tomb the voice of Nature cries,
    Even in our ashes live their wonted fires.

For thee, who mindful of the unhonored dead
    Dost in these lines their artless tale relate;
If chance, by lonely contemplation led,   95
    Some kindred spirit shall inquire thy fate,

Haply some hoary-headed swain may say,
    "Oft have we seen him at the peep of dawn
Brushing with hasty steps the dews away
    To meet the sun upon the upland lawn.   100

"There at the foot of yonder nodding beech
    That wreathes its old fantastic roots so high,
His listless length at noontide would he stretch,
    And pore upon the brook that babbles by.

"Hard by yon wood, now smiling as in scorn,   105
    Muttering his wayward fancies he would rove,
Now drooping, woeful wan, like one forlorn,
    Or crazed with care, or crossed in hopeless love.

"One morn I missed him on the customed hill,
    Along the heath and near his favorite tree;   110
Another came; nor yet beside the rill,
    Nor up the lawn, nor at the wood was he;

"The next with dirges due in sad array
    Slow through the churchway path we saw him borne.
Approach and read (for thou canst read) the lay,   115
    Graved on the stone beneath yon aged thorn."

The Epitaph

Here rests his head upon the lap of Earth
    A youth to Fortune and to Fame unknown.
Fair Science° frowned not on his humble birth,   general knowledge
    And Melancholy marked him for her own.   120

Large was his bounty, and his soul sincere,
    Heaven did a recompense as largely send:
He gave to Misery all he had, a tear,
    He gained from Heaven ('twas all he wished) a friend.

No farther seek his merits to disclose,   125
    Or draw his frailties from their dread abode
(There they alike in trembling hope repose),
    The bosom of his Father and his God.

Thom Gunn (1929 – 2004)
The Man with Night Sweats

I wake up cold, I who
Prospered through dreams of heat

Wake to their residue,
Sweat, and a clinging sheet.

My flesh was its own shield:
Where it was gashed, it healed.

I grew as I explored
The body I could trust
Even while I adored
The risk that made robust,

A world of wonders in
Each challenge to the skin.

I cannot but be sorry
The given shield was cracked,
My mind reduced to hurry,
My flesh reduced and wrecked.

I have to change the bed,
But catch myself instead

Stopped upright where I am
Hugging my body to me
As if to shield it from
The pains that will go through me,

As if hands were enough
To hold an avalanche off.

My Sad Captains

One by one they appear in
the darkness: a few friends, and
a few with historical
names. How late they start to shine!
but before they fade they stand
perfectly embodied, all

the past lapping them like a
cloak of chaos. They were men
who, I thought, lived only to
renew the wasteful force they
spent with each hot convulsion.
They remind me, distant now.

True, they are not at rest yet,
but now that they are indeed

apart, winnowed from failures,
they withdraw to an orbit
and turn with disinterested
hard energy, like the stars.

H. D. (1886 – 1961)
Helen[1]

All Greece hates
the still eyes in the white face,
the lustre as of olives
where she stands,
and the white hands.

All Greece reviles
the wan face when she smiles,
hating it deeper still
when it grows wan and white,
remembering past enchantments
and past ills.

Greece sees unmoved,
God's daughter, born of love,
the beauty of cool feet
and slenderest knees,
could love indeed the maid,
only if she were laid,
white ash amid funereal cypresses.

THOMAS HARDY (1840 – 1928)
Afterwards

When the Present has latched its postern behind my tremulous
      stay,
    And the May month flaps its glad green leaves like wings,
Delicate-filmed as new-spun silk, will the neighbors say,
    "He was a man who used to notice such things"?

If it be in the dusk when, like an eyelid's soundless blink,
    The dewfall-hawk comes crossing the shades to alight

---

[1]The beautiful wife of Menelaus. Her abduction by Paris was the cause of the Trojan War.

Upon the wind-warped upland thorn, a gazer may think,
　　"To him this must have been a familiar sight."

If I pass during some nocturnal blackness, mothy and warm,
　　When the hedgehog travels furtively over the lawn,
One may say, "He strove that such innocent creatures should
　　　　come to no harm,
　　But he could do little for them; and now he is gone."

If, when hearing that I have been stilled at last, they stand at the
　　　　door,
　　Watching the full-starred heavens that winter sees,
Will this thought rise on those who will meet my face no more,
　　"He was one who had an eye for such mysteries"?

And will any say when my bell of quittance is heard in the gloom,
　　And a crossing breeze cuts a pause in its outrollings,
Till they rise again, as they were a new bell's boom,
　　"He hears it not now, but used to notice such things"?

MICHAEL S. HARPER (b. 1938)
Nightmare Begins Responsibility[1]

I place these numbed wrists to the pane
watching white uniforms whisk over
him in the tube-kept
prison
fear what they will do in experiment
watch my gloved stickshifting gasolined hands
breathe *boxcar-information-please* infirmary tubes
distrusting white-pink mending paperthin
silkened end hairs, distrusting tubes
shrunk in his *trunk-skincapped*
shaven head, in thighs
distrusting-white-hands-picking-baboon-light
on this son who will not make his second night
of this wardstrewn intensive airpocket
where his father's asthmatic
hymns of *night-train,* train done gone
his mother can only know that he has flown

---

[1] A play on William Butler Yeats's epigraph to his volume *Responsibilities* (1913): "In dreams begin responsibilities." This poem is an elegy for Harper's son, who died one day after birth. Another son had also died shortly after birth.

up into essential calm unseen corridor
going boxscarred home, *mamaborn, sweetsonchild*
gonedowntown into *researchtestingwarehousebatteryacid*
mama-son-done-gone / me telling her 'nother
train tonight, no music, no breathstroked
heartbeat in my infinite distrust of them:

and of my distrusting self
white-doctor-who-breathed-for-him-all-night
say it for two sons gone,
say nightmare, say it loud
panebreaking heartmadness:
nightmare begins responsibility.

We Assume: On the Death of Our Son, Reuben Masai Harper

We assume
that in 28 hours,
lived in a collapsible isolette,
you learned to accept pure oxygen
as the natural sky;
the scant shallow breaths
that filled those hours
cannot, did not make you fly —
but dreams were there
like crooked palmprints on
the twin-thick windows of the nursery —
in the glands of your mother.

We assume
the sterile hands
drank chemicals in and out
from lungs opaque with mucus,
pumped your stomach,
eeked the bicarbonate in
crooked, green-winged veins,
out in a plastic mask;

A woman who'd lost her first son
consoled us with an angel gone ahead
to pray for our family —
gone into that sky
seeking oxygen,

gone into autopsy,
a fine brown powdered sugar,
a disposable cremation:

We assume
you did not know we loved you.

ROBERT HAYDEN (1913 – 1980)
Frederick Douglass[1]

When it is finally ours, this freedom, this liberty, this beautiful
and terrible thing, needful to man as air,
usable as earth; when it belongs at last to all,
when it is truly instinct, brain matter, diastole, systole,
reflex action; when it is finally won; when it is more
than the gaudy mumbo jumbo of politicians:
this man, this Douglass, this former slave, this Negro
beaten to his knees, exiled, visioning a world
where none is lonely, none hunted, alien,
this man, superb in love and logic, this man
shall be remembered. Oh, not with statues' rhetoric,
not with legends and poems and wreaths of bronze alone,
but with the lives grown out of his life, the lives
fleshing his dream of the beautiful, needful thing.

Mourning Poem for the Queen of Sunday[2]

Lord's lost Him His mockingbird,
His fancy warbler;
Satan sweet-talked her,
four bullets hushed her.
Who would have thought
she'd end that way?

Four bullets hushed her. And the world a-clang with evil.
Who's going to make old hardened sinner men tremble now
and the righteous rock?
Oh who and oh who will sing Jesus down

---

[1]Frederick Douglass (ca. 1817–1895), who escaped from slavery in 1838, became
an abolitionist, writer, and statesman.

[2]Lula Butler Hurst, gospel singer at Detroit's Second Baptist Church, murdered by
her lover.

to help with struggling and doing without and being colored
all through blue Monday?
Till way next Sunday?

> All those angels
> in their cretonne clouds and finery
> the true believer saw
> when she rared back her head and sang,
> all those angels are surely weeping.
> Who would have thought
> she'd end that way?

Four holes in her heart. The gold works wrecked.
But she looks so natural in her big bronze coffin
among the Broken Hearts and Gates-Ajar,
it's as if any moment she'd lift her head
from its pillow of chill gardenias
and turn this quiet into shouting Sunday
and make folks forget what she did on Monday.

> Oh, Satan sweet-talked her,
> and four bullets hushed her.
> Lord's lost Him His diva,
> His fancy warbler's gone.
> Who would have thought,
> who would have thought she'd end that way?

TERRANCE HAYES (b. 1971)

A Small Novel

The protagonist spends the first twenty pages
crossing a bridge wearing nothing but red
swimming trunks and sneakers with no socks.

I can remember standing naked
outside my neighbor's window at fourteen
when I read the paragraph about the placard of night

held up by pine trees.
Wherever there is a mention of solitude or desire
I think, without wanting to, of Race. Race

when the protagonist spends a page long sentence
trying to work free a knot of shoe string
in his basketball sneaker. Race

when he spends the hot seasons of his twenties
like a beggar with no mouth. Race
when he tells his wife: *"There are no Open Houses*

on Easter." Late in the book he feels himself
becoming a shadow. On page 113 just as I reach
the final sentence about traffic like the sound of wind

like the sound of water, a horn yelps somewhere.
"It was all he'd ever known of rivers . . . "
I pencil L. H.° in the margin. I think, without   *Langston Hughes*
    wanting to,

That they will find this book someday
and turn its muddy bosom all golden in the sunset.
On its blank last page I write the poem

"The Blue Langston" which begins:
"O Blood of the River songs, O songs of the River of Blood,"
and ends: "There was nothing I could do about Race."

Woofer (When I Consider the African–American)

When I consider the much discussed dilemma
of the African-American, I think not of the diasporic
middle passing,° unchained, juke, jock,   *those dispersed as slaves*
    and jiving   *across the ocean*
sons and daughters of what sleek dashikied° poets   *African tunic*
and tether fisted Nationalists commonly call Mother   5
Africa, but of an ex-girlfriend who was the child
of a black-skinned Ghanaian beauty and Jewish-
American, globetrotting ethnomusicologist.
I forgot all my father's warnings about meeting women
at bus stops (which is the way he met my mother)   10
when I met her waiting for the rush hour bus in October
because I have always been a sucker for deep blue denim
and Afros and because she spoke so slowly
when she asked the time. I wrote my phone number
in the back of the book of poems I had and said   15
something like "You can return it when I see you again"
which has to be one of my top two or three best
pickup lines ever. If you have ever gotten lucky
on a first date you can guess what followed: her smile
twizzling above a tight black v-neck sweater, chatter   20
on my velvet couch and then the two of us wearing nothing

but shoes. When I think of African-American rituals
of love, I think not of young, made-up unwed mothers
who seek warmth in the arms of any brother
with arms because they never knew their fathers   25
(though that could describe my mother), but of that girl
and me in the basement of her father's four story Victorian
making love among the fresh blood and axe
and chicken feathers left after the Thanksgiving slaughter
executed by a 3-D witchdoctor houseguest (his face   30
was starred by tribal markings)° and her   *the guest is an African*
    ruddy American
poppa while drums drummed upstairs from his
    hi-fi woofers
because that's the closest I've ever come to anything
remotely ritualistic or African, for that matter.
We were quiet enough to hear their chatter
between the drums and the scraping of their chairs
at the table above us and the footsteps of anyone
approaching the basement door and it made
our business sweeter, though I'll admit I wondered
if I'd be cursed for making love under her father's nose   40
or if the witchdoctor would sense us and then cast a spell.
I have been cursed, broken hearted, stunned, frightened
and bewildered, but when I consider the African-American
I think not of the tek nines° of my generation deployed   *guns*
by madness or that we were assigned some lousy fate   45
when God prescribed job titles at the beginning of Time
or that we were too dumb to run the other way
when we saw the wide white sails of the ships
since given the absurd history of the world, everyone
is a descendant of slaves (which makes me wonder   50
if outrunning your captors is not the real meaning
    of Race?).
I think of the girl's bark colored, bi-continental nipples
when I consider the African-American.
I think of a string of people connected one to another
and including the two of us there in the basement   55
linked by a hyphen° filled with blood;   *in the word*
linked by a blood filled baton in one great   *"African-American"*
    historical relay.

[Handwritten annotations: "Attempts to connect the African heritage to the American community — The hyphen"; "bloodlines / violence in cultural memory"]

SEAMUS HEANEY (b. 1939)
Bogland

For T. P. Flanagan

We have no prairies
To slice a big sun at evening —
Everywhere the eye concedes to
Encroaching horizon,

Is wooed into the cyclops' eye
Of a tarn. Our unfenced country
Is bog that keeps crusting
Between the sights of the sun.

They've taken the skeleton
Of the Great Irish Elk
Out of the peat, set it up,
An astounding crate full of air.

Butter sunk under
More than a hundred years
Was recovered salty and white.
The ground itself is kind, black butter

Melting and opening underfoot,
Missing its last definition
By millions of years.
They'll never dig coal here,

Only the waterlogged trunks
Of great firs, soft as pulp.
Our pioneers keep striking
Inwards and downwards,

Every layer they strip
Seems camped on before.
The bogholes might be Atlantic seepage.
The wet centre is bottomless.

Punishment

I can feel the tug
of the halter at the nape
of her neck, the wind
on her naked front.

It blows her nipples
to amber beads,
it shakes the frail rigging
of her ribs.

I can see her drowned
body in the bog,
the weighing stone,
the floating rods and boughs.

Under which at first
she was a barked sapling
that is dug up
oak-bone, brain-firkin:°   *container*

her shaved head
like a stubble of black corn,
her blindfold a soiled bandage,
her noose a ring

to store
the memories of love.
Little adulteress,
before they punished you

you were flaxen-haired,
undernourished, and your
tar-black face was beautiful.
My poor scapegoat,

I almost love you
but would have cast, I know,
the stones of silence.
I am the artful voyeur

of your brain's exposed
and darkened combs,
your muscles' webbing
and all your numbered bones:

I who have stood dumb
when your betraying sisters,
cauled in tar,
wept by the railings,

who would connive
in civilized outrage

yet understand the exact
and tribal, intimate revenge.

The Collar

    I struck the board° and cried, "No more;   *table*
        I will abroad!
    What? shall I ever sigh and pine?
My lines and life are free, free as the road,
      Loose as the wind, as large as store.
            Shall I be still in suit?
    Have I no harvest but a thorn
    To let me blood, and not restore
What I have lost with cordial fruit?
           Sure there was wine
Before my sighs did dry it; there was corn
      Before my tears did drown it.
    Is the year only lost to me?
      Have I no bays to crown it,
No flowers, no garlands gay? All blasted?
      All wasted?
    Not so, my heart; but there is fruit,
      And thou hast hands.
    Recover all thy sigh-blown age
On double pleasures: leave thy cold dispute
Of what is fit and not. Forsake thy cage,
      Thy rope of sands,
Which petty thoughts have made, and made to thee
    Good cable, to enforce and draw,
        And be thy law,
    While thou didst wink and wouldst not see.
      Away! take heed;
      I will abroad.
Call in thy death's-head there; tie up thy fears.
      He that forbears
    To suit and serve his need,
      Deserves his load."
But as I raved and grew more fierce and wild
      At every word,

Methought I heard one calling, *Child!*
                And I replied, *My Lord.*

Redemption

Having been tenant long to a rich lord,
        Not thriving, I resolvèd to be bold,
        And make a suit unto him, to afford°   *grant*
A new small-rented lease, and cancel the old.

In heaven at his manor I him sought;
        They told me there that he was lately gone
        About some land, which he had dearly bought
Long since on earth, to take possessiön.

I straight returned, and knowing his great birth,
        Sought him accordingly in great resorts;
        In cities, theaters, gardens, parks and courts;
At length I heard a ragged noise and mirth

        Of thieves and murderers; there I him espied,
        Who straight, *Your suit is granted,* said, and died.

ROBERT HERRICK (1591 – 1674)
Corinna's Going A-Maying

Get up! get up for shame! the blooming morn
Upon her wings presents the god unshorn.°   *Apollo, god of the sun*
        See how Aurora° throws her fair   *goddess of dawn*
        Fresh-quilted colors through the air:
        Get up, sweet slug-a-bed, and see   5
        The dew bespangling herb and tree.
Each flower has wept and bowèd toward the east
Above an hour since, yet you not dressed;
        Nay, not so much as out of bed?
        When all the birds have matins said,   10
        And sung their thankful hymns, 'tis sin,
        Nay, profanation to keep in,
Whenas a thousand virgins on this day
Spring, sooner than the lark, to fetch in May.

Rise, and put on your foliage, and be seen   15
To come forth, like the springtime, fresh and green,
        And sweet as Flora.° Take no care   *goddess of flowers*
        For jewels for your gown or hair;

Fear not; the leaves will strew
   Gems in abundance upon you;   20
Besides, the childhood of the day has kept,
Against you come, some orient pearls unwept;
     Come and receive them while the light
     Hangs on the dew-locks of the night,
     And Titan° on the eastern hill   *the sun*   25
     Retires himself, or else stands still
Till you come forth. Wash, dress, be brief in praying:
Few beads° are best when once we go a-Maying.   *prayers*

Come, my Corinna, come; and, coming mark
How each field turns a street, each street a park   30
     Made green and trimmed with trees; see how
     Devotion gives each house a bough
     Or branch: each porch, each door ere this,
     An ark, a tabernacle is,
Made up of whitethorn neatly interwove,   35
As if here were those cooler shades of love.
     Can such delights be in the street
     And open fields, and we not see 't?
     Come, we'll abroad; and let's obey
     The proclamation made for May,   40
And sin no more, as we have done, by staying;
But, my Corinna, come, let's go a-Maying.

There's not a budding boy or girl this day
But is got up and gone to bring in May;
     A deal of youth, ere this, is come   45
     Back, and with whitethorn laden home.
     Some have dispatched their cakes and cream
     Before that we have left to dream;
And some have wept, and wooed, and plighted troth,
And chose their priest, ere we can cast off sloth.   50
     Many a green-gown has been given,
     Many a kiss, both odd and even,
     Many a glance, too, has been sent
     From out the eye, love's firmament;
Many a jest told of the keys betraying   55
This night, and locks picked; yet we're not a-Maying.

Come, let us go while we are in our prime,
And take the harmless folly of the time.
     We shall grow old apace, and die

Before we know our liberty.   60
Our life is short, and our days run
As fast away as does the sun;
And, as a vapor or a drop of rain
Once lost, can ne'er be found again;
So when or you or I are made   65
A fable, song, or fleeting shade,
All love, all liking, all delight
Lies drowned with us in endless night.
Then while time serves, and we are but decaying,
Come, my Corinna, come, let's go a–Maying.   70

JOHN HOLLANDER (b. 1929)

By Nature

As if hopefulness
Were a kind of natural
Right instead of a
Sort of malady
Most incident to the mind,
We have looked upward
And then down again,
Looked under, and behind, for
Some acknowledgment
Of what it is we
Act as if we'd been promised.
The jack o' lantern
Grin of sunrise, noon's
Reasonable demeanor,
Night's apparently
Loving hand drawing
Her dark curtain between us
And what will come next —
These are what we get,
Having by nature both to
Take it and leave it.
The cold sky, having
Come in time to imitate
Our moods, will giggle
Or frown, as it will,
But without the convictions
We believe we have;

The relenting snow
Will yield to the gray green dark
Surface of the land;
The unforgiving
Land will leave us nothing much
To ground our hopes in;
And the water, wide
With possibility and
With desperation
At once, can take back
What was never more than our
Borrowed buoyancy.

GERARD MANLEY HOPKINS (1844 – 1889)
God's Grandeur

The world is charged with the grandeur of God.
    It will flame out, like shining from shook foil;
    It gathers to a greatness, like the ooze of oil
Crushed. Why do men then now not reck his rod?
Generations have trod, have trod, have trod;
    And all is seared with trade; bleared, smeared with toil;
    And wears man's smudge and shares man's smell: the soil
Is bare now, nor can foot feel, being shod.

And for all this, nature is never spent;
    There lives the dearest freshness deep down things;
And though the last lights off the black West went
    Oh, morning, at the brown brink eastward, springs —
Because the Holy Ghost over the bent
    World broods with warm breast and with ah! bright wings.

No worst, there is none. Pitched past pitch of grief

No worst, there is none. Pitched past pitch of grief,
More pangs will, schooled at forepangs, wilder wring.
Comforter, where, where is your comforting?
Mary, mother of us, where is your relief?
My cries heave, herds-long; huddle in a main, a chief-
woe, world-sorrow; on an age-old anvil wince and sing —
Then lull, then leave off. Fury had shrieked "No ling-
ering! Let me be fell:° force° I must be brief."   *fierce / perforce*

O the mind, mind has mountains; cliffs of fall
Frightful, sheer, no-man-fathomed. Hold them cheap
May who ne'er hung there. Nor does long our small
Durance deal with that steep or deep. Here! creep,
Wretch, under a comfort serves in a whirlwind: all
Life death does end and each day dies with sleep.

A. E. HOUSMAN (1859 – 1936)
Loveliest of Trees, the Cherry Now

Loveliest of trees, the cherry now
Is hung with bloom along the bough,
And stands about the woodland ride
Wearing white for Eastertide.

Now, of my threescore years and ten,
Twenty will not come again,
And take from seventy springs a score,
It only leaves me fifty more.

And since to look at things in bloom
Fifty springs are little room,
About the woodlands I will go
To see the cherry hung with snow.

With Rue My Heart Is Laden

With rue my heart is laden
 For golden friends I had,
For many a rose-lipt maiden
 And many a lightfoot lad.

By brooks too broad for leaping
 The lightfoot boys are laid;
The rose-lipt girls are sleeping
 In fields where roses fade.

LANGSTON HUGHES (1902 – 1967)
Dream Variation

To fling my arms wide
In some place of the sun,
To whirl and to dance
Till the white day is done.

Then rest at cool evening
Beneath a tall tree
While night comes on gently,
      Dark like me —
That is my dream!

To fling my arms wide
In the face of the sun,
Dance! whirl! whirl!
Till the quick day is done.
Rest at pale evening. . . .
A tall, slim tree. . . .
Night coming tenderly
      Black like me.

Harlem

What happens to a dream deferred?

    Does it dry up
    like a raisin in the sun?
    Or fester like a sore —
    And then run?
    Does it stink like rotten meat?
    Or crust and sugar over —
    like a syrupy sweet?

    Maybe it just sags
    like a heavy load.

    Or does it explode?

I, Too

I, too, sing America.

I am the darker brother.
They send me to eat in the kitchen
When company comes,
But I laugh,
And eat well,
And grow strong.

Tomorrow,
I'll be at the table
When company comes.
Nobody'll dare

Say to me,
"Eat in the kitchen,"
Then.

Besides,
They'll see how beautiful I am
And be ashamed —

I, too, am America.

The Weary Blues

Droning a drowsy syncopated tune,
Rocking back and forth to a mellow croon,
    I heard a Negro play.
Down on Lenox Avenue the other night
By the pale dull pallor of an old gas light
    He did a lazy sway. . . .
    He did a lazy sway. . . .
To the tune o' those Weary Blues.
With his ebony hands on each ivory key
He made that poor piano moan with melody.
    O Blues!
Swaying to and fro on his rickety stool
He played that sad raggy tune like a musical fool.
    Sweet Blues!
Coming from a black man's soul.
    O Blues!
In a deep song voice with a melancholy tone
I heard that Negro sing, that old piano moan —
    "Ain't got nobody in all this world,
    Ain't got nobody but ma self.
    I's gwine to quit ma frownin'
    And put ma troubles on the shelf."
Thump, thump, thump, went his foot on the floor.
He played a few chords then he sang some more —
    "I got the Weary Blues
    And I can't be satisfied.
    Got the Weary Blues
    And can't be satisfied —
    I ain't happy no mo'
    And I wish that I had died."

And far into the night he crooned that tune.
The stars went out and so did the moon.
The singer stopped playing and went to bed
While the Weary Blues echoed through his head.
He slept like a rock or a man that's dead.

LAWSON INADA (b. 1938)
From _West Side Songs_

XI. Japs
are great
imitators —
they stole
the Greeks'
skewers,
used them
on themselves.
Their sutras°   *religious precepts*
are Face
and Hide.
They hate
everyone else,
on the sly.

They play
Dr. Charley's°   *the white man*
games — bowling,
raking,
growing forks
on lapels.
Their tongues
are yellow
with "r's",
with "l's."°   *sounds confusing to Japanese speakers of English*

They hate
themselves,
on the sly. I
used to be
Japanese

BEN JONSON (1572 – 1637)
Come, My Celia[1]

Come, my Celia, let us prove,°   *experience*
While we can, the sports of love;
Time will not be ours forever;
He at length our good will sever.
Spend not then his gifts in vain.
Suns that set may rise again;
But if once we lose this light,
'Tis with us perpetual night.
Why should we defer our joys?
Fame and rumor are but toys.
Cannot we delude the eyes
Of a few poor household spies,
Or his easier ears beguile,
So removèd by our wile?
'Tis no sin love's fruit to steal;
But the sweet thefts to reveal,
To be taken, to be seen,
These have crimes accounted been.

LAURA KASISCHKE (b. 1961)
Argument w/ herself
Miss Consolation for Emotional Damages

When the embarrassment began, no one could see it. It lived

in the closet, the basement, the attic, the brain. It was
a moth at first, and then it was the hole a moth had made.

It had to do with unemployment: No! (Who   *Uses parentheses*
cared that my father couldn't work?) It had

to do with the boy next door, who'd
seen my mother drunk, whose
own mother had explained to him
that it wasn't our fault we were poor.

No.

It had been born
in another country. It had come to this one on a boat.
It couldn't speak the language. It had
left a wolf

moves true abstract → physical

---

on the other shore. (A tame
wolf: someone
had beaten the wildness out of it
with kindness, and a stick.) It had

to do with paradox, that space was transparent
and also dense.
It had to do with Einstein.
The curvature of the world in a third dimension. It couldn't
take the contradiction, woke
one morning as a careless
American girl, mouth
stuffed with <u>pink</u> ~~physical embodiment~~
<u>fluff</u>: When ~~of "pleasant inanities"~~

she opened it, for centuries, nothing
but <u>pleasant inanities</u> came out.

JOHN KEATS (1795 – 1821)
In drear-nighted December

In drear-nighted December,
    Too happy, happy tree,
Thy branches ne'er remember
    Their green felicity —
The north cannot undo them
With a sleety whistle through them,
Nor frozen thawings glue them
    From budding at the prime.

In drear-nighted December,
    Too happy, happy brook,
Thy bubblings ne'er remember
    Apollo's summer look;
But with a sweet forgetting
They stay their crystal fretting,
Never, never petting
    About the frozen time.

Ah! would 'twere so with many
    A gentle girl and boy —
But were there ever any
    Writh'd not of passèd joy?
The feel of not to feel it,

When there is none to heal it,
Nor numbèd sense to steel it,
    Was never said in rhyme.

La Belle Dame sans Merci[1]

O what can ail thee, Knight at arms,
ghostly Alone and palely loitering?
The sedge has withered from the Lake
    And no birds sing!

O what can ail thee, Knight at arms,
    So haggard, and so woebegone?
The squirrel's granary is full
    And the harvest's done. *end of the season*

I see a lily on thy brow
    With anguish moist and fever dew,
And on thy cheeks a fading rose
    Fast withereth too.

"I met a Lady in the Meads,°   *meadows*
    Full beautiful, a faery's child,
Her hair was long, her foot was light
    And her eyes were wild. *youth*

"I made a Garland for her head,
    And bracelets too, and fragrant Zone;°   *belt*
She looked at me as she did love
    And made sweet moan.

"I set her on my pacing steed
    And nothing else saw all day long,
For sidelong would she bend and sing
    A faery's song.

"She found me roots of relish sweet,
    And honey wild, and manna dew,
And sure in language strange she said
    'I love thee true.'

"She took me to her elfin grot°   *cave*
    And there she wept and sighed full sore,
And there I shut her wild wild eyes
    With kisses four.

---

[1]The beautiful lady without pity.

"And there she lullèd me asleep,
  And there I dreamed, Ah Woe betide!
The latest° dream I ever dreamt   *last*
  On the cold hill side.

"I saw pale Kings, and Princes too,
  Pale warriors, death-pale were they all;
They cried, 'La belle dame sans merci
  Hath thee in thrall!'

"I saw their starved lips in the gloam
  With horrid warning gapèd wide,
And I awoke, and found me here
  On the cold hill's side.

"And this is why I sojourn here,
  Alone and palely loitering;
Though the sedge is withered from the Lake
  And no birds sing."

On Sitting Down to Read King Lear Once Again

O golden-tongued Romance with serene lute!
  Fair plumèd Siren!° Queen of far away!   *enchantress*
  Leave melodizing on this wintry day,
Shut up thine olden pages, and be mute:
Adieu! for once again the fierce dispute
  Betwixt damnation and impassioned clay
  Must I burn through; once more humbly assay
The bitter-sweet of this Shakespearean fruit.
Chief Poet! and ye clouds of Albion,°   *England*
  Begetters of our deep eternal theme,
When through the old oak forest I am gone,
  Let me not wander in a barren dream,
But when I am consumèd in the fire,
Give me new Phoenix[1] wings to fly at my desire.

This living hand[1]

This living hand, now warm and capable
Of earnest grasping, would, if it were cold
And in the icy silence of the tomb,
So haunt thy days and chill thy dreaming nights

---

[1]Legendary bird that lives for centuries, then consumes itself in fire and is reborn.
[1]Written on a manuscript page of Keats's unfinished poem, "The Cap and Bells."

That thou wouldst wish thine own heart dry of blood
So in my veins red life might stream again,
And thou be conscience-calmed — see here it is —
I hold it towards you.

JANE KENYON (1947 – 1995)
Back

We try a new drug, a new combination
of drugs, and suddenly
I fall into my life again

like a vole° picked up by a storm   *fieldmouse*
then dropped three valleys
and two mountains away from home.

I can find my way back. I know
I will recognize the store
where I used to buy milk and gas.

I remember the house and barn,
the rake, the blue cups and plates,
the Russian novels I loved so much,

and the black silk nightgown
that he once thrust
into the toe of my Christmas stocking.

Otherwise

I got out of bed
on two strong legs.
It might have been
otherwise. I ate
cereal, sweet
milk, ripe, flawless
peach. It might
have been otherwise.
I took the dog uphill
to the birch wood.
All morning I did
the work I love.

At noon I lay down
with my mate. It might
have been otherwise.

We ate dinner together
at a table with silver
candlesticks. It might
have been otherwise.
I slept in a bed
in a room with paintings
on the walls, and
planned another day
just like this day.
But one day, I know,
it will be otherwise.

Surprise

He suggests pancakes at the local diner,
followed by a walk in search of mayflowers,
while friends convene at the house
bearing casseroles and a cake, their cars
pulled close along the sandy shoulders
of the road, where tender ferns unfurl
in the ditches, and this year's budding leaves
push last year's spectral leaves from the tips
of the twigs of the ash trees. The gathering
itself is not what astounds her, but the casual
accomplishment with which he has lied.

ETHERIDGE KNIGHT (1931 – 1991)
A Poem for Myself
(Or Blues for a Mississippi Black Boy)

I was born in Mississippi;
I walked barefooted thru the mud.
Born black in Mississippi,
Walked barefooted thru the mud.
But, when I reached the age of twelve
I left that place for good.
My daddy he chopped cotton
And he drank his liquor straight.
Said my daddy chopped cotton
And he drank his liquor straight.
When I left that Sunday morning
He was leaning on the barnyard gate.
I left my momma standing

With the sun shining in her eyes.
Left her standing in the yard
With the sun shining in her eyes.
And I headed North
As straight as the Wild Goose Flies,
I been to Detroit & Chicago —
Been to New York city too.
I been to Detroit and Chicago
Been to New York city too.
Said I done strolled all those funky avenues
I'm still the same old black boy with the same old blues.
Going back to Mississippi
This time to stay for good
Going back to Mississippi
This time to stay for good —
Gonna be free in Mississippi
Or dead in the Mississippi mud.

KENNETH KOCH (1925 – 2002)
Variations on a Theme by William Carlos Williams[1]

1

I chopped down the house that you had been saving to live in next
      summer.
I am sorry, but it was morning, and I had nothing to do
and its wooden beams were so inviting.

2

We laughed at the hollyhocks together
and then I sprayed them with lye.
Forgive me. I simply do not know what I am doing.

3

I gave away the money that you had been saving to live on for the
      next ten years.
The man who asked for it was shabby
and the firm March wind on the porch was so juicy and cold.

---

[1]See Williams's "This Is Just to Say," p. 634.

4

Last evening we went dancing and I broke your leg.
Forgive me. I was clumsy, and
I wanted you here in the wards, where I am the doctor!

Yusef Komunyakaa (b. 1947)
Boat People

After midnight they load up.
A hundred shadows move about blindly.
Something close to sleep
hides low voices drifting
toward a red horizon. Tonight's
a black string, the moon's pull —
this boat's headed somewhere.
Lucky to have gotten past
searchlights low-crawling the sea,
like a woman shaking water
from her long dark hair.

Twelve times in three days
they've been lucky,
clinging to each other in gray mist.
Now Thai fishermen gaze out across
the sea as it changes color,
hands shading their eyes
the way sailors do,
minds on robbery & rape.
Sunlight burns blood-orange.

Storm warnings crackle on a radio.
The Thai fishermen turn away.
Not enough water for the trip.
The boat people cling to each other,
faces like yellow sea grapes,
wounded by doubt & salt.
Dusk hangs over the water.
Seasick, they daydream Jade Mountain
a whole world away, half-drunk
on what they hunger to become.

My Father's Loveletters

On Fridays he'd open a can of Jax,
Close his eyes, & ask me to write
The same letter to my mother
Who sent postcards of desert flowers
Taller than a man. He'd beg her
Return & promised to never
Beat her again. I was almost happy
She was gone, & sometimes wanted
To slip in something bad.
His carpenter's apron always bulged
With old nails, a claw hammer
Holstered in a loop at his side
& extension cords coiled around his feet.
Words rolled from under
The pressure of my ballpoint:
Love, Baby, Honey, Please.
We lingered in the quiet brutality
Of voltage meters & pipe threaders,
Lost between sentences . . . the heartless
Gleam of a two-pound wedge
On the concrete floor,
A sunset in the doorway
Of the tool shed.
I wondered if she'd laugh
As she held them over a flame.
My father could only sign
His name, but he'd look at blueprints
& tell you how many bricks
Formed each wall. This man
Who stole roses & hyacinth
For his yard, stood there
With eyes closed & fists balled,
Laboring over a simple word,
Opened like a fresh wound, almost
Redeemed by what he tried to say.

The Towers[1]

Yes, dear son[2]
dead, but not gone,
some were good, ordinary
people who loved a pinch of salt
on a slice of melon. Good,
everyday souls gazing up
at birds every now & then,
a flash of wings like blood
against the skylights. Well,
others were good as gold
certificates in a strongbox
buried in the good earth. Yes,
two or three stopped to give
the homeless vet on the corner
a shiny quarter or silver dime,
while others walked dead
into a fiery brisance,[3] lost
in an eternity of Vermeer.
A few left questions blighting
the air. Does she love me?
How can I forgive him?
Why does the dog growl
when I turn the doorknob?
Some were writing e-mails
& embossed letters to ghosts
when the first plane struck.
The boom of one thousand
trap drums was thrown against
a metallic sky. A century of blue
vaults opened, & rescue workers
scrambled with their lifelines
down into the dark, sending up
plumes of disbelieving dust.
They tried to soothe torn earth,
to stretch skin back over the
pulse beat. When old doubts
& shame burn, do they smell
like anything we've known?
When happiness is caught off
guard, when it beats its wings
bloody against the bony cage,
does it die screaming or laughing?

No,
none,
not a single one
possessed wings as agile
& unabashedly decorous as yours,
son. Not even those lovers who
grabbed each other's hand & leapt
through the exploding windows.
Pieces of sky fell with the glass,
bricks, & charred mortar. Nothing
held together anymore. Machines
grunted & groaned into the heap
like gigantic dung beetles. After
planes had flown out of a scenario
in Hollywood, few now believed
their own feet touched the ground.
Signed deeds & promissory notes
floated over the tangled streets, &
some hobbled in broken shoes
toward the Brooklyn Bridge.
The cash registers stopped on
decimal points, in a cloud bank
of dead cell phones & dross.
Search dogs crawled into tombs
of burning silence. September
could hardly hold itself upright,
but no one donned any feathers.
Apollo[4] was at Ground Zero
because he knows everything
about bandaging up wounds.
Men dug hands into quavering
flotsam, & they were blinded by
the moon's indifference. No,
Voice,[5] I don't know anything
about infidels, though I can see
those men shaving their bodies
before facing a malicious god
in the mirror. The searchlights
throbbed. No, I'm not Daedalus,[6]
but I've walked miles in a circle,
questioning your wings of beeswax
& crepe singed beyond belief.

---

[1]The World Trade Center in New York, destroyed by terrorists on September 11, 2001.   [2]The poet's murdered infant son.   [3]How fast an explosive detonates.   [4]Greek god of poetry and medicine.   [5]Perhaps the poet's muse.   [6]Father of Icarus, whose wax wings melted when he flew too near the sun.

STANLEY KUNITZ (1905 – 2006)

The Portrait

My mother never forgave my father
for killing himself,
especially at such an awkward time
and in a public park,
that spring
when I was waiting to be born.
She locked his name
in her deepest cabinet
and would not let him out,
though I could hear him thumping.
When I came down from the attic
with the pastel portrait in my hand
of a long-lipped stranger
with a brave moustache
and deep brown level eyes,
she ripped it into shreds
without a single word
and slapped me hard.
In my sixty-fourth year
I can feel my cheek
still burning.

PHILIP LARKIN (1922 – 1985)

High Windows

When I see a couple of kids
And guess he's fucking her and she's
Taking pills or wearing a diaphragm,
I know this is paradise

Everyone old has dreamed of all their lives —
Bonds° and gestures pushed to one side   *marriage bonds*
Like an outdated combine harvester,
And everyone young going down the long slide

To happiness, endlessly. I wonder if
Anyone looked at me, forty years back,
And thought, *That'll be the life;*
No God any more, or sweating in the dark

About hell and that, or having to hide
What you think of the priest. He
And his lot will all go down the long slide
Like free bloody birds. And immediately

Rather than words comes the thought of high windows:
The sun-comprehending glass,
And beyond it, the deep blue air, that shows
Nothing, and is nowhere, and is endless.

Reasons for Attendance

The trumpet's voice, loud and authoritative,
Draws me a moment to the lighted glass
To watch the dancers — all under twenty-five —
Shifting intently, face to flushed face,
Solemnly on the beat of happiness.

— Or so I fancy, sensing the smoke and sweat,
The wonderful feel of girls. Why be out here?
But then, why be in there? Sex, yes, but what
Is sex? Surely, to think the lion's share
Of happiness is found by couples — sheer

Inaccuracy, as far as I'm concerned.
What calls me is that lifted, rough-tongued bell
(Art, if you like) whose individual sound
Insists I too am individual.
It speaks; I hear; others may hear as well,

But not for me, nor I for them; and so
With happiness. Therefore I stay outside,
Believing this; and they maul to and fro,
Believing that; and both are satisfied,
If no one has misjudged himself. Or lied.

This Be the Verse

They fuck you up, your mum and dad.
    They may not mean to, but they do.
They fill you with the faults they had
    And add some extra, just for you.

But they were fucked up in their turn
    By fools in old-style hats and coats,

Who half the time were soppy-stern
    And half at one another's throats.

Man hands on misery to man.
    It deepens like a coastal shelf.
Get out as early as you can,
    And don't have any kids yourself.

D. H. LAWRENCE (1885 – 1930)
The English Are So Nice!

[handwritten margin notes: 1. Repetition 2. Condescending/ overly inflated tone parodic tone 3. Hyperbole 4. Use al questions like conversat with yourself]

1 The English are so nice
    So awfully nice
3 They are the nicest people in the world.
    And what's more, they're very nice about being nice
5 About your being nice as well!
6 If you're not nice they soon make you feel it.

7 Americans and French and Germans and so on
    They're all very well
9 But they're not *really* nice, you know.
10 They're not nice in *our* sense of the word, <u>are they now?</u>

11 That's why one doesn't have to take them seriously.
    We must be nice to them, of course,
13 Of course, naturally.
    But it doesn't really matter what you say to them,
16 They don't really understand
    You can just say anything to them:
17 Be nice, you know, just nice
18 But you must never take them seriously, they wouldn't
        understand,
19 Just be nice, you know! oh, fairly nice,
    Not too nice of course, they take advantage
21 But nice enough, just nice enough
    To let them feel they're not quite as nice as they might be.

LI-YOUNG LEE (b. 1957)
Mother Deluxe

"We can't stay where we are,
and we don't know where else to go,"

is the first card my mother deals. We're playing
her deluxe edition of "Memories
from the 20th Century."

"Dead Baby," "Mystery Bundles," "Cleansing by Sacrifice."

Seven cards apiece and the object is to not die.

"Exodus," "Eyes Snatched Away,"
"Superstition at the Side of the Road."

All cards are good or bad depending on how you play them.
"Defeated by Wings," "Eating Forbidden Blood."

No card possesses inherent value.
"Among the Lepers," "Burial by the Solo River,"°   *the longest river*
"The Extracted Oil."   *in Java*

Every player begins in bondage.
Every player eventually dies. Everybody plays
whether they know or don't know they're playing.

Maybe this isn't a game.
Maybe it's the World Evening News.

Maybe this time I'll rescue my mother.
I can't tell if I thought that or if she said it.

Maybe this isn't the news.
Maybe this is a dream God is having
and somebody should wake Him.

Good boat, first boat, old boat, Mother,
my first night with you lasted nine months.
Our second night together is the rest of my life.

DENISE LEVERTOV (1923 – 1997)
The Ache of Marriage

The ache of marriage:

thigh and tongue, beloved,
are heavy with it,
it throbs in the teeth

We look for communion
and are turned away, beloved,
each and each

It is leviathan and we
in its belly
looking for joy, some joy
not to be known outside it

two by two in the ark of
the ache of it.

HAROLD LITTLEBIRD (b. 1951)
White-Washing the Walls

(For my mother)

"You just mix your sand with a little water . . ."

"How much?"

"Just enough to cover it, and when you put it on
always scoop enough sand in your water and keep
stirring and adding water. When you're ready to
start, at least say a few words to ask for help
and then it will go easier . . ."

this clay, sand-colored and dry, comes from a place near Laguna
the people° have known about it for a long time   *Native Americans*

in a galvanized pan, mixed with warm water, I stir
and break up small hard chunks that crush easily
in my hands
an aroma like when it rains lightly, cool and sweet
fills the sunroom, taking me back years, to my mother's
house in Paguate, the adobe walls have always been
this color and always held this same smell
and in our small home among the grey sage
below Taos Mountain, it continues

HENRY WADSWORTH LONGFELLOW (1807 – 1882)
Aftermath

When the summer fields are mown,
When the birds are fledged and flown,
  And the dry leaves strew the path;
With the falling of the snow,
With the cawing of the crow,
Once again the fields we mow
  And gather in the aftermath.

Not the sweet, new grass with flowers
Is this harvesting of ours;
    Not the upland clover bloom;
But the rowen mixed with weeds,
Tangled tufts from marsh and meads,
Where the poppy drops its seeds
    In the silence and the gloom.

The Jewish Cemetery at Newport

How strange it seems! These Hebrews in their graves,
    Close by the street of this fair seaport town,
Silent beside the never-silent waves,
    At rest in all this moving up and down!

The trees are white with dust, that o'er their sleep   5
    Wave their broad curtains in the southwind's breath,
While underneath these leafy tents they keep
    The long, mysterious Exodus of Death.

And these sepulchral stones, so old and brown,
    That pave with level flags° their burial-place,   *flagstones*   10
Seem like the tablets of the Law, thrown down
    And broken by Moses at the mountain's base.

The very names recorded here are strange,
    Of foreign accent, and of different climes;
Alvares and Rivera interchange   15
    With Abraham and Jacob of old times.

"Blessed be God! for he created Death!"°   *the kaddish*
    The mourners said, "and Death is rest and peace;"
Then added, in the certainty of faith,
    "And giveth Life that nevermore shall cease."   20

Closed are the portals of their Synagogue,
    No Psalms of David now the silence break,
No Rabbi reads the ancient Decalogue°   *Ten Commandments*
    In the grand dialect the Prophets spake.

Gone are the living, but the dead remain,   25
    And not neglected; for a hand unseen,
Scattering its bounty, like a summer rain,
    Still keeps their graves and their remembrance green.

How came they here? What burst of Christian hate,
    What persecution, merciless and blind,   30

Drove o'er the sea — that desert desolate —
    These Ishmaels and Hagars of mankind?

They lived in narrow streets and lanes obscure,
    Ghetto and Judenstrass,[1] in mirk and mire;
Taught in the school of patience to endure   35
    The life of anguish and the death of fire.

All their lives long, with the unleavened bread
    And bitter herbs of exile and its fears,
The wasting famine of the heart they fed,
    And slaked its thirst with marah[2] of their tears.   40

Anathema maranatha![3] was the cry
    That rang from town to town, from street to street;
At every gate the accursed Mordecai[4]
    Was mocked and jeered, and spurned by Christian feet.

Pride and humiliation hand in hand   45
    Walked with them through the world where'er they went;
Trampled and beaten were they as the sand,
    And yet unshaken as the continent.

For in the background figures vague and vast
    Of patriarchs and of prophets rose sublime,   50
And all the great traditions of the Past
    They saw reflected in the coming time.

And thus forever with reverted look
    The mystic volume of the world they read,
Spelling it backward, like a Hebrew book,   55
    Till life became a Legend of the Dead.

But ah! what once has been shall be no more!
    The groaning earth in travail and in pain
Brings forth its races, but does not restore,
    And the dead nations never rise again.   60

---

[1]German for "Street of Jews."

[2]The Hebrew word for "bitterness."

[3]A curse; literally, "Let him be cursed, the Lord has come" (I Corinthians 16:22).

[4]See the Book of Esther, in which Mordecai represents the Jew devoted to his people's welfare.

AUDRE LORDE (1934 – 1992)
Hanging Fire

I am fourteen
and my skin has betrayed me
the boy I cannot live without
still sucks his thumb
in secret
how come my knees are
always so ashy
what if I die
before morning
and momma's in the bedroom
with the door closed.

I have to learn how to dance
in time for the next party
my room is too small for me
suppose I die before graduation
they will sing sad melodies
but finally
tell the truth about me
There is nothing I want to do
and too much
that has to be done
and momma's in the bedroom
with the door closed.

Nobody even stops to think
about my side of it
I should have been on Math Team
my marks were better than his
why do I have to be
the one
wearing braces
I have nothing to wear tomorrow
will I live long enough
to grow up
and momma's in the bedroom
with the door closed.

ROBERT LOWELL (1917 – 1977)
Sailing Home from Rapallo[1]

[February 1954]

Your nurse could only speak Italian,
but after twenty minutes I could imagine your final week,
and tears ran down my cheeks. . . .

When I embarked from Italy with my Mother's body,
the whole shoreline of the *Golfo di Genova*[2]
was breaking into fiery flower.
The crazy yellow and azure sea-sleds
blasting like jack-hammers across
the *spumante*[3]-bubbling wake of our liner,
recalled the clashing colors of my Ford.
Mother traveled first-class in the hold;
her *Risorgimento*[4] black and gold casket
was like Napoleon's at the *Invalides.*[5] . . .

While the passengers were tanning
on the Mediterranean in deck-chairs,
our family cemetery in Dunbarton[6]
lay under the White Mountains
in the sub-zero weather.
The graveyard's soil was changing to stone —
so many of its deaths had been midwinter.
Dour and dark against the blinding snowdrifts,
its black brook and fir trunks were as smooth as masts.
A fence of iron spear-hafts
black-bordered its mostly Colonial grave-slates.
The only "unhistoric" soul to come here
was Father, now buried beneath his recent
unweathered pink-veined slice of marble.
Even the Latin of his Lowell motto:
Occasionem cognosce,[7]
seemed too businesslike and pushing here,

---

[1]A city in northern Italy.
[2]Gulf of Genoa.
[3]Italian for "sparkling," as of wine.
[4]A reference to the period of Italy's national revival in the mid-nineteenth century.
[5]The building in Paris where Napoleon is buried.
[6]A town in New Hampshire, location of family graveyard.
[7]Latin for "Recognize (your) opportunity."

where the burning cold illuminated
the hewn inscriptions of Mother's relatives:
twenty or thirty Winslows and Starks.
Frost had given their names a diamond edge. . . .

In the grandiloquent lettering on Mother's coffin,
Lowell had been misspelled LOVEL.
The corpse
was wrapped like *panettone*[8] in Italian tinfoil.

ARCHIBALD MACLEISH (1892 – 1982)
Ars Poetica

A poem should be palpable and mute
As a globed fruit,

Dumb
As old medallions to the thumb,

Silent as the sleeve-worn stone
Of casement ledges where the moss has grown —

A poem should be wordless
As the flight of birds.

A poem should be motionless in time
As the moon climbs,

Leaving, as the moon releases
Twig by twig the night-entangled trees,

Leaving, as the moon behind the winter leaves,
Memory by memory the mind —

A poem should be motionless in time
As the moon climbs.

A poem should be equal to:
Not true.

For all the history of grief
An empty doorway and a maple leaf.

For love
The leaning grasses and two lights above the sea —

A poem should not mean
But be.

---

[8]A Milanese sweet cake.

VÍCTOR MARTÍNEZ (b. 1954)
The Ledger

> *I suffer with song, yet I create them here on earth . . .*
> — CUAOAHTZIN

I waited this long I might as well stay, I said
under my lapel to no one who could listen,
and took out my boyhood collection of June-bugs,
Yellow-jackets, and other species of wing
that slept once in my cotton pillow of alcohol
before freezing into decoration:
a mantis into prayer, a bee into a lifetime of work.

I remember baiting abdomens onto needles
to lure all eyes into my glass cases.
I caught salamander and bullfrog
to scuddle° in my muddy tanks,   *scuttle*
and when the hull of a sandcrab was a lesson
in form, a mere nothing on my palm,
its death was mine, and I recorded it in my ledger.

In my ledger, I wrote how a cat kneels
stiff under the fading thread of mice,
how winds splash the poplar and a sky opens
and pours milk into a river. I was there,
I stated how paralysis took my grandpa's tongue
and through it numbed everything, carried away
with the drool in the washbasin.

Because I took account, because I knew how
to put back the words, sponged from the slate,
I was his favorite, I was my family's best —
lugging around my book of events,
telling myself over and over into my collar
that this is all there is. This cold, flat
reduction of the living is all there is. And this too
I wrote down, and about the sidewalks glowing
with rain and neons, the streets hissing with cars.

ANDREW MARVELL (1621 – 1678)

The Definition of Love

My Love is of a birth as rare
As 'tis for object strange and high:
It was begotten by Despair
Upon Impossibility.

Magnanimous Despair alone
Could show me so divine a thing,
Where feeble Hope could ne'er have flown
But vainly flapped its tinsel wing.

And yet I quickly might arrive
Where my extended soul is fixt,
But Fate does iron wedges drive,
And always crowds itself betwixt.

For Fate with jealous eye does see
Two perfect Loves; nor lets them close:
Their union would her ruin be,
And her tyrannic power depose.

And therefore her decrees of steel
Us as the distant Poles have placed,
(Though Love's whole World on us doth wheel)
Not by themselves to be embraced.

Unless the giddy Heaven fall,
And Earth some new convulsion tear;
And, us to join, the World should all
Be cramped into a planisphere.°   *a flat representation of the sky, the*
heavenly bodies, and the stars

As lines so Loves oblique may well
Themselves in every angle greet:
But ours so truly parallel,
Though infinite, can never meet.

Therefore the Love which us doth bind
But Fate so enviously debars,
Is the conjunction° of the Mind,   *terms from astronomy and*
And opposition° of the Stars.   *astrology, used in horoscopes*

The Mower's Song

My mind was once the true survey
Of all these meadows fresh and gay,
And in the greenness of the grass
Did see its hopes[1] as in a glass;°   *mirror*
When Juliana came, and she,
What I do to the grass, does to my thoughts and me.[2]

But these, while I with sorrow pine,
Grew more luxuriant still and fine,
That not one blade of grass you spied
But had a flower on either side;
When Juliana came, and she,
What I do to the grass, does to my thoughts and me.

Unthankful meadows, could you so
A fellowship so true forego,
And in your gaudy May-games[3] meet,
While I lay trodden under feet?
When Juliana came, and she,
What I do to the grass, does to my thoughts and me.

But what you in compassion ought
Shall now by my revenge be wrought,
And flowers, and grass, and I, and all,
Will in one common ruin fall;
When Juliana comes, and she,
What I do to the grass, does to my thoughts and me.

And thus ye meadows, which have been
Companions of my thoughts more green,
Shall now the heraldry become
With which I shall adorn my tomb;
When Juliana comes, and she,
What I do to the grass, does to my thoughts and me.

The Mower to the Glowworms

Ye living lamps, by whose dear light
The nightingale does sit so late,

---

[1]Green is the color of hope.

[2]The alexandrine (12-syllable line) used here is the only example of a refrain in Marvell.

[3]Festivals and merrymaking marked the first of May.

And studying all the summer night
Her matchless songs does mediate,

Ye country comets, that portend
No war nor prince's funeral,
Shining unto no higher end
Than to presage the grass's fall;

Ye glowworms, whose officious° flame   *zealous, attentive*
To wand'ring mowers shows the way,
That in the night have lost their aim,
And after foolish fires° do stray;   *will-o-the-wisps*

Your courteous fires in vain you waste,
Since Juliana here is come,
For she my mind hath so displaced
That I shall never find my home.

To His Coy Mistress

    Had we but world enough, and time,
This coyness, lady, were no crime.
We would sit down, and think which way
To walk, and pass our long love's day.
Thou by the Indian Ganges' side
Shouldst rubies find; I by the tide
Of Humber[1] would complain. I would
Love you ten years before the flood,
And you should, if you please, refuse
Till the conversion of the Jews.[2]
My vegetable love should grow
Vaster than empires and more slow;
An hundred years should go to praise
Thine eyes, and on thy forehead gaze;
Two hundred to adore each breast,
But thirty thousand to the rest;
An age at least to every part,
And the last age should show your heart.
For, lady, you deserve this state,
Nor would I love at lower rate.

---

[1]The Humber flows through Hull, Marvell's native town.
[2]Supposed to occur at the end of time.

But at my back I always hear
Time's wingèd chariot hurrying near;
And yonder all before us lie
Deserts of vast eternity.
Thy beauty shall no more be found;
Nor, in thy marble vault, shall sound
My echoing song; then worms shall try
That long-preserved virginity,
And your quaint honor turn to dust,
And into ashes all my lust:
The grave's a fine and private place,
But none, I think, do there embrace.
    Now therefore, while the youthful hue
Sits on thy skin like morning dew,
And while thy willing soul transpires
At every pore with instant fires,
Now let us sport us while we may,
And now, like amorous birds of prey,
Rather at once our time devour
Than languish in his slow-chapped power.
Let us roll all our strength and all
Our sweetness up into one ball,
And tear our pleasures with rough strife
Thorough the iron gates of life:
Thus, though we cannot make our sun
Stand still, yet we will make him run.

SHARA MCCALLUM (b. 1972)
The Incident

for my sister Natalia

We are not there.
There is no blood on my hands.
The neighbour's child,
her head suddenly a riverbed:
plaits° her mother had made,   *braids*
sticky and swimming in blood.
There is no rock
that flew like a sparrow
from my hands.
We are not there but

I am always turning
from this game gone,
in one moment, wrong,
I am always poised to run
from that look on your face,
your voice at first
countering the taunts
the right way, the way
we were taught,
then faltering midbreath,
Sticks and stones
may break my bones.
Words will never . . .
You and I later
on the verandah,
sitting in the hammock,
conspirators now,
not speaking, holding hands,
swinging into sunset,
twilight, night.

HERMAN MELVILLE (1819 – 1891)
The Berg

A Dream

I saw a ship of martial build
(Her standards set, her brave apparel on)
Directed as by madness mere
Against a stolid iceberg steer,
Nor budge it, though the infatuate ship went down.
The impact made huge ice-cubes fall
Sullen, in tons that crashed the deck;
But that one avalanche was all —
No other movement save the foundering wreck.

Along the spurs of ridges pale,
Not any slenderest shaft and frail,
A prism over glass-green gorges lone,
Toppled; nor lace of traceries fine,
Nor pendent drops in grot or mine
Were jarred, when the stunned ship went down.

Nor sole the gulls in cloud that wheeled
Circling one snow-flanked peak afar,
But nearer fowl the floes that skimmed
And crystal beaches, felt no jar.
No thrill transmitted stirred the lock
Of jack-straw needle-ice at base;
Towers undermined by waves — the block
Atilt impending — kept their place.
Seals, dozing sleek on sliddery ledges
Slipt never, when by loftier edges
Through very inertia overthrown,
The impetuous ship in bafflement went down.

Hard Berg (methought), so cold, so vast,
With mortal damps self-overcast;
Exhaling still thy dankish breath —
Adrift dissolving, bound for death;
Though lumpish thou, a lumbering one —
A lumbering lubbard loitering slow,
Impingers rue thee and go down,
Sounding thy precipice below,
Nor stir the slimy slug that sprawls
Along thy dead indifference of walls.

Monody[1]

To have known him, to have loved him,
    After loneness long;
And then to be estranged in life,
    And neither in the wrong;
And now for death to set his seal —
    Ease me, a little ease, my song!

By wintry hills his hermit-mound
    The sheeted snow-drifts drape,
And houseless there the snow-bird flits
    Beneath the fir-tree's crape:
Glazed now with ice the cloistral vine
    That hid the shyest grape.

---

[1]This poem is perhaps an elegy for Nathaniel Hawthorne, called "Vine" in Melville's long poem *Clarel*.

JAMES MERRILL (1926 – 1995)
Christmas Tree

    To be
      Brought down at last
From the cold sighing mountain
Where I and the others
Had been fed, looked after, kept still,
Meant, I knew — of course I knew —
That it would be only a matter of weeks,
That there was nothing more to do.
Warmly they took me in, made much of me,
The point from the start was to keep my spirits up.
I could assent to that. For honestly,
It did help to be wound in jewels, to send
Their colors flashing forth from vents in the deep
Fragrant sables that cloaked me head to foot.
Over me then they wove a spell of shining —
Purple and silver chains, eavesdripping tinsel,
Amulets, milagros: software of silver,
A heart, a little girl, a Model T,
Two staring eyes. The angels, trumpets, BUD and BEA
(The children's names) in clownlike capitals,
Somewhere a music box whose tiny song
Played and replayed I ended before long
By loving. And in shadow behind me, a primitive IV
To keep the show going. Yes, yes, what lay ahead
Was clear: the stripping, the cold street, my chemicals
Plowed back into the Earth for lives to come —
No doubt a blessing, a harvest, but one that doesn't bear,
Now or ever, dwelling upon. To have grown so thin.
Needles and bone. The little boy's hands meeting
About my spine. The mother's voice. *Holding up wonderfully!*
No dread. No bitterness. The end beginning. Today's
    Dusk room aglow
    For the last time
    With candlelight.
    Faces love lit,
    Gifts underfoot.
Still to be so poised, so
Receptive. Still to recall, to praise.

W. S. Merwin (b. 1927)

For a Coming Extinction

Gray whale
Now that we are sending you to The End
That great god
Tell him
That we who follow you invented forgiveness *Contrasting ideas*
And forgive nothing

I write as though you could understand
And I could say it
One must always pretend something
Among the dying
When you have left the seas nodding on their stalks
Empty of you
Tell him that we were made
On another day

The bewilderment will diminish like an echo
Winding along your inner mountains
Unheard by us
And find its way out
Leaving behind it the future
Dead
And ours

When you will not see again
The whale calves trying the light
Consider what you will find in the black garden
And its court
The sea cows the Great Auks the gorillas
The irreplaceable hosts ranged countless
And fore-ordaining as stars
Our sacrifices

Join your word to theirs
Tell him
That it is we who are important

For the Anniversary of My Death

Every year without knowing it I have passed the day
When the last fires will wave to me
And the silence will set out

Tireless traveller
Like the beam of a lightless star

Then I will no longer
Find myself in life as in a strange garment
Surprised at the earth
And the love of one woman
And the shamelessness of men
As today writing after three days of rain
Hearing the wren sing and the falling cease
And bowing not knowing to what

JOHN MILTON (1608 – 1674)
L'Allegro[1]

Hence loathèd Melancholy
    Of Cerberus and blackest midnight born,
In Stygian cave forlorn
    'Mongst horrid shapes, and shrieks, and sights unholy,
Find out some uncouth cell,   5
    Where brooding Darkness spreads his jealous wings,
And the night-raven sings;
    There under ebon shades, and low-browed rocks,
As ragged as thy locks,
    In dark Cimmerian[2] desert ever dwell.   10
But come thou goddess fair and free,
In Heaven yclept° Euphrosyne,[3]   *called*
And by men, heart-easing Mirth,
Whom lovely Venus at a birth
With two sister Graces more   15
To ivy-crownèd Bacchus bore;
Or whether (as some sager sing)[4]
The frolic wind that breathes the spring,
Zephyr with Aurora playing,
As he met her once a–Maying,   20
There on beds of violets blue,
And fresh-blown roses washed in dew,

---

[1] The title is Italian for "The Cheerful Man."
[2] A land in which, according to Homer, the sun never shone.
[3] Mirth, one of the three Graces.
[4] This genealogy is invented by Milton.

Filled her with thee a daughter fair,
So buxom, blithe, and debonair.
Haste thee nymph, and bring with thee   25
Jest and youthful Jollity,
Quips and Cranks, and wanton Wiles,
Nods, and Becks, and wreathèd Smiles,
Such as hang on Hebe's° cheek,   *goddess of youth*
And love to live in dimple sleek;   30
Sport that wrinkled Care derides,
And Laughter holding both his sides.
Come, and trip it as ye go
On the light fantastic toe,
And in thy right hand lead with thee,   35
The mountain nymph, sweet Liberty;
And if I give thee honor due,
Mirth, admit me of thy crew
To live with her and live with thee,
In unreprovèd pleasures free;   40
To hear the lark begin his flight,
And, singing, startle the dull night,
From his watch-tower in the skies,
Till the dappled dawn doth rise;
Then to come in spite of sorrow,   45
And at my window bid good morrow,
Through the sweetbriar, or the vine,
Or the twisted eglantine.
While the cock with lively din,
Scatters the rear of darkness thin,   50
And to the stack, or the barn door,
Stoutly struts his dames before;
Oft listening how the hounds and horn
Cheerly rouse the slumbering morn,
From the side of some hoar hill,   55
Through the high wood echoing shrill.
Sometime walking not unseen
By hedgerow elms, on hillocks green,
Right against the eastern gate,
Where the great sun begins his state,   60
Robed in flames, and amber light,

The clouds in thousand liveries dight;°   *clad*
While the plowman near at hand,
Whistles o'er the furrowed land,
And the milkmaid singeth blithe,   65
And the mower whets his scythe,
And every shepherd tells his tale,
Under the hawthorn in the dale.
Straight mine eye hath caught new pleasures
Whilst the landscape round it measures,   70
Russet lawns and fallows gray,
Where the nibbling flocks do stray,
Mountains on whose barren breast
The laboring clouds do often rest;
Meadows trim with daisies pied,   75
Shallow brooks, and rivers wide.
Towers and battlements it sees
Bosomed high in tufted trees,
Where perhaps some beauty lies,
The cynosure of neighboring eyes.   80
Hard by, a cottage chimney smokes,
From betwixt two aged oaks,
Where Corydon and Thyrsis[5] met,
Are at their savory dinner set
Of herbs, and other country messes,   85
Which the neat-handed Phyllis dresses;
And then in haste her bower she leaves,
With Thestylis to bind the sheaves;
Or if the earlier season lead
To the tanned haycock in the mead.   90
Sometimes with secure delight
The upland hamlets will invite,
When the merry bells ring round
And the jocund rebecks° sound   *fiddles*
To many a youth and many a maid,   95
Dancing in the checkered shade;
And young and old come forth to play
On a sunshine holiday,

---

[5]Corydon, Thyrsis, Phyllis (lines 83, 86), and Thestylis (line 88) are conventional names from pastoral poetry.

Till the livelong daylight fail;
Then to the spicy nut-brown ale,   100
With stories told of many a feat,
How fairy Mab the junkets eat;
She was pinched and pulled, she said,
And he, by Friar's lantern° led,   *will-o'-the-wisp*
Tells how the drudging goblin sweat   105
To earn his cream-bowl, duly set,
When in one night, ere glimpse of morn,
His shadowy flail hath threshed the corn
That ten day-laborers could not end;
Then lies him down the lubber° fiend,   *drudging*   110
And, stretched out all the chimney's° length,   *fireplace's*
Basks at the fire his hairy strength;
And crop-full out of doors he flings
Ere the first cock his matin rings.
Thus done the tales, to bed they creep,   115
By whispering winds soon lulled asleep.
Towered cities please us then,
And the busy hum of men,
Where throngs of knights and barons bold,
In weeds of peace high triumphs hold,   120
With store of ladies, whose bright eyes
Rain influence, and judge the prize
Of wit, or arms, while both contend
To win her grace, whom all commend.
There let Hymen° oft appear   *god of marriage*   125
In saffron robe, with taper clear,
And pomp, and feast, and revelry,
With masque, and antique pageantry;
Such sights as youthful poets dream
On summer eves by haunted stream.   130
Then to the well-trod stage anon,
If Jonson's learnèd sock[6] be on,
Or sweetest Shakespeare, fancy's child,
Warble his native wood-notes wild.

---

[6]The light shoe of ancient comic actors, a symbol of comedy.

And ever against eating cares   135
Lap me in soft Lydian airs
Married to immortal verse
Such as the meeting soul may pierce
In notes, with many a winding bout°   *turn*
Of linkèd sweetness long drawn out,   140
With wanton heed, and giddy cunning,
The melting voice through mazes running;
Untwisting all the chains that tie
The hidden soul of harmony;
That Orpheus' self[7] may heave his head   145
From golden slumber on a bed
Of heaped Elysian flowers, and hear
Such strains as would have won the ear
Of Pluto, to have quite set free
His half-regained Eurydice.   150
These delights if thou canst give,
Mirth, with thee I mean to live.

Methought I Saw My Late Espousèd Saint

Methought I saw my late espousèd saint
    Brought to me like Alcestis from the grave,
    Whom Jove's great son° to her glad husband gave,   *Heracles*
    Rescued from Death by force, though pale and faint.
Mine, as whom washed from spot of child-bed taint
    Purification in the Old Law did save,
    And such, as yet once more I trust to have
    Full sight of her in heaven without restraint,
Came vested all in white, pure as her mind.
    Her face was veiled; yet to my fancied sight
    Love, sweetness, goodness, in her person shined
So clear as in no face with more delight.
    But O, as to embrace me she inclined,
    I waked, she fled, and day brought back my night.

---

[7]Orpheus, the great musician of classical mythology, pleaded with Pluto, god of the underworld, to allow him to rescue his wife, Eurydice. Pluto consented to let Eurydice return; but Orpheus, by looking back to be sure she was following, broke the terms of his agreement with Pluto, and Eurydice remained in Hades.

On Shakespeare

What needs my Shakespeare for his honored bones
The labor of an age in pilèd stones?
Or that his hallowed reliques should be hid
Under a star-ypointing pyramid?
Dear son of Memory, great heir of Fame,
What need'st thou such weak witness of thy name?
Thou in our wonder and astonishment
Hast built thyself a livelong monument.
For whilst, to th' shame of slow-endeavoring art,
Thy easy numbers flow, and that each heart
Hath from the leaves of thy unvalued° book   *invaluable*
Those Delphic° lines with deep impression took,   *oracular*
Then thou, our fancy of itself bereaving,
Dost make us marble with too much conceiving,
And so sepúlchred in such pomp dost lie
That kings for such a tomb would wish to die.

MARIANNE MOORE (1887 – 1972)

England

with its baby rivers and little towns, each with its abbey or its
        cathedral,
with voices — one voice perhaps, echoing through the
        transept[1] — the
criterion of suitability and convenience: and Italy
with its equal° shores — contriving an epicureanism   *on either side*
from which the grossness has been extracted:

and Greece with its goat and its gourds,
the nest of modified illusions: and France,
the "chrysalis of the nocturnal butterfly,"[2]
in whose products mystery of construction
diverts one from what was originally one's object —
substance at the core: and the East with its snails, its emotional

---

[1]The part of a church that crosses the nave, to make the shape of a cross.
[2]Description of an evening gown by the French fashion designer Erté.

shorthand° and jade cockroaches, its rock crystal and its   *Chinese*
    imperturbability,   *characters*
all of museum quality: and America where there
is the little old ramshackle victoria° in the south,   *a light*
where cigars are smoked on the street in the north;   *carriage*
where there are no proof-readers, no silkworms, no digressions;

the wild man's land; grassless, linksless,° languageless   *without*
    country in which letters are written   *golf courses*
not in Spanish, not in Greek, not in Latin, not in shorthand,
but in plain American which cats and dogs can read!
The letter a in psalm and calm when
pronounced with the sound of a in candle, is very noticeable, but

why should continents of misapprehension
have to be accounted for by the fact?
Does it follow that because there are poisonous toadstools
which resemble mushrooms, both are dangerous?
Of mettlesomeness which may be mistaken for appetite,
of heat which may appear to be haste,
no conclusions may be drawn.

To have misapprehended the matter is to have confessed that one
    has not looked far enough.
The sublimated wisdom of China, Egyptian discernment,
the cataclysmic torrent of emotion
compressed in the verbs of the Hebrew language,
the books of the man who is able to say,
"I envy nobody but him, and him only,
who catches more fish than I do" —
the flower and fruit of all that noted superiority —
if not stumbled upon in America,
must one imagine that it is not there?
It has never been confined to one locality.

A Grave

Man looking into the sea,
taking the view from those who have as much right to it as you
    have to it yourself,

it is human nature to stand in the middle of a thing,
but you cannot stand in the middle of this;
the sea has nothing to give but a well excavated grave.
The firs stand in a procession, each with an emerald turkey-foot
    at the top,
reserved as their contours, saying nothing;
repression, however, is not the most obvious characteristic
    of the sea;
the sea is a collector, quick to return a rapacious look.
There are others besides you who have worn that look —
whose expression is no longer a protest; the fish no longer
    investigate them
for their bones have not lasted:
men lower nets, unconscious of the fact that they are desecrating
    a grave,
and row quickly away — the blades of the oars
moving together like the feet of water-spiders as if there were no
    such thing as death.
The wrinkles progress among themselves in a
    phalanx° — beautiful under networks of foam,   *a body of troops*
and fade breathlessly while the sea rustles in and out   *in close array*
    of the seaweed;
the birds swim through the air at top speed, emitting cat-calls
    as heretofore —
the tortoise-shell scourges about the feet of the cliffs, in motion
    beneath them;
and the ocean, under the pulsation of lighthouses and noise of
    bell-buoys,
advances as usual, looking as if it were not that ocean in which
    dropped things are
    bound to sink —
in which if they turn and twist, it is neither with volition nor
    consciousness.

Poetry

I, too, dislike it: there are things that are important beyond all this fiddle.
   Reading it, however, with a perfect contempt for it, one discovers in
   it after all, a place for the genuine.
      Hands that can grasp, eyes
      that can dilate, hair that can rise
         if it must, these things are important not because a

high-sounding interpretation can be put upon them but because they are
   useful. When they become so derivative as to become unintelligible,
   the same thing may be said for all of us, that we
      do not admire what
      we cannot understand: the bat
         holding on upside down or in quest of something to

eat, elephants pushing, a wild horse taking a roll, a tireless wolf under
   a tree, the immovable critic twitching his skin like a horse that feels a flea, the baseball fan, the statistician —
      nor is it valid
         to discriminate against "business documents and

school-books";[1] all these phenomena are important. One must make a distinction
   however: when dragged into prominence by half poets, the result is not poetry,
   nor till the poets among us can be
      "literalists of
      the imagination"[2] — above
         insolence and triviality and can present

for inspection, "imaginary gardens with real toads in them," shall we have
   it. In the meantime, if you demand on the one hand,
   the raw material of poetry in
      all its rawness and
      that which is on the other hand
         genuine, you are interested in poetry.

---

[1]Moore's note: "*Diary of Tolstoy* (Dutton), p. 84. 'Where the boundary between prose and poetry lies, I shall never be able to understand. The question is raised in manuals of style, yet the answer
to it lies beyond me. Poetry is verse; prose is not verse. Or else poetry is everything with the exception of business documents and school books.' "

[2]Moore's note: "*Yeats: Ideas of Good and Evil* (A. H. Bullen, 1903), p. 182. 'The limitation of
his view was from the very intensity of his vision; he was a too literal realist of imagination, as others are of nature; and because he believed that the figures seen by the mind's eye, when exalted by
inspiration, were "eternal existences," symbols of divine essences, he hated every grace of style that
might obscure their lineaments.' "

The Steeple-Jack

Revised, 1961

Dürer would have seen a reason for living
      in a town like this, with eight stranded whales
to look at; with the sweet sea air coming into your house
on a fine day, from water etched
      with waves as formal as the scales   5
on a fish.

One by one in two's and three's, the seagulls keep
      flying back and forth over the town clock,
or sailing around the lighthouse without moving their wings —
rising steadily with a slight   10
      quiver of the body — or flock
mewing where

a sea the purple of the peacock's neck is
      paled to greenish azure as Dürer changed
the pine green of the Tyrol to peacock blue and guinea   15
gray. You can see a twenty-five-
      pound lobster; and fish nets arranged
to dry. The

whirlwind fife-and-drum of the storm bends the salt
      marsh grass, disturbs stars in the sky and the   20
star on the steeple; it is a privilege to see so
much confusion. Disguised by what
      might seem the opposite, the sea-
side flowers and

trees are favored by the fog so that you have   25
      the tropics at first hand: the trumpet vine,
foxglove, giant snapdragon, a salpiglossis that has
spots and stripes; morning-glories, gourds,
      or moon-vines trained on fishing twine
at the back door: 30

cattails, flags, blueberries and spiderwort,
      striped grass, lichens, sunflowers, asters, daisies —
yellow and crab-claw ragged sailors with green bracts — toad-
         plant,
petunias, ferns; pink lilies, blue   35
      ones, tigers; poppies; black sweet-peas.
The climate

is not right for the banyan, frangipani, or
      jack-fruit trees; or for exotic serpent
life. Ring lizard and snakeskin for the foot, if you see fit;   40
but here they've cats, not cobras, to
      keep down the rats. The diffident
little newt

with white pin-dots on black horizontal spaced-
      out bands lives here; yet there is nothing that   45
ambition can buy or take away. The college student
named Ambrose sits on the hillside
      with his not-native books and hat
and sees boats

at sea progress white and rigid as if in   50
      a groove. Liking an elegance of which
the source is not bravado, he knows by heart the antique
sugar-bowl shaped summerhouse of
      interlacing slats, and the pitch
of the church   55

spire, not true, from which a man in scarlet lets
      down a rope as a spider spins a thread;
he might be part of a novel, but on the sidewalk a
sign says C. J. Poole, Steeple Jack,
      in black and white; and one in red   60
and white says

Danger. The church portico has four fluted
      columns, each a single piece of stone, made
modester by whitewash. This would be a fit haven for
waifs, children, animals, prisoners,   65
      and presidents who have repaid
sin-driven

senators by not thinking about them. The
      place has a schoolhouse, a post-office in a
store, fish-houses, hen-houses, a three-masted   70
         schooner on
the stocks. The hero, the student,
      the steeple jack, each in his way,
is at home.

It could not be dangerous to be living   75
      in a town like this, of simple people,

who have a steeple-jack placing danger signs by the church
while he is gilding the solid-
    pointed star, which on a steeple
stands for hope.   80

PAT MORA (b. 1942)
La Migra[1]

1

Let's play La Migra.
I'll be the Border Patrol.
You be the Mexican maid.
I get the badge and sunglasses.
You can hide and run,
but you can't get away
because I have a jeep.
I can take you wherever
I want, but don't ask
questions because
I don't speak Spanish.
I can touch you wherever
I want but don't complain
too much because I've got
boots and kick — if I have to,
and I have handcuffs.
Oh, and a gun.
Get ready, get set, run.

2

Let's play La Migra.
You be the Border Patrol.
I'll be the Mexican woman.
Your jeep has a flat,
and you have been spotted
by the sun.
All you have is heavy: hat,
glasses, badge, shoes, gun.
I know this desert,
where to rest,
where to drink.

---

[1]Border control police.

Oh, I am not alone.
You hear us singing
and laughing with the wind,
Agua dulce brota aquí, aquí, aquí,[2]
but since you can't speak Spanish,
you do not understand.
Get ready.

Rituals

Our children came for our hands,
for the last blessing, came to memorize our faces,
our wrinkled bark. One by one they returned to the *rancho*°   farm
on that grumbling bus. I felt the faces I no longer see,
traced eyebrows, nose, lips, gently pressed their eyelids,
felt their life flicker on my fingertips.

The house was noisy again, the arguing, loud pigeons
flapping. My husband shouted orders, missing the sound
of his own voice. He showed our sons the bags of cement
to seal us on all sides so we will lie clean in that hole.
He sent the youngest to Santa María for the coffins,
said to store corn and beans in them until we die.
A safe, dry place. He gave our sons his hoe and pick,
but said, "*Oigan, muchachos.*° I know my young one   *Listen, boys*
drinks too much beer. Touch him and no locks will keep me out."
My startled birds left the thorny nest again.
My husband is all bones now, even cotton pants wear him out.
All day we linger at our door. My days are nights.
I've learned to feel my way.

THYLIAS MOSS (b. 1954)
One for All Newborns

They kick and flail like crabs on their backs.
Parents outside the nursery window do not believe
they might raise assassins or thieves, at the very worst
a poet or obscure jazz musician whose politics
spill loudly from his horn.
Everything about it was wonderful, the method
of conception, the gestation, the womb opening

---

[2]Sweet water springs up here, here, here.

in perfect analogy to the mind's expansion.
Then the dark succession of constricting years,
mother competing with daughter for beauty and losing,
varicose veins and hot-water bottles, joy boiled away,
the arrival of knowledge that eyes are birds with clipped wings,
the sun at a 30° angle and unable to go higher, parents
who cannot push anymore, who stay by the window
looking for signs of spring
and the less familiar gait of grown progeny.
I am now at the age where I must begin to pay
for the way I treated my mother. My daughter is just like me.
The long trip home is further delayed, my presence
keeps the plane on the ground. If I get off, it will fly.
The propeller is a cross spinning like a buzz saw
about to cut through me. I am haunted and my mother is not dead.
The miracle was not birth but that I lived despite my crimes.
I treated God badly also; he is another parent
watching his kids through a window, eager to be proud
of his creation, looking for signs of spring.

HARRYETTE MULLEN (b. 1953)
Omnivore

Because I was afraid to lose you
I swallowed stones
chewed metal
sucked bullets through my teeth

While you licked sugar
I pocketed salt
I burned my tears
cooked my blues
and ate the smoke

And still you left me
spilling all my hungers
my belly split open
full of wonders
like an ancient fish

•Lack of punctuation
•Open letter format

FRANK O'HARA (1926 – 1966)

Ave Maria[1]

Mothers of America
                let your kids go to the movies!
get them out of the house so they won't know what you're up to
it's true that fresh air is good for the body
                                    but what about the soul
that grows in darkness, embossed by silvery images
and when you grow old as grow old you must
                                    they won't hate you
they won't criticize you they won't know
                        they'll be in some glamorous country
they first saw on a Saturday afternoon or playing hookey
they may even be grateful to you
                        for their first sexual experience
which only cost you a quarter
                        and didn't upset the peaceful home
they will know where candy bars come from
                        and gratuitous bags of popcorn
as gratuitous as leaving the movie before it's over
with a pleasant stranger whose apartment is in the Heaven on Earth
        Bldg
near the Williamsburg Bridge
                        oh mothers you will have made the little tykes
so happy because if nobody does pick them up in the movies
they won't know the difference
                        and if somebody does it'll be sheer gravy
and they'll have been truly entertained either way
instead of hanging around the yard
                        or up in their room
                                    hating you
prematurely since you won't have done anything horribly mean yet
except keeping them from the darker joys
                        it's unforgivable the latter
so don't blame me if you won't take this advice
                        and the family breaks up
and your children grow old and blind in front of a TV set
                                    seeing
movies you wouldn't let them see when they were young

---

[1]Latin: "Hail Mary," prayer to the Virgin Mary saluting her as the Mother of God.

Why I Am Not a Painter

I am not a painter, I am a poet.
Why? I think I would rather be
a painter, but I am not. Well,

for instance, Mike Goldberg
is starting a painting. I drop in.
"Sit down and have a drink" he
says. I drink; we drink. I look
up. "You have SARDINES in it."
"Yes, it needed something there."
"Oh." I go and the days go by
and I drop in again. The painting
is going on, and I go, and the days
go by. I drop in. The painting is
finished. "Where's SARDINES?"
All that's left is just
letters, "It was too much," Mike says.

But me? One day I am thinking of
a color: orange. I write a line
about orange. Pretty soon it is a
whole page of words, not lines.
Then another page. There should be
so much more, not of orange, of
words, of how terrible orange is
and life. Days go by. It is even in
prose, I am a real poet. My poem
is finished and I haven't mentioned
orange yet. It's twelve poems, I call
it ORANGES. And one day in a gallery
I see Mike's painting, called SARDINES.

WILFRED OWEN (1893 – 1918)
Anthem for Doomed Youth

What passing-bells for these who die as cattle?
    — Only the monstrous anger of the guns.
    Only the stuttering rifles' rapid rattle
Can patter out their hasty orisons.
No mockeries now for them; no prayers nor bells;
    Nor any voice of mourning save the choirs, —

The shrill, demented choirs of wailing shells;
    And bugles calling for them from sad shires.

What candles may be held to speed them all?
    Not in the hands of boys, but in their eyes
Shall shine the holy glimmers of goodbyes.
    The pallor of girls' brows shall be their pall;
Their flowers the tenderness of patient minds,
And each slow dusk a drawing-down of blinds.

Disabled

He sat in a wheeled chair, waiting for dark,
And shivered in his ghastly suit of grey,
Legless, sewn short at elbow. Through the park
Voices of boys rang saddening like a hymn,
Voices of play and pleasure after day,
Till gathering sleep had mothered them from him.

About this time Town used to swing so gay
When glow-lamps budded in the light blue trees,
And girls glanced lovelier as the air grew dim,
— In the old times, before he threw away his knees.
Now he will never feel again how slim
Girls' waists are, or how warm their subtle hands.
All of them touch him like some queer disease.

There was an artist silly for his face,
For it was younger than his youth, last year.
Now, he is old; his back will never brace;
He's lost his colour very far from here,
Poured it down shell-holes till the veins ran dry,
And half his lifetime lapsed in the hot race
And leap of purple spurted from his thigh.

One time he liked a bloodsmear down his leg,
After the matches, carried shoulder-high.
It was after football, when he'd drunk a peg,
He thought he'd better join. — He wonders why.
Someone had said he'd look a god in kilts,
That's why; and maybe, too, to please his Meg,
Aye, that was it, to please the giddy jilts
He asked to join. He didn't have to beg;
Smiling they wrote his lie: aged nineteen years.
Germans he scarcely thought of; all their guilt

And Austria's, did not move him. And no fears
Of Fear came yet. He thought of jewelled hilts
For daggers in plaid socks; of smart salutes;
And care of arms; and leave; and pay arrears;
Esprit de corps; and hints for young recruits.
And soon, he was drafted out with drums and cheers.

Some cheered him home, but not as crowds cheer Goal.
Only a solemn man who brought him fruits
Thanked him; and then inquired about his soul.

Now, he will spend a few sick years in institutes,
And do what things the rules consider wise,
And take whatever pity they may dole.
Tonight he noticed how the women's eyes
Passed from him to the strong men that were whole.
How cold and late it is! Why don't they come
And put him into bed? Why don't they come?

GRACE PALEY (1922 – 2007)

From *Detour*

I had thought the tumors
on my spine would kill me but
the tumors on my head seem to be
extraordinarily competitive this week

For the past twenty or thirty years
I have eaten the freshest most
organic and colorful fruits and
vegetables   I did not drink   I
did drink one small glass of red
wine with dinner nearly every day
as suggested by *The New York Times*
I should have taken longer walks but
obviously I have done something wrong

I don't mean morally or ethically or
geographically   I did not live near
a nuclear graveyard or under a coal
stack   nor did I allow my children
to do so   I lived in a city no worse
than any other great and famous city   I
lived one story above a street that led

cabs and ambulances to the local hospital
that didn't seem so bad and was
often convenient

        In any event I am
already old and therefore a little ashamed
to have written this poem full
of complaints against mortality which
biological fact I have been constructed for
to hand on to my children and grand–
children as I received it from my
dear mother and father and beloved
grandmother who all
ah   if I remember it
were in great pain at   leaving
and were furiously saying goodbye

CARL PHILLIPS (b. 1959)
Blue

As through marble or the lining of
certain fish split open and scooped
clean, this is the blue vein
that rides, where the flesh is even
whiter than the rest of her,° the splayed   *the poet's mother*
thighs mother forgets, busy struggling
for command over bones: her own,
those of the chaise longue, all
equally uncooperative, and there's
the wind, too. This is her hair, gone
from white to blue in the air.

This is the black, shot with blue, of my dark
daddy's knuckles, that do not change, ever.
Which is to say they are no more pale
in anger than at rest, or when, as
I imagine them now, they follow
the same two fingers he has always used
to make the rim of every empty blue
glass in the house sing.
Always, the same
blue-to-black sorrow
no black surface can entirely hide.

Under the night, somewhere
between the white that is nothing so much as
blue, and the black that is, finally, nothing,
I am the man neither of you remembers.
Shielding, in the half-dark,
the blue eyes I sometimes forget
I don't have. Pulling my own stoop-
shouldered kind of blues across paper.
Apparently misinformed about the rumored
stuff of dreams: everywhere I inquired,
I was told look for blue.

The Kill

The last time I gave my body up,

to you, I was minded
briefly what it is made of,
what yours is, that

I'd forgotten, the flesh
which always
I hold in plenty no

little sorrow for because — oh, do
but think on its predicament,
and weep.

We cleave most entirely
to what most we fear
losing. We fear loss

because we understand
the fact of it, its largeness, its
utter indifference to whether

we do, or don't,
ignore it. By then, you
were upon me, and then

in me, soon the tokens
I almost never can let go of, I'd
again begin to, and would not

miss them: the swan
unfolding
upward less on trust than

because, simply, that's
what it does; and the leaves,
leaving; a single arrow held

back in the merciless
patience which, in taking
aim, is everything; and last,

as from a grove in
flame toward any air
more clear, the stag, but

this time its bent
head a chandelier, rushing
for me, like some

undisavowable
distraction. I looked back,
and instead of you, saw

the soul-at-labor-to-break-its-bonds
that you'd become. I tensed
my bow:

one animal at attack,
the other — the other one
suffering, and love would

out all suffering —

Passing

When the Famous Black Poet speaks,
I understand

that his is the same unnervingly slow
rambling method of getting from A to B
that I hated in my father,
my father who always told me
don't shuffle.

The Famous Black Poet is
speaking of the dark river in the mind
that runs thick with the heroes of color,
Jackie R., Bessie, Billie, Mr. Paige, anyone
who knew how to sing or when to run.
I think of my grandmother, said
to have dropped dead from the evil eye,

of my lesbian aunt who saw cancer and
a generally difficult future headed her way
in the still water
of her brother's commode.
I think of voodoo in the bottoms of soup-cans,
and I want to tell the poet that the blues
is *not* my name, that Alabama
is something I cannot use
in my business.

He is so like my father,
I don't ask the Famous Black Poet,
afterwards,
to remove his shoes,
knowing the inexplicable black
and pink I will find there, a cut
gone wrong in five places.
I don't ask him to remove
his pants, since that too
is known, what has never known
a blade, all the spaces between,
where we differ . . .

I have spent years tugging
between my legs,
and proved nothing, really.
I wake to the sheets I kicked aside,
and examine where they've failed to mend
their own creases, resembling some silken
obstruction, something pulled
from my father's chest, a bad heart,
a lung,

the lung of the Famous Black Poet
saying nothing I want to understand.

Sylvia Plath (1932 – 1963)
Edge

The woman is perfected.
Her dead

Body wears the smile of accomplishment,
The illusion of a Greek necessity

5 Flows in the scrolls of her toga,
  Her bare

  Feet seem to be saying:
10 We have come so far, it is over.

  Each dead child coiled, a white serpent,
  One at each little

  Pitcher of milk, now empty.
  She has folded

  Them back into her body as petals
  Of a rose close when the garden

  Stiffens and odors bleed
  From the sweet, deep throats of the night flower.

  The moon has nothing to be sad about,
  Staring from her hood of bone.

  She is used to this sort of thing.
  Her blacks crackle and drag.

Lady Lazarus[1]

I have done it again.
One year in every ten
I manage it —
A sort of walking miracle, my skin
Bright as a Nazi lampshade,[2]   5
My right foot

A paperweight,
My face a featureless, fine
Jew linen.

Peel off the napkin[3]   10
O my enemy.[4]
Do I terrify? —

---

[1]Lazarus was raised from the dead by Jesus.

[2]The Nazis, in concentration camps, made lampshades of human skin.

[3]According to legend, the veil or napkin with which Veronica wiped Jesus' face, as he bore the Cross, was then impressed with his features.

[4]Dr. Otto Plath, Plath's father, was a native of Germany. The Plaths were not Jewish.

The nose, the eye pits, the full set of teeth?
The sour breath
Will vanish in a day.   15

Soon, soon the flesh
The grave cave ate will be
At home on me

And I a smiling woman.
I am only thirty.   20
And like the cat I have nine times to die.

This is Number Three.
What a trash
To annihilate each decade.

What a million filaments.   25
The peanut-crunching crowd
Shoves in to see

Them unwrap me hand and foot —
The big strip tease.
Gentleman, ladies,   30

These are my hands,
My knees.
I may be skin and bone,

Nevertheless, I am the same, identical woman.
The first time it happened I was ten.   35
It was an accident.

The second time I meant
To last it out and not come back at all.
I rocked shut

As a seashell.   40
They had to call and call
And pick the worms off me like sticky pearls.

Dying
Is an art, like everything else.
I do it exceptionally well.   45

I do it so it feels like hell.
I do it so it feels real.
I guess you could say I've a call.

It's easy enough to do it in a cell.
It's easy enough to do it and stay put.   50
It's the theatrical

Comeback in broad day
To the same place, the same face, the same brute
Amused shout:

"A miracle!"   55
That knocks me out.
There is a charge

For the eyeing of my scars, there is a charge
For the hearing of my heart —
It really goes.   60

And there is a charge, very large charge,
For a word or a touch
Or a bit of blood

Or a piece of my hair or my clothes.
So, so, Herr Doktor.   65
So, Herr Enemy.

I am your opus,
I am your valuable,
The pure gold baby

That melts to a shriek.   70
I turn and burn.
Do not think I underestimate your great concern.

Ash, ash —
You poke and stir.
Flesh, bone, there is nothing there —   75

A cake of soap,
A wedding ring,
A gold filling.[5]

Herr God, Herr Lucifer,
Beware   80
Beware.

---

[5]Items left in the crematoria of the Nazi concentration camps after the bodies of prisoners had been burned. (The rendered fat of the bodies was used to make soap.)

Out of the ash
I rise with my red hair
And I eat men like air.

Morning Song

1   Love set you going like a fat gold watch.
    The midwife slapped your footsoles, and your bald cry
3   Took its place among the elements.

4   Our voices echo, magnifying your arrival. New statue.
    In a drafty museum, your nakedness
6   Shadows our safety. We stand round blankly as walls.

7   I'm no more your mother
    Than the cloud that distills a mirror to reflect its own slow
9   Effacement at the wind's hand.

All night your moth-breath
Flickers among the flat pink roses. I wake to listen:
12 A far sea moves in my ear.

One cry, and I stumble from bed, cow-heavy and floral
In my Victorian nightgown.
15 Your mouth opens clean as a cat's. The window square

Whitens and swallows its dull stars. And now you try
Your handful of notes;
18 The clear vowels rise like balloons.

EDGAR ALLAN POE (1809 – 1849)
Annabel Lee

It was many and many a year ago,
    In a kingdom by the sea,
That a maiden there lived whom you may know
    By the name of Annabel Lee;
And this maiden she lived with no other thought
    Than to love and be loved by me.

She was a child and *I* was a child,
    In this kingdom by the sea,
But we loved with a love that was more than love —
    I and my Annabel Lee —
With a love that the wingèd seraphs of Heaven
    Coveted her and me.

And this was the reason that, long ago,
    In this kingdom by the sea,
A wind blew out of a cloud by night
    Chilling my Annabel Lee;
So that her highborn kinsmen came
    And bore her away from me,
To shut her up in a sepulchre
    In this kingdom by the sea.

The angels, not half so happy in Heaven,
    Went envying her and me:
Yes! that was the reason (as all men know,
    In this kingdom by the sea)
That the wind came out of the cloud, chilling
    And killing my Annabel Lee.

But our love it was stronger by far than the love
    Of those who were older than we —
    Of many far wiser than we —
And neither the angels in Heaven above
    Nor the demons down under the sea,
Can ever dissever my soul from the soul
    Of the beautiful Annabel Lee:

For the moon never beams without bringing me dreams
    Of the beautiful Annabel Lee;
And the stars never rise but I see the bright eyes
    Of the beautiful Annabel Lee;
And so, all the night-tide, I lie down by the side
Of my darling, my darling, my life and my bride,
    In her sepulchre there by the sea —
    In her tomb by the side of the sea.

ALEXANDER POPE (1688 – 1744)

From *An Essay on Man* (Epistle I)

Heav'n from all creatures hides the book of Fate,
All but the page prescrib'd, their present state:
From brutes what men, from men what spirits know:
Or who could suffer Being here below?   80
The lamb thy riot dooms to bleed to-day,
Had he thy Reason, would he skip and play?
Pleas'd to the last, he crops the flow'ry food,

And licks the hand just rais'd to shed his blood.
Oh blindness to the future! kindly giv'n,   85
That each may fill the circle mark'd by Heav'n;
Who sees with equal eye, as God of all,
A hero perish, or a sparrow fall,
Atoms or systems into ruin hurl'd,
And now a bubble burst, and now a world.   90

. . . . .

   What would this Man? Now upward will he soar,
And little less than Angel, would be more;
Now looking downwards, just as griev'd appears   175
To want the strength of bulls, the fur of bears.
Made for his use all creatures if he call,
Say what their use, had he the pow'rs of all?
Nature to these, without profusion, kind,
The proper organs, proper pow'rs assign'd;   180
Each seeming want compénsated of course,
Here with degrees of swiftness, there of force;
All in exact proportion to the state;
Nothing to add, and nothing to abate.
Each beast, each insect, happy in its own;   185
Is Heav'n unkind to Man, and Man alone?
Shall he alone, whom rational we call,
Be pleas'd with nothing, if not bless'd with all?
         The bliss of Man (could Pride that blessing find)
Is not to think or act beyond mankind;   190
No pow'rs of body or of soul to share,
But what his nature and his state can bear.
Why has not Man a microscopic eye?
For this plain reason, Man is not a Fly.
Say what the use, were finer optics giv'n,   195
T' inspect a mite, not comprehend the heav'n?
Or touch, if tremblingly alive all o'er,
To smart and agonize at ev'ry pore?
Or quick effluvia darting thro' the brain,
Die of a rose in aromatic pain?   200

. . . . .

   Far as Creation's ample range extends,
The scale of sensual, mental pow'rs ascends:
Mark how it mounts, to Man's imperial race,

From the green myriads in the peopled grass: 210
What modes of sight betwixt each wide extreme,
The mole's dim curtain, and the lynx's beam:
Of smell, the headlong lioness between,
And hound sagacious on the tainted green:
Of hearing, from the life that fills the flood,   215
To that which warbles thro' the vernal wood:
The spider's touch, how exquisitely fine!
Feels at each thread, and lives along the line:
In the nice° bee, what sense so subtly true   *exact*
From pois'nous herbs extracts the healing dew: 220
How Instinct varies in the grov'ling swine,
Compar'd, half-reas'ning elephant, with thine:
'Twixt that, and Reason, what a nice barrier,
For ever sep'rate, yet for ever near!
Remembrance and Reflection how ally'd;   225
What thin partitions Sense from Thought divide:
And Middle natures, how they long to join,
Yet never pass th' insuperable line!
Without this just gradation, could they be
Subjected these to those, or all to thee?   230
The pow'rs of all subdu'd by thee alone,
Is not thy Reason all these pow'rs in one?

EZRA POUND (1885 – 1972)
In a Station of the Metro

The apparition of these faces in the crowd;
Petals on a wet, black bough.

D. A. POWELL (b. 1963)
[autumn set us heavily to task: unrooted the dahlias]

autumn set us heavily to task: unrooted the dahlias
lay wrapped in the cellar.   cider pressing time.   grain milling
time to pick persimmons.   time to fix the leaky hayloft

slaughtering time.   rendering° time.   *melting down fat (as for lard)*
          time to put up chokecherries
take the woolens from the cedar chest: britches mending time
rabbit hunting time.   tallow candle dipping time.   soap making time

count the butter and egg money.   count the diapers in the wash
time to split wood and clean the flue.   time that the pesky swallows
in the chimney took their leave.   molasses cooking time

kids sent to glean the fields at dusk.   yams laid out to cure
and the last huckleberries balljarred in the larder.   corn husking time
clay dull red in sunlight crumbling: *the one-tenth of income*
      abundant the harvest and the tithe°   *donated to church*

[cherry elixir: the first medication. so mary poppins]

cherry elixir:° the first medication.   so mary poppins   *medicine with*
a chance to acclimate: an infant dose.   a baby step   *alcohol base*
supplanting pneumonia half a teaspoon at a time

until the tablet can be tolerated.   with adult strength
my throat constricts around unspeckled eggs: rosy boa

everybody talks about the cocktail:° sounds delicious   *of drugs for HIV*
I think in jello flavors.   picturing umbrellas in tall glass
the cocktail up.   the cocktail over.   straws and serviettes

not a steel spansule.°   *capsule containing time-*
      not a fistful of bloated tictacs.   no burn   *released medication*
in the bowels the belly & the mouth.   want my goddamn cocktail

SIR WALTER RALEGH (c. 1554 – 1618)
The Lie

Go, soul, the body's guest,
Upon a thankless errand;
Fear not to touch the best;
The truth shall be thy warrant.
Go, since I needs must die,   5
And give the world the lie.

Say to the court, it glows
And shines like rotten wood;
Say to the church, it shows
What's good, and doth no good.   10
If church and court reply,
Then give them both the lie.

Tell potentates, they live
Acting by others' action;

Not loved unless they give,   15
Not strong but by a faction.
If potentates reply,
Give potentates the lie.

Tell men of high condition,
That manage the estate,   20
Their purpose is ambition,
Their practice only hate.
And if they once reply,
Then give them all the lie.

Tell them that brave it most,   25
They beg for more by spending,
Who, in their greatest cost,
Seek nothing but commending.
And if they make reply,
Then give them all the lie.   30

Tell zeal it wants° devotion;   *lacks*
Tell love it is but lust;
Tell time it is but motion;
Tell flesh it is but dust.
And wish them not reply,   35
For thou must give the lie.

Tell age it daily wasteth;
Tell honor how it alters;
Tell beauty how she blasteth;°   *fades*
Tell favor how it falters.   40
And as they shall reply,
Give every one the lie.

Tell wit how much it wrangles
In tickle° points of niceness;   *fine*
Tell wisdom she entangles   45
Herself in overwiseness.
And when they do reply,
Straight give them both the lie.

Tell physic° of her boldness;   *medicine*
Tell skill it is pretension;   50
Tell charity of coldness;
Tell law it is contention.

And as they do reply,
So give them still the lie.

Tell fortune of her blindness;   55
Tell nature of decay;
Tell friendship of unkindness;
Tell justice of delay.
And if they will reply,
Then give them all the lie.   60

Tell arts they have no soundness,
But vary by esteeming;
Tell schools they want profoundness,
And stand too much on seeming.
If arts and schools reply,   65
Give arts and schools the lie.

Tell faith it's fled the city;
Tell how the country erreth;
Tell manhood shakes off pity;
Tell virtue least preferreth.°   *promotes one*   70
And if they do reply,
Spare not to give the lie.

So when thou hast, as I
Commanded thee, done blabbing —
Although to give the lie   75
Deserves no less than stabbing —
Stab at thee he that will,
No stab the soul can kill.

SRIKANTH REDDY (b. 1973)
Fourth Circle[1]

Fig tree stamped
on the back of a
coin. Sticky fig I
swapped for a coin
in my prime. O
coin I bought with
a coin in my age.

---

[1]In the *Inferno*, the location of the Prodigal and the Avaricious.

ADRIENNE RICH (b. 1929)
Diving into the Wreck

First having read the book of myths,
and loaded the camera,
and checked the edge of the knife-blade,
I put on
the body-armor of black rubber   5
the absurd flippers
the grave and awkward mask.
I am having to do this
not like Cousteau[1] with his
assiduous team   10
aboard the sun-flooded schooner
but here alone.

There is a ladder.
The ladder is always there
hanging innocently   15
close to the side of the schooner.
We know what it is for,
we who have used it.
Otherwise
it's a piece of maritime floss   20
some sundry equipment.

I go down.
Rung after rung and still
the oxygen immerses me
the blue light   25
the clear atoms
of our human air.
I go down.
My flippers cripple me,
I crawl like an insect down the ladder   30
and there is no one
to tell me when the ocean
will begin.

First the air is blue and then
it is bluer and then green and then   35

---

[1]Jacques Cousteau (1910–1997), French underwater explorer, inventor of the aqualung, author, and filmmaker.

black I am blacking out and yet
my mask is powerful
it pumps my blood with power
the sea is another story
the sea is not a question of power   40
I have to learn alone
to turn my body without force
in the deep element.

And now: it is easy to forget
what I came for   45
among so many who have always
lived here
swaying their crenellated fans
between the reefs
and besides   50
you breathe differently down here.

I came to explore the wreck.
The words are purposes.
The words are maps.
I came to see the damage that was done   55
and the treasures that prevail.
I stroke the beam of my lamp
slowly along the flank
of something more permanent
than fish or weed   60

the thing I came for:
the wreck and not the story of the wreck
the thing itself and not the myth
the drowned face always staring
toward the sun   65
the evidence of damage
worn by salt and sway into this threadbare beauty
the ribs of the disaster
curving their assertion
among the tentative haunters.   70

This is the place.
And I am here, the mermaid whose dark hair
streams black, the merman in his armored body
We circle silently
about the wreck   75

we dive into the hold.
I am she: I am he

whose drowned face sleeps with open eyes
whose breasts still bear the stress
whose silver, copper, vermeil cargo lies   80
obscurely inside barrels
half-wedged and left to rot
we are the half-destroyed instruments
that once held to a course
the water-eaten log   85
the fouled compass

We are, I am, you are
by cowardice or courage
the one who find our way
back to this scene   90
carrying a knife, a camera
a book of myths
in which
our names do not appear.

"I Am in Danger — Sir —"[1]

"Half-cracked" to Higginson, living,
afterward famous in garbled versions,
your hoard of dazzling scraps a battlefield,[2]
now your old snood

mothballed at Harvard[3]
and you in your variorum monument[4]
equivocal to the end —
who are you?

Gardening the day-lily,
wiping the wine-glass stems,
your thought pulsed on behind
a forehead battered paper-thin,

---

[1] Emily Dickinson to T. W. Higginson (June 7, 1862). He once referred to her as his "half-cracked poetess."

[2] Dickinson's poems were rewritten in part by her first editors, and family members disputed the possession of her manuscripts.

[3] Some of Dickinson's possessions are the property of Harvard's Houghton Library.

[4] The three-volume edition of Dickinson by Thomas H. Johnson, recording all variant readings of the poems.

you, woman, masculine
in single-mindedness,
for whom the word was more
than a symptom —

a condition of being.
Till the air buzzing with spoiled language
sang in your ears
of Perjury

and in your half-cracked way you chose
silence for entertainment,
chose to have it out at last
on your own premises.

The Middle-Aged

Their faces, safe as an interior
Of Holland tiles and Oriental carpet,
Where the fruit-bowl, always filled, stood in a light
Of placid afternoon — their voices' measure,
Their figures moving in the Sunday garden
To lay the tea outdoors or trim the borders,
Afflicted, haunted us. For to be young
Was always to live in other peoples' houses
Whose peace, if we sought it, had been made by others,
Was ours at second-hand and not for long.
The custom of the house, not ours, the sun
Fading the silver-blue Fortuny[1] curtains,
The reminiscence of a Christmas party
Of fourteen years ago — all memory,
Signs of possession and of being possessed,
We tasted, tense with envy. They were so kind,
Would have given us anything; the bowl of fruit
Was filled for us, there was a room upstairs
We must call ours: but twenty years of living
They could not give. Nor did they ever speak
Of the coarse stain on that polished balustrade,
The crack in the study window, or the letters
Locked in a drawer and the key destroyed.
All to be understood by us, returning

---

[1]Manufacturers of expensive cloth.

Late, in our own time — how that peace was made,
Upon what terms, with how much left unsaid.

ALBERTO RÍOS (b. 1952)
Teodoro Luna's Two Kisses

Mr. Teodoro Luna in his later years had taken to kissing
His wife
Not so much with his lips as with his brows.
This is not to say he put his forehead
Against her mouth —
Rather, he would lift his eyebrows, once, quickly:
Not so vigorously he might be confused with the villain
Famous in the theaters, but not so little as to be thought
A slight movement, one of accident. This way
He kissed her
Often and quietly, across tables and through doorways,
Sometimes in photographs, and so through the years themselves.
This was his passion, that only she might see. The chance
He might feel some movement on her lips
Toward laughter.

EDWIN ARLINGTON ROBINSON (1869 – 1935)
Richard Cory

Whenever Richard Cory went down town,
We people on the pavement looked at him:
He was a gentleman from sole to crown,
Clean favored, and imperially slim.

And he was always quietly arrayed,
And he was always human when he talked;
But still he fluttered pulses when he said,
"Good-morning," and he glittered when he walked.

And he was rich — yes, richer than a king —
And admirably schooled in every grace:
In fine, we thought that he was everything
To make us wish that we were in his place.

So on we worked, and waited for the light,
And went without the meat, and cursed the bread;
And Richard Cory, one calm summer night,
Went home and put a bullet through his head.

ALEIDA RODRÍGUEZ (b. 1953)
Lexicon of Exile

> *Animals seem to fill their skins, trees their bark,*
> *rivers their banks, so beautifully, that we cannot*
> *help but see in their wildness a perfect at-homeness.*
> — SCOTT RUSSELL SANDERS

There is no way I can crank a dial,
scroll back the scenery,
perch *sinsontes*° outside my windows   *tropical mockingbirds*
instead of scrub jays and mockingbirds and linnets.

There is no way the brightly lit film
of childhood's cerulean sky, fat with meringue clouds,
can play out its reel unbroken by the hypnotist's snap:
You will not remember this.

There is no way I can make that Pan American plane
fly backward, halt the tanks of the Cuban revolution,
grow old in Güines,° smelling the sour   *Cuban city south of Havana*
    blend of rice and milk
fermenting in a pan by the chicken coop.

There is no way I can pull the harsh tongue
from my mouth, replace it with lambent
turquoise on a white sand palate,
the cluck of coconuts high in the arc of palm trees.

The trees fingering their dresses outside my windows now
are live oak, mock orange, pine, eucalyptus.
Gone are the *ciruelas,*° *naranjas agrias,*°   *plum, bitter orange*
the *mamoncillos*° with their crisp green shells   *papaya*
concealing the pink tenderness of lips.

Earth's language is a continuous current,
translating the voices of my early trees along the ground.
I can't afford not to listen.
They find me islanded in Los Angeles,
surrounded by a moat filled with glare,
and deliver a lost dictionary of delight.

A lingual bridge lowers into my backyard,
where the Fuju persimmon beams in late summer
and the fig's gnarled silver limbs become conduits
for all the ants of the world; where the downy woodpecker
    teletypes

a greeting on the lightpost and the overripe sapotes° fall   *eggfruit*
with a squishy thud; where the lemon, pointillistically studded
with fruit, glows like a celebration; where the loquat drops
yellow vowels and the scrub jays nesting in the lime
chisel them noisily with their hard black beaks
high in the branches, and the red-throated hummingbird —
mistaking me for a flower — suspends just inches from my face,
deciding whether or not to dip into the nectar of my eyes
until I blink, and it sweeps all my questions into the single sky

THEODORE ROETHKE (1908 – 1963)
Elegy for Jane

My Student, Thrown by a Horse
I remember the neckcurls, limp and damp as tendrils;
And her quick look, a sidelong pickerel smile;
And how, once startled into talk, the light syllables leaped for her,
And she balanced in the delight of her thought,
A wren, happy, tail into the wind,
Her song trembling the twigs and small branches.
The shade sang with her;
The leaves, their whispers turned to kissing;
And the mold sang in the bleached valleys under the rose.

Oh, when she was sad, she cast herself down into such a pure depth,
Even a father could not find her:
Scraping her cheek against straw;
Stirring the clearest water.

My sparrow, you are not here,
Waiting like a fern, making a spiny shadow.
The sides of wet stones cannot console me,
Nor the moss, wound with the last light.

If only I could nudge you from this sleep,
My maimed darling, my skittery pigeon.
Over this damp grave I speak the words of my love:
I, with no rights in this matter,
Neither father nor lover.

The Waking

I wake to sleep, and take my waking slow.
I feel my fate in what I cannot fear.
I learn by going where I have to go.

We think by feeling. What is there to know?
I hear my being dance from ear to ear.
I wake to sleep, and take my waking slow.

Of those so close beside me, which are you?
God bless the Ground! I shall walk softly there,
And learn by going where I have to go.

Light takes the Tree; but who can tell us how?
The lowly worm climbs up a winding stair;
I wake to sleep, and take my waking slow.

Great Nature has another thing to do
To you and me; so take the lively air,
And, lovely, learn by going where to go.

This shaking keeps me steady. I should know.
What falls away is always. And is near.
I wake to sleep, and take my waking slow.
I learn by going where I have to go.

Brynn Noelle Saito (b. 1981)
Turkey People

Other familiar monsters surface along with my white republican
    uncle
to tell me what they really think about guns and art.
In their arms, they carry love and chocolate.

My capri-clad mother balances on her skinny ankles,
while searching for anything interesting to say to her frumpy
    sister-in-law
who is coughing up sincere attempts at political correctness.

The Korean matriarch crosses her long legs, fiddles with her thick
    jewelry,
and runs her bony fingers through the hair of her newly born and
    nearly blonde
grandchild. Oh the wonder of acceptance.

Everyone and their perfect english will dance on the linoleum,
    smell like cinnamon.
Everyone will nibble the bird, inhale the tamales, dissect the sushi,
and breathe through the screaming in their peculiar heads.

WILLIAM SHAKESPEARE (1564 – 1616)
Fear No More the Heat o' the Sun[1]

Fear no more the heat o' the sun,
    Nor the furious winter's rages;
Thou thy worldly task hast done,
    Home art gone, and ta'en thy wages:
Golden lads and girls all must,
As chimney-sweepers, come to dust.

Fear no more the frown o' the great;
    Thou art past the tyrant's stroke;
Care no more to clothe and eat;
    To thee the reed is as the oak:
The scepter, learning, physic, must
All follow this, and come to dust.

Fear no more the lightning flash,
    Nor the all-dreaded thunder stone;
Fear not slander, censure rash;
    Thou hast finished joy and moan:
All lovers young, all lovers must
Consign to thee, and come to dust.

No exorciser harm thee!
Nor no witchcraft charm thee!
Ghost unlaid forbear thee!
Nothing ill come near thee!
Quiet consummation have;
And renownèd be thy grave!

Full Fathom Five[1]

Full fathom five thy father lies;
    Of his bones are coral made;
Those are pearls that were his eyes:
    Nothing of him that doth fade,
But doth suffer a sea change
Into something rich and strange.
Sea nymphs hourly ring his knell:
    Ding-dong.
Hark! now I hear them — Ding-dong, bell.

---

[1]From *Cymbeline.*
[1]From *The Tempest.*

Sonnet 18

Shall I compare thee to a summer's day?
Thou art more lovely and more temperate:
Rough winds do shake the darling buds of May,
And summer's lease hath all too short a date:
Sometimes too hot the eye of heaven shines,
And often is his gold complexion dimmed;
And every fair from fair sometimes declines,
By chance or nature's changing course untrimmed;°   *divested of*
But thy eternal summer shall not fade,   *beauty*
Nor lose possession of that fair thou ow'st;°   *ownest*
Nor shall death brag thou wander'st in his shade,
When in eternal lines to time thou grow'st:
So long as men can breathe, or eyes can see,
So long lives this, and this gives life to thee.

Sonnet 116

Let me not to the marriage of true minds
Admit impediments. Love is not love
Which alters when it alteration finds,
Or bends with the remover to remove:
Oh, no! it is an ever-fixèd mark,
That looks on tempests and is never shaken;
It is the star to every wandering bark,
Whose worth's unknown, although his height be taken.
Love's not Time's fool, though rosy lips and cheeks
Within his bending sickle's compass come;
Love alters not with his brief hours and weeks,
But bears it out even to the edge of doom.
If this be error and upon me proved,
I never writ, nor no man ever loved.

PERCY BYSSHE SHELLEY (1792 – 1822)
Ode to the West Wind

1

O wild West Wind, thou breath of Autumn's being,
Thou, from whose unseen presence the leaves dead
Are driven, like ghosts from an enchanter fleeing,

Yellow, and black, and pale, and hectic red,
Pestilence-stricken multitudes: O thou,
Who chariotest to their dark wintry bed

The wingèd seeds, where they lie cold and low,
Each like a corpse within its grave, until
Thine azure sister of the Spring shall blow

Her clarion o'er the dreaming earth, and fill
(Driving sweet buds like flocks to feed in air)
With living hues and odors plain and hill:

Wild Spirit, which art moving everywhere;
Destroyer and preserver; hear, oh, hear!

2

Thou on whose stream, mid the steep sky's commotion,
Loose clouds like earth's decaying leaves are shed,
Shook from the tangled boughs of Heaven and Ocean,

Angels of rain and lightning: there are spread
On the blue surface of thine aëry surge,
Like the bright hair uplifted from the head

Of some fierce Maenad,[1] even from the dim verge
Of the horizon to the zenith's height,
The locks of the approaching storm. Thou dirge

Of the dying year, to which this closing night
Will be the dome of a vast sepulcher,
Vaulted with all thy congregated might

Of vapors, from whose solid atmosphere
Black rain, and fire, and hail will burst: oh, hear!

3

Thou who didst waken from his summer dreams
The blue Mediterranean, where he lay,
Lulled by the coil of his crystálline streams,

Beside a pumice isle in Baiae's bay,[2]
And saw in sleep old palaces and towers
Quivering within the wave's intenser day,

---

[1]Women inspired with ecstatic frenzy by the Greek god Dionysus.
[2]Near Naples, Italy.

All overgrown with azure moss and flowers
So sweet, the sense faints picturing them! Thou
For whose path the Atlantic's level powers

Cleave themselves into chasms, while far below
The sea-blooms and the oozy woods which wear
The sapless foliage of the ocean, know

Thy voice, and suddenly grow gray with fear,
And tremble and despoil themselves: oh, hear!

4

If I were a dead leaf thou mightest bear;
If I were a swift cloud to fly with thee;
A wave to pant beneath thy power, and share

The impulse of thy strength, only less free
Than thou, O uncontrollable! If even
I were as in my boyhood, and could be

The comrade of thy wanderings over Heaven,
As then, when to outstrip thy skyey speed
Scarce seemed a vision; I would ne'er have striven

As thus with thee in prayer in my sore need.
Oh, lift me as a wave, a leaf, a cloud!
I fall upon the thorns of life! I bleed!

A heavy weight of hours has chained and bowed
One too like thee: tameless, and swift, and proud.

5

Make me thy lyre, even as the forest is:
What if my leaves are falling like its own!
The tumult of thy mighty harmonies

Will take from both a deep, autumnal tone,
Sweet though in sadness. Be thou, Spirit fierce,
My spirit! Be thou me, impetuous one!

Drive my dead thoughts over the universe
Like withered leaves to quicken a new birth!
And, by the incantation of this verse,

Scatter, as from an unextinguished hearth
Ashes and sparks, my words among mankind!
Be through my lips to unawakened earth

The trumpet of a prophecy! O Wind,
If Winter comes, can Spring be far behind?

Ozymandias[1]

I met a traveler from an antique land
Who said: Two vast and trunkless legs of stone
Stand in the desert . . . Near them, on the sand,
Half sunk, a shattered visage lies, whose frown,
And wrinkled lip, and sneer of cold command,
Tell that its sculptor well those passions read
Which yet survive, stamped on these lifeless things,
The hand that mocked them, and the heart that fed:
And on the pedestal these words appear:
"My name is Ozymandias, king of kings:
Look on my works, ye Mighty, and despair!"
Nothing beside remains. Round the decay
Of that colossal wreck, boundless and bare
The lone and level sands stretch far away.

SIR PHILIP SIDNEY (1554 – 1586)
From *Astrophel and Stella*

1

Loving in truth, and fain in verse my love to show,
That she, dear she, might take some pleasure of my pain,
Pleasure might cause her read, reading might make her know,
Knowledge might pity win, and pity grace obtain,
I sought fit words to paint the blackest face of woe:
Studying inventions fine, her wits to entertain,
Oft turning others' leaves, to see if thence would flow
Some fresh and fruitful showers upon my sunburned brain.
But words came halting forth, wanting Invention's stay;
Invention, Nature's child, fled stepdame Study's blows;
And others' feet still seemed but strangers in my way.
Thus, great with child to speak, and helpless in my throes,
Biting my truant° pen, beating myself for spite: *idle*
"Fool," said my Muse to me, "look in thy heart, and write."

---

[1]Greek name for the Egyptian monarch Ramses II (1304–1237 B.C.).

. . . . .

31

With how sad steps, Oh Moon, thou climb'st the skies,
How silently, and with how wan a face!
What, may it be that even in heav'nly place
That busy archer° his sharp arrows tries?   *Cupid*
Sure, if that long-with-love-acquainted eyes
Can judge of love, thou feel'st a lover's case;
I read it in thy looks: thy languished grace,
To me that feel the like, thy state descries.
Then even of fellowship, Oh Moon, tell me,
Is constant love deemed there but want of wit?
Are beauties there as proud as here they be?
Do they above love to be loved, and yet
Those lovers scorn whom that love doth possess?
Do they call virtue there ungratefulness?

CHARLES SIMIC (b. 1938)

Charon's° Cosmology   *ferryman of the dead*

With only his feeble lantern
To tell him where he is
And every time a mountain
Of fresh corpses to load up

Take them to the other side
Where there are plenty more
I'd say by now he must be confused
As to which side is which

I'd say it doesn't matter
No one complains he's got
Their pockets to go through
In one a crust of bread in another a sausage

Once in a long while a mirror
Or a book which he throws
Overboard into the dark river
Swift cold and deep

Fork

This strange thing must have crept
Right out of hell.

It resembles a bird's foot
Worn around the cannibal's neck.

As you hold it in your hand,
As you stab with it into a piece of meat,
It is possible to imagine the rest of the bird:
Its head which like your fist
Is large, bald, beakless and blind.

A Suitcase Strapped with a Rope

They made themselves so small
They could all fit in a suitcase.
The suitcase they kept under the bed,
And the bed near the open window.

They just huddled there in the dark
While the mother called out the names
To make sure no one was missing.
Her voice made them so warm, made them so sleepy.

He wanted to go out and play.
He even said so once or twice.
They told him to be quiet.
Just now the suitcase was moving.

Soon the border guards were going
To open it up,
Unless of course it was a thief
And he had a long way to go.

CHRISTOPHER SMART (1722 – 1771)
From *Jubilate Agno*[1]

For I will consider my Cat Jeoffry.
For he is the servant of the Living God, duly and daily serving him.
For at the first glance of the glory of God in the East he worships
    in his way.
For is this done by wreathing his body seven times round with
    elegant quickness.
For then he leaps up to catch the musk, which is the blessing of
    God upon his prayer.   5

---

[1]"Jubilate Agno" was written during Smart's incarceration in a private madhouse
from 1758 to 1763. The manuscript remained unknown to the public until 1939.

For he rolls upon prank to work it in.

For having done duty and received blessing he begins to consider
    himself.

For this he performs in ten degrees.

For first he looks upon his fore-paws to see if they are clean.

For secondly he kicks up behind to clear away there.   10

For thirdly he works it upon stretch with the fore paws extended.

For fourthly he sharpens his paws by wood.

For fifthly he washes himself.

For sixthly he rolls upon wash.

For Seventhly he fleas himself, that he may not be interrupted
    upon the beat.   15

For Eighthly he rubs himself against a post.

For Ninthly he looks up for his instructions.

For Tenthly he goes in quest of food.

For having consider'd God and himself he will consider his
    neighbour.

For if he meets another cat he will kiss her in kindness.   20

For when he takes his prey he plays with it to give it chance.

For one mouse in seven escapes by his dallying.

For when his day's work is done his business more properly begins.

For he keeps the Lord's watch in the night against the adversary.

For he counteracts the powers of darkness by his electrical skin
    & glaring eyes.   25

For he counteracts the Devil, who is death, by brisking about the
    life.

For in his morning orisons he loves the sun and the sun loves him.

For he is of the tribe of Tiger.

For the Cherub Cat is a term of the Angel Tiger.

For he has the subtlety and hissing of a serpent, which in goodness
    he suppresses.   30

For he will not do destruction, if he is well-fed, neither will he spit
    without provocation.

For he purrs in thankfulness, when God tells him he's a good Cat.

For he is an instrument for the children to learn benevolence upon.

For every house is incompleat without him & a blessing is lacking
    in the spirit.

For the Lord commanded Moses concerning the cats at the
    departure of the Children of Israel from Egypt.[2]   35

For every family had one cat at least in the bag.

---

[2]No cats are mentioned in the Bible.

For the English Cats are the best in Europe.

For he is the cleanest in the use of his fore-paws of any quadrupede.

For the dexterity of his defence is an instance of the love of God
to him exceedingly.

For he is the quickest to his mark of any creature. 40

For he is tenacious of his point.

For he is a mixture of gravity and waggery.

For he knows that God is his Saviour.

For there is nothing sweeter than his peace when at rest.

For there is nothing brisker than his life when in motion. 45

For he is of the Lord's poor and so indeed is he called by benevolence perpetually — Poor Jeoffry! poor Jeoffry! the rat has
bit thy throat.

For I bless the name of the Lord Jesus that Jeoffry is better.

For the divine spirit comes about his body to sustain it in compleat
cat.

For his tongue is exceeding pure so that it has in purity what it
wants in musick.

For he is docile and can learn certain things. 50

For he can set up with gravity which is patience upon approbation.

For he can fetch and carry, which is patience in employment.

For he can jump over a stick which is patience upon proof positive.

For he can spraggle upon waggle at the word of command.

For he can jump from an eminence into his master's bosom. 55

For he can catch the cork and toss it again.

For he is hated by the hypocrite and miser.

For the former is afraid of detection.

For the latter refuses the charge.

For he camels his back to bear the first notion of business. 60

For he is good to think on, if a man would express himself neatly.

For he made a great figure in Egypt for his signal services.

For he killed the Icneumon-rat[3] very pernicious by land.

For his ears are so acute that they sting again.

For from this proceeds the passing quickness of his attention. 65

For by stroaking of him I have found out electricity.

For I perceived God's light about him both wax and fire.

For the Electrical fire is the spiritual substance, which God sends
from heaven to sustain the bodies both of man and beast.

For God has blessed him in the variety of his movements.

---

[3]The Ichneumon, which resembles a weasel, was domesticated (and highly valued)
by the ancient Egyptians.

For, tho he cannot fly, he is an excellent clamberer.   70
For his motions upon the face of the earth are more than any other
        quadrupede.
For he can tread to all the measures upon the musick.
For he can swim for life.
For he can creep.

On a Bed of Guernsey Lilies

Written in September 1763

Ye beauties! O how great the sum
        Of sweetness that ye bring;
On what a charity ye come
        To bless the latter spring!
How kind the visit that ye pay,
Like strangers on a rainy day,
        When heartiness despair'd of guests:
No neighbour's praise your pride alarms,
No rival flow'r surveys your charms,
        Or heightens, or contests!

Lo, thro' her works gay nature grieves
        How brief she is and frail,
As ever o'er the falling leaves
        Autumnal winds prevail.
Yet still the philosophic mind
Consolatory food can find,
        And hope her anchorage maintain:
We never are deserted quite;
'Tis by succession of delight
        That love supports his reign.

Dave Smith (b. 1942)
On a Field Trip at Fredericksburg[1]

The big steel tourist shield says maybe
fifteen thousand got it here. No word
of either Whitman[2] or one uncle

---

[1] Site in Virginia of a Civil War battle (December 13, 1862), a Union defeat.

[2] Although Walt Whitman (1819–1892) wrote about the Civil War, his poems do not mention the Battle of Fredericksburg, but he traveled to Fredericksburg in search of his wounded brother George.

I barely remember in the smoke
that filled his tiny mountain house.

If each finger were a thousand of them
I could clap my hands and be dead
up to my wrists. It was quick
though not so fast as we can do it
now, one bomb, atomic or worse,
one silly pod slung on wing-tip,
high up, an egg cradled
by some rapacious mockingbird.

Hiroshima[3] canned nine times their number
in a flash. Few had the time
to moan or feel the feeling
ooze back in the groin.

In a ditch I stand
above Marye's Heights, the book-
boned faces of Brady's[4] fifteen-year-old
drummers, before battle, rigid
as August's dandelions
all the way to the Potomac
rolling in my skull.

If Audubon[5] came here, the names
of birds would gush, the marvel
single feathers make
evoke a cloud, a nation,
a gray blur preserved
on a blue horizon, but
there is only a wandering child,
one dark stalk snapped off
in her hand, held out to me.
Taking it, I try to help her
hold its obscure syllables
one instant in her mouth,
like a drift of wind
at the forehead, the front door,
the black, numb fingernails.

---

[3]City in Japan where the first atomic bomb was dropped.

[4]Matthew Brady (ca. 1823–1896), Civil War photographer.

[5]John James Audubon (1785–1851), Haitian-born American ornithologist and painter of birds.

RON SMITH (b. 1949)

The Teachers Pass the Popcorn

When the mawkish Juliet
they'd come to resent
for mumbling began to wake

but the blubbering Romeo
didn't see her giant lips part, eyelids
flutter, fingers flex,

even they who said it was all about sex
endured a raw, unforeseen regret
that was nearly intolerable. And the darkness,

the jostling, whispering,
giggling darkness around them, stilled.
Breathed. Rustled.

Then shuddered through them like the massed
oblivious dead suffering a final
vision of the youth they had negligently been,

the salt and sweetness each
truly believed for a moment he, she
would never taste again.

STEVIE SMITH (1902 – 1971)

Not Waving but Drowning

Nobody heard him, the dead man,
But still he lay moaning:
I was much further out than you thought
And not waving but drowning.

Poor chap, he always loved larking
And now he's dead
It must have been too cold for him his heart gave way,
They said.

Oh, no no no, it was too cold always
(Still the dead one lay moaning)
I was much too far out all my life
And not waving but drowning.

TRACY K. SMITH (b. 1972)
Credulity

We believe we are giving ourselves away,
And so it feels good,
Our bodies swimming together
In afternoon light, the music
That enters our window as far
From the voices that made it
As our own minds are from reason.

There are whole doctrines on loving.
A science. I would like to know everything
About convincing love to give me
What it does not possess to give. And then
I would like to know how to live with nothing.
Not memory. Nor the taste of the words
I have willed you whisper into my mouth.

Diego,

Winter is a boa constrictor
Contemplating a goat. Nothing moves,
Save for the river, making its way
Steadily into ice. A state of consternation.

My limbs settle into stony disuse
In this city full of streetlamps
And unimaginable sweets.
I would rather your misuse, your beard

Smelling of some other woman's
Idle afternoons. Lately, the heart of me
Has grown to resemble a cactus
Whose one flower blooms one night only

Under the whitest,
The most disdainful of moons.

El Mar°   *The Sea*

There was a sea in my marriage.
And air. I sat in the middle

In a tiny house afloat
On night-colored waves.

The current rolled in
From I don't know where.

We'd bob atop, drift
Gently out.

I liked best
When there was nothing

That I could
Or could not see.

But I know
There was more.

A map drawn on a mirror.
Globe cinched in at the poles.

Marriage is a rare game,
Its only verbs: *am*

And *are*. I aged.
Some time ago

We sailed past bottles,
The strangest signs inside:

A toy rig. A halo of tears.
Rags like trapped doves.

Why didn't we stop?
Didn't sirens sing our names

In voices that begged with promise
And pity?

GARY SNYDER (b. 1930)
Axe Handles

One afternoon the last week in April
Showing Kai how to throw a hatchet
One-half turn and it sticks in a stump.
He recalls the hatchet-head
Without a handle, in the shop
And go gets it, and wants it for his own.
A broken-off axe handle behind the door
Is long enough for a hatchet,
We cut it to length and take it
With the hatchet head

And working hatchet, to the wood block.
There I begin to shape the old handle
With the hatchet, and the phrase
First learned from Ezra Pound
Rings in my ears!
"When making an axe handle
    the pattern is not far off."
And I say this to Kai
"Look: We'll shape the handle
By checking the handle
Of the axe we cut with — "
And he sees. And I hear it again:
It's in Lu Ji's *Wên Fu,* fourth century
A.D. "Essay on Literature" — in the
Preface: "In making the handle
Of an axe
By cutting wood with an axe
The model is indeed near at hand."
My teacher Shih-hsiang Chen
Translated that and taught it years ago
And I see: Pound was an axe,
Chen was an axe, I am an axe
And my son a handle, soon
To be shaping again, model
And tool, craft of culture,
How we go on.

How Poetry Comes to Me

It comes blundering over the
Boulders at night, it stays
Frightened outside the
Range of my campfire
I go to meet it at the
Edge of the light

EDMUND SPENSER (c. 1552 – 1599)
An Hymne in Honour of Love

1

Love, that long since hast to thy mighty powre,
Perforce subdude my poore captivèd hart,

And raging now therein with restlesse stowre,°   *tumult*
Doest tyrannize in everie weaker part;
Faine would I seeke to ease my bitter smart,
By any service I might do to thee,
Or ought that else might to thee pleasing bee.

2

And now t'asswage° the force of this new flame,°   *assuage/passion*
And make thee more propitious in my need,
I meane to sing the praises of thy name,
And thy victorious conquests to areed;°   *proclaim*
By which thou madest many harts to bleed
Of mighty Victors, with wyde wounds embrewed,°   *stained*
And by thy cruell darts to thee subdewed.

3

Onely I feare my wits° enfeebled late,   *mind*
Through the sharpe sorrows, which thou hast me bred,°   *caused*
Should faint, and words should faile me, to relate
The wondrous triumphs of thy great godhed.
But if thou wouldst vouchsafe to overspred
Me with the shadow of thy gentle wing,
I should enabled be thy actes to sing.

4

Come then, ô come, thou mightie God of love,°   *Cupid*
Out of thy silver bowres and secret blisse,
Where thou doest sit in *Venus*°   *goddess of Love, mother of Cupid*
    lap above,
Bathing thy wings in her ambrosiall° kisse,   *nectar-like*
That sweeter farre then any Nectar is;
Come softly, and my feeble breast inspire
With gentle furie,° kindled of thy fire.   *poetical rapture*

5

And ye sweet Muses, which have often proved°   *tried/felt*
The piercing points of his avengefull darts;
And ye faire Nimphs, which oftentimes have loved
The cruell worker of your kindly° smarts,   *natural*
Prepare your selves, and open wide your harts,
For to receive the triumph of your glorie,
That made you merie oft, when ye were sorie.

6

And ye faire blossomes of youths wanton° breed,   *playful*
Which in the conquests of your beautie bost,
Wherewith your lovers feeble eyes you feed,
But sterve° their harts, that needeth nourture most,   *starve*
Prepare your selves, to march amongst his host,
And all the way this sacred hymne do sing,
Made in the honor of your Soveraigne king.

7

Great god of might, that reignest in the mynd,
And all the bodie to thy hest° doest frame,   *command*
Victor of gods, subduer of mankynd,
That doest the Lions and fell° Tigers tame,   *fierce*
Making their cruell rage thy scornefull game,
And in their roring taking great delight;
Who can expresse the glorie of thy might?

8

Or who alive can perfectly declare,
The wondrous cradle of thine infancie?
When thy great mother *Venus* first thee bare,
Begot of Plentie and of Penurie,
Though elder° then thine owne nativitie;   *older, as a god*
And yet a chyld, renewing still thy yeares;
And yet the eldest of the heavenly Peares.°   *the gods*

9

For ere this worlds still° moving mightie masse,   *continually*
Out of great Chaos ugly prison crept,
In which his goodly face long hidden was
From heavens view, and in deepe darknesse kept,
Love, that had now long time securely slept
In *Venus* lap, unarmèd then and naked,
Gan reare his head, by *Clotho*° being waked.   *the Fate who spins the
thread of life*

10

And taking to him wings of his owne heate,
Kindled at first from heavens life-giving fyre,
He gan to move out of his idle seate,
Weakely at first, but after with desyre
Lifted aloft, he gan to mount up hyre,

And like fresh Eagle, make his hardie° flight   *bold*
Through all that great wide wast, yet wanting° light.   *lacking*

11

Yet wanting light to guide his wandring way,
His owne faire mother, for all creatures sake,
Did lend him light from her owne goodly ray:
Then through the world his way he gan to take,
The world that was not till he did it make;
Whose sundrie parts he from them selves did sever,
The which before had lyen confusèd ever.

12

The earth, the ayre, the water, and the fyre,
Then gan to raunge them selves in huge array,
And with contrary forces to conspyre
Each against other, by all meanes they may,
Threatning their owne confusion and decay:
Ayre hated earth, and water hated fyre,
Till Love relented° their rebellious yre.   *calmed*

13

He then them tooke, and tempering° goodly well   *adjusting*
Their contrary dislikes and lovèd meanes,
Did place them all in order, and compell
To keepe them selves within their sundrie raines,°   *reigns*
Together linkt with Adamantine° chaines;   *magnetic*
Yet so, as that in every living wight°   *person*
They mixe themselves, and shew their kindly° might.   *natural*

14

So ever since they firmely have remained,
And duly well observèd his beheast;°   *command*
Through which now all these things that are contained
Within this goodly cope,° both most and least   *canopy*
Their being have, and dayly are increast,
Through secret sparks of his infusèd fyre,
Which in the barraine cold he doth inspyre.°   *breathe into*

15

Thereby they all do live, and movèd are
To multiply the likenesse of their kynd,°   *species*

Whilest they seeke onely, without further care,
To quench the flame, which they in burning fynd:
But man, that breathes a more immortall mynd,
Not for lusts sake, but for eternitie,
Seekes to enlarge his lasting progenie.

16

For having yet in his deducted spright,°   *weakened spirit*
Some sparks remaining of that heavenly fyre,
He is enlumind with that goodly light,
Unto like goodly semblant° to aspyre: *likeness*
Therefore in choice of love, he doth desyre
That° seemes on earth most heavenly, to embrace,   *what*
That same is Beautie, borne of heavenly race.

17

For sure of all, that in this mortall frame
Contained is, nought more divine doth seeme,
Or that resembleth more th'immortall flame
Of heavenly light, then Beauties glorious beame.
What wonder then, if with such rage° extreme   *passion*
Fraile men, whose eyes seek heavenly things to see,
At sight thereof so much enravisht bee?

18

Which well perceiving, that imperious boy
Doth therwith tip his sharp empoisned darts;
Which glancing through the eyes with countenance coy,
Rest not, till they have pierst the trembling harts,
And kindled flame in all their inner parts,
Which suckes the blood, and drinketh up the lyfe
Of carefull° wretches with consuming griefe.   *careworn*

19

Thenceforth they playne,° and make ful piteous mone   *complain*
Unto the author of their balefull bane;°   *deadly ruin*
The daies they waste, the nights they grieve and grone,
Their lives they loath, and heavens light disdaine;
No light but that, whose lampe doth yet remaine
Fresh burning in the image of their eye,
They deigne to see, and seeing it still° dye.   *continually*

20

The whylst thou tyrant Love doest laugh and scorne
At their complaints, making their paine thy play;
Whylest they lye languishing like thrals° forlorne,   *slaves*
The whyles thou doest triumph in their decay,°   *destruction*
And otherwhyles, their dying to delay,
Thou doest emmarble° the proud hart of her,   *harden*
Whose love before their life they doe prefer.

21

So hast thou often done (ay me the more)
To me thy vassall, whose yet bleeding hart,
With thousand wounds thou mangled hast so sore
That whole remaines scarse any little part,
Yet to augment the anguish of my smart,
Thou hast enfrosen her disdainefull brest,
That no one drop of pitie there doth rest.

22

Why then do I this honor unto thee,
Thus to ennoble thy victorious name,
Since thou doest shew no favour unto mee,
Ne once move ruth° in that rebellious Dame,   *pity*
Somewhat to slacke the rigour of my flame?
Certes° small glory doest thou winne hereby,   *certainly*
To let her live thus free, and me to dy.

23

But if thou be indeede, as men thee call,
The worlds great Parent, the most kind preserver
Of living wights,° the soveraine Lord of all,   *men*
How falles it then, that with thy furious fervour,
Thou doest afflict as well the not deserver,
As him that doeth thy lovely heasts° despize,   *commands*
And on thy subjects most doest tyrannize?

24

Yet herein eke° thy glory seemeth more,   *also*
By so hard handling those which best thee serve,
That ere° thou doest them unto grace restore,   *before*

Thou mayest well trie if they will ever swerve,
And mayest them make it better to deserve,
And having got it, may it more esteeme,
For things hard gotten, men more dearely deeme.

25

So hard those heavenly beauties° be enfyrèd,°   *ladies / hardened by fire*
As things divine, least passions doe impresse,
The more of stedfast mynds to be admyrèd,
The more they stayed be on stedfastnesse:
But baseborne mynds such lamps regard the lesse,
Which at first blowing take not hastie fyre,
Such fancies feele no love, but loose desyre.

26

For love is Lord of truth and loialtie,
Lifting himselfe out of the lowly dust,
On golden plumes up to the purest skie,
Above the reach of loathly sinfull lust,
Whose base affect° through cowardly distrust   *passion*
Of his weake wings, dare not to heaven fly,
But like a moldwarpe° in the earth doth ly.   *mole*

27

His dunghill thoughts, which do themselves enure°   *accustom*
To dirtie drosse, no higher dare aspyre,
Ne can his feeble earthly eyes endure
The flaming light of that celestiall fyre,
Which kindleth love in generous desyre,
And makes him mount above the native might
Of heavie earth, up to the heavens hight.°   *height*

28

Such is the powre of that sweet passion,
That it all sordid basenesse doth expell,
And the refynèd mynd doth newly fashion
Unto a fairer forme, which now doth dwell
In his high thought, that would it selfe excell;
Which he beholding still with constant sight,
Admires the mirrour of so heavenly light.

29

Whose image printing in his deepest wit,
He thereon feeds his hungrie fantasy,°   *imagination*
Still full, yet never satisfyde with it,
Like *Tantale*,[1] that in store doth stervèd ly:
So doth he pine in most satiety,
For nought may quench his infinite desyre,
Once kindled through that first conceivèd fyre.

30

Thereon his mynd affixèd wholly is,
Ne thinks on ought,° but how it to attaine;   *anything*
His care, his joy, his hope is all on this,
That seemes in it all blisses to containe,
In sight whereof, all other blisse seemes vaine.
Thrise happie man, might he the same possesse;
He faines° himselfe, and doth his fortune blesse.   *imagines*

31

And though he do not win his wish to end,
Yet thus farre happie he him selfe doth weene,°   *think*
That heavens such happie grace did to him lend,
As thing on earth so heavenly, to have seene,
His harts enshrined saint, his heavens queene,
Fairer then° fairest, in his fayning° eye,   *than / longing*
Whose sole aspect he counts felicitye.

32

Then forth he casts° in his unquiet thought,   *plans*
What he may do, her favour to obtaine;
What brave exploit, what perill hardly° wrought,   *with difficulty*
What puissant° conquest, what adventurous paine,   *powerful*
May please her best, and grace unto him gaine:
He dreads no danger, nor misfortune feares,
His faith, his fortune, in his breast he beares.

33

Thou art his god, thou art his mightie guyde,
Thou being blind, letst him not see his feares,

---

[1] *Tantale*: Tantalus was punished by the gods by being made to stand in water which he was unable to drink, and to reach up towards a cluster of grapes that would be snatched away from him at the crucial moment.

But cariest him to that which he hath eyde,
Through seas, through flames, through thousand
    swords and speares:
Ne ought so strong that may his force withstand,
With which thou armest his resistlesse° hand.   *irresistible*

34

Witnesse *Leander,* in the Euxine waves,
And stout *AEneas* in the Troiane fyre,
Achilles preassing through the Phrygian glaives,°   *swords*
And *Orpheus* daring to provoke the yre°   *anger*
Of damned fiends, to get his love retyre:[2]
For both through heaven and hell thou makest way,
To win them worship which to thee obay.

35

And if by al these perils and these paynes,
He may but purchase lyking in her eye,
What heavens of joy, then to himselfe he faynes,°   *imagines*
Eftsoones° he wypes quite out of memory,   *at once*
What ever ill before he did aby:°   *suffer*
Had it bene death, yet would he die againe,
To live thus happie as her grace to gaine.

36

Yet when he hath found favour to his will,
He nathemore can so contented rest,
But forceth further on, and striveth still
T'approch more neare, till in her inmost brest,
He may embosomd bee, and lovèd best;
And yet not best, but to be lov'd alone,
For love can not endure a Paragone.°   *rival*

---

[2]In his *Heroides* Ovid describes how Leander swam across the Hellespont every night to visit his beloved Hero until one night he was drowned and Hero threw herself into the sea; Virgil (*Aen* 2) describes how Aeneas battles with the Greeks and rescues his family from burning Troy; Achilles returned to the battle of Troy to kill Hector who had slain his friend Patroclus (*Iliad* Bks. 18–22); Orpheus journeyed to Hades to retrieve his bride Eurydice who had died after being bitten by a snake. By the power of his music he made the lords of the underworld grant him his wish of bringing his wife back to the world of the living. But disobeying their orders not to turn around to look for her, he lost her forever.

37

The feare whereof, ô how doth it torment
His troubled mynd with more then hellish paine!
And to his fayning fansie° represent   *yearning imagination*
Sights never seene, and thousand shadowes vaine,
To breake his sleepe, and waste his ydle braine;
Thou that hast never lov'd canst not beleeve
Least part of th'evils which poore lovers greeve.

38

The gnawing envie, the hart-fretting feare,
The vaine surmizes, the distrustfull showes,
The false reports that flying tales doe beare,
The doubts, the daungers, the delayes, the woes,
The faynèd° friends, the unasssurèd foes,   *false*
With thousands more then any tongue can tell,
Doe make a lovers life a wretches hell.

39

Yet is there one more cursed then they all,
That cancker worme,° that   *destroyer of flowers*
    monster Gelosie,   *and fruits*
Which eates the hart, and feedes upon the gall,°   *bile*
Turning all loves delight to miserie,
Through feare of loosing his felicitie.
Ah Gods, that ever ye that monster placed
In gentle love, that all his joyes defaced.°   *destroyed*

40

By these, ô Love, thou doest thy entrance make,
Unto thy heaven, and doest the more endeere°   *make dear*
Thy pleasures unto those which them partake,
As after stormes when clouds begin to cleare,
The Sunne more bright and glorious doth appeare;
So thou thy folke, through paines of Purgatorie,
Dost beare unto thy blisse, and heavens glorie.

41

There thou them placest in a Paradize
Of all delight, and joyous happie rest,
Where they doe feede on Nectar heavenly wize,°   *of a heavenly sort*
With *Hercules* and *Hebe,* and the rest

Of *Venus* dearlings,[3] through her bountie blest,
And lie like Gods in yvorie beds arayd,
With rose and lillies over them displayd.°   *spread out*

42

There with thy daughter *Pleasure* they doe play
Their hurtlesse sports, without rebuke or blame,
And in her snowy bosome boldly lay
Their quiet heads, devoyd of guilty shame,
After full joyance of their gentle game,
Then her they crowne their Goddesse and their Queene,
And decke with floures thy altars well beseene.

43

Ay me, deare Lord, that ever I might hope,
For all the paines and woes that I endure,
To come at length unto the wishèd scope°   *object*
Of my desire, or might my selfe assure,
That happie port for ever to recure.°   *regain*
Then would I thinke these paines no paines at all,
And all my woes to be but penance small.

44

Then would I sing of thine immortall praise
An heavenly Hymne, such as the Angels sing,
And thy triumphant name then would I raise
Bove all the gods, thee onely honoring,
My guide, my God, my victor, and my king;
Till then, dread Lord, vouchsafe to take of me
This simple song, thus fram'd in praise of thee.

Sonnet 75

From "Amoretti"

One day I wrote her name upon the strand,
But came the waves and washèd it away:
Agayne I wrote it with a second hand,
But came the tyde, and made my paynes his pray.
"Vayne man," sayd she, "that doest in vaine assay,

---

[3]After his death, Hercules ascended to heaven and was married to Hebe, goddess of youth and daughter of Zeus and Hera.

A mortall thing so to immortalize,
For I my selve shall lyke to this decay,
And eek° my name bee wypèd out lykewize."   *also*
"Not so," quod I, "let baser things devize°   *contrive*
To dy in dust, but you shall live by fame:
My verse your vertues rare shall eternize,
And in the hevens wryte your glorious name.
Where whenas death shall all the world subdew,
Our love shall live, and later life renew."

WALLACE STEVENS (1879 – 1955)
The Idea of Order at Key West

She sang beyond the genius of the sea.
The water never formed to mind or voice,
Like a body wholly body, fluttering
Its empty sleeves; and yet its mimic motion
Made constant cry, caused constantly a cry,   5
That was not ours although we understood,
Inhuman, of the veritable ocean.

The sea was not a mask. No more was she.
The song and water were not medleyed sound
Even if what she sang was what she heard,   10
Since what she sang was uttered word by word.
It may be that in all her phrases stirred
The grinding water and the gasping wind;
But it was she and not the sea we heard.

For she was the maker of the song she sang.   15
The ever-hooded, tragic-gestured sea
Was merely a place by which she walked to sing.
Whose spirit is this? we said, because we knew
It was the spirit that we sought and knew
That we should ask this often as she sang.   20

If it was only the dark voice of the sea
That rose, or even colored by many waves;
If it was only the outer voice of sky
And cloud, of the sunken coral water-walled,
However clear, it would have been deep air,   25
The heaving speech of air, a summer sound
Repeated in a summer without end
And sound alone. But it was more than that,

More even than her voice, and ours, among
The meaningless plungings of water and the wind,   30
Theatrical distances, bronze shadows heaped
On high horizons, mountainous atmospheres
Of sky and sea.
              It was her voice that made
The sky acutest at its vanishing.   35
She measured to the hour its solitude.
She was the single artificer of the world
In which she sang. And when she sang, the sea,
Whatever self it had, became the self
That was her song, for she was the maker. Then we,   40
As we beheld her striding there alone,
Knew that there never was a world for her
Except the one she sang and, singing, made.

Ramon Fernandez,[1] tell me, if you know,
Why, when the singing ended and we turned   45
Toward the town, tell why the glassy lights,
The lights in the fishing boats at anchor there,
As the night descended, tilting in the air,
Mastered the night and portioned out the sea,
Fixing emblazoned zones and fiery poles,   50
Arranging, deepening, enchanting night.

Oh! Blessed rage for order, pale Ramon,
The maker's rage to order words of the sea,
Words of the fragrant portals, dimly-starred,
And of ourselves and of our origins,   55
In ghostlier demarcations, keener sounds.

The Planet on the Table[1]

Ariel[2] was glad he had written his poems.
They were of a remembered time
Or of something seen that he liked.

Other makings of the sun
Were waste and welter
And the ripe shrub writhed.

---

[1]No particular person is intended.

[1]The "planet" is an image for Stevens's *Collected Poems* (1954).

[2]Ariel, the tree spirit in Shakespeare's play *The Tempest,* here represents the poet.

His self and the sun were one
And his poems, although makings of his self,
Were no less makings of the sun.

It was not important that they survive.
What mattered was that they should bear
Some lineament or character,

Some affluence, if only half-perceived,
In the poverty of their words,
Of the planet of which they were part.

The Snow Man

One must have a mind of winter
To regard the frost and the boughs
Of the pine-trees crusted with snow;

And have been cold a long time
To behold the junipers shagged with ice,
The spruces rough in the distant glitter

Of the January sun; and not to think
Of any misery in the sound of the wind,
In the sound of a few leaves,

Which is the sound of the land
Full of the same wind
That is blowing in the same bare place

For the listener, who listens in the snow,
And, nothing himself, beholds
Nothing that is not there and the nothing that is.

Sunday Morning

1

Complacencies of the peignoir, and late
Coffee and oranges in a sunny chair,[1]
And the green freedom of a cockatoo
Upon a rug mingle to dissipate
The holy hush of ancient sacrifice.[2]
She dreams a little, and she feels the dark

---

[1]The woman in the poem does not attend a Sunday church service; instead, she remains in her peignoir and has breakfast.

[2]The death of Jesus.

Encroachment of that old catastrophe,
As a calm darkens among water-lights.
The pungent oranges and bright, green wings
Seem things in some procession of the dead,
Winding across wide water, without sound.
The day is like wide water, without sound,
Stilled for the passing of her dreaming feet
Over the seas, to silent Palestine,
Dominion of the blood and sepulchre.[3]

2

Why should she give her bounty to the dead?
What is divinity if it can come
Only in silent shadows and in dreams?
Shall she not find in comforts of the sun,
In pungent fruit and bright, green wings, or else
In any balm or beauty of the earth,
Things to be cherished like the thought of heaven?
Divinity must live within herself:
Passions of rain, or moods in falling snow;
Grievings in loneliness, or unsubdued
Elations when the forest blooms; gusty
Emotions on wet roads on autumn nights;
All pleasures and all pains, remembering
The bough of summer and the winter branch.
These are the measures destined for her soul.

3

Jove in the clouds had his inhuman birth.
No mother suckled him, no sweet land gave
Large-mannered motions to his mythy mind.
He moved among us, as a muttering king,
Magnificent, would move among his hinds,°   shepherds
Until our blood, commingling, virginal,
With heaven, brought such requital to desire
The very hinds discerned it, in a star.
Shall our blood fail? Or shall it come to be
The blood of paradise? And shall the earth
Seem all of paradise that we shall know?
The sky will be much friendlier then than now,

---

[3]The passion and entombment of Jesus.

A part of labor and a part of pain,
And next in glory to enduring love,
Not this dividing and indifferent blue.

4

She says, "I am content when wakened birds,
Before they fly, test the reality
Of misty fields, by their sweet questionings;
But when the birds are gone, and their warm fields
Return no more, where, then, is paradise?"
There is not any haunt of prophecy,
Nor any old chimera° of the grave,   *ghost*
Neither the golden underground,[4] nor isle
Melodious,[5] where spirits gat them home,
Nor visionary south, nor cloudy palm[6]
Remote on heaven's hill, that has endured
As April's green endures; or will endure
Like her remembrance of awakened birds,
Or her desire for June and evening, tipped
By the consummation of the swallow's wings.

5

She says, "But in contentment I still feel
The need of some imperishable bliss."
Death is the mother of beauty; hence from her,
Alone, shall come fulfilment to our dreams
And our desires. Although she strews the leaves
Of sure obliteration on our paths,
The path sick sorrow took, the many paths
Where triumph rang its brassy phrase, or love
Whispered a little out of tenderness,
She makes the willow shiver in the sun
For maidens who were wont to sit and gaze
Upon the grass, relinquished to their feet.
She causes boys to pile new plums and pears
On disregarded plate.° The maidens taste   *silver dishes*
And stray impassioned in the littering leaves.

---

[4]The Elysian fields — in Greek mythology, the heaven of heroes.
[5]Avalon, where King Arthur was taken after his death.
[6]The palm was the reward given to Christian martyrs in heaven.

6

Is there no change of death in paradise?
Does ripe fruit never fall? Or do the boughs
Hang always heavy in that perfect sky,
Unchanging, yet so like our perishing earth,
With rivers like our own that seek for seas
They never find, the same receding shores
That never touch with inarticulate pang?
Why set the pear upon those river-banks
Or spice the shores with odors of the plum?
Alas, that they should wear our colors there,
The silken weavings of our afternoons,
And pick the strings of our insipid lutes!
Death is the mother of beauty, mystical,
Within whose burning bosom we devise
Our earthly mothers waiting, sleeplessly.

7

Supple and turbulent, a ring of men
Shall chant in orgy on a summer morn
Their boisterous devotion to the sun,
Not as a god, but as a god might be,
Naked among them, like a savage source.
Their chant shall be a chant of paradise,
Out of their blood, returning to the sky;
And in their chant shall enter, voice by voice,
The windy lake wherein their lord delights,
The trees, like serafin,° and echoing hills,   *angels*
That choir among themselves long afterward.
They shall know well the heavenly fellowship
Of men that perish and of summer morn.
And whence they came and whither they shall go
The dew upon their feet shall manifest.

8

She hears, upon that water without sound,
A voice that cries, "The tomb in Palestine
Is not the porch of spirits lingering.
It is the grave of Jesus, where he lay."
We live in an old chaos of the sun,
Or old dependency of day and night,
Or island solitude, unsponsored, free,

Of that wide water, inescapable.
Deer walk upon our mountains, and the quail
Whistle about us their spontaneous cries;
Sweet berries ripen in the wilderness;
And, in the isolation of the sky,
At evening, casual flocks of pigeons make
Ambiguous undulations as they sink,
Downward to darkness, on extended wings.

Thirteen Ways of Looking at a Blackbird

1

Among twenty snowy mountains,
The only moving thing
Was the eye of the blackbird.

2

I was of three minds,
Like a tree
In which there are three blackbirds.

3

The blackbird whirled in the autumn winds.
It was a small part of the pantomime.

4

A man and a woman
Are one.
A man and a woman and a blackbird
Are one.

5

I do not know which to prefer,
The beauty of inflections
Or the beauty of innuendoes,
The blackbird whistling
Or just after.

6

Icicles filled the long window
With barbaric glass.
The shadow of the blackbird
Crossed it to and fro.

The mood
Traced in the shadow
An indecipherable cause.

7

O thin men of Haddam,°   *town in Connecticut*
Why do you imagine golden birds?
Do you not see how the blackbird
Walks around the feet
Of the women about you?

8

I know noble accents
And lucid, inescapable rhythms;
But I know, too,
That the blackbird is involved
In what I know.

9

When the blackbird flew out of sight,
It marked the edge
Of one of many circles.

10

At the sight of blackbirds
Flying in a green light,
Even the bawds of euphony
Would cry out sharply.

11

He rode over Connecticut
In a glass coach.
Once, a fear pierced him,
In that he mistook
The shadow of his equipage
For blackbirds.

12

The river is moving.
The blackbird must be flying.

13

It was evening all afternoon.
It was snowing

And it was going to snow.
The blackbird sat
In the cedar-limbs.

MARK STRAND (b. 1934)
Keeping Things Whole

In a field
I am the absence
of field.
This is
always the case.
Wherever I am
I am what is missing.

When I walk
I part the air
and always
the air moves in
to fill the spaces
where my body's been.

We all have reasons
for moving.
I move
to keep things whole.

ADRIENNE SU (b. 1967)
The English Canon°   *list of standard famous works*

It's not that the first speakers° left out women   *oral poets*
Unless they were goddesses, harlots, or impossible loves
Seen from afar, often while bathing,

And it's not that the only parts my grandfathers could have played
Were as extras in Xanadu,°   *exotic Asian location in*
Nor that it gives no instructions for shopping   *Coleridge's "Kubla Khan"*
    or cooking.

The trouble is, I've spent my life
Getting over the lyrics
That taught me to brush my hair till it's gleaming,

Stay slim, dress tastefully, and not speak of sex,
Death, violence, or the desire for any of them,
And to let men do the talking and warring

And bringing of the news. I know a girl's got to protest
These days, but she also has to make money
And do her share of journalism and combat,

And she has to know from the gut whom to trust,
Because what do her teachers know, living in books,
And what does she know, starting from scratch?

Female Infanticide: A Guide for Mothers
in order of expediency

I
Ultrasound, abortion.

II
Drowning; asphyxiation.

III
Hilltop abandonment.

IV
Automobile accident.

V
Failure to immunize; ill nutrition.

VI
Lack of activity; inattention.

VII
Care by little-known relations.

VIII
A mixup on a family vacation.

IX
Wait until you have a son;
put the female up for adoption.

X
Create a scandal in her adolescence.
Her options: suicide, disappearance.

XI
Raise her as one of her brother's servants;
marry her off at your convenience.

XII
Keep her unwed (use psychological torture).
In old age a daughter is fine good fortune.

MAY SWENSON (1913 – 1989)
How Everything Happens
(Based on a Study of the Wave)

                                                        happen.
                                                   to
                                           up
                                  stacking
                             is
                     something
When nothing is happening

When it happens
             something
                  pulls
                       back
                           not
                         to
                            happen.

When   has happened.
     pulling back   stacking up
           happens

         has happened   stacks up.
When it   something   nothing
                  pulls back while

Then nothing is happening.
                              happens.
                         and
                    forward
               pushes
            up
         stacks
     something
Then

I Look at My Hand

I look at my hand and see
   it is also his and hers;°   *the poet's parents*
the pads of the fingers his,

           the wrists and knuckles hers.
          In the mirror my pugnacious eye
             and ear of an elf, his;

               my tamer mouth and slant
                   cheekbones hers.
           His impulses my senses swarm,
       her hesitations they gather.
           Father and Mother
           who dropped me,

       an acorn in the wood,
      repository of your shapes
      and inner streams and circles,

    you who lengthen toward heaven,
   forgive me
     that I do not throw

  the replacing green
trunk when you are ash.
  When you are ash, no
features shall there be,
tangled of you,
  interlacing hands and faces

   through me
 who hide, still hard,
  far down under your shades —

          and break my root, and prune my buds,
             that what can make no replica
        may spring from me.

Untitled

I	will	be	earth	you	be	the	flower		
You	have	found	my	root	you	are	the	rain	
I	will	be	boat	and	you	the	rower		
You	rock	you	toss	me	you	are	the	sea	
How	be	steady	earth	that's	now	a	flood		
The	root's	the	oar's	afloat	where's	blown	our	bud	
We	will	be	desert	pure	salt	the	seed		
Burn	radiant	sex	born	scorpion	need				

ALFRED, LORD TENNYSON (1809 – 1892)
From *In Memoriam A. H. H.*

7

Dark house, by which once more I stand
    Here in the long unlovely street,
    Doors, where my heart was used to beat
So quickly, waiting for a hand,

A hand that can be clasped no more —
    Behold me, for I cannot sleep,
    And like a guilty thing I creep
At earliest morning to the door.

He[1] is not here; but far away
    The noise of life begins again,
    And ghastly through the drizzling rain
On the bald street breaks the blank day.

. . . . .

99

Risest thou thus, dim dawn, again,
    So loud with voices of the birds,
    So thick with lowings of the herds,
Day, when I lost the flower of men;

Who tremblest thro' thy darkling red
    On yon swollen brook that bubbles fast
    By meadows breathing of the past,
And woodlands holy to the dead;

---

[1]Arthur Henry Hallam (1811–1833), Tennyson's brilliantly promising friend. He died suddenly in Vienna, while on a tour of the Continent with his father.

Who murmurest in the foliage eaves
     A song that slights the coming care,
     And Autumn laying here and there
A fiery finger on the leaves;

Who wakenest with thy balmy breath
     To myriads on the genial earth,
     Memories of bridal, or of birth,
And unto myriads more, of death.

O, wheresoever those may be,
     Betwixt the slumber of the poles,
     To-day they count as kindred souls;
They know me not, but mourn with me.

. . . . .

106

Ring out, wild bells, to the wild sky,
     The flying cloud, the frosty light:
     The year is dying in the night;
Ring out, wild bells, and let him die.

Ring out the old, ring in the new,
     Ring, happy bells, across the snow:
     The year is going, let him go;
Ring out the false, ring in the true.

Ring out the grief that saps the mind,
     For those that here we see no more;
     Ring out the feud of rich and poor,
Ring in redress to all mankind.

Ring out a slowly dying cause
     And ancient forms of party strife;
     Ring in the nobler modes of life,
With sweeter manners, purer laws.

Ring out the want, the care, the sin,
     The faithless coldness of the times;
     Ring out, ring out my mournful rhymes,
But ring the fuller minstrel in.

Ring out false pride in place and blood,
     The civic slander and the spite;
     Ring in the love of truth and right,
Ring in the common love of good.

Ring out old shapes of foul disease;
    Ring out the narrowing lust of gold;
    Ring out the thousand wars of old,
Ring in the thousand years of peace.

Ring in the valiant man and free,
    The larger heart, the kindlier hand;
    Ring out the darkness of the land,
Ring in the Christ that is to be.

. . . . .

121

Sad Hesper° o'er the buried sun   *the evening star*
    And ready, thou, to die with him,
    Thou watchest all things ever dim
And dimmer, and a glory done.

The team is loosened from the wain,°   *wagon*
    The boat is drawn upon the shore;
    Thou listenest to the closing door,
And life is darkened in the brain.

Bright Phosphor,° fresher for the night,   *the morning star*
    By thee the world's great work is heard
    Beginning, and the wakeful bird;
Behind thee comes the greater light.

The market boat is on the stream,
    And voices hail it from the brink;
    Thou hear'st the village hammer clink,
And see'st the moving of the team.

Sweet Hesper–Phosphor, double name[2]
    For what is one, the first, the last,
    Thou, like my present and my past,
Thy place is changed; thou art the same.

Tears, Idle Tears

From "The Princess"

    Tears, idle tears, I know not what they mean,
Tears from the depth of some divine despair
Rise in the heart, and gather to the eyes,

---

[2]The morning star and evening star are both the planet Venus.

In looking on the happy autumn-fields,
And thinking of the days that are no more.

Fresh as the first beam glittering on a sail,
That brings our friends up from the underworld,
Sad as the last which reddens over one
That sinks with all we love below the verge;
So sad, so fresh, the days that are no more.

Ah, sad and strange as in dark summer dawns
The earliest pipe of half-awakened birds
To dying ears, when unto dying eyes
The casement slowly grows a glimmering square;
So sad, so strange, the days that are no more.

Dear as remembered kisses after death,
And sweet as those by hopeless fancy feigned
On lips that are for others; deep as love,
Deep as first love, and wild with all regret;
O Death in Life, the days that are no more!

Ulysses[1]

It little profits that an idle king,
By this still hearth, among these barren crags,
Matched with an aged wife, I mete and dole
Unequal laws unto a savage race,
That hoard, and sleep, and feed, and know not me.   5
I cannot rest from travel; I will drink
Life to the lees. All times I have enjoyed
Greatly, have suffered greatly, both with those
That loved me, and alone; on shore, and when
Through scudding drifts the rainy Hyades[2]   10
Vext the dim sea. I am become a name;
For always roaming with a hungry heart
Much have I seen and known — cities of men
And manners, climates, councils, governments,
Myself not least, but honored of them all, —   15

---

[1]This poem derives from Ulysses' description of his last voyage in Dante's *Inferno* (Canto 26).

[2]A cluster of five stars in the constellation Taurus. They were supposed to foretell rain.

And drunk delight of battle with my peers,
Far on the ringing plains of windy Troy.
I am a part of all that I have met;
Yet all experience is an arch wherethrough
Gleams that untraveled world whose margin fades   20
For ever and for ever when I move.
How dull it is to pause, to make an end,
To rust unburnished, not to shine in use!
As though to breathe were life! Life piled on life
Were all too little, and of one to me   25
Little remains; but every hour is saved
From that eternal silence, something more,
A bringer of new things; and vile it were
For some three suns to store and hoard myself,
And this gray spirit yearning in desire   30
To follow knowledge like a sinking star,
Beyond the utmost bound of human thought.
      This is my son, mine own Telemachus,
To whom I leave the scepter and the isle,
Well-loved of me, discerning to fulfill   35
This labor, by slow prudence to make mild
A rugged people, and through soft degrees
Subdue them to the useful and the good.
Most blameless is he, centered in the sphere
Of common duties, decent not to fail   40
In offices of tenderness, and pay
Meet adoration to my household gods,
When I am gone. He works his work, I mine.
      There lies the port; the vessel puffs her sail;
There gloom the dark, broad seas. My mariners,   45
Souls that have toiled, and wrought, and thought with me,
That ever with a frolic welcome took
The thunder and the sunshine, and opposed
Free hearts, free foreheads — you and I are old;
Old age hath yet his honor and his toil.   50
Death closes all; but something ere the end,
Some work of noble note, may yet be done,
Not unbecoming men that strove with gods.
The lights begin to twinkle from the rocks;
The long day wanes; the slow moon climbs; the deep   55

Moans round with many voices. Come, my friends,
'Tis not too late to seek a newer world.
Push off, and sitting well in order smite
The sounding furrows; for my purpose holds
To sail beyond the sunset, and the baths   60
Of all the western stars, until I die.
It may be that the gulfs will wash us down;
It may be we shall touch the Happy Isles,[3]
And see the great Achilles, whom we knew.
Though much is taken, much abides; and though   65
We are not now that strength which in old days
Moved earth and heaven, that which we are, we are,
One equal temper of heroic hearts,
Made weak by time and fate, but strong in will
To strive, to seek, to find, and not to yield.   70

DYLAN THOMAS (1914 – 1953)
Fern Hill

Now as I was young and easy under the apple boughs
About the lilting house and happy as the grass was green,
    The night above the dingle starry,
        Time let me hail and climb
    Golden in the heydays of his eyes,   5
And honored among wagons I was prince of the apple towns
And once below a time I lordly had the trees and leaves
        Trail with daisies and barley
    Down the rivers of the windfall light.

And as I was green and carefree, famous among the barns   10
About the happy yard and singing as the farm was home,
    In the sun that is young once only,
        Time let me play and be
    Golden in the mercy of his means,
And green and golden I was huntsman and herdsman, the calves 15

---

[3]The abode after death of those favored by the gods.

Sang to my horn, the foxes on the hills barked clear and cold,
     And the sabbath rang slowly
      In the pebbles of the holy streams.

All the sun long it was running, it was lovely, the hay
Fields high as the house, the tunes from the chimneys, it was air 20
     And playing, lovely and watery
        And fire green as grass.
     And nightly under the simple stars
As I rode to sleep the owls were bearing the farm away,
All the moon long I heard, blessed among stables, the night-jars 25
     Flying with the ricks, and the horses
       Flashing into the dark.

And then to awake, and the farm, like a wanderer white
With the dew, come back, the cock on his shoulder: it was all
     Shining, it was Adam and maiden,   30
       The sky gathered again
     And the sun grew round that very day.
So it must have been after the birth of the simple light
In the first, spinning place, the spellbound horses walking warm
     Out of the whinnying green stable   35
       On to the fields of praise.

And honored among foxes and pheasants by the gay house
Under the new made clouds and happy as the heart was long,
     In the sun born over and over,
       I ran my heedless ways,   40
     My wishes raced through the house high hay
And nothing I cared, at my sky blue trades, that time allows
In all his tuneful turning so few and such morning songs
     Before the children green and golden
       Follow him out of grace,   45

Nothing I cared, in the lamb white days, that time would take me
Up to the swallow thronged loft by the shadow of my hand,
     In the moon that is always rising,
       Nor that riding to sleep
     I should hear him fly with the high fields   50
And wake to the farm forever fled from the childless land.
Oh as I was young and easy in the mercy of his means,
       Time held me green and dying
     Though I sang in my chains like the sea.

In My Craft or Sullen Art

In my craft or sullen art
Exercised in the still night
When only the moon rages
And the lovers lie abed
With all their griefs in their arms,
I labor by singing light
Not for ambition or bread
Or the strut and trade of charms
On the ivory stages
But for the common wages
Of their most secret heart.

Not for the proud man apart
From the raging moon I write
On these spindrift pages
Nor for the towering dead
With their nightingales and psalms
But for the lovers, their arms
Round the griefs of the ages,
Who pay no praise or wages
Nor heed my craft or art.

NATASHA TRETHEWEY (b. 1966)
What Is Evidence

Not the fleeting bruises she'd cover
with makeup, a dark patch as if imprint
of a scope she'd pressed her eye too close to,
looking for a way out, nor the quiver
in the voice she'd steady, leaning
into a pot of bones on the stove. Not
the teeth she wore in place of her own, or
the official document — its seal
and smeared signature — fading already,
the edges wearing. Not the tiny marker
with its dates, her name, abstract as history.
Only the landscape of her body — splintered
clavicle,° pierced temporal° — her thin bones   *collarbone/part of skull*
settling a bit each day, the way all things do.

HENRY VAUGHAN (1622 – 1695)

They Are All Gone into the World of Light!

They are all gone into the world of light!
    And I alone sit lingering here;
Their very memory is fair and bright,
    And my sad thoughts doth clear.

It glows and glitters in my cloudy breast
    Like stars upon some gloomy grove,
Or those faint beams in which this hill is dressed
    After the sun's remove.

I see them walking in an air of glory,
    Whose light doth trample on my days;
My days, which are at best but dull and hoary,
    Mere glimmering and decays.

O holy hope, and high humility,
    High as the heavens above!
These are your walks, and you have showed them me
    To kindle my cold love.

Dear, beauteous death! the jewel of the just,
    Shining nowhere but in the dark;
What mysteries do lie beyond thy dust,
    Could man outlook that mark!

He that hath found some fledged bird's nest may know
    At first sight if the bird be flown;
But what fair well or grove he sings in now,
    That is to him unknown.

And yet, as angels in some brighter dreams
    Call to the soul when man doth sleep,
So some strange thoughts transcend our wonted themes,
    And into glory peep.

If a star were confined into a tomb,
    Her captive flames must needs burn there;
But when the hand that locked her up gives room,
    She'll shine through all the sphere.

O Father of eternal life, and all
    Created glories under Thee!

Resume° Thy spirit from this world of thrall   *take back*
    Into true liberty!

Either disperse these mists, which blot and fill
    My pérspective° still as they pass;   *telescope*
Or else remove me hence unto that hill
    Where I shall need no glass.

DEREK WALCOTT (b. 1930)
Blues

Those five or six young guys
hunched on the stoop
that oven-hot summer night
whistled me over. Nice
and friendly. So, I stop.
MacDougal or Christopher
Street in chains of light.

A summer festival. Or some
saint's. I wasn't too far from
home, but not too bright
for a nigger, and not too dark.
I figured we were all
one, wop, nigger, jew,
besides, this wasn't Central Park.
I'm coming on too strong? You figure
right! They beat this yellow nigger
black and blue.

Yeah. During all this, scared
in case one used a knife,
I hung my olive-green, just-bought
sports coat on a fire plug.
I did nothing. They fought
each other, really. Life
gives them a few kicks,
that's all. The spades, the spicks.

My face smashed in, my bloody mug
pouring, my olive-branch jacket saved
from cuts and tears,
I crawled four flights upstairs.

Sprawled in the gutter, I
remember a few watchers waved
loudly, and one kid's mother shouting
like "Jackie" or "Terry,"
"now that's enough!"
It's nothing really.
They don't get enough love.

You know they wouldn't kill
you. Just playing rough,
like young America will.
Still, it taught me something
about love. If it's so tough,
forget it.

God Rest Ye Merry, Gentlemen

Splitting from Jack Delaney's, Sheridan Square,
that winter night, stewed, seasoned in Bourbon,
my body kindled by the whistling air
snowing the Village that Christ was reborn,
I lurched like any lush by his own glow
across towards Sixth, and froze before the tracks
of footprints bleeding on the virgin snow.
I tracked them where they led across the street
to the bright side, entering the wax-
sealed smell of neon, human heat,
some all-night diner with its wise-guy cook
his stub thumb in my bowl of stew and one
man's pulped and beaten face, its look
acknowledging all that, white-dark outside,
was possible: some beast prowling the block,
something fur-clotted, running wild
beyond the boundary of will. Outside,
more snow had fallen. My heart charred.
I longed for darkness, evil that was warm.
Walking, I'd stop and turn. What had I heard,
wheezing behind my heel with whitening breath?
Nothing. Sixth Avenue yawned wet and wide.
The night was white. There was nowhere to hide.

Perhaps it exists . . .

Perhaps it exists on only one horizon —
one with windmills and belfries with questioning cranes,
meadows with supple aspens, a temperate zone,
equestrian statues and water-braiding fountains,
and, when towns break off and hedges and trees commence,
the exuberant country we see from the train
with hayricks and duck ponds and ravens on a fence
for an alderman's funeral. Deferential rain
falls ceremonially on cafés and cobbles,
umbrellas blossom and a decent haze
glazes the streets where the cathedral wobbles
in its reflection, a drizzle is quiet praise,
and the unshaven priest in his dusty soutane,°   *cassock*
protector of Latin and the widowed cypress,
sees how flocks of starlings record the annals
that preserve history in its immortal greyness,
and barges pass in stanzas along canals.
This is poetry's weather, this is its true home,°   *Europe*
not where palms applaud themselves and sails dance
in mindless delight and gulls race the foam.°   *Walcott's native*
                                            Caribbean island St. Lucia

ROSANNA WARREN (b. 1953)
In Creve Coeur, Missouri

(Pulitzer Prize for Photojournalism, 1989)

Only in Creve Coeur
would an amateur photographer
firebug snap a shot so
unconsolable: fireman bent low

over the rag of body held
like impossible laundry pulled
too soon from the line, too pale,
too sodden with smoke to flail

in his huge, dark, crumpled embrace.
He leans to the tiny face.
Her hair stands out like flame.
She is naked, she has no name.

No longer a baby, almost
a child, not yet a ghost,
she presses a doll–like fist
to his professional chest.

Her head falls back to his hand.
Tell us that she will stand
again, quarrel and misbehave.
He is trying to make her breathe.

Strong man, you know how it's done,
you've done it again and again
sucking the spirit back
to us from its lair of smoke.

We'll call it a fine surprise.
The snapshot won a prize
though it couldn't revive *her*
that night in Creve Coeur.

JOSHUA WEINER (b. 1963)
The Yonder Tree

Bought myself a ticket, the ticket freed me,
I flew through a storm to the yonder tree.
    I said to myself   *now I can see, now I can see.*

Bought myself a horse, the horse pleased me,
I rode my horse to the yonder tree.
    The horse said   *nay, nay.*
    I said to myself   *now I can see, now I can see.*

Bought myself a cat, the cat pleased me,
I chased that cat to the yonder tree.
    The cat said   *me, me.*
    The horse said   *nay, nay.*
    I said to myself   *now I can see, now I can see.*

Bought myself a dog, the dog pleased me,
I walked my dog to the yonder tree.
    The dog said   *bow down.*
    The cat said   *me, me.*
    The horse said   *nay, nay.*
    I said to myself   *now I can see, now I can see.*

Found myself a woman, the woman pleased me,
I followed my woman to the yonder tree.
    The woman said *maybe, baby.*
    The dog said *bow down.*
    The cat said *me, me.*
    The horse said *nay, nay.*
    I said to myself *now I can see, now I can see.*

Bought myself a knife, the knife pleased me,
I cut two names into the yonder tree.
    The knife said *hungry, angry.*
    The woman said *maybe, baby.*
    The dog said *bow down.*
    The cat said *me, me.*
    The horse said *nay, nay.*
    I said to myself *now I can see, now I can see.*

Bought myself a house, the house pleased me,
I built my house from the yonder tree.
    The house said *comfort, come back.*
    The knife said *hungry, angry.*
    The woman said *maybe, baby.*
    The dog said *bow down.*
    The cat said *me, me.*
    The horse said *nay, nay.*
    I said to myself *now I can see, now I can see.*

Bought myself a watch, the watch pleased me,
I checked my watch at the yonder tree.
    The watch said *tick, take.*
    The house said *comfort, come back.*
    The knife said *hungry, angry.*
    The woman said *maybe, baby.*
    The dog said *bow down.*
    The cat said *me, me.*
    The horse said *nay, nay.*
    I said to myself *now I can see, now I can see.*

Bought myself a stone, the stone pleased me,
I placed my stone beneath the yonder tree.
    The stone said *good-night, this night, all night.*
    The watch said *tick, take.*
    The house said *comfort, come back.*
    The knife said *hungry, angry.*
    The woman said *maybe, baby.*

The dog said	*bow down.*
The cat said	*me, me.*
The horse said	*nay, nay.*
I said to myself	*what did I see? I thought I could see . . .*

James Welch (1940 – 2003)
Getting Things Straight

Is the sun the same drab gold?
The hawk — is he still rising, circling,
falling above the field? And the rolling day,
it will never stop? It means nothing?
Will it end the way history ended when
the last giant climbed Heart Butte,[1] had his vision,
came back to town and drank himself
sick? The hawk has spotted a mouse.
Wheeling, falling, stumbling to a stop,
he watches the snake ribbon quickly
under a rock. What does it mean?
He flashes his wings to the sun, bobs
twice and lifts, screaming
off the ground. Does it mean this to him:
the mouse, a snake, the dozen angry days
still rolling since his last good feed?
Who offers him a friendly meal?
Am I strangling in his grip?
Is he my vision?

Harlem, Montana: Just Off the Reservation

We need no runners here. Booze is law
and all the Indians drink in the best tavern.
Money is free if you're poor enough.
Disgusted, busted whites are running
for office in this town. The constable,
a local farmer, plants the jail with wild
raven-haired stiffs who beg just one more drink.
One drunk, a former Methodist, becomes a saint
in the Indian church, bugs the plaster man
on the cross with snakes. If his knuckles broke,
he'd see those women wail the graves goodbye.

---

[1]Butte in Blackfeet Indian Reservation, Heart Butte, Montana.

Goodbye, goodbye, Harlem on the rocks,
so bigoted, you forget the latest joke,
so lonely, you'd welcome a battalion of Turks
to rule your women. What you don't know,
what you will never know or want to learn —
Turks aren't white. Turks are olive, unwelcome
alive in any town. Turks would use
your one dingy park to declare a need for loot.
Turks say bring it, step quickly, lay down and dead.

Here we are when men were nice. This photo, hung
in the New England Hotel lobby, shows them nicer
than pie, agreeable to the warring bands of redskins
who demanded protection money for the price of food.
Now, only Hutterites out north are nice. We hate
them. They are tough and their crops are always good.
We accuse them of idiocy and believe their belief all wrong.

Harlem, your hotel is overnamed, your children
are raggedy-assed but you go on, survive
the bad food from the two cafes and peddle
your hate for the wild who bring you money.
When you die, if you die, will you remember
the three young bucks who shot the grocery up,
locked themselves in and cried for days, we're rich,
help us, oh God, we're rich.

PHILLIS WHEATLEY (1753 – 1784)

To S. M. a young African Painter, on seeing his Works.

To show the lab'ring bosom's deep intent,
And thought in living characters to paint,
When first thy pencil° did those beauties give,   *brush*
And breathing figures learnt from thee to live,
How did those prospects give my soul delight,
A new creation rushing on my sight?

Still, wond'rous youth! each noble path pursue,
On deathless glories fix thine ardent view:
Still may the painter's and the poet's fire
To aid thy pencil, and thy verse conspire!
And may the charms of each seraphic theme
Conduct thy footsteps to immortal fame!
High to the blissful wonders of the skies

Elate° thy soul, and raise thy wishful eyes.   *make joyful*
Thrice happy, when exalted to survey
That splendid city,° crown'd with endless day,   *the Heavenly Jerusalem*
Whose twice six gates on radiant hinges ring:
Celestial *Salem*° blooms in endless spring.   *City of Peace*

    Calm and serene thy moments glide along,
And may the muse inspire each future song!
Still, with the sweets of contemplation bless'd,
May peace with balmy wings your soul invest!
But when these shades of time are chas'd away,
And darkness ends in everlasting day,
On what seraphic pinions shall we move,
And view the landscapes in the realms above?
There shall thy tongue in heav'nly murmurs flow,
And there my muse with heav'nly transport° glow: *rapture*
No more to tell of *Damon's* tender sighs,
Or rising radiance of *Aurora's* eyes,°   *pastoral lovers*
For nobler themes demand a nobler strain,
And purer language on th' ethereal plain.
Cease, gentle muse! the solemn gloom of night
Now seals the fair creation from my sight.

WALT WHITMAN (1819 – 1892)

A Hand-Mirror

Hold it up sternly — see this it sends back, (who is it? is it you?)
Outside fair costume, within ashes and filth,
No more a flashing eye, no more a sonorous voice or
    springy step,
Now some slave's eye, voice, hands, step,
A drunkard's breath, unwholesome eater's face, venerealee's[1]
    flesh,
Lungs rotting away piecemeal, stomach sour and cankerous,
Joints rheumatic, bowels clogged with abomination,
Blood circulating dark and poisonous streams,
Words babble, hearing and touch callous,
No brain, no heart left, no magnetism of sex;
Such from one look in this looking-glass ere you go hence,
Such a result so soon — and from such a beginning!

---

[1]Victim of venereal disease.

From *Song of Myself*

1

I celebrate myself, and sing myself,
And what I assume you shall assume,
For every atom belonging to me as good belongs to you.

I loaf and invite my soul,
I lean and loaf at my ease observing a spear of summer grass.

My tongue, every atom of my blood, formed from this soil, this air,
Born here of parents born here from parents the same, and their
      parents the same,
I, now thirty-seven years old in perfect health begin,
Hoping to cease not till death.

Creeds and schools in abeyance,
Retiring back a while sufficed at what they are, but never forgotten,
I harbor for good or bad, I permit to speak at every hazard,
Nature without check with original energy.

. . . . .

6

A child said *What is the grass?* fetching it to me with full hands;
How could I answer the child? I do not know what it is any more
      than he.

I guess it must be the flag of my disposition, out of hopeful green
      stuff woven.

Or I guess it is the handkerchief of the Lord,
A scented gift and remembrancer designedly dropped,
Bearing the owner's name someway in the corners, that we may
      see and remark, and say *Whose?*
Or I guess the grass is itself a child, the produced babe of the
      vegetation.

Or I guess it is a uniform hieroglyphic,
And it means, Sprouting alike in broad zones and narrow zones,
Growing among black folks as among white,
Kanuck, Tuckahoe, Congressman, Cuff,[1] I give them the same,
      I receive them the same.

And now it seems to me the beautiful uncut hair of graves.

---

[1]A "Kanuck" refers to a French Canadian, a "Tuckahoe" refers to a native of
Tidewater, Virginia, and a "Cuff" refers to an African American.

18 Tenderly will I use you curling grass,
It may be you transpire from the breasts of young men,
20 It may be if I had known them I would have loved them,
It may be you are from old people, or from offspring taken soon
22   out of their mothers' laps,
And here you are the mothers' laps.

24 This grass is very dark to be from the white heads of old mothers,
Darker than the colorless beards of old men,
26 Dark to come from under the faint red roofs of mouths.

27 O I perceive after all so many uttering tongues,
And I perceive they do not come from the roofs of mouths for
29   nothing.

30 I wish I could translate the hints about the dead young men and
   women,
32 And the hints about old men and mothers, and the offspring taken
   soon out of their laps.

34 What do you think has become of the young and old men?
And what do you think has become of the women and children?

36 They are alive and well somewhere,
The smallest sprout shows there is really no death,
38 And if ever there was it led forward life, and does not wait at the
   end to arrest it,
40 And ceased the moment life appeared.

42 All goes onward and outward, nothing collapses,
And to die is different from what anyone supposed, and luckier.

. . . . .

52

43 The spotted hawk swoops by and accuses me, he complains of my
   gab and my loitering.

45 I too am not a bit tamed, I too am untranslatable,
I sound my barbaric yawp over the roofs of the world.

47 The last scud of day holds back for me,
It flings my likeness after the rest and true as any on the shadowed
   wilds,
50 It coaxes me to the vapor and the dusk.

I depart as air, I shake my white locks at the runaway sun,
52 I effuse my flesh in eddies, and drift it in lacy jags.

I bequeath myself to the dirt to grow from the grass I love,
If you want me again look for me under your boot-soles.

You will hardly know who I am or what I mean,
But I shall be good health to you nevertheless,
And filter and fiber your blood.

Failing to fetch me at first keep encouraged,
Missing me one place search another,
I stop somewhere waiting for you.

Vigil Strange I Kept on the Field One Night

Vigil strange I kept on the field one night;
When you my son and my comrade dropt at my side that day,
One look I but gave which your dear eyes return'd with a look I
    shall never forget,
One touch of your hand to mine O boy, reach'd up as you lay on
    the ground,
Then onward I sped in the battle, the even-contested battle,
Till late in the night reliev'd to the place at last again I made my
    way,
Found you in death so cold dear comrade, found your body son of
    responding kisses, (never again on earth responding,)
Bared your face in the starlight, curious the scene, cool blew the
    moderate night-wind,
Long there and then in vigil I stood, dimly around me the battle-
    field spreading,
Vigil wondrous and vigil sweet there in the fragrant silent night,
But not a tear fell, not even a long-drawn sigh, long I gazed,
Then on the earth partially reclining sat by your side leaning my
    chin in my hands,
Passing sweet hours, immortal and mystic hours with you dearest
    comrade — not a tear, not a word,
Vigil of silence, love and death, vigil for you my son and my
    soldier,
As onward silently stars aloft, eastward new ones upward stole,
Vigil final for you brave boy, (I could not save you, swift was your
    death,
I faithfully loved you and cared for you living, I think we shall
    surely meet again,)
Till at latest lingering of the night, indeed just as the dawn appear'd,
My comrade I wrapt in his blanket, envelop'd well his form,

Folded the blanket well, tucking it carefully over head and care-
    fully under feet,
And there and then and bathed by the rising sun, my son in his
    grave, in his rude-dug grave I deposited,
Ending my vigil strange with that, vigil of night and battle-field dim,
Vigil for boy of responding kisses, (never again on earth responding,)
Vigil for comrade swiftly slain, vigil I never forget, how as day
    brighten'd,
I rose from the chill ground and folded my soldier well in his
    blanket,
And buried him where he fell.

RICHARD WILBUR (b. 1921)

Cottage Street, 1953

Framed in her phoenix fire-screen, Edna Ward
Bends to the tray of Canton,[1] pouring tea
For frightened Mrs. Plath; then, turning toward
The pale, slumped daughter, and my wife, and me,

Asks if we would prefer it weak or strong.
Will we have milk or lemon, she enquires?
The visit seems already strained and long.
Each in his turn, we tell her our desires.

It is my office to exemplify
The published poet in his happiness,
Thus cheering Sylvia, who has wished to die;[2]
But half-ashamed, and impotent to bless,

I am a stupid life-guard who has found,
Swept to his shallows by the tide, a girl
Who, far from shore, has been immensely drowned,
And stares through water now with eyes of pearl.

How large is her refusal; and how slight
The genteel chat whereby we recommend
Life, of a summer afternoon, despite
The brewing dusk which hints that it may end.

---

    [1]Blue-and-white patterned Chinese-export porcelain ware; in this case, the tea
service.
    [2]The poet Sylvia Plath (1932–1963) attempted suicide after her junior year at
Smith College. Later, she died by suicide, at thirty-one.

And Edna Ward shall die in fifteen years,
After her eight-and-eighty summers of
Such grace and courage as permit no tears,
The thin hand reaching out, the last word *love,*

Outliving Sylvia who, condemned to live,
Shall study for a decade, as she must,
To state at last her brilliant negative
In poems free and helpless and unjust.

The Writer

In her room at the prow of the house
Where light breaks, and the windows are tossed with linden,
My daughter is writing a story.

I pause in the stairwell, hearing
From her shut door a commotion of typewriter-keys
Like a chain hauled over a gunwale.

Young as she is, the stuff
Of her life is a great cargo, and some of it heavy:
I wish her a lucky passage.

But now it is she who pauses,
As if to reject my thought and its easy figure.
A stillness greatens, in which

The whole house seems to be thinking,
And then she is at it again with a bunched clamor
Of strokes, and again is silent.

I remember the dazed starling
Which was trapped in that very room, two years ago;
How we stole in, lifted a sash

And retreated, not to affright it;
And how for a helpless hour, through the crack of the door,
We watched the sleek, wild, dark

And iridescent creature
Batter against the brilliance, drop like a glove
To the hard floor, or the desk-top,

And wait then, humped and bloody,
For the wits to try it again; and how our spirits
Rose when, suddenly sure,

It lifted off from a chair-back,
Beating a smooth course for the right window
And clearing the sill of the world.

It is always a matter, my darling,
Of life or death, as I had forgotten. I wish
What I wished you before, but harder.

WILLIAM CARLOS WILLIAMS (1883 – 1963)
Landscape with the Fall of Icarus

According to Breughel
when Icarus fell
it was spring

a farmer was ploughing
his field
the whole pageantry

of the year was
awake tingling
near

the edge of the sea
concerned
with itself

sweating in the sun
that melted
the wings' wax

unsignificantly
off the coast
there was

a splash quite unnoticed
this was
Icarus drowning

The Raper from Passenack

was very kind. When she regained
her wits, he said, It's all right, Kid,
I took care of you.

What a mess she was in. Then he added,
You'll never forget me now.
And drove her home.

Only a man who is sick, she said
would do a thing like that.
It must be so.

No one who is not diseased could be
so insanely cruel. He wants to give it
to someone else —

to justify himself. But if I get a
venereal infection out of this
I won't be treated.

I refuse. You'll find me dead in bed
first. Why not? That's
the way she spoke,

I wish I could shoot him. How would
you like to know a murderer?
I may do it.

I'll know by the end of this week.
I wouldn't scream. I bit him
several times

but he was too strong for me.
I can't yet understand it. I don't
faint so easily.

When I came to myself and realized
what had happened all I could do
was to curse

and call him every vile name I could
think of. I was so glad
to be taken home.

I suppose it's my mind — the fear of
infection. I'd rather a million times
have been got pregnant.

But it's the foulness of it can't
be cured. And hatred, hatred of all men
— and disgust.

Spring and All

By the road to the contagious hospital°   *treating contagious diseases*
under the surge of the blue
mottled clouds driven from the
northeast — a cold wind. Beyond, the
waste of broad, muddy fields
brown with dried weeds, standing and fallen

patches of standing water
the scattering of tall trees

All along the road the reddish
purplish, forked, upstanding, twiggy
stuff of bushes and small trees
with dead, brown leaves under them
leafless vines —

Lifeless in appearance, sluggish
dazed spring approaches —

They enter the new world naked,
cold, uncertain of all
save that they enter. All about them
the cold, familiar wind —

Now the grass, tomorrow
the stiff curl of wildcarrot leaf
One by one objects are defined —
It quickens: clarity, outline of leaf

But now the stark dignity of
entrance — Still, the profound change
has come upon them: rooted, they
grip down and begin to awaken

This Is Just to Say

I have eaten
the plums
that were in
the icebox

and which
you were probably
saving
for breakfast

Forgive me
they were delicious
so sweet
and so cold

WILLIAM WORDSWORTH (1770 – 1850)

My Heart Leaps Up

My heart leaps up when I behold
    A rainbow in the sky:
So was it when my life began;
So is it now I am a man;
So be it when I shall grow old,
    Or let me die!
The Child is father of the Man;
And I could wish my days to be
Bound each to each by natural piety.

Ode

Intimations of Immortality from Recollections
    of Early Childhood

                The Child is father of the Man;
                And I could wish my days to be
                Bound each to each by natural piety.

           1
There was a time when meadow, grove, and stream,
The earth, and every common sight,
      To me did seem
      Appareled in celestial light,
The glory and the freshness of a dream.
It is not now as it hath been of yore —
      Turn whereso'er I may,
        By night or day,
The things which I have seen I now can see no more.

        2
      The Rainbow comes and goes,
      And lovely is the Rose,

The Moon doth with delight
Look round her when the heavens are bare,
  Waters on a starry night
  Are beautiful and fair;
 The sunshine is a glorious birth;
 But yet I know, where'er I go,
That there hath passed away a glory from the earth.

     3

Now, while the birds thus sing a joyous song,
  And while the young lambs bound
   As to the tabor's° sound,   *small drum*
To me alone there came a thought of grief; *grief, sadness*
A timely utterance gave that thought relief, *is back again*
   And I again am strong:
The cataracts blow their trumpets from the steep;
No more shall grief of mine the season wrong;
I hear the Echoes through the mountains throng,
The Winds come to me from the fields of sleep,
  And all the earth is gay;
    Land and sea
  Give themselves up to jollity,
   And with the heart of May
  Doth every Beast keep holiday —
Addressee Thou Child of Joy,
Shout round me, let me hear thy shouts, thou happy Shepherd-
 boy! *All sounds.*

     4

Ye blessèd Creatures, I have heard the call
  Ye to each other make; I see
The heavens laugh with you in your jubilee;
  My heart is at your festival,
   My head hath its coronal,
The fullness of your bliss, I feel — I feel it all.
   — Oh, evil day! if I were sullen
   While Earth herself is adorning,
    This sweet May morning,
  And the Children are culling
   On every side,
In a thousand valleys far and wide,
Fresh flowers; while the sun shines warm,

And the Babe leaps up on his Mother's arm —
   I hear, I hear, with joy I hear!
   — But there's a Tree, of many, one,
A single Field which I have looked upon,
Both of them speak of something that is gone:
      The Pansy at my feet
      Doth the same tale repeat:
Whither is fled the visionary gleam?
Where is it now, the glory and the dream?

5

Our birth is but a sleep and a forgetting:
The Soul that rises with us, our life's Star,
    Hath had elsewhere its setting,
     And cometh from afar:
    Not in entire forgetfulness,
    And not in utter nakedness,
But trailing clouds of glory do we come
    From God, who is our home:
Heaven lies about us in our infancy!
Shades of the prison-house begin to close
    Upon the growing Boy
But he beholds the light, and whence it flows,
    He sees it in his joy;
The Youth, who daily farther from the east
    Must travel, still is Nature's Priest,
    And by the vision splendid
    Is on his way attended;
At length the Man perceives it die away,
And fade into the light of common day.

6

Earth fills her lap with pleasures of her own;
Yearnings she hath in her own natural kind,
And, even with something of a Mother's mind,
    And no unworthy aim,
    The homely Nurse doth all she can
To make her foster child, her Inmate Man,
    Forget the glories he hath known,
And that imperial palace whence he came.

7

Behold the Child among his newborn blisses,
A six-years' Darling of a pygmy size!
See, where 'mid work of his own hand he lies,
Fretted by sallies of his mother's kisses,
With light upon him from his father's eyes!
See, at his feet, some little plan or chart,
Some fragment from his dream of human life,
Shaped by himself with newly-learnèd art;
  A wedding or a festival,
  A mourning or a funeral;
   And this hath now his heart,
  And unto this he frames his song;
   Then will he fit his tongue
To dialogues of business, love, or strife;
  But it will not be long
  Ere this be thrown aside,
  And with new joy and pride
The little Actor cons another part;
Filling from time to time his "humorous stage"
With all the Persons, down to palsied Age,
That Life brings with her in her equipage;
  As if his whole vocation
  Were endless imitation.

8

Thou, whose exterior semblance doth belie
  Thy Soul's immensity;
Thou best Philosopher, who yet dost keep
Thy heritage, thou Eye among the blind,
That, deaf and silent, read'st the eternal deep,
Haunted forever by the eternal mind —
  Mighty Prophet! Seer blest!
  On whom those truths do rest,
Which we are toiling all our lives to find,
In darkness lost, the darkness of the grave;
Thou, over whom thy Immortality
Broods like the Day, a Master o'er a Slave,
A Presence which is not to be put by;
Thou little Child, yet glorious in the might
Of heaven-born freedom on thy being's height,

Why with such earnest pains dost thou provoke
The years to bring the inevitable yoke,
Thus blindly with thy blessedness at strife?
Full soon thy Soul shall have her earthly freight,
And custom lie upon thee with a weight,
Heavy as frost, and deep almost as life!

Why in such a hurry to grow up?

Burden of adulthood

9

       O joy! that in our embers
       Is something that doth live,
       That nature yet remembers
       What was so fugitive!

Nostalgic
The thought of our past years in me doth breed
Perpetual benediction: not indeed
For that which is most worthy to be blest;
Delight and liberty, the simple creed
Of Childhood, whether busy or at rest,
With new-fledged hope still fluttering in his breast —
       Not for these I raise
       The song of thanks and praise; *Ode*
    But for those obstinate questionings
    Of sense and outward things,
    Fallings from us, vanishings;
    Blank misgivings of a Creature
Moving about in worlds not realized,
High instincts before which our mortal Nature
Did tremble like a guilty Thing surprised;
      But for those first affections,
      Those shadowy recollections,
    Which, be they what they may,
Are yet the fountain-light of all our day,
Are yet a master-light of all our seeing;
    Uphold us, cherish, and have power to make
Our noisy years seem moments in the being
Of the eternal Silence: truths that wake,
      To perish never;
Which neither listlessness, nor mad endeavor,
      Nor Man nor Boy,
Nor all that is at enmity with joy,
Can utterly abolish or destroy!
      Hence in a season of calm weather

Best evidence of preexistence — Child

Though inland far we be,
Our Souls have sight of that immortal sea
Which brought us hither,
Can in a moment travel thither,
And see the Children sport upon the shore,
And hear the mighty waters rolling evermore.

10

Then sing, ye Birds, sing, sing a joyous song!
And let the young Lambs bound
As to the tabor's sound!
We in thought will join your throng,
Ye that pipe and ye that play, *rhyme seems*
Ye that through your hearts today *playful,*
Feel the gladness of the May! *innocent*
What though the radiance which was once so bright
Be now forever taken from my sight,
Though nothing can bring back the hour *Gist of*
Of splendor in the grass, of glory in the flower; *the poem*
We will grieve not, rather find
Strength in what remains behind;
In the primal sympathy
Which having been must ever be;
In the soothing thoughts that spring
sad but Out of human suffering; *strange to put together*
not sad? In the faith that looks through death,
In years that bring the philosophic mind. *ultimately, will develop*
this philosophic mind

11

And O, ye Fountains, Meadows, Hills, and Groves,
Forebode not any severing of our loves!
Yet in my heart of hearts I feel your might;
I only have relinquished one delight *delight of pre existence?*
To live beneath your more habitual sway.
I love the Brooks which down their channels fret,
Even more than when I tripped lightly as they;
The innocent brightness of a newborn Day
Is lovely yet;
The clouds that gather round the setting sun
Do take a sober coloring from an eye
That hath kept watch o'er man's mortality;
Another race hath been, and other palms° are won.   *symbols of victory*

Thanks to the human heart by which we live,
Thanks to its tenderness, its joys, and fears,
To me the meanest° flower that blows°   *most ordinary / blooms*
    can give   Beautiful but wilting
Thoughts that do often lie too deep for tears.

The Solitary Reaper

Behold her, single in the field,
Yon solitary Highland Lass!
Reaping and singing by herself;
Stop here, or gently pass!
Alone she cuts and binds the grain,
And sings a melancholy strain;
O listen! for the Vale profound
Is overflowing with the sound.

No Nightingale did ever chaunt
More welcome notes to weary bands
Of travelers in some shady haunt,
Among Arabian sands;
A voice so thrilling ne'er was heard
In springtime from the Cuckoo bird,
Breaking the silence of the seas
Among the farthest Hebrides,

Will no one tell me what she sings? —
Perhaps the plaintive numbers flow
For old, unhappy, far-off things,
And battles long ago;
Or is it some more humble lay,
Familiar matter of today?
Some natural sorrow, loss, or pain,
That has been, and may be again?

Whate'er the theme, the Maiden sang
As if her song could have no ending;
I saw her singing at her work,
And o'er the sickle bending —
I listened, motionless and still;
And, as I mounted up the hill,
The music in my heart I bore,
Long after it was heard no more.

JAMES WRIGHT (1927 – 1980)

A Blessing

Just off the highway to Rochester, Minnesota,
Twilight bounds softly forth on the grass.
And the eyes of those two Indian ponies
Darken with kindness.
They have come gladly out of the willows
To welcome my friend and me.
We step over the barbed wire into the pasture
Where they have been grazing all day, alone.
They ripple tensely, they can hardly contain their happiness
That we have come.
They bow shyly as wet swans. They love each other.
There is no loneliness like theirs.
At home once more,
They begin munching the young tufts of spring in the darkness.
I would like to hold the slenderer one in my arms,
For she has walked over to me
And nuzzled my left hand.
She is black and white,
Her mane falls wild on her forehead,
And the light breeze moves me to caress her long ear
That is delicate as the skin over a girl's wrist.
Suddenly I realize
That if I stepped out of my body I would break
Into blossom.

Small Frogs Killed on the Highway

Still,
I would leap too
Into the light,
If I had the chance.
It is everything, the wet green stalk of the field
On the other side of the road.
They crouch there, too, faltering in terror
And take strange wing. Many
Of the dead never moved, but many
Of the dead are alive forever in the split second
Auto headlights more sudden
Than their drivers know.

The drivers burrow backward into dank pools
Where nothing begets
Nothing.

Across the road, tadpoles are dancing
On the quarter thumbnail
Of the moon. They can't see,
Not yet.

SIR THOMAS WYATT (1503 – 1542)
Forget Not Yet

Forget not yet the tried intent
Of such a truth as I have meant;
My great travail so gladly spent
    Forget not yet.

Forget not yet when first began
The weary life ye know, since whan°   *when*
The suit, the service none tell can;
    Forget not yet.

Forget not yet the great assays,°   *trials*
The cruel wrong, the scornful ways,
The painful patience in denays,°   *denials*
    Forget not yet.

Forget not yet, forget not this,
How long ago hath been and is
The mind that never meant amiss;
    Forget not yet.

Forget not then thine own approved,
The which so long hath thee so loved,
Whose steadfast faith yet never moved;
    Forget not this.

JOHN YAU (b. 1950)
Autobiography in Red and Yellow

I was born in Shanghai
peony bicycle harbor

twilight zodiacal boulevards
where all poets and their

perilous possibilities
are tossed ashore

As is the custom
I never studied

accordion bassoon
or fabled tambourine

wooden instruments
which rest above

a marble fireplace
in the minds of those

who weren't born in Shanghai
In the Year of the Adamant Aardvark°   *the Chinese associate each year*
                                                      with an animal
we dressed in the plainest idioms available
lest we found ourselves

chained to a statue of a discredited ancestor
of which I have many

according to the chart recently downloaded
from the Ancestor Registry and Radio Tracking System

I was born in Shanghai
shortly after one cylinder of war ended

and another revolution
in barnyard fashion began

In my youth I spoke
with forked tongue

and ate with forking sticks
I was born in Shanghai

during the month
obesity runs rampant

and tractor operators
embrace their tractors

and their snowshoes
but now it is almost

the Year of the Lighthearted Howitzer
Will we ever learn to wash our hair

with oils extracted
from the stones

we used to blast our enemies
I was born in Shanghai

where there is a genuine franchise
on every corner

Our wits are short
but our tongues are long

WILLIAM BUTLER YEATS (1865 – 1939)
Among School Children

I

I walk through the long schoolroom questioning;
A kind old nun in a white hood replies;
The children learn to cipher and to sing,
To study reading-books and history,
To cut and sew, be neat in everything
In the best modern way — the children's eyes
In momentary wonder stare upon
A sixty-year-old smiling public man.

II

I dream of a Ledaean body,[1] bent
Above a sinking fire, a tale that she
Told of a harsh reproof, or trivial event
That changed some childish day to tragedy —
Told, and it seemed that our two natures blent
Into a sphere from youthful sympathy,
Or else, to alter Plato's parable,
Into the yolk and white of the one shell.[2]

III

And thinking of that fit of grief or rage
I look upon one child or t'other there

---

[1]A body like Leda's. Leda was, in Greek myth, a maiden ravished by Zeus, who took the form of a swan. She bore Helen of Troy, whom Yeats identified with his beloved Maud Gonne.

[2]Plato, in *The Symposium*, suggests that man was originally both male and female in one sphere but fell into division. Each half now longs for the other half.

And wonder if she stood so at that age —
For even daughters of the swan can share
Something of every paddler's heritage —
And had that colour upon cheek or hair,
And thereupon my heart is driven wild:
She stands before me as a living child.

IV

Her present image floats into the mind —
Did Quattrocento[3] finger fashion it
Hollow of cheek as though it drank the wind
And took a mess of shadows for its meat?
And I though never of Ledaean kind
Had pretty plumage once — enough of that,
Better to smile on all that smile, and show
There is a comfortable kind of old scarecrow.

V

What youthful mother, a shape upon her lap
Honey of generation had betrayed,
And that must sleep, shriek, struggle to escape
As recollection or the drug decide,
Would think her son, did she but see that shape
With sixty or more winters on its head,
A compensation for the pang of his birth,
Or the uncertainty of his setting forth?

VI

Plato thought nature but a spume that plays
Upon a ghostly paradigm of things;
Solider Aristotle played the taws
Upon the bottom of a king of kings;[4]
World-famous golden-thighed Pythagoras
Fingered upon a fiddle-stick or strings
What a star sang and careless Muses heard:[5]
Old clothes upon old sticks to scare a bird.

---

[3]Italian name for the fifteenth century.

[4]Yeats wrote to a friend, "Here is a fragment of my last curse upon old age. It means that even the greatest men are owls, scarecrows, by the time their fame has come. Aristotle, remember, was Alexander [the Great's] tutor, hence the taws [form of birch]," i.e., Aristotle flogged his pupil into learning.

[5]Yeats is referring to the fact that Pythagoras measured the intervals between notes on a stretched string.

VII

Both nuns and mothers worship images,
But those the candles light are not as those
That animate a mother's reveries,
But keep a marble or a bronze repose.
And yet they too break hearts — O Presences
That passion, piety or affection knows,
And that all heavenly glory symbolise —
O self-born mockers of man's enterprise;

VIII

Labour is blossoming or dancing where
The body is not bruised to pleasure soul,
Nor beauty born out of its own despair,
Nor blear-eyed wisdom out of midnight oil.
O chestnut-tree, great-rooted blossomer,
Are you the leaf, the blossom or the bole?
O body swayed to music, O brightening glance,
How can we know the dancer from the dance?

A Dialogue of Self and Soul

I

MY SOUL. I summon to the winding ancient stair;
　　Set all your mind upon the steep ascent,
　　Upon the broken, crumbling battlement,
　　Upon the breathless starlit air,
　　Upon the star that marks the hidden pole;
　　Fix every wandering thought upon
　　That quarter where all thought is done:
　　Who can distinguish darkness from the soul?

MY SELF. The consecrated blade upon my knees
　　Is Sato's° ancient blade, still as it was,   *Japanese admirer*
　　Still razor-keen, still like a looking-glass   *of Yeats*
　　Unspotted by the centuries;
　　That flowering, silken, old embroidery, torn
　　From some court-lady's dress and round
　　The wooden scabbard bound and wound,
　　Can, tattered, still protect, faded adorn.

MY SOUL. Why should the imagination of a man
　　Long past his prime remember things that are

Emblematical of love and war?
Think of ancestral night that can,
If but imagination scorn the earth
And intellect its wandering
To this and that and t' other thing,
Deliver from the crime of death and birth.

MY SELF. Montashigi, third of his family, fashioned it
Five hundred years ago, about it lie
Flowers from I know not what embroidery —
Heart's purple — and all these I set
For emblems of the day against the tower
Emblematical of the night,
And claim as by a soldier's right
A charter to commit the crime once more.

MY SOUL. Such fullness in that quarter overflows
And falls into the basin of the mind
That man is stricken deaf and dumb and blind,
For intellect no longer knows
Is from the *Ought,* or *Knower* from the *Known*—
That is to say, ascends to Heaven;
Only the dead can be forgiven;
But when I think of that my tongue's a stone.

II

MY SELF. A living man is blind and drinks his drop.
What matter if the ditches are impure?
What matter if I live it all once more?
Endure that toil of growing up;
The ignominy of boyhood; the distress
Of boyhood changing into man;
The unfinished man and his pain
Brought face to face with his own clumsiness;

The finished man among his enemies? —
How in the name of Heaven can he escape
That defiling and disfigured shape
The mirror of malicious eyes
Casts upon his eyes until at last
He thinks that shape must be his shape?
And what's the good of an escape
If honour find him in the wintry blast?

I am content to live it all again
And yet again, if it be life to pitch
Into the frog-spawn of a blind man's ditch,
A blind man battering blind men;
Or into that most fecund ditch of all,
The folly that man does
Or must suffer, if he woos
A proud woman not kindred of his soul.

I am content to follow to its source,
Every event in action or in thought;
Measure the lot; forgive myself the lot!
When such as I cast out remorse
So great a sweetness flows into the breast
We must laugh and we must sing,
We are blest by everything,
Everything we look upon is blest.

Down by the Salley Gardens

Down by the salley gardens my love and I did meet;
She passed the salley gardens with little snow-white feet.
She bid me take love easy, as the leaves grow on the tree;
But I, being young and foolish, with her would not agree.
In a field by the river my love and I did stand,
And on my leaning shoulder she laid her snow-white hand.
She bid me take life easy, as the grass grows on the weirs;
But I was young and foolish, and now am full of tears.

The Lake Isle of Innisfree

I will arise and go now, and go to Innisfree,
And a small cabin build there, of clay and wattles made:
Nine bean-rows will I have there, a hive for the honeybee,
And live alone in the bee-loud glade.

And I shall have some peace there, for peace comes dropping slow,
Dropping from the veils of the morning to where the cricket sings;
There midnight's all a glimmer, and noon a purple glow,
And evening full of the linnet's wings.

I will arise and go now, for always night and day
I hear lake water lapping with low sounds by the shore;
While I stand on the roadway, or on the pavements grey,
I hear it in the deep heart's core.

Leda and the Swan[1]

A sudden blow: the great wings beating still
Above the staggering girl, her thighs caressed
By the dark webs, her nape caught in his bill,
He holds her helpless breast upon his breast.

How can those terrified vague fingers push
The feathered glory from her loosening thighs?
And how can body, laid in that white rush,
But feel the strange heart beating where it lies?

A shudder in the loins engenders there
The broken wall, the burning roof and tower
And Agamemnon dead.
                              Being so caught up,
So mastered by the brute blood of the air,
Did she put on his knowledge with his power
Before the indifferent beak could let her drop?

Sailing to Byzantium

I

That is no country for old men. The young
In one another's arms, birds in the trees
— Those dying generations — at their song,
The salmon-falls, the mackerel-crowded seas,
Fish, flesh, or fowl, commend all summer long
Whatever is begotten, born, and dies.
Caught in that sensual music all neglect
Monuments of unageing intellect.

II

An aged man is but a paltry thing,
A tattered coat upon a stick, unless
Soul clap its hands and sing, and louder sing
For every tatter in its mortal dress,
Nor is there singing school but studying[1]
Monuments of its own magnificence;

---

[1] In Greek myth, Leda was ravished by Zeus, who took the form of a swan. She gave birth to Helen. Helen left her husband, Menelaus, to go with Paris to Troy, thus causing the Trojan War.

[1] That is, "Nor is there any way to learn to sing except by studying."

And therefore I have sailed the seas and come
To the holy city of Byzantium.

III

O sages standing in God's holy fire
As in the gold mosaic of a wall,
Come from the holy fire, perne in a gyre,[2]
And be the singing-masters of my soul.
Consume my heart away; sick with desire
And fastened to a dying animal
It knows not what it is; and gather me
Into the artifice of eternity.

IV

Once out of nature I shall never take
My bodily form from any natural thing,
But such a form as Grecian goldsmiths make
Of hammered gold and gold enamelling
To keep a drowsy Emperor awake;[3]
Or set upon a golden bough to sing
To lords and ladies of Byzantium
Of what is past, or passing, or to come.

The Second Coming

Turning and turning in the widening gyre[1]
The falcon cannot hear the falconer;
Things fall apart; the centre cannot hold;
Mere anarchy is loosed upon the world,
The blood-dimmed tide is loosed, and everywhere
The ceremony of innocence is drowned;
The best lack all conviction, while the worst
Are full of passionate intensity.

Surely some revelation is at hand;
Surely the Second Coming is at hand.
The Second Coming! Hardly are those words out

---

[2]Swoop down in a whirling movement. A perne is a cone-shaped bobbin.

[3]Yeats's note: "I have read somewhere that in the Emperor's palace at Byzantium was a tree made of gold and silver, and artificial birds sang."

[1]Yeats used the image of two interlocking gyres or cones to symbolize the conflicting forces of life.

When a vast image out of *Spiritus Mundi*[2]
Troubles my sight: somewhere in sands of the desert
A shape with lion body and the head of a man
A gaze blank and pitiless as the sun,
Is moving its slow thighs, while all about it
Reel shadows of the indignant desert birds.
The darkness drops again; but now I know
That twenty centuries of stony sleep
Were vexed to nightmare by a rocking cradle,
And what rough beast, its hour come round at last,
Slouches towards Bethlehem to be born?

---

[2]Yeats's term for the collective human memory.

Appendices

Appendix 1. On Prosody

Prosody concerns the measure in which poems are written. There are three kinds of poems, prosodically speaking:

poems in counted lines (where lines have a regular number of beats);

poems in free verse (where lines have an irregular number of beats);

poems in prose (usually a short symbolic paragraph).

This appendix is concerned with poems in counted lines and poems in free verse. Since free verse is a relatively recent form (Walt Whitman is the earliest significant American poet of free verse), we will take up counted poetry first.

Poems in Counted Lines

Poems in counted lines are written in units we call feet. A foot consists of one stressed syllable (one "beat," to use the musical term), usually accompanied by one or two unstressed syllables. We represent a stressed syllable by an accent (´) and an unstressed syllable by a symbol called a breve (˘).

Here is an example of a line with four feet:

Whose woóds / these áre / I thínk / I knów

The number of feet in a line gives the line its (Greek-derived) name, and tells you how *wide* the line is. Natural intonation makes you stress some words and leave others unstressed, helping you to see how many beats are in the line. We characterize a line by how many stresses (beats) exist in it: the word "meter" (meaning measure) is the general name for the width of a counted line:

> one beat per line = *monometer* (from Greek meaning "one," as in "monologue");
>
> two beats per line = *dimeter* (from Greek meaning "two," as in "dialogue");
>
> three beats per line = *trimeter* (from Greek meaning "three," as in "triangle");
>
> four beats per line = *tetrameter* (from Greek meaning "four," as in "tetrahedron");
>
> five beats per line = *pentameter* (from Greek meaning "five," as in "Pentagon");
>
> six beats per line = *hexameter* (from Greek meaning "six," as in "hexagram");
>
> seven beats per line = *heptameter* (from Greek meaning "seven," as in "heptathlon");
>
> eight beats per line = *octameter* (from Greek meaning "eight," as in "octopus").

Most poems written in English have lines four or five beats wide. Shakespeare wrote all of his plays in pentameter lines five beats wide (though he also inserted prose and short songs from time to time).

When you are looking to see how many beats are in a line, it helps sometimes to see how many syllables are in the line. Ten-syllable lines tend to have five beats each; eight-syllable lines tend to have four beats each. But it is still natural intonation that tells you where to put the stresses:

> When Í / see bír / ches bénd / to léft / and ríght [ten syllables, five beats]
> Gólden / láds and / gírls all / múst [seven syllables, four beats]

Here are samples of six of the line-widths. It helps to read these aloud, so that you can hear the beats.

1. **MONOMETER** *(one beat per line, a rare meter),* as in the little poem called "Fleas":

   > Adam
   > Had 'em.

2. **DIMETER** *(two beats),* which is likewise rare:

   > Take her up tenderly,
   > Lift her with care,
   > Fashioned so slenderly,
   > Young and so fair.
   >
   > — THOMAS HOOD, "The Bridge of Sighs"

3. **TRIMETER** *(three beats):*

   > It is time that I wrote my will;
   > I choose upstanding men
   > That climb the streams until
   > The fountain leap, and at dawn
   > Drop their cast at the side
   > Of dripping stone; I declare
   > They shall inherit my pride.
   >
   > — W. B. YEATS, "The Tower"

4. **TETRAMETER** *(four beats):*

   > Whose woods these are I think I know
   > His house is in the village though,
   > He will not see me stopping here
   > To watch his woods fill up with snow.
   >
   > — ROBERT FROST, "Stopping by Woods"

5. **PENTAMETER** *(five beats):*

   > The woods decay, the woods decay and fall,
   > The vapours weep their burthens to the ground,
   > Man comes and tills the soil and lies beneath,
   > And after many a summer dies the swan.
   >
   > — ALFRED, LORD TENNYSON, "Tithonus"

6. **HEXAMETER** *(six beats),* which is sometimes called an Alexandrine (from the French usage) and which is rare in English verse:

   > I will arise and go now, and go to Innisfree,
   > And a small cabin build there, of clay and wattles made.
   >
   > — W. B. YEATS, "The Lake Isle of Innisfree"

The common meters (line-widths) have been trimeter, tetrameter, and pentameter, used singly or in combination.

RHYTHM

You have probably noticed that the lilts (swings) in each of the above examples of line-width differ. That is because the lines are written in different rhythms. Two dimeter poems can sound very different from each other because they are written in two different rhythms. You can see this by comparing Hood's "The Bridge of Sighs," given above as an example of dimeter, with Dorothy Parker's satirical poem on suicide, "Résumé," also in dimeter:

Táke her up / ténderly,   Rázors / páin you
Líft her with / cáre   Rívers are / dámp;
Fáshioned so / slénderly   Ácids / stáin you;
Yóung and so / fáir.   And drúgs cause / crámp.

To describe the versification of a poem, you have to say not only how wide its lines are, but also what rhythm they are written in. English rhythms are based on *stressed* and *unstressed* syllables. Each stressed syllable with its associated unstressed syllable(s) makes a single unit, which we call a foot.

There are two main kinds of rhythm in English: *rising* rhythms and *falling* rhythms. In a *rising* rhythm, a foot consists of one or more unstressed syllables leading up to a stressed syllable: ˘´ or ˘˘´.

Where the Yoúth / pined awáy / with desíre,
And the pále / Virgin shroúd / ed in snów
Aríse / from their gráves / and aspíre
Where my Sún / flower wísh / es to gó.
— WILLIAM BLAKE, "Ah Sun-flower"

In a *falling* rhythm, a foot begins with the stressed syllable, which is followed by one or more unstressed syllables: ´˘ or ´˘˘.

Týger! / Týger! / búrning / bríght
Ín the / fórests / óf the / níght,
— WILLIAM BLAKE, "The Tyger"

Metrical feet are named according to where their stress appears and how many unstressed syllables they possess. Rising rhythms are either *iambic* (with two syllables, ˘´) or *anapestic* (with three syllables, ˘˘´). We speak of an *iamb* or an *iambic foot* when we mean ˘´; an *anapest* or an *anapestic foot* when we mean ˘˘´. Falling rhythms are either *trochaic* (with two syllables, ˘´) or *dactylic* (with three syllables, ˘˘´). The corresponding nouns are *trochee* and *dactyl*.

When you read a poem in counted lines, try to see whether the general movement is a rising one or a falling one. In the two examples from Blake given above, "Ah Sun-flower" is written in rising anapestic (three-syllable) feet, and "The Tyger" in falling trochaic (two-syllable) feet.

In each *line* of "Ah Sun-flower" there are three *feet* (because there are three stressed syllables):

Where the Youth / pined awáy / with desíre

In each *line* of "The Tyger" there are four *feet* (because there are four stressed syllables):

Týger! / týger! / búrning / bríght

If you think of each *stressed* syllable as a musical beat, the lines of "Ah Sun-flower" have three beats each ("and a *one* and a *two* and a *three*"); the lines of "The Tyger" have four beats each ("*one* and *two* and *three* and *four*").

Feet can shed one or more of their unstressed syllables. You can see that at the end of each line in "The Tyger," an unstressed syllable is "missing." And in "Ah Sun-flower," in the line "Aríse / from their gráves / and aspíre," an unstressed syllable is missing in the first foot, which has only two syllables, "Arise." These irregularities do not occur so often that they destroy the general impression of the metrical scheme underlying the poem.

If you hear these rhythms in your ear as you read, you will soon recognize them. Here are two more examples, to fill out our scheme:

I found a dimpled spider, fat and white.
— ROBERT FROST, "Design"

Read aloud, this reveals itself to have five beats (five stressed syllables): "and *one* and *two* and *three* and *four* and *five*." Each of the five units consists of an unstressed syllable followed by a stressed syllable (iambic foot):

I foúnd / a dímp / led spí / der, fát / and whíte.

Listen to Longfellow's description of the original American forest:

This is the forest primeval, the murmuring pines and the hemlocks.
— HENRY WADSWORTH LONGFELLOW, "Evangeline"

Read aloud, this reveals itself to have six beats (six stressed syllables): "*one* and a *two* and a *three* and // a *four* and a *five* and a *six* and." Each foot (except the last, which has shed one unstressed syllable) consists of a stressed syllable followed by two unstressed syllables (dactylic foot):

> Thís is the / fórest prim / éval // the / múrmuring / pínes and
> the / hémlocks.

These rising and falling feet occur in lines of different widths. We have seen, above, trimeter lines ("Ah Sun-flower") and tetrameter lines ("The Tyger"). We have seen pentameter lines ("Design") and hexameter lines ("Evangeline"). *A full description of a line describes its rhythm and then its width.* "Ah Sun-flower" is written in anapestic trimeter. "The Tyger" is written in trochaic tetrameter. "Design" is written in iambic pentameter. "Evangeline" is written in dactylic hexameter.

It is less important that you know these names than that you recognize a rhythm by ear. Practice tapping out the rhythms above until they become familiar. Counting out the rhythm and width of a line is called *scanning* it.

It is often difficult, even impossible, to scan a single line taken by itself. One line can be scanned two or more ways, depending on the intonation we give it. The rule of thumb is to look at the other lines matching it. If they are all five-beat lines, then the dubious line is probably a five-beat line, too. But do not allow the prevailing rhythm, when you read a line aloud, to ride roughshod over the sense; the sense will usually tell you what syllables ought to be stressed.

In all rhythms, some feet are irregular, so that the cadence does not become intolerably inflexible. Feet of comparable length can freely substitute for each other. Shakespeare often begins one of his iambic (˘´) lines with an initial trochaic foot (´˘) to give energy to the line:

> Whý is / my verse / so bar / ren of / new pride?

Each of these metrical schemes is merely a grid underlying a line. The line itself must, by its intonation pattern, indicate the grid (or you cannot know what the basic rhythm is supposed to be), but it can depart from the grid in various ways — by substituting a different foot, by having a light foot called the *pyrrhic* (˘˘) for unimportant words, or a heavy foot called the *spondee* (´´) for important words, and so on. What you are asked to do in scanning the line is to see the underlying grid, first of all, and then to note any departures from it. Poets enjoy varying their rhythms to accord with dramatic emphasis, tone of voice, and so on. They also enjoy breaking their lines with a pause in the middle, which we call a *caesura* and represent with a double slash. An iambic pentameter line can be broken one or more times:

> I grant I never saw a goddess go;
> My mistress, // when she walks, // treads on the ground.
> And yet, // by heaven, // I think my love as rare
> As any she belied with false compare.
>
> — SHAKESPEARE, Sonnet 130

RHYMES AND STANZA-FORMS

Not all counted poetry is written in rhymes. But because lyric began as song (the name "lyric" comes from "lyre"), simple rhyming stanza-forms such as those found in the ballad or the hymn became important in the English tradition. Gradually, as oral poetry gave way to printed poetry (meant to be read rather than sung), stanza-forms of considerable complexity arose. Here are some of the most common rhyming forms in English. When rhyming units are separated by white space, they are called *stanzas*. (*Stanza,* in Italian, means "room." Poems are made up of little "rooms.")

1. A pair of rhyming lines is called a *couplet.* Couplets are frequently run together, not separated as stanzas:

> While the plowman near at hand,
> Whistles o'er the furrowed land,
> And the milkmaid singeth blithe,
> And the mower whets his scythe,
> And every shepherd tells his tale,
> Under the hawthorn in the dale.
>
> — JOHN MILTON, "L'Allegro"

These couplets are written in trochaic tetrameter. The rhyme scheme of these lines is indicated thus: *aabbcc.* That is, because the first two lines rhyme ("hand" "land"), they can be indicated by *aa,* and because the next two rhyme, they can be indicated by *bb.* We indicate the *rhyme scheme* by these abbreviated lowercase italicized letters.

The *heroic couplet* is an iambic pentameter couplet that is end-stopped (marked by a heavy pause after the second line of the couplet), and frequently pointed and witty. Alexander Pope and John Dryden used it with brio:

> Meanwhile, declining from the noon of day,
> The sun obliquely shoots his burning ray;

> The hungry judges soon the sentence sign,
> And wretches hang that jurymen may dine.
> — ALEXANDER POPE, "The Rape of the Lock"

2. A stanza of three lines is called a *tercet:*

> Light the first light of evening, as in a room
> In which we sit, and for small reason, think
> The world imagined is the ultimate good.
> — WALLACE STEVENS,
> "Final Soliloquy of the Interior Paramour"

Terza rima is a form of pentameter tercet with interlinked rhymes (*aba bcb cdc* and so on) used by Dante in the *Divine Comedy*. It is difficult to carry off in English, though Shelley used it for his "Ode to the West Wind." Many poets intend an allusion to Dante when they use loosely rhymed pentameter tercets.

3. A stanza of four lines is called a *quatrain*. The commonest quatrain is the *ballad stanza,* in which the first and third lines are unrhymed and have four beats, while the second and fourth lines rhyme and have three beats:

> It is an ancient Mariner
> And he stoppeth one of three.
> —"By thy long gray beard and glittering eye,
> Now wherefore stopp'st thou me?"
> — SAMUEL TAYLOR COLERIDGE,
> "The Rime of the Ancient Mariner"

Some tetrameter quatrains are rhymed *abba,* like those in Shakespeare's "The Phoenix and the Turtle" and Tennyson's "In Memoriam." This stanza is generally referred to as the *"In Memoriam" stanza*:

> Ring out, wild bells, to the wild sky,
>   The flying cloud, the frosty light:
>   The year is dying in the night;
> Ring out, wild bells, and let him die.

The *heroic quatrain* is an iambic pentameter quatrain, rhyming *abab*:

> I know my life's a pain and but a span;
> I know my sense is mock'd with everything;

And, to conclude, I know myself a man,
Which is a proud and yet a wretched thing.
> — SIR JOHN DAVIES, "Nosce Teipsum"

4. A stanza of six lines is sometimes called a *sixain* (its French name) or a *sestet*. The commonest sixain rhyme-form is *ababcc*. A pentameter sixain rhyming this way is called the *"Venus and Adonis" stanza,* from the poem of that name by Shakespeare:

Look how a bird lies tangled in a net,
So fast'nd in her arms Adonis lies,
Pure shame and awed resistance made him fret,
Which bred more beauty in his angry eyes.
> Rain added to a river that is rank
> Perforce will force it overflow the bank.

5. The only common seven-line stanza is *rime royal* (so called because King James I used it) — iambic pentameter rhyming *ababbcc*. This is the meter of many long poems on high themes — Chaucer's *Troilus and Criseyde,* for instance. Spenser uses it for his "Four Hymns":

For love is a celestial harmony
Of likely hearts composed of stars' consent,
Which join together in sweet sympathy,
To work each other's joy and true content,
Which they have harbored since their first descent
Out of their heavenly bowers, where they did see
And know each other here beloved to be.
> — EDMUND SPENSER, "An Hymn in Honour of Beauty"

6. The best-known eight-line form is *ottava rima* — iambic pentameter rhyming *abababcc*. The final couplet can give this stanza epigrammatic point, and Byron used it with notable wit in his long poem *Don Juan*. Its greatest modern practitioner has been W. B. Yeats:

Labour is blossoming or dancing where
The body is not bruised to pleasure soul,
Nor beauty born out of its own despair,
Nor blear-eyed wisdom out of midnight oil.
O chestnut-tree, great-rooted blossomer,
Are you the leaf, the blossom or the bole?

O body swayed to music, O brightening glance,
How can we know the dancer from the dance?
— W. B. YEATS, "Among School Children"

7. The best-known nine-line form is the *Spenserian stanza* (so called because Spenser used it in *The Faerie Queene*). Keats adopted it for "The Eve of St. Agnes." All its lines are pentameter, except the last, which is a hexameter. It rhymes in a closely linked way: *ababbcbcc.*

St. Agnes' Eve — Ah, bitter chill it was!
The owl, for all his feathers, was a-cold;
The hare limped trembling through the frozen grass,
And silent was the flock in woolly fold:
Numb were the Beadsman's fingers, while he told
His rosary, and while his frosted breath,
Like pious incense from a censer old,
Seemed taking flight for heaven, without a death,
Past the sweet Virgin's picture, while his prayer he saith.
— JOHN KEATS, "The Eve of St. Agnes"

There are many unnamed stanza-forms, some of them common ones. For instance, an extra line or two is often added to the ballad stanza, to make a five- or six-line stanza. Or a *refrain* (a line repeated after every stanza) can be added to lengthen the ballad quatrain.

TYPES OF RHYMING POEMS

1. The *sonnet* is a fourteen-line pentameter poem. There are two chief forms:

The *Italian (Petrarchan) sonnet* consists of an octave and a sestet. There are embraced rhymes in the octave (the first eight lines): *abbaabba.* The sestet of a Petrarchan sonnet can rhyme in several different ways, but the most common are *cdecde* and (as below) *cdcdee:*

Who will in fairest book of Nature know
How Virtue may best lodged in beauty be,
Let him but learn of *Love* to read in thee,
Stella, those fair lines which true goodness show.
There shall he find all vices' overthrow,
Not by rude force, but sweetest sovereignty
Of reason, from whose light those nightbirds fly,
That inward sun in thine eyes shineth so.
And, not content to be Perfection's heir

Thyself, dost strive all minds that way to move,
Who mark in thee what is in thee most fair.
So while thy beauty draws the heart to love,
    As fast thy Virtue bends that love to good.
    "But ah," Desire still cries, "give me some food."
           — SIR PHILIP SIDNEY, *Astrophel and Stella,* 71

The *English (Shakespearean) sonnet* consists of three four-line quatrains, alternately rhymed *(ababcdcdefef),* and a couplet, *gg:*

Let me not to the marriage of true minds
Admit impediments. Love is not love
Which alters when it alteration finds,
Or bends with the remover to remove.
O no, it is an ever fixèd mark
That looks on tempests and is never shaken;
It is the star to every wand'ring bark,
Whose worth's unknown, although his height be taken.
Love's not Time's fool, though rosy lips and cheeks
Within his bending sickle's compass come,
Love alters not with his brief hours and weeks,
But bears it out even to the edge of doom.
    If this be error and upon me proved,
    I never writ, nor no man ever loved.

There have been many variations on the two basic sonnet forms.
Spenser wrote sonnets that were composed of linked rhymes: *abab bcbc
cdcd ee.* Some poets (Herbert, Yeats) have made hybrid sonnets by attaching Petrarchan sestets to Shakespearean octaves, or vice versa. Others, like
George Meredith and Stevens, have written sonnet-like poems with
sixteen or fifteen lines. The odes of Keats basically form their stanzas by
combining a Shakespearean quatrain with a Petrarchan sestet (they vary
the length of line and sometimes double a rhyme, but it is clear that
their elements come from the two sonnet traditions).

2. The *sestina* is a pentameter poem consisting of six stanzas of six
lines plus a three-line coda (known as the *envoy* or *envoi).* The sestina
"rhymes" on six end-words, which must be repeated in each stanza in a
controlled order, whereby the last end-word in each stanza becomes the
first end-word of the next stanza: *abcdef, faebdc, cfdabe, ecbfad, deacfb, bdfeca.*
The envoi must employ two of the end-words in each of its three lines. A
good sestina makes this difficult pattern seem natural. The sestina is easier
seen than described. Here is one (called "Sestina") by Elizabeth Bishop.
The six end-words are "house," "grandmother," "child," "stove," "almanac,"

and "tears." It may help to know that Bishop was raised by her grandmother, since her father was dead and her mother was confined in an
asylum for the mentally ill:

> September rain falls on the house.
> In the failing light, the old grandmother
> sits in the kitchen with the child
> beside the Little Marvel Stove,
> reading the jokes from the almanac,
> laughing and talking to hide her tears.
>
> She thinks that her equinoctial tears
> and the rain that beats on the roof of the house
> were both foretold by the almanac,
> but only known to a grandmother.
> The iron kettle sings on the stove.
> She cuts some bread and says to the child,
>
> *It's time for tea now;* but the child
> is watching the teakettle's small hard tears
> dance like mad on the hot black stove,
> the way the rain must dance on the house.
> Tidying up, the old grandmother
> hangs up the clever almanac
>
> on its string. Birdlike, the almanac
> hovers half open above the child,
> hovers above the old grandmother
> and her teacup full of dark brown tears.
> She shivers and says she thinks the house
> feels chilly, and puts more wood in the stove.
>
> *It was to be,* says the Marvel Stove.
> *I know what I know,* says the almanac.
> With crayons the child draws a rigid house
> and a winding pathway. Then the child
> puts in a man with buttons like tears
> and shows it proudly to the grandmother.
>
> But secretly, while the grandmother
> busies herself about the stove,
> the little moons fall down like tears
> from between the pages of the almanac
> into the flower bed the child

has carefully placed in the front of the house.
Time to plant tears, says the almanac.
The grandmother sings to the marvelous stove
and the child draws another inscrutable house.

3. The *villanelle* is a French form that has been used with notable success
by many modern poets, among them Theodore Roethke, William Empson,
Dylan Thomas, and Bishop. A villanelle is a poem of five pentameter tercets
rhyming *aba,* followed by a pentameter quatrain rhyming *abaa.* In a villanelle, lines 1 and 3 of the first tercet are repeated alternately at the end of
each following tercet, and they close the final quatrain. Again, this is easier
seen than described, and in a good villanelle the repetitions are made to
seem natural. Here is Dylan Thomas's villanelle "Do Not Go Gentle into
That Good Night," a poem he wrote when his father was dying:

> Do not go gentle into that good night,
> Old age should burn and rave at close of day;
> Rage, rage against the dying of the light.
>
> Though wise men at their end know dark is right,
> Because their words had forked no lightning they
> Do not go gentle into that good night.
>
> Good men, the last wave by, crying how bright
> Their frail deeds might have danced in a green bay,
> Rage, rage against the dying of the light.
>
> Wild men who caught and sang the sun in flight,
> And learn, too late, they grieved it on its way,
> Do not go gentle into that good night.
>
> Grave men, near death, who see with blinding sight
> Blind eyes could blaze like meteors and be gay,
> Rage, rage against the dying of the light.
>
> And you, my father, there on the sad height,
> Curse, bless, me now with your fierce tears, I pray.
> Do not go gentle into that good night.
> Rage, rage against the dying of the light.

There are many other rhymed poem-forms, such as the *rondeau,* the *bal-
lade,* the *pantoum.* A poet using one of the rhymed poem-forms expects
the reader to recall the tradition of such forms.

4. The *ode* in English is usually a stanzaic poem, but it has no set form.
An ode is defined by its content: it is a poem of a lofty or sublime sort,

often using the figure of speech called *apostrophe,* which is an address to some divine or quasi-divine person or thing. "O wild West Wind," says Shelley; "Thou still unravished bride of quietness," says Keats addressing the Grecian urn.

Counted Verse That Does Not Rhyme

The most common form of counted unrhymed verse is *blank verse,* unrhymed iambic pentameter lines. This is the verse of Shakespeare's plays and of Milton's epic poem, *Paradise Lost:*

> That space the evil one abstracted stood
> From his own evil, and for the time remained
> Stupidly good, of enmity disarmed,
> Of guile, of hate, of envy, of revenge.

Blank verse can also be used in a lyric, as Coleridge uses it in his poem "Frost at Midnight":

> Therefore all seasons shall be sweet to thee,
> Whether the summer clothe the general earth
> With greenness, or the redbreast sit and sing
> Betwixt the tufts of snow on the bare branch.

Most of the unrhymed verse in English is blank verse, though poets have also written unrhymed four-beat poems that imitate Anglo-Saxon meter. Some poets have experimented with stanzas of unrhymed verse in imitation of Greek and Latin verse (which did not rhyme, but depended on a quantitative system contrasting long vowels with short vowels). Here are two stanzas of Thomas Campion's "Rose-Cheeked Laura," an imitation of the Greek meter called, after the poet Sappho, *sapphic.* The first line has three beats, the next two have four beats each, the fourth line two beats:

> Róse-cheeked Laúra, cóme,
> Síng thou smoóthly wíth thy beaúty's
> Sílent músic, eíther óther
> > Sweétly grácing.
>
> Lovely forms do flow
> From concent divinely framèd;
> Heav'n is music, and thy beauty's
> > Birth is heavenly.

Every so often a new poet will once again imitate classical unrhymed forms.

Free Verse

Free verse — verse in which the lines are of different widths, and which does not rhyme in any regular way — was invented by poets who had been brought up on rhymed and counted verse. Poets such as Whitman, Pound, Eliot, Stevens, Williams, Lowell, and Bishop all began by writing conventional verse. Whitman was drawn to free verse because he saw it as a primitive, "bardic" form. Eliot wrote it in imitation of the French poet Jules Laforgue. Pound wrote it in an attempt to achieve poetic effects he thought inhered in the Chinese ideogram. Williams and Stevens adopted it as a way to free themselves from the hold of English poets such as Keats. But behind their free verse there lurked always the shadow of counted verse. Eliot's "The Love Song of J. Alfred Prufrock" keeps threatening to turn into regular pentameter. Pound's largely free-verse "Cantos" include counted and rhymed segments.

The history of free verse is not yet entirely understood. The United States was a more hospitable environment for it than England, and a nativist wish to throw off inherited English forms certainly motivated many American poets. The unit of free verse seems to be the breath: there is a breath limit to the long line of free verse (reached by Whitman and Ginsberg, to give two notable examples). The theoretical appeal of free verse is that it admits an element of *chance;* it offers a model not of a tele-ological or providential universe but of an *aleatory* one, where the casual, rather than the fated, holds sway.

Free verse must justify its reasons for breaking a line here rather than there. If we look at a small free-verse poem, William Carlos Williams's "The Red Wheelbarrow," we must ask why the lines break where they do:

So much depends
upon

a red wheel
barrow

glazed with rain
water

beside the white
chickens

We might notice that in each little "stanza" the second line has only two syllables. This gives symmetry to the poem. The word "upon" literally hangs off the word "depends," acting out the meaning of something that depends (Latin: *dependere,* "to hang from") on something else. The red "wheel" turns into a "wheelbarrow" as we turn the line. Rain turns into rainwater, in the same way. After the inorganic wheelbarrow and rainwater, we may expect an inorganic object to follow the word "white" — say "the white / fences." Instead, the scene comes alive with chickens.

This very mannered little poem says that if the eye didn't see something inviting in the landscape (the shiny glaze the rain has put on the redness of the wheelbarrow; the composition of the still wheelbarrow and the living chickens; the contrast of red and white), there would be nothing to write about. "So much depends" on there being something out there to gratify and focus the eye. When we understand the poem, we understand its line-breaks. A free-verse poem that doesn't justify its line-breaks hardly deserves the name "poem."

Summary

When you come across a new poem, look at the way it displays itself on the page. Is it a skinny poem or a wide poem? A short poem or a long one? Are all the lines the same width, or are some shorter than others? Does it rhyme? Does it have stanzas?

Think of the look of the poem as its body. Is it a symmetrical body or a ragged body? A solid-looking body or an emaciated one?

As you read it aloud and listen to its rhythms, feel what it is telling you. Is it serious or even ponderous? Or does it move with a lilt and a skip? Does it change its manner of walking, from indolent to hurried? Does it manifest leisure or anxiety in its rhythms?

These are questions to ask even before you begin to note a rhyme scheme or count how many beats there are in a line. After you have done the technical noticing and counting, ask yourself how these formal features match up with the sentiments and emotions that the poem is expressing. Do the formal features align with those sentiments, or do they contradict them? It is always worthwhile to pay attention to the technical work the poet has done on the external form of the poem; it is, after all, the body the poet has chosen to live in for a determined period.

For a more complete survey of metrical forms, see Paul Fussell, *Poetic Meter and Poetic Form* (New York: Random House, 1965; revised 1979); or John Hollander, *Rhyme's Reason* (New Haven, Conn.: Yale University Press, 1981). For fuller definitions of terms used here, see the *Princeton Encyclopedia of Poetry and Poetics,* ed. Alex Preminger et al. (Princeton, N.J.: Princeton University Press, 1965; rpt. 1993).

Appendix 2. On Grammar

A familiarity with grammatical terms can help you to analyze and to describe poetry. This appendix provides a brief review of some of the most common and useful grammatical terms.

Noun

A word that names a person, place, thing, or idea. Examples: "Adam," "garden," "chair," "destiny." In short, a noun names an *essence*.

Adjective

A word that tells you something about that essence. An adjective modifies a noun by limiting or describing it. Examples: "the *early* bird," "a *false* alarm." An adjective expresses something present with or connected to a noun, but not essential: "a *red* wheelbarrow" (not all wheelbarrows are red). Adjectives are the chief resource of descriptive language, as when Shakespeare says (Sonnet 129) that lust is "perjur'd, murderous, bloody, full of blame, / Savage, extreme, rude, cruel, not to trust." The plainness of nouns is fleshed out by adjectives; and the complexity of life is such that poems need a wealth of adjectives to describe their essential nouns.

Pronoun

A word that stands in for a noun. Pronouns can be used as subjects (nominative case, as in "On a cloud *I* saw a child") or as objects (objective case, as in "And he laughing said to *me*"). In what follows I'll give the objective case in brackets after the nominative case.

The *first-person singular* is "I" [objective: "me"]; the *first-person plural* is "we" ["us"].

The modern *second-person pronoun* is "you" in both the singular and plural, nominative and objective, though in the past it was more complex. Then, the second-person singular was "thou" ["thee"], and the plural was "ye." "Thou" was used both in familiar address and in an exalted form of address to God or a monarch; over time, "you" took its place.

The *third-person singular* pronouns are "he" ["him"], "she" ["her"], and "it"; the plural is "they" ["them"].

A change in person ("I" to "you") or in number ("I" to "we") in a poem is always of profound significance, since, on the general principle of inertia, a speaker tends to continue in the same person rather than change, unless the change is somehow provoked. In the poem "In Memory of Eva Gore-Booth and Con Markiewicz," Yeats himself changes significantly from "I" to "we," as he finally makes common cause with the sisters he had begun by opposing; and his reference to the sisters changes from "one or the other" (third-person, people other than the poet) to "you" (people he addresses) to "we" (part of a group that also includes the poet):

> Many a time *I* think to seek
> *One or the other* out. . . .
>
> Dear shadows, now *you* know it all. . . .
>
> *We* the great gazebo built. . . .

A reader who misses the changes in person and number here misses the essential drama of the poem, as the poet changes his mind about the sisters and his relation to them.

Verb

A word that usually conveys either action ("My mother *bore* me in the southern wild") or state ("And I *am* black"). Verbs may be

> *Linking* verbs, which join two things that are equivalent ("He *seems* tired"; "I *will become* a teacher"; "Mary *is* a doctor");
>
> *Transitive* verbs, which take objects both direct and indirect ("I *gave* him the book"); or
>
> *Intransitive* verbs, which do not take an object ("The building *fell* down").

Verbs can appear in two *voices:*

> *Active:* "I *do* this."
>
> *Passive:* "This *is done* to me."

They can take on different *tenses* (past, present, future, and so on):

> *Simple present:* "I *sing* of heaven."
>
> *Present of habitual action:* "Whenever it *rains*, I *take* my umbrella."
>
> *Present of perpetual truth:* "Water *boils* at 212°F."
>
> *Present of state:* "I *am* a lawyer."
>
> *Present progressive:* "It *is raining*."
>
> *Simple past:* "I *knew* him, Horatio."
>
> *Compound past:* "I *have known* him a long time."

Past progressive: "It *was snowing.*"

Pluperfect: "I *had known* him for several years before I met his wife."

Simple future: "I *will call* him tomorrow."

Future perfect: "I *will have called* him by Wednesday."

Future progressive: "I *shall be telling* this with a sigh."

They can appear in different *moods* (statement, question, wish, and so on):

Indicative (states an assertion): "I *like* him."

Interrogative (asks a question): "*Do* you *like* him?"

Imperative (gives a command): "*Do* this."

Subjunctive (often contrary to fact or hypothetical): "If I *were to do* this, I would be prosecuted."

Optative (wish): "Oh, if I *could* only *do* [*have done*] this!"

Hortatory (enjoining something): "*Let us kiss* and part."

Conditional: "I *should like* to come if you *would let* me."

Poems can achieve multiple effects by changing tenses and moods as they go along.

Adverb

A word that characterizes (limits or describes) a verb, just as an adjective characterizes a noun. Adverbs answer the questions "Where?" "How?" "In what manner?" "When?" "Why?" and so on. Examples: "Till noon we *quietly* sailed on"; "my collar mounting *firmly* to my chin." Since verbs, like nouns, tend to be bare things, the poet uses adverbs to put a halo of circumstance around the verbs of the poem. Verbs are also amplified by adverbial phrases: "From you have I been absent *in the spring.*"

Appendix 3. On Speech Acts

There are numberless speech acts in which a lyric speaker may engage. The list that follows is merely a sampling of common ones in lyric. It is always a good idea to name the successive speech acts in a poem. Does it begin with an apology? Is that followed by a plea? Is that followed by a claim? Is that followed by a boast? This classifying helps you to track the emotions that structure a poem.

ACKNOWLEDGING	The darkness drops again, but now I know. . . .
ADDRESS	Old trooper, I see your child's red crayon pass.
ADMISSION	Alas, 'tis true, I have gone here and there, And made myself a motley to the view.
APOLOGY	Sweet Love of youth, forgive, if I forget thee.
APOSTROPHE	O wild West Wind!
BANISHING	Hence, loathèd Melancholy!
BOAST	Not marble, nor the gilded monuments Of princes, shall outlive this powerful rhyme.
CELEBRATION	I celebrate myself, and sing myself.
CLAIM	Mine — by the Right of the White Election!
COMMAND	Irish poets, learn your trade, Sing whatever is well made.
CONJECTURE	Thou mayst be false, and yet I know it not.
CONSOLATION	Fear no more the heat o' the sun.
DEFINITION	Remorse – is Memory – awake –
DESCRIPTION	No cloud, no relique of the sunken day Distinguishes the West.
DIALOGUE	Does the road wind uphill all the way? Yes, to the very end.
DREAMING	I dream of a Ledaean body, bent Above a sinking fire.

EXCLAMATION	What a piece of work is a man!
EXHORTATION	Be shellèd, eyes, with double dark And find the uncreated light.
EXPOSTULATION	Up, up, my friend, and quit your books!
GENERALIZATION	All this the world well knows, yet none knows well To shun the heaven that leads men to this hell.
IMPRECATION	For God's sake hold your tongue, and let me love.
INSTRUCTION	He who binds to himself a joy Does the wingèd life destroy.
INVITATION	Come live with me and be my love.
INVOCATION	But come, thou goddess fair and free.
LAMENT	Alas! I have nor hope nor health.
NARRATION	
PRESENT	It is an ancient Mariner And he stoppeth one of three.
PAST	I wandered lonely as a cloud.
HABITUAL	For oft, when on my couch I lie . . . They flash upon that inward eye.
HISTORICAL	Calvert and Wilson, Blake and Claude, Prepared a peace for the people of God.
OATH	I will not harm her, by all saints I swear.
PLEA	Say, may I be for aye thy vassal blest?
PRAYER	Mine, O thou Lord of life, send my roots rain.
PROPHECY	Therefore all seasons shall be sweet to thee.
QUESTION	Did he who made the Lamb make thee?
REBUTTAL	Love's not Time's fool.
REMINISCENCE	I was thy neighbor once, thou rugged Pile!
REQUEST	Permit me voyage, love, into your hands.
RESOLVE	Despair I will not.
RETRACTION	But I am by her death (which word wrongs her) . . .

Rhetorical question	O chestnut-tree, great-rooted blossomer, Are you the leaf, the blossom or the bole?
Scorning	How vainly men themselves amaze To win the palm, the oak, the bays.
Self-blame	I see The lost are like this, and their scourge to be As I am mine, their sweating selves, but worse.
Self-correction	Alas, but Morrison fell young: He never fell, thou fall'st, my tongue. He stood, a soldier to the last right end.
Self-presentation	I am the mower Damon.
Spell	No exorciser harm thee! Nor no witchcraft charm thee!
Supposition	Had we but world enough, and time.
Surmise	I cannot see what flowers are at my feet . . . But, in embalmèd darkness, guess each sweet.
Vow	Yes, I will be thy priest.

Appendix 4. On Rhetorical Devices

These devices, sometimes called "figures of speech," appear in all speech and writing (you can find them in advertising, political speeches, and newspapers, as well as in essays, letters, and poems). It helps, if you wish to give a brief description of what a writer is doing at a given moment, to know some of these shorthand terms for frequent practices.

ALTERNATIVE ORDERING

A man that looks on glass,
On it may stay his eye,
Or, if he pleaseth, through it pass,
And then the heaven espy.

ANALOGY
(comparison of A and B)

No more be grieved at that which thou
    hast done:
Roses have thorns, and silver fountains
    mud.

ANAPHORA
(repetition of opening word)

All shuffle there, all cough in ink,
All wear the carpet with their shoes,
All think what other people think;
All know the man their neighbor knows.

ANTICLIMAX

In silk, in crepes, in Garters, and in rags.

ANTITHESIS
(opposition of A and B)

For I have sworn thee fair, and thought
    thee bright,
Who art as black as hell, as dark as night.

APPOSITION
(list of different formulations of the same thing)

        The Mind of Man,
My haunt, and the main region of my
    song.

CATALOGUE

The leaden-eyed shark, the walrus, the
    turtle, the hairy sea-leopard.

CHIASMUS
(an X-like arrangement)

By brooks too broad for leaping
        The lightfoot boys are laid;
The rose-lipt girls are sleeping
        In fields where roses fade.
[brooks : boys :: girls : fields]

HIERARCHICAL ORDERING	Such sweet neglect more taketh me Than all th' adulteries of art.
METAPHOR *(comparison without "like" or "as")*	Church bells beyond the stars heard, the soul's blood, The land of spices; something understood.
METONYMY *(assemblage by parts)*	Four beating wings, two beaks, a swirling mass.
ONOMATOPOEIA *(imitative sound)*	And murmuring of innumerable bees.
PARADOX *(union of dissimilar qualities)*	There is in God, some say, A deep but dazzling darkness.
PARALLELISM	These are thy wonders, Lord of Power . . . These are thy wonders, Lord of Love.
PERIPHRASIS *(circumlocution)*	The Peer now spreads the glittering forfex wide [= opens scissors]
PERSONIFICATION *(an abstraction made into a person)*	Love is swift of foot, Love's a man of war.
PUN *(a play on two meanings of one word)*	Therefore I lie with her, and she with me, And in our faults by lies we flattered be.
QUOTATION	My flesh began unto my soul in pain, "Sicknesses cleave my bones."
SIMILE *(comparison with "like" or "as")*	Like as the waves make toward the pebbled shore, So do our minutes hasten to their end.
SYNECDOCHE *(use of the part for the whole)*	Diadems – drop – and Doges – surrender
ZEUGMA *(two dissimilar objects of same verb)*	Or stain her honor, or her new brocade.

Appendix 5. On Lyric Subgenres

This is a summary of the kinds of poems that lyric poets return to most frequently. It is convenient to be able to name a poem by its kind, because you can then compare it to others of the same kind.

ADDRESS TO THE READER	Pray thee, take care, that tak'st my book.
BALLAD	There lived a wife at Usher's well, And a wealthy wife was she; She had three stout and stalwart sons, And sent them o'er the sea.
CHILD'S POEM	"The Little Black Boy" (Blake)
DAWN POEM *(aubade)*	Get up! get up for shame! the blooming morn Upon her wings presents the god unshorn.
DEATHBED POEM	I heard a Fly buzz – when I died –
DEBATE-POEM	*Body* O who shall me deliver whole From bonds of this tyrannic soul? . . . *Soul* What magic could me thus confine Within another's grief to pine?
ECHO-POEM	Then tell me, what is that supreme de-light? Light. Light to the mind, what shall the will en-joy? Joy.
EKPHRASIS *(poem on an art object)*	"Ode on a Grecian Urn" (Keats)
ELEGY	Felix Randal the farrier, O is he dead then, my duty all ended?
EMBLEM-POEM *(allegorical object)*	"The Sick Rose" (Blake)

Epigram *(short, pointed poem)*	I am his Highness' dog at Kew: And pray, good sir, whose dog are you?
Epitaph	Underneath this stone doth lie All of beauty that could die.
Epithalamion *(wedding song)*	And evermore they *Hymen Hymen* sing, That al the woods them answer and theyr eccho ring.
Hymn	Jerusalem, Jerusalem, Lift up your gates and sing, Hosanna in the highest . . .
Inscription	I the poet William Yeats . . . Restored this tower for my wife George: And may these characters remain When all is ruin once again.
Letter	This is my letter to the World That never wrote to me.
Lover's complaint	And wilt thou leave me thus?
Lullaby	Lullay, lullay, thou tiny child.
Muse-poem	"The Solitary Reaper" (Wordsworth)
Nocturne	'Tis the year's midnight, and it is the day's.
Pastoral *(rustic poem)*	The shepherds' swains shall dance and sing For thy delight each May morning.
Political poem	"Easter, 1916" (Yeats)
Praise-poem	Shall I compare thee to a summer's day? Thou art more lovely and more temperate.
Quest-poem	"Childe Roland" (Browning)
Religious poem	I saw eternity the other night.
Romance *(fairy-tale poem)*	"The Eve of St. Agnes" (Keats)
Seasonal poem	Sumer is icumen in, Lhude sing cuccu!

SELF-REFLEXIVE POEM	I sing of brooks, of blossoms, birds, and bowers.
SHAPED POEM	"Easter Wings" (Herbert)
SONG	It was a lover and his lass, With a hey and a ho and a hey nonny no . . .
TWIN POEMS	"The Lamb" and "The Tyger" (Blake)
VALEDICTION	Adieu, farewell earth's bliss.
VARIATIONS ON A THEME	"Thirteen Ways of Looking at a Black-bird" (Stevens)

There are many other such that one could name: the *bird poem,* the *eclogue* (a dialogue of shepherds), the *georgic* (a poem on farming), the *testament* (a poem making a will), the *conversation poem* (a poem of a middle, or familiar, style recounting a conversation among friends), and so on. The essential thing is to realize that almost any poem is a repeat of a preceding genre, perhaps an answer to it, perhaps a revision of it. Thinking "What kind of a lyric is this?" makes you more aware of its place in a genre tradition, and of its response to that tradition.

Acknowledgments

Paula Gunn Allen. "Zen Americana." From *Coyote's Daylight Trip.* Copyright © 1978 by La Confluencia. Reprinted with the permission of the author.

Elizabeth Alexander. "Nineteen." From *The Venus Hottentot.* Copyright © 1990 by Elizabeth Alexander. Reprinted with the permission of the author.

Sherman Alexie. "Evolution" and "Reservation Love Song." From *The Business of Fancydancing.* Copyright © 1992 by Sherman Alexie. "On the Amtrak from Boston to New York City." From *First Indian on the Moon.* Copyright © 1993 by Sherman Alexie. Reprinted with the permission of Hanging Loose Press.

Julia Alvarez. Excerpt from "33," and "Homecoming." From *Homecoming.* Copyright © 1984, 1996 by Julia Alvarez. Published by Plume, an imprint of The Penguin Group (USA); originally published by Grove Press. Reprinted with the permission of Susan Bergholz Literary Services, New York, NY and Lamy, NM. All rights reserved.

A. R. Ammons. "The City Limits." From *The Selected Poems, Expanded Edition.* Copyright © 1971 by A. R. Ammons. "Easter Morning." From *A Coast of Trees.* Copyright © 1981 by A. R. Ammons. Used by permission of W. W. Norton & Company, Inc.

John Ashbery. "Paradoxes and Oxymorons." From *Shadow Train.* Copyright © 1980, 1981 by John Ashbery. "Street Musicians." From *Houseboat.* Copyright © 1975, 1976, 1977 by John Ashbery. Reprinted with the permission of Georges Borchardt, Inc.

Margaret Atwood. "Footnote to the Amnesty Report on Torture." From *Two-headed Poems.* Copyright © 1978 by Margaret Atwood. Reprinted with the permission of Margaret Atwood. First published in the United States by Simon and Schuster and in Canada by Oxford University Press. Reprinted by permission of Larmore Literary Agency. "Habitation." From *Selected Poems, 1965–1975* Copyright © 1976 by Margaret Atwood. Reprinted by permission of Houghton Mifflin Harcourt Publishing Company. All rights reserved. From *Selected Poems 1966–1984.* Copyright © Oxford University Press Canada 1990. Reprinted by permission of the publisher. "This is a photograph of me." From *The Circle Game.* Copyright © 1966, 1998 by Margaret Atwood. Reprinted by permission of House of Anansi Press, Toronto. "Up." From *Morning in the Burnt House.* Copyright © 1995 by Margaret Atwood. Reprinted by permission of Houghton Mifflin Harcourt Publishing Company and McClelland & Stewart Ltd. All rights reserved.

W. H. Auden. "As I Walked Out One Evening" and "Musée des Beaux Arts." From *Collected Poems* by W. H. Auden. Copyright 1940 and renewed © 1968 by W. H. Auden. Used by permission of Random House, Inc.

John Berryman. "Dream Song #4," "Dream Song #45," "Dream Song #384" (1 line each), and excerpt from "Prelude V." From *The Dream Songs.* Copyright © 1969 by John Berryman. Copyright renewed 1997 by Kate Donahue Berryman. Reprinted by permission of Farrar, Straus & Giroux, LLC.

Frank Bidart "An American in Hollywood," and "If See No End In Is." From *Watching the Spring Festival*. Copyright © 1990 by Frank Bidart. "To My Father." From *In the Western Night: Collected Poems 1965–1990*. Copyright © 1990 by Frank Bidart. Reprinted by permission of Farrar, Straus & Giroux, LLC.

Elizabeth Bishop. "At the Fishhouses, "One Art," "Poem," and "Sestina." From *The Complete Poems 1927–1979*. Copyright © 1979, 1983 by Alice Helen Methfessel. Reprinted by permission of Farrar, Straus & Giroux, LLC.

Richard Blanco. "Letters for Mamá." From *Little Havana Blues: A Cuban-American Literature Anthology*, edited by Delia Poey and Virgil Suarez. © 1996 Arte Publico Perss–University of Houston. Reprinted with the permission of the publisher.

Michael Blumenthal. "Early Childhood Education." From "Correctng the World: Selected Poetry and Writings of Michael Blumenthal" in *Legal Studies Forum* 31.1 (2007): 373. Originally published in *Dusty Angel* (BOA Editions, page 89). Copyright © 1999 by Michael Blumenthal. Reprinted with the permission of BOA Editions, Ltd., www.boaeditions.org. "A Marriage." From *Against Romance*. Copyright © 1987 by Michael Blumenthal. Used by permission of Viking Penguin, a division of Penguin Group (USA) Inc.

Lucie Brock-Broido. "Carrowmore." From *The Master Letters*. Copyright © 1995 by Lucie Brock-Broido. "Domestic Mysticism." From *A Hunger*. Copyright © 1988 by Lucie Brock-Broido. "Self-Deliverance by Lion." From *Trouble in Mind: Poems*. Copyright © 2004 by Lucie Brock-Broido. Used by permission of Alfred A. Knopf, a division of Random House, Inc.

Gwendolyn Brooks. "The Bean Eaters, "Beverly Hills, Chicago," and "We Real Cool." From *Blacks*. Copyright © 1991 by Gwendolyn Brooks. Reprinted by permission of Brooks Permissions.

Lorna Dee Cervantes. "Freeway 280." From *Emplumada*. Originally published in *The Latin-American Literary Review* 5, no. 10 (1977). Reprinted with the permission of Latin American Literary Review Press. "Poema para los Californios Muertos." From *Emplumada*. Copyright © 1981 by Lorna Dee Cervantes. Reprinted by permission of the University of Pittsburgh Press.

Victoria Chang. "$4.99 All You Can Eat Sunday Brunch." From *Circle*. Copyright © 2005 by Victoria Chang. Reprinted with the permission of Southern Illinois University Press.

Marilyn Chin. "Autumn Leaves." From *The Phoenix Gone, The Terrace Empty* (Minneapolis: Milkweed Editions, 1994). Copyright © 1994 by Marilyn Chin. Reprinted with the permission of Milkweed Editions, www.milkweed.org.

Lucille Clifton. "the lost baby poem." From *100 Essential Modern Poems by Women*, edited by Joseph Parisi and Kathleen Welton (Chicago: Ivan R. Dee, 2008). Previously published in *Good Woman: Poems and a Memoir 1969–1980*. (Rochester, New York: BOA Edition, 1987). Reprinted with the permission of BOA Editions Ltd., www.boaeditions.org.

Henri Cole. "40 Days and 40 Nights." From *The Look of Things*. Copyright © 1994 by Henri Cole. Used by permission of Alfred A. Knopf, a division of Random House, Inc. "Carwash." First published in *The New Republic* (March 28, 2008): 54. Copyright © 2008. Reprinted with the permission of the author.

Eduardo C. Corral. "Monologue of a Vulture's Shadow." Originally published in *Three Candles Journal*, www.threecandles.org/archive/ecorral.html. Reprinted with the permission of the author.

Robert Creeley. "When I think." From *The Collected Poems of Robert Creeley, 1975–2005*. Copyright © 2005 by The Regents of the University of California. Reprinted with the permission of the University of California Press.

Mark Ford. "The Long Man." From *Soft Sift*. Copyright © 2001 by Mark Ford. Reprinted by permission of Houghton Mifflin Harcourt Publishing Company and Faber & Faber, Ltd.

Robert Frost. "After Apple-Picking," "Design," "Mending Wall," and "Unharvested." From *The Poetry of Robert Frost*, edited by Edward Connery Lathem. Copyright 1930, 1939, 1969 by Henry Holt and Company. Copyright 1936, 1958 by Robert Frost. Copyright 1964, 1967 by Lesley Frost Ballantine. "Birches," "The Gift Outright," "Stopping by Woods on a Snowy Evening" and "The Road Not Taken." From *The Poetry of Robert Frost*, edited by Edward Connery Lathem. Copyright 1916, 1923, 1969 by Henry Holt and Company. Copyright 1942, 1944, 1951 by Robert Frost. Copyright 1970 by Lesley Frost Ballantine. Reprinted by permission of Henry Holt and Company, LLC.

Allen Ginsberg. "America." From *Collected Poems 1947–1980*. Copyright © 1956, 1959 by Allen Ginsberg. "Sunflower Sutra." From *Collected Poems 1947–1980* by Allen Ginsberg. Copyright © 1955 by Allen Ginsberg. Reprinted by permission of Harper-Collins Publishers.

Louise Glück. "All Hallows," "The School Children," and "Mock Orange." From *The First Four Books of Poems (Firstborn, Descending Figure, House on Marshland, Triumph of Achilles)*. Copyright © 1968, 1971, 1972, 1973, 1974, 1975, 1976, 1977, 1978, 1979, 1980, 1985, 1995 by Louise Glück. "The Balcony." From *The Seven Ages*. Copyright © 2001 by Louise Glück. Reprinted by permission of HarperCollins Publishers. "Midsummer." From *Poetry* 191.5 (February 2008): 379. Forthcoming in *A Village Life* (New York: Farrar, Straus & Giroux, 2009). Copyright © 2008 by Louise Glück. Reprinted with permission of The Wylie Agency.

Albert Goldbarth. "The Novel That Asks to Erase Itself," and "Unforeseeables." From *The Kitchen Sink: New and Selected Poems 1972–2007*, pages 298, 320. Copyright © 2007 by Albert Goldbarth. Reprinted with the permission of Graywolf Press, Saint Paul, Minnesota, www.graywolfpress.org.

Jorie Graham. "What the End Is For," "Of Forced Sightes and Trusty Ferefulness." From *The End of Beauty*. Copyright © 1987 by Jorie Graham. "Soul Says." From *Regions of Unlikeness*. Copyright © 1991 by Jorie Graham. "The Strangers." From *The Errancy*. Copyright © 1997 by Jorie Graham. Reprinted by permission of HarperCollins Publishers. "San Sepolcro." From *Erosion*. Copyright © 1983 by Princeton University Press. Reprinted by permission of Princeton University Press.

Thom Gunn. "The Man with Night Sweats." From *The Man with Night Sweats*. Copyright © 1992 by Thom Gunn. "My Sad Captains." From *My Sad Captains*. Copyright © 1961 and copyright renewed 1989 by Thom Gunn. Reprinted by permission of Farrar, Straus & Giroux, LLC and Faber and Faber Limited.

H. D. (Hilda Doolittle). "Oread," and "Helen." From *Collected Poems 1912–1944*. Copyright © 1982 by The Estate of Hilda Doolittle. Reprinted by permission of New Directions Publishing Corp.

Thomas Hardy. "Afterwards." From *The Complete Poems of Thomas Hardy*, edited by James Gibson. Copyright 1925 by The Macmillan Company. Copyright renewed © 1953 by Lloyds Bank Ltd. Reprinted with the permission of Scribner, a Division of Simon & Schuster, Inc. All rights reserved.

Joy Harjo. "Song for Deer and Myself to Return On." From *In Mad Love and War*. Copyright © 1990 by Joy Harjo. Reprinted by permission of Wesleyan University Press.

Michael Harper. "American History." From *Dear John, Dear Coltrane*. Copyright © 1970, 1985 by Michael S. Harper. Reprinted with the permission of the author. "Nightmare Begins Responsibility," and "We Assume: On the Death of Our Son, Reuben Masai Harper." From *Songliness in Michaeltree: New and Collected Poems*. Copyright © 2000 by Michael S. Harper. Used with the permission of the poet and the University of Illinois Press.

permission of Farrar, Straus & Giroux, LLC and Faber and Faber Ltd. "Reasons for Attendance." From *The Less Deceived*. Copyright © 1958 by Philip Larkin. Reprinted with the permission of The Marvell Press.

D. H. Lawrence. "The English Are So Nice!" From *The Complete Poems of D.H. Lawrence*, edited by V. deSola Pinto and F. W. Roberts. Copyright © 1964, 1971 by Angelo Ravagli and C. M. Weekley, Executors of the Estate of Frieda Lawrence Ravagli. Used by permission of Viking Penguin, a division of Penguin Group (USA) Inc.

Li-Young Lee. "Mother Deluxe." From *Behind My Eyes*. Copyright © 2008 by Li-Young Lee. Used by permission of W. W. Norton & Company, Inc.

Denise Levertov. "The Ache of Marriage." From *Poems 1960–1967*. Copyright © 1966 by Denise Levertov. Reprinted by permission of New Directions Publishing Corp.

Harold Littlebird. "White-Washing the Walls." From *On Mountains Breath* (Tooth of Time Books, 1982). Copyright © 1982 by Harold Littlebird. Reprinted by permission.

Audre Lorde. "Hanging Fire." From *The Black Unicorn*. Copyright © 1978 by Audre Lorde. Used by permission of W. W. Norton & Company, Inc.

Robert Lowell. "Epilogue." From *Day by Day*. Copyright © 1977 by Robert Lowell. "For the Union Dead." From *For the Union Dead*. Copyright © 1959 by Robert Lowell. Copyright renewed by Harriet Lowell, Caroline Lowell, and Sheridan Lowell. "The March I." From *History*. Copyright © 1973 by Robert Lowell. "Sailing Home from Rapallo" and "Skunk Hour." From *Life Studies*. Copyright © 1959 by Robert Lowell. Copyright renewed 1987 by Harriet Lowell, Sheridan Lowell, and Caroline Lowell. Reprinted by permission of Farrar, Straus & Giroux, LLC.

Archibald MacLeish. "Ars Poetica." From *Collected Poems 1917–1982*. Copyright © 1985 by The Estate of Archibald MacLeish. Reprinted by permission of Houghton Mifflin Harcourt Publishing Company. All rights reserved

Dionisio Martínez. "History as a Second Language." From *History as a Second Language*. Copyright © 1982 by Dionisio Martínez. Reprinted with the permission of the author.

Victor Martínez. "The Ledger." From *Caring for a House*, published by Chusma House Publications in 1992. Copyright © 1992 by Victor Martínez. By permission of Susan Bergholz Literary Services, New York, NY and Lamy, NM. All rights reserved.

Shara McCallum. "The Incident." From *Song of Thieves* by Shara McCallum. © 2003. Reprinted by permission of the University of Pittsburgh Press.

James Merrill. "The Christmas Tree." From *Collected Poems* by James Merrill, edited by J. D. McClatchy and Stephen Yenser. Copyright © 2001 by the Literary Estate of James Merrill at Washington University. Used by permission of Alfred A. Knopf, a division of Random House, Inc.

W. S. Merwin. "The Asians Dying," "For a Coming Extinction," and "For the Anniversary of My Death." From *The Second Four Books of Poems*. Copyright © 2000 by W. S. Merwin. Reprinted with the permission of The Wylie Agency, LLC.

Marianne Moore. "England," "A Grave," "Poetry," and "The Steeple-Jack." From *The Collected Poems of Marianne Moore* by Marianne Moore. Copyright 1935 by Marianne Moore. Copyright renewed © 1963 by Marianne More & T. S. Eliot. Reprinted with the permission of Scribner, a Division of Simon & Schuster, Inc. All rights reserved.

Pat Mora. "La Migra." Currently appears in *Agua Santa: Holy Water*, published by University of Arizona Press. Copyright © 1995 by Pat More. Reprinted with the permission of Curtis Brown, Ltd. "Rituals." From the publisher of *Communion*. © 1991 by Arte Publico Press (University of Houston). Reprinted with permission from the publisher.

Thylias Moss. "One for All Newborns." From *Small Congregations: New and Selected Poems*. Copyright © 1983, 1990, 1991, 1993 by Thylias Moss. Reprinted by permission of HarperCollins Publishers.

Harryette Mullen. "Omnivore." From *Blues Baby* (Bucknell University Press, 2002). Copyright © 2002 by Harryette Mullen. Reprinted with the permission of the author.

David Mura. "An Argument: On 1942." From *After We Lost Our Way*. Copyright © 1989. Reprinted with the permission of the author.

Marilyn Nelson. "Live Jazz, Franklin Park Zoo." From *The New Bread Loaf Anthology of Contemporary American Poetry*, edited by Michael Collier and Stanley Plumly. Copyright © 1999. Reprinted with the permission of the author.

Frank O'Hara. "Ave Maria." From *The Selected Poems of Frank O'Hara*. Copyright © 1964. Reprinted with the permission of City Lights Books. "Why I Am Not a Painter." From *The Collected Poems of Frank O'Hara* by Frank O'Hara, edited by Donald Allen. Copyright © 1958 by Maureen Granville-Smith, Administratrix of the Estate of Frank O'Hara. Used by permission of Alfred A. Knopf, a division of Random House, Inc.

Simon J. Ortiz. "Bend in the River." From *Going for the Rain*. Copyright © 1976. Reprinted with the permission of the author.

Grace Paley. Excerpt from "Detour." From *Fidelity*. Copyright © 2008 by Grace Paley. Reprinted by permission of Farrar, Straus & Giroux, LLC.

Carl Phillips. "Blue." From *In the Blood*. Copyright © 1992 by Carl Phillips. Reprinted with the permission of University Press of New England. "The Kill." from *Pastoral*. Copyright © 2000 by Carl Phillips. Reprinted with the permission of Graywolf Press, St. Paul, Minnesota, www.graywolfpress.org.

Sylvia Plath. "The Applicant," "Daddy," "Edge," "Lady Lazarus," and "Morning Song." From *Ariel: Poems* by Sylvia Plath. Copyright © 1961, 1962, 1963, 1964, 1965, 1966 by Ted Hughes. "Metaphors" From *Crossing the Water* by Sylvia Plath. Copyright © 1960 by Ted Hughes. Reprinted by permission of HarperCollins Publishers. "Metaphors." from *Collected Poems*. Reprinted by permission of Faber and Faber Ltd.

Ezra Pound. "In a Station of the Metro," and "The River Merchant's Wife: A Letter." From *Personae*. Copyright 1926 by Ezra Pound. Reprinted by permission of New Directions Publishing Corp.

D. A. Powell. "autumn set us heavily to task: unrooted the dahlias" and "cherry elixir: the first medication. so mary poppins" from *Lunch*. © 2000 by D. A. Powell. Reprinted by permission of Wesleyan University Press.

Srikanth Reddy. "Fourth Circle." From *Facts for Visitors*. Copyright © 2004 by Srikanth Reddy. Reprinted with the permission of the University of California Press.

Henry Reed. "Naming of Parts." From *Henry Reed's Collected Poems*, edited by Jon Stallworthy. Reprinted by permission of Oxford University Press Ltd.

Adrienne Rich. "The Middle-Aged." From *Collected Early Poems: 1950–1970*. Copyright © 1993, 1955 by Adrienne Rich. "Mother-in-Law." From *A Wild Patience Has Taken Me This Far: Poems 1978–1981*. Copyright © 1981 by Adrienne Rich. "Diving into the Wreck." Copyright © 2002 by Adrienne Rich. Copyright © 1973 by W. W. Norton & Company, Inc. "I Am in Danger – Sir" and "Necessities of Life." Copyright © 2002 by Adrienne Rich. Copyright © 1966 by W. W. Norton & Company, Inc. "Prospective Immigrants Please Note." Copyright © 2002, 1967, 1963 by Adrienne Rich. From *The Fact of a Doorframe: Selected Poems: 1950–2001*. Used by permission of the author and W. W. Norton & Company, Inc.

Alberto Rios. "Teodoro Luna's Two Kisses. From *Teodoro Luna's Two Kisses*. Copyright © 1990 by Alberto Rios. Used by permission of W. W. Norton & Company, Inc.

Aleida Rodríguez. "Lexicon of Exile." From *Lengua Fresca: Latinos Writing on the Edge*, edited by Harold Augenbraum and Ilan Stavans. Copyright © 1999 by Aleida Rodríguez. Reprinted with the permission of Sarabande Books, Inc., www.sarabandebooks.org.

Theodore Roethke. "Elegy for Jane," My Papa's Waltz," and "The Waking." From *The Collected Poems of Theodore Roethke*. Copyright © 1942 by Hearst Magazines, Inc. Copyright © 1950, 1953 by Theodore Roethke. Used by permission of Doubleday, a division of Random House, Inc.

Brynn Saito. "Turkey People." From *From Totems to Hip-Hop: A Multicultural Anthology of Poetry Across the Americas*, edited by Ishmael Reed. Reprinted with the permission of the author.

Carl Sandburg. "Grass." From *Cornhuskers*. Copyright 1918 by Holt, Rinehart & Winston, and renewed 1946 by Carl Sandburg. Reprinted by permission of Houghton Mifflin Harcourt Publishing Company.

Anne Sexton. "Her Kind." From *To Bedlam and Part Way Back*. Copyright © 1960 by Anne Sexton, renewed 1988 by Linda G. Sexton. Reprinted by permission of Houghton Mifflin Harcourt Publishing Company. All rights reserved.

Charles Simic. "Charon's Cosmology," "Fork," and "A Suitcase Strapped with Rope." From *Selected Early Poems*. Copyright © 1999 by Charles Simic. Reprinted with the permission of George Braziller, Inc. "Old Couple." From *The Weather Forecast for Utopia and the Vicinity*. Copyright © 1983 by Charles Simic. Reprinted with the permission of Station Hill Press.

Dave Smith. "On a Field Trip at Fredericksburg" and "The Spring Poem." From *Floating on Solitude: Three Volumes of Poetry*. Copyright © 1976 by Dave Smith. Reprinted with the permission of the author.

Ron Smith. "The Teachers Pass the Popcorn." From *Moon Road: Poems 1986–2005*. Copyright © 2007 by Ron Smith. Reprinted with the permission of Louisiana State University Press.

Stevie Smith. "Not Waving But Drowning." From *The Collected Poems of Stevie Smith*. Copyright © 1972 by Stevie Smith. Reprinted by permission of New Directions Publishing Corp.

Tracy K. Smith. "El Mar" and "Diego." From *Duende*. Copyright © 2007 by Tracy K. Smith. "Credulity." From *The Body's Question*. Copyright © 2003 by Tracy K. Smith. Reprinted with the permission of Graywolf Press, St. Paul, Minnesota, www.graywolfpress.org.

Gary Snyder. "Axe Handles." From *Axe Handles*. Copyright © 2005 by Gary Snyder. Reprinted by permission of Counterpoint. "How Poetry Comes to Me." From *No Nature*. Copyright © 1992 by Gary Snyder. Used by permission of Pantheon Books, a division of Random House, Inc.

Gary Soto. "History." From *New and Selected Poems*. Copyright © 1995 by Gary Snyder. Used with permission of Chronicle Books, LLC, San Francisco. Visit ChronicleBooks.com.

Heidy Steidlmayer. "Knife-Sharpener's Song." From *Poetry* 177 (February 2001). Copyright © 2001 by The Modern Poetry Association. Reprinted with the permission of the Editor of *Poetry* and the author.

Wallace Stevens. "The Idea of Order at Key West." Copyright 1936 by Wallace Stevens and renewed 1964 by Holly Stevens. "The Plain Sense of Things," "The Planet on the Table," "Poetry Is a Destructive Force," and "A Primitive Like an Orb." From *The Collected Poems of Wallace Stevens* by Wallace Stevens. Copyright © 1954 by Wallace Stevens and renewed 1982 by Holly Stevens. Used by permission of Alfred A. Knopf, a division of Random House, Inc.

Mark Strand. "Courtship," and "Keeping Things Whole." From *Selected Poems*. Copyright © 1979, 1980 by Mark Strand. Used by permission of Alfred A. Knopf, a division of Random House, Inc.

Adrienne Su. "The English Canon" and "Female Infanticide: A Guide for Mothers." From *Sanctuary*. Copyright © 2006 by Adrienne Su. Reprinted with the permission of Manic D Press, San Francisco.

May Swenson. "Untitled," "I Look at My Hand," and "How Everything Happens (Based on a Study of the Wave)." From *Nature: Poems Old and New*. Copyright © 1994 by May Swenson. Reprinted with the permission of The Literary Estate of May Swenson.

Sheila Ortiz Taylor. "The Way Back." From *Slow Dancing at Miss Polly's*. Copyright © 1989 by Sheila Ortiz Taylor. Reprinted with the permission of Naiad Press.

Dylan Thomas. "Fern Hill." Copyright © 1945 by The Trustees for the Copyrights of Dylan Thomas. "In My Craft or Sullen Art." Copyright © 1946 by New Directions Publishing Corp. "Do Not Go Gentle Into That Good Night." Copyright © 1952 by Dylan Thomas. From *The Poems of Dylan Thomas*. Reprinted by permission of New Directions Publishing Corp.

Natasha Trethewey. "What Is Evidence." From *Native Guard*. Copyright © 2006 by Natasha Trethewey. Reprinted with the permission of Houghton Mifflin Harcourt Publishing Company. All rights reserved.

Derek Walcott. "Blues," "God Rest Ye Merry, Gentlemen," "The Gulf," and "The Season of Phantasmal Peace." From *Collected Poems 1948–1984*. Copyright © 1986 by Derek Walcott. Reprinted by permission of Farrar, Straus & Giroux, LLC. "Perhaps it exists." From *Agni* 67 (2008). Copyright © 2008 by Derek Walcott. Reprinted with the permission of the author.

Rosanna Warren. "In Creve Coeur, Missouri." From, *Stained Glass*. Copyright © 1993 by Rosanna Warren. Used by permission of W. W. Norton & Company, Inc.

Joshua Weiner. "The Yonder Tree." From *The World's Room*. Copyright © 2001 by Joshua Weiner. Reprinted with the permission of the author and The University of Chicago Press.

James Welch. "Getting Things Straight." From *Riding the Earthboy 40*. Copyright © 1971, 1976, 1990 by James Welch. Used by permission of Penguin, a division of Penguin Group (USA) Inc. "Harlem, Montana: Just Off the Reservation." From *Riding the Earthboy 40*. Copyright © 1971, 1976, 1990 by James Welch. Used by permission of Confluence Press.

Richard Wilbur. "Cottage Street, 1953" and "The Writer." From *The Mind-Reader*. Copyright © 1971, 1972 by Richard Wilbur. Reprinted by permission of Houghton Mifflin Harcourt Publishing Company.

William Carlos Williams. "The Raper from Passenack," "Spring and All," and "This Is Just to Say." Copyright 1938 by William Carlos Williams. "Poem." Copyright © 1953 by William Carlos Williams. From *The Collected Poems: Volume I: 1909–1939*. "The Dance" [When the snow falls] and "Landscape with the Fall of Icarus." Copyright © 1962 by William Carlos Williams. From *Collected Poems: 1939–1962, Volume II*. All reprinted by permission of New Directions Publishing Corp.

Charles Wright, "Self-Portrait." From *The World of the Ten Thousand Things: Poems 1980–1990*. Copyright © 1990 by Charles Wright. Reprinted by permission of Farrar, Straus & Giroux, LLC.

James Wright. "A Blessing." From *The Branch Will Not Break*. Copyright © 1963 by James Wright. "Small Frogs Killed on the Highway." From *Collected Poems*. Copyright © 1971 by James Wright. Reprinted by permission of Wesleyan University Press.

John Yau. "Autobiography in Red and Yellow." From *Borrowed Love Poems*. Copyright © 2002 by John Yau. Used by permission of Viking Penguin, a division of Penguin Group (USA) Inc.

William Butler Yeats. "The Lake Isle of Innisfree." Copyright © New York: Scribner, 1997. "Among School Children," "Leda and the Swan," and "Sailing to Byzantium." Copyright © 1928 by The Macmillan Company. Copyright renewed © 1956 by Georgie Yeats. "Crazy Jane Talks to the Bishop" and "A Dialogue of Self and Soul." Copyright © 1933 by The Macmillan Company. Copyright renewed © 1961 by Bertha Georgie Yeats. "Meru." Copyright © 1934 by The Macmillan Company. Copyright renewed © 1962 by Bertha Georgie Yeats. From *The Complete Works of W.B. Yeats, Volume I: The Poems, Revised*, edited by Richard J. Finneran. Reprinted with the permission of Scribner, a division of Simon & Schuster, Inc. All rights reserved.

Index of Authors, Titles, and First Lines

Index of Terms